Wisdom With Understanding is Better Than Rubies

Lurine Karon Greenberg
Fine Arts Collection

THE LANDMARKS OF NEW YORK III

THIS BOOK IS DEDICATED TO CARL D. SPIELVOGEL

AND ALL THE OWNERS, OCCUPANTS, FRIENDS,

AND SUPPORTERS OF THE LANDMARKS OF NEW YORK

THE LANDMARKS

BARBARALEE DIAMONSTEIN

OF NEW YORK III

HARRY N. ABRAMS, INC., PUBLISHERS

PROJECT MANAGER: ADELE WESTBROOK
EDITOR: AMY L. VINCHESI
DESIGNERS: JUDITH MICHAEL WITH BETH TONDREAU DESIGN

Page 2 (left to right): Ellis Island, Main Building interior; Standard Oil Building, Manhattan; Brooklyn Bridge
Page 3 (left to right): Dime Savings Bank interior, Brooklyn; Chrysler Building, Manhattan; The Unisphere, Queens

LIBRARY OF CONGRESS CATALOGING–IN–PUBLICATION DATA

Diamonstein, Barbaralee.
The landmarks of New York III / Barbaralee Diamonstein.
p. cm.
Updated ed. of: The landmarks of New York II.
Includes index.
ISBN 0–8109–3594–5
1. Historic buildings—New York (State)—New York. 2. Historic buildings—New York (State)—New York—Pictorial
works. 3. New York (N.Y.)—Buildings, structures, etc. 4. New York (N.Y.)—Pictorial works. I. Diamonstein, Barbaralee.
Landmarks of New York II.
II. Title.
F128.7.D57 1998
974.7' 1— dc21   97–23865

Printed and bound in Hong Kong

Harry N. Abrams, Inc.
100 Fifth Avenue
New York, N.Y. 10011
www.abramsbooks.com

CONTENTS

INTRODUCTION

I pray let us satisfy our eyes—with the memorials and the things of fame that do renown this city. —WILLIAM SHAKESPEARE

For most of our history, Americans have been fervent believers in progress, which has often meant, in the realm of architecture, tearing down the old and building again—bigger, bolder, and taller than before. This is particularly true of New Yorkers, whose city, in its ceaseless ebb and flow, is a monument to transience, a moveable feast. New York City's quintessential characteristic is its quicksilver quality, its ability to transform itself not just from year to year but almost from day to day. Cast your eyes upward almost anywhere in the city: a forest of cranes challenges the sky. The French architect Le Corbusier saw New York as a white cathedral that is never finished, a geyser whose fountains leap and gush in continual renewal. He said of our city: "It has such courage and enthusiasm that everything can be begun again, sent back to the building yard, and made into something greater. . . . A considerable part of New York is nothing more than a provisional city. A city which will be replaced by another city." This is New York: its motion perpetual, its details a blurred collage.

Yet amidst this constant change, we have managed to preserve at least part of the city's legacy of great architecture. Until relatively recently, it seemed that this would not be possible. During the first three centuries of the city's existence, many of its fine buildings were destroyed. Not until the 1960s did an urban preservation movement emerge whose objective was to conserve the best of our past—architecturally, historically, culturally.

Preservationists have long argued the intangible social benefits of protecting the past from the wrecker's ball: by conserving our historical and physical heritage, preservation provides a reassuring chain of continuity between past and present. And a sense of continuity, an awareness that some things last longer than mortal existence, is important to most people. Cities, as the greatest communal works of man, provide the deepest assurance that this is so. This may be the city's most valuable cultural function. Lewis Mumford put it most succinctly when he said, "In the city, time becomes visable."

Down through the centuries, many of mankind's greatest buildings have been destroyed: some by acts of outright vandalism, others by not-always-benign neglect. The ongoing saga of destruction and construction, the endless clash between old and new, between tradition and progress, has always engaged poets and politicians. But in the last few decades, the delicate mesh that weaves the new into the old, continuing the layering process that creates a culture, has captured the interest of far larger, and still-growing, numbers of people. Lately, public attention has been focused not only on the protection of our fast-vanishing wilderness, but also on the urgent need to protect our architectural environment—from its irreplaceable structures to its cherished open spaces and parks—which faces a daily threat of extinction. These natural and cultural resources, it has been said, are inherited from our ancestors and borrowed from our children. We are challenged to honor this pact and protect our legacy from human, industrial, and aesthetic pollution. Fortunately, we Americans have grown in our appreciation of our historical environment as both beautiful and useful. For nearly a quarter of a century, a dedicated army of women and men, some holding official positions in public and private preservation organizations, some laboring in far less visible capacities, has had a remarkable impact on the character and appearance of our cities.

HISTORIC PRESERVATION IN THE UNITED STATES

The need to protect and preserve our cultural resources had been recognized by various groups of private citizens as far back as the early 1800s, when voices began to be raised against the demolition of buildings identified with the nation's history. Perhaps the most significant nineteenth-century effort was the fight to save Virginia's Mount Vernon, spearheaded by Ann Pamela Cunningham, a remarkably dedicated and persevering woman. Her success in saving that national monument inspired other efforts at protecting and preserving historic sites, and gave rise to a number of pioneering organizations and societies. In 1888, the Association for the Preservation of Virginia Antiquities was formed to protect Jamestown. Such patriotic societies as the Daughters of the American Revolution and the National Society of the Colonial Dames of America began to center their efforts on preservation. The Society for the Preservation of New England Antiquities, begun in 1910, rescued many important landmarks in that region. The idea of preserving larger areas, though later subject to revisionist criticism, gained ground: the model was John D. Rockefeller's reconstruction of Colonial Williamsburg in the 1920s.

The first official federal legislation came with the Antiquities Act of 1906, which authorized the president to designate as national monuments those areas of the public domain containing historic landmarks, historic and prehistoric structures, and objects of historical importance situated on federal property. A decade later, in 1916, the National Parks Service was created to protect historical and national parks. Local governments, too, started to enact preservation laws authorizing the designation and preservation of local buildings and neighborhoods of value: New Orleans adopted its laws in 1925; Charleston in 1937; San Antonio in 1939. States also began to support preservation efforts.

With the Historic Sites Act of 1935, Congress proclaimed "a national policy to preserve for public use historic sites, buildings, and objects of national significance." Unfortunately, the declared national policy was by no means the standard national practice, and precious structures were demolished apace. Aware that its earlier efforts had been insufficient, Congress chartered the National Trust for Historic Preservation in 1949 to foster awareness and advocacy. In 1966, the National Historic Preservation Act called for preserving the integrity of cultural property of national, state, and local importance; at the same time, the National Register was created to encourage the identification and protection of the nation's historic buildings by conducting an ongoing inventory of such landmarks.

Preservation's coming-of-age is most evident in the expansion of activity at the local government level. By 1966, approximately 100 communities had established historic district commissions; a decade later, the figure was 500, and by 1982, roughly 1,000. Today they number more than 1,200. Clearly, preservation has come a long way from the early days of limited, ad hoc activity.

HISTORIC PRESERVATION IN NEW YORK CITY

As far back as 1831, New Yorkers had begun to fret that many important structures were being destroyed to make way for new ones. In March of that year, the New York *Mirror* carried a picture of an old Dutch house on Pearl Street, in Lower Manhattan, with the caption: "Built in 1626, Rebuilt 1647, Demolished 1828," accompanied by a ringing editorial criticizing the destruction. Just seven years later, Mayor Philip Hone had this to say about the city's penchant for tearing itself apart: "The city is now undergoing its usual metamorphosis; many stores and houses are being pulled down and others altered to make every inch of ground productive to its utmost extent. It looks like the ruins occasioned by an earthquake." Not a bad way to describe the situation more than one hundred and fifty years later.

In its early history, the city grew by moving uptown in Manhattan and outward in the other boroughs. But by the early 1900s the land, at least in Manhattan, was largely taken. In most cases, the only way to build something new was to tear down something else, or to build on top of it. At first, most New Yorkers accepted the destruction of the past as the price to be paid for progress. They had little use for Victor Hugo's injunction: "Let us, while waiting for new monuments, preserve the ancient monuments." Instead, they relished what Walt Whitman referred to in the mid-1840s as the "pull-down-and-build-over-again" spirit that seemed to epitomize their city, and, indeed, all of America.

Yet some citizens fully endorsed Mayor Hone's appeal to resist the temptation to "overturn, overturn, overturn." During the prosperous post–Civil War years, Americans who had traveled throughout Europe on the grand tour came home with a new awareness and appreciation of the indigenous American culture that had taken root, particularly its architecture. In 1904 Henry James returned from Europe to find that his home in Boston had been demolished. "This act of obliteration had been breathlessly swift," he wrote, "and if I had often seen how fast history could be made, I had doubtless never so felt that it could be unmade still faster." About the same time, the American writer Edith Wharton warned that if New York kept tearing down its great old buildings and putting up inferior replacements, one day it "would become as much a vanishing city as Atlantis or the lowest layer of Schliemann's Troy." In the October 23, 1869, issue of *Harper's Weekly*, a caption read: "In a city where new construction is constantly in progress, demolition of the old and the excavation of the site are a commonplace to which New Yorkers have long been accustomed."

Indeed, much of older New York's most treasured architecture—in SoHo, in parts of Greenwich Village, in Little Italy—has survived only by chance. At critical moments, the development climate simply was not vigorous enough to make it worthwhile to knock down the older buildings in those areas and put up new ones. In fact, we owe it to accident alone that some of the most valuable artifacts of our past have survived. But accidents are, by definition, sometime things. The unhappy truth is that of all the works of architecture in this country still standing in 1920 that we would now find worth saving for historic or aesthetic reasons, almost 90 percent have been wantonly destroyed. Today, preserving our built environment—not just the exteriors of structures but their interiors as well—is less a matter of chance. All about us, in New York, are buildings that have been saved, in large measure due to the dedicated work of the New York City Landmarks Preservation Commission, as well as the Municipal Art Society and the New York Landmarks Conservancy.

The emergence of the New York City Landmarks Preservation Commission came about as the result of years of work by concerned citizens. Among them were members of two groups that helped to educate the public about the city's architectural heritage, the Municipal Art Society and the New York Community Trust, as well as lobbyists for such organizations as the Brooklyn Heights Association. Between the late 1950s and the mid-1960s, the city lost some of its finest architecture to one glass-and-steel tower after another in a building binge that threatened to wipe out whatever old and good structures remained. Public concern was so great that one of the leading practitioners of the International Style, the modernist architect Philip Johnson, joined other marching protesters to mourn the loss of Pennsylvania Station in 1963.

Other important buildings were lost during the same period, but it was Penn Station's destruction that accelerated the creation of the New York City Landmarks Preservation Commission. The original Pennsylvania Station, one of the acknowledged monuments of our century, was designed in 1910 by Charles Follen McKim of the preeminent architectural firm of McKim, Mead & White, and modeled after the Roman baths of Caracalla and the basilica of Constantine. "In our history there was never another building like Penn Station," wrote Philip Johnson. "It compares with the great cathedrals of Europe." In 1962 its fate was determined when the financially ailing Pennsylvania Railroad sold the air rights above the station to permit construction of a new Madison Square Garden (a building utterly lacking in distinction or quality). The fifty-two-year-old railroad station was torn down and replaced with a new, "smaller" one. What planners did not imagine at that time was that intercity and commuter rail service would bounce back and that, in fewer than twenty years, the new station would be impossibly congested. The current Penn Station facility has recently completed another in a long series of renovations to accommodate its 250,000 daily passengers. The result does not suffice at peak periods, and even at regular levels, traffic is impeded by accessways that do not work.

Preservationists, architects, and humanists were stunned that such a desecration could take place. By the time they had rallied to save the building, however, it was too late; no legal mechanism existed, nor was sufficient public pressure generated, to fight for its survival. "Until the first blows fell," wrote the *New York Times* on October 30, 1963, over a quarter-century ago, "no one was convinced that Penn Station really would be demolished or that New York would permit this monumental act of vandalism.

. . . Any city gets what it admires, will pay for, and ultimately deserves. Even when we had Penn Station, we couldn't afford to keep it clean. We want and deserve tin-can architecture in a tin-horn culture. And we will probably be judged not by the monuments we build but by those we have destroyed." In reply to mounting public criticism, the president of the Pennsylvania Railroad Company wrote a letter to the *New York Times* asking, "Does it make any sense to preserve a building merely as a 'monument'?" As Nathan Silver states in *Lost New York*, "The station was sacrificed through the application of real-estate logic that often dictates the demolition of the very building that makes an area desirable." The absurdity and the iconoclasm of the act were noted by many constituencies: how could a city as civilized and culturally oriented as New York permit the annihilation of one of its most important physical legacies?

Soon thereafter, the most important legislative and regulatory institution to preserve New York's built heritage was born: on April 19, 1965, Mayor Robert F. Wagner signed the bill that brought the New York City Landmarks Preservation Commission into existence. Over the last thirty-three years, the law has helped transform the process of preservation from a series of brushfire rescue operations into an integral part of city government. Despite the fact that a hundred cities were already ahead of it, having established preservation commissions by 1965, New York has since become the pacesetter in preservation work. By one estimate, New York has succeeded in designating at least three times as many landmarks and four times as many historic districts as fourteen major cities whose combined population is twice New York's.

Numbers, of course, cannot tell the whole story: it is neither feasible nor desirable to measure the success of the preservation effort merely by the number of old buildings that have been saved. Nor, for that matter, does it make sense to preserve structures by restricting their functions to what they had been in the past; the effect would be to create a city of mausoleums rather than functioning, evolving buildings that people actually use. With its mandate to conserve New York's architectural past, the Landmarks Preservation Commission is justifiably proud that it "has not wanted to make museums of all its historic treasures," but has vigorously promoted the recycling of carefully selected buildings instead. For example, at least five new uses were proposed for the Astor Library, but it was producer Joseph Papp's vision and imagination—in combination with the New York City landmarks preservation ordinance—that in the mid-1960s succeeded in saving the elegant structure from destruction and transformed it into the Joseph Papp Public Theater, a thriving cultural institution.

LANDMARKS AND THE DESIGNATION PROCESS

The New York City Landmarks Preservation Commission is charged with identifying and designating landmarks and with regulating their preservation. The identification of structures and sites is an important part of guarding New York City's rich past. Some sites represent events of historical significance, people's association with the city's history, or a certain style or period of architecture. Others are designated because they represent a way of life, a way of doing business, or a way of maintaining a community in an ever-changing world.

Of the 960,000 tax lots in the city, the roster of landmarks thus far numbers more than 20,300. Among these landmarks are banks, bridges, apartment houses, piers, theaters, streets, churches, factories, schools, cemeteries, parks, clubs, museums, office towers, and even trees. As of November 1997, this includes more than 1,054 exteriors, 70 historic districts (which themselves include more than 19,000 sites), 100 interiors, and 9 scenic landmarks. The vast majority of both landmarks and districts is in Manhattan: 752 landmarks and 41 districts. Brooklyn has 127 landmarks and 16 districts; The Bronx has 62 landmarks and 8 districts; Staten Island has 98 landmarks and 2 districts; while Queens has 43 landmarks and 3 districts. This may sound like a great deal; actually it accounts for approximately 2 percent of the property in New York City. *The Landmarks of New York III* contains 76 new individually designated entries—buildings that have been designated between December 1992 and July 1997. There are also 11 new historic districts, 1 new historic district extension, and 15 new interiors; there have been no new scenic landmarks designated.

What makes a "landmark" a landmark? The New York City Landmarks Preservation Commission law defines a landmark as a structure at least thirty years old that has "a special character or special historical or aesthetic interest or value as part of the development, heritage or cultural characteristics of the city, state or nation." The chief criterion for designating landmarks is architectural integrity; approximately 6 percent have been designated for their historical significance. Buildings and scenic landmarks are also designated for cultural reasons, such as associations with celebrated people or events. The law further states:

It is hereby declared as a matter of public policy that the protection, enhancement, perpetuation and use of improvements and landscape features of special character or special historical or aesthetic interest or value is a public necessity and is required in the interest of the health, prosperity, safety and welfare of the people. The purpose is to effect and accomplish the protection, enhancement and perpetuation of such improvements and landscape features and of districts which represent or reflect elements of the city's cultural, social, economic, political and architectural history; safeguard the city's historic, aesthetic and cultural heritage; stabilize and improve property values; foster civic pride in the beauty and noble accomplishments of the past; protect and enhance the city's attractions to tourists and visitors and the support and stimulus to business and industry; strengthen the economy of the city; promote the use of historical districts, landmarks, interior landmarks, and scenic landmarks for the education, pleasure and welfare of the city.

An interior landmark is defined as the interior of a structure, in whole or part, that is customarily open and accessible to the public and that has special qualities of design. Some examples include the Bartow-Pell Mansion in The Bronx, the Woolworth Building in Manhattan, and the Gage & Tollner restaurant in Brooklyn. The law prohibits the designation of the interiors of places of worship.

A scenic landmark is defined as a landscape feature that is of special character or historical or aesthetic interest and is at least thirty years old. It must also be situated on city-owned property. Some examples include all of Central Park, Verdi Square on Broadway and 73rd Street, and Prospect Park in Brooklyn.

Distinct from individual landmarks, a historic district is an area that has a special character or special historical or aesthetic interest representing one or more architectural styles or periods and that constitutes a distinct section of the city. For example, the Charlton-King-Vandam Historic District, on the site of what was once Aaron Burr's estate, Richmond Hill, contains fine Federal and Greek Revival houses. The St. Mark's Historic District, on land that was Peter Stuyvesant's, contains very early Federal and fine Anglo-Italianate row houses. The Ladies' Mile Historic District, the fashion center of New York's Gilded Age, had a concentration of the city's first department stores, including Lord & Taylor, B. Altman & Co., and Tiffany & Co. Its best-known residents included Edith Wharton, Isabella Stewart Gardner, Samuel F. B. Morse, and Emily Post.

The Landmarks Preservation Commission consists by law of eleven members, one of whom is now a full-time paid chairman. The law states that the Commission is required to include at least one resident of each borough, three architects, one historian, one realtor, and one city planner or landscape architect. Members are appointed by the mayor for three-year terms, and the chairman and vice-chairman are selected at the pleasure of the mayor from among the commissioners. There has been an extraordinary continuity of informed and courageous leadership in the last thirty-three years, thanks to the five men and two women who have chaired the Commission: Geoffrey Platt (1965–68); Harmon Goldstone (1968–73); Beverly Moss Spatt (1974–78); Kent Barwick (1978–83); Gene Norman (1983–89, the first full-time paid commissioner); David F. M. Todd (1989–90); Laurie Beckelman (1990–94); and Jennifer Raab (1994 to the present). The Commission has enjoyed the support of the elected leaders of New York over the last two and a half decades: Mayors Wagner, Lindsay, Beame, Koch, Dinkins, and Giuliani.

The commissioners are assisted by a full-time, paid professional staff, including researchers, historians, lawyers, administrators, and secretaries. While in 1990 the staff had been comprised of 79 persons, by the summer of 1992, due to budget cuts, it was reduced to 57, a decrease of more than 20 percent. Over the same period, the workload increased by more than 200 percent. The number of applications has risen dramatically, from 500 in 1981 to 2,000 in 1986. By 1992 there were almost 4,000 applications annually. To further offset budget cuts, the City's Office of Management and Budget mandated that the Commission establish a schedule of fees for applications and permits. The proposed fees ranged from $25 to $1,500 and would have fractured the broad public support and cooperation needed for landmark regulation. After widespread and vehement public disapproval, the Commission unanimously rejected the proposal on March 3, 1992.

The work of the Commission is divided into three main functions: 1) to identify; 2) to designate; and 3) to regulate. The identification function consists of research—determining the histories of individual buildings—as well as a survey, which is an inventory of all the building lots in the city's five boroughs. The regulation and preservation function consists of considering and approving or disapproving changes to already designated landmark structures. For the first decade of its existence, from 1965 to 1974, public hearings for designations were held every six months and the Commission designated clearly important and obvious architectural works. In 1974, its jurisdiction was extended to include scenic and interior landmarks, which necessitated more frequent designation hearings. Over the last fifteen years or so, the emphasis of the Commission has shifted away from designation to preservation and regulation and, most important, to the determination of appropriateness of new and extended construction on landmark sites—thus influencing land development in New York City. Recommendations that the Commission establish preservation policy statements and guidelines that address the character of a specific historic district as well as individual building elements have been successfully implemented (for example, the Riverdale Guidelines and the Window Guidelines). These regulations have not only provided the public with clear directions for applications but have expedited the Commission's regulatory process.

In New York City, a landmark achieves official designation only after a process that was deliberately designed to be as painstaking and exhaustive as possible. The five stages of the designation process are: 1) identification; 2) evaluation and prioritization; 3) calendaring; 4) public hearing and further research; 5) designation.

Six sources are relied upon for identification: the general public; property owners; Commission staff; commissioners; public officials; and the survey of properties conducted by the Commission. The survey is considered the most important source. Regardless of who proposes a building, the Commission staff undertakes to evaluate its significance, which often involves a field visit, photographs, and research. The staff presents its findings, with its recommendations of buildings to be considered, to the commissioners in a public executive session, and the Commission decides which buildings should be researched further. Whenever possible, the commissioners visit those buildings or sites that are advanced for further consideration. At a subsequent public executive session, they vote on which buildings to calendar for a public hearing held at City Hall, usually six to eight weeks later. A letter of notification advising of this hearing is sent to the owner, to community boards, to public officials, and to the Buildings Department; printed calendars are mailed to the same people and those members of the general public on the Commission's mailing list.

At the City Hall public hearing, the Commission decides whether to: 1) close the hearing and the record, and then act; 2) take no action until the record closes at a later meeting; or 3) continue the hearing until a later date. A decision is not usually made at this public hearing. Rather, staff members are instructed to continue research and report back with their findings. Commissioners often hear the owner's point of view and receive additional information from any other sources that testify. Assuming the building or site is still proceeding toward landmark status, all of the research is then summarized in a draft of a designation report prepared by the research department and discussed by the Commission at a later public executive session. A vote is then taken at this session; to declare the proposed site a landmark, six affirmative votes are needed, no matter how many (or few) of the Commission's eleven members are present. Once the vote to designate is taken, a building is protected; all subsequent changes to it must be approved by the Commission before a building permit may be issued.

In recent years, the importance of the public hearing process has gradually eroded. Since 1994, there have been sixty-four sites proposed, of which all but two were designated. It seems clear that sites with potential to generate long and acrimonious debate, and which are not certain to be designated, are not calendared for public hearing. This results in what appears to be a commendable success rate for the Landmarks Preservation Commission's designation process, and it may have the welcome effect of abbreviating what sometimes feels like the endless process of public review, but it also stifles debate and raises questions about the value of public hearings. Also, there is the risk that a site that deserves landmark status may not be heard if the owner objects, and therefore not be designated in a timely manner. If calendaring a site for public hearing is tantamount to designation, then the public is effectively denied full access to the process, and many important decisions are limited to city officials, property owners, and/or real-estate developers. By implicitly giving political and economic issues higher priority than preservation concerns, a situation is created that threatens to undermine historical preservation in New York City.

A public hearing, however, is by no means the end of the approval process. Up until the 1989 revision of the Landmarks Preservation Commission's charter, the Board of Estimate was the final decision-maker on designations. Recognizing that the validity of a designation is more readily defended in any litigation if it is approved by an elected legislative body, the charter revision made the Board of Estimate defunct, and its role in the landmark designation process was given to the City Council. To handle these new responsibilities the Council created a fifteen-member Land Use Committee with three separate subcommittees: Landmarks and Zoning, Franchises, and Siting Approval. In addition, all landmarks decisions are required to go through a public committee process, as are any other land use matters.

Thus, the final steps in the current designation process are as follows: after designation, the Landmarks Preservation Commission must file reports with the Department of Buildings, the City Planning Commission (CPC), the Board of Standards and Appeals, the Fire and Health Departments, and the City Council. The CPC then submits to the City Council a report on the designation and its potential impact, if any, on the zoning resolutions, projected public improvements, and plans for development, growth, improvement, or renewal of the area involved. (In the case of a historic district designation, the CPC also holds a public hearing.) Next commences a 120-day period during which the City Council may, by majority vote, either approve, modify, or disapprove a designation. Its subcommittees hold hearings and make recommendations to the Land Use Committee, which in turn refers a resolution or a designation to the full Council for a vote. Finally, the vote is filed with the mayor, and the designation—as modified by the City Council—becomes final unless disapproved by the mayor within five days. (A mayoral veto may be overridden by two-thirds vote of the Council.)

Only rarely has either the Board of Estimate or the City Council rejected or amended landmark designations in the past; the Commission attributes the limited number of denials to its careful process of review and to detailed discussions with owners before a designation is made. There are, of course, a few exceptions: in June 1991 the Council did overturn the designation of Dvořák House, home to the renowned Czech composer Antonín Dvořák when he wrote the *New York* Symphony in the 1880s. The house's 1991 owner, Beth Israel Medical Center, opposed the designation. The hospital wanted to tear it down in order to build an AIDS hospice. Interestingly, many AIDS activists opposed the hospital's plans—and supported the designation—claiming that the proposed facility would be substandard. Nonetheless, the designation was overturned. In response to the overwhelming public demand for a memorial to the composer, East 17th Street between First and Second avenues was co-named Dvořák Place. The Council also slightly modified the Tribeca West Historic District during its review of that designation in September 1991. More recently, in September 1992 the designation of the former Jamaica Savings Bank in Queens was overturned, and the landmark site of the former Knickerbocker Field Club was rescinded after the building was badly damaged in a fire and subsequently demolished.

On the average, the Commission holds hearings on about 60 to 100 individual buildings or sites a year, writes up to 50 reports, reviews about 3,500 applications for requested architectural changes in already designated buildings (which may range from the repair of door moldings in Brooklyn Heights to the construction of office towers in Manhattan), and receives and reviews requests from the public to designate approximately 100 new individual landmarks, and several historic districts.

Once a building or site is designated, it is subject to specific laws and protected against any further changes without public review. The owner must consult with the Commission to have any proposed changes approved. Moreover, plans for changes must take into account not only the owner's specific needs but also the retention of the architectural and/or historical integrity of the building/site and its surroundings. How the modified building or site may be used is not within the purview of the Commission. When a change is approved, the Commission issues a Certificate of Appropriateness and the owner is then permitted to proceed with the work. If an owner wishes to demolish a landmark, there are provisions in the law that ensure his or her right to claim economic hardship; the law also gives the Commission a specific time frame in which to seek a feasible solution. In the history of the Commission, six landmarks have been demolished, ten individual designations rejected by the Board of Estimate, and four landmarks rescinded.

A concern in recent years has been the decline in the overall quality and condition of proposed designations, and a trend toward what appears to be equivocal or politicized "evenhandedness" of landmark distribution. Structures and districts of sometimes questionable or dubious architectural significance outside of Manhattan and in nonwhite areas are designated, while fine architectural examples may be ignored. Recent individual designations of wood-framed workers' housing on Staten Island; Lewis Latimer's unexceptional, modest, and relocated house in Queens; and the much-renovated and currently stripped-down house at 12 West 129th Street in Harlem reflect this trend. Similarly, recent district designations primarily fall into two categories: neighborhoods with sociological or historical importance (including districts in the South Bronx and Queens), and disputed areas which the Commission wants a hand in administering (including Ellis and Governors Islands Historic Districts, the African Burial Ground/the Commons Historic District, and the numerous individual designations in the Financial District). Although many of these items deserve some sort of protection, it is not readily apparent that they merit landmark status.

Of the sixty-two sites that the Commission has designated since 1994, more than half of them were drawn from the backlog of items that had not been designated previously, either because they were too controversial or of questionable merit. The Landmarks Preservation Commission has been in existence since 1965, and there is a body of opinion that holds that nearly all of the truly important, historic, and iconic New York City structures and spaces (excepting those constructed in the last thirty years) have already been designated. The Commission also has to consider that many potential designations may be of questionable merit or in poor repair, and thus no longer of "landmark quality," including many buildings of communal importance. One possible solution to several of these problems would be to expand the scope of landmark purview by introducing an additional category that reflects neighborhood "status:" "designation of cultural/historical importance" or "special design district," for example. A new category could allow structures such as the numerous turn-of-the-century lower Manhattan office towers and the middle- and low-income housing districts in The Bronx and Queens to be identified as important and thus worthy of preservation, without conferring on them landmark status which they may or may not merit. Such a category could facilitate preservation efforts and be responsive to community needs.

COMPETING INTERESTS: PRESERVATIONISTS, DEVELOPERS, OWNERS, AND THE COURTS

As preservation activity has grown, so has resistance from some owners and real-estate developers who objected to the often stringent limitations that the law was increasingly placing on land use. But a milestone court decision more than a decade ago gave tremendous impetus to further preservation efforts by endorsing such limitations. The case grew out of efforts by the Penn Central Transportation Co. to abolish the restrictions put on landmark buildings and property owners in New York City. Penn Central sought to construct a high-rise office tower above Grand Central Station. In 1978, the U.S. Supreme Court affirmed the designation of the terminal as a landmark, noting that cities had the right to enhance their quality of life by preserving aesthetic features.

In 1992 a ruling by the Appellate Division of the Supreme Court in Manhattan signified that landmark designations cannot be compromised for political reasons. Peter S. Kalikow, owner of the *New York Post*, planned to replace four of the fourteen designated City and Suburban Homes Company York Avenue Estate buildings with a very large apartment tower. Four months after they were designated (April 1990), the Board of Estimate stripped the four easternmost buildings of their designation to accommodate Mr. Kalikow's building plans, and in August of the following year, the board's decision was upheld by the New York Supreme Court, thus setting a precedent of negotiating designations that, it was feared, could be perpetuated by the City Council. In overturning the ruling, the appellate court sent a clear message affirming landmark designation as a process with reason and integrity, not one to be diluted to satisfy the competing political demands of powerful landowners. The Commission designated the complex—the largest low-income housing project in the world at the time it was built, 1901–13—as a "landmark site" instead of fourteen individual buildings. The position that a single element of the complex should on its own be considered worthy of designation as a landmark for its historical, architectural, cultural, and aesthetic value is inherently inconsistent. On July 1, 1992, Chemical Bank began foreclosure on ten of the buildings at that site owned by Mr. Kalikow.

In another case, the Supreme Court's action over St. Bartholomew's landmark appeal enhanced the credibility of preservation laws across the country. St. Bartholomew's had wanted to raze its community house and build a forty-seven-story, glass-walled office building in its place, saying that the church would lose more than $100 million in property value if it could not build the office tower. The long battle ended four years later, March 4, 1991, when the Supreme Court refused to hear the church's challenge to the designation of the church complex as a landmark.

Though these battles were won, others have been less successful. In the 1980s, the processes and procedures of the Landmarks Preservation Commission were put to the test in the Coty-Rizzoli designation, Bryant Park's renovation, and Grand Central Terminal's office tower at 383 Madison Avenue, to mention but a few controversies. The debate continues to rage over the best way to keep worthy buildings from falling victim to the demolition crews before the Commission can designate them.

The central question is how we can preserve the past without jeopardizing a vital future for a vibrant city. Simply stated, developers argue that the Commission process interferes with the laissez-faire workings of the market; they contend that many opportunities are lost because of the Commission's overly rigorous scrutiny. Property owners, for their part, argue against landmark restrictions and resent the lack of freedom to do as they please with their structures. Preservationists must strike a balance between saving the public patrimony and yielding to the imperatives of progress.

As a further assistance to significant—and imperiled—landmark buildings, the Department of City Planning recently proposed the Grand Central Subdistrict in order to expand design opportunities in the area of Grand Central Station, which is a designated landmark. This proposal offers a more flexible system of distributing the terminal's unused air rights than does current zoning and takes measures to protect and enhance the distinctive character of the neighborhood.

Francis Bacon wrote that "the monuments of wit survive the monuments of power." Unfortunately, when "wit" is a charming eighteenth-century frame house that lends an air of scale and civility to an already crowded neighborhood, and when "power" is a block-square behemoth that promises to generate thousands of jobs and millions in sales and property taxes, Bacon's dictum is placed in jeopardy. The looming fate of Broadway's theaters was a case in point. They had been under increasing pressure for years as large office towers, whose construction was made possible by a 1982 revision of the zoning law that permits larger buildings on the West Side, sprang up in the area. The loss of older buildings was gradual and occurred in relative silence until 1982. In that year, the Morosco and Helen Hayes, two of the district's most beloved older theaters, were demolished to make way for the Marriott Marquis Hotel. Those theaters are sometimes referred to as "sacrificial lambs," for their demolition galvanized support for saving the ones that remained. What should have been obvious all along became clear only belatedly: the more than forty older theaters that still stand in the Broadway district represent the heart and soul of the American theater; they are cultural resources without peer. Between November 1987 and January 1988, after protracted hearings and negotiations, the exterior, interior, or both of twenty-eight theaters were designated. Upon their designation, the Broadway theater owners filed a lawsuit to overturn the designation of twenty-two of these playhouses. Their efforts finally concluded on May 27, 1992, when the U.S. Supreme Court refused to hear their case. In turning back the owners' challenge without comment, the high court effectively let stand a 1991 ruling by a New York State appeals court that upheld the designation. This case definitively showed that the designations by the New York City Commission could survive judicial scrutiny. According to Jack Goldstein, director of Save the Theaters, of the forty-four extant theaters, only those protected by landmark laws are expected to survive the down cycles that have always plagued the commercial theater business.

The effect of landmark designation on the value and use of properties owned by nonprofit and religious institutions has also become a contentious issue in recent years. These groups are often housed in older, architecturally distinctive structures. Since designation can prohibit demolition and redevelopment to a higher intensity of use, leaders of these groups have charged that designation compels them to remain in buildings that are no longer suitable to their needs—that are, in short, no longer economically viable. In response, preservationists claim that the suitability of property to an organization's needs has little bearing on designation. But they acknowledge that problems can indeed arise and, in some instances, preservation advocates have devised provisions within the designation system to offer necessary relief. The Hardship Panel, which is independent of the Commission, was created in 1991 to review denials of hardship applications to nonprofit institutions by the Landmarks Preservation Commission. The Panel, made up of five City Council members appointed by the mayor, will uphold the Commission's decision unless it finds that the decision is not supported on a reasonable or rational basis. After finding owner hardship, the Commission, as an alternative to demolition, can look for a new owner to alleviate the burden on the present owner. To date there have been no appointments to the Hardship Panel.

Many of the city's religious properties are the work of America's finest architects, constructed at a time when craftsmanship was at its height. Today, many of these properties face an uncertain future due not only to changing demographic patterns and evolving family and religious practices, but also to the high maintenance costs of older structures. Deferred maintenance is a problem common to both thriving houses of worship and those with dwindling congregations. Rising land values and, in some cases, development pressures further endanger the survival of these buildings and sites. Many institutions wish to preserve their properties, but restoration work is costly, and financial and technical resources are limited.

Fortunately, community preservation groups are emerging that seek to restore and revive older structures that can no longer meet their expenses. The restoration of the Eldridge Street Synagogue on the Lower East Side by a community group and the S.O.U.L. project for the Universalist Church on Central Park West at 76th Street have helped to encourage others to restore religious structures. These and similar efforts stand as a clear and positive response to all that the St. Bartholomew's controversy has come to symbolize.

It was, however, the partial destruction of the Willkie Memorial Building at 20 West 40th Street that was the catalyst for the most recent change in the procedures for landmark designation. The structure, a beautiful building by the architect Henry J. Hardenbergh (who also designed the Dakota Apartments, the Art Students League Building, and the Plaza Hotel), was identified by the Commission staff as being of landmark quality but was never scheduled for formal consideration. While the Willkie Building stood unprotected, one Friday night in February 1985 a work permit went out from the Buildings Department. Scaffolding went up, work commenced immediately, and by Monday, without any notice ever having been given to the Commission, the elaborate stone moldings and carvings on the facade had been stripped away—and the building's architectural beauty permanently lost.

At about the same time, the Commission designated the Coty and Rizzoli buildings on Fifth Avenue, after learning that a developer planned to replace them with a forty-four-story office and residential tower. The Commission's action, however, angered the real-estate community, and Mayor Koch established the Cooper Committee in February 1985 to review the concerns of owners, developers, and preservationists with the city's landmarks designation process. The Cooper Committee, a five-member group chaired by Alexander Cooper, an architect and planner, was directed to pay particular attention to the objectives of the landmarks law, the calendaring procedures of the Landmarks Preservation Commission, the Building Department's procedures for issuing permits in connection with structures that may be of landmark quality, and communications between the Buildings Department and the Commission.

The resulting procedural recommendations focused on two concerns: that the landmark designation process include reasonable time limits for action by the Commission, in order to make the development process more predictable; and that buildings being considered for designation be protected from last-minute stripping, damage, or demolition before the Commission could, within newly prescribed time limits, decide whether to designate.

The Cooper Committee also suggested that the Commission be given enough money to accelerate its citywide survey and establish a new category, a "protected buildings list" of potential designations. Such a list could alleviate the antagonisms between developers and preservationists and possibly save many structures from untimely disaster. The owner of a building on this list would have to go before the Commission for approval to renovate or demolish. A number of the recommendations of the Cooper Committee have been adopted, including the establishment of the Commission as a separate agency, a reduction in the designation process time frame, and published rules and guidelines.

On May 12, 1988, Mayor Koch announced a series of initiatives that he believed would enhance the ability of the Commission to protect potential landmark buildings before destructive alterations could occur. Discussed at public hearings on June 30, 1988, some of these proposals allowed the Commission to create large geographic "study areas;" buildings included within them would come under the jurisdiction of the Commission for the term of one year. Study areas would be established where there are structures of special historic or aesthetic interest whose continued survival might be threatened by the potential for development. The proposal states that after one year, the Commission would compile a list of protected buildings from which individual structures to be considered for designation would be drawn. After the one-year period, owners would have the right to request a determination of a building's landmark status, to which the Commission would have to respond within ninety days. On the preservation side, these proposals are meant to enable the Landmarks Preservation Commission to study a predetermined area systematically, and to ensure through civil and legal penalties that no inappropriate alteration or demolition can occur in that area during the study period. On the development side, once the protected list is published, owners will know whether their property is being considered for landmark status.

During the years of its existence numerous proposals to strengthen, clarify, and sometimes limit the landmarks law have emerged. Thus far, the only change in the law occurred in 1974, when the Commission was empowered to designate individual scenic and interior landmarks, and to amplify its authority to designate on a regular, nonrestricted basis. Further proposals to strengthen the Landmarks Preservation Commission emerged from the Historic City Commission (sometimes known as the Conklin Commission) in the fall of 1988. On July 1, 1990, the Landmarks Preservation Commission was separated administratively from the Department of Parks and became an independent mayoral agency of the City of New York. The need for increased staffing and funding was partially addressed upon the Commission's separation, but subsequent budget cuts have rolled back resources to the lowest level in the past ten years.

ADAPTIVE REUSE

Preservation was long seen as an "elitist" concern—something best left to ladies' lunches and the organizers of walking tours. No longer. Never before in modern history have so many people been aware of and involved in the design of the places where they live and work as they struggle with the forces of change. Thanks to this awareness, choice is now available: it is no longer a given that an older building or entire neighborhood will be razed for the construction of a huge, new monolith—a monument of power, as Bacon would put it. The technique of adaptive reuse—recycling old buildings to different uses from the ones for which they were originally intended—has made a practical means of preservation available to everyone.

Changes in the federal tax code also make recycling economical. Chief among the incentives that now exist are tax credits for restoring landmarks, and direct appropriations to attract developers and investors. By means of such incentives, historic rehabilitation has been placed on an equal footing with new construction. It is now economically feasible through recycling to prolong the usefulness of buildings that otherwise would suffer continuing decline or demolition.

The first of the federal incentives was included in the Tax Reform Act of 1976, which provided five-year amortization of costs for projects certified as appropriate historic rehabilitations. The 1978 Revenue Act added a provision allowing a 10 percent investment tax credit for certain rehabilitation costs. The Economic Recovery Act of 1981 repealed the earlier incentives and instituted a 25 percent investment tax credit for certified historic rehabilitation. Even under the 1986 Tax Reform Act, which eliminated many tax credits, substantial incentives were retained for historic rehabilitation work.

Though the 25 percent investment credit was cut to 20 percent and abolished for those with incomes exceeding $250,000, the tax code still provides a substantial incentive to those who are interested in undertaking rehab work. Together, the various tax incentives have triggered private investment whose public benefits—in housing, new jobs, and increased property, sales, and income taxes—far outweigh the public cost. Perhaps the greatest benefit has been to enhance the stability of neighborhoods, and in some cases to make possible their survival.

New York City gave a striking demonstration in the 1970s of just how well incentives can work. A nationwide economic recession and an even worse situation on the local level had the city reeling. At that time the city enacted its J–51 legislation, designed to offer significant incentives so that builders, who were doing very little new construction, would be encouraged to reclaim old structures. Wisely, and immediately, the development community pounced on J–51 and put it to excellent use. Suddenly scores of loft buildings and tin-ceilinged interiors in SoHo, Tribeca, Chelsea, and elsewhere were being rehabilitated and recycled into artists' apartments or shops or restaurants. Much of this rehab work had an unintended or at least unforeseen consequence: the process we now know as gentrification, the unfortunate effect of which has often been to squeeze out of changing neighborhoods poorer residents and mom-and-pop stores whose longtime operators could no longer afford the sky-high rents that were being charged.

THE ARCHITECTURE OF NEW YORK CITY

Through the accomplishments of several organizations, primarily the New York City Landmarks Preservation Commission, we have learned to revere and guard our past by carefully and systematically conferring landmark status on deserving structures. Many architectural assets have been restored to their original state, and many old buildings have been recycled to serve new, vital functions. This has had a pronounced and beneficial influence on the attitudes of contemporary architects, who are now faced with the challenge of building alongside older structures. Rather than ignoring the existing context, much contemporary design celebrates the historic tapestry of our city and incorporates in its scheme many historic elements and allusions.

And what a brilliant, richly textured tapestry New York is! The city's architecture is the richest in the entire country with respect to the diversity of buildings. There are farmhouses, brownstones, cast-iron buildings, Art Deco towers, glass-and-steel skyscrapers. One can journey to the boroughs and travel back in history: from the early-nineteenth-century wood-frame houses of Brooklyn's Hunterfly Road, to the late-nineteenth-century brownstones of Longwood in the Bronx, to the early-twentieth-century attached brick row houses in Ridgewood, Queens. Then there are the better-known structures that have come to symbolize New York: the great Flatiron Building standing in majestic isolation at the corner of Fifth Avenue and 23rd Street, the Dakota Apartments at Central Park West and 72nd Street, the Empire State Building, the Chrysler Building, the Statue of Liberty, St. Patrick's Cathedral, Rockefeller Center.

New York is also the richest in the diversity of styles that have survived three hundred and fifty years of construction and demolition: Federal, Georgian, Greek and Gothic Revival, Italianate and French-inspired, Victorian, International, Post-Modern, and Post-Post-Modern. Between 1830 and 1930, more architectural styles were employed in New York than at any other place or point in history. It was a period of rapid growth and change due to the technological, economic, and ideological revolutions that were transforming America from a spread-out, agricultural society to a highly urbanized, industrial one. Although its roots still reached back to Europe, the new republic spent a century putting down indigenous ones. Bursting with the innocence and impatience of youth, the new nation was willing and eager to try anything. In architecture, styles such as the Greek Revival, Gothic Revival, and Italianate came and went as swiftly as did fashions in clothing. Styles were revived, abandoned, revived again. Sometimes a building's appearance changed in mid-construction because a new look had become fashionable overnight.

Different building periods have lent New York its great variety of colors and forms, and within a single block we may encounter many styles, shapes, and textures. For the first two centuries of the city's history, beginning with the steep-roofed houses of the founding Dutch, New York was characterized by thousands of beautiful red-brick buildings and farmhouses, some of which survive today. In the middle of the nineteenth century, a brownish-violet coating seemed to descend like a cloak over everything: "brownstone," a soft, fine-grained sandstone easily shaped into the pedestals and oriels, consoles, and ornamental touches that the Italianate style of the period demanded. In *Things As They Are In America*, William Chambers, the Edinburgh publisher of *Chambers' Encyclopedia*, said this about the New York of 1853: "Wherever any of [the] older brick edifices have been removed, their place has been supplied by tenements built of brown sandstone; and it may be said that at present New York is in process of being renewed by this species of structure." The choice of brownstone for cladding the grandiose Vanderbilt mansions along Fifth Avenue (built from 1880 to 1884 and since demolished) finally confirmed the material's supremacy. By the 1880s, New York had become a red-and-brown city, as Bath was cream and Jerusalem gold.

Architecturally, cast-iron construction, whose development was impelled by the growth of industry and manufacturing in the city, represented one of the most important building innovations of the nineteenth century and was a giant step toward modern skyscraper construction. The building type was modeled after the Italian Renaissance–style palazzo, a spacious, rectangular building of several stories, suited to a functional commercial structure.

While the great European cities were showplaces for royalty and pageantry, New York was always a merchants' city. By the late nineteenth century, however, the successful merchants had formed a distinctly American aristocracy of their own. They had the money and the manners. Now they wanted their city to be as grand as any in Europe. So one by one, they hired the finest architects of their time and, in the sumptuous style of the day, they built palaces befitting their empires. The district known as Ladies' Mile, from Union Square to the old Madison Square, exemplifies this trend, as do some surviving structures along Fifth Avenue as far north as the nineties.

Perhaps it is the towering skyscrapers of the 1920s and 1930s, replete with dramatic Art Deco adornment, that embody "classic" New York: the Empire State Building, Rockefeller Center, the Chrysler Building. The post–World War II years brought the glass curtain walls and sleek boxes that line the midtown avenues, the most distinguished example being Ludwig Mies van der Rohe's Seagram Building of 1958. By the twenty-first century, who knows? Perhaps these are the structures that will be considered "classic" as New York, in its time-honored fashion, replaces them with even newer styles.

THE LANDMARKS PRESERVATION COMMISSION:
LIMITED RESOURCES AND AN OVERBURDENED STAFF

On May 7, 1987, I appeared before the Charter Review Commission and issued a call for "an act of civic maturity"—namely, that Section 2204 of the New York City Charter be amended to put several changes into effect. During my testimony, I noted that over the Landmarks Preservation Commission's twenty-two-year existence, "the workload of the agency has grown enormously. Not only is the Commission responsible for research, public review, and designation of new city landmarks, but also for review and approval of applications to alter previously designated properties. . . . The number of applications has risen dramatically from about 600 five years ago to 1,000 last year and to more than 2,000 in the current year. The Commission must also review applications for new construction in historic districts, for demolition, and for hardship; assess the impact of public projects on landmark properties; advise on changes to city-owned landmarks; and approve proposals to transfer development rights from landmark sites." And, I noted, there is more, including the citywide survey of property to identify possible future designations, two grant programs, and the continual development of policies and guidelines for preservation.

"Given the range and scope of its activities," I continued, "the Commission at this time is not adequately equipped, either structurally or economically, with the resources necessary to carry out its appointed tasks. In addition, officially establishing the Commission as a separate municipal body, and removing it from under the jurisdiction of the Department of Parks and Recreation, will bring the Commission more in line with the structure of other city agencies. (In keeping with this change we would hope that in the future, the Commission's growing responsibilities will also be recognized with an increase in its budget that will allow for adequate staffing and operations.)"

The need for such changes was all too clear. For the Landmarks Preservation Commission's unpaid, volunteer appointees, as I testified, the "demanding workload is not compatible with career responsibilities and is, in fact, unfair to those who care deeply about our city." I concluded: "These are necessary steps if the Commission is to be endowed with the resources, both professional and financial, that will enable it to carry out its mandate to preserve and protect our city's landmark buildings and districts. This proposed charter amendment is past due. It will permit our city to remain in the vanguard of the challenge to enhance the urban texture and further economic progress."

Ten years later, these issues persist, and low levels of funding continue to hinder the Commission. Historic districts become problematic because violations within them are frequent. This is also true, to a lesser degree, of individual designations. Owners often make changes, ranging from repainting or making desirable renovations to fully replacing facades or even demolishing structures, without consulting the Commission. And while the Commission can issue a violation after the fact, it has no mechanism to discover, prevent, or punish changes. So long as the Commission is limited by a lack of effective regulation, a modest budget, and a small staff, it cannot hope to effectively ensure the integrity of historic districts and landmark sites. This further undermines efforts toward historic preservation.

What is remarkable is how much the Landmarks Preservation Commission has been able to accomplish since 1965 with its severely limited resources and its overburdened staff. Thanks to the workings of the often-embattled Commission, it is no longer easily or entirely possible to destroy great works of architecture. The Commission has allowed for the delicate equilibrium that must exist between new and old, between economics and aesthetics, between progress and history.

At a time when humankind's massive damage to the planet—fuel spills, oil fires, chemical pollution, and deforestation—seems overwhelming, and global thinking is the order of the day, writer and avid gardener Michael Pollan offers some simple, almost archaic advice: "The place to start repairing our relationship with nature is in our backyard. Think locally, act locally, and the global will take care of itself." Preserving historic landmarks has many virtues. In some cases—but not all, of course—it restores to commercial viability properties that had been falling into disuse and disrepair. Preservation ensures variety. It provides a sense of continuity. It guarantees access to light and air.

Cities are most interesting when they combine the new with the old, the traditional with the avant-garde. New York juxtaposes high rises with church spires, crammed spaces with green vistas, streets of shops with streets of houses, glass-and-steel towers with cast-iron buildings or houses of brick and timber. The older buildings of our cities give us the possibility of visualizing the past, for they are, in a very real sense, time capsules. The capitol of Virginia in Richmond brings Robert E. Lee to life, Louis XIV is best understood amid the carefully calculated grandeur of Versailles, the remnants of the Parthenon give voice to Demosthenes. The original Pennsylvania Station is gone, as are the Bartholdi Hotel and the Atheneum Club building and the old Metropolitan Opera House. No generation has the right to make the city a monotonous monument to a single moment. Daily living was as varied in the past three centuries as it is for us in the closing years of the twentieth century. And our schools, churches, and commercial structures testify to this diversity and remind us where we have been and how far we have come in a few hundred years. The architecture of New York must be saved so that future generations will have the chance to experience the magic of strolling down Fifth Avenue to Madison Square, and stepping into the past. In the many buildings, parks, and districts that survive in New York City and are recorded in this book, we can see the history of the city and its architecture. We see the untouchable past with the unspoken beginning, new spires rising alongside the old.

THE THIRD EDITION OF *THE LANDMARKS OF NEW YORK*

This book tries to give a brief indication of the history and significance of each of the designated properties in New York City through July 1997. The text has been based in part on the designation reports of the Landmarks Preservation Commission. Initially, my assistants and I systematically gathered and catalogued each report. Next we communicated, orally and in writing, with property owners, city officials, historical societies, architects, preservationists, and citizens, requesting historical and anecdotal material. Then began the elaborate process of documenting the designated landmarks: cross-checking and authenticating the historical information, architectural descriptions, photographs, and fresh anecdotal material that we had gathered about each of them. The exhaustive research involved interviews, conversations, and digging in archives so that each building or site would be presented with its own story, its own intricate history. We not only wrote to every individual landmark owner/occupant to gather information, but all of them were sent follow-up letters as well. Exhaustive and repeated efforts to verify the accuracy of the material were made. This was not possible in every instance. Therefore, it is our hope that if you have, or are aware of, verifiable data, or emendations, that relate to any of these landmarks, you will share them with us. We hope to continue our researches and incorporate appropriate changes in future editions of this work. In an attempt to unfold New York's architectural history, the landmarks in this book have been organized chronologically, by date of construction. In several instances, to accommodate all of the material, the order is not strictly followed.

Hundreds of responses came back, many of them detailed and filled with fresh verifiable information. The letters show the depth of people's concern about the places in which they live and work. Among the proud responses was one from a woman who wrote that her house had been in her family for more than five generations. "I have the deed attesting to such fact," she said, "and have had it framed." A man wrote that he has lived in his house for some thirty years and had worked there for some fifteen years before that with his father-in-law, who bought it in 1928. "It's my home in a very meaningful sense," he wrote with pride. A man who has owned a house in Greenwich Village since 1937 wrote that the structure "was supposed to be an example of Greek Revival architecture, but it's hard to see exactly why," since it has "no real pillars!" The present owner of one of the houses that William Rhinelander built in the nineteenth century for his family from 146 to 156 East 89th Street wrote of the "nightmare aspects" of such a cozy grouping: "Five daughters-in-law and parents cheek-by-jowl sounds pretty dismal."

Such letters convinced me that there is a far higher level of citizen awareness of the places we inhabit than is generally appreciated. Indeed, one of my motivations for writing this book was to enhance that level of awareness and to encourage even more citizens to get involved in helping to revitalize their communities—and not simply for aesthetic reasons. I firmly believe that landmark preservation improves the well-being of a community's citizens, not just by means of the "product"— the rescued buildings and sites—but also the process: involving large numbers of people and nurturing a growing constituency for civic concern and pride.

Another reason for writing this book was to attempt to correct some misconceptions regarding landmark preservation, in particular the notion that a building is "frozen" once it receives landmark status. Hardly! As we accumulated data, in fact, our greatest problem was keeping track of all the changes that had taken place in a landmark since designation, and determining to what use the landmark was currently being put. Effecting changes in landmark structures is not only wholly possible but has been vast, constant, and widespread. Due to repairs, renovations, and adaptations to landmarks, even their appearance can change—which proves that a landmark is not static and museumlike but, as is true of almost any building in active use, constantly evolving.

Far from seeking simply to preserve a bygone world, the members of the New York City Landmarks Preservation Commission accept the circumstances of a changing world, and attempt to preserve the past without jeopardizing the future. But while giving progress and change their due, we must not permit the best of our past to be buried or otherwise lost. Some time ago, when I visited Cliveden, a historic house in Buckinghamshire, England, I noticed some lovely blue-and-white Dutch tiles surrounded by bronze frames. When I looked closer, I saw a plaque that read: "Tiles out of the Apthorp site, Bdwy 78th and 79th Street"—a New York City vestige preserved in a great historic house in England! Which only points to the need to preserve our indigenous history: if we don't do it, we can only hope that others will do it for us.

BARBARALEE DIAMONSTEIN
July 27, 1997

THE LANDMARKS OF NEW YORK, 1965 TO 1988

PIETER CLAESEN WYCKOFF HOUSE, before 1641
Clarendon Road and Ralph Avenue, Brooklyn
Architect: Unknown
Designated: October 14, 1965

The Pieter Claesen Wyckoff House, at Clarendon Road and Ralph Avenue in the Flatlands section, is the oldest building in New York State and one of the oldest wooden structures in this country. The one-story building has a full attic reached by a boxed-in stair. The earliest part of the house is the lower part of the building lying to the west. The "ski-jump" curve of the overhanging roof is characteristic of the Dutch Colonial vernacular. Pieter Claesen was a wealthy landowner and superintendent of Peter Stuyvesant's estate. The house stands on land that four men, including Wouter Van Twiller, Peter Stuyvesant's predecessor as director general of New Netherland, bought in 1636 from the Canarsie Indians. Van Twiller injudiciously put the property in his own name instead of that of the Dutch West India Company; Stuyvesant confiscated the land and turned the farm over to Claesen.

After 1664, Claesen adopted the surname Wyckoff (a combination of *wyk*, meaning "parish," and *hof*, meaning "court") as a fitting name for a local magistrate. The original homestead remained in his family until 1901. In 1969 the Wyckoff House Foundation donated the house to the City of New York, and it has since been completely restored.

OLD GRAVESEND CEMETERY, including the Van Sicklen Family Cemetery, established c. 1650
Village Road South, Gravesend Neck Road, Van Sicklen Avenue, and McDonald Avenue, Brooklyn
Designated: March 23, 1976

A picturesque old cemetery, Gravesend is the most tangible reminder of the village of the same name. The village patent was the first land document in the New York area written in English. An unusual example of early town planning in America, Gravesend was reminiscent of cities in sixteenth- and seventeenth-century Europe, with the town center, residences, and other buildings all contained within protective walls. The community was also the first town charter in the colonies to list a woman patentee, Lady Deborah Moody, an Anabaptist leader who had fled the intolerant climate of the Massachusetts Bay Colony to seek religious freedom. Lady Moody is believed to be buried in the cemetery.

Occupying an irregularly shaped 1.6-acre lot, the cemetery, which has been recently restored, is one of the smallest in the city. Many of the headstones are brownstone. Some have inscriptions in Dutch and English, while others depict angel heads with wings. Among the legible gravestones are those of Revolutionary War veterans, most of the original patentees, and many prominent families of the community. The Van Sicklen family maintained their own burial plot in the northwest corner of the site, which is still separately fenced.

STREET PLAN OF NEW AMSTERDAM AND COLONIAL NEW YORK,
c. 1660–present
Beaver, Bridge, Broad streets, Broadway, Exchange Place, Hanover Square, Hanover and Marketfield streets, Mill Lane, New, Pearl, South William, Stone, Whitehall, Wall, and William streets, Manhattan
Designated: June 14, 1983

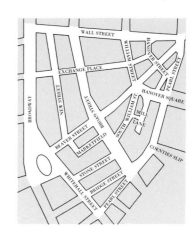

The street plan of lower Manhattan south of Wall Street, within the confines of the Dutch settlement of New Amsterdam, is a striking reminder of New York's colonial past, and provides virtually the only above-ground physical evidence in Manhattan of the Dutch presence in New York during the seventeenth century.

The Dutch arrived in Manhattan (whose name means "hilly island" in the Algonquin language) in the early seventeenth century; there is evidence that Indians had lived on the island since 10,000 B.C. From Henry Hudson's 1609 voyage until 1624, the Dutch sailed the Hudson River and other waterways such as Long Island Sound, slowly establishing a fur trade with the many local Indian nations in the region. In 1624 Dutch families established their claim to the land by settling Nut Island (now Governors Island) under the sponsorship of the Dutch West India Company. In the same year, some of these people may also have settled in Lower Manhattan. In 1626, Peter Minuit purchased the island of Manhattan from some local Algonquin Indians for European trade goods "the value of sixty guilders." Nieuw Amsterdam, as the new Dutch settlement was called, began to take shape under the guidance of Crijn Fredericksz, who in 1625 had been assigned the task of laying out the city by the Dutch West India Company. In 1664, the English captured the city and colony and renamed it New York.

A detailed plan of the city in 1660, known as the Castello Plan, is the earliest and most detailed guide to the city's street pattern just prior to English conquest in 1664. (The original was lost or destroyed, but a copy, redrawn by an unknown draftsman, has survived.) Most of the streets shown in the Castello Plan are still evident today in roughly the same configuration, and even their very names evoke the city's early physical character. For example, Beaver Street was named for the animal that was central to the city's fur trade—the major source of the colony's early wealth; Bridge Street marks the location of one of the three bridges built by the Dutch settlers to cross the canal at Broad Street. Broadway was originally an Indian thoroughfare called Wickquasgeck, meaning "birch-bark country"; the route led through the Bronx and Westchester to the north of present-day Albany, and remains the oldest thoroughfare in New York City and one of the oldest in North America. Exchange Place was given this name in 1827 after the construction of the Merchant's Exchange Building at Wall and William streets. Marketfield Street was the location of the first Dutch livestock market; during the English period the street was known as Petticoate Lane, for it was here that New York's prostitutes gathered. Mill Lane was named after a mill built in 1628 to grind bark used by tanners. Pearl Street's name is a reference to the oysters that were found in abundance in the waters of the East River, whose pearls—the colonists hoped— would make their fortune instantly. South William Street was known by several early Dutch names—Glaziers' Street, Muddy Lane, Mill Street, and Jews' Alley—that reflected its industries, character, and the presence of a Jewish synagogue. Stone Street was the first paved street in the city—surfaced with cobblestones in 1655. Wall Street was named for a wall built by the Dutch to defend the city against attacks from the north by Indians or the English.

After the English took over, another survey—the Nicolls Map—was made in 1668, and by the eighteenth century, city plans were plentiful. The streets in these maps are nearly identical to those in the earlier Castello Plan, but some additions include New Street—the first street added by the British to the Dutch street plan—and Hanover Street and Square, named for the royal family of England.

The street patterns of Lower Manhattan, unlike the formal grid used later, were determined by the natural terrain and the city's primary functions: defense and trade. In contrast to many European towns, New Amsterdam did not have a religious focus. Indeed, when the first church was built in 1633, it was erected within the walls of the defensive fort that shaped the layout of the town.

Only modest alterations to the original street plan have been made over the last two centuries. These include the demolition of colonial buildings and changes in the grade, composition, and paving of the streets. Today, the street plan of New Amsterdam and colonial New York is the last visible remnant of a major colonial city. Despite its age and its narrow, curving roadways, the plan of Lower Manhattan has somewhat miraculously accommodated change and growth for almost 360 years.

Christopher House

Parsonage

Eltingville Store

RICHMONDTOWN RESTORATION, 1670–1860
Richmondtown, Staten Island
Architects: Unknown
Designated: August 26, 1969

Britton Cottage, c. 1670; additions,
c. 1755, c. 1765, c. 1800
Designated: November 9, 1976

Voorlezer's House, c. 1695

Treasure House, c. 1700; additions,
c. 1740, c. 1790, c. 1860

Rezeau–Van Pelt Family Cemetery,
established eighteenth century

Christopher House, c. 1720; addition,
c. 1730

Guyon-Lake-Tysen House, c. 1740;
additions, c. 1820, c. 1840

Boehm House, 1750; addition, c. 1840

Kruser-Finley House, c. 1790; additions,
c. 1820, c. 1850–60

Basketmaker's House, c. 1810–20

Sylvanus Decker Farm, c. 1810
435 Richmond Hill Road (off site)

Visitors Center, formerly Third County
Courthouse, 1837

Stephens-Black House, c. 1838–40

Bennett House, 1839; addition, c. 1854

The Historical Museum, formerly Richmond
County Clerk's and Surrogate's Office, 1848;
additions to c. 1918

Parsonage, 1855

Eltingville Store, c. 1860

From 1729 until 1898—when New York's five boroughs were united—Richmondtown served as the county seat of Staten Island. The movement to preserve local heritage, begun in the 1930s, resulted in the establishment of the Richmondtown Restoration.

At its founding about 1690, Richmondtown was humbly known as Cocclestown—presumably a reference to the mollusks abundant nearby. Here, about 1695, the Dutch erected the Voorlezer's House, their first meetinghouse, used as both a church and a school. Subsequently a town hall and a jail were built. By 1730 the town was thriving; it had a new courthouse, one tavern, about a dozen homes, and the Church of St. Andrew. This tiny town had become the

Britton Cottage

Boehm House

Kruser-Finley House

Voorlezer's House

Treasure House

Guyon-Lake-Tysen House

largest and most important on the island, and the name Cocclestown—no longer appropriate—was changed to the more solid-sounding Richmondtown. By the time of the Revolution, when the British occupied it, the town had a blacksmith shop, a general store, a poorhouse, a tanner's shop, a Dutch Reformed church, a gristmill, and several private homes.

Surviving buildings in situ have been joined by others, moved here from elsewhere on the island to save them from demolition. The restoration and reconstruction provide a fascinating picture of life on Staten Island over the course of more than two centuries. In all, there are about thirty-six buildings, the earliest dating back to the 1670s, not all of which are designated landmarks.

The Britton Cottage, built in four stages from 1670 to about 1800, is an outstanding example of the island's early civic and domestic architecture. The Voorlezer's House is a two-story, clapboard-sheathed building erected about 1695 as a school, church, and home for the lay minister and teacher; it is this country's oldest surviving elementary school, and its restoration in 1939 initiated the Richmondtown Restoration. The Treasure House is a modest clapboard structure built about 1700, with additions between about 1740 and 1860; a $7,000 cache of British coins was discovered within its walls about 1860—hence the name. The Rezeau–Van Pelt Family Cemetery is a tiny eighteenth-century family graveyard of a type known as a homestead burial plot. The Christopher House is a vernacular stone farmhouse whose oldest sections date from about 1720. The Guyon-Lake-Tysen House, built about 1740 for a French Huguenot, is a fine example of a Dutch Colonial–style farmhouse with gambrel roof and spring eaves. The Boehm House is a simple clapboard building with brick end chimneys dating from 1750; it was enlarged in about 1840. The Kruser-Finley House is a simple, one-and-one-half-story clapboard house of about 1790 with a cooper's workshop attached. The Basketmaker's House, of about 1810, is a clapboard and shingle house with a veranda sheltered by spring eaves. The Sylvanus Decker Farm, also of about 1810, is a fine clapboard and shingle farmhouse, of a type once quite common on the island. The Visitors Center, formerly the Third County Courthouse, of 1837, is an imposing Greek Revival structure with pedimented portico and square cupola erected of local stone and wood. The Stephens-Black House of about 1838–40 has a fascinating reconstruction of a nineteenth-century general store attached. Built in 1839,

Basketmaker's House

Bennett House

Sylvanus Decker Farm

Visitor's Center

The Historical Museum

Stephens House

the Bennett House is a two-story, clapboard-sheathed house with Greek Revival elements. The Historical Museum, formerly the Richmond County Clerk's and Surrogate's Office, is a charmingly scaled, red-brick building in a simplified Italianate style built in 1848. The Parsonage was erected in 1855 for the nearby Dutch Reformed Church, and is a clapboard house with Gothic Revival ornamentation. The Eltingville Store dates from about 1860 and is a typical country store that is now furnished as a nineteenth-century printshop.

The Richmondtown Restoration is a unique project in the New York metropolitan region. Since 1958, it has been maintained by the Staten Island Historical Society under contract from the New York City Department of Parks.

BOWNE HOUSE, 1661; additions, 1680, 1691
37–01 Bowne Street, Queens
Builder: John Bowne (original structure); additions, unknown
Designated: February 15, 1966

The oldest surviving dwelling in Queens, the Bowne House is both an extremely important example of early, wood-frame English Colonial architecture and a monument to religious freedom in America. Little changed since its construction in 1661, the earliest portion of the house, containing a kitchen with bedroom upstairs, was built by John Bowne. Additions were made in 1680 and 1691, and in the 1870s the roof was raised and the north wing added. The steeply sloping roof, medieval in both tone and influence, has three shed dormers across the front that contribute to the picturesque quality of the façade.

The historical importance of the house stems from John Bowne's defiance of Governor Stuyvesant's ban on Quaker worship. Challenging Stuyvesant's opinion of Quakers as "an abominable sect," Bowne refused to sacrifice his religious freedom and instead invited fellow Quakers to meet in his house. His trial and subsequent acquittal helped to define the American value of religious freedom, later articulated in the Bill of Rights. The house continued to be used as a place of worship until 1694, when the Friends Meeting House of Flushing was built.

Nine generations of Bownes lived in the house. In 1946 the house became a museum, and today it is owned by New York City and operated by the Bowne House Historical Society as a shrine to religious freedom.

BILLIOU-STILLWELL-PERINE HOUSE, c. 1679;
additions, 1700, 1750, 1790, 1830
1476 Richmond Road, Staten Island
Architect: Unknown
Designated: February 28, 1967

The original portion of the Billiou-Stillwell-Perine House was built by Captain Thomas Stillwell, a prominent resident of Staten Island. After his death in 1704, it was passed down to his son-in-law, Nicholas Britton. At some point, the Perine family acquired the farmhouse and occupied it until it was purchased in 1915 by the Antiquarian Society, now the Staten Island Historical Society.

The original one-and-one-half-story farmhouse, built of rough-cut fieldstone about 1679, is distinguished for its steep, medieval-style roof and an immense Dutch fireplace with a huge chimney head supported by two wooden posts. This structure, which is now the rear wing, overlaps in an unusual way the stone addition nearer to Richmond Road. A tree stood at one end of the original house and, to avoid having to cut the tree down, the newer structure was placed against only a portion of the side of the older dwelling. Both stone sections are built of undressed rubble fieldstone known as Dutch construction (the roughly squared stone of a later date is called English construction). The section added in 1700 is notable for its fine paneled fireplace, transitional type panel, and feather-edge partition. Later stone and frame additions of the same height were built about 1750, 1790, and 1830.

CONFERENCE HOUSE, formerly the
Christopher Billopp House, 1680–88
Foot of Hylan Boulevard, Staten Island
Architect: Unknown
Designated: February 28, 1967

The former Christopher Billopp House, now called Conference House, is the only surviving seventeenth-century manor house on Staten Island. The building was the setting for a fruitless peace conference held on September 11, 1776. The two-and-one-half-story fieldstone residence was built in 1680–88 by Christopher Billopp, a captain in the British navy; a wood-frame lean-to was added some years later.

After the British seized New York in the Battle of Long Island on August 27, 1776, Admiral Richard Howe, the King's Commissioner, invited members of the Continental Congress to discuss terms of surrender. Benjamin Franklin, John Adams, and Edward Rutledge, the Congress's three representatives, traveled from Philadelphia to the manor house, the home of Christopher Billopp, the great-grandson of Captain Billopp and a Tory colonel. In this house, the patriots refused the king's offer of an honorable return to British rule in exchange for renunciation of their demand for independence, reaffirming their constituency's desire for independence, and fixing the course of American history.

After the Revolution, the Billopps' Tory connections prompted the state of New York to confiscate the house. Over the next century and a half, a succession of private owners lived there, and for a short time it was used as a rat-poison factory.

In 1925 the Conference House Association was formed to preserve the house as a model of colonial architecture. Since 1929, the association has maintained the dwelling. The house is open to visitors.

FIRST SHEARITH GRAVEYARD, established 1683
55–57 St. James Place, Manhattan
Designated: February 1, 1966

The First Shearith graveyard is a tiny remnant of the Congregation Shearith Israel, the oldest Jewish congregation in the United States. Shearith Israel dates from September 12, 1654, when a group of recently landed Spanish and Portuguese Jews who had fled the Inquisition held a New Year's service in New Amsterdam.

The small, quaint burial ground is marked by handsome tombstones; interspersed are marble sarcophagi with simple, flat-slab tops. The oldest gravestone dates from 1683, just a few years later than the earliest legible stone in Trinity Churchyard.

Over the years, surrounding streets have been widened and new ones cut through; the congregation established other graveyards on West 11th and West 21st streets.

PROSPECT CEMETERY, established before 1688
159th Street and Beaver Road, Queens
Designated: January 11, 1977

Established by 1688, Prospect Cemetery is Queens's oldest public burial ground. Several revolutionary war veterans are buried here, as are members of many prominent families of early New York, including the Sutphins and Van Wycks.

Many of the older headstones are made of brownstone and carved with motifs of angels' heads and skulls; more recent nineteenth- and twentieth-century graves are marked with granite obelisks.

The cemetery was originally affiliated with the Presbyterian congregation whose Old Stone Church, built in the 1690s, stood near present-day Union Hall Street. The church served as the town hall, and its cemetery was accordingly considered to be town property.

The cemetery expanded during the first half of the nineteenth century as individual plots were purchased from surrounding land. Small plots were purchased for family use, but larger tracts, which held a profit incentive, were purchased, subdivided, and resold by several people, including Nicholas Ludlum, whose Romanesque Revival chapel now stands as the focal point of this historic burial ground. On his own land, Ludlum erected a memorial to his three young daughters. Today the cemetery is maintained by the Prospect Cemetery Association of Jamaica Village.

FRIENDS MEETING HOUSE, 1694; additions, 1716–19
137–16 Northern Boulevard, Queens
Architect: Unknown
Designated: August 18, 1970

The Friends Meeting House is not only the oldest house of worship standing in New York City, but also one of the oldest in the country. The building has been used continuously by the Society of Friends since 1694, except for the years 1776 to 1783 when the British used it successively as a prison, a storehouse for hay, and a hospital. The meetinghouse was built on land held in the names of John Bowne and John Rodman, two prominent Quakers. Their ownership of the property, however, was a legal convenience: The Society of Friends was forbidden to own land in the province of New York, but the property and the meetinghouse belonged in spirit, if not in fact, to the Friends.

Simplicity is the keynote of the meetinghouse, both inside and outside. The interior, with its hardwood benches and total lack of adornment, is typical of the restraint and austerity that have always characterized the Quakers, who desired that no worldly ostentation should distract their attention from worship.

The original meetinghouse—a small frame structure comprising the eastern third of the present building—dates from 1694. The plain, shingled, rectangular building, erected on a frame of forty-foot-long oak timbers, each hand-hewn from a single tree, is notable for the rustic European character of its proportions, framing system, and tiny windows. The unusually steep, hipped roof is almost as high as the two stories below it—a feature that can be traced to seventeenth-century Holland.

Between 1716 and 1719, the building was enlarged to its present size; the original chimney, removed for the construction, was not rebuilt. The division between the two construction periods is evident in the internal structuring and in the spacing of the windows on the south side. There are separate double doors for men and women on the south side; the south porch was added in the nineteenth century.

The pleasant, landscaped setting of the meetinghouse was formerly set apart from Northern Boulevard by a picket fence; it now has a stone wall. The building still faces south, with its back to the street. A feeling of inherent peace survives, in perfect accord with the simple charm of the gray-shingled building and the sense of a long and continuous history.

MANEE-SEGUINE HOMESTEAD, late seventeenth century
509 Seguine Avenue, Staten Island
Architect: Unknown
Designated: September 11, 1984

Located on the shore of Prince's Bay near the southern tip of Staten Island, the Manee-Seguine Homestead, later known as the Homestead Hotel or Purdy's Hotel, is characteristic of the rubblestone and clapboard or shingle dwellings built by Staten Island's earliest settlers. There are fewer than twenty houses remaining on Staten Island that were built before 1750. The Manee-Seguine Homestead is one of the oldest, probably built about 1690.

The house consists of two main sections, both of which were constructed in several stages. The larger, one-story rubblestone section was built first and a smaller, two-story gabled wood-frame addition was attached to the west side of the original house in the early eighteenth century. One of the distinctive features of the house is the spring eave, a mid-eighteenth-century addition to the north eave; deriving from northern France, it reflects the construction techniques of French Huguenots—such as Abraham Manee—who settled in the area.

The house was originally built for Manee; his family occupied the structure for three generations, until Manee's grandson's death in 1780. A few years later the house became the property of the Seguine family. The Seguines made a great deal of money in oystering, and by 1840 Joseph Seguine had built himself a much finer residence on what is now Seguine Avenue. In 1867 Joseph's widow sold the old house, and in 1874 it was acquired by Stephen Purdy, who converted it into a hotel to serve Staten Island's burgeoning tourist trade. Today the house is a private residence.

RICHARD CORNELL GRAVEYARD, established 1700s
Adjacent to 1457 Gateway Boulevard (Greenport Road), Queens
Designated: August 18, 1970

The Richard Cornell Graveyard is the oldest burial ground in the Rockaways and one of the few surviving eighteenth-century cemeteries in New York City. Enclosed by a high iron picket fence, the graveyard measures seventy-five feet wide and sixty-seven feet deep. It is named for the first European settler in the Rockaways, Richard Cornell, who had immigrated from England with his parents by 1638.

In 1687 Richard Cornell purchased most of the area now known as Far Rockaway from John Palmer, who had acquired the land two years earlier from the Indians for £31. The cemetery was established sometime in the early eighteenth century, and used into the nineteenth as a private burial ground for the Cornell family. Family members interred here include Thomas Cornell, who served as a representative from Queens in the New York State Colonial Assembly for twenty-seven years. Among Richard Cornell's distinguished descendants were Ezra Cornell, the founder of Cornell University, and his son Alonzo Cornell, governor of New York from 1879 to 1882.

POILLON-SEGUINE-BRITTON HOUSE,* c. 1695;
additions, 1730, 1845, 1930
361 Great Kills Road, Staten Island
Architect: Unknown
Designated: August 25, 1981

Dating from the late seventeenth century, the Poillon-Seguine-Britton House is one of Staten Island's oldest surviving houses. Originally an isolated country farmhouse situated on 130 acres of land, the house is, today, an urban residence. It is named for its various owners, the first being Jacques Poillon, who came to America from France in 1671.

The house is situated a short distance from the seashore and commands a view to the south across the water of the Great Kills Bay to the distant hills of the New Jersey Highlands. Built in a local vernacular style, the stone and wood structure is two and one-half stories high. The first-story stone portion of the house is the oldest; the western part of the stone section was probably built in the late seventeenth century, as evidenced by the large floor beams, enormous chimney base, and relieving arches above the first-floor windows, all details of vernacular construction at the time. The stone wall of the west end is carried up about one-third of the height of the gable, and the area above is covered with clapboard. The original roof was very steep: the hand-hewn collar beams that once connected the long rafters now lie unattached above the ceiling of the second floor. The wood portions of the house, including the colonnaded veranda and the abundant Greek Revival woodwork, represent mid-nineteenth-century additions and alterations, with the exception of the large sunroom on the western end, which was added in 1930.

*See page 529

LAWRENCE FAMILY GRAVEYARD, established 1703
20th Road and 35th Street, Queens
Designated: April 19, 1966

The Lawrence Family Graveyard, situated in the center of a residential block, is chiefly important for its social heritage. The grounds of this half-acre plot do have aesthetic merit: the graveyard is enclosed by a brick wall, surmounted by a wrought-iron fence and entrance gate. The brown slate gravestones have remained legible through the centuries, and a hand-carved statue of an angel overlooks the burial ground. Nonetheless, it is the Lawrences' distinguished record of civic service that qualifies their family graveyard as a landmark.

Buried here are Major Thomas Lawrence, an officer in Her Majesty's army and the first to be buried in 1703, and Major Jonathan Lawrence, a soldier, statesman, and patriot who aided General George Washington in obtaining additional forces for the revolutionary army at Brooklyn. Among the other family members interred were twelve ranking military officers, whose service spanned the period from Dutch colonial rule in New York to the Civil War, and seven major government officials of the state of New York. Oliver Lawrence, who died in 1975, was the last of the Lawrence family to be buried here.

The Admiral's House

Castle Williams

The Governor's House

Fort Jay

GOVERNORS ISLAND
Designated: September 19, 1967

The Governor's House,
early eighteenth century
Architect: Unknown

Fort Jay, 1794–98; rebuilt, 1806
Architect: Unknown

Castle Williams, 1807–11
Architect: Lieutenant Colonel
Jonathan Williams

The Admiral's House, 1840
Architect: Unknown

The Block House, 1843
Architect: Martin E. Thompson

After the English captured New Amsterdam, Governors Island was used for "the benefit and accommodation of His Majestie's Governors for the time being"—hence the name. This little piece of land has also been used as a quarantine station, a pheasant preserve, a garrisoned fortress, a summer resort, a recruiting depot, a prison, an embarkation port, and a flying field. The island was an army installation for over 150 years and since 1966 has been the headquarters of the Coast Guard's Eastern Area.

Built in the early 1700s, the austere red-brick Governor's House was designed in a modified Georgian style. It was erected during the era of rule by British colonial governors and was reputedly the home of Lord Cornbury, the first British governor of the new colony. Two stories high, it is symmetrical in plan, with the original portion designed in the form of a Greek cross.

Fort Jay was begun in 1794 when war with France was threatened. It was completed by 1798 using volunteer labor and named for John Jay, then secretary of foreign affairs. It was rebuilt in 1806 and renamed Fort Columbus in 1808; in 1904 the old name was restored.

Like so many other fortifications in this country, Fort Jay owes its inspiration to the great French architect Sébastian de Vauban, military engineer to Louis XIV. Impressive in size and design, the pentagonal breastworks occupy a knoll and dominate the northern end of the island; in combination with other forts on the island, it made invasion from the sea unlikely. The fort was originally equipped with batteries of powerful guns and well-trained men; its might has gone untested, however; Fort Jay has never been called into action against an enemy.

The fort's imposing Federal-style stone entrance gateway shows considerable French influence; monumental in size and scale, a low-arched opening set within a tall blind arch is flanked by four large Doric pilasters. Surmounting the cornice is a handsome carved sculptural composition of flags, cannon, weapons, banded fasces with liberty cap, and a spread eagle.

In 1811 Castle Williams—originally called "The Tower" and nicknamed "The Cheesebox"—was erected. This impressive, circular red sandstone bastion was built to guard the waterway between Governors Island and New York City. It was named after its designer, Lieutenant Colonel Jonathan Williams, chief engineer of the army and Benjamin Franklin's nephew. Its walls are some forty feet high and eight feet thick. The stones in the outer walls are dovetailed so that no stone can be removed without first being broken to pieces.

The Admiral's House, formerly the Commanding General's Quarters, is an elegant late Federal-style manor house resembling a southern plantation. Built in 1840, it is rectangular in plan and two stories high with a basement; both the front and rear of this brick house have wide verandas dominated by six-columned Doric porticoes. The regal entrance doorway, centered between four full-length windows with large, paneled shutters, is noted for its intricate leaded transom and sidelights with four handsome pilasters capped with ornate acanthus leaves.

The Block House, built in 1843, is a severely simple house. Almost square, this two-story Greek Revival structure has superb architectural character, deriving its austere dignity from the strict, disciplined scale expressed in its proportion and components, and from the large, unadorned surfaces of brick interspersed with evenly spaced, well-proportioned openings.

Now used by the U.S. Coast Guard, Governors Island is not open to the public, but can be visited by special appointment.

ALICE AUSTEN HOUSE, c. 1700; additions, c. 1730, 1846
2 Hylan Boulevard, Staten Island
Architect: Unknown; additions, James Renwick, Jr.
Designated: November 9, 1971

Notable for its seventeenth-century construction, the Austen House was the longtime residence and workshop of Elizabeth Alice Austen (1866–1952), a pioneer photographer who lived here for over seventy years.

Built sometime between 1691 and 1710 by a Dutch merchant, the house originated as a one-room dwelling erected parallel to the shoreline of Staten Island's Narrows. A southern extension, which later became the Austens' parlor, was added to the house before 1730. A wing, featuring three-foot-thick walls and including a kitchen, was constructed before the Revolution, changing the house's plan to an L shape.

When John Austen purchased the house in 1844, he immediately began a series of renovations on Clear Comfort (as his wife fondly called it). The house's plan changed once more when Austen built a north room, which later became a bedroom shared by Alice and her mother. Austen hired his friend James Renwick, Jr., who had recently completed Grace Church (1846), to execute further renovations.

By inserting Gothic Revival dormers into the Dutch-style roof, adorning the roof with a ridge crest and scalloped shingles, and decorating the entire structure with intricate gingerbread trim, Renwick transformed the matter-of-fact Dutch Colonial house into an exemplar of Victorian architectural romanticism. Japanese wisteria and Dutchman's pipe vines once trailed down from the house's roof and complemented its lacy aspect.

From the 1880s through the 1930s, John's daughter Alice made more than 7,000 glass negatives, many of which feature her house in its magnificent natural setting. Austen's images are marked by a sensitive but unsentimental realism, which provides us with a valuable glimpse of nineteenth-century Staten Island. The house was recently restored.

FRAUNCES TAVERN, 1719; reconstruction and renovation, 1907
54 Pearl Street, Manhattan
Architect: Unknown; restoration, William Mersereau
Designated: November 23, 1965

American taverns in the eighteenth century were centers of communication, transportation, business, and politics. Today, Fraunces Tavern Museum includes the only surviving public house of colonial New York. The Fraunces Tavern building, which occupies a site that was one of the earliest landfill developments in the city, is a good example of a fashionable eighteenth-century Georgian residence.

The tavern is a 1907 reconstruction by William Mersereau of what the original may have been. The house was first built about 1719 as a residence for Etienne Delancey but apparently was not occupied. Samuel Fraunces, a well-known West Indian innkeeper, purchased the building in 1762 and opened it as a tavern the following year. Originally called At the Sign of Queen Charlotte, the tavern became a fashionable meeting place for colonists: several organizations, including the New York Chamber of Commerce, were founded there. It was not until after the Revolution that Fraunces renamed the tavern after himself. The place then became the site of several celebrations, including General George Washington's farewell to his officers on December 4, 1783.

In 1785 Fraunces sold the building to George Powers, who leased it to the new Department of Foreign Affairs for three years. In the ensuing years, the tavern was used for many purposes, including a hotel, a meeting place, and a tavern, and it was almost totally destroyed by fires in 1832, 1837, and 1852. The earliest visual record of the building—a print from Bryant and Gay's *Popular History of the United States* (1854)—shows that two floors had been added to the original eighteenth-century structure. By the beginning of the twentieth century, very little of the original structure was left.

In 1904 the Sons of the Revolution in the State of New York purchased the building; the restoration they undertook was one of the earliest in this country. Now the Fraunces Tavern building is a well-maintained site, one of five historic structures comprising Fraunces Tavern Museum. The ground-floor restaurant and upper-story meeting rooms are leased by the museum's board.

The structure reproduces the principal elements of the Georgian style. Restored to its original height of three and one-half stories, the rectangular, red-brick building has a centrally placed, ornately carved classical main doorway, with an arched semicircular fanlight. Above the door the entablature is supported with columns, and each side of the building has three rows of double-hung windows, shed dormers, and a balustrade running along the top. The high basement helped to keep the house warm and dry, and allowed for an imposing flight of steps, with hand railings, to the front entrance.

Fraunces Tavern Museum, the eighth-oldest museum in the city, opened to the public in 1907; it interprets the history and culture of early America through its permanent collection of prints, paintings, decorative arts, and artifacts.

POILLON HOUSE, c. 1720; additions, 1837, 1848
4515 Hylan Boulevard, Staten Island
Architect: Unknown; 1848 addition, Frederick Law
Olmsted
Designated: February 28, 1967

The first owner of the Poillon House property was Dominic Petrus Tesschenmaker, who built a one-room stone shelter here in 1685; the foundations of his house now form half of the present building's basement. Jacques Poillon, a road commissioner, purchased the property in 1696 and enlarged the shelter into a farmhouse. Many generations of the Poillon family resided here, including John Poillon, who, during the revolutionary war, was a member of the Committee of Safety for Richmond County.

The farmhouse was remodeled twice: first in 1837, when it was enlarged to thirteen rooms, and again in 1848, when noted landscape architect Frederick Law Olmsted added a one-and-one-half-story wooden extension. The exterior of the 1837 addition features massive stone arches over the windows in the basement and first-story areas. In 1848, porches were added on three sides of the house. The original stone door arches were enclosed and two pairs of windows were added in each arched opening. Above the narrow porch, the house was sided with wide clapboard.

KREUZER-PELTON HOUSE, 1722; additions, 1770, 1836
1262 Richmond Terrace, Staten Island
Architect: Unknown
Designated: August 24, 1967

Two additions, built from varying textures and materials, reflect the three stages of construction governing the Kreuzer-Pelton House. The original one-room cottage was built in 1722 by Cornelius Van Santvoord, a native of Holland and minister of the Dutch Reformed church. It is composed of random fieldstone. Inside, a trapdoor led from the kitchen to a so-called dungeon and adjacent wine cellar.

The larger steep-roofed, one-and-one-half-story central section, built from rough-cut stone, was joined to the cottage by Cornelius Kreuzer about 1770. During the revolutionary war, General Cortlandt Skinner used the residence as his commanding headquarters for the American Loyalist party. In 1836, a two-story brick extension to this central structure was completed. The addition was supervised by Daniel Pelton, whose son, Daniel Pelton, Jr., was a noted poet at the turn of the century.

LENT HOMESTEAD, c. 1729
78–03 19th Road, Queens
Architect: Unknown
Designated : March 15, 1966

Lent Homestead is one of the oldest remaining private residences in Queens. This Dutch Colonial stone farmhouse with its steeply sloping roof was built about 1729 by Abraham Lent, the grandson of Abraham Riker. The house faces Rikers Island, once owned by the Riker family and now the site of several city prisons.

A prominent family, the Rikers were among the first Dutch settlers in this area. They obtained the land grant from Governor Peter Stuyvesant in 1654 and built this house several decades later. The larger family homestead that once stood nearby burned down in 1938. The property includes a family cemetery in which many generations of Rikers and Lents are buried.

Damaged by fire in 1955, the house was intermittently occupied until 1979; the present owners, Michael and Marion Smith, began exhaustive renovations in that year to restore their house to its original colonial charm.

HOUSMAN HOUSE, c. 1730; addition, c. 1760
308 St. John Avenue, Staten Island
Architect: Unknown
Designated: October 13, 1970

The earliest part of this structure is a small, one-room stone house built about 1730 on the estate of Governor Thomas Dongan. In 1760 Peter Housman, a prosperous millwright, purchased forty-six acres of the Dongan manor and built an addition to the house.

The building combines stone and frame construction. One notable feature of the older section is the unusually deep overhang of the steeply pitched roof. The larger, three-bay addition has a clapboard front and a slightly less steep roof, broken by two dormer windows. A four-paneled Greek Revival door serves as the entrance. Both sections of the roof are covered with shingles, and wood siding has replaced shingles at the gable ends. A rustic porch built of logs shelters the doorway and runs along the end of the house.

The house and twenty-five acres were sold in 1887, and the property was divided into smaller lots for a summer resort; this resort became the residential neighborhood now known as Westerleigh. The Housman House is still a private residence.

SCOTT-EDWARDS HOUSE, c. 1730; addition, 1840
752 Delafield Avenue, Staten Island
Architect: Unknown
Designated: August 24, 1967

This one-and-one-half-story structure with a stone basement dates from the early eighteenth century; a Dutch Colonial country residence with Greek Revival alterations, it was built on a parcel of Governor Dongan's grant of 1677. Throughout the eighteenth century, the structure was probably a tenant house on the Dongan estate. During the 1840s it became the home of Judge Ogden Edwards; a descendant of Jonathan Edwards and a cousin of Aaron Burr, Edwards was the first New York supreme court justice from Staten Island. The house was later owned by Adam Scott, a florist, and then by Samuel Henshaw, an employee of the New York Botanical Garden in the Bronx, who was responsible for the skillful planting of the shrubbery, which enhances the overall appeal of the structure.

The house is constructed of quarry-faced ashlar masonry and sandstone at the ground floor, with clapboard above. The 1840 additions include a Greek Revival portico. The long sweep of the roof is supported by seven box columns forming a veranda that extends the width of the façade. Floor-to-ceiling, double-hung windows are complemented by paneled shutters; above these windows is a row of low attic windows set under eaves. The two entrance doors are framed with plain pilasters and flanked by narrow sidelights. The rear of the house features a bay window; the insets of tinted English glass are considered to be over two hundred years old.

CORNELIUS VAN WYCK HOUSE, c. 1735; additions, before 1770
37–04 Douglaston Parkway, Queens
Architect: Unknown
Designated: April 19, 1966

The Van Wyck house is one of two surviving Dutch Colonial farmhouses in the Douglaston section of Queens. It is considered by some authorities to be one of the finest of its kind on Long Island. The earliest part of the house was built by Cornelius Van Wyck in about 1735 in a vernacular rural style and consisted of what serve today as the dining room, the master bedroom, and the living hall—each retaining its original oak beams. Between 1735 and 1770, the house was expanded to the south and west. There are handsome Georgian mantelpieces in the present living room and in the downstairs bedroom. The scalloped shingles on the exterior west and south walls are original; the asphalt roof shingles are a recent addition.

The history of this house is intimately linked with that of early Dutch settlers in New York. Cornelius Van Wyck was the eldest son of Johannes Van Wyck, whose father had emigrated from Holland in 1660. Cornelius had three sons, Stephen, Cornelius II, and Gilbert; Stephen, who inherited the property and added to the house, was a delegate to the Continental Congress. The Van Wyck family sold the house in 1819 to Winant Van Zandt, who added his adjoining 120 acres, including an area to the north known as The Point, to the property.

In 1835, all of this land was sold to George Douglas, a wealthy Scottish merchant; in 1876 his son William donated land for the Long Island Railroad station nearby, and the area became known as Douglaston. In 1906, the Van Wyck House and its property were sold to the Douglas Manor Company, which began to develop the community of Douglaston Manor, and the Van Wyck House became the first home of the Douglaston Club. In 1921 the club moved, and Mr. and Mrs. E. M. Wicht bought the house; they undertook major restoration of the structure. Mr. and Mrs. L. K. Larson purchased the Van Wyck House in 1933, and sold it to their son, Stallworth M. Larson, and his wife in 1980.

STOOTHOFF-BAXTER-KOUWENHOVEN HOUSE,
small wing, c. 1747; addition, 1811
1640 East 48th Street, Brooklyn
Architect: Unknown
Designated: March 23, 1976

The Stoothoff-Baxter-Kouwenhoven House is named for a succession of related families who occupied it from the time of its construction until the 1920s. The first member of the Stoothoff family arrived in New Netherland from Holland in 1633 as a ten-year-old Dutch farmboy named Elbert Elbertsen. He later assumed the name "Stoothoff" when the British required distinctive surnames. This wood-frame Dutch Colonial building type is quite different from the styles of Manhattan and the Hudson River Valley, where a masonry tradition prevailed. A shingled dwelling, this house was built in two sections; the small wing, which dates from about 1747, was moved and consolidated with the new house of 1811. Both parts were shifted and oriented to their present position around 1900.

One and one-half stories high, the building's profile features pitched roofs, end chimneys, and projecting eaves. The windows on the front façade at the main floor have paneled shutters; those at the upper floor of the newer section are set directly under the eaves. The Dutch-style front door has a rectangular glass transom.

SLEIGHT FAMILY GRAVEYARD, the Rossville (Blazing Star) Burial Ground, established c. 1750
Arthur Kill Road at Rossville Avenue, Staten Island
Designated: January 17, 1968

Located just east of Rossville, on the north side of Arthur Kill Road, the Sleight Family Graveyard was one of the earliest burial grounds on Staten Island. Such early burial grounds were referred to as homestead graves; often deeds to property containing homestead graves included a restriction stating that the graves were not to be moved.

The Sleight Family Graveyard is located on a narrow strip of land on rising ground that lies between a highway and a steep bank leading to a salt meadow. The plot was originally used solely for members of the Sleight family; it came to be shared by other families. Peter Winant (whose father was one of the first permanent settlers of Staten Island, in 1661) was buried here in 1758. In addition to the Sleights and Winants, some other well-known Staten Island families represented here include the Seguines, Perines, and Poillons. This graveyard is widely known as the Rossville or the Blazing Star Burial Ground (after the Blazing Star Ferry, which used to sail to New Jersey). The earliest graves date from 1750.

VAN CORTLANDT MANSION, 1748
Broadway and West 242nd Street, The Bronx
Architect: Unknown
Designated: March 15, 1966; interior designated July 22, 1975

The freestanding landmark houses and mansions still remaining in the Bronx provide excellent illustrations of all the important styles of architecture that captured American taste from the colonial period to the Civil War. One of the earliest is the splendid Georgian-style Van Cortlandt Mansion. Dating from 1748, the Van Cortlandt Mansion is a handsome manor house, almost square, built of rough fieldstone with fine brick trim around the windows. The stone was quarried and dressed locally. The bricks, also made locally, form a neat transition between the irregular shapes of the stonework and the multipaned double-hung windows. The carved heads that form the keystones over the principal windows are a touch of unexpected whimsy in this otherwise very staid and English-looking house. The roof is pierced by regularly spaced dormer windows.

Unlike other Georgian houses in the city, whose interiors were updated in the nineteenth century, the Van Cortlandt Mansion retains most of its handsome original interior architectural features. Departing from the typical Georgian design of two rooms on each side of a central hall, the plan of the mansion is L shaped, perhaps reflecting the Dutch Colonial influence. The interior combines the formal elegance and symmetry of the Georgian style with practical features incorporated to best withstand the climate. Among the mansion's original architectural detail are the floorboards, fireplaces, and paneled and plaster walls in their original colors; a U-shaped staircase in the front hall; eared moldings and window cornices; and beautiful examples of eighteenth-century English and American furniture, some of which belonged to the Van Cortlandts.

Oloff Van Cortlandt arrived in New Amsterdam in 1638 and founded a dynasty that at one time owned almost 200 square miles of land. The Van Cortlandts were traders, merchants, and shipbuilders, and they married into such wealthy and influential families as the Schuylers, the Philipses, and the Livingstons. Oloff's son Stephanus was appointed mayor in 1677, the first native-born American to hold that post. Oloff's grandson Frederick built the family mansion just a few years before his death. During the Revolution, General George Washington kept campfires burning around the house for several days to fool the British while he withdrew his troops across the Hudson. Members of the family lived in the house continuously until 1889, when the building and grounds were donated to the city as a public park. The National Society of Colonial Dames in the State of New York has maintained the house as a museum since 1897.

KING MANSION, c. 1730, c. 1755, c. 1805
King Park, Jamaica Avenue and 153rd Street, Queens
Architect: Unknown
Designated: April 19, 1966; interior designated March 23, 1976

Three stages of construction reflect architecturally diverse styles—Georgian, Federal, and Greek Revival—in this large, two-and-one-half-story, L-shaped residence. The western section was added to the original rear portion (which dated from about 1730) by the Reverend Thomas Colgan, rector of Grace Episcopal Church, in 1755. In 1805, Rufus King—a member of the Continental Congress, ambassador to Britain, and U.S. senator from New York—purchased the estate from one of Colgan's daughters and enlarged the house.

The main, gambrel-roofed portion of the building is symmetrical in plan, with rooms on each side of a central hallway. An elaborate ceiling cornice containing several rows of molding, plus a row of Greek fretwork and dentils, decorates the hall. From here, four doorways lead to the principal rooms. In the western section is the parlor, which was renovated several times; it features an ornate ceiling cornice in addition to its elegant Greek Revival mantelpiece of dark gray and white marble. A mantel with pulvinated frieze and paneled overmantel is found in the library, above a fireplace surrounded by blue-and-white Dutch tiles depicting landscape scenes. Both the library and Rufus King's bedroom on the second story have plaster walls painted to simulate wood-grained paneling that, in combination with a chair rail, resembles a wainscot.

The eastern part of the house, built about 1805, contains a dining room with an inscribed, curved end wall and a Federal-style fireplace. The large sitting room on the second floor retains architectural features that date from 1755, including an ornate chimney piece. On the second floor, sunk slightly below the level of the other rooms, is the children's playroom.

Cornelia King was the last family member to occupy the house. The building is now owned by the city and maintained as a museum by the King Manor Association of Long Island.

ADRIANCE FARMHOUSE, formerly Creedmoor (Cornell)
Farmhouse, c. 1770; additions, c. 1840, 1875, c. 1885, 1932, 1945–46
73–50 Little Neck Parkway, Queens
Architect: Unknown
Designated: November 9, 1976

The earliest part of the Adriance Farmhouse dates from the mid-eighteenth century; it is believed that Jacob Adriance built the house on about eighty acres of land purchased from his brother, Elbert. The essentially Dutch Colonial house had two unusual characteristics: the north façade, rather than the south, was intended to be the front; and the fireplace was located in the center rather than on the end wall, suggesting an English influence. Set on a basement of dressed fieldstone, the house originally contained a parlor, bedroom, and kitchen, surmounted by an unfinished attic. It was covered in shingles, and the north eave has a typical Dutch overhang.

About 1840, after Peter Cox purchased the house, two rooms and a one-story wing were added. This portion was built on a brick foundation laid in common bond. In 1875 a wing was added to the north, and around 1885, after Daniel Stattel's purchase of the property, a narrow porch was added to the east and south façades, the north wing roof was raised, and three eyebrow windows put in.

In 1926, what was then the Creedmoor branch of the Brooklyn State Hospital acquired the property. The farm then served as a vegetable garden for the hospital's psychiatric patients, some of whom worked in the gardens as part of their therapy. A minor fire in 1932 necessitated repair work, and a nearby one-room building was moved and joined to the main house by a shed. The state added a pantry and extended the east porch in 1945. In 1982, the title of the property, now encompassing about forty-eight acres, passed to New York City. It is operated as the Queens County Farm Museum.

THE VALENTINE-VARIAN HOUSE, c. 1758
3266 Bainbridge Avenue, The Bronx
Architect: Unknown
Designated: March 15, 1966

The Valentine-Varian House exemplifies the vernacular Georgian style popular before the emergence of professional architects in America. Built by Isaac Valentine, a blacksmith and farmer, it is a fieldstone farmhouse bonded with a mud-based mortar.

Four rooms on both the first and second floors are arranged symmetrically around a central hallway to form the straightforward rectangular plan. In contrast to the simple pitched roof that crowns the entire structure, the doorway—with its pediment and fluted pilasters—follows the tenets of classical architecture. Within the house are hand-hewn beams and Valentine's hand-forged nails.

From 1792 to 1905, the house was owned and occupied by the Varian family, one member of which, Isaac L. Varian, served as mayor of New York between 1839 and 1841. Purchased by William F. Beller shortly thereafter, the house was entrusted to caretaker tenants until 1960. In 1965, it was moved from its original site on Van Cortlandt Avenue, east of Bainbridge, to property owned by the New York City Department of Parks and Recreation. Ownership and administration of the house were transferred to the Bronx County Historical Society, which continues to operate it as the Museum of Bronx History.

ST. PAUL'S CHAPEL AND CHURCHYARD, 1764–66; tower, 1794
Broadway at Fulton Street, Manhattan
Architects: Attributed to Thomas McBean (church); James Crommelin Lawrence (tower)
Designated: August 16, 1966

St. Paul's Chapel is the oldest church building in continuous use in Manhattan. Although it is commonly attributed to Thomas McBean, there is no evidence among church records to support this, and the chapel may have been designed by Andrew Gautier and others.

Modeled on James Gibbs's famous St. Martin-in-the-Fields (London), St. Paul's Chapel is built of small stone blocks reinforced at the window openings by brownstone frames. Giant pilasters flank the two stories of windows with Gibbs surrounds, and a stone belt course is topped by a continuous balustrade. The spire was built in 1794 by James Crommelin Lawrence. It is topped by a replica of Athens's Choragic Monument of Lysicrates, and decorated with consoles and pediments. The entire chapel, whose main entrance originally faced west, is surrounded by a handsome iron fence.

George Washington worshiped here for nearly two years, and was officially received in the chapel in 1789 following his inauguration. The revolutionary war hero Brigadier General Richard Montgomery was interred underneath the east porch after his death in 1775, and Benjamin Franklin, acting for the Second Continental Congress, commissioned the Italian sculptor Jacques Caffieri to design a memorial in Montgomery's honor, which was erected in 1789.

MORRIS-JUMEL MANSION, 1765
West 160th Street and Edgecombe Avenue, Manhattan
Architect: John Edward Pryor
Designated: July 12, 1967; interior designated May 27, 1975

Situated in a one-and-one-half-acre park, the Morris-Jumel Mansion is Manhattan's only surviving prerevolutionary house; the mansion and its grounds were originally part of a 160-acre estate that spanned the width of Manhattan at Harlem Heights.

The house was built in 1765 by Colonel Roger Morris, a member of the British Executive Council of the Province of New York; his wife was Mary Philipse, who was rumored to have been romantically involved with George Washington before her marriage. Morris was the son of a well-known British Palladian architect, and his knowledge of the Palladian style is reflected in the double-storied portico and the octagonal wing, both among the first of their type in America.

The Morrises used the house as a summer villa until increasing hostilities endangered both Morris and his property. He then fled to England, entrusting the estate to his wife's care. Before Morris returned to New York in 1777, Mount Morris had served as General Washington's headquarters, as the post of General Sir Henry Clinton and his British officers, and as the home of Baron von Knyphausen and his Hessian troops. When peace was declared in 1783, the Morris property was confiscated and sold. For a short period—before Stephen and Eliza Jumel bought it in 1810—the house was a fashionable inn, the first stop north of New York City on the Albany Post Road.

Madame Jumel, whose social aspirations were checked by an unsavory past, sought to enter New York society by redecorating the mansion in the finest French style, which she had seen in Paris. After her husband died in 1832, Eliza Jumel married Aaron Burr, the former vice-president, then seventy-seven and notorious for his duel with Alexander Hamilton. Burr died in 1836, and his widow became a recluse; she died in the house in 1865, and her heirs occupied it until 1887.

In 1903, the last private owners of the house persuaded the city to purchase the property; it was made a museum under the custodianship of the Washington Headquarters Association, which continues to maintain, furnish, and administer the interiors.

WYCKOFF-BENNETT HOMESTEAD, c. 1766
1669 East 22nd Street, Brooklyn
Architect: Unknown
Designated: January 17, 1968

The Wyckoff-Bennett Homestead is considered the finest example of Dutch Colonial architecture in Brooklyn. It is believed to have been built by Henry and Abraham Wyckoff, descendants of Pieter Claesen Wyckoff, whose house in the Flatlands section of Brooklyn is the oldest building in New York State. The date 1766, carved into a beam of the old barn, is the basis for dating the house to that year. Other souvenirs of the past include two little glass windowpanes, into which were scratched the names and ranks of two Hessian soldiers quartered in the house during the Revolution.

One and one-half stories high, the rectangular frame house has an extension on the northern end containing a kitchen and what was once a milk house. In the late 1890s, the structure was turned around to face the west and placed upon a brick foundation; dormers were then added. A long porch extends the width of the south exposure, and six slender columns support the roof, which is swept down over the porch area in a gentle curve. The upper half of the horizontally divided front door still has its two thick, bluish green bull's-eye windows. The interior retains much of its original paneled woodwork.

In 1835 the house was purchased by Cornelius W. Bennett, and four generations of Bennetts lived here. It has recently been sold to a new owner.

NEVILLE HOUSE, c. 1770
806 Richmond Terrace, Staten Island
Architect: Unknown
Designated: November 15, 1967

This large country house is one of the few remaining colonial houses in New York City; it stands as a reminder of a time when the city stopped at Chambers Street and when farms and villages populated the rest of Manhattan and the outer boroughs. The house was built as a retreat for Captain John Neville, a retired officer of the British navy. Later, it passed into the hands of the family of Judge Jacob Tysen, whose son Raymond wrote a brief history of Staten Island. Many of the city's country houses were used as taverns at some point after the Revolution; their large size suited the purpose well. The Neville House was no exception—as The Old Stone Jug, it served the retired sailors at nearby Snug Harbor for many years.

The house is built of quarry-faced red sandstone ashlar, unusual for a time when skilled masons were in short supply. In marked contrast to the rough surface of the walls is the dressed ashlar used for lintels and door surrounds. A broad flight of stairs in the center of the façade leads to another distinguishing feature of this Georgian vernacular house—the three-bay-wide, two-story veranda. A West Indian convention, the veranda may have been inspired by Neville's travels with the navy.

BOWLING GREEN FENCE, 1771
Bowling Green Park, Manhattan
Designated: July 14, 1970

One of the oldest landmarks in Lower Manhattan is small and inconspicuous—the simple iron fence at Bowling Green. The fence was erected in 1771 to protect the gilded equestrian statue of George III of England, and to ensure that the green (which was—not surprisingly—used for bowling) should not become a neighborhood dumping ground; the cost was £843. The statue became a hated symbol of tyranny during the Revolution and was pulled down and hacked apart by a crowd of soldiers and civilians on July 9, 1776—the day the Declaration of Independence reached New York from Philadelphia. It is said that pieces of the statue were melted down and molded into 42,000 bullets by the patriotic wife and daughter of the governor of Connecticut. The fence, too, was partially destroyed, and the ornaments that capped the posts (variously described as iron balls and royal crowns) were broken off by patriots and melted down for ammunition.

The iron fence was repaired in 1786, and old prints show that graceful lamps once adorned it. During the course of the nineteenth century, the surrounding neighborhood became completely commercial, and in 1914 the fence was dismantled to allow construction of the subway beneath the green. The iron railings were removed to Central Park and lay there, forgotten, until 1919, when most of the fence was rediscovered and restored to Bowling Green. In the 1970s, the fence was again restored.

KINGSLAND HOMESTEAD, 1774
143–35 37th Avenue, Queens
Architect: Unknown
Designated: October 14, 1965

The Kingsland Homestead is Flushing's only remaining eighteenth-century dwelling and the second-oldest house in the area, predated only by the historic Bowne House. It was built by Charles Doughty during the prerevolutionary period and named for Captain Joseph King, a British seaman and Doughty's son-in-law. Kingsland Homestead was built in a style that might be characterized as Dutch-English Colonial. The wooden, two-story structure with basement and attic has the divided front door and bold, even proportions of Dutch architecture; but the gambrel roof, central chimney, and round-headed and quadrant windows are typical of the English Colonial style. As with many Dutch-influenced dwellings (once common in western Long Island), the front elevation is dominated by a narrow porch covered by a column-supported roof. The door on one side is offset by two windows on the other, an asymmetrical arrangement that is repeated by the windows of the second floor. With the exception of some minor interior alterations and a modern replacement of the original service wing, the house retains its original structure and form.

DYCKMAN HOUSE, c. 1783
Broadway between West 204th and West 207th streets, Manhattan
Architect: Unknown
Designated: July 12, 1967

A charming little one-and-one-half-story structure on upper Broadway, the Dyckman House was built about 1783. Once the center of a prosperous farm, it is a typical Dutch Colonial farmhouse and the last surviving one in Manhattan.

The Dyckman family settled in the northern end of Manhattan Island in 1661 and helped to build the Free Bridge—sometimes called Dyckman's Bridge—over the Harlem River in 1758. During the Revolution, the Continental army, in its retreat from Harlem Heights, occupied the original Dyckman farmhouse, and subsequently the British used it during their occupation of Manhattan. When the British withdrew in 1783, they burned the building; the Dyckman family returned and reconstructed the house, reusing the materials from their former house.

The building as it stands today is of fieldstone, brick, and wood, with a sweeping, low-pitched gambrel roof, spring eaves, and a porch. On the grounds are a smokehouse and a military hut that were used during the British occupation.

In 1915, when the house was threatened by demolition, Dyckman family descendants purchased the building and restored it, filling it with family heirlooms. They presented it to the city, which now, in conjunction with the Metropolitan Historic Structures Association, runs the house as a museum.

EDWARD MOONEY HOUSE, 1785–89
18 Bowery, Manhattan
Architect: Unknown
Designated: August 23, 1966

Dating from 1785—shortly after the British evacuated New York but before Washington was inaugurated as the first president—the structure at 18 Bowery is one of the city's most interesting town houses and its oldest row house. It formed the end of Pell Street and the Bowery, on the edge of what is now Chinatown. Built by Edward Mooney, a well-to-do merchant in the wholesale meat trade, the house still contains its original hand-hewn timbers.

Two windows in the gable end on Pell Street are particularly interesting for their quarter-round shape and interlacing muntins, which also appear in a round-headed central window. These features are characteristic of the incoming Federal style, whereas the splayed lintels and splayed double keystones at the heads of the other windows are typically Georgian.

The house has been restored to its original state by a recent owner. Among other tenants, it currently houses an off-track betting parlor—appropriately, since Mooney was a breeder of racehorses.

ERASMUS HALL MUSEUM, 1786
Courtyard of Erasmus Hall High School,
911 Flatbush Avenue, Brooklyn
Architect: Unknown
Designated: March 15, 1966

This wood-frame, clapboard Federal building of two and one-half stories stands in the center of an ivy-towered quadrangle of brick and stone Collegiate Gothic buildings. One of the oldest schools in the country, and the first secondary school to be chartered by the Regents of New York State, Erasmus Hall began as a private academy in 1787 with funds contributed by John Jay, Alexander Hamilton, Aaron Burr, and others. The land was donated by the Flatbush Dutch Reformed Church, located across the street.

The rectangular structure's façade is divided into three equal sections, with the center section defined by sharply cut corner blocks. It has a stone basement and four-columned porch with a low-pitched pediment set into the hipped roof. The Palladian window on the second floor is centered in a row of eight evenly spaced, double-hung windows. Likewise the sidelights and delicate pilasters of the front door divide the symmetrically balanced first-floor windows.

The building, no longer used for classrooms, houses a museum and administrative offices.

REMSEN CEMETERY, established c. 1790
Between Alderton Street and Trotting Course Lane, Queens
Designated: May 26, 1981

Located between Alderton Street and Trotting Course Lane in
Queens, the Remsen Cemetery is the burial ground of one of New
York City's earliest families, whose members played a vital role in
the American Revolution.

The Remsen family ancestors emigrated from northern Germany to
America and eventually settled in Queens County in the seventeenth
century. The founding father of the clan in America was Rem Jansen
Van der Beeck; his sons changed the name to Remsen. The original
cemetery, believed to have been used from the mid-eighteenth
century through the nineteenth, lay solely within the property of the
Remsen family. The oldest known grave is that of Jeromus Remsen,
who died in 1790.

The oldest memorials in the cemetery are a group of three
brownstone gravestones near Alderton Avenue, two more along the
northwesterly perimeter, and the remnants of another tombstone
along the southern property line. Commemorative marble gravestones
have been recently erected by the Veterans Administration in honor
of Colonel Jeromus Remsen, Major Abraham Remsen, and their two
brothers, Aert and Garrett, who were officers in the Revolution. A
memorial honoring the community's participation in World War I
occupies the center of the cemetery. The graveyard and memorials
are preserved and maintained by various local organizations and
citizens within the community.

COE HOUSE, 1793–94
1128 East 34th Street, Brooklyn
Architect: Unknown
Designated: November 19, 1969

This late-eighteenth-century Dutch Colonial farmhouse is a striking
contrast to the ordinary twentieth-century houses that now surround
it. Sometimes referred to as the Van Nuyse House, after Joost Van
Nuyse's eighty-five-acre farm, the house was rented to Ditmas Coe by
Johannes Van Nuyse, Joost's son. Today the building is better known
as the Coe House.

The one-and-one-half-story frame house stands behind a white
fence of an unusual design, known as an Adams fence. A low, brick
stoop leads to the paneled Dutch door with transom above. The main
portion of the house, two bays wide, has low windows at floor level
under the eaves of a steeply pitched roof with a cantilevered
overhang. The smaller wing of the house is similar in design; it has
an immense walk-in cooking fireplace and a beamed ceiling. Two
windows and one door wide, the wing has a covered porch supported
by five square posts.

FLATBUSH DUTCH REFORMED CHURCH
Brooklyn

Flatbush Dutch Reformed Church, 1793–98;
addition, 1887
866 Flatbush Avenue
Architect: Thomas Fardon
Designated: March 15, 1966

Graveyard, established late 17th century
890 Flatbush Avenue
Designated: January 9, 1979

Parsonage, 1853
2101–2103 Kenmore Terrace
Architect: Unknown
Designated: January 9, 1979

The Church House, 1922
890 Flatbush Avenue
Architects: Meyer & Mathieu
Designated: January 9, 1979

In 1654, under orders from Director General Peter Stuyvesant, the first Dutch Reformed church was built in Flatbush. By 1698, as the neighborhood prospered, a more substantial building was financed by local inhabitants. In August of 1793, in the mood of expansion that followed the Revolution, they voted to erect still another church, this one to be designed by Thomas Fardon.

Three courses of squared sandstone blocks rest above the foundation of gray Manhattan schist. The octagonal wooden lantern with Tuscan columns supports entablature blocks topped by graceful urns. The tall, wooden steeple is also octagonal; at the top is a gilded weather vane. An extension of the apse was added in 1887 to accommodate the organ and choir loft.

Thirteen years after the church was designated, the landmark site was expanded to include the Parsonage, Church House, and graveyard. The Parsonage, a large, imposing wood-frame residence at 2101–2103 Kenmore Terrace, was built south of the church in 1853. The structure—two and one-half stories high with four chimneys and a peaked roof—is five bays wide with a center hall, in the Greek Revival tradition with some Italianate details. A porch extends across the front of the house, with a roof supported by ten wooden, fluted Corinthian columns, connected by a railing of delicately turned wooden balusters. The floor-length parlor windows on each side of the front door retain exterior wooden louvered shutters. The front door has a three-light transom and flanking sidelights. In 1918 the parsonage was moved to its present location across from the cemetery.

Meyer & Mathieu designed the Church House of 1922. Two stories high and nine bays wide, the Georgian-style structure is built of red brick laid in Flemish bond. The five central bays project slightly to create a pavilion with six fluted Corinthian pilasters supporting a heavy entablature. The four round-arched window openings and main entrance contain stone lunettes with oval medallions in the center and draped swags on either side. The building rests on a high basement of cast stone blocks that project forward to create a broad terrace.

Members of the early Dutch families are interred in the cemetery adjoining the church, which is included in the expanded landmark site.

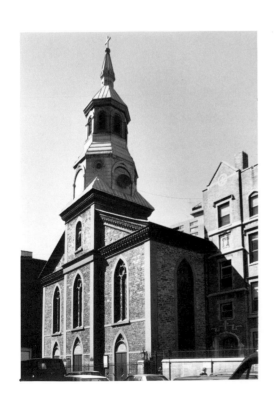

CHURCH OF THE TRANSFIGURATION, 1801
25 Mott Street, Manhattan
Architect: Unknown
Designated: February 1, 1966

The English Lutheran congregation built this charming and unpretentious church in 1801. Called the Lutheran Zion Church, it was constructed of the same rubble masonry as St. Paul's Chapel, but this early church is far less sophisticated in its detailing. It is Georgian in style, with steeply pitched end gables, rich entablature and quoins, and rectangular plan with the tower set forward. Decidedly not Georgian, however, and somewhat unexpected in the early 1800s, are the pitched window heads reminiscent of English Gothic parish churches.

The church was partially destroyed by the Great Fire of 1835. In 1853, the Roman Catholic Church of the Transfiguration, known as the Church of Immigrants, bought this building and moved to 25 Mott Street, at which time the church was remodeled and the bell tower replaced.

SHRINE OF THE BLESSED ELIZABETH SETON,
formerly the James Watson House, right portion, 1793; left portion, 1806;
restored, 1965
7 State Street, Manhattan
Architects: Attributed to John McComb, Jr.;
restoration, Shanley & Sturges
Designated: November 23, 1965

The Shrine of Elizabeth Ann Seton is the last of an elegant row of houses that once faced the Bowery on State Street. The easternmost, older part of the house, two windows wide, was built in 1793 and is Georgian in feeling, except for the typically Federal detail of two marble plaques inserted in the brickwork over the second-story windows. The house is more famous for the Federal wing of 1806, attributed to American architect John McComb, Jr. The addition is noted for its curved porch with delicate Ionic columns rising two stories from the second floor; graceful oval windows enhance the west wall. The attenuation of columns, always a characteristic of the Federal style, is particularly exaggerated here because the columns were made from ships' masts.

Built as a gentleman's home, this building demonstrates that even when pressed together in rows, such houses retained elegance and individuality. Surrounded today by sheer glass walls of modern office towers, the house still stands out. On the basis of a print from Valentine's Manual of 1859, the house has been restored to its original appearance, with its fine cornice, distinctive second-floor porch windows, and attractive balustrade at the edge of the roof.

ST. MARK'S-IN-THE-BOWERY CHURCH, 1795–99; steeple, 1828; portico, 1854
East 10th Street at Second Avenue, Manhattan
Architects: Unknown (church); Ithiel Town (steeple)
Designated: April 19, 1966

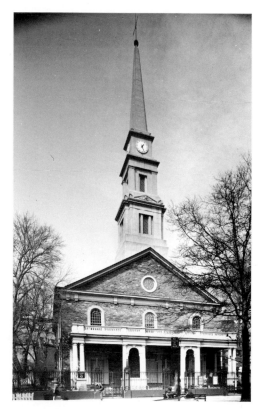

St. Mark's-in-the-Bowery, an Episcopalian church and once part of the parish of Trinity Church, was erected in 1799 on the site of a 1660 Dutch chapel on Peter Stuyvesant's farm, or *bouwerie*; funds for the construction of the new church were donated by Stuyvesant's great-grandson. Peter Stuyvesant's remains, along with those of his heirs and his English successor, Governor Sloughter, are buried in the church's vault. The architect of the church remains unknown.

Just months after its consecration in 1799, the vestry of St. Mark's considered setting up its own parish. By the terms of its charter, Trinity was supposed to be the only parish in the city, and churches built before St. Mark's—such as St. Paul's Chapel—were in fact part of Trinity and administered by the Trinity parish. Two prominent members of St. Mark's, Alexander Hamilton and Richard Harrison, found a legal detour around this part of Trinity's charter and were able to establish their church as the second independent Episcopal parish in New York. This precedent enabled other Episcopalian congregations to create new parishes as the city grew.

The church itself, with a west tower over a colossal portico, was probably modeled after James Gibbs's London masterpiece, St. Martin-in-the-Fields. Gibbs published engravings of his church, and his design, with a lofty tower rising over a pediment, was imitated all over the eastern seaboard.

The most distinctive features of these Gibbsian, colonial designs are the steeple, a translation of Gothic into classical forms, and the prominent quoins used to subdivide the elevation. In 1828 Ithiel Town altered the steeple, making the Gibbsian type into a Greek Revival tower. The colossal cast-iron portico is in a Renaissance mode. A chancel was added in 1836, and the present altar in 1891. The mosaics above the reredos are based on the lions outside St. Mark's in Venice. In the mid-nineteenth century, the rough fieldstone exterior received a coat of smooth plaster, which was removed in the 1930s.

After a fire in 1978, the Preservation Youth Project—a work-training program sponsored by the church—undertook the building's restoration.

Octagon Tower

Blackwell House

Good Shepherd Community Ecumenical Center

Smallpox Hospital

ROOSEVELT ISLAND
Designated: March 23, 1976

Blackwell House, 1796–1804
Blackwell Park, adjacent to Main Street
Architect: Unknown

Octagon Tower, 1839;
additions, 1847–48, 1879
North of Northtown
Architect: Alexander Jackson Davis

Smallpox Hospital, 1854–56
Southwest of Strecker Laboratory
Architect: James Renwick, Jr.

Lighthouse, 1872
North tip of island
Architect: James Renwick, Jr.

Good Shepherd Community Ecumenical
Center, formerly Chapel of the Good
Shepherd, 1888–89
543 Main Street
Architect: Frederick Clarke Withers

Strecker Laboratory, 1892
Southeast of City Hospital
Architects: Withers & Dickson

Across the East River from midtown Manhattan lies Roosevelt Island, a sliver of land two and one-half miles long. The island was not always known by that name. In the 1630s, the Dutch called it Varken Island, some years later the English renamed it Manning's Island, and after the Revolution, it became Blackwell's Island. Jacob Blackwell's restored Federal-style mansion remains a link to the last private owner.

In 1828, the city of New York paid Blackwell a mere $30,000 for the 120-acre island and began populating it with vast institutions—some penal, others humanitarian, and many a combination of both. The quality of the architecture was uncompromising: in that era of strong civic pride, city officials rejected the commonplace and chose top architects to ensure the excellence of the design. The result was an extraordinary collection of some of New York City's finest historical landmarks. The six landmark structures, dating from the late eighteenth century to the late nineteenth century, illustrate the transformation of 107 acres of open farmland to institutional use.

The oldest structure on the island, the Blackwell House is a modest clapboard farmhouse built in the vernacular style in 1796–1804 by the Blackwell family, who farmed the island from the late seventeenth century until they sold it to the city in 1828. Restored in 1973, the house is one of the few farmhouses dating from the years following the Revolution; it is now used as a community center.

Surrounded by an attractive plaza, the Chapel of the Good Shepherd was designed by Frederick Withers and built in 1888–89. Late Victorian Gothic in style, the chapel is in the tradition of English parish churches. The richly textured and subtly polychromatic wall surfaces enrich the simply massed structure. The chapel was the gift of banker George M. Bliss and was intended for use by inmates of the city's almshouse, which stood nearby. The chapel closed in 1958 and reopened in 1975 following restoration. It is now one of the island's community centers and an ecumenical place of worship.

On the southern end of the island stand two exceptional landmarks. The older, and for many the most romantic, is James Renwick, Jr.'s original Smallpox Hospital. When it was officially opened in 1857, it was a miraculous haven, the first public facility in the United States to provide professional care for those afflicted with that dreaded contagious disease. Today, the bare and weathered Gothic walls are reminiscent of ancient English ruins.

Faced with gray gneiss quarried on the island, the hospital is three stories high and U-shaped in plan. The dramatic focal point of the building is the entry: a heavy stone porch is surmounted by a crenellated bay and enhanced by a massive towerlike structure above, with recessed Gothic pointed arch on corbels. The whole is crowned by crenellations and a smaller, freestanding pointed arch. Additions were made in 1903–04 (York & Sawyer, architects) and in 1904–05 (Renwick, Aspinwall & Owen, architects).

The second building on the southern end is the Strecker Laboratory, also considered one of the most advanced facilities of its kind when it opened in 1892. Frederick Clarke Withers, the principal architect, is best known in the New York area for his earlier Jefferson Market Courthouse in the Gothic Revival style. This petite yet elegant Romanesque Revival building reflects the late-nineteenth-century shift of mood to the more restrained neo-Renaissance tradition popularized by McKim, Mead & White.

The picturesque silhouette of the Octagon Tower is still a prominent feature of the island's skyline. It is the sole surviving portion of the city's Lunatic Asylum, which opened in 1839, and was the central core of a much larger structure planned by architect Alexander Jackson Davis in 1834–35, partially completed in 1848, and added to in 1879. The Davis plan reflected a change in attitude toward mental illness: the recognition that patients required medical assistance, not merely custodial care. The bold geometry of the building, carried out in smooth, crisply faced walls of gneiss, is enhanced by simple detail and a "modern" treatment of fenestration: paired windows appear at each floor, separated by heavy mullions and by simple stone transverse members, creating a very modern feeling of continuous verticality. The domelike convex mansard roof and entrance were additions of 1879. Following the transfer of the indigent insane to Ward's Island in 1894, the name of the facility was changed to Metropolitan Hospital. It was closed in 1950.

Standing on a point of land that was once a separate, tiny island, the fifty-foot-tall lighthouse was built in 1872 under the supervision of James Renwick, Jr. The octagonal shaft of rock-faced random ashlar is enlivened by boldly scaled Gothic-style detail. According to legend, it was built by John McCarthy, an inmate of the nearby Lunatic Asylum.

In the 1920s, the island's name was changed again, to Welfare Island, and in 1973 to Roosevelt Island, in honor of Franklin Delano Roosevelt. Redevelopment plans for the island began in the late 1960s under the direction of the New York State Urban Development Corporation, and some of the abandoned and dilapidated landmarks were restored. Restoration of the structures was undertaken by New York architect Giorgio Cavaglieri, who had earlier adapted the old Astor Library to a new use as the Shakespeare Festival Theater, and the Jefferson Market Courthouse to a branch of the New York Public Library.

Lighthouse

VAN NUYSE-MAGAW HOUSE, c. 1800–03
1041 East 22nd Street, Brooklyn
Architect: Unknown
Designated: February 11, 1969

After his marriage to Nellie Lott on April 2, 1800, Johannes Van Nuyse constructed this Dutch Colonial–style frame farmhouse on the west end of his father's eighty-five-acre farm. Robert Magaw bought the house at some time between 1844 and 1852; Frederick, one of his three sons, sold it in 1909. George C. Case purchased the house in 1916; at about the same time he moved it to its present site, removed the kitchen wing, and added the new dormer windows.

The rectangular, two-and-one-half-story, shingled dwelling is on a lot bounded by two driveways. There are two large double-hung windows on the first floor, two paired windows on the floor above, and a single round-arched window in the attic in the west gable end of the house. A gambrel roof with out-sweeping curves projects beyond the two long sides, forming cantilevered overhangs. A brick path leads to a raised platform in front of the main entrance, which is flanked by two freestanding, fluted Doric columns supporting a low entablature.

HARRISON STREET HOUSES
Manhattan
Designated: May 13, 1969

317 Washington Street, 1797
Architect: John McComb, Jr.

Jonas Wood House, 1804
314 Washington Street
Architect: Unknown

315 Washington Street, 1819
Architect: John McComb, Jr.

Ebenezer Miller House, 1827
33 Harrison Street
Architect: Unknown

Jacob Ruckle House, 1827
31 Harrison Street
Architect: Unknown

Sarah R. Lambert House, 1827
29 Harrison Street
Architect: Unknown

Joseph Randolph House, 1828
329 Washington Street
Architect: Unknown

William B. Nichols House, 1828
331 Washington Street
Architect: Unknown

Wilson Hunt House, 1828
327 Washington Street
Architect: Unknown

This unique group of nine restored Federal-style brick town houses—forming an L-shaped enclave surrounded by the apartment towers of Independence Plaza—were erected between 1796 and 1828 on Harrison and Washington streets for specific owners. Two houses were designed by John McComb, Jr., New York's first native-born architect, and 317 Washington Street served as his residence for many years. All display the scale and craftsmanlike attention to detail characteristic of the Federal style; each is two and one-half stories high, built of Flemish bond brickwork, and retains its original pitched roof and dormers. Though built for people of considerable means, these houses nonetheless have discreet and modest interiors.

As the city grew and Washington Market moved northward, the houses became engulfed in a busy commercial environment; they were used for warehousing and deteriorated rapidly. By 1968, the houses were threatened with demolition. The Landmarks Preservation Commission worked with the Housing and Development Administration to secure funding to incorporate the landmarks within the redevelopment area and to pay for their restoration. This work has recently been completed by the firm of Oppenheimer, Brady & Vogelstein, and the houses have been sold to private owners.

ABIGAIL ADAMS SMITH MUSEUM, 1799
421 East 61st Street, Manhattan
Architect: Unknown
Designated: January 24, 1967

The Abigail Adams Smith Museum, also known as Smith's Folly and Mount Vernon on the East River, was designed as the coach house for the elaborate estate of Colonel William Stephens Smith and his wife, Abigail Adams Smith, daughter of John Adams and sister of John Quincy Adams. Before the Smiths finished the buildings on their property, they were forced by financial troubles to sell the estate to William T. Robinson, who completed the work in 1799.

The original manor house was destroyed by fire in 1826; the stable and several acres were purchased by Joseph Coleman Hart, who remodeled the stable as an inn. In 1833 the inn and land were purchased by Jeremiah Towle, and sold by his daughters to the Standard Gas and Light Company in 1905. The house soon fell into neglect. In 1919, Jane Teller, president of the Society of American Antiquarians, leased the house and opened a shop for antiques and colonial crafts here. In 1924, the Colonial Dames of America purchased the building; they have operated a museum here, open to the public, since 1939.

The architectural interest of the Federal stone stable lies in its superb masonry construction and excellent proportions. The low-pitched, pedimented gable roofs are cut in sharp profiles. Originally, large arched openings accommodated horse and carriage traffic; these were filled in with brick when the Harts converted the stable to an inn. They also added the Greek Revival porticoes and interior details, subdivided the large rooms, and added six fireplaces. The eighteenth-century-style garden that now surrounds the building was planted by the Colonial Dames, who furnished nine rooms of the house in the Federal style.

HAMILTON GRANGE, 1801
287 Convent Avenue, Manhattan
Architect: John McComb, Jr.
Designated: August 2, 1967

John McComb, Jr., New York's finest Federal architect, designed the Grange as a country home for Alexander Hamilton. The two-story clapboard house originally had elegant verandas and a shallow hipped roof masked by a balustrade. Doric columns carried the veranda roof; the order was repeated in the main cornice. Two of the four large chimneys were false, made of wood, an unusual manifestation of the period's obsession with symmetry.

Originally located on a thirty-five-acre tract along the Old Albany Post Road (now Kingsbridge Road), the Grange was moved to its present site in 1889 to escape demolition. One side now faces the street, so the front door and porch were moved to create a more impressive entrance. After its relocation, the Grange served as a chapel and rectory for St. Luke's Church; since 1962 it has been a National Monument, administered by the National Park Service.

Alexander Hamilton served George Washington during the Revolution as secretary and as aide-de-camp. Following the war, he was a member of the Continental Congress and the New York State Legislature. As secretary of the treasury he proposed a national bank in 1791 and the U.S. Mint in 1792. Hamilton, always a staunch Federalist, passionately held political convictions that led to his 1804 duel with Aaron Burr, in which Hamilton was mortally wounded.

GRACIE MANSION, 1799
East End Avenue at 88th Street in Carl Schurz Park, Manhattan
Architect: Unknown
Designated: September 20, 1966

New York's official mayoral residence, Gracie Mansion, is the only Federal-style country seat in Manhattan still used as a home. Archibald Gracie, a Scottish immigrant and successful New York merchant, built this house in 1799 on Horn's Hook, the site of loyalist Jacob Walton's 1774 dwelling. Walton's house was destroyed during the revolutionary war, and the American army then confiscated the site for use as a fort, which was also destroyed by British bombardment. Gracie used some of the old Walton house foundations for his two-story, three-chimneyed house.

In 1809, Gracie moved the entrance from the southeast to the northeast and created an entrance hall at the center of the house. He also added two bedrooms. Although the building's architect is unknown, it is possible that the designer was Ezra Weeks, who had become notorious in 1800 for his involvement in a murder trial.

Despite the threat of British attack, Gracie and his family summered in the house during the War of 1812; Gracie's business, however, was crippled by the war and never recovered. In 1823, Archibald Gracie & Sons was dissolved, and Rufus King, Gracie's longtime friend and trustee, sold the mansion to Joseph Foulke in the same year.

Prompted by the population increase downtown, Foulke made Gracie's summer estate his permanent residence, where he remained for nearly twenty-seven years. Noah Wheaton, a house builder, purchased the mansion and twelve surrounding lots in 1857; in their thirty-nine years there, the Wheatons decorated lavishly.

The Parks Commission purchased the house in 1896 and renamed the grounds Carl Schurz Park, in honor of the distinguished German immigrant, who had arrived in New York in 1852 and settled in Yorkville in 1881. Among other accomplishments, Schurz served as a U.S. senator and editor of the *Nation* and the *New York Evening Post*. It is fitting that the land surrounding Gracie's mansion was named in Schurz's honor, for Gracie had helped to establish the *New York Evening Post*, ninety-five years earlier.

The house was neglected for several years, but in 1927 the city undertook a first restoration; the house was restored again in 1942, when Mayor Fiorello La Guardia moved in. A reception wing was skillfully added in 1966. In the 1980s, extensive renovations, funded by private contributions from the Gracie Mansion Conservancy, were completed. Today, the mayor shares his home with the 25,000 New Yorkers and out-of-towners who visit it annually.

STUYVESANT-FISH HOUSE, 1803–04
21 Stuyvesant Street, Manhattan
Architect: Unknown
Designated: October 14, 1965

The house at 21 Stuyvesant Street, a three-story brick residence, exhibits the restraint and beauty of proportion that were hallmarks of the Federal period. The house was built by Peter Stuyvesant on a tract of land granted in 1651 to his great-grandfather, also Peter Stuyvesant, the last Dutch director general of New Netherland. The younger Peter Stuyvesant constructed the house for his daughter, Elizabeth, at the time of her marriage to Nicholas Fish, a close friend of Alexander Hamilton and General Lafayette. Fish entertained Lafayette here on the evening of September 10, 1824, during Lafayette's return to America in anticipation of the fiftieth anniversary of the Revolution. Hamilton Fish, Nicholas and Elizabeth's son, was born at 21 Stuyvesant Street in 1808; he continued the family tradition of public service as governor of New York, U.S. senator, and secretary of state.

The three-bay façade remains intact, with its high New York stoop, splayed brownstone lintels, and arched dormer windows with double keystones. Inside as well, numerous features remain unchanged, including the archway in the entrance hall, the stairway, and the elaborate plaster ceiling ornament.

OLD ST. PATRICK'S CATHEDRAL
Manhattan

Old St. Patrick's Cathedral, 1809–15;
restored, 1868
Mott and Prince streets
Architect: Joseph F. Mangin
Designated: June 21, 1966

Old St. Patrick's Convent and
Girls' School, 1826
32 Prince Street
Architect: Unknown
Designated: June 21, 1966

St. Michael's Chapel, 1858–59
266 Mulberry Street
Architects: James Renwick, Jr., and
William Rodrigue
Designated: July 12, 1977

Old St. Patrick's Cathedral

The original St. Patrick's Cathedral and its companions—St. Michael's Chapel and the Convent and Girls' School—are among the oldest ecclesiastical structures in the city. The cathedral was begun in 1809, a year after the Diocese of New York was established by Pope Pius VII. The War of 1812 interrupted the work, but architect Joseph Mangin, co-architect of City Hall, was able to complete the church by 1815. The original church, with its tripartite Gothic façade, was among the first Gothic Revival churches in this country; half a century after its completion, it was destroyed by a disastrous fire. All that we see today, with the exception of the pointed windows along the nave, was added in 1868 when the church was rebuilt; yet the rebuilt church is an impressive, if severely plain, masonry structure.

Around the corner from the cathedral is the Convent and Girls' School. Completed in 1826, the convent and school were conservatively designed in the late Federal style; the main doorway is one of the finest surviving examples in the city of this restrained yet elegant style.

St. Michael's Chapel was built in 1858–59 as a chancery office; designed by James Renwick, Jr., in association with William Rodrigue, it is a Gothic Revival masterpiece. Three stories high and built of red brick, this small building is noted for its central projecting stone entrance vestibule with pointed-arched doorway outlined by a drip molding. It is currently used for worship by Catholics of the Russian Rite.

St. Michael's Chapel

CITY HALL, 1803–12; restored, 1954–56
Broadway at City Hall Park, Manhattan
Architect: John McComb, Jr., and Joseph F. Mangin
Designated: February 1, 1966; interior designated January 27, 1976

New York's City Hall, built between 1803 and 1812, ranks among the finest architectural achievements of its period in America. The exterior is a wonderfully orchestrated blend of Federal and French Renaissance styles; the interior, dominated by the cylindrical, domed space of the Rotunda, reflects the American Georgian manner. Serving today—as it has since 1812—as the center of municipal government, City Hall continues to recall the spirit of the early years of the new Republic, when both the nation and the city were setting forth on new paths.

The building, actually New York's third city hall, is the result of the successful collaboration of John McComb, Jr., the first American-born architect, and Joseph Mangin, a French emigré. There still exists considerable controversy over the exact nature of the contribution of each man. Trained in the master-builder tradition of his father, John McComb, Jr., was the leading architect in New York after the American Revolution, and is often credited with the majority of the interior design. Joseph Mangin was, some feel, probably the principal designer of the exterior, particularly in view of the French look of City Hall. McComb and Mangin carried off first prize and a $350 award following the open architectural contest in 1802. The cornerstone was laid by Mayor Edward Livingston on May 26, 1803, and after numerous financial setbacks, the building was dedicated on July 4, 1811. City Hall, which Henry James described as a "divine little structure," was ready for use the following year.

At the time of City Hall's construction, no one expected the city to extend north of Chambers Street. To cut costs, only the front and side façades were covered in marble; the rear received a less dignified treatment in New Jersey brownstone. The building is a clearly defined central structure with projecting side wings, elegantly articulated by a parade of windows decorated with pilasters and, on the top story, typical French Renaissance swags. A one-story Ionic portico sits atop a broad sweep of entry steps. Its roof, bordered by a balustrade, forms an open deck in front of large, arched windows set between Corinthian columns. Above the attic rises the clock tower (1831), whose cupola is crowned by a copper figure of Justice. The two-story building was sheathed in durable Alabama limestone during a complete restoration in 1954–56.

The interior is dominated by the Rotunda. Its grandeur is the product of an impressively simple spatial organization (extending back to the Roman Pantheon), the colors and light emanating from the coffered dome's oculus, and the refined decorative detail throughout. The central space encloses a magnificent double stairway that unfolds and circles up to the landing at the second floor, itself surrounded by ten Corinthian columns supporting the great dome. It was at the top of this staircase, just outside the Governor's Room, that the body of Abraham Lincoln lay in state on April 24 and 25, 1865.

Although repeatedly threatened with demolition, City Hall stands within its park, beautifully restored and maintained. Its scale and style provide a dramatic contrast to the buildings that have grown up around it in the last century and a half.

BROOKLYN NAVY YARD
Brooklyn

Commandant's House, 1805–06
Hudson Avenue and Evans Street, New York
Naval Shipyard
Architects: Attributed to Charles Bulfinch
and John McComb, Jr.
Designated: October 14, 1965

U.S. Naval Hospital, 1830–38
Hospital Road between Squibb Place and
Oman Road, New York Naval Shipyard
Architect: Martin E. Thompson
Designated: October 14, 1965

Dry Dock #1, 1840–51
Dock Street at Third Street
Engineer: William J. McAlpine
Architect and master of masonry: Thornton
MacNess Niven
Designated: September 23, 1975

Surgeon's House, 1863
Third U.S. Naval District, Flushing Avenue
opposite Ryerson Street
Builders: True W. Rollins and
Charles Hastings
Designated: November 9, 1976

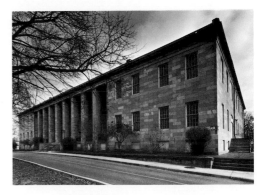

U.S. Naval Hospital

In 1801 the U.S. Navy purchased this property from John Jackson, owner of a small private shipyard; by 1812, the yard had become an important servicing facility, and it remained so for over a century. During the Civil War, the yard's 5,000 workers fitted out 400 merchant-marine vessels as cruisers; and during World War II, 70,000 workers were employed here, turning out battleships and destroyers for the war effort.

The property, now closed to the public, includes four designated landmarks. The earliest of these is the former Commandant's House, a three-story Federal structure attributed to Charles Bulfinch with John McComb, Jr. The elaborately carved front entrance—which is actually on the second floor—has a leaded fanlight; the attic is crowned by dormer windows and a widow's walk, and there is an ornate cornice at the level of the roof.

Surgeon's House

Built in 1830–38, the U.S. Naval Hospital (formerly the U.S. Marine Hospital) is a two-story, 125-bed Greek Revival structure in the shape of an E. The refined granite building contains a recessed portico with eight classical piers of stone that reach the full height of the building.

Occupying the same property as the hospital, the Surgeon's House follows the style of the French Second Empire with its low, concave mansard roof and dormer windows. It is a two-story brick structure divided into two main sections, the house proper and a servant's wing, together totaling sixteen rooms. The symmetrical entrance façade has a central doorway flanked by segmental arches and low balustrades. Also on the first floor is a handsome, projecting three-sided bay window; on the second floor, segmental-arched windows rest on small corbel blocks. The side elevations of the house show both segmental-arched and square-headed windows.

Commandant's House

The first permanent dry dock in the New York area was primarily engineered by William J. McAlpine. He solved several massive problems posed by the excavation site, which included a faulty cofferdam and flooding underground springs. The successful masonry superstructure, still active today, consists primarily of 23,000 cubic yards of granite facing. Designed to withstand the uplifting forces, the stone at the bottom of the dry dock forms a great inverted arch below a flat, thirty-foot-wide floor. The sides of the dock are stepped. The dock's landward end terminates in a curve, while the seaward end is an inverted arch set back to accommodate a large metal floating gate. This gate can be raised and floated free to one side, thus eliminating the need for hinges and allowing large ships to enter. Among the ships that have been built or serviced here are the *Monitor*, of Civil War fame, and the *Niagara*, which laid the first transatlantic cable. The city of New York purchased the navy yard in 1966; much of the property has fallen into disuse, but the dry dock is operated by the New York Dry Dock Company.

Dry Dock #1

CASTLE CLINTON, 1807
The Battery, Manhattan
Architect: John McComb, Jr.
Designated: November 23, 1965

Castle Clinton once promised great security to Manhattan, although none of its twenty-eight guns were ever fired in battle. Once three hundred feet from the tip of the island and connected by a causeway, but since incorporated into Manhattan by landfill, the rock-faced brownstone fort designed by John McComb, Jr., is a formidable presence, with massive walls measuring eight feet thick at the gun ports. The more refined rusticated gate reflects the influence of French military engineer Sébastian de Vauban.

The federal government ceded the fort to the city in 1823, when it was converted to Castle Garden, a fashionable gathering place that was the scene of some spectacular social events, notably Jenny Lind's 1850 American debut. In 1855 it became an immigrant landing depot; over 7.5 million people were processed at the fort during the center's forty-five years of operation. Remodeled again by McKim, Mead & White in 1896, the fort became the New York Aquarium, remaining a popular attraction until it closed in 1941. Thwarted in his desire to construct a Brooklyn-Battery bridge on the site, Robert Moses retaliated by attempting to demolish the building in 1946. Only a public outcry stopped him, but not before McKim, Mead & White's addition had been destroyed.

The federal government recognized Castle Clinton as a National Monument in 1946; it has since been under the jurisdiction of the National Park Service. It stands today as an outstanding example of nineteenth-century American military architecture and as a testament to the rich cultural patrimony of southern Manhattan.

2 WHITE STREET, 1809
Manhattan
Builder: Gideon Tucker
Designated: July 19, 1966

A modest, two-story building that has surprisingly survived the times is the tiny house at 2 White Street. It was erected as a residence by and for Gideon Tucker, a prominent New Yorker in his day. He was the assistant alderman of the Fifth Ward, a school commissioner, and commissioner of estimates and assessments.

Although it was completed in 1809, this house is really eighteenth century in its feeling and style. The gambrel roof, splayed lintels, and double keystones of the second story are Georgian. The very flat, pedimented dormers containing elliptical-headed openings are rare Federal survivors. There has probably always been a shop on the ground floor.

SCHERMERHORN ROW, 1811–12
2–18 Fulton Street, 91–92 South Street,
and 189–195 Front Street, Manhattan
Architects: Unknown
Designated: October 29, 1968

Schermerhorn Row, one of the earliest commercial developments in
New York City, consists of twelve red-brick warehouses erected
between 1811 and 1812 by Peter Schermerhorn, one of New York's
leading merchants, who ran a ship chandler's business at 243 Water
Street. Designed in the Federal style, and originally of equal height,
the group is made up of nine row houses on Fulton Street, and houses
at 195 Front Street and 91 and 92 South Street around the corner.
The buildings were used as warehouses and stores for cargo in an era
when New York Harbor was a busy port for sailing ships. The row on
the south side of Fulton Street runs from number 2 at South Street to
number 18 at Front Street. The building at 92 South Street, which
adjoins 2 Fulton Street at the corner, was converted into a hotel in the
late nineteenth century; at this time, the original cornice was
removed, and two stories, with mansard roof and dormers, were
added.

The row is today part of the South Street Seaport Museum, an
institution that oversees the preservation of the structures in this part
of the city.

POE COTTAGE, c. 1812; restored, 1913
2640 Grand Concourse at Kingsbridge Road, The Bronx
Architect: Unknown; restoration, John Harden
Designated: February 15, 1966

Poe Cottage, named for its most famous resident, Edgar Allan Poe, is
one of the few extant nineteenth-century wood-frame residences in
the Bronx. Built for John Wheeler, the simple clapboard farmhouse
with attic and porch stands one and one-half stories tall. The siding
and shutters are original; the doors and windows, while period
originals, were added in 1913 by architect John Harden. Initially
located on Kingsbridge Road, the cottage was moved once in 1895 to
allow for the widening of the road, and again in 1913 to occupy a two-
and-one-half-acre plot designated Poe Park by New York City.

When Poe lived here, the cottage was still at Kingsbridge Road.
He rented the small farmhouse from 1846 to 1849 in the hope of
providing his dying wife, Virginia, with therapeutic country air. The
treatment failed, and Virginia died here in 1847. It is generally
believed that Poe wrote "Annabel Lee"—a memorial to his young
wife—and his last great work, "Eureka," while he lived here.

Poe Cottage is operated as a historic home museum by the Bronx
County Historical Society; it is jointly administered by the society
and the New York City Department of Parks and Recreation.

STEELE HOUSE, c. 1812
200 Lafayette Avenue, Brooklyn
Architect: Unknown
Designated: March 19, 1968

This two-and-one-half-story Greek Revival frame house, with later Italianate embellishments, dates from the first quarter of the nineteenth century. An ornate iron fence encloses the corner lot, and a flight of wooden steps—complete with newel posts, turned spindles, and a wide handrail—projects from the front of the house. The doorway supports an entablature with a modillioned cornice, a feature repeated at the shuttered, octagonal cupola rising above the roof. Adjoining the main façade but set back is a wing with a narrow porch raised several feet above the ground; French doors lead into the first floor. An engaged pilaster and two fluted Ionic columns support an entablature and low-pitched roof, and a dentiled cornice crowns the wing.

OLD WEST FARMS SOLDIER CEMETERY, established 1815
2103 Bryant Avenue, The Bronx
Designated: August 2, 1967

The remains of forty soldiers lie in this small cemetery, the oldest veterans' graveyard in the Bronx. Samuel Adams, a veteran of the War of 1812, was the first buried here; Valerino Tulosa, a veteran of World War I, was the last. Veterans of the Civil and Spanish-American wars are also interred here. A bronze statue of a Union soldier once stood in the cemetery.

The neighborhood around the cemetery was given the name West Farms in 1663 by Edward Jessup and John Richardson, who hoped to distinguish their recently acquired property from the nearby Westchester Village. John Butler founded the cemetery in 1815 on property that he had laid out as a private burial ground the year before. The Butler family retained control of the site until 1954, when New York City assumed responsibility for the cemetery's upkeep.

STEPHEN VAN RENSSELAER HOUSE, 1816; moved, 1841
149 Mulberry Street, Manhattan
Architect: Unknown
Designated: February 11, 1969

The Stephen Van Rensselaer House is a lonely reminder of the small Federal-style row houses built in Lower Manhattan during the early nineteenth century. Its high-shouldered gambrel roof and round-headed dormers with delicate pilasters are typical of the period, as are the lintels, with their flat, incised panels.

Built at 153 Mulberry in 1816 for Stephen Van Rensselaer and assessed at $3,750, the building was moved to 149 Mulberry Street in 1841. The basement and first floor have been occupied for nearly forty years by a restaurant; the upper stories are residential and are currently being restored to a semblance of their original architectural design.

JAMES BROWN HOUSE, 1817
326 Spring Street, Manhattan
Architect: Unknown
Designated: November 19, 1969

Several small residences, remnants of the city's early history, are found today in densely developed manufacturing sections of New York. One of the earliest is the James Brown House at 326 Spring Street. Built in 1817—when it was assessed for the considerable sum of $2,000—it is a charming, modest Federal-style structure with the high gambrel roof characteristic of many little Federal houses. It has a brick façade, laid up in Flemish bond, three windows wide with stone sills. The splayed lintels and double flared keystones are a throwback to the earlier Georgian style. The two dormers are a later modification.

In the nineteenth century, the house was a brewery; it became a restaurant at the turn of the century. During Prohibition, it was a speakeasy, with a boardinghouse, brothel, and smugglers' den upstairs. Later on, the establishment became a sailors' bar. Today it is a popular, casual night spot; the present owner, who bought the building in 1977, runs the bar and resides in the building. The house offers an unexpected sense of scale and intimacy.

FIRST CHINESE PRESBYTERIAN CHURCH,
formerly Church of Sea and Land, 1817
61 Henry Street, Manhattan
Architect: Unknown
Designated: January 18, 1966

Colonel Henry Rutgers, the American revolutionary war patriot, donated land for the construction of this attractive church, whose design shows a Georgian influence. In 1866, when the church began to serve seamen, it was named the Church of Sea and Land.

Ashlar quoins, horizontal stone belt courses, and stone window and door frames animate this simple brick church. Full-length windows flank the sides of the building; on the interior, the windows are backed by balconies. The pointed-arched windows anticipate the Gothic Revival by some thirty years.

MOORE-MCMILLEN HOUSE,
formerly Rectory of the Church of St. Andrew, 1818
3531 Richmond Road, Staten Island
Architect: Unknown
Designated: August 24, 1967

The Moore-McMillen House, completed in 1818, is one of the few nineteenth-century Federal-style farmhouses surviving on Staten Island. This modest, two-story wood-shingle house is characterized by a low-pitched, high-shouldered gambrel roof. Among its beautifully executed architectural details are the entry door, highlighted by well-proportioned pilasters, panels, sidelights, and transom; a dentilled cornice; and flush siding beneath the veranda. The simple floor plan consists of a central hall and staircase with two rooms extending from each side.

The Moore-McMillen House was built by the Episcopal Church of St. Andrew, located in the nearby village of Richmondtown. Set on a sixty-acre farm known as Little Glebe, the house was the home and rectory for the church's minister, the Reverend David Moore. He served the parish for forty-eight years and eventually received the house from the church; it remained in the Moore family until 1943. In 1944, Loring McMillen, borough and county historian for Richmond, who still owns and maintains the house, sympathetically restored this architecturally significant home.

83, 85, 116 SULLIVAN STREET, 1819–32
Manhattan
Architects: Unknown
Designated: May 15, 1973

Sullivan Street—named for John Sullivan, the revolutionary general—has three surviving Federal-style town houses built on what was once part of the farm belonging to Nicholas Bayard, Peter Stuyvesant's brother-in-law. A later Nicolas Bayard sold the land in 1789, and over the next three decades the property was subdivided into lots and changed owners four times. In 1819 the houses at 83 and 85 were built; in 1832, number 116 was erected.

Modest yet elegantly charming, these houses typify the Federal style—sometimes referred to as "the architecture of good breeding." Among their most distinctive features are their original Federal doorways, Flemish bond brickwork, six-over-six pane windows, and wrought-iron stoop railings.

The house at 116, built over a decade later than its neighbors, has an unusual and elaborate Federal doorway enframement. Flanked by plain brownstone pilasters, with a semicircular band of brownstone defining the simple, round-arched masonry opening, the doorway has perhaps the most unusual sidelights in the city. Instead of the leaded-glass treatment typical of the period, each sidelight is divided into three oval sections, formed by a richly carved wood enframement that simulates a cloth sash curtain drawn through a series of rings.

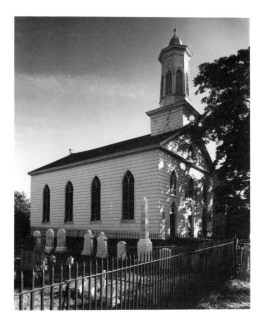

NEW LOTS COMMUNITY CHURCH, 1823
630 New Lots Avenue, Brooklyn
Architect: Unknown
Designated: July 19, 1966

The New Lots Community Church, formerly the New Lots Reformed Dutch Church, is one of New York's oldest standing wooden churches. Built in 1823 during the late Federal period, the church is an example of a rural clapboard structure. Local oaks were cut and hand-shaped in order to frame the building, and a raising bee was held to construct it. The timbers themselves were jointed and secured by pegs.

The church includes details in the early Gothic Revival style. The front elevation is dominated by a plain, low-pitched pediment with three windows above three doors, all framed with pointed wooden arches. The center window is a triple Palladian window. Four pointed-arched windows are included in both of the identical side elevations. The low-pitched gable roof supports a square tower base with an octagonal belfry, which is topped by a cupola-style roof. The church has a provincial character and, as a wooden church of this period, is architecturally unique to New York City.

BIALYSTOKER SYNAGOGUE, formerly Willett Street Methodist Church, 1826
7–13 Willett Street, Manhattan
Architect: Unknown
Designated: April 19, 1966

The Bialystoker Synagogue, originally the Willett Street Methodist Church, is a severely plain late Federal building. With its cheerful fieldstone façade, the structure is a fine example of masonry construction in the vernacular tradition. Its simple exterior is marked by three windows over three doors, framed with round arches; a base course with a low flight of brownstone steps; a low-pitched, pedimented roof pierced by a lunette window; and a very plain wooden cornice.

In 1905 the building was purchased by the Bialystoker Synagogue, whose congregation was composed chiefly of Polish immigrants from the province of Bialystok (now in the U.S.S.R.).

51 MARKET STREET, 1824–25
Manhattan
Architect: Unknown
Designated: October 14, 1965

The house at 51 Market Street exemplifies the architecture of the newly created Republic. This four-story brick building is an admirable urban example of the late Federal style; well preserved, it sets a standard by which other houses of the period may be judged today.

The front entrance is one of the few fine, complete late Federal doorways in the city; both original outer and inner entryways are intact. An eight-paneled door is flanked by fluted Ionic columns, leaded-glass sidelights, and similar half-columns; the whole is surrounded by a molded, elliptical-arched stone frame. A handsome leaded-glass fanlight is set above the door. The basement windows are framed with a rusticated architrave composed of alternating smooth and textured blocks of stone; the windows on the first three floors retain their original lintels, which are elaborately decorated with panels and rosettes. Much of the exterior ironwork is also original; in the Federal tradition, it is predominantly wrought iron, in contrast to the cast iron that was used later in Greek Revival architecture.

FORT HAMILTON, 1825–31
Fort Hamilton Parkway at 101st Street, Brooklyn
Architect: Unknown
General designer: Simon Bernard
Designated: March 8, 1977

No shot was ever fired from this fort in battle; nonetheless, it remained in a constant state of military readiness from 1831 until World War II, and the original structure is still part of an active army base—the third-oldest continuously garrisoned federal post in the nation. When vertical-walled masonry defenses became obsolete during the Civil War, old Fort Hamilton became a barracks, then the post stockade, and finally—after 1938—an officers' club. A large function room was added at that time, another in 1958, and a third in 1985.

Built of granite blocks in random ashlar, the fort today takes the form of an elongated C, since the wall facing the Verrazano Narrows was destroyed in the 1890s for newer coastal guns. At the rear of the fort, the original casemates—a series of chambers for cannon that were fired through embrasures in an outer wall or scarp—face another wall or counterscarp across the dry ditch, now used for parking. This system, developed by the French engineer Montalembert in the 1780s, provided greater protection to guns and crews and made possible multiple-gun tiers.

Today the main fort is a private club, but the original architecture is on view at the fort's nearby caponier, or flank defense, now the Harbor Defense Museum of New York City, almost unchanged; the main fort, however, in addition to its new rooms, has been lined with stucco, and its embrasures have been enlarged to form windows.

HENRY STREET SETTLEMENT
Manhattan
Architects: Unknown
Designated: January 18, 1966

263 Henry Street, 1827

265 Henry Street, 1827

267 Henry Street, 1834

Founded in 1893 by Lillian Wald to alleviate the living conditions of slum dwellers on the Lower East Side, the Henry Street Settlement occupies three well-preserved early-nineteenth-century houses in Manhattan. The modified Federal houses at 263 and 265 Henry Street were built in 1827; number 267, which is Georgian Eclectic in style, was built in 1834. The eight-paneled front door of number 265 is a rare survivor of the Federal period; it is flanked by attenuated Ionic columns and surmounted by a transom that once held leaded glass. The sidelights (also once of leaded glass) are framed by richly carved moldings, and just over the front door itself is a break in the entablature, a typical Federal detail. Other Federal features that have survived include the wrought-iron railings, open box newel, and the acorn and pineapple finials—symbols of hospitality—that top the areaway posts of 265 and 263, respectively. The cornice over the doorway and the window lintels of number 265 are later additions. The houses at 263 and 267, while practically contemporary with number 265, have been much modified by later changes.

The Henry Street Settlement was one of the earliest social programs of its kind in the United States. Miss Wald, a nurse and settlement worker from a privileged, middle-class Jewish family in Rochester, was struck by the intolerable filth and desperation that were the immigrant's lot on the Lower East Side. She persuaded some wealthy friends—notably philanthropist Jacob Schiff—to finance a small establishment on Henry Street to serve as a volunteer nursing service and social center.

In 1895, Schiff acquired number 265 Henry Street for the use of the Henry Street Settlement/Visiting Nurse Service; numbers 267 and 263 were added to the settlement in 1903 and 1934. Schiff's estate included a gift of $300,000 to the settlement for the construction of a central administration building for the Visiting Nurse Service.

Over the years, some of the country's most fundamental health and social programs were generated here, among them district nursing, school nurses, the U.S. Children's Bureau, and the whole concept of public-health nursing. Henry Street Settlement is still operating from the three landmark buildings, where the executive and administrative offices are located.

NEW UTRECHT REFORMED CHURCH, 1828
18th Avenue at 83rd Street, Brooklyn
Architect: Unknown
Designated: March 15, 1966

The Reformed Protestant Dutch Church of New Utrecht was organized in October 1677, and by 1699 a fieldstone church building had been erected on this site. During the American Revolution, the British used the original church as a hospital and cavalry-training school. The present church, an early Gothic Revival meetinghouse, was built with fieldstone from the 1699 building, which was destroyed to make way for this structure. Surrounded by trees and boxwood, it has a countrified aspect today.

The structure has painted brick arches and a handsome stone tower with wooden Gothic pinnacles. A round, late Federal-style window pierces the wall over the main entrance, and a cornice extends around the building. A liberty pole, marking the spot over which the American flag first waved after the departure of the British from New Utrecht, stands on the church grounds, the sixth one erected in succession on this site.

ST. AUGUSTINE'S CHAPEL, formerly All Saints' Free Church, 1828–29; additions, 1850, 1871
290 Henry Street, Manhattan
Architect: Attributed to John Heath
Designated: August 16, 1966

St. Augustine's Chapel—originally known as All Saints' Free Church—was founded in 1827 by a group of wealthy clipper-ship owners and builders. In 1850 the chancel was added to the original building, and the tower was built in 1871. The motto "All Saint's Church Free" was carved over the entrance when pew rent was abolished.

Built of Manhattan schist in a random ashlar pattern with wooden cornices, the church has a simple, boxlike mass with a slightly projecting central tower that breaks the front façade into three bays. The tower cuts through the pediment of the roof and is embellished with a smaller pediment, sharing the same horizontal cornice. Although a wooden spire was planned, it was never built. Classical motifs are kept to the pediments; the windows follow the Gothic tradition with their pointed arches. Each bay of the front façade has a door surmounted by a window. Windows pierce the side elevations too, as well as the tower.

In 1946, with a dwindling parish and bleak financial situation, All Saints' merged with Trinity Church, which assumed full financial responsibility. Renamed St. Augustine's, it is now one of Trinity's four chapels.

REFORMED DUTCH CHURCH OF NEWTOWN AND FELLOWSHIP HALL
85–15 Broadway, Queens
Architect: Unknown
Designated: July 19, 1966

Reformed Dutch Church, 1831

Fellowship Hall, 1860; moved and expanded, 1906

One of the oldest wooden churches in New York City, the white clapboard Reformed Dutch Church was built in 1831. Its cornerstone originally was part of an earlier church, erected in 1735.

The Georgian-style church features a flat-roofed porch with seven Neoclassical columns. Three round-headed windows (originally square-headed) are located above the porch, one above each of three doorways. Five similar windows adorn the sides of the sanctuary. A square base supports the church's octagonal bell tower, which straddles the west end of the roof.

Constructed in 1860 as a chapel, Fellowship Hall was built in the Greek Revival style. It, too, features a fine portico of wooden columns. These are surmounted by an entablature and a pedimented gable with a circular window.

In 1906, Fellowship Hall was aligned with the church; an addition now used as a wayside chapel was built to connect the two buildings.

HUNTERFLY ROAD HOUSES, c. 1830
1698, 1700, 1702–04, 1706–08 Bergen Street, Brooklyn
Architect: Unknown
Designated: August 18, 1970

Four wooden houses remain along the old Hunterfly Road, within the boundaries of what was once Weeksville, a nineteenth-century free black community that is now known as Bedford-Stuyvesant. A refuge for black families during the draft riots of the Civil War, the area became a predominantly black community with the abolition of slavery in New York in 1827. The road, documented as early as 1662, was an avenue of communication under British rule; it fell into disuse with the installation of a grid system in 1838.

The houses at 1698 and 1700 Bergen Street are two and one-half stories tall and three bays wide. On the latter, casement windows occupy the second-floor front. The pitched roof is covered with shingles on the north side and by clapboard at the south side. Similar in style, the houses at 1702–04 and 1706–08 are one story and one and one-half stories, respectively.

The Society for Preservation of Weeksville and Bedford-Stuyvesant History now owns the houses and is attempting to restore the properties for use as a historical museum.

NEW YORK MARBLE CEMETERY, established 1830
Interior of block between East 2nd and East 3rd streets,
Second Avenue and the Bowery, Manhattan
Designated: March 4, 1969

Manhattan's first nonsectarian burial ground open to the public was begun as a joint business enterprise on July 13, 1830. The founders Perkins Nichols, Anthony Dey, and George W. Strong purchased 156 underground vaults of Tuckahoe marble, sold them, and then charged a ten-dollar fee for opening and maintaining them.

There are no monuments or individual tombstones in the cemetery; only marble plaques set in the north and south walls, which bear the names of the 156 original owners and their vault numbers.

Among those buried here are David Olyphant, a China trade merchant who refused to deal in opium; Uriah Scribner and his son Charles, the publishers; and James Tallmadge, one of the founders and first presidents of New York University.

An endowment fund was established by 1915, run by descendants of the original vault owners, to preserve the cemetery from deterioration.

NEW YORK CITY MARBLE CEMETERY, established 1831
52–74 East 2nd Street, Manhattan
Designated: March 4, 1969

The New York City Marble Cemetery was established in 1831, by Evert Bancker, Samuel Whittemore, Henry Booraem, Garret Storm, and Thomas Addis Emmet, as the second public, nonsectarian burial ground in the city. The land originally belonged to Samuel Cowdrey, who owned a vault in the first New York Marble Cemetery nearby. Among those interred here are James Lenox, whose library was to be incorporated into the New York Public Library, and several members of the Roosevelt family.

The cemetery was considered a fashionable burial place; monuments and markers were used to signal the locations of the marble vaults, laid out along parallel walks. It is surrounded by a high brick wall on three sides and bordered on its south side by a handsome iron fence with gate.

OLD MERCHANT'S HOUSE, formerly the Seabury Tredwell House, 1831–32
29 East 4th Street, Manhattan
Builder: Joseph Brewster
Designated: October 14, 1965; interior designated December 22, 1981

Home to prosperous merchants during the nineteenth century, the row houses near Astor Place attest to the rapid growth of early New York. Owned by the Seabury Tredwell family for 98 years, the Old Merchant's House—in its mixture of Federal and Greek Revival elements—preserves both the conservative and flamboyant sides of this transitional period in industrial society. The builder was Joseph Brewster, who was influenced by Minard Lafever.

This tall, red-brick house has a steep, slate roof with dormer windows. The fanlighted doorway and wrought-iron stoop railings mark the otherwise restrained, predominantly Federal façade; the fluted Ionic columns flanking the door hint at the Greek Revival opulence within.

The floor plan is typical of early-nineteenth-century homes; the comfortable basement contains a kitchen and a dining or family room, while the first floor houses a pair of formal parlors. Spacious bedrooms are located on the second and third floors, with finer woodwork and marble chimneypieces found on the former. The top floor contains smaller rooms for servants.

The increased availability of architectural items at the beginning of the Industrial Revolution made possible the extravagant interior, with its simulated Siena marble walls and highly decorative plasterwork, such as a rosette in the entranceway and cornice with egg-and-dart moldings; details that are repeated throughout. The front and rear parlors are identical, with fourteen foot ceilings, eight panel mahogany doors, and six-over-six windows at the front and rear walls. Each room is bounded by wide paneled baseboards and carpeted from wall to wall with a reproduction French moquette carpet, whose pattern imitated the mosaic floors discovered at Pompeii and Herculaneum. On the second floor, the two large bedrooms are also identical in plan. The hallways sustain the Greek Revival style; the mahogany stairways are partially carved with acanthus leaves in high relief, and the woodwork here, as elsewhere in the house, is painted off-white.

All the furnishings originally belonged to the Tredwell family. Gertrude Tredwell, Seabury's reclusive youngest daughter, continued to live in the house until her death in 1933 at the age of 93. Heavy mortgages were incurred as finances dwindled, and arrangements were made to sell the house and its contents upon her death. But George Chapman, a New York lawyer and Gertrude's nephew, persuaded the assignee to cancel the mortgages, forming the Historic Landmark Society, which runs the house as a museum.

DANIEL LEROY HOUSE, 1832
20 St. Mark's Place, Manhattan
Architect: Unknown
Designated: November 19, 1969

The Daniel LeRoy House is one of an entire blockfront of gracious houses erected on the south side of St. Mark's Place (formerly 8th Street), one of the most elegant residential streets in early-nineteenth-century New York. Daniel LeRoy was the son-in-law of Elizabeth and Nicholas Fish, who lived in nearby 21 Stuyvesant Street—also a landmark.

The LeRoy House is constructed in Flemish bond brickwork trimmed with stone. It is one of four houses on the block that retain the ornately decorated iron handrails at the stoop, low, bird-cage newel posts, and iron railings in the windows of the parlor floor. The arched stone entrance has a triple keystone and a Gibbs surround. Utilitarian doors and a plain transom have replaced the original entrance and its beautiful fanlight.

203 PRINCE STREET, 1833–34; additions, 1888
Manhattan
Architect: Unknown
Designated: February 19, 1974

A characteristic upper-class residence of the 1830s, this house was built in an area originally known as Richmond Hill—after Aaron Burr's eighteenth-century estate, which was eventually purchased, subdivided, and sold off by John Jacob Astor. As a favored area for well-to-do New Yorkers until the mid-nineteenth century, its population doubled between 1815 and 1825. The original owner of this house, John P. Haff, was a leather inspector; his family retained the building until the 1860s.

The house exhibits both Federal and Greek Revival stylistic elements. Set above a high stoop, an impressive Federal-style entrance features a semielliptical arched doorway with Ionic columns enframing three-paned sidelights. The façade is red Flemish bond brickwork with a brownstone basement. The third floor and the metal roof cornice were added in 1888.

COLONNADE ROW, formerly LaGrange Terrace, 1832–33
428–434 Lafayette Street, Manhattan
Architect: Attributed to Alexander Jackson Davis
Designated: October 14, 1965

These four town houses were once part of a group of nine such buildings that extended south along Lafayette Street. The buildings were the first row-house development in New York to be unified behind a single monumental façade—a long colonnade of the Corinthian order, executed in white Westchester marble cut by Sing Sing prisoners. It is possible that Davis was inspired by his partner, Ithiel Town, who, during his European trip of 1829–30, wrote admiringly of the unified treatment of mid-eighteenth-century row houses he had seen in France and England.

The chance to execute such lavish designs came in 1832 when Seth Geer commissioned Davis to design the row on land bordering on the Astor estate, well outside the fashionable Washington Square area. Contemporaries thought that no one would live so far east and dubbed the complex "Geer's Folly." The unique design and rich appointments soon attracted buyers, however, including Franklin Delano, grandfather of Franklin D. Roosevelt; within a decade, many other elegant town houses had been erected in the area of Astor Place.

The individual unit plans were unusual in their day, as were the elevations. In the typical New York City row house, the main parlor was entered directly from the stoop and was only half a floor above street level. Here, the rusticated ground floor served as an entry from the street. Inside, a grand stair rose to the main floor (the second story, or *piano nobile*) in the European fashion. Geer accentuated the European associations by calling the row La Grange Terrace, after General Lafayette's country house.

STATE UNIVERSITY OF NEW YORK MARITIME COLLEGE formerly Fort Schuyler, 1833–56; **alterations, 1934, 1967**
Throgs Neck, The Bronx
Architect: Unknown
Designated: April 19, 1966

Named for Philip J. Schuyler, a general of the American Revolution, this structure was designed, along with Fort Totten, to protect New York City. A square-headed main entrance announces the restrained simplicity of detail that characterizes this fort. The pentagonal structure was built from horizontally coursed, rock-faced granite ashlar. Small arches are cut out of single pieces of ashlar; the larger openings are composed of voussoirs with a keystone at the top. An armament of 312 guns could be aimed through the fort's five- to eleven-foot-thick walls.

Used as a prison camp during the Civil War, the fort was finally abandoned in 1870. In 1934, it was restored by the WPA for use by the New York State Merchant Marine Academy, currently the State University of New York Maritime College. The gun galleries were converted into a library in 1967.

SAILORS' SNUG HARBOR
Richmond Terrace, Staten Island

Gatehouse

Main buildings, general view

Veterans Memorial Hall

Building C, 1831–33; interior redecorated, 1884
Architect: Minard Lafever
Designated: October 14, 1965; interior designated October 12, 1982

Building B, 1839–40
Builder: Samuel Thompson, after plans by Minard Lafever
Designated: October 14, 1965

Building D, 1840–41,
Builder: Samuel Thompson, after plans by Minard Lafever
Designated: October 14, 1965

Iron Fence, 1842; later additions
Architect: Frederick Diaper
Designated: May 15, 1973

Veterans Memorial Hall, formerly the Chapel, 1855–56
Architect: James Solomon
Designated (interior and exterior): October 14, 1965

Building A, 1879
Architect: Samuel Thompson
Designated: October 14, 1965

Building E, 1880
Architect: Samuel Thompson
Designated: October 14, 1965

Gatehouse, third quarter, nineteenth century
Architect: Richard P. Smythe
Designated May 15, 1973

The breadth of scale and stylistic uniformity of Sailors' Snug Harbor mark this complex as one of the finest essays in Greek Revival architecture in the country. Sailors' Snug Harbor was founded with an 1801 bequest from New York merchant Robert Randall to care for "aged, decrepit and worn out sailors." Nineteenth-century medical theory suggested that health care was best provided in locations where patients would not be taxed by the difficulties of urban life. Many New York institutions, notably Leake and Watts's Orphan Asylum and the Bloomingdale Insane Asylum, adhered to this notion; in 1831, Sailors' Snug Harbor, too, followed suit with its purchase of eighty acres on Staten Island. Construction began immediately, and the complex continued to expand throughout the nineteenth century, eventually comprising over twenty buildings that were home to 900 men in 1900. It operated as a home for retired sailors until the mid-1960s, when New York City purchased the buildings. Since 1976, Sailors' Snug Harbor has been home to the Snug Harbor Cultural Center, a multidimensional project serving all members of the artistic community. Plans are progressing under SHCC supervision for the construction of a recital hall, the first significant addition to the complex since the turn of the century.

The first building at Snug Harbor was Minard Lafever's administration building, now known as Building C; it established the stylistic and formal model for the rest of the complex. While the body of the two-story building is brick, its main façade is sheathed in Westchester marble quarried by prisoners at Sing Sing. The monumental Ionic order of the façade, derived from the Little Temple of Ilyssus near Athens, carries a full entablature and shallow pediment. This, Lafever's earliest extant work, is his only surviving essay in the Greek Revival and bears a strong resemblance to the design for a courthouse he included in *The Young Builder's General Instructor*, the first of his influential works on building. The interior, also designated, was redecorated toward the end of the nineteenth century and is distinguished by the nautical theme of its ornament.

Buildings B and D are identical and were built almost simultaneously about 1840 as dormitories to accommodate the growing population of Snug Harbor. Rising two stories above a high basement, each has a three-bay façade dominated by a broad, shallow pediment. The central bay of the first story is the entrance, distinguished by a small Ionic porch. These

Veterans Memorial Hall

dormitories connect with Building C by four-bay-wide hyphens that Lafever designed, anticipating just such an expansion of his original plan.

Built in 1879–80 as the terminal phase of the central complex, buildings A and E are also identical. These dormitories are identified by their hexastyle Ionic porticoes. They, too, are two stories above a raised basement with a three-bay façade.

The chapel, built in 1856, was expanded in 1883 with the addition of a tower. This small Italianate brick building has round-arched windows and a bracketed cornice. Its interior is extremely simple, with a coved ceiling and trompe l'oeil Ionic pilasters. This building has been rehabilitated to house an intimate recital hall, known as Veterans Memorial Hall.

The gatehouse on Richmond Terrace is a vernacular synthesis of Romanesque, Italianate, and Second Empire influences. It was intended as a pedestrian entrance, providing a formal entry to the Snug Harbor complex. The elevation is composed of a large central arch flanked by a window in a lower wing on each side. The composition is completed with a square cupola above the vaulted tunnel that leads through the gatehouse. Each side of the cupola has a pair of round-arched windows with red glass panes.

A cast-iron fence marks the northern boundary of the original Snug Harbor property; its pickets are topped by spikes, supported by X-shaped cross-members, and ornamented with cast rosettes. This design was inspired by the Cumberland Gates of London's Hyde Park.

Building C

131 CHARLES STREET, 1834
Manhattan
Builder: David Christie
Designated: April 19, 1966

This small, red-brick Federal row house in Greenwich Village was built in 1834 and remains original in almost every detail. It was built by David Christie, a stonemason, one of thirty or so speculative houses built (each for about $2,600) on an old tobacco farm that once belonged to the Earl of Abingdon.

This modest yet charming house is twenty-four feet wide and two stories high and is graced by white lintels and a denticulated cornice. The eight-paneled oak door is flanked by slender Ionic columns and topped by a rectangular, leaded fanlight. The frames of the six-over-six windows, lintels, and cornice outlining the roof are all intact. The steep-pitched roof with delicate dormers, and the low brownstone stoop with wrought-iron rails and fence, add to the delicate simplicity of the house.

Each floor contains two rooms and a small cubicle. The house was well maintained by its many occupants, and the original doors, moldings, and yellow pine floorboards have survived. The interior is sparsely ornamented; the window and door moldings in the parlor, however, form pilasters with acanthus-leaf and acorn or pineapple trim, and two of the five fireplaces have decorative clipper-ship mantels, inset with carved wooden panels.

The house remained in the Christie family for thirty-one years; since 1865, approximately ten different families have lived here.

ELIAS HUBBARD RYDER HOUSE,
1834; alterations, 1929
1926 East 28th Street, Brooklyn
Architect: Unknown
Designated: March 23, 1976

The Elias Hubbard Ryder House is located in Gravesend, one of the six original townships of Kings County (later included in the city of Brooklyn). Gravesend was the only English settlement to receive a patent from the Dutch director general and council; the patentee was Lady Deborah Moody, the first woman so included. The patent also contained a proviso permitting freedom of worship "without magisterial or ministerial interference."

The house is a typical early-nineteenth-century Dutch Colonial farmhouse, distinguished by a projecting roof eave that may initially have acted as an overhang to protect the masonry walls from rain and snow. Two stories high and with a wood frame, this vernacular structure was built on the edge of the farmland inherited by Elias Hubbard Ryder, member of a prominent Gravesend family. The Hubbard Ryder family occupied the house until 1966.

BAYLEY-SETON HOSPITAL, formerly Seamen's Retreat
131 Bay Street, Staten Island
Designated: April 9, 1985

Main Building, 1834–53
Architect: Abraham P. Maybie

Physician-in-Chief's Residence, 1842
Architect: Unknown

For more than 150 years, the Seamen's Retreat has provided care for merchant seamen. Established by the New York State Legislature in 1831, "to provide for sick and disabled seamen," the retreat has won recognition for medical research related to its maritime mission.

The retreat's Main Building, dating from 1834–53, is a Greek Revival granite ashlar structure built by Abraham P. Maybie. The center pavilion is five bays wide and three stories high, with a basement and attic. The center bay is emphasized by wide window openings, a pediment fanlight, and a projecting portico with a tall, granite-block podium and fluted Doric columns. The end bays are essentially identical to the center. The wings linking the end pavilions have colonnades of large stuccoed piers that rise through two stories to support double porches. Tall door openings on the second floor of the wings provide direct access from the wards to the porches. Copper detailing is used throughout.

The Physician-in-Chief's Residence is also constructed of local granite ashlar. It, too, has columned porches and a concentration of Greek Revival detailing at the doorway.

In 1882 the retreat became the U.S. Marine Hospital, which was disbanded in 1981. Today it functions as the Bayley-Seton Hospital.

Main Building

Physician's House

CALEB TOMPKINS WARD MANSION, c. 1835
141 Nixon Avenue, Staten Island
Builder: George B. Davis
Designated: August 22, 1978

The Caleb Tompkins Ward Mansion is an imposing Greek Revival structure built about 1835 on the crest of Ward's Hill, Staten Island. It commands a magnificent view of the New York harbor and the metropolitan area. Originally surrounded by an estate of 250 acres, the Ward mansion is one of the last great houses from a time when the north shore of Staten Island was a fashionable resort for wealthy New Yorkers.

The builder, George B. Davis, was probably influenced by the building guide of Minard Lafever, whose writings were responsible in part for the popularization of the Greek Revival style throughout the country.

FEDERAL HALL NATIONAL MEMORIAL, 1834–42
28 Wall Street, Manhattan
Architects: Ithiel Town, Alexander Jackson Davis, Samuel Thompson, John Frazee
Designated: December 21, 1965; interior designated May 27, 1975

Rich in historical associations, Federal Hall National Memorial occupies the site of New York's second city hall. Remodeled and enlarged in 1789 by the expatriate French architect Pierre L'Enfant, this city hall was renamed Federal Hall and served as the seat of the federal government until 1790. It was here, on the balcony, that George Washington took the oath of office as first president of the United States on April 30, 1789. L'Enfant's Federal Hall reverted to use as a city hall in 1790 and was demolished in 1812 when the current City Hall was opened.

The present building on the site, Federal Hall National Memorial, was built between 1834 and 1842 as the U.S. Custom House. The original design of the marble building was a product of the partnership of Ithiel Town and Alexander Jackson Davis, two of New York's most influential early-nineteenth-century architects. In 1862, the building became the U.S. Sub-Treasury and acted as the center of the government's fiscal operations in the Northeast. From 1920 to 1939, it housed a variety of federal offices. In 1939, the building was taken over by the National Park Service in conjunction with the Federal Hall Memorial Associates. Renamed Federal Hall National Memorial in 1955, the former Custom House/Sub-Treasury is now a museum devoted to early American and New York history as well as a center for civic functions.

With its austere Doric porticoes, the building is the finest example in New York of a Greek Revival temple. The original Town and Davis plans had called for a crowning dome in the Roman tradition, but the dome was eventually removed from the design owing to stylistic, spatial, and structural inconsistencies. The interior design, derived from Greek and Roman prototypes, is dominated by a two-story rotunda. The most impressive feature of this space is the circular colonnade that supports the deep entablature and the low, paneled dome decorated by anthemion motifs. The Corinthian columns (modeled after those of the Roman temple of Jupiter Stator) are simple shafts of white marble from Tuckahoe, New York; the richly foliated capitals were imported from Italy. Behind the colonnade runs a cast-iron balcony whose railing is supported by a series of slender caryatids. The bronze finish of this ornamental ironwork was restored in 1987.

Samuel Thompson, appointed superintendent of construction at Town's suggestion, is believed to have been responsible for the revised plan of the building. It has also been documented that Robert Mills was involved in advising the Treasury Department on the design changes of 1834. Most of the interior ornamental detail was the work of sculptor John Frazee, who became architect and superintendent after Thompson resigned in 1835. It has long been believed that William Ross, a British architect and magazine correspondent living in New York in the 1830s, was responsible for many of the alterations to the original Town and Davis design. According to recent research done by the National Park Service, however, Ross was a draftsman for Thompson and made no official contribution to the design. The only attribution for Ross's involvement came from his own article in London's *Architectural Magazine* in 1835.

The classical traditions of architecture that flourished in America's early years epitomized the ideals of Greek democracy and Roman republicanism that had inspired this nation's Founding Fathers. These ideals lived on into the middle decades of the nineteenth century, typified by public buildings such as this one. In Federal Hall National Memorial, the outstanding architecture of that age is preserved.

GARDINER-TYLER HOUSE, c. 1835
27 Tyler Street, Staten Island
Architect: Unknown
Designated: April 12, 1967

This two-story frame house demonstrates how pervasive the Greek Revival had become by the second quarter of the nineteenth century. The design of the Gardiner-Tyler House must certainly have come from its builder rather than a trained architect. Yet with the aid of pattern books, he was able to include, albeit in greatly simplified form, many of the elements essential to the style. The five-bay façade has four columns with Corinthian capitals but no bases. The exterior walls are shingled, in contrast to the plainer surfaces found in high-style models of the Greek Revival.

Elizabeth Racey built the house about 1835 on land once farmed by Nathaniel Britton. Juliana and David Gardiner purchased the house for their daughter Julia, who married President John Tyler in 1844. Mrs. Tyler rarely visited the house before 1868, when, as a widow, she returned to Staten Island with Tyler's seven children from a previous marriage. Julia Tyler left the house in 1874, and it was later owned by William M. Evarts, who served as attorney general under Andrew Johnson and as secretary of state under Rutherford B. Hayes.

390 VAN DUZER STREET, 1835
Staten Island
Architect: Unknown
Designated: December 18, 1973

This frame house, built in modified Greek Revival style, is located in the old village of Stapleton. Of the original structure built in 1835, only the kitchen wing still remains. A tetrastyle portico, with Corinthian columns rising two stories to an entablature, projects from the front façade. Above the entablature is a spring eave—unusual in Greek Revival houses, which more often have a triangular gable. A classical enframement opens onto the portico. A doorway with sidelights and balustered railings lend interest to the simple front façade.

The house was built by Richard G. Smith, whose wife was a member of an important Staten Island family; her father, Daniel D. Tompkins, was governor of New York State and vice president of the United States under James Monroe.

CHURCH OF ST. JAMES, 1835–37
32 St. James Street, Manhattan
Architect: Attributed to Minard Lafever
Designated: January 18, 1966

One of the oldest Roman Catholic church structures in Manhattan, the Church of St. James displays the handsome proportions and extreme refinement of the Greek Revival style. In a modification of the classical temple, the walls were extended forward to enclose the sides of the portico; enclosed stairs appear on each side, with doors opening onto the street. This construction places the entire front under one great gable or pediment. The front entrance, in line with the side entrances, stands between two massive columns on the recessed porch. All three doorways are decorated by Tuscan porticoes with pilasters. The attribution to Lafever is based on the ornament above the entrance door and on the interior balcony, which is similar to designs published by the architect in one of his books.

JOHN KING VANDERBILT HOUSE, c. 1836
1197 Clove Road, Staten Island
Architect: Unknown
Designated: October 6, 1987

The John King Vanderbilt House dates from the beginning of the urbanization of Staten Island in the early 1830s. Built about 1836 by John King Vanderbilt, first cousin of "Commodore" Cornelius Vanderbilt, the house is representative of the Federal and Greek Revival styles that were popular at the time.

The most common characteristic of Greek Revival architecture was the colonnade, made up of columns that spanned the façade of the house. These columns were grafted into the spring eave, a continuation of the front roof slope. The house's other distinguishing characteristics are its two-and-one-half-story height, a departure from the more common one and one-half stories; the Greek Revival–inspired entranceway; and the façade-wide porch with twin end-wall chimneys.

In 1825, John King Vanderbilt moved to Staten Island with his family and many other relatives. Listed as a farmer in census records, Vanderbilt was also active in the local real-estate market. His business dealings prospered, yet his house—while stately—is simple in comparison to other, more ostentatious temple-fronted houses of the period. The house remained in the Vanderbilt family until 1908, when it was sold by Joseph Mortimer Vanderbilt. In 1955 the house was purchased and restored by Dorothy Valentine Smith, a member of the Vanderbilt extended family.

LATOURETTE HOUSE, c. 1836; additions, 1936
Latourette Park, Staten Island
Architect: Unknown
Designated: July 30, 1968

At the end of the nineteenth century, the Latourette farm—with this large Greek Revival house at its center—was considered the finest on Staten Island. David Latourette, who built the house, was descended from a family that had been active on Staten Island since 1702, when Jean Latourette's name appeared in records as a witness and a freeholder. The farm, which the family began in the early 1800s, continued to operate until 1928, when the family sold it to New York City; the grounds became a park with a golf course, and the house a clubhouse.

Added during a 1936 restoration were a stone staircase leading to a veranda that dominates the façade. The veranda roof is supported by six square columns, joined by a balustrade; the pattern of the balustrade is repeated in the railing around the edge of the porch roof. The entrance door is a model of Greek Revival design, with paneled pilasters, narrow sidelights, and a glazed transom. No spandrel panel separates the windows of the first story from those of the second, an effect that creates the appearance of a single-story building.

ST. PETER'S CHURCH, 1836–40
22 Barclay Street, Manhattan
Architects: John R. Haggerty and Thomas Thomas
Designated: December 21, 1965

Built in the Greek Revival style, St. Peter's Church belongs to the oldest Roman Catholic parish in New York. The present building's predecessor was a Georgian church, constructed on this site in 1785, that partially collapsed after the great New York fire of 1835.

Both the façade on Barclay Street and the west wall on Church Street are faced with gray granite. The structure has a handsome, six-column Ionic portico and a shallow pediment; a niche holds a statue of St. Peter. The building's style expresses classic Roman monumentality.

BARTOW-PELL MANSION MUSEUM, 1836–42; restored, c. 1914
Pelham Bay Park, Shore Road, The Bronx
Architect: Unknown
Designated: February 15, 1966; interior designated May 27, 1975; expanded landmark designated January 10, 1978

The Bartow-Pell Mansion is noteworthy for the history of its site and for its association with some of New York's most prominent families. Thomas Pell, an English physician who settled in Connecticut, purchased nine thousand acres of land from the Siwanoy Indians in 1654; in 1666 he received a charter from Charles II to create the Manor of Pelham. In 1675 his heir, Sir John Pell, built the house that was to be occupied by his family until its destruction in the Revolution.

In 1813 Hannah LeRoy, wife of the Dutch diplomat Herman LeRoy, purchased the estate from John Bartow, a Pell descendant, for use as a summer home. In 1836 John Bartow's grandson Robert bought back the property. The house that now stands here—the third house to occupy the site—was completed by Bartow in 1842. It has a distinguished Greek Revival interior that features elaborate over-door pediments, graceful pilasters, and an elegant, freestanding elliptical staircase.

In 1888, the Bartows sold their estate to the city, and for a short while at the turn of the century the house was used as a home for crippled children. The mansion gradually deteriorated, however, until 1914, when the International Garden Club was established there and restorations were made by the firm of Delano & Aldrich. Opened as a museum in 1947, the mansion has been furnished with fine Greek Revival objects, many on loan from the Metropolitan Museum of Art, the Brooklyn Museum, and the Museum of the City of New York.

St. John's Residence Hall

FORDHAM UNIVERSITY
East Fordham Road and East 191st Street, The Bronx
Designated: February 3, 1981

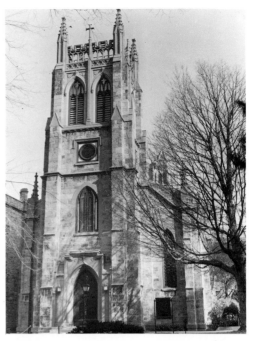

Chapel

Administration Building,
formerly Rose Hill, 1836–38
Architect: Unknown

Alumni House, 1840
Architect: William Rodrigue

Our Lady, Mediatrix of All Graces, 1845;
transept completed 1929
Architect: William Rodrigue

St. John's Residence Hall, 1845
Architect: William Rodrigue

Fordham University takes its name from the Manor of Fordham, granted in 1671 to John Archer by the British royal governor of New York, Francis Lovelace. Robert Watts acquired the property in 1787 and named it Rose Hill, after the former residence of his father. After changing hands several times, the estate was purchased in 1839 by the Right Reverend John Hughes (later New York's first Catholic archbishop) for use as a seminary and college. The first six students arrived for classes at St. John's College, Fordham, on June 24, 1841. In 1905 the institution became Fordham University.

The Greek Revival manor house, Rose Hill—now the Administration Building—is superbly sited on a semicircular tree-lined driveway. It is a two-and-one-half-story random-ashlar structure. The entrance porch, standing on a raised platform with wide steps, Ionic columns, and square corner posts supporting a full entablature, is one of the finest in New York. A full wooden entablature with a dentiled cornice crowns the house and an octagonal cupola surmounts the roof.

Administration Building

The former Greek Alumni House, which now serves as the housing office, is a small fieldstone house by architect William Rodrigue, who worked with James Renwick, Jr., on St. Patrick's Cathedral. A stone plaque beneath the central attic window bears the date 1840, two years after the completion of the Administration Building, but the house displays certain earlier details, such as the window lintels that appear to be a holdover from the Federal period. The house is constructed of random-laid, dark-colored fieldstone, with fieldstone quoins; keyed red brick frames the windows. The wooden attic story has three small, rectangular windows inset on both the front and back façades. The entrance door is framed by wooden pilasters and sidelights. The end walls are simple planes of fieldstone, in and in the rear is a double door, flanked by paired windows.

The university's chapel, constructed of rough-hewn stone in the Gothic Revival style, is adjacent to St. John's Residence Hall; together these buildings frame Queen's Court. The dominant feature of the chapel is a tall, square tower with large stepped buttresses projecting from the corners that rises to a louvered belfry, terminating in graceful pinnacles, and decorated with crockets and finials. In 1928–29, a large transept was added. Marking the crossing of the transept and the nave is a heavily decorated copper lantern that features small flying buttresses. The stained-glass windows were donated by King Louis Philippe of France; the altar, installed in 1943, was once part of St. Patrick's Cathedral and was donated by Cardinal Spellman.

Alumni House

LAWRENCE GRAVEYARD, established c. 1830
216th Street and 42nd Avenue, Queens
Designated: August 2, 1967

A plot of land originally known as Pine Grove was granted by Dutch Governor Kieft of New Amsterdam to John and William Lawrence in 1645. For years the land was a favorite picnic ground, but the Lawrence family converted it to a burial plot about 1830. It was used for this purpose until 1925.

Members of the Lawrence family included many notables in the spheres of politics and commerce. Among those buried here are Cornelius W. Lawrence, the mayor of New York from 1834 to 1837; Effingham Lawrence, a county judge; and Frederick Newbold Lawrence, president of the New York Stock Exchange from 1882 to 1883. There are forty-eight graves in total, and each has been carefully restored.

Many of the gravestones are Gothic in design. One particularly interesting example is a twin marker for two children, Margaret and Clarence, who died in their infancy. The stones have a trefoil pointed arch surrounded by a foliate carving and surmounted by the carved head of a child enfolded in an angel's wings.

Today the graveyard is maintained by public-spirited Bayside residents, descendants of the Lawrence family, and the Bayside Historical Society.

TRINITY CHURCH AND GRAVEYARD, 1839–46
Broadway at Wall Street, Manhattan
Architect: Richard Upjohn
Designated: August 16, 1966

Established on land granted by Queen Anne in 1705, Trinity was the first Episcopalian parish in New York; the current church, however, is actually the third built on this site. The first, built in 1698, was burned in 1776; it was rebuilt in 1787 but razed in 1839 on the advice of Boston architect Richard Upjohn, who had emigrated from England in 1829, and who had been called in to correct the building's structural defects. Before the year was over, Upjohn submitted designs for the present building, which was one of the grandest American churches of its day. Upjohn specialized in Gothic Revival churches, but his early works were inaccurate, rather provincial versions of the English Gothic; Trinity was his first convincing application of Gothic forms in a truly massive and richly decorated structure. As such, it marks the beginning of the mature Gothic Revival in the United States.

Executed in New Jersey brownstone, Trinity is now black from city grime. A recent study has shown that this surface dirt helps to protect this unusually soft, poorly weathering stone; where rainwater has washed the stone clean, spalling is evident. In both massing and detail, Trinity shows the influence of the late Decorated style of the later fourteenth century. The steeple is decorated with crocketed ogee arches and shallow, tracery-paneled buttresses. At just over 280 feet, it was the tallest structure in the city until the late 1860s. The bell was presented to the church by the bishop of London in 1704 and installed in the original church in 1711, when the steeple was completed. It is topped by an octagonal spire with flying buttresses, crocketed finials (echoed on the nave roof), and an early-fifteenth-century-style paneled parapet (repeated at the cornice levels of the three remaining elevations). The chancel wall, from which the sacristy and chapel project, is supported by flying buttresses.

The side-aisle window tracery is repeated in the clerestory above, while the proportions and moldings of the windows reappear in the nave arcades. The sexpartite rib vaults are executed in plaster and lath rather than stone.

Richard Morris Hunt was responsible for the overall design of the three sculpted bronze doors. To achieve variety, he assigned each portal to a different sculptor. The west door is the work of Karl Bitter and the north door was designed by J. Massey Rhind; both show biblical scenes. The

south door, sculpted by Charles H. Niehaus, shows the history of Trinity Church. All three constitute a memorial to John Jacob Astor III.

The furnishings and decorative details are average by European standards, but remarkable for a country that was then an artistic backwater. All Saints' Chapel was constructed in 1913 as a memorial to the Reverend Dr. Morgan Dix, rector from 1862 to 1908; he is buried under the chapel altar.

Many well-known New Yorkers have been members of Trinity parish; interred in the graveyard, which recounts this history, are such notables as Alexander Hamilton, Captain James Lawrence, Robert Fulton, and Francis Lewis—the only signer of the Declaration of Independence buried in Manhattan. Trinity Church's present congregation is drawn from all parts of the metropolitan area; members worship at weekday and Sunday services.

HIGH BRIDGE AQUEDUCT AND PEDESTRIAN WALK, 1838–48
Harlem River at West 170th Street, The Bronx, to High Bridge Park, Manhattan
Engineer: John B. Jervis
Designated: November 10, 1970

High Bridge, designed by engineer John B. Jervis, is a monument to the water system that brought to New York its first adequate public water supply. The elegant masonry of the structure and the severity of its lines constitute a triumph of architecture as well as engineering. Resembling a Roman aqueduct, the High Bridge consists of fifteen arches that span the river 84 feet above high water. The High Bridge was part of the Croton Aqueduct, opened in 1842, which carried drinking water from the Croton Reservoir in Westchester County to New York City. In 1923 navy engineers replaced the central piers in the Harlem River with the steel arch we see today to allow larger ships to pass up the river. The bridge is no longer used as an aqueduct, and the pedestrian walk is closed.

5910 AMBOY ROAD, 1840
Staten Island
Architect: Unknown
Designated: March 19, 1974

This simple Greek Revival frame house, erected in 1840, is situated on a low, grassy knoll; it is set back from Amboy Road, which was laid out in 1709 and is one of the oldest roads on Staten Island.

The structure is composed of three clapboard-sided sections. The central portion is three windows wide and one and one-half stories high, and the two stepped-down flanking wings are two windows wide. The porch at the center has four square, paneled columns with molded capitals that support a projecting roof decorated with dentils. Two square engaged pilasters flank the ground floor of the main section. The doorway still retains its original small-paned transom and sidelights.

440 CLINTON STREET, 1840
Brooklyn
Architect: Unknown
Designated: July 14, 1970

This Greek Revival mansion was built in 1840, when the area was rural farmland and clipper ships sailed into New York harbor. Its original owner, John Rankin, was an affluent merchant; his home on a corner lot had a magnificent view of the bay.

Imposing in size, the austere-looking, almost square, three-story house is distinguished by classical orderliness and symmetry. The façade is divided into three sections; the middle section, projecting forward from the two sides, contains a centrally located doorway with stoop. Stone pilasters around the doorway support an entablature enriching the entrance. Crowning the dwelling is a simple but dominant entablature with moldings and dentils below the cornice.

170–176 JOHN STREET, 1840
Manhattan
Architect: Attributed to Town & Davis
Designated: October 29, 1968

Hickson W. Field, a successful commission merchant, had this exceptional warehouse constructed in 1840 to house his business. The building's all-granite façade is nearly unique in New York, where, for reasons of economy, granite was rarely used above the ground story. The regularity of the twelve-bay façade and the near-total absence of ornament emphasize the utilitarian nature of the building and at the same time provide a model of Greek Revival restraint.

John Street has long been associated with maritime activity. The area where 170–176 John Street stands was originally Burling Slip, a docking area for ships. Filled in about 1835, the new street retained the extra width of the former berth. Originally a warehouse for seagoing cargo, the building later housed Baker, Carver & Morrell, a renowned ship's chandlery. In 1983 the building was refurbished as an apartment house by the architect Samuel White, its fortunes improved by the rebirth of the area after the development of South Street Seaport by the Rouse Company.

SEGUINE HOUSE, c. 1840
440 Seguine Avenue, Staten Island
Architect: Unknown
Designated: May 25, 1967

Built as a waterfront residence and situated on the highest point overlooking Prince's Bay, this eighteen-room mansion is a monument to the Greek Revival period of architecture. Formerly the focus of the extensive 200-acre Seguine estate, the house gives evidence of the grand life of Staten Island's past. The Seguines, who first settled on the island in 1706, were one of the most prominent families on Staten Island during the eighteenth and nineteenth centuries.

The two-and-one-half-story stone structure is covered with white clapboard, The low-pitched, pedimented gable of the attic story is supported by six two-story pilasters. Centered in the pediment beneath the peak of the roof is a handsome fanlight. The main entrance is framed by an arrangement of pilasters, in which plain moldings and blocks serve as capitals and bases.

The mansion remained in the Seguine family until 1969, whereupon it fell into disrepair. Over the last decade or so the home has been restored to its former grandeur by its current owner.

CITIBANK, formerly First National City Bank, 1842; addition, 1907
55 Wall Street, Manhattan
Architects: Isaiah Rogers; McKim, Mead & White
Designated: December 21, 1965

Occupying an entire city block at 55 Wall Street, the Citibank building is a monumental structure representing the zenith of the Greek Revival in New York City. It is the result of two building campaigns. The lower portion, with its monolithic Ionic columns, was originally built as the Merchants Exchange and later housed the U.S. Custom House. After the National City Bank acquired the building in 1907, the architects McKim, Mead & White, in accordance with classical precedent, added a Corinthian colonnade to the upper portion, completing the addition without marring the integrity and proportion of the original structure.

One of the few truly classical buildings in New York City, this is an important example of great commercial power expressed in stone and mortar.

STEINWAY HOUSE, c. 1850
18–33 41st Street, Queens
Architect: Unknown
Designated: February 15, 1967

Originally surrounded by tennis courts, stables, lawns, and orchards, this rambling, asymmetrical structure was home to the Steinway family until the 1920s. Although built for Benjamin Pike, it was acquired by the famous piano manufacturer William Steinway during the 1870s.

A two-story, T-shaped section forms the building's central portion. The first floor contains several parlors, a dining room, and a kitchen; the bedrooms are on the second floor. The west end of the cross section is connected to a striking, four-story tower with additional living quarters. A combination library and den occupies the western section of the T; at the opposite end is an open porch. Other porches and terraces are located on the southern and eastern sides.

An imaginative combination of classical and medieval elements decorates the twenty-seven-room house. Typical classical features include four cast-iron Corinthian columns supporting the main entrance porch, modillions, and the triangular, pedimentlike gable in both the central hall and eastern elevation. The double-arched window in the main hall and the several rows of round-arched tower windows are reminiscent of those of an Italian villa; the rough-surfaced stonework resembles medieval domestic architecture.

JOHN STREET UNITED METHODIST CHURCH, 1841
44 John Street, Manhattan
Architect: Unknown
Designated: December 21, 1965

John Street United Methodist Church, with its pleasing, austere brownstone façade, is a fine, small church that has survived untouched in the heart of the city's financial district. Built in 1841, the church is contemporary with the Greek Revival churches in the city, but it shows the incoming Anglo-Italianate style. The windows, like those of their Renaissance prototypes, are crowned with semicircular arches. The Palladian window dominating the façade—a round-headed window flanked by two narrow square-headed ones—is a Northern Italian detail that reached America after a long period of popularity in England.

The present building is the third Methodist church erected on the site (earlier buildings were constructed in 1768 and 1817) and houses the oldest Methodist congregation in the United States, organized in 1766 under the leadership of two Irish cousins, Philip Embury and Barbara Heck. Peter Williams, a slave and one of the first members of the congregation, worked as the church sexton. To save him from the auction block, the church trustees purchased him for £40; he was given his freedom and later, as a tobacco merchant, helped to found the city's first Methodist church for blacks, the African Methodist Episcopal Zion Church.

The church library contains volumes dating from the library's organization in the 1790s; there is also a museum collection with early American items, including a 1767 clock, a painting of the 1768 church, and a 1767 Windsor chair.

ST. ANN'S CHURCH OF MORRISANIA AND GRAVEYARD, 1841
295 St. Ann's Avenue, The Bronx
Architect: Unknown
Designated: June 9, 1967

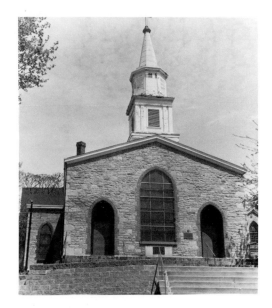

Gouverneur Morris, Jr., commissioned St. Ann's Church as a memorial to his mother, Ann Cary Randolph Morris, a direct descendant of Pocahontas, and a member of one of the most influential families in Virginia. She is buried here, in a vault in front of the altar; with her are other members of the Morris family, notably Judge Lewis Morris, first lord of the Manor of Morrisania, and Major General Lewis Morris, a member of the Continental Congress and a signer of the Declaration of Independence. Gouverneur Morris, Sr., is buried in the adjacent graveyard. A close friend of George Washington, the elder Morris was a member of the Constitutional Convention, ambassador to France, and a member of Congress.

This fieldstone Greek Revival parish church reflects the increased influence of the Gothic Revival. While the detail of the steeple is classically inspired, all of the window and door openings are brick-framed pointed arches. The south façade has a large, central stained-glass window with tracery. The church complex includes a large parish house connected to the sanctuary by a covered walkway, notable for its Gothic-style arcade.

WOODROW UNITED METHODIST CHURCH, 1842
1109 Woodrow Road, Staten Island
Architect: Unknown
Designated: November 15, 1967

This small Greek Revival church is a model of simplicity. The body of the church is a four-bay-deep rectangular structure, its rhythm defined by tall windows along the length of the nave. A flight of steps spanning the width of the building leads to the entrance portico, which has four fluted Doric columns, a simple entablature, and a plain pediment. A pair of well-proportioned paneled portals, with eared surrounds below pediments, leads into the sanctuary. The building is crowned by a later bell tower with an octagonal spire.

The church was built on the site of the first Methodist church on Staten Island, established in 1787. It is also associated with two of New York's most influential Methodist missionaries, Bishop Francis Asbury and the Reverend Henry Boehm.

MARINERS' TEMPLE, 1842
12 Oliver Street, Manhattan
Architect: Minard Lafever
Designated: February 1, 1966

This superb Greek Revival church in brownstone with fluted Ionic columns was built in 1842 according to designs by Minard Lafever. Like the nearby St. James Church (1835), which is attributed to Lafever, the Mariners' Temple has a recessed entrance loggia with a central pair of columns flush with the front wall. The flanking extensions contain stairs to the gallery.

The Mariners' Temple was organized by Baptists in 1795 to serve seamen when their ships were in port, and moved here from Cherry Street in 1842. During the period of heavy European immigration, the temple opened its doors to immigrants of all faiths. Among the congregations organized here were the First Swedish Church, the First Italian Church, the First Latvian Church, the Norwegian-Danish Mission, the First Russian Church, and the First Chinese Church. From the turn of the century until World War II, its main concern was working with homeless men of the Bowery. Today the older members of the church tutor the youngsters in after-school programs that provide remedial help and stress social skills and community involvement.

Grace Church School

GRACE CHURCH COMPLEX
Manhattan

Grace Church and Rectory, 1843–47;
800–804 Broadway
Architect: James Renwick, Jr.
Designated: March 15, 1966

Grace Church School Clergy House, 1902
92 Fourth Avenue,
Architects: Heins & La Farge
Designated: February 22, 1977

Grace Church School
Memorial House, 1882–83
94–96 Fourth Avenue
Architect: James Renwick, Jr.
Designated: February 22, 1977

Grace Church School
Neighborhood House, 1907
98 Fourth Avenue
Architects: Renwick, Aspinwall, & Tucker
Designated: February 22, 1977

The Grace Church complex is a remarkably coherent Gothic Revival ensemble, even though its building history spans sixty years. The congregation's first church was a modest structure at the corner of Rector Street and Broadway across from the second Trinity Church (which was replaced between 1839 and 1845 by Richard Upjohn's Gothic Revival masterpiece). In 1843, the New York City architect James Renwick, Jr., received the commission for the new Grace Church and rectory on this site north of the Astor estate. The congregation purchased the land from Renwick's uncles, Henry and Elias Brevoort, whose prosperous farm extended to 23rd Street. Renwick himself was a lifelong member of the congregation.

Like the more famous Trinity, Grace Church was one of the first Gothic Revival buildings in the United States to accurately reflect Gothic—in this case, fourteenth-century—forms. The rose window in the west façade recalls the curvilinear tracery of the Flamboyant style; the windows and buttresses are mixtures of French and English details; the openwork spire, which now lists noticeably and has recently undergone extensive repairs, is a common German type.

Grace Memorial House, at 94–96 Fourth Avenue, was built as a memorial to Mrs. Levi P. Morton, whose husband was vice president of the United States under Benjamin Harrison. It became a day nursery for children of working mothers, along with the Neighborhood House. The latter building and the Clergy House, as well as the gate facing the Vestry House on Fourth Avenue, blend seamlessly with Renwick's work. These later buildings originally served as the choir school and as housing for associated clergy. In 1973 the congregation considered replacing these to provide more space for community programs, but in the wake of a public outcry, the buildings were adapted to satisfy the church's needs. Since 1942, all three buildings have been part of the Grace Church School.

Grace Church

WAVE HILL HOUSE, center section, 1843; north wing, late nineteenth century; armor hall, 1928; south wing, 1932
675 West 252nd Street, The Bronx
Architects: Dwight James Baum (armor hall); otherwise unknown
Designated: June 21, 1966

Built in 1843 as a summer residence for jurist William Lewis Morris, Wave Hill House has been the residence over the years of such notables as Theodore Roosevelt, Samuel Clemens, and Arturo Toscanini. Purchased from the Morris family in 1866 by publisher William Henry Appleton, the property was subsequently incorporated into an eighty-acre estate in 1903 by financier George W. Perkins. Perkins's daughter and son-in-law, Mr. and Mrs. Edward U. Freeman, owned Wave Hill until 1960, when they donated it to the Parks Department of the City of New York. Today, the property serves as a botanic garden and cultural and educational institution.

The house is a fieldstone structure with white wood trim. Constructed over a ninety-year period, the building is an amalgam of architectural styles: Morris's original central portion is designed in the Federal style; the entrance doorway, added during a twentieth-century remodeling, has the heavy columns and broken pediment of Georgian architecture; the armor hall, built by Metropolitan Museum of Art curator Bashford Dean in 1928 to house his collection of armor, is predominantly Gothic in character.

MCFARLANE-BREDT HOUSE, formerly the New York Yacht Club, c. 1845
30 Hylan Boulevard, Staten Island
Architect: Unknown
Designated: October 12, 1982

This Victorian villa was built in the mid-1840s as a residence for Henry McFarlane, an early Staten Island developer. The house later served as the second clubhouse of the New York Yacht Club from 1868 to 1871. In 1870, the start of the first race for the America's Cup took place in the Narrows in front of the clubhouse.

The long, low house—a two-story, clapboard-covered, wood-frame cottage with brick-filled walls—was designed to resemble an Italian-Swiss villa, in a short-lived style that was popular in the 1840s. The main entrance, centered on the southern side, features a hood above paneled double doors. Narrow, latticed posts support a sharply concave tin roof with a wooden valance of pointed jigsaw ornament. Above the main entrance, a shallow balcony rests on a pair of console brackets with a wooden railing of diamond design. The broad cornice is supported by elaborate brackets ornamented with wooden acorn pendants. The northern façade features a long, open veranda with flat, wooden posts of diamond trelliswork. The west wing is nearly square and rises three stories above a red-brick foundation to a pyramidal hipped roof.

In the mid-1970s, the New York City Department of Parks and Recreation assumed ownership of the house; the Parks Department currently administers the building as a multifamily rental dwelling.

CHURCH OF THE HOLY COMMUNION BUILDINGS
47 West 20th Street, Manhattan
Architect: Richard M. Upjohn
Designated: April 19, 1966

Rectory, 1844–46

Sisters' House, 1850

Chapel, 1879

Belonging stylistically to the Gothic Revival, the buildings of the Church of the Holy Communion are nonetheless simple and symmetrical in form. They are constructed with random brownstone ashlar, in a way reminiscent more of a rural parish than an urban construction. The rectory is one of the finest masonry town houses in New York City. The gable ends of the rectory and the Sisters' House face the street, the steep pitch of their roofs emphasized by stone caps and horizontal returns at the eaves. This exaggerated outline is echoed above the entrance doors in the porch roofs.

Known as the first free church in the city, the Church of the Holy Communion Chapel offered open pews to all worshipers. In line with the rectory, it features a similar design with an additional tower and rose windows. The Sisters' House, which resembles both buildings, has its own smaller tower, gable, and gabled entrance door.

Noted activities throughout the church's history include the first "boy choir" in the city and the first Anglican sisterhood in the country. More importantly, the plans for St. Luke's Hospital were originated under the rectorship of the Reverend William Muhlenberg. Now located on Amsterdam Avenue, the hospital was originally administered in the Sisters' House by the Sisters of Charity.

26, 28, 30 JONES STREET, 1844
Manhattan
Architect: Unknown
Designated: April 19, 1966

Very similar in overall design, these three small brick row houses, each with three stories over a low basement, are good examples of the urban expression of the Greek Revival style. Their warm brick, with limited use of brownstone, is typical of the period.

The doors and sidelights at 26 and 28 are slightly recessed within pilastered door frames. At number 30, the entrance is a double door with a vestibule. A dentiled cornice capping the original wood frieze board at the roofline successfully completes the design.

The buildings are owned by a small cooperative of eight families that was formed in 1920 to purchase them from Greenwich House, a well-known settlement house founded in 1902 at 26 Jones Street.

GARIBALDI MEUCCI MUSEUM, c. 1845
420 Tompkins Avenue, Staten Island
Architect: Unknown
Designated: May 25, 1967

General Giuseppe Garibaldi, the charismatic military leader of the nineteenth-century wars that liberated and unified Italy, occupied this modest Country Gothic house from 1850 to 1851 as a guest of the Italian-American inventor Antonio Meucci.

Driven into temporary exile, Garibaldi worked for Meucci in his candle factory on Staten Island until he was able to resume his career as a merchant-ship captain while waiting to take up the struggle for freedom in Italy.

In this house, Meucci spent the remainder of his life; he developed a wide range of inventions, but his greatest achievement was an early prototype of the telephone, for which he received a U.S. patent in 1871.

A marker commemorating Garibaldi's residence was placed on the house in 1884, five years before Meucci's death. The house was relocated just two blocks from its original site and enclosed in a memorial pantheon; it became the responsibility of the Order of the Sons of Italy in America in 1907. The pantheon was removed in 1956 and the exterior of the house has been restored to its original condition in almost every detail.

The structure is three windows wide, clapboarded, and has a wood shingle roof. On both the front and rear of the house, a single pointed-arched window is located in the center of the roofline gable. Beneath these, three "tummy-on-the-floor" windows run across the front and façades. Verges with a fleur-de-lis motif and crowning pendants, which were depicted in an 1882 view of the house in *Leslie's Illustrated Weekly*, had been removed before the death of Meucci in 1889, but the house retains the main lines evident in this early illustration.

SAMUEL TREDWELL SKIDMORE HOUSE, 1845
37 East 4th Street, Manhattan
Architect: Unknown
Designated: August 18, 1970

This house was built for Samuel Tredwell Skidmore, cousin of Seabury Tredwell, whose house at 29 East 4th Street survives in much better condition. Both buildings suggest the type and scale of residential development that filled the area adjacent to the Astor family estate in the 1840s. Seth Geer's development of La Grange Terrace (Colonnade Row) on Lafayette Street began to attract wealthy New Yorkers here in the 1830s. Their row houses were generally of brick, and detailed in the style of the day—at this time, the Greek Revival. The Skidmore House is a perfect, though somewhat poorly preserved, example of this mode. A stoop over a high basement, which has traces of the original rustication, leads to a door marked by a pair of Ionic columns with entablature. Although the door's original sidelights are now blocked up, the three-paned transom remains with traces of carved molding surrounding it. The low attic windows (which marked the servants' quarters) and simple wood cornice with fascia below are characteristic of the Greek Revival. No original ironwork survives, but traces of it found by the present owners suggest it was identical to the ironwork on the Tredwell House.

Skidmore was involved in the wholesale drug business, later served as president of the Howard Insurance Company at 66 Wall Street, and finally became a trustee of the U.S. Trust Company. He served as a vestryman and senior warden for Trinity Church. He died in 1881; his large family remained here until 1883. By that time, light industry and printing houses had transformed this once-fashionable block into a commercial district, pushing residential areas farther north. The house at number 37, however, has continued to function as a private residence.

SUN BUILDING, 1845–46; additions, 1850–51, 1852–53, 1872, 1884
280 Broadway, Manhattan
Architects: Joseph Trench and John B. Snook, Frederick Schmidt
and Edward D. Harris
Designated: October 7, 1986

Originally the A. T. Stewart Store, the Sun Building is one of the most influential erected in New York City during the nineteenth century, significant both in terms of architectural and social history. It initiated a new architectural mode based on the palazzo of the Italian Renaissance. In this building, Alexander Turney Stewart began the city's first department store, a type of commercial enterprise that was to have a great effect on the city's economic growth as well as on merchandising throughout the entire country. From 1919 until 1952, the building housed one of the oldest dailies, the *New York Sun;* the paper's motto ("The Sun—It Shines For All") is still visible on the façade.

The building's present configuration is the result of a series of additions over a forty-year period, but the whole is visually unified. The structure is faced with a light-colored marble, intended to convey a sense of wealth, luxury, and extravagance. The Broadway façade, always intended as the main façade, has a colonnade of smooth pilasters on the ground floor. The exterior is profusely ornamented with Corinthian columns and pilasters, quoins, embossed spandrels, and windows framed with architrave moldings.

The building was acquired by the city in 1970 and has been used to house a variety of agencies. Under a forty-nine-year lease with the city, the Starrett Corporation will now rebuild and operate the second-floor retail space. The building is slated to reopen in late 1999 with one or more large stores at its base and the headquarters of the City Buildings Department upstairs.

33–37 BELAIR ROAD, formerly Woodland Cottage, c. 1845;
addition, 1900
Staten Island
Architect: Unknown
Designated: October 12, 1982

The 33–37 Belair Road House is one of the few surviving Gothic Revival cottages dating from the early period of Staten Island's suburban development. Constructed about 1845 by a developer as a rental residence known as Woodland Cottage, it was one of the many Gothic Revival villas and cottages built in the east shore suburb of Clifton after the late 1830s. Although its architect is unknown, the cottage reflects the influence of Alexander Jackson Davis, whose work included a number of residences designed for Staten Island clients.

The property on which the cottage stands was once part of the farmland that the Simonson family had owned since the 1700s. Between 1834 and 1841, the land changed hands several times before being acquired by David Abbott Hayes, a Newark, New Jersey, lawyer, in 1841. In 1849 Hayes sold the cottage to a Manhattan pottery merchant. Between 1858 and 1869 the cottage served as the rectory for St. John's Episcopal Church. Since that time it has been a private residence.

The original portion of the house is a cross-gabled structure of clapboard with a prominent center chimney. The steep center and end gables, with wide eaves, are ornamented by sturdy baseboards. A broad porch, with fluted and turned posts set on tall bases, extends across the front façade. The main doorway on the west end of the façade, with upper and lower panels of thin, turned spindles fronting tall panes of glass, is surrounded by French windows with diamond-shaped panes. The gabled section of the western end of the house, added in 1900, repeats the Gothic Revival bargeboard of the original structure but adds Queen Anne features such as the decoratively treated window sash.

ANDREW NORWOOD HOUSE, 1845–47
241 West 14th Street, Manhattan
Architect: Unknown
Designated: May 9, 1978

This elegant house was built for Andrew Norwood, a prosperous merchant, in 1845–47. A handsome, generously proportioned four-story building set above a brownstone basement and subtly accented with brownstone trim, the Norwood House was designed in a transitional style that combined Greek Revival and Italianate features. At the first floor are two full-height French doors with eared Greek Revival frames; these doors open onto the original Italianate cast-iron balcony. The doorway, above a high stoop, has an elegant Doric entablature carried on Doric pilasters. The windows grow progressively smaller at each ascending level; those at the second, third, and fourth floors have distinctive Italianate enframements and sills, and each sill is supported by two corbels. The wooden roof cornice, with its fascia board below a series of modillions, is a familiar feature of the Greek Revival style.

The well-preserved and recently restored house remained in the Norwood family until the turn of the century. The interior retains all the original crown moldings as well as the oculus in the hall ceiling; the thirteen fireplaces are all in working order. Listed on the National Register of Historic Places, the house survives as a striking remnant of the fashionable 14th Street residential area of the 1840s; it is still a private residence.

17 WEST 16TH STREET, c. 1846
Manhattan
Builder: Attributed to Edward S. Mesier
Designated: November 9, 1976

Built about 1846, this handsome Greek Revival house was one of a row of nine town houses, only four of which survive today. Located in the once-fashionable Union Square area—part of the proposed Ladies' Mile historic district—the houses were planned and most likely built by Edward S. Mesier, whose goal was to make West 16th Street between Fifth and Sixth avenues a first-class residential street. The house at number 17 is interesting because of its bowed front, a feature more commonly seen in Boston architecture; this house and its neighbors at numbers 5–9 West 16th Street are among the very few bow-fronted survivors in New York. Another handsome feature is the original Greek Revival doorway, with its eared architrave, frieze, modillioned cornice, and crisp details. The recessed double doors are framed with an egg-and-dart molding, flanked by sidelights, and surmounted by a three-light transom that, in turn, is crowned by a decorative frieze supporting a rich cornice.

The house was purchased in 1846 by George S. Fox, and after 1876 was the residence of Mr. and Mrs. William B. Rice, a socially prominent family. From 1930 to 1973, it served as the clinic of Margaret Sanger (1883–1966), the pioneer of family planning in the United States.

POLYTECHNIC UNIVERSITY, formerly the First Free Congregational Church, 1846–47
311 Bridge Street, Brooklyn
Architect: Unknown
Designated: November 24, 1981

The former First Free Congregational Church, with its simple, rectangular shape and temple front, is one of the few remaining examples of the vernacular Greek Revival building popular in the mid-nineteenth century. The "Free" in its name refers to the church's policy of not charging a rental fee for its pews. Popularly known as the Bridge Street Church, the building has changed hands many times since its construction. By 1854 it housed the oldest black congregation in Brooklyn, the African Wesleyan Methodist Episcopal Church, which used the basement to hide escaping slaves.

Despite a fire in 1885 that burned part of the interior, the church appears today as it did when it was constructed. The two fluted wooden columns, the low-pitched, full-width pediment, and the lack of applied ornament were stylistic statements then considered fitting for a religious structure. Although the architect is unknown, the style was made popular by architect Minard Lafever, who designed similar churches in Manhattan at the time.

THE PLAYERS, 1845; remodeled 1888
16 Gramercy Park, Manhattan
Architect: Unknown; alterations, Stanford White of McKim, Mead & White
Designated: March 15, 1966

This Gothic Revival town house was built for the New York banker Elihu Townsend in 1845. In 1888, the American actor Edwin Booth bought it to house a club where "actors and dramatists could mingle in good fellowship with craftsmen of the fine arts, as well as those of the performing arts." Booth commissioned Stanford White to transform the brownstone into a clubhouse, which he then called the Players.

Though established exclusively as a men's club, the Players has recently voted to admit women beginning May 31, 1989.

Executed in the Italian Renaissance style, the distinguished front porch at the second-story level, supported by square uprights below, displays a fine series of Tuscan columns; the handsome roof deck is topped by an iron railing. White's new front was an ingenious way to disguise the conversion of the original raised stoop to a basement-type entrance in the English style.

BROOKLYN BOROUGH HALL, 1846–51
209 Joralemon Street, Brooklyn
Architect: Gamaliel King
Designated: April 19, 1966

The oldest of Brooklyn's public buildings, Borough Hall was designed by architect Gamaliel King and built between 1846 and 1851. To this day, it remains a monument to the civic pride and immense growth and prosperity that characterized the newly incorporated city of Brooklyn in the mid-nineteenth century.

Until Brooklyn's consolidation as part of greater New York in 1898, the building served as the city hall and housed many governmental and judicial offices. Its elegant and stately Greek Revival architecture, typical of public buildings of the period, appropriately recalls the spirit of democracy and civic duty associated by America's founders with ancient times. Conceived as Brooklyn's response to New York's City Hall (1802–11), Borough Hall has symbolized from its inception both independence and unity of purpose.

Brooklyn received its charter as a city in 1834. Soon thereafter the search began for an architect to design a city hall on a one-and-one-half-acre triangle of land that had been sold to the city by two of Brooklyn's preeminent families, the Pierreponts and the Remsens. A grandiose plan was prepared by the well-known New York City architect Calvin Pollard, and the cornerstone was laid in 1836; but the financial panic of 1837 and ensuing depression of 1841 halted all work on the building, which had not advanced beyond the foundation stage.

The project was resumed in 1845. King, who had been a runner-up in the 1835 competition and superintendent and resident architect of the Pollard design, became principal architect. His new design, loosely based on Pollard's, was much reduced and more severe by comparison. King also designed the former King's County Courthouse, just behind Borough Hall on Joralemon Street (built 1861–68; now destroyed).

Architecturally, Borough Hall is one of the most splendid of the many Greek Revival buildings that sprang up in Brooklyn during its boom years. Rectangular in plan, it has two stories

cadenced above and below by a high basement and a low attic. An impression of solemn dignity is created by the symmetrical ordering of the façades. At the northern end an imposing Greek portico, consisting of six fluted Ionic columns rising above a steep flight of steps, commands a view out over Cadman Plaza and the commemorative statue of Henry Ward Beecher. A simple pediment surmounts the columns.

The rear and side façades echo this front portico in low relief. The slightly projecting central bay of the sides is accentuated by pilasters between the windows, which extend the full height of the façade above the basement level, ending in a low-pitched pediment. This arrangement is repeated on the two end wings of the rear façade. The whole is sheathed in Westchester County Tuckahoe marble.

The present cupola, constructed of cast iron and built in an eclectic and decorative Beaux Arts style, was designed in 1898 by Stoughton & Stoughton; the original wooden structure was destroyed by fire in 1895. The allegorical figure of Justice that crowns the cupola was part of the building's original design, but the statue was first executed and installed in 1987.

In 1980 the renewal of Borough Hall was begun. Aiming to restore both the exterior and interior of Gamaliel King's original city hall, the project has recovered the architectural grandeur of a building that, for over a hundred years, has been Brooklyn's seat of government.

ST. GEORGE'S CHURCH, 1846–56; restored, 1867
Rutherford Place at 16th Street, Manhattan
Architects: Blesch & Eidlitz
Designated: June 20, 1967

St. George's Church is one of the finest examples of early Romanesque Revival architecture in New York City. It ranks among architect Leopold Eidlitz's major works, and it was, in fact, his first building; he designed it in 1846, at age twenty-three, in collaboration with the older Bavarian architect Charles Blesch. The parish house to the west of the church was Eidlitz's last work; the stylistic development of his entire career can be read on 16th Street. The church burned in the 1860s, but in 1867 it was restored according to Eidlitz's original plans.

A bold demonstration of the celebrated unity between architecture and engineering, the style of the church may be identified with the sturdy Romanesque of southern Germany. The massive exterior radiates solidity and an impression of permanence. A fine rose window is a conspicuous feature of the heavily decorated end gable of the nave. The church houses what was once the largest interior space in New York, with the huge roof beams elegantly exposed. Stone spires, damaged by fire in 1865, were removed in 1889, but the towers today have lost none of their powerful thrust.

Fonthill

COLLEGE OF MOUNT ST. VINCENT
West 261st Street, The Bronx

Fonthill, 1848
Architect: Unknown
Designated: March 15, 1966

Cottage and Stable, 1848–52
Architect: Unknown
Designated: July 28, 1981

Administration Building, 1857–59;
additions, 1865, 1883, 1906–08, 1951
Architects: Henry Englebert;
1906 addition, E. Wenz
Designated: February 8, 1979

Fonthill, a Gothic castle overlooking the Hudson River at the extreme northwest corner of Riverdale, was built in 1848 as the home of Edwin Forrest, a famous Shakespearean actor, and his wife, Catherine. This extravagantly romantic building was inspired by William Beckford's Fonthill Abbey in England, as was much Gothic Revival architecture in America. Though the exact identity of the architect remains unknown, the design has been attributed to Alexander Jackson Davis, one of the most important architects of the time, who corresponded with Forrest about Fonthill. The connection of Davis with the design of Fonthill and its outbuildings is of particular interest because it was Davis who initiated the Picturesque Cottage tradition, of which the castle and its cottage and stable are a part.

Built of dark, hammer-dressed fieldstone, the castle consists of six octagonal turrets of different heights and dimensions, joined together. The highest, the staircase tower, rises seventy feet from the base; the window styles include round-arched, flatheaded, and ogival. The towers are battlemented and machicolated in the Gothic tradition. The cottage and stable were built in

Administration Building

The Cottage

The Stable

1848 as outbuildings for Fonthill and combine elements of the Gothic and Italianate modes in a typically picturesque manner. The cottage is a small, two-story building crowned by a half-hipped roof with deep eaves projecting out over ornately carved wooden brackets. The stable, a rambling structure with peaked roof gables of various sizes that create a picturesque roofline, functions today as the archives of the Sisters of Charity.

The Forrests never occupied the residence. During lengthy divorce proceedings, Fonthill and its surrounding property were bought by the Sisters of Charity of New York (the first Roman Catholic religious community in this country); the sisters were looking for a new location for their Academy of Mount St. Vincent, which was forced to relocate to make way for the expansion of Central Park. In 1911, the academy's charter was amended and the College of Mount St. Vincent was incorporated. Fonthill has served numerous functions for Mount St. Vincent since 1856.

The Administration Building is the main campus building, containing classrooms and departmental offices. It was constructed in 1857 in an Early Romanesque Revival/Byzantine style. The first college building to be erected on the Forrest estate, it was designed by Henry Engelbert, an architect active in New York City from 1852 to 1879. Extensions were added to the first building in 1865, 1883, 1906–08, and 1951; together, they form an imposing asymmetrical group, with the main façade facing west and overlooking the Hudson.

The original structure is red brick and rises four stories with an attic fifth story pierced by dormers; a central six-story tower is crowned by a copper lantern and spire. The major focus is the square tower, screened at its base by a two-story-high wooden porte cochere and porch flanked by gabled sections. The central tower of the building rises 180 feet and houses a bell that is rung on special occasions. A south wing was added in 1865, followed by a north wing in 1883, both by Engelbert. The extension to the complex in 1906–08, by architect E. Wenz, is a Neoclassical structure. The chapel, built in 1859 and located on the second floor, features a fresco by the American artist Constantino Brumidi.

ODD FELLOWS HALL, 1847–48; addition, 1881–82
165–171 Grand Street, Manhattan
Architects: Trench & Snook; addition, John Buckingham
Designated: August 24, 1982

Located on a prominent site on Grand Street, the Odd Fellows Hall was designed by the firm of Joseph Trench and John Butler Snook. Built in 1847–48, it is an early and particularly fine example of the austere and restrained Anglo-Italianate style that these architects helped introduce to New York. Moreover, it is one of the few surviving institutional buildings from the 1840s. John Snook later became one of the city's most renowned architects of the nineteenth century; the Odd Fellows Hall stands as one of his most striking and important buildings.

The Independent Order of Odd Fellows was one of the many mutual aid societies and fraternal organizations established in New York to contribute to the welfare of the city's populace. Faced in brownstone and four stories high, the original building was distinguished by its emphasis on planar surfaces, accented by a rusticated base, central projections, and colossal pilasters. The second owner of the building, R. Hoe and Co., holds an important place in the city's commercial history as one of the most innovative manufacturers of printing presses in the country. The two uppermost floors, designed in a reserved Queen Anne style with characteristic chimneys enlivened by vertical patterns of indented brick, were added by the architect John Buckingham.

WEEPING BEECH TREE, 1847
37th Avenue between Parsons Boulevard and Bowne Street, Flushing, Queens
Designated: April 19, 1966

While traveling through Europe in 1847, a Flushing nurseryman named Samuel Parsons purchased a small section from a tree on the estate of Baron DeMan in Beersal, Belgium. Today, the mature tree that took root from that cutting stands over sixty feet high. The circumference of the trunk is fourteen feet, and the spread of the crown is about eighty-five feet.

Protected by an iron fence one hundred feet in diameter, the tree is surrounded by a small residential park. A walkway lined with benches follows the circumference of the fence, providing a comfortable and pleasant place for a stroll.

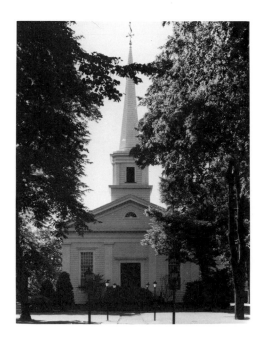

FLATLANDS DUTCH REFORMED CHURCH, 1848
Kings Highway and East 40th Street, Brooklyn
Architect: Unknown
Designated: July 19, 1966

Flatlands Dutch Reformed Church, erected in 1848, stands in a spacious churchyard enclosed by a fine wrought-iron fence. Buried in the adjacent cemetery is the Reverend Ulpianus Van Sinderen, the outspoken revolutionary war minister known as The Rebel Parson. Beneath the pulpit lie the remains of Pieter Claesen Wyckoff, who founded the church in 1654 and whose house is the oldest still standing in New York City.

This Greek Revival church, set on a stone foundation, is built of white clapboard. The stately front contains a handsome door and two tall triple-sash windows. The cornice is simple and crowned by a low-pitched pediment. Four pilasters on the front are repeated in the simple belfry, which supports a graceful spire topped with a gold ball and weather vane.

THE ARSENAL, 1847–51
Central Park at 64th Street, Manhattan
Architect: Martin E. Thompson
Designated: October 12, 1967

Standing serenely in a slight hollow west of Fifth Avenue, this five-story structure was erected "to house and protect the arms of the State of New York." Until 1848, the state's armaments were located at Centre and Franklin streets; but concern for the security of the arms and ammunition kept there prompted a move uptown. The building was used as an arsenal for less than ten years. In 1857, New York City purchased the site and converted the arsenal into the headquarters of the 11th Police Precinct. In 1869, the second and third stories housed the American Museum of Natural History; the upper story contained the Municipal Weather Bureau, and until 1914 the parks commissioner also had his office here. In 1934, the structure was renovated to accommodate the consolidated New York City Department of Parks (now Parks and Recreation), which is located here today.

The façade is organized around crenellated octagonal towers that rise a full story above the fourth-floor cornice. The massing and the square-headed windows with simplified hood moldings recall fortified Tudor castles. The basement is faced with rough-cut granite blocks; the floors above are of plain orange brick. Ornamental carving is kept to a minimum—due perhaps as much to a lack of architectural sculptors at the time as to the building's original function. The simply articulated brick masses are nonetheless elegant and provide a pleasant backdrop to the carved door frame with eagle resting on cannon balls above.

291–299 State Street

290–324 State Street

STATE STREET HOUSES, c. 1847–c. 1871
290–324 State Street, Brooklyn
Builder: Michael Murray
Designated: November 20, 1973

Located in the Boerum Hill neighborhood of the old town of "Breukelen," State Street was developed between the 1840s and 1870s as a neighborhood for merchants and professionals working in the Wall Street and Fulton Street areas. Standing upon what was once the farmland of Dutch colonist Jacob Van Brunt, the twenty-three State Street Houses exemplify the transition in style from Greek Revival to Italianate that was taking place in the architecture of the period.

Although completed over a thirty-year period, the block is remarkably uniform. Each three-story house is constructed of brick and brownstone and stands upon a rusticated brownstone or stuccoed basement (with the sole exception of number 322, which has a wood frame on a brick foundation). All have high stoops leading to arched double doorways framed in either engaged columns and pilasters or decorative moldings. The houses have projecting cornices embellished with modillions and dentils; most are fenced in by elaborate wrought-iron and cast-iron railings.

The block, however, is preserved from a dull homogeneity by the decorative details that distinguish one façade from another. Numbers 291 through 299 have engaged wooden columns with Italianate Corinthian capitals framing the doors; the architect of houses 310 through 316 chose instead to use Greek Revival pilasters with Doric capitals. The projecting lintels above the windows of number 298 decrease progressively in size; those of houses 290–294 and 304 are flush and uniform, and the window lintels of the others all have decorative cap moldings.

710 BAY STREET, formerly the Boardman-Mitchell House, 1848
Staten Island
Architect: Unknown (after a design by A. J. Downing)
Designated: October 12, 1982

The well-preserved Boardman-Mitchell House at 710 Bay Street was built in 1848 in the village of Edgewater, now part of Stapleton. This house, situated atop a steep bluff bordering Bay Street with an extensive view across the Narrows to the Manhattan skyline, was the home of Dr. James R. Boardman, resident physician at the nearby Seaman's Retreat Hospital, and later Captain Elvin Eugene Mitchell, founding member and hero of the Sandy Hook Pilots Benevolent Association. Mitchell bought the house with prize money awarded him by Cunard Lines for having saved 176 passengers and crew members from the Cunard liner SS *Oregon*, which sank off Fire Island in 1886.

This early Italianate villa is covered with gray-painted cedar shingles with contrasting buff trim. The twelve-inch-wide overhanging eaves of the roof are supported by broad, curvilinear double volute brackets. A low, triangular pediment intersecting the roofline shelters a pair of central arched windows that light the small, third-floor room that Captain Mitchell maintained as a lookout. At each side of the pediment, set below the eaves, are narrow, horizontal windows with three panes each, flanking a projecting central bay. At the second-floor level, a pair of French doors opens onto a low, square, balustraded balcony above a large, enclosed, pilastered entrance pavilion. The entrance is flanked by wide, balustraded first-floor balconies (extending in front of the living room and dining room) and fronted by a balustraded stoop with flanking entrance steps. The sides of the house, visible from Bay Street, are identical in design, each with four Italianate-framed, double-hung windows. An Italianate cornice continues around the sides of the house and across the rear roofline.

Fort Tompkins

Battery Weed

FORT WADSWORTH RESERVATION
Hudson Road, Staten Island
Architects: Unknown

Battery Weed, formerly Fort
Richmond, 1847–61
Designated: October 12, 1967

Fort Tompkins, 1861–c. 1870
Designated: September 24, 1974

Battery Weed and Fort Tompkins are the two major fortifications in the Fort Wadsworth Reservation. Fort Tompkins is built at the crest of the hill above Battery Weed, located at the water's edge on the Narrows. Both were part of the third system of U.S. coastal fortifications constructed between 1817 and 1864, although Fort Tompkins was not actually completed until years after the Civil War. Unlike the first system, which was initiated when it seemed the United States might be drawn into the European wars that followed the French Revolution, and the second, started during the threat of war with Britain, the construction of the third system came chiefly during periods of peace.

At the height of its glory, Battery Weed (then called Fort Richmond) was one of the most powerful forts on the eastern seaboard. In 1862, it mounted between 140 and 150 cannon and was manned by a large force of U.S. volunteer artillery. Battery Weed, like Fort Tompkins, is a superb example of a granite masonry structure. The battery is laid out in the form of an irregularly shaped trapezoid, with the shorter side facing the water. The open inner courtyard is framed on all three sides by tiers of segmental arches resting on heavy piers with octagonal towers at the corners.

A long, low, polygonal structure, Fort Tompkins stands on a platform carved out of the eastern side of the hill. The eastern façade, an uninterrupted stretch of smooth-faced granite, is barely visible from the water's edge. In contrast, the rear, or western, façade of the fort, covered with rough-hewn granite, rises up in front of a deep, dry moat. Fort Tompkins served primarily as a barracks for Battery Weed.

The reservation as a whole is extraordinary, both as an example of the military architecture of the mid-nineteenth century and for the historical associations, national in scope, attached to the site.

THEODORE ROOSEVELT BIRTHPLACE NATIONAL HISTORIC SITE, 1848; reconstructed, 1923
28 East 20th Street, Manhattan
Architect: Unknown; renovation, Theodate Pope Riddle
Designated: March 15, 1966

The original of this handsome town house was built in 1848 and demolished in 1916; in 1923, Roosevelt's boyhood home was replicated by Theodate Pope Riddle, the first woman architect in the United States. Constructed of brownstone, the house is distinguished by its shutters, decorative balcony and railings, entrance door with transom above and a delivery entrance under the stoop, Gothic Revival blind arcade-supported cornice, and drip moldings above the windows and front door—all typical of other houses on 20th Street built during the mid-nineteenth century. A fourth story with dormers and a slate-shingled mansard roof crown this handsome building.

A descendant of one of the old Dutch families of Manhattan, Theodore Roosevelt is the only native of New York City to be elected president. The family moved to a larger house uptown in 1872, and the former Roosevelt home was severely altered for commercial purposes. In 1919, a few months after Roosevelt's death, the Woman's Roosevelt Memorial Association (later to merge with the Roosevelt Memorial Association) bought it and the adjoining house where Roosevelt's uncle lived (number 26), the two buildings were demolished and the present building reconstructed by Riddle. In 1962, the house was named a National Historic Site, and today it is administered by the National Park Service as a museum.

CHURCH OF THE TRANSFIGURATION, 1849–61; lych-gate, 1896; chapels, c. 1906–08
1 East 29th Street, Manhattan
Architects: Frederick C. Withers (lych-gate); otherwise unknown
Designated: May 25, 1967

This is the Little Church Around the Corner—also called the Actors' Church, but officially known as the Church of the Transfiguration. Reminiscent of an English parish church, it stands serene in its miniature garden, in the shadow of the Empire State Building.

The main entrance to the church is through the tower, which is reinforced at the corners by diagonally placed, stepped buttresses and crowned by a small, peaked roof. At the base of the tower and to the left are the three arched windows of the Lady chapel. The main body of the church, which lies to the right, is divided into four sections of unequal size by squat buttresses. Small dormers serve as clerestory windows above the nave. The octagonal crossing tower contains St. Joseph's mortuary chapel. The lych-gate, an unusual feature in an American churchyard, is a pagodalike structure supported by stone Gothic arches. Usually found at the entrance to a churchyard, a lych-gate (from the Old English *lich*, meaning corpse) was intended to provide a covered resting place for a coffin before the start of the burial service.

The great American actor Joseph Jefferson made popular the church's sobriquet in 1870. An actor friend, George Holland, had died, and Jefferson went to a fashionable church in the neighborhood to arrange for the funeral service. When the rector learned that the deceased had been an actor, he politely declined but suggested that there was a "little church around the corner where the matter might be arranged." Whereupon Jefferson, with deep feeling, replied, "Thank God for the little church around the corner." From that day, there has been a special bond between the stage and this church. Sir Henry Irving, Dame Ellen Terry, and Sarah Bernhardt attended services here, and there are memorial windows to some of the most distinguished American actors: Richard Mansfield, John Drew, and Edwin Booth.

The rectory of the Little Church was designed as a subsidiary part of a larger composition and is an excellent example of domestic Gothic Revival architecture. The brick and brownstone building's strong architectural character blends well with the adjacent church, forming one of the most picturesque ecclesiastical enclaves in the city.

ALLEN-BEVILLE HOUSE, c. 1848–50
29 Center Drive, Queens
Architect: Unknown
Designated: January 11, 1977

Attractively situated on spacious grounds, the Allen-Beville House is a handsome Greek Revival dwelling erected about 1848–50 in what is now known as Douglaston, Queens. One of the few remaining nineteenth-century farmhouses in New York City, the structure retains many of its fine details. Resting on a low basement, the symmetrical, rectangular house is sheathed in white clapboard. It is five bays wide and three bays deep, with front and rear porches extending the full width of the house. Characteristic of the Greek Revival style are the elegant fluted Doric columns that support the porch entablature, which in turn is highlighted by dentils and Italianate paired brackets. A pair of later Queen Anne doors replace the original entry. Set beneath the projecting cornice, the fascia board is accented by alternating panels, small, shuttered attic windows, dentils, and paired brackets. A striking bracketed, octagonal cupola crowns the house.

It is believed that Benjamin P. Allen erected the house soon after he acquired the property in 1847 from a relative. Allen and his wife, Catherine, the parents of seven, reportedly opened a school for local children in the house in 1865. The property later became part of the William P. Douglas estate and was probably used as a guesthouse. Douglas, for whom the village of Douglaston is named, is best known for his yacht *Sappho*, which defeated the British challengers and won the America's Cup in 1876. In 1905 and 1906 the land of the Douglas estate was sold and subdivided as a real-estate development. In 1946, the house was sold to Hugh and Eleanor Beville.

CHURCH OF THE HOLY APOSTLES, 1848; transept, 1858
300 Ninth Avenue, Manhattan
Architects: Minard Lafever (church); Richard Upjohn & Son (transept)
Designated: October 19, 1966

While simple in style, the Church of the Holy Apostles features a handsome square, brick tower skillfully connected to a copper-clad, octagonal steeple. Round-arched windows rhythmically punctuate the building's surface, while others, with a bull's-eye design, appear in the arched pediments.

Inside the church, a Tuscan order and groin vaults echo the external touches of classic Italianate design. These details are exceptions for Lafever, generally noted for his work in Greek Revival and Gothic Revival styles.

The nave has a series of original stained-glass windows by William Jay Bolton, with simple, sepia-toned round panes illustrating Biblical and early Christian scenes, surrounded by stylized panels of geometric and floral glass. They are the only American example of this style that Bolton designed.

The church is notable not only for its architecture, but also for the distinguished rectors who have served it: the Reverend Robert Shaw Howland, second rector of the church, later founded the Church of the Heavenly Rest on Fifth Avenue; the Reverend Lucius A. Edelblute, rector for thirty years, wrote *The History of the Church of the Holy Apostles (A Hundred Years in Chelsea)*, published in 1949. For five years the church has operated a nationally known soup kitchen, which now feeds more than 1,200 hungry people each day.

SON-RISE INTERFAITH CHARISMATIC CHURCH,
formerly Asbury Methodist Church, 1849; remodeled, 1878
2100 Richmond Avenue, Staten Island
Architect: Unknown
Designated: March 19, 1968

This simple, mid-nineteenth-century Federal church was named after Bishop Francis Asbury, a preacher who first came to Staten Island in 1771. During the forty-five years of his stay, Bishop Asbury saw, largely through his own efforts, the five hundred Methodists under his jurisdiction grow to 214,000. The first Asbury Methodist Church, then called the North End Church, was constructed in 1802 near the site of the present building. It was removed from the property in 1850. The gravestones in the cemetery that remains date from 1813.

The present church is rectangular in plan. The front elevation consists of a square tower, projecting forward from the front wall and containing an entranceway with plain double doors in a round arch with a fanlight above the doors. The entrance is surrounded by windows, one centered above the door and one in each flanking wall. The tower supports a belfry with angular side openings and a single bell. The bonded side walls, dating from 1849, are pierced by four square-headed windows with plain lintels and sills. A wide fascia board and cornice adorn the building at roof level.

CONGREGATION ANSHE SLONIM, formerly
Congregation Anshe Chesed, 1849–50
172–176 Norfolk Street, Manhattan
Architect: Alexander Saeltzer
Designated: February 10, 1987

Congregation Anshe Slonim, located on the Lower East Side of Manhattan, was the largest congregation in the city at the time of its construction in 1849–50. Established in 1828, the German congregation was the third Jewish congregation in New York, after Shearith Israel and B'nai Jeshurun, and the second to practice Reform Judaism. The Gothic Revival building was designed by German architect Alexander Saeltzer, who was also responsible for the Astor Library at 425 Lafayette Street, now the New York Shakespeare Festival Public Theater.

Saeltzer's background influenced the pronounced Gothic style of the synagogue, said to be inspired by the Cologne Cathedral. The tripartite façade of the building is of brick covered with stucco. Two square towers border the recessed central section. These towers have a lancet window at each level; now truncated above the second story, they were originally three stories tall with concave, pyramidal roofs. The three main doors of the building are surmounted by pointed-arched windows. A large central window dominates the façade and is flanked by two smaller windows. A pointed gable frames the top of the façade and includes the remains of a foliate cornice.

During its history, the synagogue has housed three congregations: Anshe Chesed, from 1850 until 1874; Ohab Zedek, from 1886 until 1921; and Anshe Slonim, a Polish congregation, from 1921 until 1974. Today it is owned by Spanish sculptor Angel Orensanz, who plans to renovate it into an arts space.

JOSEPH PAPP PUBLIC THEATER, formerly the New York Shakespeare Festival Public Theater, 1849–53; 1856–59; 1879–81; renovated, 1966
425 Lafayette Street, Manhattan
Architects: Alexander Saeltzer (south wing); Griffith Thomas (center wing); Thomas Stent (north wing); renovation, Giorgio Cavaglieri
Designated: October 26, 1965

Funds for the Astor Library were bequeathed by John Jacob Astor, a German-born entrepreneur who made his fortune first in the western fur trade and later in New York City real estate. The Astor collection would eventually become, with the Lenox and Tilden collections, the core of the New York Public Library. When it was opened in 1854, the Astor was the first free library in New York—but it was open only during daylight hours, and so was inaccessible to most of the working public. The aged Washington Irving was the Astor's first librarian.

With the $400,000 bequest, Astor's son William B. Astor hired German-born Alexander Saeltzer to design and build what is now the southern third of the structure. The façade is divided into three bays by two slightly projecting pavilions. The rusticated base is of brownstone, as are the early Renaissance–style windows above. The whole is capped by a strapwork cornice, Ionic frieze, and solid parapet. The arches set in a plain brick surface are marks of the German *Rundbogenstil*, literally "round-arched style," used for civic structures in the German states from the early to mid-nineteenth century. This particular design draws on early Renaissance forms.

In 1856, William commissioned Griffith Thomas, who was well known for his cast-iron façades in what is now SoHo, to extend the library to the north. In turn, William's sons, John Jacob and William B. Astor, Jr., hired Thomas Stent to add the northernmost section as a memorial to their father. Stent also built an attic story over Thomas's 1856 annex to give the long, unbroken façade a central emphasis. What is most interesting about the entire complex is the care with which the efforts of the two later architects matched the original building in design as well as materials. Indeed, the three separate building campaigns merge seamlessly.

In 1920, the Hebrew Immigrant Aid Society (HIAS) purchased the building, but by 1965 it was again in disuse and facing demolition. Joseph Papp's New York Shakespeare Festival convinced the city to buy it and Giorgio Cavaglieri designed and superintended the 1966 renovation to theaters, offices, and auditoriums. At the time, this area—the westernmost border of the East Village—was run down. As the neighborhood grew more popular in the 1970s, the Public Theater and Cooper Union have provided the focus for redevelopment to the east and south.

WEST 24TH STREET HOUSES, 1849–50
437–459 West 24th Street, Manhattan
Architects: Unknown
Designated: September 15, 1970

This long, handsome row of paired three-story houses was built in 1849–50 by Philo V. Beebe, in association with the attorney Beverly Robinson and George F. Talman, to provide housing for merchants and professionals of the expanding Chelsea community. Set behind landscaped yards, they possess an appealing sense of human scale, and generally retain their original ironwork and architectural character, transitional between the Greek Revival and the Italianate.

The basic proportions are Greek Revival, with later modifications in the Neo-Grec, Queen Anne, and Federal Revival styles. Thus the houses represent more than a century of architectural development. In general, they retain their setbacks behind front yards, original height, bold modillioned roof cornices, and ironwork—features that unify this charming row.

SERBIAN ORTHODOX CATHEDRAL OF ST. SAVA
15 West 25th Street, Manhattan
Architect: Richard M. Upjohn
Designated: April 18, 1968

Cathedral of St. Sava and Clergy House, 1850–55

Parish House, 1860

A large English-style Gothic Revival church, this brownstone structure is celebrated for its fine proportions and for the great length of its nave. Designed by Richard M. Upjohn, the church was consecrated in 1855 as a chapel of Trinity Church to serve uptown communicants of the parish. It was purchased by the Serbian Orthodox Church in 1945 and renamed the Cathedral of St. Sava.

The lofty nave is situated below a steep-pitched slate roof; the angular gable of the south elevation faces 25th Street. Centered in this gabled wall is a large wheel window. Directly below and flanked by buttresses a pointed-arched portal, accented with slender columns and graceful arches within its deep reveal, serves as the main entrance to the cathedral. The side walls of the long nave are pierced by slender pointed-arched windows; the seven-bay apse is topped by an octagonal slate roof.

The Clergy House forms the short leg of the L-shaped plan of the ensemble. Adjacent to the chancel, its steep pyramidal roof contains one triangular dormer window. A pair of leaded-glass, pointed-arched windows pierce the center of the buttress-supported south wall, and an entrance door on the east side is topped by an arched molding and pointed gable.

The Parish House, about forty feet east of the church, was completed about five years after the cathedral. A high, pointed-arched, leaded-glass window contains fine stone tracery, and an open-arched belfry rises above the gable of the south elevation.

Cathedral of St. Sava and Clergy House

BETH HAMEDRASH HAGODOL SYNAGOGUE,
formerly the Norfolk Street Baptist Church, 1850
60–64 Norfolk Street, Manhattan
Architect: Unknown
Designated: February 28, 1967

Originally built as the Norfolk Street Baptist Church in 1850, this austere building is a restrained example of the Gothic Revival style. In 1860, when the Baptists moved north, Methodists took it over for the next quarter century; they were replaced by Russian Jews, who had been settling on the Lower East Side for some time. The church was rededicated as Beth Hamedrash Hagodol Synagogue in 1885 and still serves the oldest congregation of Russian Orthodox Jews (founded 1852) to have been organized in this country.

Raised on a platform of steps above the street, the recessed central section of the symmetrical façade is flanked by square towers pierced by coupled, pointed-arched windows that light the side vestibules. The focus of the façade is the main double entrance door with over-door panel joining it to the tall, tripartite arched window. The whole is surmounted by a pedimented roof affixed with the Star of David. At the top of each tower is a square decorative panel of Gothic quatrefoil design. An early print published in the *New York Almanac* of 1851 shows that the towers originally had battlements or crenellations, which were later removed.

DR. SAMUEL MACKENZIE ELLIOTT HOUSE, c. 1850
69 Delafield Place, Staten Island
Architect: Dr. Samuel MacKenzie Elliott
Designated: April 12, 1967

The Dr. Samuel MacKenzie Elliott House is said to be one of more than twenty-two houses designed by Dr. Elliott, an eye surgeon of wide repute and an enthusiastic amateur architect. The house was built around 1850 in a country version of the Gothic Revival. Constructed of locally quarried random ashlar, the two-and-one-half-story house, with twenty-three-inch walls, has eight rooms, an attic, and a large cellar. The entrance, situated at the gable end of the building, is framed by blue and amber diamond-shaped glass sidelights and surmounted by a polychrome fan-patterned glasswork transom. On one side of the entrance, the first-floor windows are double-hung with wide, vertical, central muntins that simulate casements, and are topped by sandstone lintels. On the second floor, a Gothic pointed-arched window, designed to light the attic through its upper portion, accents the façade. Above, scalloped wooden vergeboards trim the gables of the roof.

Dr. Elliott, who emigrated from Scotland in the 1830s, was a citizen of enormous prestige; his influence was so great that the area around his estate on Staten Island's north shore was often called "Elliottville." One reason for Elliott's popularity was his devotion to the abolitionist cause. This house was reputedly part of the Underground Railroad, and the cellar was fitted with a special fireplace for cooking. Today the house is still a private residence.

167–171 JOHN STREET, 1849–50
Manhattan
Architect: Unknown
Designated: October 29, 1968

Abiel Abbot Low, one of the foremost merchants of the China trade, commissioned this granite Greek Revival building, which commanded an impressive view of the harbor—including his own clipper ships, offices, and warehouses. Inhabited by Low and his brother, Josiah, the building was meant to symbolize the success and importance of their firm.

Although the brownstone front, Corinthian capitals, and molded sills have been removed, the building's imposing scale still conveys a sense of grandeur. The eight-bay, five-story structure stands on a raised brownstone basement. Tall windows on the second, third, and fourth floors contrast with shorter windows on the top story. The restrained façade is completed by a simple cornice.

MARBLE COLLEGIATE CHURCH, 1851–54
275 Fifth Avenue, Manhattan
Architect: Samuel A. Warner
Designated: January 11, 1967

The Collegiate church, founded by the Dutch in 1628, is the oldest Protestant congregation in America, and it has had a continuous ministry since its inception.

To house this venerable congregation, Samuel A. Warner designed a distinguished marble structure that synthesized European and American styles. Succeeding the "Stone Church in the Fort" of 1642, the Marble Collegiate Church has the rounded arches, heavy buttresses, and massive planes of thirteenth- and fourteenth-century Romanesque architecture, as well as the soaring spires, delicately carved finials, and decorative detail of the Gothic style of the fifteenth and sixteenth centuries. The most impressive feature is the spire- and weather vane–topped central tower that contains the belfry and clock. This tower is flanked at its base by tall double windows; it is supported by graduated buttresses that are in turn used to support the walls of the main building. The sides of the building are punctuated by five Romanesque arched windows. Octagonal turrets and pinnacles capped with molded cornices and carved finials complete the structure.

While European architecture informs much of the detail of Warner's design, the overriding impression is nonetheless that of a New England–style, American church, complete with tower, spire, and weather vane.

PRITCHARD HOUSE, c. 1850
66 Harvard Avenue, Staten Island
Architect: Unknown
Designated: March 19, 1968

This brick Italianate mansion with stucco and stone trim was erected about 1850 for C. K. Hamilton. Two and one-half stories high, the house features a rectangular floor plan with a short wing projecting from the southwestern corner, accented by round-arched windows embellished with fanlights and an elaborate cornice. Dominating the main structure is the imposing hipped roof with generous overhang, supported by paired brackets. The roof is crowned by two large chimneys and a monitor roof containing low windows that provide the attic with light.

A second-story horizontal stringcourse surrounds the mansion, cutting through the sharply beveled quoins that highlight the corners of the structure. Enframed with Greek ears at the top, the main block windows are square-headed, including the first-floor French doors with muntins. A flight of wooden steps leads up to the porch and main entrance on the west side. The low-pitched porch roof is supported by slender, turned columns. The entrance is a double-paneled door with sidelights set between plain pilasters; the doorway is crowned by a molded entablature.

Today the house continues to serve as a private residence.

INDIA HOUSE, formerly Hanover Bank, 1851–54
1 Hanover Square, Manhattan
Architect: Unknown
Designated: December 21, 1965

Reminiscent of a Florentine palazzo, India House is typical of many brownstone commercial buildings that once dotted this area. Built for the Hanover Bank between 1851 and 1854, the Anglo-Italianate structure is a prototype of the New York brownstone row house that was to be built on a large scale in the latter half of the nineteenth century.

Three stories high and symmetrically composed, India House contains details typical of brownstone residences. Above a rusticated basement, smooth masonry walls rise to a well-detailed cornice supported by closely spaced brackets. The windows are defined by the use of triangular and segmental arched pediments on the first and second stories, and brackets beneath the sills on the second and third stories. Handsome Corinthian columns and a fine balustrade create a distinguished doorway entrance.

India House played an important role in the city's commercial life in the latter part of the nineteenth century; from 1870 to 1886 it served as the New York Cotton Exchange, and later it housed the offices of W. R. Grace & Co. Today it serves as a clubhouse, harboring a fine maritime museum, and continues to provide a warm intimacy amidst the austere concrete and steel structures of lower Manhattan.

SOUTH CONGREGATIONAL CHURCH
253–269 President Street and 358–366 Court Street, Brooklyn
Designated: March 23, 1982

Chapel, 1851	Ladies' Parlor, 1889
Architect: Unknown	Architect: Frederick Carles Merry
Church, 1857	Rectory, 1893
Architect: Unknown	Architect: Woodruff Leeming

The South Congregational Church is located on a prominent corner in Carroll Gardens, one of Brooklyn's oldest residential neighborhoods. The church is a brick structure enhanced by a series of recessed arches expressive of the finest and most sophisticated early Romanesque Revival designs of the pre–Civil War period. The founding of the church is attributed to Henry Ward Beecher, the well-known abolitionist and minister of the nearby Plymouth Church. He is reputed to have stood on this spot in 1850 and said, "Here the next Congregational church should be built."

The South Congregational Church is notable for the extraordinary manner in which the brick is modeled on the façade. The main gable with inset arches and a corbeled cornice contains a rectilinear entrance with a stone lintel below. It is flanked by square towers with pinnacles. The chapel exhibits a rectangular entrance, round arches, and recessed panels. A continuous corbeled cornice links the two buildings.

An addition, built in 1889 for use as a ladies' parlor and Sunday school, was designed in the Richardsonian Romanesque style by architect Frederick Carles Merry. A red-brick and terra-cotta structure, its massive forms and Byzantine carving are typical of this phase of the Romanesque Revival. The focal point of this two-story building is the entrance bay, which is in the form of a tower.

In 1893 the church built a rectory adjoining the ladies' parlor. This four-story, Gothic Revival structure, designed by Brooklyn architect Woodruff Leeming, forms a transitional link between the church and the mid-nineteenth-century row houses to the west.

Above: South Congregational Church and Rectory

ROSSVILLE A.M.E. ZION CHURCH CEMETERY, established 1852
Crabtree Avenue, Staten Island
Designated: April 9, 1985

The Rossville A.M.E. Church Cemetery, located near the western tip of Staten Island, commemorates the history of Sandy Ground, a community established in the mid-nineteenth century by free black oystermen and their families, most of whom moved northward from Snow Hill, Maryland, one of a number of settlements in the Chesapeake Bay area where blacks had prospered in the oystering industry. The mid-century relocation to Staten Island was a logical step, for the island at that time was the center of a flourishing oyster trade.

The area that eventually became Sandy Ground was a plateau on the outskirts of Woodrow, a small farming community. The A.M.E. Zion Church, incorporated in 1850, provided a spiritual center for the new settlement.

The community's growth and prosperity continued until the first years of the twentieth century, when water pollution dramatically altered the oyster industry. Despite such major disasters as the condemnation of the oyster beds in 1916 and a destructive fire in 1963, Sandy Ground has survived. Today, the Rossville A.M.E. Zion Church and its cemetery remain in use, a link with history. The cemetery bears the markers and stones of some thirty-four families, many associated with Sandy Ground's beginnings, and the family plots provide a visual record of the network of relationships that constituted the community.

LIGHT OF THE WORLD CHURCH
formerly New England Congregational Church, 1852–53
179 South Ninth Street, Brooklyn
Architect: Thomas Little
Designated: November 24, 1981

One of the earliest Congregational churches in Brooklyn, this rectangular Italianate church was organized on March 18, 1851, under the popular minister Thomas Kinnicut Beecher. Although Congregationalism was the dominant Protestant sect in New England, it was a latecomer to New York. Here it became closely associated with Thomas's brother, the Reverend Henry Ward Beecher, the outspoken abolitionist who took over the Plymouth Church in Brooklyn. Their sister, Harriet Beecher Stowe, was the author of *Uncle Tom's Cabin*.

Between 1845 and 1850, Williamsburg tripled in population; this fact, coupled with the popularity of Congregational worship, caused a number of Congregational churches in Williamsburg to be built in the decades before the Civil War. Thomas Little, principally a commercial architect, was selected to design this church, a choice that reflected Williamsburg's strong connections to commercial New York.

While the body of the church is brick, the façade is clad in brownstone, articulated with metal and wood trim, and flanked by large quoins. Courses of quarry-faced stone form a basement level. Within, the structure's generous galleries allow as much seating with as little obstruction as possible between the congregation and the preacher. The town house immediately to the west was built in 1868 to serve as the church rectory and is linked to the church by the return molding on the church's side elevation. The design of the gable front is repeated in the doorways and fenestration, with sharply projecting triangular pediments on the console brackets.

SALMAGUNDI CLUB, formerly the Irad Hawley House, 1853
47 Fifth Avenue, Manhattan
Architect: Unknown
Designated: September 9, 1969

The Salmagundi Club is the last of the brownstone mansions that once lined Fifth Avenue almost solidly from Washington Square to Central Park—"Two Miles of Millionaires." The mansion was built for Irad Hawley, president of the Pennsylvania Coal Company. The club, which was organized in 1871 for "the promotion of social intercourse among artists and the advancement of art," bought the building in 1917 and has maintained it. *Salmagundi* was the name given to Washington Irving's satirical periodical of 1807–08; the word originally denoted a spicy potpourri of chopped meat, anchovies, eggs, onions, and oil.

The building was erected in 1853 in the newly fashionable Italianate style. The characteristics of the style show clearly in the heavy pediment over the arched doorway, the richly carved consoles that support this pediment, and the little brackets that carry the individual cornices over each of the French windows of the main floor. The moldings around the windows were later stripped off, but the main cornice along the top of the building is still supported on its original heavy, paired brackets.

326, 328, and 330 EAST 18TH STREET, 1852–53
Manhattan
Architect: Unknown
Designated: March 20, 1973

These three relatively modest brick row houses—the oldest buildings surviving on this block—were built between 1852 and 1853 on land that was once part of Peter Stuyvesant's bouwerie, or farm. They recall a period when rows of one-family dwellings were beginning to line the city's "uptown" side streets, from the Harlem River to Avenue A.

Reflecting a vernacular interpretation of the Italianate style popular during the mid-nineteenth century, their outstanding features include unusually deep front yards and the original cast-iron work of the stoops and verandas.

Number 326 was home for many years to Henry Wilson, a stonecutter. Wilson and John Edwards, a builder, were partners and apparently were associated with these houses' construction.

2876 RICHMOND TERRACE, c. 1853
Staten Island
Architect: Unknown
Designated: July 13, 1976

This simple brick house, built for oysterman Stephen D. Barnes, is one of few surviving structures on "Captain's Row," an area of predominantly Greek Revival designs along the Shore Road. Unlike most of the other houses, Barnes's home combines elements from the Italianate and Gothic Revival styles, with the Italianate dominating the two-and-one-half-story square house. The broad, symmetrical façade contains a central doorway with square-headed windows on each side. Flanking the doorway are paneled pilasters that support an arched transom with rope molding.

On the second story, a cast-iron balcony ornaments a simple central window with segmental arch. Windows at the sides and rear of the house have flat brick arches and plain granite sills. Beneath the roof at the center of the house is a pair of small, arched windows sharing a common sill. The roof itself, flat with overhanging eaves, is supported on four sides by paired, vertical brackets. Stylized ornament in low relief marks these brackets, along with foliate terminations.

In the 1880s, following the death of Judith Barnes, the house was bought at auction by William Wheeler. He transferred it to Jane Van Pelt Wheeler, the last known owner.

COOPER UNION FOR THE ADVANCEMENT OF SCIENCE AND ART, 1853–59; renovation, 1975–76
Cooper Square between Astor Place and East 7th Street, Manhattan
Architect: Frederick A. Peterson; renovation, John Hejduk
Designated: March 15, 1966

Cooper Union embodies the ideals of its founder, Peter Cooper—a self-made entrepreneur who built the Tom Thumb locomotive, participated in laying the first transatlantic cable, and owned iron and steel-rolling mills in Trenton, New Jersey. In 1859, he established it as one of the first institutions in the country to offer a free education for the sons and daughters of the working class. Cooper wanted to provide students—men and women alike—with the means to earn a living, just as Charles Pratt was to do later in the century.

The six-story brownstone displays some of the first wrought-iron beams used in New York City, which were designed and produced in Peter Cooper's plant. Rolled instead of cast, these beams were produced on machinery that made possible the later development of the skyscraper. The structure also contains the prototype for the modern elevator.

The predominant style is Anglo-Italianate, demonstrated in the building's heavily enframed round-arched windows and handsome round-arched loggias. A long arcade of cast-iron arches appearing on both the Third Avenue and Lafayette Place façades is the work of Daniel D. Badger, who ran the largest iron foundry in New York City.

The building was extensively restored and renovated in 1975 and 1976; John Hejduk, the current dean of Cooper Union's Irwin S. Chanin School of Architecture, was the architect. The project entailed glazing the ground-floor arcades, encasing Cooper's wrought-iron columns in smooth plaster, and extending the elevator shaft through the roof. Dean Hejduk also corrected structural weaknesses that had threatened to destroy the building.

REFORMED CHURCH OF SOUTH BUSHWICK, 1853;
additions, 1885, 1903
855–867 Bushwick Avenue, Brooklyn
Architect: Unknown
Designated: March 19, 1968

The Reformed Church of South Bushwick is a Greek Revival church surmounted by a Georgian tower. Built in 1853, the Reformed Church, with central tower and steeple, was modeled after the great Georgian churches of Wren and Gibbs in London. The original congregation was made up of families from the rural farming community; the cornerstone was laid in 1852, a late date for Greek Revival architecture.

Among its dominant features are the classical portico and the soaring tower, which rises from a square base through a handsome octagonal belfry to an octagonal spire. The influence of the Greek Revival is seen in the pilasters of the steeple and in the two fine fluted Ionic columns of the portico, with delicately carved capitals, that are set between slender pilasters. Their capitals are noteworthy for their delicate carving.

In 1885 the church was enlarged to include the church house (dedicated in 1881), and the side wings were added. In 1903 the gallery and north and east extensions were added to the church house.

Today the Reformed Church of South Bushwick continues to function as a part of the Reformed Church in America, a descendant of the church that the Dutch settlers established in New Amsterdam.

364 VAN DUZER STREET, c. 1855
Staten Island
Architect: Unknown
Designated: December 18, 1973

Part of the property surveyed and subdivided by Minthorne Tompkins and William J. Staples in 1834, the year after they bought it, the land at 364 Van Duzer Street was originally sold to and developed by Captain Robert M. Hazard. Currently owned by Mr. and Mrs. Edward Tylonski, the house is undergoing extensive restoration.

The Greek Revival structure features classical double porticoes with two-story Doric columns. In place of the traditional triangular gable, the entablature of the frieze rests below an overhanging spring eave characteristic of the Dutch Colonial style. This curious combination is enhanced by the elegant windows opening onto the portico and by the delicate railings that decorate the parlor floor and second floor.

NEW DORP LIGHT, c. 1854
New Dorp Heights, Altamont Avenue, Staten Island
Architect: Unknown
Designated: November 15, 1967; amended to include the entire surrounding lot,
December 18, 1973

The New Dorp Light, also known as the New Dorp Beacon or the Moravian Light, was once a sentinel to ships in New York Bay. Well situated on a commanding perch in New Dorp Heights, the light was placed under the jurisdiction of the federal Lighthouse Service in 1856 and was operated by that agency until 1939. At that time, the light was acquired by the U.S. Coast Guard. Then on June 15, 1964, after almost ninety years of operation, the New Dorp Light was decommissioned. Today the lighthouse and the surrounding property are being restored and developed as a private residence, accessible to the public.

The architect of this one-and-one-half-story, rectangular lighthouse used a simple vernacular design to build a utilitarian structure. A low brick foundation supports a clapboard frame pierced by plain, double-hung sash windows, and a steeply pitched gable roof. The low, square lighthouse tower, covered by a low-pitched, pyramidal roof supporting a light beacon, rises from the center of the building and is flanked by a brick chimney at each end of the roof. The ground-level wing was added, with a covered entrance and screened-in porch for the caretaker.

W. S. PENDLETON HOUSE, c. 1855
22 Pendleton Place, Staten Island
Architect: Unknown
Designated: March 4, 1969

The two-and-one-half-story Gothic Revival Pendleton House, built about 1855, is situated on a lot overlooking the stream Kill Van Kull. The house is a charming shingle structure with a square, spire-topped tower, steeply pitched gable roofs, and windows of varying shapes and sizes. A gabled vestibule doorway projects forward from the southern elevation, adorned with scalloped scrollwork. Similar motifs are repeated in the roof dormers and in those of the spire. A special feature of the west elevation is an oriel with paired windows. Two one-story extensions and a greenhouse were added to the west side of the building at a later date.

ST. PETER'S CHURCH, CEMETERY, AND FOSTER HALL
2500 Westchester Avenue, The Bronx
Designated: March 23, 1976

St. Peter's Church, 1855;
restored 1879 Architect: Leopold Eidlitz;
restoration, Cyrus L. W. Eidlitz

Foster Hall, formerly the Chapel, 1867–68
Architect: Leopold Eidlitz

Cemetery, established c. 1700

The Parish of St. Peter's was organized in 1693 but it was not until 1700 that the town meetinghouse, previously used for religious services, was abandoned and a church was erected. Its Czech architect Leopold Eidlitz came to New York in 1843. Eidlitz, along with Henry Hobson Richardson and Frederick Law Olmsted, is noted for redesigning and completing the New York State Capitol in Albany in 1875–85. After a fire in 1879, the church was restored by his son Cyrus.

St. Peter's Church is a Gothic structure with a bold profile, dominated by a steeply pitched roof and a towering spire at the corner of the nave. Cruciform in plan, it has a high nave with clerestory, narrow side aisles, and shallow transepts. The clerestory was added by Cyrus Eidlitz and is the only feature of the church that is different from the original design.

The chapel, now called Foster Hall, was built as a Sunday school. This modest, one-story Victorian Gothic structure is made of the same rough-faced stone as the church, with windows and other details in contrasting sandstone. There are entrance doors on each side of the gable tower, beneath a low, sloping slate roof. The tower terminates in a freestanding bell cot with a pointed-arched opening. Two small engaged colonnettes with foliate capitals flank the entrance. Two slender chimneys with gable capstones pierce the lower edge of the roof on one side.

The cemetery, which surrounds the church and chapel, contains gravestones dating from the 1750s and '60s; headstones of soldiers killed during the Revolution can be seen near the chapel. There are also a Romanesque Revivial vault, a Victorian Gothic tomb, and several large twentieth-century mausoleums.

271 NINTH STREET, formerly William B. Cronyn House, 1856–57
Brooklyn
Architect: Unknown
Designated: July 11, 1978

An impressive suburban residential house in the French Second Empire style, 271 Ninth Street was built on four farm lots in 1856–57 for William B. Cronyn, a prosperous Wall Street merchant. The three-story house is constructed of wood and brick and covered with stucco. It features a central half-story cupola with clerestory, below which is a slate mansard roof with end pavilions pierced with dormers, ornamental iron crestings, and handsome detail.

The house remained in the Cronyn family until 1862, and in 1879 it became the residence of Daniel H. Gray, who was in the sulfur-refining business. Gray's daughter lived there until 1896, and Charles M. Higgins acquired the property two years later. Like many former residences in this changing neighborhood, the house was converted to commercial use, serving as the headquarters for Higgins's India Ink Company. Today the house is again a private residence.

WATCH TOWER, c. 1855
Center of Mount Morris Park, opposite East 122nd Street, Manhattan
Architect: Attributed to James Bogardus
Designated: July 12, 1967

James Bogardus, the self-styled "originator and constructor of cast-iron buildings," is credited with having built this skeletal cast-iron fire lookout tower for New York City. It stands on the tall, rocky outcropping in Mount Morris Park at the northernmost end of Fifth Avenue. From the little cupola four stories high on the octagonal tower, the watchman gazed across the roofs of Harlem, striking the bell to signal local fire companies when he spotted a fire. Before the first alarm-box system was installed in 1871, and before the advent of the telephone, fire watchtowers played a vital role in the city's fire control system. Although its fire-alarm purpose was discontinued in 1878, the bell at Mount Morris continued to ring daily, at 9:00 A.M. and noon, for years afterward, for the benefit of citizens who liked maintaining the tradition.

The slender iron columns of the watchtower are delicately fluted, and the sweep of the staircase spiraling up around the bell creates a lacy silhouette against the sky. The Mount Morris fire tower is, in the 1980s, an unexpected and rare souvenir.

FRIENDS MEETING HOUSE, 1857
110 Schermerhorn Street, Brooklyn
Master builder: Attributed to Charles T. Bunting
Designated: October 27, 1981

The Friends Meeting House at 110 Schermerhorn Street beautifully reflects the restrained character of Quaker architecture. The meetinghouse, which replaced an earlier structure located at Henry and Clark streets in Brooklyn Heights, is a transitional blend of the Greek Revival and Italianate styles; Charles T. Bunting is generally credited with its design.

The main façade rises through three and one-half stories to a peaked roof with a low gable that contains a bisected lunette window. The walls are constructed of hard-pressed red brick, laid in running bond. The window lintels and sills are of brownstone, as are the foundations. The restrained ornamentation consists of a porch with a triangular pediment supported by plain, wooden Doric columns and a raking cornice faced with simple moldings.

The building continues to be used as a meetinghouse by the Brooklyn Monthly Meeting of the Religious Society of Friends.

311–313 EAST 58TH STREET
Manhattan

311 East 58th Street, 1856–57
Architect: Unknown
Designated: May 25, 1967

313 East 58th Street, 1856–57
Builder: Hiram G. Disbrow
Designated: July 14, 1970

No more startling contrast can be imagined than that provided by the towering skyscrapers that now surround these two charming vernacular houses. Today the buildings are situated below the sidewalk level—the result of the construction of a new approach to the Queensboro Bridge in 1930.

In 1676, the land on which the houses stood was granted by Governor Edmund Andros to John Danielson. In colonial times, a tavern called The Union Flag, which served travelers on the Eastern Post Road (now replaced by the approach to the bridge), occupied part of the property.

Two stories high with a basement, and constructed of brick with stone trim, both houses have small wooden stoops raised above the sidewalk and a sunken front yard. Number 313 was built by mason-builder Hiram G. Disbrow as his own residence, and is chiefly vernacular in style, with Greek Revival elements. The simple, square-paneled pilasters, plain window treatment, and row of dentils under the porch's roof recall the Greek Revival, while the brackets over the doorway, frieze section, larger paired console brackets supporting the roof cornice, and muntined windows on the second story are typical of the Italianate mode of the 1850s.

ST. MONICA'S CHURCH, 1856–57
94–20 160th Street, Queens
Builder: Anders Peterson, under the supervision of the Reverend Anthony Farley
Designated: March 13, 1979

In response to the influx of Irish Catholic immigrants around 1850, a building program was initiated by the prominent archbishop John Hughes in such areas as Jamaica, New York. St. Monica's Church was built as part of this project. It retained an active congregation until 1973, when the structure was incorporated into York College's Urban Renewal Site.

With its tall central campanile, round-arched openings, corbel tables, and pilaster strips, the basilica-shaped church exemplifies the early Romanesque Revival, a turn-of-the-century style developed by Robert Dale Owen and James Renwick as "Arch Architecture." Veering away from the Anglican ecclesiological movement's decorative use of Gothic Revival, other denominations turned toward the earlier and simpler forms of the Romanesque. St. Monica's three-bay façade is marked by a four-story entrance tower. The tower is linked to the church by a double belt course with crossbars running above the entrance portals; a round-arched triad decorates its gabled top. Thin pilaster strips separate the building's bays, providing a strong vertical emphasis. The corbel table running along the eaves emphasizes corners.

254–260 CANAL STREET, 1856–57
Manhattan
Architect: Attributed to James Bogardus
Designated: March 12, 1985

Located at the southwest corner of Canal and Lafayette streets, this is one of the earliest surviving cast-iron buildings in New York City, and one of the largest remaining examples of its type from the early days of cast-iron architecture. Its design has been attributed to James Bogardus, through whose pioneering efforts cast iron became a popular material for the façades of commercial buildings from the 1850s to the '90s.

The building was erected for George Bruce, a prominent figure in the printing industry who was regarded as the "father and chief" of typography in America. His technological innovations in the printing field were largely responsible for the rapid and efficient advancement of newspaper and book publishing in America during the latter part of the nineteenth century.

As was the vogue at the time for commercial buildings, its façade was rendered in the Italianate palazzo style and sought to give the effect of being a solid masonry structure. Its Venetian-inspired design includes a storefront level punctuated by columns; four stories of arched and rectangular-edged windows, rhythmically spaced and separated by fluted columns; and ornamental details such as the Medusa-head keystones on the fourth level.

This was one of the first commercial structures erected in a neighborhood that was quickly being transformed from an industrial area to a center of retail trade. The building continues to be in commercial use today, its ground floor devoted to shops and its upper floors to lofts and offices.

CARY BUILDING, 1856–57
105–107 Chambers Street, Manhattan
Architects: Gamaliel King and John Kellum
Designated: August 24, 1982

The Cary Building, built in 1856–57, is one of New York's most important nineteenth-century cast-iron commercial structures. It was designed by architects Gamaliel King and John Kellum, a prominent firm that specialized in commercial architecture, with cast-iron fronts fabricated by the city's preeminent foundry, Daniel Badger's Architectural Iron Works. The structure was built for the firm of Cary, Howard & Sanger, dry-goods merchants, as both a store and a warehouse.

The building exemplifies three contemporary developments that set major patterns for the economic growth of post–Civil War New York: the commercial development of the area north and west of City Hall; the introduction of the Italianate palazzo; and the invention of the cast-iron façade. The five-story façade consists of a series of arched windows set between Corinthian columns and crowned with a heavy bracketed cornice and a large triangular pediment. The design shows the historic combination of the Italianate style with cast-iron architecture.

E. V. HAUGHWOUT BUILDING, 1857
488–492 Broadway, Manhattan
Architect: John P. Gaynor; iron components by Daniel D. Badger
Designated: November 23, 1965

The Haughwout Building is an outstanding example of early cast-iron commercial architecture in New York City. Designed in 1857 by J. P. Gaynor and built by Daniel Badger and his firm, Architectural Iron Works, it was the first cast-iron-façade structure to be declared a landmark. It was originally designed as a department store that sold cut glass, silverware, clocks, and chandeliers, and it was the first building to have an Otis passenger elevator equipped with a safety device (patented 1861).

The five-story building elegantly displays the Venetian palazzo style that was quickly gaining popularity as a mercantile idiom in the 1850s and '60s. Above the ground level, arched windows are set between colonnettes flanked by crisply detailed Corinthian columns in a manner reminiscent of Sansovino's great library in Venice. The Haughwout Building represented the state of the art in architectural design when it was built. Not only was it made from a very new building material—easier to use and more economical than traditional stone—but it was also bold in design; its Italianate style was considered avant-garde, since it consciously rejected the conservative Greek Revival manner often adopted for government buildings.

One of the major advantages of cast-iron architecture—in addition to ease of construction, greater strength, and economy—is that it allows an opening up of the façade. As Badger stated in his influential 1865 publication, *Illustrations of Iron Architecture* (which acted as a pattern book of sorts):

> A light and ornamental edifice of iron may be safely substituted for the cumbrous structures of other substances, and sufficient strength be secured without exclusion of light—which is often highly desirable for mercantile and mechanical purposes.

The Haughwout Building may appear outmoded today, particularly because it masks functionalism behind a highly decorative façade. Nonetheless many of the architectural details resulting from the cast-iron construction had a significant influence on the development of the skyscraper aesthetic. First of all, the load-bearing potential of metal-frame construction allowed for an expansion upward, a trend that was further encouraged by the elevator. Stylistically, the rhythmic and repetitive orientation of the façade—standardized units without any central or peripheral focus—fostered the growth of the mechanical precision associated with the skyscraper.

For the most part, the very decorative style of cast-iron construction exemplified by the Haughwout Building had been eclipsed by the 1870s, when a more functional and declarative approach became popular. But its importance to New York, as one of the earliest and finest examples of cast-iron architecture, is still felt today.

HANSON PLACE SEVENTH-DAY ADVENTIST CHURCH, 1857–60
88 Hanson Place, Brooklyn
Architect: Unknown
Designated: October 13, 1970

This building was originally erected as the Hanson Place Baptist Church, an outgrowth of the Atlantic Street Baptist Church. Since 1963, the church has been owned by the Seventh-Day Adventists. Constructed of brick above a brownstone base and trimmed with wood, this Italianate church gives distinction to a neighborhood that still retains much of its nineteenth-century atmosphere.

A flight of stone steps leads up to an elevated portico with a steeply pitched pediment supported on four tall Corinthian columns. The portico's upper entablature is enriched with modillions and dentils. The details of the door enframements are distinctly Greek Revival; above each doorway is an eared rectangular frame; those to the left and right are filled with stained glass. Slightly projecting corner pavilions flank the entrance portico, and the classical entablature is carried along the sides of the church. A projecting section, facing South Portland Avenue, was built as a lecture hall and is now used for classes. Its four tall, segmental-arched windows are crowned by similar segmental arches in the architrave. The windows are separated by fluted, wood pilasters with Corinthian capitals and crowned by a pediment similar to the one at the front of the church.

152 EAST 38TH STREET, 1858; altered, 1934–35
Manhattan
Architect: Unknown
Designated: May 25, 1967

Typical of the hundreds of modest semisuburban houses that once dotted the uptown cross streets of mid-nineteenth-century Manhattan is the charming house at 152 East 38th Street, in Murray Hill. Originally built as a gatehouse for an estate that belonged to a member of President Martin Van Buren's family, the house is set back from the street by a forecourt and a landscaped garden. It was sold by Van Buren's descendants in 1929 to the publisher Cass Canfield, who remodeled it in 1934–35, giving it a Federal Revival look, with modified Greek architectural details.

One of the house's most handsome features is the superb doorway with glass sidelights framed by delicate pilasters supporting a molded entablature and a handsomely designed transom. Delicate iron trellises support a graceful, scalloped bronze canopy covering the stoop, and a frieze over the third-floor windows is decorated with rosettes. The simple cornice is crowned by a low brick parapet, and the handsome double-hung sash windows have attractive black shutters.

FIRST REFORMED CHURCH OF JAMAICA, formerly First Reformed Church, 1858–59; extension, 1902
153–10 Jamaica Avenue, Queens
Architect: Sidney J. Young
Designated: March 13, 1979

This site was previously occupied by the Dutch Reformed Church of Jamaica for almost 150 years. Brick was selected for the new building after a fire destroyed one of the original church buildings in 1857. Its design follows the tenets of "Arch Architecture," based on a German adaptation of the round-arched Romanesque style (*Rundbogenstil*).

Slightly projecting towers—four stories high on the west side, three stories on the east—flank the building's broad, gabled facade. A belt course runs above the first story, emphasized by dentils in the center section. A triad of round-arched windows rests above this course; two round-arched portals pierce the floor below it. The openings in both these sections are outlined by square-cut reveals.

On the towers, brownstone courses mark the separate levels. A blind rondel appears on the third floor of the larger, western tower; its fourth floor is pierced by a triad of louvered openings, flanked by octagonal turrets, and crowned by crenellation. Above the third- and fourth-story levels are rows of corbel tables. The smaller, eastern tower follows a similar design. The main body of the church behind the towers is five bays long, with a two-bay addition attached to the south end.

A memorial chapel, built in 1902 and since demolished, inaugurated a broader building program, under which architect Cuyler B. Tuthill extended and refurbished the main church. Emil Zundel, a member of the congregation, designed and executed all but one of sixteen stained-glass windows as part of the renovation. Although seventeen feet high, the main windows employ a minimum number of construction bars, and their multiple layers of glass are combined to produce an opalescent effect.

In 1973, the church was incorporated into the Central Jamaica Urban Redevelopment Project. While the community has proposed plans for a performing arts center, the building is still being used by the Reformed Church of America for regular Sunday services.

ST. MARY'S EPISCOPAL CHURCH, 1858–59
230 Classon Avenue, Brooklyn
Architect: Richard T. Auchmuty
Designated: October 27, 1981

St. Mary's Church, located just north of the Pratt Institute in the Clinton Hill section of Brooklyn, is a beautiful Gothic Revival structure reminiscent of an English rural parish church. Built in 1858, it was designed by a relatively obscure architect, Richard T. Auchmuty, in accordance with the religious philosophy of ecclesiology. This movement, which originated in England in the 1830s, called for a doctrinaire interpretation of Christian teachings. It laid out a strict set of rules for the design of Episcopal churches; the more dogmatic style drew its inspiration from medieval Gothic parish churches.

According to the rules of the movement, as established by the New York Ecclesiological Society, the chancel is the most important design element of a church. At St. Mary's, the chancel is twenty-four feet deep, and a handsome square tower with polygonal extension and a broached spire is located to the south of it, giving added emphasis to the portion of the building facing Classon Avenue. The nave, which extends to the west, has a steep sloping roof that is clearly separated from the shallower slope of the side aisle roofs—all originally covered with slate shingles. To the north of the chancel is a low, polygonal vestry room that connects the chancel and side aisle. An unusually picturesque pointed-arched gateway that takes the form of a stepped flying buttress serves as an ingenious method of channeling the parishioners to the southwest entrance porch. In addition to its handsome structural design, St. Mary's has beautiful ornamentation and attractive pointed-arched and rose windows.

The Conservatory Garden

CENTRAL PARK, 1857–present
Bounded by Frawley Circle, West 110th Street, Cathedral Parkway,
Frederick Douglass Circle, Central Park West, Columbus Circle,
Central Park South (West 59th Street), Grand Army Plaza, and
Fifth Avenue to Frawley Circle, Manhattan
Architects: Frederick Law Olmsted and Calvert Vaux
Designated: April 16, 1974

America's first great planned public park, the 840-acre Central Park masterfully integrates landscape and architectural elements. Now flanked on four sides by sandstone walls, Central Park reflects the foresight of its mid-nineteenth-century proponents.

When, in the mid-nineteenth century, an already staggering rate of urban growth was complicated by an outbreak of cholera, concerned citizens began to articulate the city's need for an open space where they could seek relief from the pressures of urban life. Originally envisioned along the East River, the park was moved west because of the opposition of East Siders, and the site was purchased in 1856. This tract extended far to the north, into an area then only sparsely settled; shortly thereafter, a real-estate boom occurred, and the lots surrounding the site were quickly purchased for the construction of villas.

When the Board of Park Commissioners was established in 1857, it announced a competition for the park's design. Frederick Law Olmsted and Calvert Vaux, whose joint plan was selected in 1858, had proposed a seemingly unrestricted garden landscape, suggestive of the Romantic garden so popular in eighteenth-century England.

The site's uneven topography was the heritage of Ice Age glaciers. Olmsted and Vaux's design made use of this unevenness, creating an apparently "natural"—but carefully cultivated— landscape. For the initial construction alone, 10 million cartloads of dirt were moved from one location to another; plantings included 4 to 5 million trees, representing 632 species, and 815 varieties of vines, plants, and flowers. To enrich the thin glacial soil, half a million cubic yards of topsoil were introduced to the site.

Olmsted and Vaux's plan incorporated architecture into their wild garden. Gates dedicated to groups of citizens—such as scholars, engineers, and inventors—mark the park's twenty-one entrances. The design also accommodated two existing architectural features that predate the park: the red-brick Arsenal and the Croton Reservoir. Paths surrounding the reservoir and the carriage lanes throughout the park were deliberately curved to discourage racing on the newly landscaped public grounds.

Among the few works commissioned specifically for the park were the Bethesda Fountain and its sculpture, *Angel of the Waters*; they were designed by Emma Stebbins and completed in 1873. Situated on a formal terrace near the lake, the fountain serves as the focus of its immediate surroundings. Other sculptures include the bronze figures of Alice in Wonderland and Samuel F. B. Morse. The seventy-one-foot-tall Egyptian obelisk was built about 1600 B.C. by Thutmose III, given to the City of New York in 1877, and installed in its present location in 1881.

Central Park's true genius resides in its careful integration of landscape and architectural elements that direct and enhance the visitor's experience. Each of the park's circuit routes, for example—pedestrian walks, bridle paths, sunken transverse roads, and a circular loop—is visually and effectively distinct from the others. Where routes cross, a series of underpasses and overpasses, nearly all different, permits a continuous traffic flow without the need for intersections. The cast-iron Bow Bridge, designed, like the other bridges, by Calvert Vaux, was completed in 1879; it spans the lake and connects the heavily wooded Ramble with the more open slope of Cherry Hill.

Throughout Central Park, the visitor moves from one landscape experience to another within a relatively small area. Hills and paths follow a rising and sinking route, while the masonry and towers that now delineate the park's periphery offer a sense of distant constancy. The towers and façades that border the park help to create a stage set that amplifies the drama of the park's ever-shifting natural vistas.

Belvedere Castle

Cop Cot

Bethesda Fountain

BROTHERHOOD SYNAGOGUE, formerly Friends Meeting House, 1859; renovation, 1974
144 East 20th Street, Manhattan
Architects: King & Kellum; renovation, James Stewart Polshek
Designated: October 26, 1965

In 1859 the fashionable firm of King & Kellum, who designed the Cary Building, designed a meetinghouse, "exactly suited for a Friends Meeting, entirely plain, neat and chaste, of good proportions, but avoiding all useless ornament, so much so as to not wound the feelings of the most sensitive among us." Anglo-Italianate in style, the original building is three stories high with a large basement and attic; simple and austere, it is decorated with Renaissance-style cornices and segmental-arched windows. A beautifully proportioned triangular pediment crowns the building; the exterior, which looks like brownstone, is constructed of blocks of Dorchester olive stone quarried in Ohio.

In 1974, the Brotherhood Synagogue purchased the building and James Stewart Polshek was asked to undertake its renovation. His additions include the Garden of Remembrance, a serene courtyard to the east of the building with a limestone wall, on which are engraved the names of Holocaust victims and members of the congregation who have died; a memorial mosaic at the far end symbolizes the synagogue's goal of peace. On the west side, a Biblical garden was added.

ST. PATRICK'S CATHEDRAL
Manhattan
Designated: October 19, 1966

St. Patrick's Cathedral, 1858–79;
towers, 1888; Lady Chapel, 1900–08
Fifth Avenue between 50th and 51st streets
Architect: James Renwick, Jr. (Cathedral);
Charles T. Mathews (Lady Chapel)

Archbishop's Residence, 1882
452 Madison Avenue
Architect: James Renwick, Jr.

Parish House, 1884
460 Madison Avenue
Architect: James Renwick, Jr.

The largest Catholic cathedral in the United States, St. Patrick's stands as a monument to the faith of New York City's immigrant Irish population of the mid-nineteenth century, and represents an American adaptation of the cathedral building, which was not an established type in the architectural canon at the time.

The Gothic Revival cathedral, Archibishop's Residence, and Parish House were designed by James Renwick, Jr., who had completed Grace Church in 1846. The Lady Chapel was designed by Charles T. Mathews and added to the cathedral's east end in 1900–08. Distinctly American in its eclecticism and adaptation to New York's grid street plan, St. Patrick's recalls the elements of the English, French, and German styles that inspired it.

Two identical towers rise 330 feet from the cathedral's entrance façade on Fifth Avenue. Completed in 1888, they have spires decorated with foliated tracery that suggests the English Decorated style. Such tracery recurs in the façade's rose window (designed by Charles Connick), which is surmounted by a gable and flanked by pinnacles. The transept doors also echo these motifs. The cathedral's cruciform plan is oriented, in the traditional manner, to the east; the Lady Chapel was inspired by thirteenth-century French Gothic, complementing Renwick's somewhat heavier, English masses.

St. Patrick's was formally opened in 1879 by His Eminence John Cardinal McCloskey, the first American cardinal. Pope Paul VI prayed before the Blessed Sacrament here during the first papal visit to the United States in 1965, as did Pope John Paul II in 1979. Both were guests in the Archbishop's Residence. Today, St. Patrick's is the seat of New York's Roman Catholic archdiocese and the place of worship for between 5,000 and 8,000 people each Sunday.

75 MURRAY STREET, c. 1859
Manhattan
Architect: Attributed to James Bogardus
Designated: December 10, 1968

The building at 75 Murray Street has one of the earliest and most handsome cast-iron fronts in Manhattan. In the manner of late-fifteenth-century Venetian palazzi, the building—which was commissioned in 1857 to house the glassware business of Francis and John Hopkins—is enlivened with rich Italianate detail.

On each floor of the five-story structure, four engaged fluted columns, which probably once had Corinthian capitals, support full entablatures with ornate modillions and leaf moldings. Cast-iron units formed by twelve contiguous, semicircular arches supported by small engaged columns on paneled pedestals fill the spaces between the columns. In contrast to the verticality of these colonnades, elaborate cornices at each floor and a crowning cornice with large, decorative brackets provide strong horizontal emphasis.

The building has arched, double-hung windows surmounted by bull's-eye openings and flanked by trefoil openings on the upper two floors. The windows of the second and fourth floors have volute-shaped keystones, and those of the third and fifth floors have Medusa-head keystones, identical to those found on two other buildings by Bogardus. An original iron step in the entrance bears the legend "James Bogardus originator and patentee of iron buildings Pat. May 7, 1850," further supporting the attribution.

BRIGHT TEMPLE A.M.E. CHURCH, formerly Sunnyslope, c. 1859–64
812 Faile Street, The Bronx
Architect: Unknown
Designated: July 28, 1981

Originally a manor house, Sunnyslope was built in the early 1860s in the Hunts Point section of the Bronx on a 14.6-acre estate belonging to Peter S. Hoe. The neighborhood was then a rural district of Westchester County, and Hunts Point was part of the town of West Farms, a quiet area of estates and manor houses.

The house was designed in the mid-nineteenth-century Picturesque Gothic tradition, which produced many of the most handsome estates in New York City. A square, compact, high-style villa, it is in the manner of Calvert Vaux, the English-born associate of Andrew Jackson Downing and Frederick Law Olmsted. There is no known connection between the Hoe house and Vaux, but the house greatly resembles several of the designs published in Vaux's *Villas and Cottages*.

Sunnyslope is a two-and-one-half-story stone residence with light stone trim and a tiled gabled roof, above which rise two broad chimneys with pointed chimney pots. It is the arrangement of the gables and gable-dormers that gives the house its characteristic Picturesque look; the Gothic style is evident primarily in the treatment of the windows and doors. Each gable has a pointed-arched attic window in its center, while the first- and second-floor windows are treated as paired or tripled lancets grouped together under a stone label lintel. The pointed-arched entrance, articulated by a heavy stone enframement, is situated on a projecting porch. To the right of the entrance, an angular, three-sided bay with multiple trefoil panels is crowned with an elaborately carved crenellation. A small, one-story extension at the rear is not part of the original house.

Peter S. Hoe sold Sunnyslope in 1864, but it remained a country estate long after the annexation of West Farms to New York City. By the turn of the century, however, West Farms was becoming increasingly urban; in 1912, Stephen Jenkins, in *The Story of the Bronx*, described the area as being "in a transition state; for, though there are a great many apartments and flats, there are still more vacant lots. The old estates have been cut up, and very few of the elegant mansions of the middle of the last century remain to show us how the well-to-do

merchants of that epoch used to live." Sunnyslope was one of the few mansions that survived. The estate lands were eventually sold off, and Sunnyslope itself was sold in 1919 to Temple Beth Elohim to serve the area's Jewish community. Today the house is occupied and maintained by the Bright Temple A.M.E. Church, and serves as a religious center for the area of which it was once the manor house. It is one of the most unusual, and finest, of the few country houses surviving within the city limits.

EAST 92ND STREET HOUSES
Manhattan
Architects: Unknown
Designated: November 19, 1969

120 East 92nd Street, 1859

122 East 92nd Street, 1871; addition, 1927

Survivors from a time before this neighborhood became fashionable, these two quaint wooden houses on East 92nd Street between Park and Lexington avenues were constructed in 1859 and 1871. Both houses have great charm, mirroring in clapboard some of the details of the more elaborate brick houses that were being built during this period.

Each house is slightly Italianate in feeling, with large brackets supporting the cornice, a handsome, columned porch, and two French doors on either side of a paneled entry door. In 1927, a penthouse was added to 122, providing a fourth floor; an earlier, two-story addition with a service entrance is found set back to the left.

HAMILTON PARK COTTAGE, 1859–72
105 Franklin Avenue, Staten Island
Architect: Unknown
Designated: October 13, 1970

Hamilton Park Cottage was one of the original houses in New Brighton, an important early residential suburban park that was derived from the Romantic landscapes of Andrew Jackson Downing. In addition to its significance in planning history, the house is also notable as a pleasing example of a brick Italianate cottage. Thomas E. Davis, a speculative builder, conceived the idea for New Brighton. Named for the English seaside resort, it was only twenty minutes from the Battery by ferry.

Picturesquely sited, with a fine view of the Kill Van Kull from the rear, the house was constructed sometime between 1859 and 1872. The dominant architectural feature is a central triple-arched porch over the main entrance that links the bay windows of the parlor and dining room. A window above the main entrance has a sill resting on corbels and is crowned by a triangular sheet-metal pediment. Other decorative features include carved console brackets, ornamental modillions, and window moldings with keystone arches.

Within the tract of land assembled by Davis, Charles K. Hamilton and his wife purchased thirty-two acres in 1851 and 1852, where Hamilton built at least four houses as a planned group. The community was developed as a single-ownership residential district, with houses approached by winding carriage roads. There was a common stable, and common quarters were reportedly provided for the servants. Hamilton defaulted on his mortgage in 1878 and the lots were put up for sale individually in 1894.

Still in use as a private residence, Hamilton Park Cottage is listed on the National Register of Historic Places. It represents with great integrity the original character of Hamilton Park.

EAST 73RD STREET BUILDINGS
Manhattan
Designated: May 12, 1980

171 East 73rd Street, 1860s
Architect: Electus D. Litchfield

175 East 73rd Street, 1860s
Architect: Unknown

166 East 73rd Street, 1883–84
Architect: Richard M. Hunt

168 East 73rd Street, c. 1890–91
Architect: Charles W. Romeyn

170 East 73rd Street, c. 1890–91
Architect: Frank Wennemer

172–174 East 73rd Street, c. 1890–91
Architect: Frank Wennemer

178 East 73rd Street, c. 1890–91
Architect: John H. Friend

180 East 73rd Street, c. 1890–91
Architects: William Schickel & Co.

182 East 73rd Street, c. 1890–91
Architect: Andrew Spense Mayer

Dalcroze School of Music, c. 1900;
remodeled, 1950
161 East 73rd Street
Architects: Thomas Rae;
remodeling, Edward Larrabee Barnes

163 East 73rd Street, c. 1900
Architect: Thomas Rae

165 East 73rd Street, c. 1900
Architect: George L. Amoroux

167 East 73rd Street, c. 1900
Architect: George L. Amoroux

173 East 73rd Street, c. 1900
Architect: Hobart H. Walker

177–179 East 73rd Street, 1906
Architect: Charles F. Hoppe

This group of buildings is a reminder of a time when the transportation needs of New Yorkers were served by horses instead of automobiles. In the 1860s the north side of East 73rd Street was built up with brick row houses of simple Italianate design; only the houses at 171 and 175 survive from that period. At about the turn of the century, however, the others were replaced by carriage houses and stables serving the fashionable mansions of Upper Fifth Avenue; these structures include 161, 163, 165, 167, and 173 East 73rd Street. Another series of stables and carriage houses adorns the south side of the street at numbers 168, 170, 172–174, 178, 180, and 182; these are somewhat earlier, most dating from 1890–91. The handsome building at number 177–179 was built specifically as an "auto garage" in 1906. Although designed by several different architects, the buildings on East 73rd Street have a unity and coherence of design—a result of the short time span in which they were built, the use of similar materials and ornamental details, and a relatively uniform cornice line.

While the carriage houses no longer accommodate horses, many of them have been converted for use as garages, with living quarters on the upper floors. The house at 161, which formerly belonged to the Harkness family, was acquired in 1950 by the Dalcroze School of Music and remodeled by Edward Larrabee Barnes.

85 LEONARD STREET, 1860–61
Manhattan
Architect: James Bogardus
Designated: November 26, 1974

The building at 85 Leonard Street is uniquely significant as the only remaining structure in the city known for certain to be the work of James Bogardus, the self-described "inventor of cast-iron buildings." Built as a storehouse for dry-goods merchants Kitchen, Montross & Wilcox, this five-story structure stands as one of a row of similar buildings, many with façades made largely of stone. Most of the buildings on both sides of Leonard Street west of Broadway were built in 1860–61 for commercial purposes, replacing residences that had previously stood on the block. The building at 85 Leonard stands out as one of the few surviving cast-iron structures designed in the so-called sperm candle style, which became popular in the city in the late 1850s. (The name derives from the use of two-story columns that resemble candles made from sperm whale oil.)

Designed in the form of an Italian Renaissance palazzo, the building emphasizes verticality, lightness, and openness—intrinsic qualities of cast-iron architecture. The structure is three bays wide with two tiers of elongated columns that span the second to the third and the fourth to the fifth stories; spandrel panels separate the floors of each two-story grouping. Rope moldings and foliate motifs enhance the surface. An impressive entablature, composed of a paneled frieze formed by a rope molding, a row of dentils, and a modillioned cornice, crowns the façade.

FRIENDS MEETING HOUSE AND FRIENDS SEMINARY
Manhattan
Architect: Attributed to Charles T. Bunting
Designated: December 9, 1969

Friends Meeting House, 1861	Friends Seminary, 1861
15 Rutherford Place	226 East 16th Street

The Friends Meeting House and Seminary on Rutherford Place, facing Stuyvesant Square, were built in 1861 by a group of Quakers known as the Hicksites. Designed in a restrained, austere Greek Revival style, the buildings reflect the simplicity and architectural conservatism of the Quakers. Charles T. Bunting, a member of the meeting and a builder, was responsible for the construction and probably also for the design.

The three-story brick meetinghouse is distinguished by its spare, pedimented entrance porch and double-hung, muntined sash windows with plain sills and lintels. The T-shaped Seminary building, to the north on 16th Street, replicated the meetinghouse as much as possible, with the entrance porch and gable also facing the square.

BROOKLYN CITY RAILROAD COMPANY BUILDING, 1860–61
8 Cadman Plaza West and 8–10 Fulton Street
Architect: Unknown
Designated: February 20, 1973

The building at 8 Cadman Plaza West was erected in 1860–61 as the office of the Brooklyn City Railroad Company, which was created in 1853 to replace the former stagecoach line and to provide modern transportation linking the Manhattan ferry with principal points on Long Island. Remnants of the old railroad's tracks are still visible next to the building, in a cobblestone parking area.

The five-story building is constructed of brick above cast-iron piers at the street level on Fulton Street. Granite quoins define the wall surface, which is distinguished by stone sills, lintels, and pediments. Carved console brackets, corbels, dentil molding, and paneled pilasters in the Italianate style further enrich the stonework.

With the end of ferry service, the building was converted to manufacturing and warehousing. Later, it was occupied by the Berglas Manufacturing Co. In 1975, architect David Morton purchased the building and converted it to loft apartments.

NICHOLAS KATZENBACH HOUSE,
formerly Stonehurst, 1860–61
5225 Sycamore Avenue, The Bronx
Architect: Unknown
Designated: October 13, 1970

Originally known as Stonehurst, the Nicholas Katzenbach House is one of the most elegant mid-nineteenth-century country residences along the Hudson. It was built in 1861 for Robert Colgate, manufacturer and philanthropist and the eldest son of William Colgate, the pioneer soap manufacturer; it was later the home of Nicholas de B. Katzenbach, a former U.S. attorney general and undersecretary of state. As the name suggests, Stonehurst continued the Bronx tradition of great stone mansions—this time in superbly cut random ashlar of smoothly dressed gray granite imported from Maine.

Stonehurst is quite different from other Anglo-Italianate villas in the Hudson River valley. It has a classical quality and symmetry that are most unusual in romantic, picturesque architecture. Its most notable features include a bold, semicircular, two-story projection, a low-pitched roof with broad eaves, round-arched windows, a bull's-eye window set beneath a low-pitched central gable, and a massive pair of paneled doors in an arched opening.

Stonehurst offers a sensitive response to its beautiful setting. The rooms in the projecting portions all have large windows, providing spectacular views in three directions—characteristic of the interest in landscape that typified the age of Emerson and transcendentalism.

GRACE EPISCOPAL CHURCH
155 Jamaica Avenue, Queens
Designated: May 25, 1967

Grace Episcopal Church, 1861–62; chancel
1901–02
Architects: Dudley Field (nave and tower);
Cady, Berg & See (chancel)

Graveyard, established c. 1734

Grace Episcopal Church was founded in
1702, when members of the congregation
requested a minister from the Society for the
Propagation of the Gospel in Foreign Parts, an
English missionary association. The widow
and heirs of Colonel C. Heathecote of New
York deeded about half an acre of land to the
rector, Thomas Colgan, in 1733; the first
church on the site was completed in the
following year. The graveyard dates largely
from this time, although the presence of
several seventeenth-century graves suggests
that an earlier church stood here.

A second building from the late eighteenth
century replaced the 1734 structure and was
in turn replaced by the present structure,
built by Dudley Field, an obscure New York
City architect. Field worked in an Anglo-
American version of the Gothic Revival,
established as the dominant style for
Episcopal church design by Upjohn's Trinity
Church (1839–45). The specific sources,
however, are earlier than the fourteenth-
century models used for Trinity. Here, the
basis for the design is twelfth-century English
Gothic, characterized by narrow, single lancet
windows without tracery and a feeling for
heavy forms, which Field rendered in a local
rough-cut sandstone. The steeply pitched roof
and heavy, gabled steeple with broached spire
are also typical. The New York City firm of
Cady, Berg & See added the chancel between
1901 and 1902; in material and style, it
matches the earlier structure perfectly.

The most famous person buried in the
graveyard is Rufus King, a member of the first
U.S. Senate in 1789 and an active member of
the congregation.

GREEN-WOOD CEMETERY GATES, including attached Comfort Station and Office, 1861–65
Fifth Avenue and 25th Street, Brooklyn
Architect: Richard Upjohn & Son
Designated: April 19, 1966

The 25th Street gateway of the Green-Wood Cemetery, constructed between 1861 and 1865, is an imposing main entrance to the 478-acre Sunset Park Cemetery. Designed by noted church architect Richard Upjohn, the gateway is a masterful synthesis of late Gothic Revival and High Victorian Gothic architecture.

The central motif of the red sandstone entryway is a clock tower flanked by spiked arches that extend over the cemetery gates. The tower's steeple—the apex of the gateway—rises above an open niche and is supported on each side by flying buttresses; these in turn are anchored by massive pinnacled piers that form the outer sides of the arches. Openwork gables surmount the bas-relief sculptures that lie within the recesses of the arches. In keeping with the gate's ecclesiastical Gothic architecture, these decorative features—carved in Nova Scotia sandstone—present religious themes, including the resurrections of Jesus, Lazarus, and the widow's son, as well as allegorical scenes representing Faith, Hope, Love, and Memory, conceived and executed by John Moffit.

The central motif is adjoined on one side by a cemetery office building and on the other side by a visitors' comfort station. These low, slate-roofed structures complete the entryway. The tower bell announces the approach of a funeral procession to this day.

At the time of its opening, Green-Wood Cemetery offered an alternative to the traditional churchyard cemetery: the rural graveyard. The first such cemetery was the Mount Auburn, in Cambridge, Massachusetts, which opened in 1831. Green-Wood opened a decade later in a picturesque landscape of rolling hills, winding paths, streams, and ponds situated on the highest land in suburban Brooklyn. During the mid-nineteenth century, the privately owned cemetery was a popular recreational site and tourist attraction; guidebooks and guided tours celebrated Green-Wood's natural setting, historical monuments, and tombs. Today's visitors to the cemetery can see the graves of such famous Americans as Nathaniel Currier, James Ives, De Witt Clinton, Horace Greeley, and Henry Ward Beecher.

208–218 EAST 78TH STREET, 1861–65
Manhattan
Architect: Unknown
Designated: May 9, 1978

Six of the original fifteen row houses on East 78th Street between Second and Third avenues serve as a representative example of New York City row house development during the 1860s. At the time of their construction, the block was considered part of the village of Yorkville. The city's residential section had gradually moved northward from the lower tip of the island, although the block was still undeveloped in 1861, when Howard A. Martin purchased the property for the houses, which he subdivided into fifteen lots, each exactly thirteen and one-third feet wide. The houses were erected by Warren and Ransom Beman and John Buckley, and it is likely that they were identical. William H. Brower, an investment broker, bought the property while the houses were still under construction and sold to several different owners before building was completed. The four-year construction period was long, but work was no doubt hampered by the Civil War.

The builders were probably responsible for the design of the three-story brick residences. The row houses all share an Italianate style, popular in New York at this time, but the elliptically arched door and window openings are exceptional.

52 CHAMBERS STREET, formerly New York County Courthouse, 1861–81; alterations, 1911, 1913, 1942, 1978–79
Manhattan
Architects: Thomas Little, John Kellum, and Leopold Eidlitz
Designated (including first-floor interior): October 16, 1984

Working with his infamous ring of cronies, William M. ("Boss") Tweed, whose name is synonymous with political corruption in New York City, misappropriated nearly $9 million from the construction budget of this building. As a member of the Courthouse Commission, Tweed could skim funds with impunity, and in 1861 he bought a stone quarry, from which he sold building materials at an enormous profit to the courthouse contractors. Variations on this procedure were repeated for every piece of hardware and all the building materials. The exposure of the kickbacks and other illegalities brought about the downfall of the Tweed ring in 1871, and this building has since been popularly known as the Tweed Courthouse.

John Kellum, the principal architect, died in 1871. Before his death, he completed the east and west wings, most of the north façade, and the central hall. All are executed in the Italianate style and were partly inspired by the design of the U.S. Capitol in Washington, D.C. The four-story façade on Chambers Street contains a pedimented portico with four engaged Corinthian columns and two flanking bays. Foliated brackets and pilasters ornament its smooth-faced marble walls. Each window is supported by consoles on paneled pilasters; the molded sills rest on corbels. On the upper floor, the windows are separated by pilasters with molded capitals. Eyebrow casement windows pierce the frieze. In addition to crowning triangular pediments, three bays with three windows each characterize the identical east and west façades.

After the death of Kellum and the simultaneous breakup of the Tweed ring, construction halted in 1871. In 1876, Leopold Eidlitz was commissioned to finish the north (Chambers Street) porch, to replace the south porch, and to complete the rotunda, skylight, and interior main hall. Eidlitz departed from Kellum's earlier design, employing round-arched windows and bands of rich foliate carving characteristic of the Romanesque Revival. Throughout his additions, ornamental details such as arches, foliation, and octagonal shapes unify the external and internal divisions.

Each floor of Eidlitz's south wing varies in design. On the first floor, a cluster of three arched windows appears on the east and west façades; a door with two windows on each side decorates the south façade. The

latter resembles Kellum's main façade, minus the portico. It is three windows wide and three windows deep with marble ashlar facing, similar in color to that of the main portion of the building. On the second floor of the south wing are clusters of three arched windows; rectangular windows with foliated banding are separated by pilasters on the third floor. Pilasters also separate the top floor's round-arched windows.

A gray asphalt roof, installed in 1978–79, replaced the building's original corrugated iron roof. Other changes include the construction of two elevator penthouses in 1911 and 1913 and the destruction of the main façade's grand stairway to allow for the widening of Chambers Street in 1942. Functional changes have also occurred: in 1927, county pleadings were transferred to New York City's new courthouse. From that year until 1961, City Court was held here; and since that time, the building has provided overflow office space for the Municipal Building and City Hall.

157, 159, 161, 163–165 EAST 78TH STREET, 1860–61
Manhattan
Builder: Henry Armstrong
Designated: April 18, 1968

Just prior to the Civil War, the area above 42nd Street developed as a residential district for working-class and lower-middle-class New Yorkers. These red-brick row houses are among the few remnants of this earliest development.

John Turner, described as a painter, hired Henry Armstrong, a local builder, to erect the houses in 1861. The prices of lots on this block were rising more rapidly than they had in the previous fifty years, and Turner apparently decided to build these speculative houses then, when he could be assured of making a profit. Work began in the fall of 1860 and finished in March, 1861, in time for the city's moving day on May 1, when leases were traditionally renewed.

Developer architecture in the mid-nineteenth century—although often well built—was "designed" in a watered-down version of the style of the day. (The same is true today.) The predominant style since the 1850s, following the Federal and Greek Revival, was Italianate. In such modest structures as these, the style manifests itself only in slightly distended proportions, especially of the main floor, where the formal parlor was located. The molded lintels and pressed metal cornices stand in marked contrast in detail to Greek Revival fascia and the short attic story. The cornice has four acanthus brackets with three modillions between each pair. The unmolded brownstone stringcourse is a vestigial base molding, historically marking the lower rustication in an Italian palazzo. The original stoops on each, which were probably of brownstone or wood, are now gone. The houses are still in good condition; number 159 retains the most original features, both inside and out.

ST. PATRICK'S CHURCH, 1862
St. Patrick's Place, Staten Island
Architect: Unknown
Designated: February 20, 1968

St. Patrick's Roman Catholic Church is an early example of the simplicity of design and elegance of proportion that characterized the best of Romanesque Revival architecture. The body of this brick church is rectangular, almost a double cube, with its corners reinforced by square buttresses. Below the gable roof, at the cornice line, is a running arched corbel. Centered on the main façade is a projecting tower; in each wall next to it is a round-arched stained-glass window. At the base of the tower is the entrance door, recessed below a large round arch. Above the arch, set in a recessed panel, are a pair of narrow, round-arched stained-glass windows beneath a blind rondel. The transition from the tower to the belfry is marked by the same running arched corbel found on the body of the building. A pair of louvered arched openings fills each side of the square belfry, which is capped by a polygonal spire carrying a cross.

This church replaced an earlier, smaller frame structure; the cornerstone for this building was laid on St. Patrick's Day, 1862.

FORT TOTTEN BATTERY, 1862–64
Willets Point, Queens
Supervising engineer: William Petit Trowbridge
Designated: September 26, 1974

The Fort Totten Battery was constructed between 1862 and 1864 opposite Fort Schuyler in the Bronx as part of the seacoast fortification system developed by Joseph G. Totten. Totten, chief engineer of the army and an internationally known military engineer, developed the Totten System of U.S. seacoast fortifications to replace two earlier systems. The Totten System featured brick and stone construction and casemate emplacements—that is, vaulted chambers from which guns are fired through embrasures. Totten's innovations determined the form of the superbly constructed battery built on Willets Point.

Built of stone, the battery was constructed in the shape of a shallow V with a polygonal bastion at the vertex of the two ramparts. Today the most striking features of the fortification are its sense of weight and the visual rhythm of the openings in the massive walls. The embrasures on the seaward side are square-faced, contrasting with the more gentle segmental arches of the inner face of the embrasures. The series of tall, narrow openings on both tiers and the broad, segmentally arched openings of the lower tier create sharp contrasts of light and dark.

The Fort Totten Battery is an impressive monument of superior stone construction rarely equaled in the United States. Carefully cut granite blocks, rough-hewn on the seaward face, make up the thick walls. The second tier, which was never completed, today recalls the romantic ruins of post-Renaissance Europe. The battery is still owned by the U.S. Army.

17 EAST 128TH STREET, c. 1864
Manhattan
Architect: Unknown
Designated: December 21, 1982

The house at 17 East 128th Street is one of a few surviving frame houses in Harlem that date from the period when Harlem was still a rural village and not legally part of the City of New York. Constructed about 1864, this two-and-one-half-story, three-bay house was once one of many similarly styled frame houses built in Harlem—particularly between 110th and 130th streets—immediately after the Civil War.

Although its architect is unknown, the house exemplifies a pleasing and picturesque synthesis of Second Empire and Italianate elements. Among its more prominent features are a polychromatic, slate-covered mansard roof and a covered porch that runs the width of the façade at the parlor-floor level. The house is significant primarily because it has managed to survive and remains remarkably intact.

RIVERDALE PRESBYTERIAN CHURCH, 1863
4765 Henry Hudson Parkway West, The Bronx
Architect: James Renwick, Jr.
Designated: April 19, 1966

Resembling the parish churches scattered throughout England, the Riverdale Church was constructed of small stones capped by a steep, slate roof. Side wings embrace a small, square tower set within the reentrant angle. The copper steeple was added to the tower at a later date. Following the style of the late Gothic Revival, a projecting stone vestibule and a pointed-arched doorway, with a niche above, decorate the main entrance. The main gable rises directly behind the entrance and contains a triangular window with three traceried trefoils of stone.

GREYSTON CONFERENCE CENTER, TEACHERS' COLLEGE, COLUMBIA UNIVERSITY, 1863–64
690 West 247th Street (4675 Hadley Avenue), The Bronx
Architect: James Renwick, Jr.
Designated: October 13, 1970

Erected during the Civil War, Greyston was commissioned by William Earl Dodge, Jr., a prominent merchant closely associated with Phelps, Dodge & Company, international dealers in copper and other metals.

Built as a country residence, this large mansion designed by James Renwick, Jr., was influenced by early English Victorian country houses, which combined Tudor features with earlier Gothic traditions. Its present appearance, however, particularly at the north (entrance side), is largely changed by the addition of a large dining-room wing and other modifications. Part of the wooden porch remains, but much of the original arched openwork and Gothic bracing have gone.

The mansion's balanced design is largely the result of later additions to the more Picturesque, asymmetrical original design. Constructed of gray granite laid up in random ashlar, Greyston rises three stories to a polychrome slate roof. The main entrance, its door near the center of the north façade, is enframed by paired Gothic trefoil niches cut into smooth stone. A wood porch continues the Gothic trefoil design in its carved balusters. The river side of the structure is dominated by a polygonal porch, of which a portion has been glazed. The southern roofline is partially hidden by pointed gables and chimneys. Paired and tripled window openings on each façade reflect a variety of decorative elements—pointed Gothic arches, cusping, trefoil and quatrefoil motifs, and mullioned windows—derived from English Gothic and Tudor traditions.

The eldest of Dodge's six children, Grace Hoadley Dodge (1856–1914), was a social worker with an interest in education; she founded Teachers' College in 1887 as an outgrowth of her formation of the Kitchen Garden Association for domestic industrial arts among the laboring classes. Her nephew, Cleveland E. Dodge, was a chairman of the Board of Trustees of Teachers' College and donated Greyston to that institution in 1961.

FLUSHING MUNICIPAL COURTHOUSE,
formerly Flushing Town Hall, 1862
137–35 Northern Boulevard, Queens
Architect: Unknown
Designated: July 30, 1968

The Flushing Courthouse, the only remaining small town hall of the 1860s in New York City, is a fine example of the early phase of the Romanesque Revival, a style that became popular in the United States just before the Civil War. From 1862 to 1900, the building was the Flushing Town Hall, and during the Civil War, Flushing's Volunteer Artillery Unit was housed here. Teddy Roosevelt gave one of his presidential campaign speeches from the steps of the portico, and the building later served as an office for municipal bureaus and as a police precinct for the 1964 World's Fair.

The masonry structure appears today much as it did when first built. The front façade is divided vertically into three sections by tall, thin buttresses that rise above the roofline. The walls are topped by continuous bands of diminutive, round-arched corbels and a simple cornice. Pairs of windows under larger, rounded arches adorn the façade. Dominating the front from its position on a platform five steps above the street, the triple-arched entrance carries a full classical entablature on massive pilasters.

BRIGHTON HEIGHTS REFORMED CHURCH, 1863–64;
addition, 1881
St. Mark's Place, corner of Fort Place, Staten Island
Architect: Unknown
Designated: October 12, 1967

The Brighton Heights Reformed Church was established as a missionary enterprise by the Port Richmond Church in 1817 and was the first missionary church on Staten Island. Donations of money and farmland from Daniel D. Tompkins, governor of New York and later vice president of the United States under James Monroe, aided its construction. In 1823 it became independent of the Port Richmond Church and became known as the Dutch Reformed Church of Tompkinsville. At that time a school was started by the church; this was the beginning of the Tompkinsville school system. The original church was located on a triangular lot in the Quarantine section; the congregation relocated to the present site during the Civil War.

The Gothic Revival structure, built in 1863–64, features at the front façade two pairs of stepped wooden buttresses supporting an octagonal steeple. A paneled central doorway and flanking side-aisle entrances are crowned by paneled tympana with pointed arches. Similar pointed-arched stained-glass windows top each of the three doorways, and paired, pointed-arched louvers surround the belfry, below which runs a pointed-arched corbel band. A series of six stained-glass windows pierce the side walls. In 1881 the addition of a terminal transept at the rear of the church was made possible by the sale of the Tompkinsville property, the site of the earlier church.

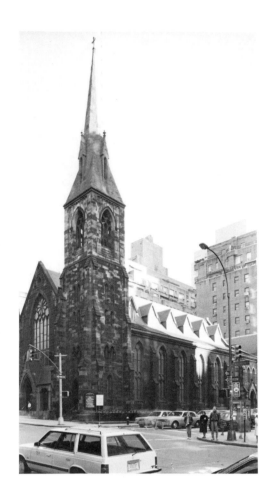

CHURCH OF THE INCARNATION AND PARISH HOUSE
205–209 Madison Avenue, Manhattan
Designated: September 11, 1979

Church of the Incarnation, 1864–68;
restored, 1882; spire, 1896
Architects: Emlen T. Littel; restored by
D. & J. Jardine

Parish House, 1864–68; remodeled 1905–06
Architects: Emlen T. Littel; remodeled by
E. P. Casey

Built as an uptown chapel of Grace Church, the Church of the Incarnation continues to serve the Murray Hill community for which it was erected. Architect Emlen Littel had a large practice, and he specialized in Protestant Episcopal churches in the Pennsylvania, New York, and New Jersey area. The brownstone ashlar structure has a broached Early English spire (completed to Littel's designs only in 1896). The coping and trim are executed in a lighter sandstone, although city grime has obscured the original contrast in materials. The masonry, tracery, and shallow buttresses, along with the asymmetrical placement of the tower, are characteristic of English thirteenth-century Gothic style, often called the Decorated.

In 1882 a fire destroyed sections of the south and west windows and the east end. David Jardine rebuilt these, lengthened the nave, and added a shallow north transept with additional pews. The interior contains outstanding furnishings: an oak communion rail carved by Daniel Chester French, a reredos by Heins & La Farge, and windows designed by Edward Burne-Jones, William Morris, John La Farge, and Louis Tiffany. The chancel mural that depicts the Adoration of the Magi is also by John La Farge. The H. E. Montgomery Memorial, dedicated to the second rector, is the only such work by H. H. Richardson to be found in New York City.

E. P. Casey gave Littel's rectory to the north a neo-Jacobean façade in 1905–06. This building became the Parish House in 1934, when the old parish house and mission chapel at 31st Street and Third Avenue was abandoned. The small scale and rural character of the church complex are dramatic reminders of the character of the earliest residential settlement of the former country estate of Robert and Mary Murray.

WOODS MERCANTILE BUILDINGS, 1865
46, 48–50 White Street, Manhattan
Architect: Unknown
Designated: September 11, 1979

The Woods Mercantile Buildings at 46 and 48–50 White Street are handsome examples of mid-nineteenth-century commercial architecture, representative of a period in the city's history when White Street was part of the country's textile and dry-goods center. Built of marble with a cast-iron ground floor, these two buildings were designed as a single unit in a simplified style based on Renaissance architecture. They were erected in 1865 by Samuel and Abraham Wood as first-class storehouses.

Five stories high and ten windows wide with a pedimented roof, the buildings were designed in the form of a cube, flat-roofed and nearly flat-surfaced. The unit had the practical advantages of providing large window areas for better interior lighting, as well as more floor space. A simple, straightforward design with little surface ornamentation, the Woods Buildings are distinguished by their cast-iron storefront with Tuscan columns on polygonal pedestals supporting an unadorned fascia and modillioned cornice, single-window bay units repeated across each floor in disciplined regularity in the upper stories, and a handsome dentiled roof entablature.

ST. JAMES EPISCOPAL CHURCH
2500 Jerome Avenue, The Bronx
Designated: November 25, 1980

St. James Episcopal Church, 1864–65   Parish House, 1891–92
Architect: Henry Dudley   Architect: Henry Kilburn

St. James Episcopal Church is a picturesque stone building designed in 1863 for a rural parish in what was then part of Westchester County. The design of the church reflects the ecclesiological movement, which called for a more dogmatic style of architecture inspired by medieval Gothic parish churches. St. James is among New York City's finest Gothic Revival religious structures.

English emigré Henry Dudley, a leading architect of the ecclesiological movement in North America, designed St. James. Ecclesiological principles required the honest use of the best materials; it was also considered important that the exterior design reflect the plan and construction of the interior, and that the church be oriented on an east-west axis. The importance of the chancel, the steep slope of the roof, the transepts, and the placement of the entrance porch on the southwest corner of the building were also important. Constructed of stone with timber arcades and an open-beamed ceiling on the interior, St. James carefully illustrates these ideas in a simple, beautifully massed structure. The polychromatic effect and various idiosyncratic details of the façade demonstrate that the Victorian Gothic movement was beginning to influence American church design in the early 1860s. The neighborhood of the church is now a heavily urbanized section of the Bronx, only one block north of commercial Fordham Road. With its landscaped grounds, situated next to St. James Park, the church is one of the few surviving reminders of the more rural past of this part of the city.

ST. ALBAN'S EPISCOPAL CHURCH, formerly Church of the Holy Comforter, 1865; moved and enlarged, 1872
76 St. Alban's Place, Staten Island
Architect: Richard M. Upjohn
Designated: September 9, 1980

Located in the old village of Eltingville near the southern tip of Staten Island, this mid-nineteenth-century rural church, constructed of board-and-batten siding, takes full advantage of the versatility of wood as a building material. Originally known as the Church of the Holy Comforter, it was designed in 1865 by the prominent Victorian architect Richard Upjohn. In 1872 the small church was moved to its present site and enlarged, probably also by Upjohn.

The structure, with its vertical members sawed to form a zigzag pattern, has a steeply pitched roof. Under the gable is the entrance porch, with a pitched roof and wooden struts. A polygonal apse is lit by pointed-arched windows with frames constructed of sticks. The transepts and a square bell tower in three sections were added later.

The congregation was first organized in 1865 by Albert Journeay, who donated the land for the first church. He had the assistance and support of many members of the surrounding community.

Soldiers' and Sailors' Memorial Arch

Lefferts Homestead

PROSPECT PARK
Brooklyn

Prospect Park, design begun, 1865;
construction begun 1866
Bounded by Prospect Park West, Bartel-
Pritchard Circle roadway, Prospect Park
Southwest, Park Circle roadway, Parkside
Avenue, Ocean Avenue, Flatbush Avenue,
and Grand Army Plaza roadway
Architects: Frederick Law Olmsted and
Calvert Vaux
Designated: November 25, 1975

Lefferts Homestead, 1777–83, moved 1918
Prospect Park (Flatbush Avenue at Empire
Boulevard)
Architect: Unknown
Designated: June 21, 1966

Litchfield Villa, completed 1856
Prospect Park (Prospect Park West
at 5th Street)
Architect: Alexander Jackson Davis
Designated: March 15, 1966

Soldiers' and Sailors' Memorial Arch,
1889–92
Grand Army Plaza
Architect: John H. Duncan
Designated: October 16, 1973

Grecian Shelter, completed 1905
Prospect Park (near Parkside Avenue)
Architects: McKim, Mead & White
Designated: December 10, 1968

Boathouse, 1904
Prospect Park (on the Lullwater)
Architects: Helmle & Huberty
Designated: October 14, 1968

Brooklyn's Prospect Park, 526 acres of picturesque landscape dotted by flower gardens, meandering pathways, and historic buildings, is one of the largest and most scenic urban parks in the United States. It was designed, starting in 1865, by Frederick Law Olmsted and Calvert Vaux, the landscape architects who had earlier been responsible for Central Park in Manhattan, begun in 1857. Like Central Park, Prospect Park offered the urban dweller a pastoral escape from the congestion of city life. As Egbert L. Viele, chief topographical engineer of the project, remarked: "The primary object of the park [is] as a rural resort where the people of all classes, escaping from the glare and glitter, and turmoil of the city, might find relief for the mind, and physical recreation."

Construction of the park began in 1866, although planning by the city's commissioners had been initiated as early as 1859, when an act was passed authorizing the selection and location of the park grounds. The outbreak of the Civil War in 1861 delayed any further work until 1865, when Vaux, later to be joined by Olmsted, was appointed. Their plan, based on the popular English-garden mode, called for three very distinct regions: a large open meadow, a hilly wooded area planted with an extensive variety of native and exotic plants and trees, and a vast lake district. A traffic circulation system like that used in Central Park artfully segregated vehicles, pedestrians, and equestrian traffic; the flow of roads and paths connected these regions without disturbing the natural scenery.

In addition to the park's natural landscape, Olmsted and Vaux designed a number of formal spaces, including the Concert Grove, now referred to as the Flower Garden, and the great elliptical Plaza, renamed the Grand Army Plaza, at the main entrance to the park. Dominating the plaza is the monumental Neoclassical Soldiers' and Sailors' Memorial Arch; built in 1889–92 by John H. Duncan (who was also responsible for Grant's Tomb on Riverside Drive), it is dedicated to the men who fought in the Union forces during the Civil War.

Olmsted and Vaux felt that any buildings within the park should be subordinated to the natural setting. Many structures built in the nineteenth century were—they provided rustic architecture in keeping with the rural environment. A number of structures dating from the early twentieth century, however, were products of a renewed interest in classicism and tend to dominate the landscape. The Boathouse, designed by Helmle & Huberty and completed in 1904, is a graceful two-story terra-cotta building recalling Sansovino's magnificent (and very urban) library in Venice. The firm of McKim, Mead & White designed the Grecian Shelter, which was completed in 1905. Like the Boathouse, it is a masterpiece of Neoclassical inspiration. The flowing rhythm of its twenty-eight Corinthian columns, topped by a balustraded terra-cotta entablature, evokes poetic associations of the Greek temple and the grandeur of classical antiquity.

There are two historic residential buildings located in the park. The Lefferts Homestead, built between 1777 and 1783 (architect unknown) and moved down Flatbush Avenue to Prospect Park in 1918, is a charming Dutch Colonial farmhouse with a low-pitched roof, arched dormer windows, and a colonnaded porch. The Litchfield Villa, already contained within the precincts of the park, was completed in 1856 after a design by Alexander Jackson Davis. It is one of the finest extant imitations of a romantic Italian villa, with its irregular towers, arched doorways and windows, and balustrades.

Since its beginning, Prospect Park has been the prime recreational site of Brooklyn and its most notable green space. Enjoyed by millions of city residents and visitors each year, the park continues to provide a much-needed respite from the brick and concrete of the urban environment.

Litchfield Villa

Grecian Shelter

Boathouse

CHRIST CHURCH RIVERDALE, 1866
5030 Riverdale Avenue, The Bronx
Architect: Richard M. Upjohn
Designated: January 11, 1967

Built in 1866 solely with funds donated by its founders, Christ Church is an example of the Victorian Gothic style. The combination of locally quarried stone and colorful brick creates the patterned façade characteristic of this style.

The west elevation has a pointed-arched stained-glass window framed in stone tracery; a pierced wall belfry rises above this elevation. The windows around the altar were executed by the English artist Wailes; a large window in the transept depicting the *Supper at Emmaus* is by the French artist Oudinot, and the oldest windows in the church were made in Montclair, New Jersey, by Doremus.

The wood framing and the doorway are characteristic of architect Richard Upjohn's later work with Gothic detail. The church, which is a parish of the Episcopal diocese of New York, has remained unaltered since its consecration, except for the addition of windows in the nave and the construction of a parish house in 1923.

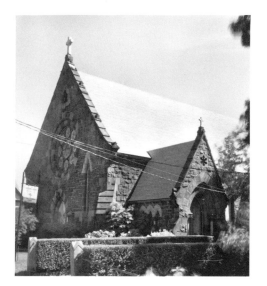

ST. PAUL'S MEMORIAL CHURCH AND RECTORY, 1866–70
225 St. Paul's Avenue, Staten Island
Architect: Edward T. Potter
Designated: July 22, 1975

These two buildings, dating from 1866–70, are the sole surviving works in New York City by the distinguished church architect Edward T. Potter. Examples of the High Victorian Gothic style, they are noted for their subdued polychromy and excellent use of local stone.

As a freestanding structure situated on a hill, the church is not only readily seen from all four sides, but also has a view of the Narrows. Constructed of rough-faced, irregularly cut blocks of Staten Island traprock and Connecticut brownstone, the building is distinguished by its broad gable ends and buttressed side walls, which are surmounted by a steeply pitched roof. The pointed-arched entrance is set beneath a gable and a central rose window. Slender stained-glass lancet windows are set in the side walls between the buttresses, and the end gables are crowned by crosses.

An example of post–Civil War domestic architecture, the rectory adjoins the church to the south and complements the earlier building in its overall design and use of materials. It is reminiscent of many country gate lodges of the period.

The congregation was organized in 1833, and the first church building consecrated in 1835. Caleb Tompkins Ward—for whom Ward's Hill was named—was the first donor of land for the church.

312 EAST 53RD STREET, 1866
Manhattan
Architect: Unknown
Designated: June 12, 1968

An enchanting little wooden structure, 312 East 53rd Street was built for R.V.J. Cunningham in 1866. Its mansard roof and heavy door and window enframements—all displaying cornices carried on brackets—recall the French Second Empire style, popular in post–Civil War architecture. The arrangement of the windows is somewhat unusual: the two long ones at the left of the door follow an asymmetrical pattern, while the two above, as well as the dormers, are situated symmetrically. They are all double-hung, with the broad central muntin intended to simulate casement windows. This arrangement was characteristic in buildings that were meant to look French but retain the practicality of double-hung windows.

PUBLIC SCHOOL 111, formerly
Public School 9, 1867–68; additions, 1887
249 Sterling Place, Brooklyn
Architect: Samuel B. Leonard
Designated: January 10, 1978

Prominently sited at the northwest corner of Sterling Place and Vanderbilt Avenue near Grand Army Plaza, this handsome red-brick schoolhouse was designed in early Romanesque Revival style by Samuel B. Leonard, the superintendent for education of the City of Brooklyn, who was responsible for many schoolhouse designs in the latter half of the nineteenth century.

The school was built to accommodate the growing population of the Prospect Heights area; it was originally called P.S. 9 and served as a grammar school. The central, oldest portion of the building is gable-fronted and two stories high. The centrally placed entrance, approached by a flight of steps, has a handsome brownstone enframement with Italianate detail. Among the school's other features are paneled pilasters flanking the doorway, round-arched windows, and a raking cornice outlining the gable. The flanking two-story wings were added to the gabled section in 1887.

In the last years of the nineteenth century, P.S. 9 moved across the street and this building was renamed P.S. 111. It is used today as a special high school.

PUBLIC SCHOOL 34, 1867; extensions, 1870, 1887–88
131 Norman Avenue, Brooklyn
Architects: Samuel B. Leonard; extensions, James W. Naughton
Designated: April 12, 1983

Public School 34—known as the Oliver H. Perry School, for the hero of the Battle of Lake Erie during the War of 1812—occupies the entire block front on the north side of Norman Avenue between Eckford Street and McGuiness Boulevard in Brooklyn. The school was built in 1867 to meet the needs of the expanding school system in Greenpoint, which—thanks to the efforts of industrialist Martin Kalbfleisch—was flourishing. Dissatisfied with the quality of public education, Kalbfleisch established a school for his own children and others in the Greenpoint area after 1842; he initiated the construction of several similar school buildings, of which this was one.

Brick with stone trim, the school was designed in the Romanesque Revival style with Italianate ornamental motifs by Samuel B. Leonard. The gabled central section rises two and one-half stories above a rusticated brownstone base, with a central round-arched entrance enframed by brownstone. The flanking two-story pavilions on the Norman Avenue side were added by James W. Naughton between 1887 and 1888.

BROOKLYN BRIDGE, 1867–83
East River from City Hall Park, Manhattan, to Cadman Plaza, Brooklyn
Architects: John A. Roebling and Washington A. Roebling
Designated: August 24, 1967

The first bridge built to span the East River, the Brooklyn Bridge remains today the most picturesque of all the bridges in New York City. Embodying the ingenuity of the American spirit, the bridge tied two shores and united two cities. It has inspired more painters, poets, and photographers than any other bridge in America.

This great structure was the largest suspension bridge in the world from the time of its completion in 1883 until 1903, spanning 1,595 feet and rising 135 feet from the river below. The construction took sixteen years and claimed more than twenty lives. The ultimate triumph of the bridge's construction can be attributed to two men, designer John A. Roebling and his son, builder Washington A. Roebling. The cablework is strung across two stone towers and is anchored at both sides by an inventive system of supports embedded in stone. Among the significant engineering feats that marked its construction was the pulley-and-reel system that made it possible to weave the enormous supporting cables.

In addition to the awesome stone towers, the elegant sweep of the cables, buttresses, pointed Gothic arches, and Italian Renaissance arches of the land approaches, the bridge has an elevated promenade. A walk on the promenade guarantees a spectacular view of the skyline, the river, and the shimmering cables and romantic arches of the bridge. A milestone in the history of American engineering, the Brooklyn Bridge is an immediately recognizable symbol of New York City and a structure of beauty.

FIRST UKRAINIAN ASSEMBLY OF GOD,
formerly the Metropolitan Savings Bank, 1867
6 East 7th Street, Manhattan
Architect: Carl Pfeiffer
Designated: November 19, 1969

The Metropolitan Savings Bank built this fireproof commercial building—whose Second Empire masonry skin conceals a structural iron frame—in 1867, and occupied it for sixty-eight years. Since 1937, it has been owned and used for religious purposes by the Ukrainian Church.

The building presents two impressive façades; one with five bays on Third Avenue, the other with eight bays on 7th Street. A horizontal band at each floor unifies the composition, as do the boldly rusticated base and the ornate cornice. The vertical emphasis of the pilasters framing the windows contrasts with an otherwise horizontal composition. A series of dormer windows, crowned with segmental arches, appears in the mansard roof. A handsome doorway, framed by a central arch and flanked by Corinthian columns, marks the entrance to the building.

GRAND HOTEL, 1868
1232–1238 Broadway, Manhattan
Architect: Henry Engelbert
Designated: September 11, 1979

The Grand Hotel, built for Elias S. Higgins, an important manufacturer and vendor of carpets, was designed by Henry Engelbert in 1868 at the beginning of the transformation of Broadway, between Madison and Herald squares, into the heart of a glittering entertainment district.

Stylistically, the marble building is an example of the Second Empire style of the new *hôtels particuliers* lining the side streets of the redesigned Paris of Napoleon III. Among its prominent characteristics are slightly projecting end and central bays, with quoins and rich window enframements, that add verticality to the façade; square-headed windows at the second and third floors; segmental-arched windows at the fourth and fifth floors; and full, round-arched windows at the sixth floor, creating an arcade effect below the roof. The sophisticated restraint of the façade contrasts with the elaborate two-story towered mansard roof above the heavily bracketed roof cornice. The towers are boldly embellished with dormers that, unfortunately, have been stripped of their ornament.

Both the Grand Hotel and its landmark neighbor, the Gilsey House, are symbols of the prosperous post–Civil War era when the hotels of the Ladies' Mile sought to exceed one another in opulence and elegance.

POPPENHUSEN INSTITUTE, 1868
114–04 14th Road, Queens
Architects: Mundell & Teckritz
Designated: August 18, 1970

The Poppenhusen Institute, a symmetrical three-story brick building with mansard roof, was erected in 1868. The architects combined features from the Italianate style with a French Second Empire roof, in a manner typical of civic architecture in the period following the Civil War.

Conrad Poppenhusen, a German immigrant and pioneer of the American hard rubber industry, founded the institute as an adult evening school. Here a newly arrived immigrant could both study English and learn a trade. For the children of working mothers, the Poppenhusen Institute provided a kindergarten—the first free kindergarten in the United States. Services provided by the institute were eventually expanded to include a library, a savings bank, a youth center, and a town jail.

KINGS COUNTY SAVINGS BANK BUILDING, 1868
135 Broadway, Brooklyn
Architects: King & Wilcox
Designated: March 15, 1966

The Kings County Savings Bank, built by architects King & Wilcox in 1868, is an impressive four-story French Second Empire building. A cast-iron balustrade flanks the structure on the property line enclosing the bank. The main entrance doorway is dominated by a porch with elaborate carving in the pediment. Arched windows at the ground-floor level, with carved keystone blocks, support the strong, horizontal, stone belt course extending around the building. Belt courses supported by columns at the front of the second and third floors also extend around the structure. The ornate bracketed cornice is topped by a mansard roof. Quoins at the corners of the building are a strong unifying element and add to the solidity and dignity of a bank that has served the banking needs of Williamsburg for 120 years.

AMSTER YARD, 1869–70
211–215 East 49th Street, Manhattan
Architect: Harold Sterner
Designated: June 21, 1966

Amster Yard, a picturesque, L-shaped courtyard in the heart of midtown Manhattan, is one of the most charming and inventive enclosures in the city. It is named for James Amster, a designer who had the idea in 1945 to take this oddly shaped lot and convert it into a pleasant oasis.

Offices and a private home are grouped around an attractive, landscaped garden set down among slate-covered walks. The buildings vary in height, style, and materials but blend harmoniously together. The brick walls of the courtyard are extremely simple in style and are distinguished by wall brackets with sculpture, hanging lamps, iron grillwork, and trees. From the street, an arch leads into the yard, and the easternmost building projects forward as a bay. Access to Amster Yard is by special permission only.

U.S. COAST GUARD STATION ADMINISTRATION BUILDING, formerly Third District U.S. Lighthouse Depot, 1868–71; additions, 1901
1 Bay Street, Staten Island
Architect: Alfred B. Mullett
Designated: November 25, 1980

Constructed in 1868–71, this French Second Empire building was designed by Alfred B. Mullett, supervising architect of the Treasury Department from 1865 to 1874. Built in granite and red brick, the three-story structure was enlarged in 1901, with the additions also in the French Second Empire style. Occupying a central location on the grounds of the former Coast Guard Station at the foot of Bay Street, the building has a long history of government service; for nearly seventy years it was the main office of the Lighthouse Service Depot for the Third Lighthouse District.

Originally the building had the same basic arrangement of openings on all four sides. Today only the front façade remains totally unaltered, with a central square entrance porch built of rock-faced granite. The sloping mansard roof has metal-framed dormer windows with decorative Flemish scrolls. The wings, added in 1901, are joined to the original building by small, square entrance bays that fill the corners and rise the height of the building. The rear façade was redone in the same year.

The Coast Guard moved to Governors Island in 1966; the building is now vacant.

LANGSTON HUGHES HOUSE, 1869
20 East 127th Street, Manhattan
Architect: Alexander Wilson
Designated: August 11, 1981

This modest brownstone row house was designed in the Italianate style by Alexander Wilson. Typical of row houses built in Harlem during the period after the Civil War, it was constructed in 1869 by James Meagher and Thomas Hanson. For twenty years, this building was the home of Langston Hughes, one of the foremost figures of the Harlem Renaissance.

The 127th Street house is three stories above a basement and faced with brownstone. Cast-iron railings lead to the entrance at the parlor-floor level. The entranceway and windows all have arched brownstone enframements. The façade is crowned by a bracketed and modillioned sheet-metal cornice.

Langston Hughes was born in Joplin, Missouri, on February 1, 1902. After a childhood of frequent moves, he came to New York to attend Columbia College in 1921–22. At Columbia, Hughes began to write, and he established friendships with young Harlem writers. His first publications—*The Weary Blues* (1926) and *Fine Clothes to the Jew* (1927)—date from this period. During the 1930s, he published four books and a play, and also established the Harlem Suitcase Theater.

Although Hughes traveled widely, he always returned to Harlem, which he claimed was the source of his literary inspiration. It was in Harlem during the 1930s that he met Emerson and Ethel Harper; when the Harpers purchased this house in 1947, Hughes moved in with them, occupying the top floor as a workroom. Here he spent the last twenty years of his life, writing poetry, nonfiction, humor, and libretti.

ST. JOHN'S CHURCH, 1869–71
1331 Bay Street, Staten Island
Architect: Arthur D. Gilman
Designated: February 19, 1974

St. John's Church sits on the corner of Belair Road and what is now called Bay Street. The first church on the site was consecrated in 1843. This larger and more elaborate structure accommodated a growing congregation.

The church is noted for its beautifully colored stained-glass windows. Reminiscent of an English parish church in both style and setting, St. John's was designed by the prominent architect Arthur D. Gilman in a Victorian Gothic style. The handsome rose-colored granite structure is dominated by a tower surmounted by a high spire above the crossing. Flanking buttresses on the western and eastern ends and at the transepts accentuate the large pointed-arched windows, distinguished by their tracery. Cruciform in plan, the church has three aisles and a steep, peaked roof that extends the length of the nave and above the transepts. Windows, each consisting of three Gothic arches under a segmental arch, are set in the clerestory walls above the low-angled roofs of the side aisles. The square belfry tower above the crossing has a louvered pointed-arched opening on each side and is crowned by a crenellated parapet. The pointed, eight-sided spire was added in the 1960s after wind damage had destroyed the original one.

The front churchyard is set behind a handsome cast-iron fence of the period. The spire has always been a prominent landmark for ships coming through the Narrows along the shore of Staten Island, and the church bells tolled a welcome to troopships returning from Europe after World War I.

901 BROADWAY, formerly the Lord & Taylor Building, 1869–70
Manhattan
Architect: James H. Giles
Designated: November 15, 1977

The former Lord & Taylor Building is a vivid reminder of the architectural splendor of the Ladies' Mile, where many commercial emporiums were built in the grandest and most impressive styles. Designed in the French Second Empire style, the building was constructed in cast iron and glass. The slender structural system of the façade allowed for eye-catching display windows, which became a chief attraction.

The structure, four stories with attic, is dominated by its diagonal corner tower, which is flanked by a single bay facing Broadway. The long 20th Street side is crowned by a mansard roof with dormers. Above the ground floor the cast-iron façade displays a profusion of decorative features; the play of projections and recessions, the contrast of light and shadow, skillfully combine to give the building a highly ornate and distinctive character.

Lord & Taylor moved to new quarters on Fifth Avenue in 1914.

PUBLIC SCHOOL 65K, 1870; front and rear extensions, 1889
158 Richmond Street, Brooklyn
Architects: Unknown; James W. Naughton (extension and façades)
Designated: February 3, 1981

Built in 1870, Public School 65K was given its present Romanesque Revival façade by James W. Naughton in 1889. The brick two-story school rises high over a stone basement, with a slightly projecting three-story central tower. The round-arched entrance at the base of the tower is enhanced by a molded archivolt. The second-story tower windows are square-headed with stone lintels, and the tympana are decorated with Gothic-derived trefoils; the third-story windows are round-arched. The tower-roof entablature is decorated by a frieze with terra-cotta plaques in the Queen Anne style and is crowned by a balustrade.

The windows of the main section of the school are arched with brick voussoirs and stone archivolts. There are compound segmental-arched windows on the first floor and round-arched windows with terra-cotta tympana on the second. The frieze of the roof entablature is ornamented with terra-cotta plaques.

FORT TOTTEN OFFICERS' CLUB, c. 1870
Fort Totten Road, Queens
Architect: Unknown
Designated: September 24, 1974

The first Fort Totten Officers' Club was a modest, frame building topped with late Gothic crenellations. To the original one-story, single-tower structure were added two additional stories and a second, identical polygonal tower; today, these towers flank a symmetrical façade. Growth of the fort and garrison resulted in a larger structure; the rear section and back porch were among the later additions. Both entrance and side porches feature Tudor arches. Other details from this style include hood or drip moldings over the windows and roof-level parapets that suggest the building's military affiliation.

During the Civil War the reservation site served as a depot for recruits, as a camping ground for volunteer units, and, at one point, as a hospital for wounded Union soldiers. In 1868, an engineering school (which became the U.S. Engineer Depot in 1870) was established by the War Department. In 1898, the "Fort at Willets Point," as it had come to be known, was renamed for General Joseph G. Totten, who had been instrumental in the planning of seacoast defenses.

In recent years the old club building served as a New York City Job Corps center. Today it houses the Bayside Historical Society, which has undertaken the restoration of the structure.

GILSEY HOUSE, 1869–71
1200 Broadway, Manhattan
Architect: Stephen Decatur Hatch
Designated: September 11, 1979

The last surviving farmhouse in midtown off Broadway was demolished to make way for the Gilsey House, one of the city's most imposing French Second Empire cast-iron and marble buildings. Erected in 1869–71, it was designed as a hotel by Stephen Decatur Hatch for Peter Gilsey, a prominent real-estate developer and an alderman for the city. Although expensive to build, Gilsey House became highly profitable when the theater district moved up Broadway. It is now used for retail stores, with cooperative apartments on the upper floors. Except for the ground-floor modernization, the exterior remains to a considerable degree as it was when built more than a century ago.

Its Baroque, modulating surface is very different from many flat-fronted cast-iron buildings, and this difference is emphasized by two recessed pavilions topped by a mansard tower with a curved roof. These pavilions are distinguished by flat pilasters bordering Palladian windows at every story. Flat marble areas along the 29th Street façade, now removed, once separated narrower windows that still have a hierarchy of pediments: urns and broken arches at the lower level, pediments at the next, segmental arches above, and finally, round-headed windows. In its heyday, the Gilsey House was painted a gleaming white. The three-story, curved, crowning tower of the flamboyant mansard roof calls attention to the grand front entrance on the corner of 29th Street and Broadway.

The hotel attracted coal magnates, railroad operators, congressmen, and army and navy officers. After it opened on April 15, 1871, the *New York Times* called it "one of the most imposing of our metropolitan palace hotels." Gilsey House later became a center for theater luminaries and such notables as the opera impresario Oscar Hammerstein (grandfather of the lyricist) resided there. The hotel temporarily closed on December 10, 1904, and finally ceased operation in 1911.

102–45 47TH AVENUE, c. 1871
Queens
Architect: Unknown
Designated: February 10, 1987

Built for Edward E. Sanford in about 1871, this small, two-story frame house is one of the last intact nineteenth-century houses in the former village of Newton, one of western Long Island's oldest settlements. Typical of suburban and rural nineteenth-century dwellings in this region, the building was probably designed on site by the contractor. Fine detailing on the porch, eaves, and property-line fence reflects both the nineteenth-century carpenter's skill and the scope of individual expression in routine construction. Additional decorative ornaments, such as window frames and foliate brackets, were mass-produced and available to both carpenter and patron in local lumberyards.

EASTERN PARKWAY, 1870–74
Brooklyn
Landscape architects: Olmsted & Vaux
Designated: August 22, 1978

Eastern Parkway, begun in 1870 and completed in 1874, was the first of Frederick Law Olmsted's parkways to see completion. His new concept of road building consisted of a mall, to be divided down the center by a road to be used for "pleasure riding and driving." Although his original plan—to go "through the rich country lying back of Brooklyn . . . to approach the East River"—was never carried out, Olmsted's parkway concept and its encouragement to suburban development within the bounds of the city became a recurring theme in his attempts to fulfill the need for open spaces shared by many American cities.

Designed as an extension of Prospect Park, the roadway featured a central pleasure drive flanked by picturesque lawns bordered by residential streets. When completed in 1874, Eastern Parkway ran from Grand Army Plaza west to the City of Brooklyn's boundary.

Today, Eastern Parkway is divided into three roadways by two broad, tree-lined pedestrian malls. Concrete and wooden park benches have been placed along the mall walkways, now shaded by trees and paved with asphalt tiles. Although the parkway's main role today is that of a major artery within the city's transportation system, the character of the original road has been maintained by the generous path it cuts through the early twentieth-century neighborhoods it helped to stimulate.

The formal elegance of the parkway attracted such prestigious cultural institutions as the Brooklyn Museum, the Brooklyn Botanic Garden, and the Brooklyn Public Library—all of which continue to enhance the area.

NEW BRIGHTON VILLAGE HALL, 1871
66 Lafayette Avenue, Staten Island
Architect: Unknown
Designated: October 14, 1965

This once-elegant three-story brick building was constructed in the style of the French Second Empire, adapted for use in a rural setting. A small porch, now destroyed, led to an arched front door on the main floor; the whole floor is lighted by high, arched windows. The door is contained within a projecting central bay or vestibule. Gabled dormers pierce the steep mansard roof.

Once a model of Second Empire simplicity, the building has since fallen into a state of dilapidation. It was bought in 1970 by Heritage House, a community group on Staten Island. Unable to secure funding for its proposed programs, the group was compelled to leave the building unoccupied.

CHURCH OF ST. ANDREW, 1872
Old Mill Road and Arthur Kill Road, Staten Island
Architect for final rebuilding: William H. Mersereau
Designated: November 15, 1967

Set in a rolling, verdant churchyard, the little stone Church of St. Andrew is reminiscent of an English Norman parish church of the twelfth century.

The church was established in 1705 by the Reverend Aeneas MacKenzie; its charter was granted by Queen Anne in 1713. The original small, stone church with gambrel roof was built in 1709–12; over the next century and a half, it was damaged by fires and rebuilt several times, in 1743, 1770, 1807–10, 1867, and finally in 1872. During the last rebuilding, architect William H. Mersereau, using the original stone walls, constructed the present edifice. Wall openings ranging in type from round-arched windows to circular oculi are framed by keyed brickwork; they contrast in color and texture with the rough-cut random fieldstone of the walls. The steeple consists of a square tower and a belfry with paired, louvered openings on each of the four sides, surmounted by a plain octagonal spire. The stone wall surrounding the churchyard was constructed in 1855.

During the Revolution, the church functioned as a hospital for the wounded British; it was the scene of battle in 1777, when Americans attacked the British troops who had barricaded themselves inside the building.

CENTRAL SYNAGOGUE, formerly Congregation Ahawath Chesed, 1870–72
652 Lexington Avenue, Manhattan
Architect: Henry Fernbach
Designated: June 7, 1966

Central Synagogue houses one of the oldest Reform congregations in continuous service in New York State. It was founded on Ludlow Street in Lower Manhattan as Ahawath Chesed in 1846, when one rabbi, Max Lilienthal, began to share his services with the Shaar Hashomayim, a congregation of German Jews founded in 1839. The present building was designed by Henry Fernbach, a German Jew, and was occupied in 1872.

Although nineteenth-century architects felt that the Gothic style was suitable for Christian edifices, there was little agreement on the proper architecture for synagogues. Gradually, what might loosely be called a "Moorish-Islamic Revival" came to be favored. The chief characteristics of this style were the banded horseshoe arch and twin onion domes in vestigial minarets applied to either side of a synagogue—the latter conceived of as references to the two columns that stood in front of Solomon's Temple. The Central Synagogue conforms to this type.

The unusual identification of Islamic forms with Jewish religious architecture came about in the early nineteenth century. Historians believed that mosques had incorporated the forms of earlier Jewish architecture, and that the banded arch was the precursor of the pointed Gothic arch. What more appropriate style was there, then, for a synagogue than a literally pre-Christian—i.e. pre-Gothic—style? The Islamic-Jewish typology was set largely by two buildings: Friedrich von Gartner's Munich Synagogue (1832), and Gottfried Semper's Dresden Synagogue (1837), which was widely known through publication in the *Allgemeine Bau-Zeitung* of 1847. Fernbach could have known the building through publication or directly: he was born in Prussian Silesia and studied at the Berlin Building Academy. After he immigrated to the United States in 1855, he used the Moorish Revival and the German *Rundbogenstil* in several other important synagogues.

The exterior coloration of Central Synagogue is muted, twentieth-century grime notwithstanding. The interior, arranged on a Gothic plan, is a riotous explosion of colorful Near Eastern motifs. The designs and color are indebted to Semper's interior, and to the brilliant color plates of the Alhambra that were published in the mid-nineteenth century by English designer and color theorist Owen Jones.

FORMER 30TH POLICE PRECINCT STATION HOUSE,
formerly 32nd Police Precinct, 1871–72
1854 Amsterdam Avenue, Manhattan
Architect: Nathaniel D. Bush
Designated: July 15, 1986

The former 30th Police Precinct Station House, a highly representative and fine example of the French Second Empire style, was built in 1871–72 as part of a citywide reconstruction and renovation campaign to modernize police facilities, and was often cited in its own day as being one of the finest of the new station houses. By the early 1860s, the Police Department had retained a full-time official architect, Nathaniel D. Bush, with offices at Police Headquarters on Mulberry Street. Over the next two decades, Bush was to design more than twenty new or renovated station houses. These larger and more architecturally commanding buildings reflected not only the growth and prosperity of the city, but also the increased professionalism of its police force.

The 32nd Police Precinct (to which this building originally belonged) erected its first documented station house on land acquired in 1864. By 1869, plans were laid for a "new and more commodious building to meet the requirements of the 32nd Precinct." The new station had a handsome stable building and also included an annex with a jail and lodging space for vagrants—the nineteenth-century solution to sheltering New York's homeless. The building is boldly massed in a compact block with strictly symmetrical tripartite elevations. The slate-shingled mansard roof has delicate metal crestings. Constructed of brick, which was originally painted off-white, the building's classical detail is executed in a contrasting brownstone.

Now owned by the St. Luke A.M.E. Congregation, the building is vacant.

614 COURTLANDT AVENUE, 1871–72; renovated, 1882
The Bronx
Architects: Unknown; alterations, Hewlett S. Baker
Designated: February 10, 1987

This early multi-use building was constructed in 1871–72 for Julius Ruppert; when erected, it contained a saloon, public rooms, meeting rooms, and a residential flat. Although the original architect is unknown, the building most likely represents the work of a builder-contractor. A variety of French Second Empire–style motifs are successfully combined to evoke the several uses of the building. The structure was renovated in 1882 by Hewlett S. Baker, who further enriched the façade.

The building is a monument to the first stages of urbanization within the South Bronx, helping by its presence to establish a sense of place in the new village of Melrose South. In many features it resembles the buildings along Manhattan's Bowery, in the area known as Kleine Deutschland, where Ruppert first established his business before following his fellow Germans to the Bronx.

Among the most interesting features of the three-story structure are the tall second-story windows; the heavy, Neo-Grec galvanized metal cornice with brackets and modillions; the Italianate cast-iron segmental window heads with foliate corbels and Queen Anne fan-motif ornament; and the raised decorative ornament of the roof dormers.

WATER TOWER, 1872
Highbridge Park, opposite Amsterdam Avenue at West 173rd Street, Manhattan
Architect: Attributed to John B. Jervis
Designated: July 12, 1967

This slender and graceful water tower in Highbridge Park was once an essential link in the system that supplied New York City with Croton Reservoir water. It was built in 1872 from a design attributed to engineer John B. Jervis, who designed the adjoining High Bridge. Resembling a medieval campanile, the tower is a vigorous Romanesque Revival structure that originally supported a 47,000-gallon tank. Water flowed from the tank with adequate pressure to supply the upper parts of the city—in fact, as far south as Murray Hill.

The octagonal tower originally consisted of a base, a simple but high shaft, a louvered belfry, and a conical roof surmounted by a lantern, spire, and weather vane which were recently destroyed in a fire. The arched doorway is crowned by a massive horseshoe arch with heavy voussoirs carried on corbels at each side.

Similar water towers were later built in other parts of the city, but the Highbridge tower, the first, is the only one that remains, although it has not been used as a water tower for many years. In 1958 the Altman Foundation donated a carillon—since removed—for the belfry as a memorial to Benjamin Altman, the department-store owner and art collector.

BOUWERIE LANE THEATRE, formerly the Bond Street Savings Bank, 1874
330 Bowery, Manhattan
Architect: Henry Engelbert
Designated: January 11, 1967

The old Bond Street Savings Bank, which later became the German Exchange Bank and after 1963 became the Bouwerie Lane Theatre, was completed in 1874 on a conventional 2,500-square-foot building lot at the northwest corner of the Bowery and Bond Street. Architect Henry Engelbert was faced with the problem of creating an impressive bank building with only a twenty-five-foot façade on the more important of the two streets, the Bowery. He solved this by designing an elaborate entrance on the Bowery and also giving the Bond Street side a façade of considerable elegance. He devised a lavish French Second Empire creation with Corinthian columns, single and coupled, divided into bays that stressed its verticality but were offset by cornices at every floor level.

The entire impression of the cast-iron building is of a great stone structure, with its heavy quoins apparently bracing the corners, its pediments, its ponderous cornice, and its emphasis on the horizontal. There is a subtle balance between the narrow façade on the Bowery and the long façade on Bond Street. The columns flanking the windows alternate between single and double, and rusticated piers recall the quoins. The central second-story windows are emphasized with pediments, and round-headed windows are played against flat-headed ones—which are all surface imitations in cast iron to create the effect of a masonry-bearing wall building. The wealth of almost sculptural ornamental detail makes this building an unusually fine example of the elaborate style of the French Second Empire.

When the bank became a theater, the windows on the Bond Street side were blocked in to darken the interior, as was a secondary entrance marked by coupled columns and by a second-floor pediment. Having served first as a bank, then as a loft building, and finally as a theater, 330 Bowery demonstrates how a century-old building can meet varied needs without the destruction of its architectural integrity.

OCEAN PARKWAY, 1874–76
Prospect Park to Coney Island, Brooklyn
Architects: Concept by Olmsted & Vaux
Designated: January 28, 1975

Ocean Parkway, stretching some six miles from Coney Island to just south of Prospect Park, was the first landscaped parkway with adjoining recreation space to be built in the United States. Frederick Law Olmsted and Calvert Vaux, as part of their plans for Prospect Park, suggested that a pleasure drive be extended from the west side of the park to the ocean. This parkway plan was influenced by Baron Haussmann's Avenue Foch in Paris and the Unter den Linden in Berlin.

Construction of the parkway began in 1874 and it was opened two years later. Two hundred and ten feet wide, it was divided into a central roadway, two malls, two side roads, and two sidewalks. The entire construction cost was initially borne by property owners whose property lay within 1,050 feet on either side of the parkway, and reimbursement did not occur until 1882. Lined with trees, the parkway is also provided with benches, playing tables, and a bicycle path. For many Brooklyn residents, Ocean Parkway is the only readily accessible large, open space with trees and grass.

Olmsted and Vaux's original intention that the parkway should serve as a promenade and greenbelt has to a great degree been realized.

RIVERSIDE PARK AND DRIVE, proposal completed 1875; construction begun 1877
West 72nd Street to West 129th Street, Manhattan
Architects: Frederick Law Olmsted, Calvert Vaux, Samuel Parsons, Julious Munkwitz, and others
Designated: February 19, 1980

Riverside Park is a long strip of green that runs along the Hudson River from 72nd Street to 129th Street on Manhattan's West Side. A successful neighborhood park encompassing 293 acres, it also represents an innovative use of land that otherwise would have been difficult to work into the city's grid plan. Riverside Drive is a significant variation of the Olmsted and Vaux parkway concept. The park was extensively redesigned under the Robert Moses administration in the 1930s, and its appearance today is radically different from the original plan.

The park and a separate drive, known as Riverside Avenue until 1908, were first proposed in 1867; in 1875 Olmsted completed a plan that combined the roadway with the park. The park today contains four basic levels: the drive, the hillside, the plateau constructed over the New York Central railroad tracks, and the landfill at the water's edge, which was added in 1934–37. Moses's restructuring added 132 acres of land, 140,000 feet of paths, and eight new playgrounds to the park.

Distinctive features of the park and drive include Grant's Tomb and the Soldiers and Sailors Monument (both designated landmarks), the beautiful 79th Street marina, the outcroppings of Manhattan schist throughout the park, the promenade that reaches from 100th to 110th streets, and the tree-lined, serpentine drive, with a green island between the two stretches of road on the upper drive. Some of the original walkways and plantings within the park were designed by Vaux, others by Samuel Parsons and Julious Munkwitz after Olmsted was fired. The walkways follow the contours of the hillside and employ the Olmsted and Vaux device of sequencing, allowing glimpses of the drive, the river, and various statues.

AMERICAN MUSEUM OF NATURAL HISTORY, 1874–present
77th to 81st streets and Central Park West, Manhattan
Architects: Calvert Vaux and Jacob Wrey Mould (south central wing, 1877);
Cady, Berg & See (77th Street façade and west wing on Columbus Avenue, 1908);
Trowbridge & Livingston (east wing, 1924, north wing of Roosevelt Memorial
Hall, 1933, and Hayden Planetarium, 1935); John Russell Pope (Roosevelt
Memorial Hall interior, 1933)
Designated: August 24, 1967; interior designated July 22, 1975

Built chiefly between 1875 and 1985, the American Museum of Natural History consists of twenty-two interconnected units on the site formerly known as Manhattan Square and currently called Theodore Roosevelt Park. The museum's early collections were first housed in the old Arsenal in Central Park. In 1869 a group of distinguished New Yorkers, including J. P. Morgan and Theodore Roosevelt (the president's father), donated funds for a new museum. From 1874 to 1877, Calvert Vaux and Jacob Wrey Mould, collaborators on many structures in Central Park, designed a five-story building of pressed red brick with brownstone trim. This structure, now visible only from Columbus Avenue, is in the High Victorian Gothic style. J. C. Cady of Cady, Berg & See designed the central section of the 77th Street façade, whose warm-toned, expressively worked, pink Vermont granite refers to the work of H. H. Richardson. Equally Richardsonian are the towers and smaller tourelles, as well as the feeling for broad masses with subtle picturesque accents. Cady added the east and west ranges in a matching style between 1894 and 1900.

In 1912, plans were made to extend the museum along Central Park West after designs by Trowbridge & Livingston. Begun in 1920, the new construction included several wings, courts, and the American Museum–Hayden Planetarium. The monumental entrance front planned to face Central Park was left unfinished, and in 1924 John Russell Pope won the competition for this entrance pavilion. Completed in 1933, the pavilion is a memorial to President Theodore Roosevelt, who had a lifelong interest in natural history and environmental conservation. Pope, a New York City–based architect, was noted for such grand Neoclassical designs as the National Archives Building, the National Gallery of Art, and the Jefferson Memorial, all in Washington, D.C. The Roosevelt Memorial Hall design is a testament to Pope's feeling for the power of pure mass and his self-professed admiration for the work of Charles Follen McKim. The building is of gray granite and is based loosely on a monumental Roman triumphal arch. Freestanding Ionic columns rise on sculpted plinths above the broad entrance plaza and stairs. The decoration is sparse; the broad wall planes are relieved only by the masonry jointing and the Corinthian aedicules with segmental pediments. The Spartan character of the design is entirely appropriate for a memorial. Above the cornice are larger-than-lifesize figures of Meriwether Lewis, George Rogers Clark, Daniel Boone, and John James Audubon. The bas-relief on the columnar plinths depicts various animals. The parapets on each side list President Roosevelt's attainments, and the whole serves as an elaborate backdrop for an equestrian statue of Roosevelt accompanied by an African tribesman and an American Indian. James Earle Fraser executed the sculpture.

The ample interior hall has a coffered, barrel-vaulted ceiling. At each end are colossal Corinthian columns of red Alcanti and Verona marbles on bases of Botticini marble. The rich materials are further enhanced by elaborate murals, executed by William Andrew MacKay in 1933, that depict scenes from Roosevelt's life.

The Roosevelt Memorial Hall, 1940

METROPOLITAN MUSEUM OF ART, including the
Assay Office façade, 1874–present
Fifth Avenue at 82nd Street, Manhattan
Architects: Calvert Vaux and Jacob Wrey Mould; Theodore Weston; Arthur L.
Tuckerman; Richard Morris Hunt; Richard Howland Hunt and George B. Post;
McKim, Mead & White; Brown, Lawford & Forbes; Kevin Roche/John Dinkeloo &
Associates. Assay Office façade, 1824, by Martin E. Thompson
Designated: June 9, 1967; interior designated November 15, 1977

Since it opened in Central Park in 1880, the Metropolitan Museum of Art has undergone
expansions that have made it one of the largest museum complexes in the world. Situated
majestically on Fifth Avenue, the Metropolitan Museum offers its millions of annual visitors a
collection that is remarkable both in scope and quality.

The original building, designed by Calvert Vaux and Jacob Wrey Mould and built between
1874 and 1880 in the Victorian Gothic style, was oriented toward Central Park. Adjoining wings
of red brick, stone bases, and high-pitched slate roofs were completed in 1888 and 1894 after
plans by Theodore Weston and Arthur L. Tuckerman. This composite structure was virtually
hidden by the monumental Beaux Arts Fifth Avenue façade, which was designed by Richard
Morris Hunt, opened in 1902, and added to by McKim, Mead & White between 1911 and 1926.
Henceforth, the building was oriented toward an urban, rather than bucolic, setting.

Richard Morris Hunt's imposing entrance centers on three monumental arches set between
four pairs of freestanding Corinthian columns on high pedestals, each with its own heavy
entablature. These columns support massive blocks of stone which were intended to be carved as
sculptural groups. The wings on each side (by McKim, Mead & White) offer a more restrained
classical vocabulary that harmonizes with Hunt's central section. In 1924, the Federal-style
marble façade of the old Assay Office building, which had been located on Wall Street from 1824
to 1912, was moved to its present location as a part of the American Wing.

As the museum's collections increased and the institution expanded its activities, more space
was required, and another series of additions was initiated with the building of the Thomas J.
Watson Library in 1964, designed by the firm of Brown, Lawford & Forbes. In the late 1960s,
Kevin Roche/John Dinkeloo & Associates redesigned the staircase at the main Fifth Avenue
entrance; their building program has extended into the 1980s and has included restorations of
the Fifth Avenue façade and Great Hall, and the additions of the Robert Lehman Wing (1975),
the Sackler Wing (1978) with its Temple of Dendur, the American Wing (1980), the Michael C.
Rockefeller Wing (1982), and the recently completed Lila Acheson Wallace Wing (1987), which
houses the twentieth-century art collection. This complex of wings presents an austere,
modernistic façade to Central Park and creates a dialogue of continuing architectural and
historical interest with the original Fifth Avenue exterior.

The interior of the museum accentuates this dialogue between the classical, Beaux Arts idiom
and the modern aesthetic. The entrance vestibule that opens into the Great Hall, designed by
Richard Howland Hunt with the aid of George B. Post after Richard Morris Hunt's death in
1895, is a vast, two-story space that rises beneath three saucer domes with circular skylights; a
gallery in the form of a balcony at the second-floor level intensifies the sense of spaciousness, as
do the colonnades at each side of the room on the main floor. The Grand Staircase, contained
within a long, narrow hallway, sweeps up to the second level, creating a compelling visual axis.
Hunt's grandiose, Roman-inspired spatial schemes give way in more modern rooms to the
angular, somewhat less monumental spaces of the modern style. There is in this progress a logic
of movement and harmony of conception.

Since its beginning, the museum has sought to encourage and develop the study of fine arts
and the applied arts at every level of society. With its continuing expansion and growing
historical collections of truly superb paintings, sculpture, furniture, objects, and architectural
elements, the Metropolitan Museum of Art has become one of the most important and successful
museums in the world.

The Main Hall, 1936

FLATBUSH TOWN HALL, completed 1875
35 Snyder Avenue, Brooklyn
Architect: John Y. Culyer
Designated: October 16, 1973

Constructed on historic ground—near the site of the August, 1776, Battle of Long Island—the Flatbush Town Hall has served as a police headquarters and the seat of the Seventh District Magistrates Court, as well as the locale of social and cultural functions.

The red-brick Victorian Gothic building has buff stone trim accentuated by a series of pointed window arches with carved drip moldings ornamented with bosses. The triple-arched entrance is enhanced by a large central gable, a structural device that crowns the side façades as well. The striking corner tower also has arched windows and a peaked roof above a cornice that rests on corbels. An open terrace, formed by the frontal extension of the building's rusticated granite base, is decorated with limestone balustrades with pierced circular motifs.

A rear addition, consisting of a simple, brown-brick exterior with large, round-arched Georgian Revival windows, was built to house the Homicide Court in 1929–30. Since the relocation of the 67th Police Precinct in 1972, attempts have been under way to transform the building into a civic and cultural center for community use.

WILLIAMSBURGH SAVINGS BANK, 1875; alterations, 1905, 1945
175 Broadway, Brooklyn
Architect: George B. Post
Designated: May 17, 1966

With its massive entrance portico and towering dome, the Williamsburgh Savings Bank in the Williamsburg section of Brooklyn is an impressive and powerful structure. Constructed in the style of the Classical Revival, this four-story building of limestone, sandstone, and marble displays magnificent architectural detail and ornament, such as bronze candelabra flanking the entrance stairs, massive stone quoins at the corners, a rich cornice and lantern, an ornate cast-iron railing extending around the building at street level, and, surmounting the unusual dome, an elaborate cupola topped by a delicate weather vane.

In designing this building, architect George B. Post anticipated by a full generation the American classical resurgence, which was not to come into full flower until after the World's Columbian Exposition of 1893. The structure is one of the finest in Brooklyn.

GAGE & TOLLNER, mid-1870s
372–374 Fulton Street, Brooklyn
Architect: Unknown
Designated: November 12, 1974; interior designated March 25, 1975

A four-story building houses the restaurant Gage & Tollner, which had its beginnings in 1879 when Charles M. Gage opened an eating establishment at 302 Fulton Street. In 1880 Eugene Tollner joined Gage, and in 1882 the restaurant was renamed Gage & Tollner. In 1892 the restaurant moved to 372–374 Fulton Street, in the center of downtown Brooklyn, where it remains today. When Charles M. Gage and Eugene Tollner retired in 1911 they sold the business with the proviso that the new owners maintain the customs established by the founders; that condition was met, and today Gage & Tollner carries on the traditions of 1890s elegance.

The unusually high, Neo-Grec painted wooden storefront that adorns this Italianate building was probably added when the restaurant opened here. The entrance is protected by a portico with modified Doric columns. Secondary entrances set at each side of the front are flanked by slender colonnettes with stylized foliate capitals. A continuous cornice above the ground floor is carried on closely spaced angular brackets with incised motifs, alternating with raised, eight-pointed star motifs in the frieze. A brownstone façade rises above the storefront and a simple modillioned roof cornice with wide fascia crowns the whole.

The interior projects the atmosphere of the Gay Nineties. Patrons wait for their tables in two bays, created by projecting wood-framed windows, that flank the entrance. The ceilings of these bays have a Lincrusta Walton covering, embossed with a sunburst design. The walls have swirling patterns of a more classical type. Arched mirrors with dark red cherry trim lend a sense of spaciousness to the room, which measures only twenty-five by ninety feet. The paneled bar and mahogany tables were transferred from the old restaurant at 302 Fulton Street.

The restaurant uses both gas and electricity for illumination, and it is possibly the only restaurant in New York to do so. This unusual lighting scheme is accomplished by means of the original combination gas-electric fixtures installed from front to rear along the ceiling in 1888.

8 THOMAS STREET, 1875–76
Manhattan
Architect: Jarvis Morgan Slade
Designated: November 14, 1978

Described by the prominent architectural historian Henry-Russell Hitchcock as "one of the handsomest specimens of High Victorian Gothic architecture which survives in the city," the building at 8 Thomas Street was erected in 1875–76 after the designs of a gifted young architect, Jarvis Morgan Slade. Slade was commissioned through the New York Real Estate Association to design a new store for the soap-manufacturing firm of David S. Brown Co., which had selected a site on the new extension of Thomas Street.

Characterized by a red-brick façade with contrasting stone arcades adorned with banded voussoirs, the style of the building is clearly derived from the Venetian Gothic style made popular by the English writer and critic John Ruskin. This narrow, five-story building is three bays wide and is ornamented with a variety of colors and patterns. The ground floor retains the original cast-iron storefront with trabeated bays separated by slender, iron colonnettes and flanked by coursed piers; this motif of the piers is carried into the brickwork of the remaining stories. Other distinguishing features are round arches with pointed extrados, a brick gable crowning the façade, and the abstract, zigzag patterning of the brick.

Although New York once boasted several fine examples of this style, very few survive today. In addition, the building is an interesting reminder of the first large-scale commercial development of the area following the destruction of the grounds of the New York Hospital, which had occupied the site between Broadway, Duane, Church, and Worth streets since 1773.

HENRY BRISTOW SCHOOL, formerly Public School 39, 1876–77
417 Sixth Avenue, Brooklyn
Architect: Attributed to Samuel B. Leonard
Designated: March 8, 1977

Erected in 1876–77 as Public School 39, this building was renamed in 1916 to honor Henry Bristow, whose home had served as a temporary schoolhouse during the building's construction. Believed to have been designed by Samuel B. Leonard, the three-story brick structure is transitional in style, combining distinctive Italianate features—such as round-arched windows, cornices with modillions, and paired brackets—with mansard roofs typical of the French Second Empire style.

The dominant feature of the principal Sixth Avenue façade is a central tower with a rusticated first floor. The recessed, arched main entranceway is surmounted on the second floor by two corbel-headed windows beneath a common lintel. These, in turn, are topped by Venetian windows and, finally, by a pair of round-arched windows joined by a central column and framed by a single stone arch. Flanking this tower are elongated corner pavilions with stone quoins on the first floor and truncated pyramidal roofs. Steep slate mansard roofs with iron crestings extend from these to the tower, and a bold roof cornice with modillions and paired brackets crowns the structure.

STATUE OF LIBERTY NATIONAL MONUMENT,
design begun 1871; constructed 1875–86
Liberty Island, Manhattan
Designers: Frédéric-Auguste Bartholdi (statue); Richard Morris Hunt (pedestal);
Gustave Eiffel (internal bracing)
Designated: September 14, 1976

The Statue of Liberty has welcomed millions of immigrants to the New World. It has become known, worldwide, as the quintessential American monument. The idea for the statue, however, was born in France where, in the constrained climate of the Second Empire, America was seen as the embodiment of liberty and republicanism. Edouard-René Lefebvre de Laboulaye, a scholar of American history and a moderate republican intellectual activist, first suggested the statue at a dinner in 1865: "If a monument to independence were to be built in America, I should think it very natural if it were built by united effort, . . . a common work of both nations." Frédéric-Auguste Bartholdi, an eminent French sculptor, was present at the gathering and soon began collaborating with de Laboulaye on the project.

As a result of a series of political setbacks at home—notably the disastrous defeat of the French in the Franco-Prussian War—Bartholdi was not able to set sail for New York until the summer of 1871. He arrived armed with instructions to study America and to propose a joint monument to liberty. While there he chose the site—Bedloe's Island (renamed Liberty Island in 1956) in New York Harbor—and by the time he returned to France in the fall of 1871, Bartholdi had pretty well decided upon the program of his monument. One contemporary historian described it as "a sublime phrase which sums up the progress of modern times: Liberty Enlightening the World," represented "by a statue of colossal proportions which would surpass all that have ever existed since the most ancient times."

Funding drives began in both countries in 1875: France was to raise the capital to pay for the statue, and the United States would contribute the cost of the pedestal. By 1881 France had raised her contribution of $400,000, and French enthusiasm even inspired Charles Gounod to create his 1876 cantata, *Liberty Enlightening the World*. In the United States, however, the public's response was not so favorable, and by 1885, only half of the required money had been raised. In March, Joseph Pulitzer, publisher of the New York *World*, declared the inability to raise the funds a disgrace and severely chastised this country's rich. Through Pulitzer's efforts, the necessary $100,000 was generated in less than five months.

Bartholdi began the statue in 1875, making a series of clay models and various enlargements in the form of plaster cast fragments, until the projected size of 151 feet was reached. For the final statue wooden molds were made from full-scale plaster fragments, then more than three hundred sheets of copper were riveted and hammered into shape over the molds. The internal structure of wrought-iron bracing was designed by Gustave Eiffel, who entered the project in 1879, ten years before his famous tower opened in Paris. The Statue of Liberty was assembled and displayed in Paris before being shipped, in parts, to New York for reconstruction. The 98-foot granite pedestal and its 65-foot concrete base were designed by Richard Morris Hunt, one of America's most prominent architects and the first American to study at the Ecole des Beaux-Arts in Paris.

On October 28, 1886, the statue was unveiled to the American people. Bartholdi's grandiose project, uniting France and the United States in the common pursuit of freedom and liberty, was finally realized after fifteen years. A century later, on October 28, 1986, Liberty was rededicated after an ambitious renovation financed by the American public, restored to her youthful glory.

PUBLIC SCHOOL 15, 1877
4010 Dyre Avenue, The Bronx
Architect: Simon Williams
Designated: January 10, 1978

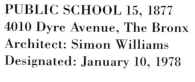

About 1875 Simon Williams, head teacher at a single-room frame schoolhouse near the intersection of Kingsbridge Road and the old White Plains Road in the Bronx, drew up designs for a new schoolhouse. In 1877 his building was erected a few blocks southwest of the former schoolhouse. For the first two years after the school's construction, Williams served as the principal of this school, now known as Public School 15.

Public School 15 stands on a large grassy lot that slopes down behind the building to Rombouts Avenue; its main entrance faces Dyre Avenue. Like many nineteenth-century schoolhouses in metropolitan areas, it has an H-form plan. The façades consist of a gabled pavilion at each end with a lower recessed central section. The pavilions, two stories high with the second story under the gables, stand on rough-faced stone bases. The ground floor of each pavilion is pierced by three segmental-arched windows on the front and rear façades and four identical windows on the sides. At the second story there is a single segmental-arched window in the front and rear gable and bull's-eye windows in the gable sides. A chimney rises through the gable of the side façade of the north pavilion.

Raking cornices carried on paired brackets and returned slightly under the ends of the gables crown the building. Over the central entrance is a dormer window with a gable supported on two brackets; above this and crowning the central section is a bell tower with pyramidal roof topped by a weather vane.

The building is now a community cultural center known as the Little Red Schoolhouse.

175 BELDEN STREET, c. 1880
The Bronx
Architect: Unknown
Designated: July 28, 1981

Cottage architecture, developed during the mid-nineteenth century for simple but comfortable living, is seldom found in urban areas. The house at Belden Street is one of only a few cottages known to exist in New York City. Hundreds of architectural pattern books on cottage building, which had a tremendous impact on nineteenth-century American taste, were published; the design of the Belden Street house was clearly inspired by these books. A prototype appears in *Bicknell's Victorian Architecture*, published in 1878.

The main section of the clapboard, two-and-one-half-story structure abuts a wing on the north side; there is a one-story porch with jigsaw brackets on both sides of the house. The gable windows, decorative bargeboard marking the eaves, bay windows with bracketed shed roofs, crossed stick-work, corbeled brick chimney, and imbricated slate roof are also typical of cottage architecture and closely resemble Bicknell's composition. The small porches, bay windows, and dormers express the domestic purpose of the cottage.

SEVENTH REGIMENT ARMORY, 1878–80; additions, 1909, 1930
643 Park Avenue, Manhattan
Architect: Charles W. Clinton
Designated: June 9, 1967

The Park Avenue façade of the Seventh Regiment Armory evokes the fortified palazzi of north Italian city-states from the thirteenth and fourteenth centuries. The proportions of the three square towers (the central tower was originally topped by a two-story, open bell tower) as well as the insistently flat surfaces of pressed red brick and granite trim mark the building as a High Victorian production. The architect was Charles W. Clinton, a veteran of the regiment and a student of Richard Upjohn, and the premier Gothic revivalist in the United States. Clinton's later work, executed in partnership with William Hamilton Russell, centered on skyscraper design influenced to a certain extent by the Chicago architect Louis Sullivan.

This is the only armory in the United States to be built and furnished with private funds. The interior is distinguished by two features: a large drill floor, covered by an impressive iron roof, and the lavish Veterans' Room and adjoining library (known today as the Trophy Room), designed by a group of artists working under the direction of Louis Comfort Tiffany. Other designers who contributed to the building included the Herter brothers, Alexander Roux, Pottier & Stymus, Kimbel & Cabus, and Marcotte & Co.

In 1909, a floor was added to the administration area; in 1930 a fifth floor was added and the third and fourth floors were redone. The first and second floors, however, are unchanged. A landscaped areaway behind a low railing surrounds the building on all but the Lexington Avenue side. The armory is a National Historic Landmark.

The Seventh Regiment was formed in 1806. It has a long list of battle honors (including service in the War of 1812, the Civil War, and both world wars). During public disturbances (such as the civil riots of the 1830s and '40s) the regiment controlled and subdued civilian crowds and protected private and city property from looting and vandalism. Prior to the armory's construction, several companies of the regiment were dispersed around the city. In 1880, the regiment marched into its permanent home; a grand ball for New York's affluent citizens followed this splendid ceremony.

BROOKLYN HISTORICAL SOCIETY BUILDING INTERIOR,
formerly Long Island Historical Society, 1878–81
128 Pierrepont Street, Brooklyn
Architect: George B. Post
Designated: March 23, 1982

Modern techniques employed in conjunction with a stylistic unity produced the most striking internal feature of this building—a light-filled library with sufficient stack space. On three sides, windows extend from the reading-room level to the balcony level. The north and south walls display three round-headed windows with geometrically patterned stained glass attributed to Charles Booth; five similar windows are located on the east wall. The room itself contains an octagonal gallery, punctuated by alternating rectilinear and curvilinear posts.

Throughout the structure, black ash bookcases, tables, columns, and railings provide a subtle contrast to this essentially bright and open space. The massive bookcases are ornamented with diagonally arranged panels and a delicate sunburst motif suggestive of the Queen Anne style. Even the twenty-four columns at the ends of the bookcases on the main level, which enhance the massive quality of the room with bracket-capped pilasters, were carefully designed to avoid impeding the flow of light. By using iron columnar supports enclosed in newly developed machine-carved casings, George Post was able to make the structures less bulky.

Another interesting feature of the library is a freestanding paneled wainscot railing with entrances at each corner of the main room. Both the walls and the ceiling are finished in white, to contrast with the dark wood. Through such continual balance of texture and form, Post—whose work includes the New York Hospital, City College, and the Wisconsin State Capitol—created a structure that reflects the prestige of cultural institutions at the turn of the century, and the consequent attention to detail displayed by these institutions.

ROBBINS & APPLETON BUILDING, 1879–80
1–5 Bond Street, Manhattan
Architect: Stephen Decatur Hatch
Designated: June 19, 1979

This splendid five-story cast-iron building, one of the finest of its period, was built for Henry Robbins and Daniel Appleton, proprietors of the American Waltham Watch Company, which manufactured watch cases here (and carried on most of its watch business next door in the big cast-iron building at 7 Bond Street). The words "Waltham Watches" appeared in gold letters over the two arched windows of 1 Bond Street's center dormer, while above them was once a large clock face. The high-ceilinged ground floor provided headquarters for D. Appleton & Co., publishers, who also occupied two other floors.

Architect Stephen Decatur Hatch used the French Second Empire style for the building, giving it a mansard roof, the dormered end towers of which suggest symmetrical pavilions. A cast-iron cresting ran along the top of the roof.

When the Landmarks Preservation Commission designated the structure an official landmark, research revealed that an earlier cast-iron-front building on the site had been destroyed by fire in 1877. It is interesting to note that an 1876 woodcut shows this earlier Bond Street building to be nearly identical with the present 1 Bond Street, and records prove that it was also designed by Stephen Hatch for Robbins and Appleton. It is thought that many of the original wooden patterns were reused in making the casts for the new building.

COACHMAN'S RESIDENCE, H. F. SPAULDING HOUSE, 1879–80; moved, 1909; remodeled, 1914
4970 Independence Avenue, The Bronx
Architect: Charles W. Clinton
Designated: July 28, 1981

The Spaulding coachman's house was built as part of an exclusive rural community of private country villas and gardens called The Park, Riverdale. Designed by Charles W. Clinton, the Stick style house was originally part of Henry Foster Spaulding's estate, Parkside.

Head of the woolens firm of Spaulding, Vail & Fuller and the commissions business of Spaulding, Hunt & Co., Spaulding was a prominent community leader and a member of Governor Samuel J. Tilden's committee that overthrew the notorious Tweed ring. Together with New York businessmen William E. Dodge and Percy Pyne, he founded The Park, Riverdale, in 1856. Parkside came into the possession of Percy Pyne, Jr., after Spaulding's death in 1893 and was subsequently incorporated into George Walbridge Perkins's estate, Wave Hill, about 1900. During the 1930s, Parkside and the neighboring estate Oaklawn were made available by Mrs. Perkins to the Riverdale Country School, although the Spaulding coachman's house was retained as part of the Perkins estate.

Originally located on the west side of Independence Avenue—then a carriage route named Palisade Avenue—the coachman's house was moved across the street in 1909 and remodeled in 1914. Another cottage had also been moved to the site in 1909, and the two were joined by an extension added in 1968. Despite these modifications, the picturesque cottage retains much of its original structure and appearance. Its two-story façade is sheathed with board-and-batten siding on the first floor; the second floor has crisscrossed exterior boards which suggest a structural purpose, as if revealing the framing that lies behind them. A steep roof of polychrome slate tops intersecting and overhanging gables with bracketed eaves and jigsaw-ornamented dormer windows. There is a bracketed porch at the entrance. The house is now a private residence.

CENTURY BUILDING, 1880–81
33 East 17th Street and 38–46 East 18th Street, Manhattan
Architect: William Schickel
Designated: October 7, 1986

The Century Building is one of the few surviving commercial examples of the Queen Anne style in the city. The style is distinguished by the picturesque mixture of seventeenth- and eighteenth-century English motifs. The tall oriel window, gambrel roof, prominent chimneys, and molded terra-cotta ornament that we find here are all characteristic of the style. Although classical details are commonly used (such as the Jacobean doorway), these are combined in an unusual and thoroughly unclassical way.

The building takes its name from the Century Co., publishers of *The Century* and *St. Nicholas* magazines, which had offices there. *The Century* was a noted literary publication, carrying work by Twain, James, Whitman, and Melville. Another prominent tenant of the building was the architect George B. Post.

Schickel might have used the Queen Anne style, which was common in domestic suburban designs but almost unknown in urban commercial structures, to draw attention to what was essentially a speculative office building. The Union Square area was booming in the last quarter of the nineteenth century. Unusual or distinctive building design would have been one way of appealing to potential tenants, especially those who thought themselves socially or artistically progressive. Championed by such artists and writers as James McNeill Whistler and Oscar Wilde, the Queen Anne style developed along with the English aesthetic movement.

ASTOR ROW
West 130th Street between Fifth and Lenox avenues, Manhattan
Designated: August 11, 1981

8–22 West 130th Street, 1880–81
Architect: Charles Buek

40–62 West 130th Street, 1883
Architect: After Charles Buek

24–38 West 130th Street, 1882–83
Architect: After Charles Buek

The group of buildings known as Astor Row is made up of twenty-eight houses, effectively grouped in pairs, that extend along most of the south side of 130th Street between Fifth and Lenox avenues. Built as a speculative development in the 1880s on land owned by William Astor, the group forms a splendid street front, recalling the period when Harlem was evolving from a rural country town to an urbanized area. The Astor Row houses were designed by Charles Buek, who was known for creating elaborate private homes and apartments for wealthy clients. The style Buek chose to employ in the Astor Row houses was not only distinct from his other structures, but was also unlike that of most other row houses being built at the time.

The houses were constructed in three groups: 8–22 were built in 1880–81, 24–38 in 1882–83, and 40–62 in 1883. Only the first group was constructed under Buek's supervision; the last two were built without the help of an architect but were almost identical to those in the first group. The most significant difference is that 24–62 stand as a single row, rather than as freestanding pairs of houses. This difference is minimized by the deep recesses between each pair of houses, which give the effect of separated buildings.

Neo-Grec details distinguish the Astor Row houses. These details, typified by the simple, linear incised design in the lintels, were commonly found on commercial cast-iron buildings. Three stories high, the buildings are constructed of brick with light stone trim. Each pair is symmetrical, with the center indicated by a projecting brick pier topped by a stone triglyph at the cornice line. Each house is two bays wide and has double doors and a full-height window on the first floor. On the upper stories, each bay has a double-hung window surmounted by a broad, shouldered stone lintel whose midpoint is emphasized by a small triangular extension that points down in front of the window molding. A simple, projecting stringcourse wraps around the building at each sill line, with footed sills located just below. A complete entablature crowns the front of these houses. It is composed of a simple projecting stone architrave surmounted by a brick frieze with recessed quatrefoil motifs. A cornice with brick dentils finishes the roofline.

Originally, each house had a large wooden porch running the full width of the building. Many of the porches are still in place, although some have been either rebuilt, replaced, or removed.

THE DAKOTA APARTMENTS, 1880–84
1 West 72nd Street, Manhattan
Architect: Henry J. Hardenbergh
Designated: February 11, 1969

In 1884 the Dakota Apartments opened its doors at 72nd Street across from a still-unlandscaped section of Central Park. The rather desolate area around the Dakota was dotted with squatters' shacks, and the odd goat, cow, and chicken could be seen in the neighborhood. Many New Yorkers were astounded, most were skeptical, but Singer Sewing Machine magnate Edward S. Clark's dreams for developing the Upper West Side soon proved well founded. His building, designed by Henry J. Hardenbergh, was fully rented even before it opened its doors, and this at a time when apartment houses, like hotels, were looked upon as "architectural inducements to immorality." Clark's prosperous tenants, unconcerned with the lack of East Side fashionability, had no difficulty overcoming that prejudice. The Dakota, after all, "guaranteed . . . comforts which would require unlimited wealth in a private residence."

"Clark's Folly," as it was dubbed soon after building began in 1880, was not the first luxury apartment building in New York City, but it quickly became the most famous. Clark defiantly resisted public opinion and called his building the Dakota after the remote U.S. Indian territory of the same name. Hardenbergh was instructed to make full decorative use of the Wild West metaphor throughout: motifs such as arrowheads and sheaves of wheat embellish both exterior and interior. A carved Indian head looks out over 72nd Street from above the main entrance.

The imposing eight-story yellow brick and stone-trimmed structure reflects the romanticism of the German Renaissance style. The principal façades—the north, south, and east (the west, overlooking a lawn which later became a tennis court, was unembellished)—are divided horizontally and vertically into three sections. Horizontally the divisions between the basement, the main body, and the roof are boldly accented by cornices, balconies, and railings. Vertically the building is defined by a simple series of bays. The central bay is slightly recessed from the end bays, which on the south façade are stressed by seventh-story rounded oriel windows. The elaborate roof, with turrets, gables, chimneys, and dormers, continues the tripartite symmetry.

The Dakota offered the some 200 inhabitants of its sixty-five ornate apartments complete seclusion from the bustle of New York City. The exterior walls at the base are approximately twenty-eight inches thick, and the three-foot-deep floors were constructed of alternating layers of brick and Central Park mud. A moat, bordered by an iron fence punctuated with the heads of sea gods intertwined with sea urchins, surrounds the exterior. The building has an inner courtyard, originally conceived as a carriage turnaround. In order to give tenants a sense of the privacy of the single dwelling, Otis hydraulic passenger elevators were installed in the small lobbies of the four courtyard corner entrances. Another set of elevators serviced the kitchens.

The Dakota soon became the conversation piece of New York, not merely as an architectural oddity, but also, and increasingly, because of its famous tenants. Boris Karloff's ghost is said to roam the corridors, and its past and present inhabitants include Lauren Bacall, Leonard Bernstein, Roberta Flack, John Lennon, and Yoko Ono.

677–679 Lafayette Avenue

Magnolia grandiflora

THE MAGNOLIA GRANDIFLORA HOUSES
Lafayette Avenue, Brooklyn

678 Lafayette Avenue, 1880–83
Architect: Unknown
Designated; July 12, 1977

679 Lafayette Avenue, 1880–83
Architect: Unknown
Designated: July 12, 1977

Magnolia grandiflora, c. 1885
679 Lafayette Avenue
Designated: May 12, 1970

677 Lafayette Avenue, 1890
Architect: L. C. Holden
Designated; July 12, 1977

Some twenty species of the genus *Magnolia* are distributed throughout Japan, China, the Himalayas, and the southeastern United States. The most beautiful of the North American species is the *Magnolia grandiflora*, an evergreen that grows with a straight trunk to a height of over seventy feet. The species *grandiflora*, bearing large, white, lemon-scented flowers that are the official state flowers of both Louisiana and Mississippi, rarely flourishes north of Philadelphia. It is remarkable, therefore, that the seedling that William Lemken received from North Carolina in the mid-1800s and planted in the front yard of his house at 679 Lafayette Avenue should have survived so long.

The person who, almost singlehandedly, has been responsible for arousing local appreciation of the tree is Hattie Carthan, affectionately known as "the tree lady." The movement she began in the early 1950s resulted in its designation as a landmark and in the construction of a protective wing-wall of masonry to the north.

Three houses, also designated landmarks, surround the tree. Number 677 Lafayette Avenue was built in 1890 from designs by the New York architect L. C. Holden. Three stories high above a basement, this Romanesque Revival town house combines rock-faced brownstone at the lower stories with brick and terra-cotta trim at the upper stories. An attractive feature of the front façade is a shallow corbel, placed in the top course of stonework, and adorned at each end by handsome bas-relief foliate carving that supports the projecting sill of the wide second-floor window. Numbers 678 and 679 Lafayette Avenue are nearly identical, three-story Neo-Grec residences built in the early 1880s.

JAMES WHITE BUILDING, 1881–82
361 Broadway, Manhattan
Architect: W. Wheeler Smith
Designated: July 27, 1982

Number 361 Broadway, at the southwest corner of Broadway and Franklin streets, was constructed in 1881–82. Built for James White, who had inherited the property from his father, who had been in the hat trade, it is one of the few late stylized cast-iron structures in an area largely built up before the Civil War, and is one of the largest cast-iron structures in the city. Designed by W. Wheeler Smith, a well-respected New York architect, this building is one of his few forays into the field of cast-iron architecture.

Based on the design of the Italian palazzo, the house has two façades composed of columns supporting heavy entablatures, and adorned with some of the finest and most inventive cast-iron ornamentation based on abstract floral forms that change from floor to floor. The building is six stories high, six bays wide on Broadway, and eighteen bays wide along Franklin Street. The six Broadway bays are defined by a row of columns terminated at each end by square piers; attached to each pier is a quarter-pilaster, creating the illusion of a row of columns that continues into the piers—a convention dating back to fifteenth-century Italy. The architrave, cornice, and panel-linked pedestals at each floor combine to form a powerful horizontal effect.

For over a century this building has been connected with the textile trade, which is concentrated at nearby Worth Street. The building is still in use commercially, and survives as an example of the country's most extraordinary indigenous artistic developments—cast-iron architecture.

ST. VINCENT FERRER COMPLEX
869 Lexington Avenue and 141–151 East 65th Street, Manhattan

Priory, 1880–81
Architect: William Schickel
Designated: May 19, 1981

Holy Name Society Building, 1930
Architect: Wilfrid E. Anthony
Designated: May 19, 1981

Church, 1918
Architect: Bertram G. Goodhue
Designated: February 28, 1967

School, 1948
Architects: Elliot L. Chisling-Ferrenz & Taylor
Designated: May 19, 1981

The St. Vincent Ferrer complex was developed by the Roman Catholic order of the Dominican fathers, who purchased the site in 1867. The first church here, finished in 1869, was the work of Patrick C. Keely, the noted Roman Catholic Gothic Revivalist. Bertram G. Goodhue's church replaced this. In plan, the more recent structure is a long rectangle with chancel and friar's chapel to the east. The style is the architect's own distinctive version of late Gothic. The exterior facing is rough-cut, split Plymouth granite with limestone trim. The crucifixion panel over the entrance and the figures that emerge from the octagonal turrets are the work of Goodhue's frequent collaborator, Lee Lawrie. Inside, Guastavino tile vaulting fills the area between the ribs that connect the nave arcades; the whole is a kind of abstracted Gothic design.

The Priory was influenced by English Gothic Revival designs, especially in the use of pointed arches in the ground story and central pavilion. The flat-headed windows with light, brownstone lintels above are close to the commercial designs (the so-called Neo-Grec) developed by Richard Morris Hunt in the 1860s. In 1930, Wilfrid E. Anthony designed the six-story Holy Name Society Building for various charities. The stone and brick structure is symmetrically massed about a recessed central section. The shallow buttresses through the second story are copied from Goodhue's church, as is the wonderfully imaginative reticulated panel tracery in the eastern pavilion. Anthony's design combines elements of those earlier works without being a pastiche. The design of the 1948 school, although less successful, is also mindful of the earlier Gothic Revival work.

HENRY VILLARD HOUSES, 1882–86
457 Madison Avenue and 24–26 East 51st Street, Manhattan
Architect: McKim, Mead & White
Designated: September 30, 1968

A Bavarian émigré, Henry Villard started his career as a journalist for English- and German-language dailies; he would eventually have a controlling interest in the New York *Evening Post*. In 1872, he was hired by a group of German businessmen to look after their investments in an Oregon railroad operation. At the same time, he acquired an interest in East Coast shipping firms, and before long he was a millionaire. In 1881, he purchased the Madison Avenue site for his city mansion opposite St. Patrick's Cathedral, and commissioned McKim, Mead & White to design six luxury town houses, most of which he hoped eventually to sell.

Responsibility for the design fell to White's chief assistant, Joseph Morrill Wells, who transformed White's preliminary plans into a powerful, Renaissance-inspired complex, using the Palazzo della Cancelleria in Rome as a model. This choice of a model signaled the firm's move away from Richardsonian Romanesque and Queen Anne work toward the classicism that became the foundation of its reputation. Wells died of tuberculosis in 1890; the Villard Houses hint that he might have become a true architectural genius.

Wells placed the six four-story houses in a U shape around a central courtyard. This novel arrangement was ideally suited to the site, across Madison Avenue from St. Patrick's Cathedral, because the church also had an open area facing the street. Together, these spaces gave the feeling of a large expanse of green. The town houses were designed to appear as a single building. They have a rusticated ground story separated from the upper stories by a small cornice. Quoins tie the second and third stories together. Above the heavy main cornice was an attic story and a tile roof. Villard's house, occupying the entire south wing, was the largest of the six. Two houses filled the east courtyard side, and two more, the north. The fifth house was entered not from the courtyard but from 51st Street, and occupied the northeast corner of the complex.

Shortly after the building was completed, Villard's financial difficulties forced him to sell his home. His wing was purchased by Mrs. Whitelaw Reid, wife of the publisher of the New York *Tribune*. That suite and the others continued to be used as residences until after World War II, when the changing character of Madison Avenue led to their conversion into offices. The Villard Houses served for many years as the headquarters of the Roman Catholic Archdiocese of New York, Random House, and the Capital Cities Broadcasting System. All but Capital Cities eventually outgrew the space, however, and by the 1970s the houses were facing demolition.

In early 1980, after complicated and lengthy negotiations, the Helmsley Corporation purchased the houses' air rights to build the fifty-one story Helmsley Palace Hotel. The two houses on the east side of the courtyard were destroyed to build the hotel, which incorporates the main public rooms of the Villard suite as a tea room and lounge. Capital Cities/ABC and the Urban Center, with its tenants the Municipal Art Society and the New York Chapter of the American Institute of Architects, now occupy what remains of the rest of the buildings.

ASSOCIATION RESIDENCE FOR WOMEN, originally the Association Residence for Respectable Aged Indigent Females, 1881–83; addition, 1907–08
891 Amsterdam Avenue, Manhattan
Architect: Richard Morris Hunt; addition, Charles A. Rich
Designated: April 12, 1983

This building was erected in 1881–83 for one of New York's oldest charitable institutions, the Association for the Relief of Respectable Aged Indigent Females. Chartered in 1814, the association was founded by a group of socially prominent women to aid the less fortunate— specifically, those women who were left poor widows by the War of 1812 or the Revolution. The association's first building was at 226 East 20th Street, and was erected in 1837–38.

Richard Morris Hunt, one of the most influential American architects of the nineteenth century, was chosen as the designer of the new building. The Victorian Gothic style shows Hunt's hand, particularly in the picturesque mansard slate roof with dormers and the Gothic pointed arches, as well as Neo-Grec detail. The addition, by architect Charles A. Rich, extends and duplicates the original Hunt elevation on Amsterdam Avenue for an additional five bays.

After 1965, when the interior was remodeled, the building became known as the Association Residence for Women. Closed in 1974, the building was severely damaged by fire in 1977. It is now being restored as a youth hostel.

GORHAM BUILDING, 1883–84; alterations, 1893
889–891 Broadway, Manhattan
Architect: Edward Hale Kendall
Designated: June 19, 1984

The Gorham Building, built in 1883–84, was designed by the noted architect Edward Hale Kendall and is one of his few surviving buildings. Erected for Robert and Ogden Goelet when this section of Broadway was a fashionable shopping district, the building housed the store of the Gorham Manufacturing Co., a producer of fine silver, in its lower two floors.

An unusual remaining example of the Queen Anne style, the Gorham Building is noted for its picturesque massing and rich ornamental detail. The structure is eight stories high and constructed of pink brick with brick and light gray Belleville sandstone trim; the high-pitched slate roof with green copper elements adds to the building's appeal. Stepped gables, dormers, and small windows with copper hoods project from the roof. The ornament of the building, its most characteristic Queen Anne feature, becomes more elaborate at the top, and includes decorated segmental arches and panels embellished with sunflowers and other floral motifs.

The alterations made to the structure were carried out by its original architect, in the same basic style, in 1893. Although primarily associated with the Gorham company's silver store, the building is unusual for its early combination of commercial and residential use. Today, after many decades as a strictly commercial building, the Gorham is once more residential.

CHELSEA APARTMENTS, formerly Chelsea Hotel, 1883
222 West 23rd Street, Manhattan
Architects: Hubert, Pirsson & Co.
Designated: March 15, 1966

The flamboyant Chelsea Hotel is one of the oldest surviving cooperative apartment houses in New York City. Designed by P. G. Hubert, the building was planned in collaboration with artists who wished to have studio space adjacent to their living quarters. Although converted to a hotel for permanent and transient residents in 1905, it has maintained associations with the arts, as home to many artists, writers, and musicians, including Thomas Wolfe, Dylan Thomas, Edgar Lee Masters, John Sloan, Robert Flaherty, Samuel Clemens, Eugene O'Neill, Janis Joplin, Andy Warhol, Sam Shepard, Bob Dylan, and Tennessee Williams.

The most striking architectural features of this eleven-story building are the wrought-iron balconies decorated with interlaced sunflowers. This motif and the high, clustered brick chimneys and patterned brick gables were inspired by the Queen Anne style, while the flattened segmental arches and horizontal granite divisions were a later American development from French Neo-Grec designs. Richard Morris Hunt was the first to combine aspects of contemporary English and French designs, particularly in his Presbyterian Hospital on 70th Street between Madison and Park avenues (1869–72; demolished).

In addition to his role as an innovator in fireproof building technology, Hubert was an ardent supporter of apartment house (then called "French flats") reform. He advocated masonry walls, thick floors, and duplex arrangements with spacious rooms as an alternative to the speculatively built, overcrowded middle-class apartment. Hubert built eight apartment buildings in New York City. In the first cooperative apartments, the tenants—in exchange for cheaper rents and larger rooms—did without costly plumbing and other less essential luxury features. Restaurants and private kitchens were located on lower floors, as no apartments had permanent cooking facilities. The ground floor was let to commercial establishments, all to defray the cost of building quiet, ample apartments. In addition, tenants contributed toward the maintenance of the building itself. The movement had declined by the turn of the century.

NEW YORK PUBLIC LIBRARY, OTTENDORFER BRANCH, 1883–84
135 Second Avenue, Manhattan
Architect: William Schickel
Designated: September 20, 1977; interior designated August 11, 1981

The Ottendorfer is the oldest branch library in Manhattan and the first one built specifically as a library. In 1884, even before the building was completed, the Ottendorfers turned the library over to the New York Free Circulating Library, with which the Lenox and Tilden libraries were soon to combine to form the branch system of the New York Public Library. At the time of the building's construction, the Lower East Side was filled with German immigrants; Oswald Ottendorfer, himself a German-American, wanted to help recent immigrants to assimilate into American culture and educate themselves. With this purpose in mind, he personally selected the first library volumes, which were equally divided between German and English titles.

It is not surprising, then, that these German-American philanthropists should do as the Astors had done nearly forty years before at the Astor Library (now the Public Theater), and hire a German-born and -trained architect. William Schickel immigrated to New York in 1870 and worked as a draftsman in several important city firms, the most prominent being that of Richard Morris Hunt. The design of the Ottendorfer Library reflects Schickel's varied design background. The Renaissance-inspired, arched entry porch and terra-cotta arcading above belong to the German *Rundbogenstil* tradition. The flattened arches with alternating voussoirs of brick and ornamental terra-cotta blocks, on the other hand, are closer to the commercial style developed by Hunt in the late 1860s.

Originally, the library's cast-iron stacks were closed to the public; books were brought to the main circulation desk. During a remodeling in the 1890s, in response to contemporary ideas of library design, the library converted to an open-shelf system.

The terra-cotta ornamentation includes many symbols of the library's function: urns and books fill the spandrel panels beneath the windows, and the frieze above the elliptical entry arch is embellished by owls and globes, which stand for wisdom and knowledge; over the door is the inscription "Freie Bibliothek u. Lesehalle" (Free library and reading room). The ornamentation and attractive coloration distinguish the library from the surrounding nineteenth-century tenements and more recent undistinguished commercial structures.

CROTON AQUEDUCT GATE HOUSE, 1884–90
135th Street and Convent Avenue, Manhattan
Architect: Frederick S. Cook
Designated: March 23, 1981

Constructed in the manner of a medieval fortress, the Croton Aqueduct Gate House was built as part of a plan to alleviate poor sanitary conditions in New York City. Its massive appearance symbolically relays the importance of its dual role—to provide safe drinking water and to serve as a reservoir for local fire brigades.

The gate house conceals a complex series of water chambers, sluice gates, stop planks, and stopcocks designed to contain and convey water from the old and new Croton aqueducts. Arched granite piers form the eight small pipe chambers used to send water both north of the reservoir and south, to Central Park. The water flowed easily from the building's elevated location. In the meantime, it was held in a chamber over forty-three feet deep with eighteen-inch granite floors and two-foot-thick granite walls.

The exterior is unusually picturesque. An entrance pavilion, an octagonal tower, and an open terrace emphasize its rectangular shape, and massive voussoirs decorate the window and doorway openings, complemented by granite parapets with inset diamonds.

Although the interior is closed to the public, its decoration too is noteworthy. The walls inside the gate house combine yellow brick with buff and black trim. All in all, their hidden yet intensely colorful coordination reflects the level of design possible in a utilitarian structure.

STUYVESANT POLYCLINIC, formerly the German Dispensary, 1883–84
137 Second Avenue, Manhattan
Architect: William Schickel
Designated: November 9, 1976

The building at 137 Second Avenue, designed by William Schickel, was commissioned by Anna and Oswald Ottendorfer, philanthropists who concerned themselves with the welfare of the German immigrant community in the city.

Dispensaries were the nineteenth-century equivalent of health clinics, providing medical care free of charge. The German Dispensary, or health clinic, which was founded in 1857, became a branch of the German Hospital (today's Lenox Hill) at Park Avenue and East 77th Street. In 1906 the building was sold to the German Polyklinik, and renovated and repaired. The name was changed to Stuyvesant Polyclinic as a result of the anti-German sentiment that was rampant during World War I. In the 1970s, the dispensary became affiliated with the Cabrini Medical Center.

The building is a handsomely ornate version of Italian Renaissance Revival design. It is constructed of Philadelphia pressed brick above a stone basement, with ornamental detail executed in molded terra-cotta. The façade is especially noted for its portrait busts of famous physicians and scientists, including the English physiologist William Harvey, Swedish botanist Carolus Linnaeus, German scientist and explorer Karl Wilhelm von Humboldt, French chemist Antoine Laurent Lavoisier, and German physician and author Christoph Wilhelm Hufeland.

DEVINNE PRESS BUILDING, 1885
393–399 Lafayette Street, Manhattan
Architects: Babb, Cook & Willard
Designated: October 19, 1966

A bold example of architectural inventiveness, the DeVinne Press Building exerted enormous influence on turn-of-the-century commercial architecture. This eight-story brick and terra-cotta structure was named after Theodore DeVinne, who in his time was an expert without equal in the history of the art of printing and in its practice. Among his products were *Scribner's Monthly*, *St. Nicholas Magazine*, and *Century Illustrated Monthly Magazine*.

Designed by Babb, Cook & Willard in the Romanesque style, the building's elevations display interesting contrasts of round- and segmental-arched windows. It has a low-pitched roof and quoins at the rounded corner of the building. Brick gable-end and round-arched attic windows contribute a distinctive note.

THE NATIONAL ARTS CLUB, formerly Samuel J. Tilden Residence, 1881–84
15 Gramercy Park South, Manhattan
Architect: Calvert Vaux
Designated: March 15, 1966

Samuel J. Tilden purchased the house at 15 Gramercy Park South in 1863. He hired Griffith Thomas to remodel the structure, and took residence there in 1866. The house soon became a center of power, where Tilden—who was to become governor of New York in 1874 and the Democratic contender for the presidency in 1876—entertained politicians, businessmen, and friends.

Tilden bought the adjoining house at 14 Gramercy Park South in 1874, but it was not until 1881 that he asked Calvert Vaux to combine the two structures into a single home. Construction was completed in 1884 at a cost of $500,000. The exterior of the two houses was finished in the Gothic Revival style. Griffith Thomas's Renaissance Revival rooms were left intact, but the whole of the parlor floor at number 14 was redesigned in the new Aesthetic style of the 1880s. Three rooms were combined to make a magnificent library, with oak carvings, a blue tiled ceiling, and a backlighted stained-glass dome, with brass frame, by Donald MacDonald. The front two parlor rooms had great sliding doors designed to close off the windows; Tilden, who had helped to bring about the downfall of the Tweed ring, was fearful of an assassination attempt. The stained glass in the front parlor of number 15 was designed by John La Farge for the vestibule doors of the front entranceway.

Tilden died in 1886, and the bulk of his estate was combined with the Lenox and Astor libraries to form the New York Public Library. The house was bought in 1906 by the National Arts Club, which occupies it today. The building is a National Historic Landmark.

ST. CECILIA'S CHURCH AND CONVENT
Manhattan
Designated: September 14, 1976

St. Cecilia's Church, 1883–87	St. Cecilia's Convent, 1883–84 and 1885–86;
120 East 106th Street	additions, 1887; façade, 1907
Architects: Napoleon LeBrun & Sons	112 East 106th Street
	Architects: Unknown; Neville & Bagge (façade)

The cornerstone of St. Cecilia's was laid in 1883, and the following year the congregation held its first service in the completed basement chapel. Napoleon Le Brun & Sons provided the plans, working drawings, and specifications for the construction of the church. The Reverend Michael J. Phelan, pastor of the parish (and known throughout the diocese as "The Builder of Churches"), served as general contractor for construction.

St. Cecilia's Church, faced with textured red brick and terra-cotta, follows a simplified basilica plan in the Romanesque tradition. A large arch in the central gable frames a high-relief terra-cotta panel depicting the patron saint of music, St. Cecilia, playing an organ, accompanied by a cherub. The portico has three arches surmounted by gables. Situated between the relief and the portico is a band of seven stained-glass windows. Octagonal towers flank the façade.

The building that is now St. Cecilia's Convent was originally two separate buildings; number 112–114, a four-family tenement house built in 1883–84, and 116–118, a two-story schoolhouse built in 1885–86 and expanded to four stories in 1887. In 1907 the firm of Neville & Bagge united the two buildings behind a single façade, faced with brick, brownstone, and terra-cotta. The Romanesque detailing of the church was repeated for the convent, which has the same decorative terra-cotta moldings and round-arched windows. The building is four stories high above a raised basement and has a central bay with a cross mounted on the roof above it.

PIER A, 1884–86; additions, 1900, 1908
Battery Park, Manhattan
Engineer: George Sears Greene, Jr.
Designated: July 12, 1977

Pier A, a picturesque structure jutting into Upper New York Bay, is the last survivor of a maritime complex that once included a firehouse, a wharf for its fireboats, a breakwater, a boat landing, and Pier New 1 (which had magnificent granite arches). For many years distinguished visitors to the city who arrived by sea were officially greeted at Pier A; today it is the headquarters of the marine division of the New York Fire Department. The clock on the tower, installed in 1919, was donated by Daniel G. Reid as a memorial to the soldiers, sailors, and marines who lost their lives in World War I. It is one of only two clocks on the eastern seaboard whose chimes ring the hours in ship's time (the other is located at the U.S. Naval Academy in Annapolis, Maryland).

Pier A was built by the New York City Docks Department in 1884–86 under the direction of its chief engineer, George Sears Greene, Jr. Structurally, the pier consists of eight subpiers, connected iron girders and concrete arches. The inshore end of the building was built of brick and terra-cotta with a tin roof, while the offshore end of the building was built with a conventional wood-frame skeleton and clad with galvanized iron siding. In 1900 and 1908 additions were made at the inshore end. This complex makes a handsome boundary for the northern end of Battery Park.

THE TOWERS NURSING HOME, formerly the New York Cancer Hospital, 1884–86; additions, 1889–90, 1925–26
Central Park West at 106th Street, Manhattan
Architect: Charles Coolidge Haight
Designated: August 17, 1976

Prominently sited on Central Park West and West 106th Street, the former New York Cancer Hospital was built in three sections between 1884 and 1890 from plans by the noted New York City architect Charles Coolidge Haight.

The hospital was founded in 1884 to further the study and treatment of cancer. The original building, funded by John Jacob Astor and known as the Astor Pavilion, housed female cancer patients. In 1889–90 an addition for male patients was built on the adjoining site on West 105th Street, also given by Astor in memory of his wife, Charlotte Augusta Astor. A chapel was added at the same time as a memorial for founder Elizabeth Hamilton Cullum. In 1899 the hospital became the General Memorial Hospital for the Treatment of Cancer and Allied Diseases. An X-ray building, attached to the 1889–90 addition, was constructed in 1925–26. In the 1950s after the hospital ceased operation the building was converted for use as a nursing home. It is presently vacant.

Built to resemble a French château, the structure is a complex arrangement of masses dominated by its five corner towers. Constructed of red brick with sandstone trim, its distinguishing features include the mansard roof, conical tower roofs, decorative gabled dormers, colonnettes, and late English Gothic detail and surface ornament. The building's unusual design features included circular wards, which allowed for generous amounts of light and pure air and prevented the accumulation of dirt in corners. Its technological advances, originating in nineteenth-century medical theory, made the hospital a model of its kind.

GIRLS' HIGH SCHOOL, 1885–86; addition, 1912
475 Nostrand Avenue, Brooklyn
Architect: James W. Naughton; addition, C.B.J. Snyder
Designated: June 28, 1983

Girls' High School at 475 Nostrand Avenue was one of the first public secondary schools in Brooklyn. It was designed in a striking and dynamic combination of the Victorian Gothic and French Second Empire styles by James W. Naughton, who as superintendent of buildings for the Board of Education in Brooklyn from 1879 to 1898 designed all the schools built there during this period. A later addition along the Macon Street side was designed by C.B.J. Snyder in the Collegiate Gothic style and opened in 1912.

Girls' High School is a symmetrically massed structure composed of three pavilions. Use of a dramatic central tower, first seen in the Chelsea section of Manhattan, was typical of school design in New York City until the twentieth century. Here, the tower has a tall pyramidal roof topped by a square belfry, with a stone Corinthian portico capped with a balustrade over the main entrance.

This is an outstanding example of school architecture by one of its leading practitioners. Together with Boys' High School it served as the prototype for many schools in the city.

KREISCHER HOUSE, c. 1885
4500 Arthur Kill Road, Staten Island
Architect: Unknown
Designated: February 20, 1968

This two-and-one-half-story Victorian residence was named for its first owner, Balthasar Kreischer, owner of a brick-manufacturing company. The frame house was executed in the so-called Stick style; the extensive decorative patterns and forms have evoked comparisons to both Mississippi riverboats and nineteenth-century Swiss chalets.

The house is partially encircled by an old-fashioned veranda that follows the polygonal form of the base of a three-story tower, asymmetrically placed at the corner. The porch roof is supported by widely spaced posts carrying an ornate railing. A top-floor balcony with a projecting gable overhang is supported by two diagonal brackets. This gable and the triangular panels beneath it are enhanced by jigsaw filigree designs.

ASTRAL APARTMENTS, 1885–86
184 Franklin Street, Brooklyn
Architects: Lamb & Rich
Designated: June 28, 1983

The Astral Apartments is a massive, six-story apartment house faced with brick and terra-cotta, occupying an entire block on the east side of Franklin Street between India and Java streets in the Greenpoint section of Brooklyn. In 1885–86, Charles Pratt, oil merchant and philanthropist, built the apartments for workers in the Greenpoint area. Designed by the New York architectural firm of Lamb & Rich, the building was considered highly innovative at the time of its construction, incorporating a number of features that improved on contemporary standards for workers' housing, including a kitchen in each apartment with scullery alcove from which a separate room with toilet opened, a substantial rear courtyard providing light and air to the rear of the apartments, bathrooms with large tubs with hot and cold water, steam heat, marble floors and wainscoting, and polished ash woodwork. Among other innovative features were dumbwaiters in the halls at each floor, a large lecture room in the basement, and ground-floor stores that were organized on a cooperative basis to reduce apartment rents.

Designed in the Queen Anne style, the building is notable for the projecting central entrance section on the main façade with a four-story-high, round-arched recess. The façade is decorated with rich Byzantine-inspired floral ornament. The exceptional interior arrangement of space, the integration of communal and private space, and the abundance of amenities distinguish the Astral as a major example of its type.

Main Building

Memorial Hall

Library, rear view

PRATT INSTITUTE
Clinton Hill, Brooklyn
Designated: December 22, 1981

Main Building, 1885–87
215 Ryerson Street
Architects: Lamb & Rich

Library, 1896
224–228 Ryerson Street
Architect: William B. Tubby

South Hall, 1889–91
215 Ryerson Street
Architect: William B. Tubby

Memorial Hall, 1926–27
215 Ryerson Street
Architect: John Mead Howells

The Pratt Institute Main Building, including the attached South Hall and Memorial Hall, is the focal point of the Pratt Institute campus, located in the Clinton Hill section of Brooklyn. Built in three stages, the Main Building and its two wings were designed in two harmonious and interrelated styles: Romanesque Revival and Renaissance Revival. The Pratt Institute was founded by Charles Pratt for the training of artisans and technicians, as an outgrowth of his interest in manual training and his belief in self-help.

The six-story Romanesque Revival Main Building, designed by Lamb & Rich, has picturesque corner towers and a central clock tower. A projecting portico with paired brownstone arches that rests on colonnettes is approached by a double staircase. The corner towers terminate in decorative parapets with small towers, and the side elevations of the building are punctuated by regularly spaced arched and rectangular window openings.

The attached Renaissance Revival South Hall, designed by William B. Tubby, is a three-story red-brick building with a sunken areaway enclosed by a railing. The first story, faced with brick simulating rustication, is punctuated by large, rectangular openings. Arched windows outlined by brick and stone moldings accent the second floor, while the third-story windows are rectangular. A modillioned cornice surmounted by a balustraded parapet extends around the building at the roofline.

Memorial Hall, designed by John Mead Howells in a Romanesque Revival style, is linked to the Main Building by a one-story sandstone gabled entrance containing a recessed, round-arched entrance with engaged colonnettes. The entrance section, with its gilded central portion, is flanked by two flat-roofed wings. A large arched opening incorporates three smaller round-arched openings with engaged colonnettes at the first floor.

The Renaissance Revival Pratt Institute Library, designed by William B. Tubby, was the first free, public library in the City of Brooklyn. Pratt's belief in self-help led him to an interest in the public library movement. The freestanding three-story red-brick structure has slightly projecting end pavilions and a two-story stacks wing at the western end. The base of the building, faced with rusticated brick, is set off by brownstone belt courses. Round-arched windows, outlined by brick and brownstone moldings, accent the second story. The building is surmounted by a modillioned cornice supporting a balustraded parapet. A small arcaded porch was removed from the south side in 1980 and has been relocated as a freestanding sculpture elsewhere on campus.

METROPOLITAN BAPTIST CHURCH, formerly
New York Presbyterian Church, 1884–85 and 1889–90
151 West 128th Street, Manhattan
Architects: John R. Thomas and Richard R. Davis
Designated: February 3, 1981

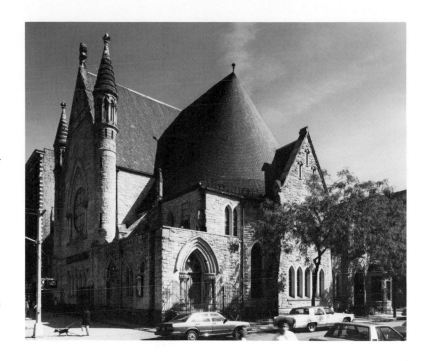

The New York Presbyterian Church was built when Harlem was a
fashionable haven for New Yorkers of affluence and elegance.
Prominent architect John R. Thomas completed the initial portion of
the existing structure—the small lecture room and chapel facing
West 128th Street—in 1885. The Seventh Avenue façade and
northern section housing the main auditorium were subsequently
added in 1890 by Harlem architect Richard R. Davis.

Davis's extension complemented the Thomas design by
incorporating many details from the earlier structure. The work of
both men is characterized by the low proportions and massive
volumes typical of Romanesque Revival architecture. Dwarf columns
flank doorways and entrances; heavy, rough-cut stone increases the
feeling of mass and weightiness. These Romanesque stylistic features
exist in contrast to such Gothic Revival devices as pointed arches,
trefoil decoration, and trefoil-arched lancets; the flying buttress of
the later addition; the stone window tracery; and the free and
generous use of windows to pierce the wall surfaces.

PUCK BUILDING, 1885–86; addition, 1892–93
295–309 Lafayette Street, Manhattan
Architects: Albert Wagner, Herman Wagner
Designated: April 12, 1983

The Puck Building, originally the home of *Puck* magazine, occupies
the block bounded by East Houston, Lafayette, Mulberry, and Jersey
streets on the edge of Manhattan's old printing district, which
centered around the Astor Library. It is distinguished by a large
statue of Puck situated at the northeast corner. The building was
erected in three stages, all supervised by Albert Wagner. The first
two were designed by Wagner, and the third by Herman Wagner, a
distant relative who took over Albert's practice in the late 1880s. The
original building is seven stories high, and the addition nine.

The building is executed in an adaptation of the German *Rundbogenstil*. The varying rhythm of the arches, the handsome courses of
pressed red brick, and the brick corbels at the cornice combine to
create a neat and coherent design. Cast-iron window enframements,
statuary, and wrought-iron entrance gates provide an attractive
contrast in materials. A porch of paired Doric columns marks the
main business entrance.

Puck magazine, founded by caricaturist Joseph Keppler and
printer/businessman Adolph Schwarzmann, first appeared in German
in 1876 and was equivalent in style and tone to the London-based
Punch. An English-language edition was launched in 1877; the
magazine shut down in 1918. *Puck* was noted for its comic and
satirical writers, most notably Henry Cuyler Bunner, and for its color
lithographs. The J. Ottman Lithography Company, which printed
these illustrations, was located in the building.

GENERAL POST OFFICE, 1885–91; addition, 1933
271–301 Cadman Plaza East, Brooklyn
Architect: William A. Freret,
after plans by Mifflin E. Bell
Designated: July 19, 1966

The General Post Office, which displays a wealth of skillfully blended Romanesque Revival and Renaissance Revival details, is a reminder of Brooklyn's illustrious past. The older section of the building was begun in 1885 and completed in 1891; the original plans of Mifflin E. Bell were modified by William A. Freret, Bell's successor as supervisory architect of the Treasury Department, while the building was under construction.

The post office is faced in polished and rough rock-faced granite; the rougher stone is found in the basement and first floor, and smooth stone rises above it. Notable features include projecting half-round turrets; a steep, slate-covered roof and dormers; and a massive, squat ground-story arcade.

The well-designed extension to the north, completed in 1933, adheres faithfully to the design of the older part of the building.

68TH POLICE PRECINCT STATION HOUSE AND STABLE, 1886
4302 Fourth Avenue, Brooklyn
Architect: Emile M. Gruwe
Designated: April 12, 1983

The Sunset Park section of Brooklyn, a planned community developed during the late nineteenth century to accommodate the middle- and lower-class industrial workers who had been migrating to Brooklyn's waterfront since after the Civil War, is home to the former 68th Police Precinct Station House and Stable. These buildings, vacant since the mid-1970s, were designed by New York architect Emile M. Gruwe in a Romanesque Revival style.

The front elevation of the three-story brick station house is dominated by a massive projecting corner tower with a stepped, corbeled cornice. The tower is decorated on the first floor by a limestone Byzantine band course carved with dogs' faces and foliate motifs, and on the third by a series of brick arches supported by carved foliate impost blocks and flanked by curvilinear wrought-iron tie washers. To the left of the tower, a Norman-inspired portico projects over the main entrance. Its arches are supported by truncated polished granite columns and surmounted by a corbel table of carved heads. To the left of the entrance is a first-floor extension topped by a sloping roof over a window arcade. Above this is a projecting pavilion, with a pair of round-arched windows on the second story and a Venetian-inspired interlaced colonnade of windows set beneath a diapered panel on the third.

From the station house, a one-story brick passage leads to the stable. This two-story building has a simple rectangular entrance, surmounted on the second floor by round-arched windows and hayloft doors topped by a crenellated cornice and rectangular pediment.

EAST 89TH STREET HOUSES, 1886–87
146, 148, 150, 152, and 156 East 89th Street, Manhattan
Architect: Hubert, Pirsson & Co.
Designated: March 13, 1979

These six, small town houses built for William Rhinelander, a wealthy sugar merchant whose family had purchased the property in 1812, were designed by Hubert, Pirsson & Co., a firm recognized for its residential work. Built in response to the real-estate opportunities created by the 1878 extension of the Third Avenue Elevated Railroad, all but one of these town houses stand on exceptionally narrow lots—just twelve and one-half feet wide.

The group is notable for the consistent use of materials—brick with stone and terra-cotta ornament—that unifies it, as well as for the richly textured surfaces that these materials create. The seemingly capricious placement of the projecting window bays contrasts with the recessed entrance loggias to animate the picturesque façades of the four-story structures. Formally, as speculative East Side row houses, and aesthetically, as accomplished essays in the Queen Anne style, these buildings are pleasing survivors of a once widespread building type.

ELDRIDGE STREET SYNAGOGUE,
Congregation Khal Adath Jeshurun with Anshe Lubz, 1886–87
12–16 Eldridge Street, Manhattan
Architects: Herter Brothers
Designated: July 8, 1980

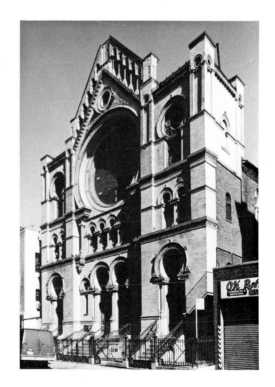

The Synagogue of Khal Adath Jeshurun, known as the Eldridge Street Synagogue, was the first major synagogue established on the Lower East Side by the Orthodox Eastern European Ashkenazi Jews, and one of New York City's finest houses of worship. Although the congregation's early history remains obscure, we know that Khal Adath Jeshurun resulted from the union of two Ashkenazi congregations, Beth Hamedrash (House of Study) and Holche Josher Wizaner (Those who Walk in Righteousness).

By 1890 more than 200,000 Jews settled in New York City, compared to the Jewish population of 13,000 in 1847. As a consequence, approximately sixty synagogues existed, and there was some competition among them for prominence in the Jewish community.

While earlier Lower East Side synagogues had been built by Western European Jews, the Eldridge Street Synagogue was the first to be established by Eastern European Jews. Determined to assert its presence in the community, the congregation commissioned Peter and Francis Herter to design a synagogue that would stand as a testament to its continued faith in the New World.

Rising from a side street of low buildings, the Herters' building is an imposing presence. Like other synagogues of the period, the Eldridge Street Synagogue's façade mixes Moorish, Gothic, and Romanesque elements, representing the trend from Euro-Christian elements to Oriental motifs.

The synagogue's most remarkable feature is its immense sanctuary, an opulent barrel-vaulted space. Stained-glass windows and brass chandeliers with Victorian glass shades illuminate the interior. Ornate walnut carving covers the front of the balcony and the ark where the sacred Torah scrolls are preserved. Small domes rest over the balcony and along the sides of the large room. The interior's paneling was marbelized and painted in 1894.

This great sanctuary was sealed in the 1930s after the flight of Jews from the Lower East Side. In the mid-1970s the sanctuary was entered for the first time in three decades. Since then the congregation has formed a preservation committee and established plans for the restoration of its sanctuary, which stands as a poignant reminder of Eastern European Jewish immigration to America.

ST. GEORGE'S PROTESTANT EPISCOPAL CHURCH,
1886–87; addition, 1889
800 Marcy Avenue, Brooklyn
Architect: Richard M. Upjohn
Designated: January 11, 1977

St. George's Church in the Bedford section of Brooklyn is a fine Victorian Gothic structure erected in 1886–87 by the architect Richard M. Upjohn, son of the noted Gothic Revivalist Richard Upjohn, who founded, with his father, the American Institute of Architects, and served as the president of the New York Chapter for two years. In the opinion of his grandson, the architectural historian Everard M. Upjohn, he was "one of the several successful practitioners of the High Victorian manner."

Designed in the dramatic polychromatic tradition of Victorian Gothic, St. George's is a striking red-brick building with light stone trim. Noted for its picturesque massing of elements, the church is sited facing Marcy Avenue with the nave running along Gates Avenue; the nave, with its steep, slate roof, is flanked by broad side aisles. A shallow clerestory with square windows rises lightly above the roofs of the side aisles. To the left of the nave from the porch, in place of a buttress, there is a polygonal tower that serves as a chimney. Adorned with slender stone colonnettes and supporting gablets and pointed arches at the top, it is the most distinctive feature of the building.

EMMANUEL BAPTIST CHURCH, 1887
279 Lafayette Avenue, Brooklyn
Architect: Francis H. Kimball
Designated: November 12, 1968

With its square twin towers and triple entrance porch, Emmanuel Baptist Church is reminiscent of a small French Gothic cathedral. Built in 1887 and designed by Francis H. Kimball, it was inspired by Romanesque and early Gothic prototypes. Its two richly decorated principal elevations are imposing, monumental, and somber, yet enlivened by a variety of fanciful carved ornament and structural forms.

The impressive front elevation is skillfully composed; the twin towers with massive stepped buttresses at the corner are divided vertically into five sections. The main entrance comprises three arched and pedimented portals, and a large, pointed-arched window is centered in the middle section above the doors; a low arcade with a pediment above crowns the front. The tympanum above the central doorway contains a beautiful bas-relief of Christ blessing the children. In the diapered surface of the gable crowning the building is a bas-relief of John the Baptist.

BAILEY HOUSE, 1886–88
10 St. Nicholas Place, Manhattan
Architect: Samuel B. Reed
Designated: February 19, 1974

This picturesque residence, designed by Samuel B. Reed, was built in 1886–88 for James Anthony Bailey, partner in the famed Barnum & Bailey Circus, which he founded with Phineas T. Barnum in 1881. The house, a fine example of domestic architecture influenced by the popular Romanesque Revival style, is one of Manhattan's few surviving freestanding mansions.

Situated on a corner site, it has an impressive three-story corner tower surmounted by a conical roof and spiked finial, rising high above the curvilinear Flemish gables found on each of the four façades. The theme of the central tower is echoed by the small turrets at the three remaining corners of the house. The gray, slate roof, with dormer windows on all four sides, is crowned by a wrought-iron railing at the truncated apex. The rough-faced random-coursed ashlar, typical of the Romanesque Revival, is relieved by smooth-faced stone, notably at the window and door enframements, the main porch, and the spandrels above the third-story tower windows. Other notable features include projecting porches, arched windows, bays, high chimneys, and delicate ornamental detail associated with the Romanesque Revival style.

The neighborhood was largely rural until the 1880s, when the Bailey residence was erected. Although much of the area today is dominated by apartment buildings, the survival of this house and other neighborhood buildings of the same period help to retain a pleasant nineteenth-century residential atmosphere. The building is currently occupied by a funeral home.

WASHINGTON BRIDGE, 1886–89
Harlem River from West 181st Street, Manhattan, to University Avenue, The Bronx
Architects: Charles C. Schneider and Wilhelm Hildenbrand; modified by Union Bridge Company, William J. McAlpine, Theodore Cooper, and DeLemos & Cordes
Chief engineer: William R. Hutton
Consulting architect: Edward H. Kendall
Designated: September 14, 1982

Constructed shortly after the completion of the Brooklyn Bridge, the Washington Bridge is a monument in the history of nineteenth-century American engineering. Made of steel, cast-iron, and wrought-iron arches with arched masonry approaches, the Washington Bridge was constructed over the Harlem River in 1886–89 to connect the Washington Heights section of Manhattan with the Bronx. It has long been considered one of the nation's finest nineteenth-century steel-arch bridges, perhaps second only to the famous Eads Bridge in St. Louis, built in 1867–74. With its two immense archways and general boldness of design, the Washington Bridge remains an ornament to the city.

ST. MARTIN'S EPISCOPAL CHURCH AND PARISH HOUSE, 1887–88
230 Lenox Avenue, Manhattan
Architect: William A. Potter
Designated: July 19, 1966

St. Martin's, built in 1887–88, is one of New York's finest Richardsonian Romanesque churches. The dominant high tower houses one of only two carillons in Manhattan—a forty-two-bell instrument brought from Holland in 1949. A copper pyramidal steeple is adorned at each corner with simple square pinnacles. At the base of the tower a pair of handsome, arched doorways leads into the church, punctuating the gabled end wall of the main aisle.

The Parish House stands between the west end of the church and Lenox Avenue. This two-story structure with its steep gables is faced with the same rock-faced sandstone blocks and smooth-faced stone trim as the church itself.

376–380 LAFAYETTE STREET, 1888
Manhattan
Architect: Henry J. Hardenbergh
Designated: May 17, 1966

This six-story commercial building was designed by Henry J. Hardenbergh, the architect of such elegant structures as the Plaza Hotel, the Dakota Apartments, and the Art Students League building.

Handsome dark-brown brick piers form five bays for the windows on Great Jones Street and four on Lafayette Street. The four-story tier arrangement of windows terminates in brick segmental arches, above which are paired windows on the fifth floor and a row of round-arched windows on the sixth. The piers, supported at the first floor by dwarf columns of sandstone, rest on polished gray granite bases. Sections of light-colored brick wall terminate the succession of arched bays, marking entrances, stairs, and elevators. A richly decorated metal cornice crowns the entire composition, and two structures with pointed roofs form end-of-building accents.

BETH JACOB SCHOOL,
formerly Public School 71K, 1888–89
119 Heyward Street, Brooklyn
Architect: James W. Naughton
Designated: February 3, 1981

The Beth Jacob School—originally Public School 71K—was erected when Brooklyn was still a separate city with an independent education system. All the school buildings built in Brooklyn in the twenty years prior to incorporation with New York City were designed by James W. Naughton, superintendent of buildings for the Board of Education from 1879–98. The school was built in the French Second Empire style, adopted in America when the building market in New York began to recover from the economic effects of the Civil War. Pavilions, which emphasize verticality on the façade, and mansard roofs, which elaborate the pavilions, were characteristic of the style.

The symmetrical, three-story brick structure with stone trim has a round-arched entrance at the base of an elaborately embellished central tower. Recessed three-window sections connect the tower to the end pavilions, which are topped by pediments with raking cornices. Stone bands at sill and impost level, brick and stone quoins, grooved piers, and stone and brick window lintels further decorate the building, which is crowned by a high mansard roof that retains its original iron crestings.

CARROLL STREET BRIDGE, 1888–89
Gowanus Canal, Brooklyn
Builder: Brooklyn Department of City Works
Chief engineer: Robert Van Buren
Designated: September 29, 1987

The Carroll Street Bridge, spanning Brooklyn's Gowanus Canal, is one of the oldest bridges in the New York City area. It was built in 1888–89 to replace the original Carroll Street Bridge, a change made necessary by the expansion of lower Brooklyn in the mid-nineteenth century, when the Gowanus Canal was constructed to accommodate the rapidly developing commercial waterfront.

The bridge is the oldest of four known surviving retractile bridges built in the United States during the late nineteenth and early twentieth centuries. The movable bridge rolls horizontally on wheels set on steel rails, allowing traffic to pass freely through the canal. It was constructed by the New Jersey Steel and Iron Company, a subsidiary of Cooper, Hewitt & Company, one of the leading producers of iron and steel at that time. Robert Van Buren, a descendant of President Martin Van Buren, was the chief engineer of the project for the Brooklyn Department of City Works. The Carroll Street Bridge survives as a reminder of a comparatively rare type of bridge that had become obsolete by the 1920s.

EDGEHILL CHURCH OF SPUYTEN DUYVIL,
formerly Riverdale Presbyterian Chapel, 1888–89
2550 Independence Avenue, The Bronx
Architect: Francis Hatch Kimball
Designated: November 25, 1980

A remnant of the Bronx's bucolic past, the Edgehill Church of Spuyten Duyvil was originally a mission of the Riverdale Presbyterian Church and was built to serve the workers of the nearby Johnson Iron Foundry. Isaac G. Johnson, the foundry's owner and a devout Baptist, sought to impart religious teachings to his workers; he initiated the construction of the chapel, and Mary E. Cox, his partner's wife, donated the land. For its design, they commissioned prominent New York City architect Francis Hatch Kimball, who incorporated Gothic, Tudor, and Richardsonian features in an eclectic style.

A massive stone base laid in random ashlar provides support for lighter shingled and stone walls and half-timbered gables. The entrance is on the east side, through a peaked-roof porch that projects from a large gable, and is lined on either side by three trefoil-arched windows. The south side has a series of projections, including a rounded extension lit by Gothic arched windows, a short nave with trefoil windows, and a shallow transept with two signed Tiffany stained-glass windows. The chancel is on the west side; a nave and transept with two Tiffany Studio stained-glass windows mark the north. Also on the north side is a tall stone chimney that, together with the variously sloped roofs of the other architectural members, adds to the chapel's picturesque character.

For almost half a century, Edgehill has been affiliated with the Congregational Church, now part of the United Church of Christ.

CHURCH OF ST. LUKE AND ST. MATTHEW, 1888–91
520 Clinton Avenue, Brooklyn
Architect: John Welch
Designated: May 12, 1981

The Church of St. Luke and St. Matthew on Clinton Avenue (once the "Gold Coast" of Brooklyn) is among the largest and finest of the ecclesiastical structures built in the city during the nineteenth century, and, like the other major buildings from the period, it reflects a sense of optimism in Brooklyn's future. The church is the masterpiece of Brooklyn architect John Welch, who established himself as a church architect, designing a number of notable Greek Revival and Gothic Revival churches in Brooklyn and New Jersey. Welch's designs for St. Luke's are loosely based on twelfth-century Romanesque churches of Northern Italy but adapted for use by a nineteenth-century urban congregation in America. The superb design also shows the influence of Henry Hobson Richardson's pioneering Romanesque Revival designs, but Richardson's forms are used in a fresh and original manner.

Its façade is distinguished by a projecting round-arched entrance porch, large wheel window, corbeled cornice, and small octagonal towers. The varieties of rough and smooth stone and terra-cotta serve to create a subtle drama on the building. The beautifully modeled tower of the chapel, a sophisticated essay in the use of round arches, is based on the campaniles found on Italian Romanesque churches.

The interior has fine double-lancet stained-glass windows produced by the Tiffany Studios and a stained-glass window in the ceiling of the chancel.

The church has continued to serve a neighborhood that has seen great changes in the last decades. The congregation of the church is now largely drawn from the West Indian population of the area, which has reinvigorated the church, allowing it to maintain its magnificent edifice.

PUBLIC SCHOOL 73, 1888; addition, 1895
241 MacDougal Street, Brooklyn
Architect: James W. Naughton
Designated: September 11, 1984

An impressive brick and stone structure, Public School 73 is an
excellent example of nineteenth-century school architecture by one
of the major practitioners in that field, James W. Naughton, the
superintendent of buildings for the Board of Education of the City of
Brooklyn. The school was built in two sections: the first, at the corner
of Rockaway Avenue and MacDougal Street, was begun in 1888; the
extension to the east was added in 1895.

Public education in New York dates back to the settlement of the
area by the Dutch; the first school was established in 1638 on
Manhattan Island, then the center of population. By the early
nineteenth century, each of Brooklyn's six towns developed a
separate though similar public education system, with the first
village school opening in 1816. Public School 73, located near the
eastern boundary of Brooklyn and the Town of New Lots, was erected
to meet the needs of a growing population.

The main (1888) section is characterized by a projecting central
entrance tower and flanking end pavilions. The 1895 extension, of
the same height and materials, has a four-bay-wide, recessed central
section and flanking end pavilions. The structure has a number of
architectural references to previous styles: the long horizontal
window arrangement suggests the Italianate palazzo style; the
projecting end pavilions that divide the façade vertically are features
of the French Second Empire; and the heavy pedimented entrance
and rendering of the tower are late Romanesque Revival.

EDGEWATER VILLAGE HALL, 1889
Tappan Park and Canal Street, Staten Island
Architect: Unknown
Designated: July 30, 1968

Edgewater Village Hall was built at the end of the nineteenth century
as a Municipal and City Magistrate's Courthouse. Originally serving
the village of Edgewater, the Romanesque Revival hall stands on a
small, landscaped public square called Tappan Park; it presently
houses offices of the Health Department of the City of New York.

The first floor of the one-and-one-half-story, T-shaped brick
building has paired, square-headed windows, set in brick arches
surmounted by circular lights and joined at the spring lines of those
arches by a brick band course. Above, the second floor is encircled
by wide eaves with a pronounced molded cornice set on evenly
spaced, fluted brackets that alternate with rosette-decorated square
panels. This pattern is interrupted at intervals by double-hung
dormer windows, enframed by large brackets and resting on a brick,
corbel-supported sill. Dominating the façade is a square tower that
rises just above the hall's hipped, slate roof. The tower is
embellished by brick corbels beneath its cornice and is crowned by a
flagpole surmounting a low, concave-roofed spire with a pedestal cap.

FOURTEENTH WARD INDUSTRIAL SCHOOL, Astor Memorial School, 1888–89
256–258 Mott Street, Manhattan
Architects: Vaux & Radford
Designated: July 12, 1977

A splendid example of Victorian Gothic architecture, the Fourteenth Ward Industrial School was built in 1888–89 for the Children's Aid Society. Founded in 1853 by Charles Loring Brace, the society was the first organization established in this country to improve the living conditions of indigent children. By the end of the century, nearly all of the older buildings that were used by the society had been replaced by newer, more modern ones built specifically for its use—the majority of which were designed by the firm of Vaux & Radford.

This polychromatic four-story structure is dominated by a three-sided, centrally placed oriel on the façade, set on a convex sandstone corbel extending up through the second and third stories, and an impressive crow-stepped gable roof. Other prominent features include foliate terra-cotta ornament, arched windows, and a series of dormers set at the roofline.

The school—built with funds contributed by John Jacob Astor as a memorial to his wife, who was a longtime supporter of the activities of the society—was built to serve the needs of the poor in the large Italian community in the neighborhood. It was the first society structure planned solely as a school. Dedicated in March 1889, it was used as an industrial and night school until 1913, when a larger structure was built nearby. It has recently been converted into cooperative apartments.

MECHANICS TEMPLE, INDEPENDENT UNITED ORDER OF MECHANICS OF THE WESTERN HEMISPHERE, formerly the Lincoln Club, 1889
65 Putnam Avenue, Brooklyn
Architect: Rudolph L. Daus
Designated: May 12, 1981

The former Lincoln Club was designed in 1889 by Brooklyn-based architect Rudolph L. Daus. Located in the affluent Clinton Hill section, the Lincoln Club was one of a number of large, sumptuous clubhouses erected in Brooklyn and Manhattan in the last two decades of the nineteenth century.

One of the finest of Daus's buildings and one of the most sophisticated Queen Anne–style structures in New York City, the Lincoln Club is distinguished by its rich variety of subtly contrasting textures and colors and asymmetrical massing—hallmarks of Queen Anne design. The Roman brick and brownstone façade is enlivened by smooth brownstone bands and rich terra-cotta ornament. Other notable features are a highly decorative roof gable, a round tower capped by a large, flamboyant cornice, and an unusual, asymmetrical arrangement of windows, all of which contrast sharply with the austere simplicity of the building.

Founded in 1878 by a small group of men who banded together for social purposes and to further the interests of the Republican Party, the Lincoln Club was dissolved in 1931 as many of Brooklyn's elite moved away. The clubhouse was purchased in the 1940s by the Independent United Order of Mechanics of the Western Hemisphere, a private philanthropic society that has taken great pride in restoring this dignified building.

PUBLIC SCHOOL 11, formerly Public School 91, 1889;
additions, 1905, 1930
1257 Ogden Avenue, The Bronx
Architect: George W. Debevoise
Designated: August 25, 1981

Built in 1889, this Romanesque Revival schoolhouse was designed
by George W. Debevoise, the superintendent of public school
buildings for the New York City Board of Education between 1884
and 1891. Little is known of Debevoise, but during the seven years
he held tenure as superintendent, over twenty schools of his design
were constructed in the Bronx and Manhattan, all in the Romanesque
Revival or Queen Anne styles. Debevoise introduced a number of
structural innovations into school buildings, including the use of iron
girders instead of wood to enlarge classroom space and the addition
of metal-lined steam pipes in classrooms to improve ventilation
and heating.

Public School 11 is built of brick and Harlem River stone. A
projecting central entrance tower incorporates a porch consisting of
banded stone piers carrying a round arch with a gable hood supported
by corbels. The tower's second floor is pierced by three narrow
round-arched windows and the third is marked by a bull's-eye
window. Above the corbeled cornice is a pyramidal roof with a
peaked dormer. Walls on each side of the tower are pierced by
secondary entrances with segmental arches. These entrances are
flanked by round-arched windows. At the southern end of the
structure, a two-window-wide pavilion has square-headed pediment
openings on the ground floor; two tiers of windows at the level of the
second floor are flat and round-arched. The pavilion, like the
entrance tower, is crowned by a steep-pitched dormer roof. There is a
narrow extension set back from the street at the northern end. In
1905 a large wing was added to the school along Ogden Avenue.
Three stories high, it is of red brick with stone trim above a rough-
faced stone base. A building housing a gymnasium auditorium was
built along Merriam Avenue in 1930.

ALHAMBRA APARTMENTS, 1889–90; altered, 1923
500–518 Nostrand Avenue and 29–33 Macon Street,
Brooklyn
Architect: Montrose W. Morris
Designated: March 18, 1986

The Alhambra Apartments, in the heart of Bedford-Stuyvesant, is
one of Brooklyn's major apartment houses. Designed by Montrose W.
Morris, it was built in 1889–90 by developer Louis F. Seitz and was
one of a number of commissions Morris executed for Seitz, including
two other exceptional apartment houses, the Renaissance and the
Imperial (both also designated landmarks). Although the Alhambra's
ground floor was converted into storefronts in 1923, the building
remains distinguished—a romantic and picturesque combination of
the Romanesque Revival and the Queen Anne styles.

Built of Roman brick, stone, metal, and terra-cotta, the building is
divided in the center, creating two separate but identical structures
connected at each upper story by open, columned bridges. Each
building rises five stories with a slate mansard roof. At each corner of
the two buildings is a polygonal tower. The central bay of each
building projects slightly and is characterized by deeply recessed,
square-headed loggias with Corinthian columns (some recently
removed) at the second and third floors, and an arcaded loggia at
the fourth.

The use of brick patterns, arched windows, carved brackets,
foliate band courses, and quoins gives continuous movement to the
façade, and the ingenious use of open loggias and arcades relieves
the strong horizontal massing of the building, as does the upward
thrust of the towers. The subtle, polychromatic effect created by the
various materials contributes an essential element to the
architectural success of the building. Although alterations have been
made, the upper floors are vacant, and the stores only partially
occupied, the building has maintained its architectural dignity and
remains, in form, detail, and massing, an outstanding example of
turn-of-the-century apartment-house design.

CARNEGIE HALL, 1889–91; addition, 1894–96
57th Street at Seventh Avenue, Manhattan
Architect: William B. Tuthill
Designated: June 20, 1967

Andrew Carnegie, one of America's best-known industrialists and philanthropists, was, by the time of his death in 1919, the epitome of the self-made man. From his humble origins in Scotland and his modest beginnings in America as a thirteen-year-old bobbin boy in a cotton mill, through his spectacular career as an industrial magnate, Carnegie kept sight of the need for intellectual and artistic self-improvement. Totally self-educated, he frequented theaters and concert halls assiduously and sought out the company of intellectuals such as Matthew Arnold and Herbert Spencer. In order to effect "the improvement of mankind," Carnegie was the founder and benefactor of several leading cultural institutions, among them the Carnegie Institute in Pittsburgh and New York City's jewel of concert halls, Carnegie Hall.

On May 13, 1890, the cornerstone was laid to the strains of music from Wagner's *Das Rheingold*. Carnegie said on that occasion: "Who shall venture to paint its history or its end? It is built to stand for ages, and during these ages it is probable that this hall will intertwine itself with the history of our country. . . . From this platform men may be spurred to aims that end not with the miserable self; here an idea may be promulgated which will affect the world. . . ."

Originally called, quite modestly, Music Hall, Carnegie Hall officially opened on the evening of May 5, 1891, with the American premiere appearance of Peter Ilich Tchaikovsky. Until this day it has continued to be a forum for musical discovery and excellence, at times presenting new artists and works of a decidedly controversial nature. For almost a century the acoustical magic of the hall has been hailed worldwide. William Burnet Tuthill, the architect, made as detailed a study of acoustics as science permitted in 1890. The interior of the hall was painted white and sumptuously adorned with velvet, which would act as an absorbent for reverberations and echoes; the boxes, decoratively laid out in sweeping curves, allowed sound to curve rather than bounce off sharp angles; and an elliptical ceiling avoided the pitfall of collecting and swallowing sound.

The exterior of the six-story building, of less historical importance than the interior, is an excellent example of a modified Italian Renaissance style, with its reddish-brown Roman brick, belt courses, arches, pilasters, and terra-cotta decorations. Originally the building had a mansard roof in the French tradition, but this was removed in 1894 to build the crowning studio floor. A somewhat awkward architectural massing results from the ten-story tower for offices and studios that was added to the building.

Carnegie Hall reopened in December 1986 after a $50 million renovation. Included in that renovation was the rebuilding of the stage ceiling, whose legendary hole, created during the filming of *Carnegie Hall* in 1946 and masked by canvas and curtains ever since, had purportedly contributed advantageously to the hall's acoustics. By all recent accounts the magnificent sound of the concert hall has changed, but it has not altered the hall's potential or the audience's expectation of musical brilliance.

149–151 EAST 67TH STREET, formerly the Mount Sinai Dispensary, 1889–90
Manhattan
Architects: Buchman & Deisler and Brunner & Tryon
Designated: January 29, 1980

The Mount Sinai Dispensary, or health clinic, reflected Mount Sinai Hospital's pride in its efforts to bring medical care to a large urban population. The hospital was founded in 1852 by eight prominent Jewish citizens. The dispensary began its life in 1875 in two rooms of the hospital's basement. It expanded rapidly as the hospital became more specialized, a trend in medicine that was only then beginning. The new dispensary building of 1889–90 was attached to the hospital by a tunnel that ran under 67th Street.

Although the exact contributions of the two architectural firms is uncertain, Buchman & Deisler, because of their prominence in the design of commercial buildings, are generally credited with the dispensary's iron structural frame. The Italian Renaissance–style building, six stories high and five bays wide, is distinguished by its handsomely proportioned Quattrocento details in contrasting colors and textures. At the ground floor the central three bays have round-arched windows, and the upper stories are of closely-laid pressed brick set off by white terra-cotta trim. The entire building is enframed by a border of vines and medallions.

PARK EAST SYNAGOGUE, 1889–90
163 East 67th Street, Manhattan
Architects: Schneider & Herter
Designated: January 29, 1980

Park East Synagogue was organized by the Rabbi Bernard Drachman, who aimed to create a place of worship in which the principles of Orthodox Judaism would not bow to the pressures of Reform Judaism. Previously rabbi at Beth Israel Bikkur Cholem, a synagogue at Lexington Avenue and 72nd Street, Drachman resigned rather than vote to have men and women seated together. The Orthodox congregation at the Park East Synagogue was largely German, but included many Polish, Russian, and Hungarian Jews as well.

The Moorish style of the building conforms with the late nineteenth-century notion of what constituted appropriate synagogue architecture. The brick and terra-cotta building is distinguished by a central rose window, asymmetrically flanking tower, and rich ornamental detail reminiscent of Byzantine architecture.

ST. ANDREW'S CHURCH, 1889–91
2067 Fifth Avenue, Manhattan
Architect: Henry M. Congdon
Designated: April 12, 1967

The congregation of St. Andrew's, organized in 1829, grew slowly at first because the church was located so far out of town. Its first church was at Park Avenue and East 128th Street. By the time the present building was completed in 1889–91 the population of the area had grown, as had the congregation.

The church is constructed of random quarry-faced granite ashlar in the Gothic tradition. Adjacent to the south transept, on 127th Street, is a clock tower with a slate-covered spire, adorned at each corner with delicate turrets. On each side of the belfry are two pointed-arched openings. The plan of the church follows a cruciform shape, with galleries in the transept and side aisles in the nave. Covering the nave and the transept is a steeply pitched roof sheathed with slate. The west façade is highlighted by buttresses opposite the nave walls, two tall, narrow windows, and a small rose window; the main doorway has its own gable. Another entrance to the church, located on the south façade, is marked by a stone vestibule and slate-covered gable.

PROTESTANT WELFARE AGENCIES BUILDING, formerly Church Missions House, 1892–94
281 Park Avenue South, Manhattan
Architects: Robert Williams Gibson and Edward J. Neville Stent
Designated: September 11, 1979

The Church Missions House was the joint project of Robert Williams Gibson, an English-born architect who built many Episcopal churches, and Edward J. Neville Stent, who specialized in church decoration. The style is a loose adaptation of Northern European Gothic of the fifteenth and early sixteenth centuries.

Gibson was one of the first New York architects to work in this mode, which is here applied in a very inventive way. Medieval arcading, clustered shafts, corner tourelles, and sculpted tympanum and roof dormers are organized into a rectilinear framework that conceals a steel-frame structure. This treatment accommodates the ample glazing made possible by this structural innovation. The inherently sculptural values of the Gothic shafts and moldings transform the grid's regularity into a positive virtue. Stent's low-relief terra-cotta decoration and modeling introduces lively surface patterns. Particularly noteworthy is the image of Christ the Consoler over the Park Avenue tympanum; the subject matter is perfectly suited to a charitable institution. The design also marks an early stage in the development of the Gothic cladding applied to a tall building. This cladding can be found on later Gothic "pier" skyscrapers, such as Cass Gilbert's Woolworth Building.

The church missions movement in the United States dates from the early nineteenth century; it received its greatest impetus at the 1821 General Convention of the Episcopal Church in Philadelphia. In 1835, the Missionary Society relocated to New York. Two other charitable organizations, the United Charities and the New York Society for the Prevention of Cruelty to Children, were located nearby.

GILBERT KIAMIE HOUSE, formerly Grolier Club, 1890
29 East 32nd Street, Manhattan
Architect: Charles W. Romeyn
Designated: August 18, 1970

The former Grolier Club at 29 East 32nd Street was designed by Charles W. Romeyn in an imaginative interpretation of the Romanesque Revival style. The three-story building is notable for its restrained use of ornament and its feeling for texture, evident in the skillful juxtaposition of Roman brick and stone. Two linked arches distinguish the first floor, and the top floor has a handsome row of windows with columns between, extending the width of the building and supporting a stone lintel with ornamented cap molding. At the second floor an arched central window is flanked by high, narrow windows. A slim, molded sill joins them at the base, and a richly ornamented but slender band course divides the two side windows at mid-height. The first-floor arches display handsome carving.

The Grolier Club, which derived its name from the sixteenth-century bibliophile Jean Grolier, was formed in 1884 for literary study and promotion of the publishing arts. The club has relocated to 47 East 60th Street, and the house at 29 East 32nd Street is now owned by a New York City real-estate concern.

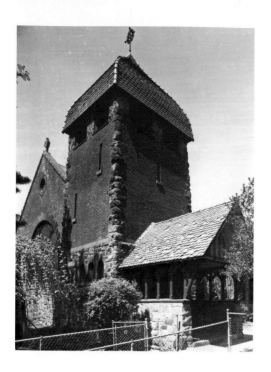

ST. BARTHOLOMEW'S CHURCH, 1890
1227 Pacific Street, Brooklyn
Architect: George P. Chappell
Designated: March 19, 1974

St. Bartholomew's Church, near Grant's Square in the Crown Heights section of Brooklyn, was designed by the Brooklyn architect George P. Chappell and completed in 1890.

A Romanesque Revival church executed in red brick with a rough-faced red granite base, its most picturesque features include a wide gable containing a large, round-arched, stained-glass window and a one-story semicircular projection at the west corner with a semi-conical roof. Rising from the east corner is a massive, square tower with battered brick walls, a belfry, and a low convex tile roof. The nave has a clerestory with stained-glass windows above the sloping roofs of the buttressed side aisles. The nave terminates in two projecting gable-roofed end sections; each contains a chancel and vestry set at right angles to the end section. Each of these sections has its own peaked roof and each gable has a large round-arched window like that of the front section.

AMERICAN FINE ARTS SOCIETY BUILDING,
housing the Art Students League of New York, 1891–92; addition, 1921
215 West 57th Street, Manhattan
Architect: Henry J. Hardenbergh
Designated: May 10, 1966

The building that now houses the Art Students League of New York was designed in 1891 by the noted New York architect Henry J. Hardenbergh. It is a dignified adaptation of the type of French Renaissance town house built during the reign of François I. A formally balanced and well-proportioned composition, it projects an air of restrained elegance that reflects the architect's sensibility as much as it does his historical sources. Four stories high (with a fifth story, not visible from the street, added in 1921), the façade is divided into three major horizontal sections separated by plain and decorated band courses; a heavily decorated cornice with balustrade crowns the composition. The arched main entrance is flanked by tall, ornate candelabralike spindles, a motif also carried out in the second-floor windows in a way that unifies the decoration. A red-tiled roof adds a touch of color to this building's formal harmonies.

An addition to the building on 58th Street was also designed by Hardenbergh; originally meant to serve as galleries for George Vanderbilt, it was completed more or less at the same time as the main building on 57th Street, and was modeled after the Galeries Georges Petit in Paris.

The American Fine Arts Society was founded in 1889 by the Society of American Artists, the Architectural League, and the Art Students League; the groups' objective was to provide facilities for their activities, including exhibitions. Practically all major art exhibitions were held in the Fine Arts Society galleries for many years. In 1906, the Society of American Artists merged with the National Academy of Design; the New York Architectural League moved into its own building in 1927. The National Academy of Design acquired its own building and galleries on Fifth Avenue in 1938. Thus, only the Art Students League remained, and has been the sole occupant of the building since the 1930s. The league and the building's owner, the Fine Arts Society, have had a significant influence on fine arts in this country.

JUDSON MEMORIAL CHURCH AND JUDSON HALL
Washington Square at Thompson Street, Manhattan
Architects: McKim, Mead & White

Judson Memorial Church, 1890–92   Judson Hall, 1890–92
Designated: May 17, 1966   Designated: April 12, 19(

Small and rectangular, Judson Memorial Church, with its sharply defined, low-pitched gable roof, sits on a corner lot of Washington Square Park, adjacent to the ten-story tower of Judson Hall, now used as a dormitory by New York University. An architectural composition in the Italian Renaissance style, the church and hall were commissioned by the church's first pastor, Edward Judson, to complement the Washington Square Arch.

A raised entrance doorway is set between the buildings; five half-round steps lead gracefully up to a pair of dark, wood-paneled doors, recessed within a richly decorated terra-cotta frame. Terra-cotta ornament continues around the first floor of the north and east elevations of the church, and again at the second, third, and fifth floors of the hall, alternating with horizontal bands of recessed yellow Roman brick. Arches envelop the round-headed windows, while splayed brick lintels span the square-headed windows of the lower three stories.

The stained-glass windows of the church are the work of John La Farge, and the altar statuary is by Augustus Saint-Gaudens. The impressive tower rising above the brick ground floor contains the same masonry work as the walls of the hall and terminates with two slender columns supporting the triple arches of the belfry.

1321 MADISON AVENUE, 1890–91
Manhattan
Architect: James E. Ware
Designated: July 23, 1974

Easily identified by its pyramidal roof among flat cornices, 1321 Madison remains a lively and attractive presence on the Upper East Side. This turn-of-the-century row house, one of an original row of five, is located in the fashionable Carnegie Hill district—named in reference to Andrew Carnegie's mansion on the corner of Fifth Avenue and 91st Street. The developer, James V. S. Woolley, commissioned these particular row houses in a growing neighborhood of middle-class residences.

The house was designed in the Queen Anne style once popular for domestic architecture. The three-sided bay window with a paneled parapet on the third floor and three round-arched windows with engaged colonnettes on the fourth floor are typical Queen Anne characteristics. Just beneath the roofline runs a bracketed cornice with a sheet-metal frieze containing swags and scallops. Other elements include a round-topped attic window with a dormer and, on 93rd Street, an impressive brownstone stairway leading to a wide stoop and arched doorway.

CENTURY ASSOCIATION, 1889–91
7 West 43rd Street, Manhattan
Architects: McKim, Mead & White
Designated: January 11, 1967

One of the purest examples of the Italian Renaissance style built
in late-nineteenth-century New York is the Century Association.
Stanford White of McKim, Mead & White was the partner in charge
of this project, which was the firm's first clubhouse design. The firm
was well regarded for its interpretation of Renaissance elements, and
White in particular was known for masterfully combining textures,
materials, and details to create unity and balance in a building.

The Century's building combines granite, terra-cotta, and
yellow brick in a free and elegant adaptation of an Italian palazzo.
Its Renaissance character is expressed by a two-story rusticated
masonry base; a monumental arched entrance doorway; four
handsomely wreathed round windows above the rectangular ones on
the third floor; an elaborate cornice; and a crowning balustrade. The
Palladian window above the main doorway was originally an open
loggia, and the appearance of the building was weakened when this
space was enclosed.

Long considered the city's most prominent cultural club, the
Century was founded in 1847 by William Cullen Bryant and Asher B.
Durand, among others, as a gathering place mainly for authors and
artists to convene in high-ceilinged parlors for amiable intellectual
conversation. The organization was named the Century because its
membership was originally supposed to be limited to one hundred—
a figure long since exceeded. Among its members have been Stanford
White, Charles McKim, and many of the city's most important and
influential scholars, jurists, and architects, although no women have
been admitted as members. The building also houses the club's art
collection, which includes works by Winslow Homer, Frederic
Remington, and Albert Bierstadt.

HARLEM COURTHOUSE, 1891–93
170 East 121st Street, Manhattan
Architects: Thom & Wilson
Designated: August 2, 1967

While essentially Romanesque Revival in style, this onetime
detention facility is highlighted by romantic overtones from the
Victorian Gothic. Red brick, bluestone belt courses, and decorative
terra-cotta are strikingly combined in a variety of forms.

A five-story gabled roof bay projects from both the west and the
north façades. Almost symmetrical in construction, each of these
fronts contains a paneled truck entrance framed by large rectangular
windows with metal grilles. Four deeply-set, arched windows on
the second floor rest above these entrances. While handsomely
constructed with banded pilasters, these arches are surpassed by the
large two-story arched windows on the third, or courtroom, floor.
Steep gables, dormers, and bold finials complete the design.

At the corner of the north and west elevations, a round tower with
an octagonal belfry rises above the four-story structure. Each portion
of the octagonal section contains a steep gable with a semicircular
arch that in turn enframes a decorative panel. Two of the arches
also enframe clocks, while the remaining arches contain circular
windows. Exemplary of the building's Gothic theme are the gargoyle
animal heads perched on top of the columns separating each paneled
section. Carved figures of cherubs holding scrolls ornament the
spandrels of the main entrance. Foliate ornament is displayed
in the frieze of the entablature, while a low balustrade caps the
entrance's classic cornice.

Once known as the Fifth District Prison, the structure served as a
temporary detention facility, although its primary role was to house
one of the many magistrates courts. Today, the structure is occupied
by city agencies, including the Department of Air Pollution Control,
the Sanitation Department, and the Parole Board.

BOYS' HIGH SCHOOL, 1891
832 Marcy Avenue, Brooklyn
Architect: James W. Naughton
Designated: September 23, 1975

This splendid Romanesque Revival building was erected in 1891, when the style was at the height of its popularity in Brooklyn. It was designed in the mature phase of the style, which originated with American architect Henry Hobson Richardson. Richardsonian Romanesque was characterized by a picturesque silhouette, the use of round-arched openings, contrasting smooth- and rough-faced stonework, and a strong massing swollen with round bays and towers. All of these features are found in this building.

The school faces three streets and each façade has certain elements in common: round-arched windows, doors, gables, dormer windows, and a wealth of terra-cotta ornament. The Marcy Avenue façade is the most impressive, with each end terminated by an imposing tower—one crowned with a conical roof and the other extending beyond the roofline in height and crowned by a pyramidal roof. There is a deeply recessed, ribbed round arch at the main entrance. On the first two floors is a projecting four-window-wide section from which rises a three-story, round-arched bay framing the windows of the upper floors. The spandrels of this bay and its crowning gable are adorned with terra-cotta ornament.

The building now houses the high school division outreach program of the city's Board of Education.

NEW YORK ARCHITECTURAL TERRA-COTTA WORKS BUILDING, 1892
42-10–42-16 Vernon Boulevard, Queens
Architect: Unknown
Designated: August 24, 1982

Built in 1892, this two-story building with stepped gables, round-bottomed roof tiles, and decorative chimneys served as the office headquarters for the New York Architectural Terra-Cotta Works. New York's only such firm, the company produced decorative tiles for many New York buildings, including Carnegie Hall, the Ansonia Hotel, and Brooklyn's Venetian-style Montauk Club.

The New York Architectural Terra-Cotta Works was established in 1886 during Manhattan's skyscraper boom, shortly after the decorative tiles began to appear in the United States. Strategically located in Queens on the East River, the company enjoyed easy river access to the construction under way in Manhattan.

Shifting architectural convention and the replacement of terra-cotta by cast concrete slowly eroded the company's success, and the firm declared bankruptcy about 1928. Today the structure awaits restoration and preservation.

FLEMING SMITH WAREHOUSE, 1891–92
451–453 Washington Street, Manhattan
Architect: Stephen Decatur Hatch
Designated: March 14, 1978

Renowned commercial architect Stephen Decatur Hatch designed this large loft building for Fleming Smith. Hatch's use of neo-Flemish detail—chiefly the stepped gables—reflects the increased interest in colonial American history at the end of the nineteenth century. While the original use of the building is not recorded, by 1898 it held a shoe factory and a storehouse for wine.

The longer façade on Watts Street is five bays wide, with a slightly projecting central bay marking the entrance. A complex pattern of windows, arches, cornices, and columns, ending in gables, is organized around the central bay. The Washington Street façade, three bays wide, is similar, except that the first story is more open, with large window bays sheltered by a canopy and protected by an iron fence.

23RD REGIMENT ARMORY, 1891–95
1322 Bedford Avenue, Brooklyn
Architects: Fowler & Hough
Designated: March 8, 1977

Designed to resemble a medieval fortress, the 23rd Regiment Armory was one of eight armories constructed in Brooklyn before 1900. The 23rd Regiment, part of the Second Brigade of the National Guard, served briefly in the Civil War during the summer of 1863. An armory for the regiment was constructed on Clermont Street in 1872–73, but as the regiment grew in size and status, plans for the new building were formulated. Colonel John N. Partridge, head of the regiment and president and general manager of the Brooklyn City and Newton Railroad Company, was instrumental in obtaining a state grant of $300,000 for the new armory.

On November 14, 1891, the cornerstone was laid, and a fair was held to raise funds for furnishing the interior. The Council Room is especially elaborate, containing an enormous twenty-four-foot-high fireplace. A newspaper article of 1898 commented, "The members of 23, if they are looking for consolation over their failure to get a call for duty at the front can find it in the thought that they are staying at home in the armory whose company rooms are the best in all the armories of the state."

The massive Romanesque Revival structure is composed of an administration building and a vast drill hall. Executed in deep red pressed brick and rough-faced, brownish red Potsdam stone, with red terra-cotta detail, the building has a series of circular corner towers. The main façade has a gabled entrance bay flanked by seventy-foot crenellated towers with rusticated first stories. The round-arched entrance, two stories high, is ornamented by terra-cotta friezes with the regimental motto and coat of arms. A large sculpted bronze plaque on the Bedford Avenue façade honors the soldiers of the regiment who fought in World War I.

GENERAL GRANT NATIONAL MEMORIAL, 1891–97
122nd Street and Riverside Drive, Manhattan
Architect: John H. Duncan
Designated (exterior and interior): November 25, 1975

On August 8, 1885, an estimated one million people watched as the funeral procession of Ulysses S. Grant—including some sixty thousand marchers—passed by. Grant was buried in a temporary tomb, but for the former president and hero of the Civil War, a more lasting tribute was demanded. Thus in 1886 the Grant Monument Association was created, and architect Napoleon LeBrun announced a competition in 1887 for a granite monument with figural sculpture to honor him.

Oddly enough, the association did not consider any of the designs submitted satisfactory; nonetheless the judges—LeBrun, George B. Post, William R. Ware, James Renwick, Jr., and James F. Ware—awarded top prizes to five memorial columns. A public outcry followed; press and public were united in their objection to what was considered a tired and outmoded type of memorial (virtually all the monuments to Civil War heroes had been in the form of memorial columns). The press suggested a building, modeled on two sources—the tomb of King Mausolus at Halicarnassus, which had recently been restored by James Fergusson, and George Kellum's Garfield Memorial, erected in 1884–90 in Cleveland, Ohio. In 1890, with the Congress and the public impatient to see Grant's memorial complete, five firms took part in a second competition; the winner was John Duncan, who had just received the commission for the Soldiers' and Sailors' Memorial Arch at Grand Army Plaza in Brooklyn.

In the disposition of its mass, Duncan's design for the Grant memorial recalls Kellum's Garfield Memorial; the circular colonnade was inspired by Fergusson's restoration of the Mausoleum at Halicarnassus. The colossal Doric entrance colonnade and pilastrade are based on Viollet-le-Duc's reconstruction of the Doric order from the Temple of Olympian Zeus at Agrigento.

On April 27, 1892, President Benjamin Harrison laid the cornerstone of the memorial. Five years later the bodies of President and Mrs. Grant were moved to the memorial and placed in the crypt, directly beneath the high, coffered dome. A circular cut in the floor that permits visitors to the tomb to see the crypt was inspired by Ludovico Visconti's tomb for Napoleon at Les Invalides. The bronze busts in the crypt were executed in 1938 under the supervision of the WPA. In the pendentives above are low-relief allegorical figures that depict different phases of Grant's life; outside are two recumbent figures representing Peace and Justice. All the figural sculpture is the work of J. Massey Rhind.

In the 1920s, John Russell Pope expanded the plaza and approach, adding two eagles. Pope wanted to complete Duncan's original program, which called for more extensive figural sculpture, but the advent of the Depression put an end to further construction. The exterior of the memorial is of Maine granite; the interior is executed in Lee and Carrara marbles.

IMPERIAL APARTMENTS, 1892
1327–1339 Bedford Avenue and 1198 Pacific Street,
Brooklyn
Architect: Montrose W. Morris
Designated: March 18, 1986

The Imperial Apartments was designed in 1892 by Montrose W. Morris for Louis F. Seitz. Located in Grant Square, the Imperial is among several distinguished buildings that recall the area's prestige at the turn of the century. It is one of a number of commissions Morris carried out for Seitz, including two other apartment buildings, the Alhambra and the Renaissance, both designated landmarks. The Imperial was also one of the earliest apartment houses in Brooklyn built for the middle class.

The design of the Imperial is based on the sixteenth-century châteaus of Renaissance France, executed in a skillful combination of buff-colored Roman brick, terra-cotta, slate, and metal. Rising from a stone base for four stories, the structure is crowned with a picturesque slate mansard fifth floor. Its three round corner towers with conical roofs create a romantic silhouette.

In scale and massing, the Imperial blends well with its row house neighbors, and the building is an important element of Grant Square, one of the most prestigious areas of Brooklyn in the early twentieth century.

RENAISSANCE APARTMENTS, 1892
140–144 Hancock Street and 488 Nostrand Avenue,
Brooklyn
Architect: Montrose W. Morris
Designated: March 18, 1986

The Renaissance Apartments, a striking 1892 building at the intersection of Nostrand Avenue and Hancock Street in the Bedford-Stuyvesant area, was commissioned by Louis F. Seitz, a local realtor. The Renaissance is one of a number of commissions that Brooklyn architect Montrose W. Morris executed for Seitz, including two apartment buildings nearby, the Alhambra and the Imperial, that are also designated landmarks.

Like the Imperial, the Renaissance combines buff Roman brick, terra-cotta, metal, and slate in a design inspired by the châteaus of sixteenth-century France. The building rises four stories from a stone base, with a picturesque slate mansard fifth story; the façade is designed in a striped pattern of continuous bands of terra-cotta separated by five courses of buff Roman brick. Among its distinguishing features are three round corner towers, classical arches, and a monumental Palladian arch joining the second, third, and fourth stories. The tall pedimented dormers, conical roofs with finials crowning the three towers, and picturesque, steep mansards all recall its French Renaissance antecedents and create a striking contrast to the angular, flat-roofed brownstones of the area.

The building is currently vacant.

520 WEST END AVENUE, 1892
Manhattan
Architect: Clarence F. True
Designated: March 17, 1987

The house at 520 West End Avenue, built in 1892 for cotton broker John B. Leech and his wife, Isabella, is an early and unusual work in the career of architect Clarence F. True. A seminal figure in establishing the initial architectural character of the Upper West Side, True was particularly active in the area west of Broadway.

The Leech residence, originally a large single-family town house, was built during the first period of development of West End Avenue, when the street was lined with handsome residences for prosperous upper-middle-class New Yorkers. In the bold form of its rusticated red sandstone, the complex massing of its tan Roman iron-spotted brick upper stories (now painted), and the subtle handling of its carved stone details of Romanesque and Gothic derivation, it is a fine example of the picturesque eclectic architecture of the late nineteenth century that once characterized West End Avenue as one of the city's most desirable residential avenues.

The building's corner site both enhances and emphasizes its status as one of the most significant surviving individually designed large town houses on the Upper West Side. One of the largest houses ever constructed on West End Avenue, it is now an apartment building.

Number 520 West End Avenue was designated a landmark on March 17, 1987. On June 9, 1988, Judge Walter M. Schackman of the New York Supreme Court overturned the designation. The city's Law Department is planning to appeal the decision.

351–355 CENTRAL PARK WEST, 1892–93
Manhattan
Architect: Gilbert A. Schellenger
Designated: November 10, 1987

These five row houses, built in 1892–93, are early survivors of the initial development of Central Park West. Before the 1880s that avenue was lined with a mixture of wooden shacks, small apartment houses, and single-family homes. As public transportation spread into the Upper West Side, intense real-estate development began, but progress lagged along Central Park West because of the high price of land. This block of houses is significant because it precedes the belated development of the avenue and was built when large portions of land were still undeveloped.

The Renaissance-style houses were designed by Gilbert Schellenger for developer Edward Kilpatrick in light-colored Roman brick, stone, and terra-cotta. The five houses are built in an alternating pattern of two different façades, distinguished by their window placement. Each stands four stories tall with the exception of the corner house, which is five stories. A restrictive agreement with the adjacent Scotch Presbyterian Church prevented the height of the houses from exceeding that of the church tower, and also insured their long-term survival. The houses remain intact today, still private residences, and recall a time when they were unique in their surroundings.

KNICKERBOCKER FIELD CLUB, 1892–93
114 East 18th Street, Brooklyn
Architects: Parfitt Brothers
Designated: July 11, 1978

In 1889, fifteen years after tennis was introduced to the United States, a small group of enthusiasts from Flatbush organized the Knickerbocker Field Club. In 1890 the club members erected a wood and stone building with bowling alleys in the basement and a dance floor and stage above. The small clubhouse soon proved inadequate, and in 1892 construction began on a Colonial Revival building designed by a prominent Brooklyn firm, the Parfitt Brothers.

The new club building was erected in part on the foundation of the earlier one, incorporating the bowling alley. The clapboard and shingle field house was a long, two-story building with a gambrel roof. A deep porch, carried on Doric columns, extended across the principle façade and around the southern end of the building. The main doorway was at the northern end; to its left, full-height double French windows opened onto the porch.

Under the picturesque roofline were dormer windows, each elegantly crowned by a broken-scroll pediment with central urn. The flat-roofed, one-story addition at the rear housed the billiard rooms and lounge.

In February 1988 the Knickerbocker Field Club was badly damaged by fire. An application for demolition was approved by the Landmarks Preservation Commission.

BROOKLYN FIRE HEADQUARTERS, 1892
365–367 Jay Street, Brooklyn
Architect: Frank Freeman
Designated: April 19, 1966

The old Brooklyn Fire Headquarters is one of New York City's finest examples of the Romanesque Revival style. Resplendent with the influence of the Chicago School, it is notable for its harmonious blending of tones and interesting juxtaposition of contrasting textures, including red sandstone trim with granite, terra-cotta details against the dark brown, Roman brick walls, and copper edging on the red tile roof. The careful proportioning of the structure's elements—a key to the success of Brooklyn architect Frank Freeman's design—is strikingly evident in the balancing of the high, broad, richly decorated arch of the fire engine exit with the imposing solidity of the watchtower that flanks it.

The Jay Street firehouse was used as a headquarters for just six years after its construction. When Brooklyn became part of Greater New York in 1898, the fire headquarters was moved to Manhattan and the Jay Street structure became a neighborhood firehouse. Today the building is owned by the city and was approved for conversion to low-income housing in 1987.

THE ARCHIVE, formerly the
U.S. Federal Building, 1892–99
641 Washington Street, Manhattan
Architect: W. J. Edbrooke
Designated: March 15, 1966

Located far to the west in Greenwich Village and occupying an entire city block is the former U.S. Federal Building, a handsome brick structure designed in the Romanesque Revival style by W. J. Edbrooke. Built in 1899 as the Appraisers' Warehouse by the U.S. government, it is ten stories high, with masonry bearing walls; its great arches and massive piers at street level are expressive of the load they carry. This extremely simple yet powerful structure, almost totally devoid of detail, relies on the rhythm and differentiation of its arches to achieve a quality of architectural integrity.

The great arches spring from the ground level, embracing both first- and basement-floor windows. Above these arches are paired, square-headed windows beneath a powerful horizontal stone belt course that extends around the structure. Above this, the windows are impressively carried up for five stories and arched at their tops. The immense scale of the building is skillfully diminished by means of paired windows extending up two stories and again arched; the topmost floor has a series of small, arched windows that rhythmically carry around the curved corners of the building and simulate the effect of the battlements of medieval castles.

After ten years of complex negotiations with city, state, and federal offices, the Rockmore Development Corporation reopened the building in May of 1988 as the Archive, a 479-unit rental apartment complex.

WEST END COLLEGIATE CHURCH AND SCHOOL,
1892–93
West 77th Street and West End Avenue, Manhattan
Architect: Robert W. Gibson
Designated: January 11, 1967

West End Collegiate Church and School was designed by Robert W. Gibson in 1892 in his own romantic combination of Dutch and Flemish Renaissance elements—appropriate to a church with deep roots in Dutch New Amsterdam. In fact, the Collegiate Church, an arm of the Dutch Reformed Church, was organized in New Amsterdam in 1628; the Collegiate School, begun in 1638, may be the oldest private secondary school in the country.

The design is both fresh and flamboyant and provides an old-world charm to the surrounding residential area. The yellow-brown brick church is distinguished by the elaborate gable of its façade. Its windows, its doorways, its corners, and the eighteen steps of the central gable are all enriched with stonework, frequently alternating with stripes of brick. The steps of the main gable and the dormer windows that thrust out from the red-tile roof erupt into terra-cotta brackets and pinnacles. Quoins define the building's corners and underscore the zigzag outlines of the gables. A handsome, lacy spire thrusts up from the center of the structure's high-pitched roof.

METROPOLITAN CLUB BUILDING, 1891–94; addition, 1912
1–11 East 60th Street, Manhattan
Architects: McKim, Mead & White; addition, Ogden Codman, Jr.
Designated: September 11, 1979

The Metropolitan Club Building, designed in the Italian Renaissance style by Stanford White, was the largest and most imposing clubhouse of its day. The purpose of the club was to give its members—some of New York's wealthiest citizens, including J. P. Morgan, the club's president, and Cornelius Vanderbilt—a place from which to enjoy a view of Central Park and the procession of society along Fifth Avenue.

The club is marked by a seven-bay façade, balanced asymmetrically on the east by a three-bay, two-story wing fronted by a courtyard. An elaborately modeled marble and copper cornice that projects six feet beyond the plane of the façade caps the building. Other prominent features include a restrained rusticated base, horizontal bands, and quoins that strengthen the corners. While the exterior is purposely restrained, the interior is extravagantly decorated, with a vaulted vestibule and monumental entrance hall constructed of expensive marbles.

The 1912 addition by Ogden Codman, Jr., is a six-story building containing bachelor apartments.

In the spring of 1987 a public debate was stirred by the plans of a developer to build a thirty-seven-story apartment tower over the club. The proposal was defended by other developers as a modest one that would respect the integrity of the landmark and enhance its courtyard. Preservationists argued that the proposed skyscraper would overwhelm the palazzo-style clubhouse and its asymmetrical courtyard, destroying the essence of the McKim, Mead & White design. The plans were ultimately rejected by the Landmarks Preservation Commission, and new ones are being prepared.

THE GERARD, 1893–94
123 West 44th Street, Manhattan
Architect: George Keister
Designated: July 27, 1982

The Gerard is an exceptionally fine brick, limestone, and terra-cotta residence hotel designed by George Keister. Erected in 1893–94, the building marks a transition in both American architectural taste and in the development of the western Midtown area.

The Gerard is notable for an unusual combination of Romanesque and Northern Gothic and Renaissance details found on very few other buildings in America, with carefully executed brickwork, curving bays, and striking gables and dormers. When it was erected, this thirteen-story apartment hotel was one of the tallest buildings in a predominantly low-rise residential area, and it heralded the enormous change that the neighborhood was to undergo as it became the heart of the city's theater district. Never a luxury hotel, the Gerard catered to respectable people who wished to stay in New York for an extended period. When completed, it had 132 suites and twenty-five studio apartments. Named after its manager, William G. Gerard, the hotel included an extremely elegant, one-hundred-foot-long dining room done in the Italian Renaissance manner, which now houses a restaurant. In 1920 the hotel was renamed the Hotel Langwell and later the Hotel 1-2-3. Today the building is used for residential rentals.

UNITED SYNAGOGUE OF AMERICA BUILDING,
formerly the Scribner Building, 1893–94
153–157 Fifth Avenue, Manhattan
Architect: Ernest Flagg
Designated: September 14, 1976

This steel-frame Beaux Arts office building once served as the corporate home of Charles Scribner's Sons and today is owned by the United Synagogue of America. In 1846, Charles Scribner founded a publishing house, Scribner & Baker, and the company soon distinguished itself as the leading publisher of books on theology and philosophy. By 1878, Scribner's sons had taken over the company and renamed it; the company moved to this building in 1894. The architect was Ernest Flagg, Charles Scribner's brother-in-law.

The base of the composition is rusticated limestone, with a wide storefront at the center beneath an entablature supported on brackets. The middle four stories have a tripartite vertical organization; the lowest of the four, like the base, is of rusticated limestone. The sixth story begins with a low parapet, behind which rises the slate mansard roof. The windows of the middle section are divided into three parts by slender colonnettes, set off from the level beneath them by a wide stone belt course with a balustrade carried forward on console brackets with lions' heads.

Charles Scribner's Sons moved uptown to a new building on Fifth Avenue in 1913.

BOWERY SAVINGS BANK, 1894
130 Bowery, Manhattan
Architects: McKim, Mead & White
Designated: April 19, 1966

This limestone structure is the first of McKim, Mead & White's three large bank buildings, all designed under the direction of Stanford White. L shaped in plan, with richly articulated entrance façades on Grand Street and the Bowery, it literally wraps around the old Butchers' and Drovers' Bank—the Bowery's rival—which had refused to sell its lot on the corner of Grand and Bowery.

On Grand Street, a sculpted pediment is raised on colossal Corinthian columns with a blank attic story above. The Corinthian order is carried around the building as a shallow pilastrade; the detailing is finely cut, and the architectural elements well-articulated.

On the Bowery, White exploited the narrow frontage, crowding together massive Corinthian columns *in antis* and a large triumphal arch. A densely carved pediment, floral frieze, and anthemia cover this arrangement. The blank surfaces of the square antae and attic provide an austere and satisfying counterpoint, focusing the energy of this powerful composition.

The building, once the Bowery's headquarters, is now a branch office. The Bowery is one of the few New York City banks to have kept its original banking hall in continuous use; as a result, the building is in excellent repair.

HIGH SCHOOL OF THE PERFORMING ARTS, formerly
Public School 67, 1893–94
120 West 46th Street, Manhattan
Architect: C.B.J. Snyder
Designated: May 19, 1981

The former Public School 67 is a rare surviving late-nineteenth-century Romanesque Revival school building. It was C.B.J. Snyder's first known building; he continued as architect to the New York City Board of Education for thirty years. During World War II, this elementary school housed the U.S. Maritime Commission.

In 1948 the principal of the Metropolitan Vocational School, Dr. Franklin J. Keller, needed a permanent location for the fledgling program for the performing arts; Public School 67 was chosen primarily for its Times Square location. Since the program's inception, many famous performers have graduated from the school, including Rita Moreno, Ben Vereen, Liza Minnelli, and Edward Villela. The school is probably best known as the setting for the popular movie and television series *Fame*.

Architecturally, the building is a fine example of Snyder's work for the public school system. It is a five-story stone and brick structure, symmetrically massed, with a projecting central three-bay pavilion taking the form of a tower rising above the roofline, and smaller projecting pavilions at each end. The Romanesque Revival features include an arch above the main entrance flanked by two columns, portrait busts, and an architrave frieze with a curving floral motif.

The High School of the Performing Arts moved in September 1984. The 46th Street building was being used as a special school when it was gutted by fire on February 13, 1988.

DOROTHY VALENTINE SMITH HOUSE, 1893–95
1213 Clove Road, Staten Island
Architect: Unknown
Designated: October 6, 1987

The Dorothy Valentine Smith House, built in 1893–95 on Staten Island, is noteworthy for both its architecture and its owners. The Smith house is recognized as a restrained example of the usually ornate Queen Anne style, especially when compared to similar houses built on Staten Island during the late nineteenth century. Such characteristics as the wraparound porch, tall chimney, ornamental shingles, and decorative window treatment, as well as the L-shaped plan and asymmetrical massing of architectural elements, are integral parts of the Queen Anne style.

The house was constructed for John Frederick Smith, a leading figure in banking and insurance and an active participant in Staten Island cultural and civic life. It eventually became the residence of Dorothy, the younger of his two children, who was deeply involved in the civic affairs and history of Staten Island. She wrote several books and articles, served as a trustee of the Staten Island Historical Society, and was a contributor to the historic village of Richmondtown. Now vacant, the Dorothy Valentine Smith house is a monument to an important figure in Staten Island's history.

CHURCH OF THE IMMACULATE CONCEPTION AND CLERGY HOUSES, formerly Grace Chapel and Hospital, 1894
406–414 East 14th Street, Manhattan
Architects: Barney & Chapman
Designated: June 7, 1966

The Church of the Immaculate Conception on East 14th Street is one of only two churches in the city inspired by the charming style of François I. Built in 1894, it was originally a Protestant church known as Grace Chapel and Hospital; the church was intended to provide free pews for those less fortunate financially than the members of nearby Grace Church itself.

A boldly severe building built of stone and Roman brick, the structure is distinguished by a freestanding tower, a steeply pitched gable roof, a large rose window embellishing the plain, asymmetrical façade, and a handsome doorway with a decorated arched portal. To the right of the doorway is a chapel of intimate charm, enriched with beautifully scaled details. Set between six pinnacled buttresses are paired, pointed-arched windows separated by small columns.

Adjacent to and contiguous with the church are the Clergy Houses, a pair of three-and-one-half-story brick and stone structures also designed in the François I style. The two structures are joined by a wide, low, sweeping arch, framing an entranceway to a small courtyard.

What was once a little neighborhood church provided a much-needed service for immigrant Protestants during the latter part of the nineteenth century. The influx of Protestant immigrants began to subside, and in 1943 the church and clergy houses were bought by Roman Catholics, who now make use of them to serve a new community.

83RD PRECINCT POLICE STATION AND STABLE, formerly 20th Precinct Station House, 1894–95
179 Wilson Avenue, Brooklyn
Architect: William B. Tubby
Designated: March 8, 1977

The imposing 83rd Precinct Police Station and connecting stable, dominating the corner site at the intersection of DeKalb and Wilson avenues in the Bushwick section of Brooklyn, was built in 1894–95 as the 20th Precinct Station House. A fine Romanesque Revival structure designed by William B. Tubby, it was hailed at the time of its construction as one of the best-equipped and handsomest police stations in the world.

Its most prominent feature is its corner tower, which effectively dominates the three-story brick building. Small, brick arches carried on a series of corbels ornament the flared top of the crenellated tower, which is crowned by a conical roof. The polychromatic use of red brick for the walls, with narrower yellow and ocher Roman brick for trim and base, enlivens the façade and adds rich texture and interest. The limestone entrance portico is composed of four columns supporting a console-bracketed entablature. Centered in the frieze is the seal of the City of Brooklyn with the Dutch motto, Eendraght Maakt Magt (Unity Makes Might).

The small stable, a common feature of nineteenth-century police stations, is connected to the station house by a one-story cell-block wing. A broad segmental-arched doorway marks its façade. The gabled roof is topped by a limestone finial.

The city-owned building is now administered by the Department of Housing Preservation and Development. One of the few intact and vacant police stations, it has been widely used as a location for shooting films and television shows.

FORMER NEW YORK LIFE INSURANCE BUILDING, 1894–98
346 Broadway
Architects: Stephen D. Hatch; McKim, Mead & White
Designated (exterior and interior): February 10, 1987

The former home office of the New York Life Insurance Company (which was organized in 1841 and is one of the oldest life insurance companies in America) was constructed between 1894 and 1898. A monumental freestanding skyscraper in the Italian Renaissance style, it was designed by Stephen D. Hatch and McKim, Mead & White. The building's history is interesting and complicated. The eastern rear section was designed by Hatch, and it was originally intended to harmonize with the old New York Life building of 1868–70, then located at the western end of the block. When Hatch suddenly died, the commission was turned over to McKim, Mead & White, and under their supervision the project took on new dimensions—the old building was demolished and the new building, now culminating in a palazzolike tower on Broadway, was carried to completion.

Built to project an image of prosperity, integrity, and permanence, 346 Broadway is an impressive white marble building that stands twelve stories high at the western end and thirteen at the eastern, in conformity with the slope of the site. A long, narrow structure with end pavilions, the Broadway tower pavilion is marked by a monumental portico entrance and crowning clock and bell tower. A thirty-three-foot-tall finial by Philip Martiny topped the tower until about 1928.

The elevations are noted for their handsome cornices and late Italian Renaissance–inspired detail. Crowning the building are four impressive large stone eagles, the emblem of New York Life. The clock tower (now the home of an art gallery) rises two stories. The four-sided striking clock by E. Howard & Co. has twelve-foot faces with Roman numerals—one of the few remaining in the city that have not been electrified.

The interiors of the building were designed using the finest craftsmanship and lavish materials—marble, bronze, mahogany—and incorporating rich classical motifs. Interestingly, the designated spaces bear the personal stamp of the architects—of Hatch most notably in the second-story executive offices, and of McKim, Mead & White in the presidential suite and the magnificent general office, which still contains three enormous walk-in safes.

In 1967, the building at 346 Broadway was acquired by the City of New York, and since then has housed courts and other city agencies.

UNIVERSITY HEIGHTS BRIDGE, 1893–95; addition, 1905–08
Harlem River from West 207th Street, Manhattan, to West Fordham Road, The Bronx
Consulting engineers: William H. Burr, Alfred P. Boller, and George W. Birdsall
Chief engineer: Othniel F. Nichols (addition)
Designated: September 11, 1984

The University Heights Bridge, which remains in use over the Harlem River, is a significant achievement in engineering as well as an aesthetically pleasing example of utilitarian architecture. This steel-truss bridge, consisting of a central swing (double) span and three deck-truss approach spans, is one of New York City's oldest major bridges and oldest extant swing bridges—a type that was employed primarily along the Harlem River between 1870 and 1910. The design, construction, move, and reconstruction of the bridge represent the collaboration of a distinguished group of American engineers.

Originally known as the Harlem Ship Canal Bridge, the structure, with a swing span and two flanking spans, bridged the Harlem River at Broadway. In 1905–08, in a complex bridge flotation operation, these spans were moved to 207th Street to form the University Heights Bridge over the Harlem River. The bridge is distinguished by its ornamental ironwork, handsome truss outline, and steel latticework, and its shelters of cast iron, copper, and stone.

LYCEE FRANÇAIS DE NEW YORK,
formerly the Henry T. Sloane Residence, 1894–96
9 East 72nd Street, Manhattan
Architects: Carrère & Hastings
Designated: January 11, 1977

By 1900, East 72nd Street was lined with the opulent town houses of rich New Yorkers, although only a few of these, such as the former Gertrude Rhinelander Waldo and Oliver Gould Jennings residences, remain today. Henry T. Sloane, a carpet and upholstery merchant, commissioned Carrère & Hastings to construct this Beaux Arts town house, which the *New York Times* called "one of the handsomest of the newer uptown residences." In 1899, after only two years of marriage, Sloane and his wife, the former Jessie Robbins, divorced. He never again lived at 9 East 72nd Street. Joseph Pulitzer occupied the house briefly before moving to 11 East 73rd Street; James Stillman purchased it in 1901. The building is currently occupied by the Lycée Français de New York.

The four-story limestone façade has four bays, unusually wide for New York, and is elaborately deocorated with classical details. Above the rusticated first story, an engaged composite colonnade divides the bays on the upper stories. The second story is the main floor, or "piano nobile," and contains tall segmental-arched French windows set behind low balustrades. Four dormer windows project from the high mansard roof.

The magnificence of the exterior is also reflected in the lavish interior. A porte cochère leads to an arcaded Court of Honor and main entrance, from which a stairway leads to the Grand Salon, stretching fifty feet across the façade.

Hall of Languages

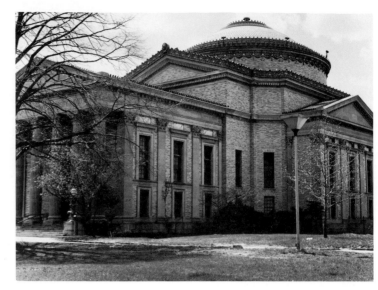

Gould Memorial Library

Hall of Fame

BRONX COMMUNITY COLLEGE,
C.U.N.Y., formerly New York University
University Heights Campus
Hall of Fame Terrace at Sedgwick Avenue
The Bronx
Architects: McKim, Mead & White

Hall of Languages, 1894
Designated: February 15, 1966

Hall of Fame, 1900
Designated: February 15, 1966

Gould Memorial Library, 1897–99
Designated: February 15, 1966: interior
designated August 11, 1981

Cornelius Baker Hall of Philosophy, 1912
Designated: February 15, 1966

In 1890 Henry MacCracken, vice-chancellor of New York University, decided to move the undergraduate students and faculty from the increasingly commercial Washington Square area to a more rustic setting. He approached Stanford White to design and plan a new campus, and by 1892, thanks to a large donation from the daughter of railroad baron and financier Jay Gould, the university had purchased the forty-acre H. W. T. Mali estate on Sedgwick Avenue in the Bronx. Construction at the new site began in 1894.

White's buff-colored brick and limestone buildings are symmetrically arranged around a cross axis, with the Gould Library at the center. Situated on a steep hillside above the Harlem River, the Gould Library is one of White's masterpieces. The drum is pushed far back onto an enormous granite and limestone base that supports the building dramatically. The entrance to the library is a portico facing the campus. The transition from the long, low stair to the three-story rotunda of the reading room, with its shallow saucer dome of Guastavino tile, is breathtaking. Sixteen green Connemara marble columns, considered to be the most extensive display of this type in the world, add a rich color accent to the interior.

Surrounding the library and set on a plateau above the Harlem River is the splendid Hall of Fame, an elegant semicircular arcade containing bronze busts of famous Americans. Two symmetrical classical-style buildings, the Hall of Languages and the Cornelius Baker Hall of Philosophy, stand at each end of the Hall of Fame. Each has an imposing flight of steps leading to an Ionic portico at the entrance. The third-floor windows of both are decorated with carved stone garlands; above, an ornate cornice is set on each low roof.

The subsidiary buildings, used as dormitories and for individual disciplines, are more modest.

Although the rural qualities of the area that first attracted MacCracken are long gone, the library still offers a remarkable view of the Harlem River.

In the 1960s New York University gradually returned to the Washington Square area, and in 1973 the Harlem River site became home to the Bronx Community College of the city university system.

Cornelius Baker Hall of Philosophy

McGOVERN-WEIR GREENHOUSE, formerly Weir Greenhouse, 1895
Southwest corner of Fifth Avenue and 25th Street, Brooklyn
Architect: C. Curtis Gillespie
Designated: April 13, 1982

The charming McGovern-Weir Greenhouse is the only Victorian commercial greenhouse known to survive in the city. Built by horticulturist James Weir, Jr., it was one of several greenhouses to serve visitors to neighboring Green-Wood Cemetery and is the only one remaining today.

Although the forms and massing of the greenhouse are extremely bold and impressive, the detailing is simple and straightforward. The building has a rectangular plan enlivened by projecting bays and domes. The greenhouse is a wood-frame structure enclosing glass panes, and has glass and galvanized-iron roof surfaces. The main entrance takes the form of an octagon. The double entry doors are flanked by wide window expanses with transoms; a cornice separates the transoms from a narrow clerestory. The sloping roof above is capped by an octagonal cupola with a ball finial.

The Weir Greenhouse, now called the McGovern-Weir Greenhouse, has been in continuous use for almost a century and continues to grace the approach to the historic cemetery.

ASSOCIATION OF THE BAR OF THE CITY OF NEW YORK, 1895
42 West 44th Street, Manhattan
Architect: Cyrus L. W. Eidlitz
Designated: May 10, 1966

The Association of the Bar of the City of New York was founded in 1870, "for the purpose of maintaining the honor and dignity of the profession of the Law, of cultivating social relations among its members and increasing its usefulness in promoting the due administration of justice."

This stately limestone building, with its skillful handling of the classical orders, was considered an appropriate symbol of the power and dignity of the law. Designed by noted architect Cyrus L. W. Eidlitz, the building has an imposing façade with a recessed porch and two magnificent fluted Doric columns. A strong horizontal stone band extends the entire width of the building, separating the base from the second floor. Above this, four pairs of well-proportioned Corinthian pilasters form three distinct bays, the center one wider than those on each side. The third-floor windows are small, but those on the fourth story are wide and flanked by Ionic columns. A Corinthian cornice with beautifully detailed brackets crowns the building and gives it a fitting termination.

The building contains one of the largest law libraries in the country. The club numbers among its past members distinguished lawyers who have helped to shape the opinions and policies of the Bar Association and the practices of the legal profession in New York, as well as throughout the country.

THE HARVARD CLUB OF NEW YORK CITY, 1893–94; additions, 1903, 1915, 1946
27 West 44th Street, Manhattan
Architects: McKim, Mead & White
Designated: January 11, 1967

The Harvard Club was organized in 1865 and incorporated in 1887 "to advance the interest of the University, and to promote social intercourse among the alumni resident in New York City and vicinity." In 1893–94, the second and present home of the Harvard Club of New York City was designed by architect Charles Follen McKim of McKim, Mead & White. Significant additions were made to the club by the same firm in 1903, 1915, and 1946.

The architects—who also designed the Harvard Union in 1902 and the Harvard Business School in 1926—planned a New York club building that would fit comfortably within the scale of its midtown Manhattan site and recall the Georgian architecture of the Harvard campus.

Limestone detail accents the red-brick façade; a limestone ledge supports two Ionic columns that in turn flank a central round-headed window and support a third-floor cornice. The finely carved shield of Harvard surmounts the cornice.

The intimate-looking building is actually quite large and continues through the block to 45th Street, where dormer windows punctuate the roof. Here, the exterior wall contains three-story round-headed windows set between brick pilasters that illuminate the great lounge inside. This room, considered by many architectural historians to be America's finest club room, rises the height of the entire building.

PUBLIC SCHOOL 108, 1895
200 Linwood Street, Brooklyn
Architect: James W. Naughton
Designated: February 3, 1981

Public School 108 was built in 1895 in the Cypress Hills section of Brooklyn. An imposing Romanesque Revival building, it was designed by James W. Naughton, who designed virtually all of Brooklyn's public schools in the late nineteenth century. Built of brick and Lake Superior sandstone, the structure rises above a rough-faced stone basement for three stories and is crowned by an attic fourth floor pierced with dormers.

The building is symmetrical in plan and divided into three parts: the three-bay-wide end pavilions are connected by recessed wings to the seven-bay-wide central entrance section. The pavilions add verticality, plasticity, and a play of light and shadow to the composition. Another picturesque feature is the modillioned roof cornice, broken by gabled dormer windows.

The building still functions as a public school.

CITY COLLEGE OF NEW YORK, C.U.N.Y., NORTH CAMPUS, 1895–1908
West 138th and West 140th streets, between Amsterdam Avenue and St. Nicholas Terrace, Manhattan
Architect: George B. Post
Designated: May 26, 1979

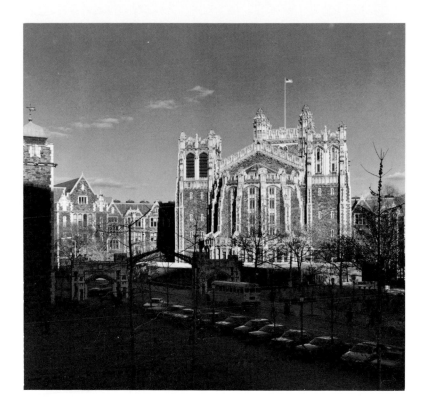

The City College of New York, C.U.N.Y., North Campus includes many fine examples of English Perpendicular Gothic style, also known as Collegiate Gothic. Designed as one complete project by the American architect George B. Post, these buildings comprised one of the first entire campuses in the United States to be built in this style.

The City College of New York was founded in 1847 by Townsend Harris as the Free Academy, originally located on Lexington Avenue between 22nd and 23rd streets. James Renwick, Jr., designed the building—a handsome Gothic Revival edifice that stood for seventy-nine years, until it was demolished in 1928. In 1866 the Free Academy was incorporated as the College of the City of New York. In 1897, the present site for a new campus was purchased, and George B. Post was selected to design it.

The impressive site at St. Nicholas Terrace was a massive stone outcropping of Manhattan schist, popularly referred to as the Acropolis. Post used schist and terra-cotta in the construction of the buildings, and the contrast created a dramatic effect. The new complex included six halls and three gates, including Townsend Harris Hall, Wingate Hall, Compton Hall, Goethals Hall, Baskerville Hall, Shepard Hall, the main gate, and two other entrance gates. The architecture is distinguished by its dramatic contrast of surface and elaborate Gothic detailing, including more than six hundred terra-cotta gargoyles and grotesques.

PUBLIC SCHOOL 111 ANNEX,
formerly Public School 9 Annex, 1895
251 Sterling Place, Brooklyn
Architect: James W. Naughton
Designated: January 10, 1978

The annex of Public School 111 presents a novel combination of Romanesque and classical ornament. A limestone basement supports three and one-half stories of brick and terra-cotta. The central pavilion contains the main entrance on the first story, marked by a large round arch flanked by paired columns, and a front-facing gable above the cornice line. On each side of the central pavilion are three-bay-wide wings with alternating rows of square and round-arched windows linked vertically by colonnettes. Elaborate terra-cotta panels ornament the spandrels, and large, ornate dormers punctuate the roofs. The terminal pavilions are more classical in detail; their two-bay façades are flanked by colossal fluted Corinthian pilasters, while the windows are ornamented with elaborated terra-cotta columns and lintels carried on brackets.

The annex was built as an extension of P.S. 111 (originally P.S. 9) across the street, whose facilities were taxed at the turn of the century by the rapid growth of its Prospect Heights neighborhood.

CHURCH OF ST. PAUL AND ST. ANDREW,
formerly St. Paul's Methodist Episcopal Church, 1895–97
540 West End Avenue, Manhattan
Architect: Robert H. Robertson
Designated: November 24, 1981

Erected between 1895 and 1897, the Church of St. Paul and St. Andrew exemplifies the eclecticism that spread throughout American architecture in the late nineteenth century. In his design, architect Robert H. Robertson merged a particularly unusual combination of forms drawn from early Christian, German Romanesque, and early Italian Renaissance precedents.

Situated at the juncture of two of the Upper West Side's widest streets, West End Avenue and 86th Street, the church is constructed in pale yellow Roman brick. The front façade on West End Avenue is raised above the street by a short flight of marble stairs and is dominated by a projecting entrance porch divided into three bays by monumental Corinthian pilasters of terra-cotta. Within each bay is a round-arched entrance enframement with paired rectangular doors and an arched transom filled with intricate grillwork, surmounted by an ornate ocular window flanked by terra-cotta reliefs of classically draped angels, each standing on a console above the entablature. At the north end of the front façade is a low, square tower set at an angle to the street. At the opposite corner a tall octagonal tower firmly anchors the church to its corner site.

The arcade of the 86th Street side is extremely regular in the rhythm of its six bays, each composed of a rectangular window and round-arched window separated by a terra-cotta plaque of foliate design. Set back and above the arcade is the tall clerestory with round-arched openings and unusual flying buttresses.

1857 ANTHONY AVENUE, 1896
The Bronx
Architects: Neville & Bagge
Designated: July 15, 1986

Located at the corner of Anthony Avenue and Mount Hope Place, this house is a handsome French Renaissance Revival structure designed for Edwin Shuttleworth by the New York firm of Neville & Bagge. Constructed in 1896, the residence is a reminder of the affluent suburban character of the Bronx at the turn of the century.

Occupying a corner site, the large two-and-one-half-story freestanding house is constructed in light gray rough-faced ashlar laid in a regular pattern of wider and narrower courses, with contrasting red mortar. The one-story veranda has wooden columns with stone capitals of unconventional design. The balustrade of the veranda, originally of wood, has been replaced by wrought-iron railings. The façade is marked by two full-length corner towers, each with a conical roof; the main body of the house is crowned by a hipped roof with a broad projecting square central bay at the first and second stories. The carved detail—griffins, fleurs-de-lis, and foliate ornament—is typical of the French Renaissance châteaux on which this design is based.

Representing a phase in the transformation of the Bronx from a sparsely populated rural area to a huge urban community, 1857 Anthony Avenue is a symbol of historical continuity, neighborhood pride, and architectural beauty.

MADISON AVENUE FRONT OF THE
SQUADRON A ARMORY, 1895
Madison Avenue between 94th and 95th streets, Manhattan
Architect: John A. Thomas
Designated: October 19, 1966

A wall with towers at each corner is all that remains of the Squadron
A Armory on Madison Avenue. The armory was completed in 1895
for use by the squadron, a volunteer unit that originated as a private
group of gentlemen riders called the First New York Hussars or First
Dragoons in 1884. The group adopted the name Troop A in 1889 and
Squadron A in 1895. Squadron A was active as a National Guard unit
until World War I, when it was called into service; it was reorganized
in 1917 as the 105th Machine Gun Battalion.

Reminiscent of a twelfth-century French medieval fortress, the
outline of the monumental brick edifice is clearly etched against the
sky. Square towers rise alongside round turrets, which are capped by
a neatly crenellated parapet wall that continues across the façade.

Today the armory is the castlelike backdrop of the schoolyard of
Hunter High School, built in 1969, and designed by Morris
Ketchum, Jr., a former vice-chairman of the New York City
Landmarks Preservation Commission.

CHURCH OF ST. IGNATIUS LOYOLA, 1895–1900
980 Park Avenue, Manhattan
Architects: Schickel & Ditmars
Designated: March 4, 1969

This Roman Catholic church is an amalgam of the features of
sixteenth- and seventeenth-century Roman Baroque churches. The
two-story façade is articulated by superposed Tuscan and Corinthian
pilastrades whose linear clarity is accented by the regular and
pleasing rhythm of the rusticated masonry facing. The Palladian
window and shallow pediment above, however, derive from the
Federal period. These features place this design squarely in the
Colonial Revival of around 1900. The lack of strong sculptural
articulation and rather squat proportions, which seem now to mar the
design, would have been offset by the twin two-hundred-foot towers
that were designed for the façade but never executed.

Although the 84th Street elevation is not especially notable, it
bears tantalizing remnants of an earlier structure. The rough-cut gray
masonry at the foot of this elevation was the foundation for the lower
chapel of a Gothic Revival church that was begun in 1884 but left
unfinished in 1886. This earlier church was dedicated to St.
Lawrence O'Toole, the titular saint of this parish, which was formed
in 1851. When the Jesuits took control of the parish in 1866, they
petitioned Rome for a new dedication to St. Ignatius Loyola, the
sixteenth-century missionary and founder of the Society of Jesus (the
Jesuits). The request for dedication change was granted in 1898.
The interior, although it is not a landmark, is richly decorated;
particularly noteworthy is the exquisite apse mosaic, made in 1915–
16 by Salviati and Co. of Venice.

POLO/RALPH LAUREN, formerly the
Gertrude Rhinelander Waldo Mansion, 1895–98
867 Madison Avenue, Manhattan
Architects: Kimball & Thompson
Designated: July 13, 1976

When Polo/Ralph Lauren opened its doors in April of 1986, New York was at last given the chance to see the grandeur of the historic Rhinelander Mansion, and be reminded of the lavish scale on which wealthy New Yorkers lived in the nineteenth century. In spite of its prime location on the Upper East Side, the building had been empty—and inaccessible—for much of its century-long life.

In 1895 Gertrude Rhinelander Waldo, a leading society matron and member of one of New York's old and established families, commissioned the architects Kimball & Thompson to create an imposing French Renaissance château in the style of François I on the corner of Madison Avenue and East 72nd Street. Although modeled on sixteenth-century French châteaux of the Loire valley, the reduced scale and urban setting of the Rhinelander Mansion result in an exceptionally fine adaptation of this style to American urban domestic architecture of the later nineteenth century. Introduced to New York by the renowned Paris-trained architect Richard Morris Hunt and used primarily for private residences, the style enjoyed a great vogue that led to its adoption by many architects, including Kimball & Thompson, despite the fact that the firm was closely associated with British architectural currents.

The mansion's four and one-half stories are constructed in limestone; the red roofs are accented by copper dormers, crestings, and finials. The main façade on Madison Avenue is symmetrically designed in a tripartite composition with projecting end bays and a slightly projecting central bay at the second and third stories. Other features include French Renaissance–style round-arched windows and handsome, elaborate carved ornaments.

The mansion was completed in 1898, but it remained unoccupied; Mrs. Waldo continued to live across the street in her sister's house until her death in 1911. Her sister, Laura Rhinelander, inherited the property, but one year later, the bank foreclosed on the mansion. Olivotti & Co., antique dealers, leased the building in 1920, and they became its first occupants, twenty-two years after its completion. Since that time, the mansion has been occupied by retailers, art auctioneers, and the nearby St. James Episcopal Church.

In 1986, the mansion was adapted for use as the Polo/Ralph Lauren shop, and both the interior and exterior have been handsomely renovated.

BROOKLYN MUSEUM, 1895–1924; altered, 1934–35
200 Eastern Parkway, Brooklyn
Architects: McKim, Mead & White
Designated: March 15, 1966

An imposing building designed by McKim, Mead & White in the Neoclassical style, the Brooklyn Museum was begun in 1895, adjacent to the site of the future Botanic Garden on Eastern Parkway. Of the four planned façades, the only one that was completed was the Eastern Parkway elevation. It was originally dominated by a monumental staircase reaching to the main entry on the present third floor, but the stairs were removed in 1934 in an attempt at modernization. The façade still retains its impressive six-column entrance portico, with a heavy Roman entablature, cornice, steep pediment filled with sculpted figures, and rich ornament. Not only is the pediment crowned by a confection of scrolls, fronds, and rosettes, but the cornice of the typically Roman attic behind it is adorned with alternating lions' heads and swags. Also impressive are the thirty heroic statues atop the cornice on each side of the portico, as well as the two sculpted female figures by Daniel Chester French representing Manhattan and Brooklyn; these were moved to the museum in 1964 when their pedestals at the Brooklyn end of the Manhattan Bridge were destroyed in a roadway improvement plan.

In the rear is the Frieda Schiff Warburg Memorial Sculpture Garden, designed in 1966 by Ian White. Here pieces of the former Pennsylvania Station are preserved, along with other architectural ornaments salvaged from demolished New York City buildings of note.

The museum is planning to add an extension, to be designed by the architectural team of Arata Isozaki & Associates/James Stewart Polshek & Partners.

ENGINE COMPANY 31, 1895
87 Lafayette Street, Manhattan
Architect: Napoleon Le Brun & Sons
Designated: January 18, 1966

Engine Company 31 is perhaps the best of the many eclectic firehouses built by the Le Brun firm, at a time when first-class architecture for civic purposes was considered as much of a necessity as fire protection itself. Located at 87 Lafayette Street, the Le Brun building was designed in the early French Renaissance style and looks very much like the châteaus of the time of François I. The entire spirit of the building—with its corner tower, its steep roof, its rich and varied dormers, and its stone and iron crestings—recalls a romantic fairy tale. Today it seems almost incredible that as recently as 1895 such an imaginative design was used for so utilitarian a structure.

The building was sold in 1986 to two community groups—the Chinatown Planning Council and the Downtown Community TV Center. They plan to spend large sums to rehabilitate the property and to use the building for community service activities.

APPELLATE DIVISION OF THE SUPREME COURT
OF THE STATE OF NEW YORK, 1896–99
Madison Avenue at East 25th Street, Manhattan
Architect: James Brown Lord
Designated: June 7, 1966; interior designated October 27, 1981

The Appellate Division of the New York State Supreme Court was established in 1894; the justices themselves chose the courthouse site on Madison Square and commissioned James Brown Lord to design the building.

The influence of English Palladian country house designs from the early eighteenth century is apparent in the colossal columns on the 25th Street and Madison Avenue façades, and in the high base and flat, unmolded walls; yet the decorative treatment is richer than that of any Palladian Revival building. In this elaborate decorative ensemble, featuring mural painting and freestanding sculpture, Lord was certainly responding to the vision of public architecture presented at the 1893 World's Columbian Exposition in Chicago.

Like other major cities in the 1890s, New York had artistic societies that promoted classically inspired, highly decorated architecture. In consultation with artists from the newly formed Municipal Art Society, the National Sculpture Society, and the National Society of Mural Painters, Lord worked out the elaborate iconographic scheme of the building, which deals with the attributes and historical development of justice and the law.

Seated figures of *Wisdom* and *Strength* by Frederick Ruckstuhl flank the main entry on 25th Street. The pediment sculpture by Charles Niehaus is an allegorical representation of the Triumph of Law; above is Daniel Chester French's *Justice, Power and Study*. The Corinthian portico on Madison Avenue is topped by caryatids representing the four seasons; the large figure group above is Karl Bitter's *Peace*. Above the cornice line, nine over-lifesize statues depict figures associated with the historical development of the law; they range from Philip Martiny's *Confucius* to Henry K. Bush-Brown's *Justinian*.

The courthouse was renovated in 1954. At this time, a tenth figure, *Mohammed*, was removed from above the cornice line at the request of religious leaders, Lord's original translucent Massachusetts marble was replaced with opaque Alabama marble, and a solid marble band was substituted for the original open-worked balustrade at street level.

The decorative program on the interior is more complex, but still in keeping with the themes developed outside. John La Farge oversaw the execution of all the interior paintings, ensuring that the painters adhered to a consistent figure scale and color scheme. The American mural tradition is seen here in its golden age. The interiors represent a zenith in the synthesis of architecture, decorative arts, and fine arts. The walls of the main hall, which functions as a lobby and waiting room, are lined with Siena marble and divided into bays by fluted marble piers and Corinthian pilasters. Above the original, leather-covered Herter Brothers chairs, a bronze and glass chandelier hangs from the gilded coffered and paneled ceiling. At frieze level are murals depicting allegorical figures related to the Law. Henry Siddons Mowbray's *The Transmission of the Law* fills the north wall, Robert Reids's *Justice* the east wall and eastern portion of the south wall, and Willard L. Metcalf's *Justice* the west wall and western portion of the south wall. Above the entrances on the south wall are *Law* and *Equity* by Charles Yardley Turner.

The courtroom is also lined with Siena marble, with piers and pilasters similar to those used in the main hall. A central, stained-glass dome, designed by Maitland Armstrong, dominates the gilded coffered and paneled ceiling. A balustered wooden railing separates the spectators from the proceedings in the courtroom. The front of the curved judges' bench has ornamental panels flanked by colonnettes, while the high back of the bench is distinguished by the scallop-shell tympana that mark each judge's seat. As in the main hall, allegorical murals complete the decorative plan. On the east wall, facing the judges' bench are three panels: Edwin Blashfield's *Power of the Law*, Edward Simmons's *Justice of the Law*, and Henry O. Walker's *Wisdom of the Law*. Above the judges' bench is Kenyon Cox's *The Reign of Law*. In sixteen panels between stained-glass windows on the north and south walls, Joseph Lauber depicted *Judicial Virtues*.

CONGREGATION SHEARITH ISRAEL, 1896–97
2 West 70th Street
Architects: Brunner & Tryon
Designated: March 19, 1974

Shearith Israel, whose name means "Remnant of Israel," is the oldest Jewish congregation in the United States. It dates from September 12, 1654, when a group of recently landed Spanish and Portuguese Jews held a Rosh Hashanah service in New Amsterdam. The earliest Jewish settlers in New York were mostly descendants of those exiled from Spain and Portugal in 1492. They first took refuge in Holland, and later in Brazil, when the Dutch established colonies there. But by 1654 the Portuguese had moved into Brazil and the Jews fled back to Holland. One ship carrying twenty-three refugees was captured by pirates, who stranded its passengers in the West Indies. The captain of a French ship, the *Saint Charles*, picked up the unfortunate group and brought them to the nearest Dutch settlement —New Amsterdam. Peter Stuyvesant was strongly opposed to the immigration of these refugees from Portuguese Brazil but, because the Jews were successful traders for the Dutch West India Company, he was overruled. In 1672, the Jews were playing an active role in the civic and commercial affairs of the colony, although they were still allowed neither to hold public office nor to build a synagogue.

The first building of the congregation, located on what is today South William Street and built in 1729, provided a permanent house of worship for the Jewish settlers. Parts of this building are preserved in the present synagogue at 2 West 70th Street, the fifth one built by the congregation.

Designed by the architects Arnold W. Brunner and Thomas Tryon and built in 1896–97, the synagogue was the first designed in the monumental Neoclassical style popular at the time for public and ecclesiastical structures at the turn of the century. Overlooking Central Park, the masonry façade is composed of four large engaged composite columns that embrace three round-arched openings, enclosed by elaborate bronze gates and three round-arched windows with balustrades. The openings, which resemble a loggia, lead to a porch containing the two main entrances. The front columns are crowned by an entablature with a modillioned cornice. Above this is a high attic with smooth-faced pilasters that enframe panels with classical wreath motifs. The attic also supports a handsome low pediment with foliate detail in the tympanum, which is crowned by the conventional anthemion-shaped acroteria. The 70th Street façade has end pavilions, the easternmost of which forms a part of the main massing on the Central Park façade. It is composed of large double doors and a transom with a handsome grille surmounted by a full entablature with foliate consoles.

WEST 54TH STREET HOUSES
Manhattan
Designated: February 3, 1981

13 West 54th Street, 1896–97
Architect: Henry J. Hardenbergh

5 West 54th Street, 1897–99
Architect: Robert H. Robertson

15 West 54th Street, 1896–97
Architect: Henry J. Hardenbergh

7 West 54th Street, 1899–1900
Architect: John H. Duncan

9–11 West 54th Street, 1896–98
Architects: McKim, Mead & White

These five town houses are examples of the elegant residential architecture that once characterized the West Fifties between Fifth and Sixth avenues—a neighborhood that developed in style and popularity after the landscaping of Central Park and during the building boom that followed the Civil War.

The house at 5 West 54th Street was built for neurologist Dr. Moses Allen Starr, designed by R. H. Robertson in the Renaissance Revival style using principles of Beaux Arts composition. Number 7 is an elegant French Beaux Arts house built for New York banker Philip Lehman, son of Emanuel Lehman, a founder of Lehman Brothers. The six-story twin residence at 9–11 West 54th was designed in the Georgian Revival style by McKim, Mead & White for businessman James Junius Goodwin; it now houses the U.S. Trust Company. Numbers 13 and 15 were built as a pair for businessman William Murray by New York architect Henry J. Hardenbergh in a Renaissance-inspired style using detail in a picturesque manner.

In the years following World War I, the superb residences of this neighborhood began to give way to commercial and apartment house development; this portion of 54th Street was a rare and fortunate exception to this trend.

PUBLIC SCHOOL 31, 1897–99
425 Grand Concourse, The Bronx
Architect: C. B. J. Snyder
Designated: July 15, 1986

During the second half of the nineteenth century, the Bronx experienced a wave of immigration from Europe as well as from other parts of New York. To accommodate this increased population, C. B. J. Snyder, then superintendent of school buildings for the Board of Education of New York, designed and developed a large number of public schools. Among these was the William Lloyd Garrison School, Public School 31. An early Collegiate Gothic building with Tudor-arched doorways, arched and square-headed windows, stone tracery, and gabled bays, P.S. 31 was a model for the style that would influence academic architecture for many years.

The school is a five-story, light brick and limestone building. Projecting from the center of the main façade is a tower, set off by two octagonal piers, with slit windows, figurehead-carved moldings and belt courses, and turrets on the fifth floor. Snyder included the tower as tribute to a tradition of New York City school building, begun in 1868 when the first tower adorned a school in Manhattan. The main entrance to the building is through the tower's base. Flanking the tower on each side are three symmetrically arranged gabled bays; the bays are pierced with groups of five narrow windows on the first four levels and with small double-turret windows on the gables of the fifth floor. Similar fenestration marks the western façade.

Low Memorial Library

COLUMBIA UNIVERSITY
West 116 Street between Broadway and Amsterdam Avenue, Manhattan

Low Memorial Library, 1895–97
Architects: McKim, Mead & White
Designated: September 20, 1966; interior designated, February 3, 1981

St. Paul's Chapel, 1904–07
Architects: Howells & Stokes
Designated: September 20, 1966

Casa Italiana, 1926–27
Architects: McKim, Mead & White
Designated: March 28, 1978

Columbia University, chartered in 1754 by King George II as King's College, is the oldest college in New York State. In 1894 Charles Follen McKim of McKim, Mead & White drafted a master plan for the university's new Morningside Heights campus. (The university had been previously housed in a group of buildings on Madison Avenue designed by Charles C. Haight in an academic Gothic mode.) McKim's design was quite a departure from the Collegiate Gothic style that was widely preferred for academic designs in the nineteenth century, and it was chosen precisely for its monumental classical forms derived from principles that he had learned at the Ecole des Beaux-Arts in Paris.

Low Memorial Library

St. Paul's Chapel

Casa Italiana

The Low Memorial Library was the first building erected. Situated on a slight rise, this gray Indiana limestone structure is planned as a Greek cross. Compared with later Beaux Arts–inspired structures, there is little ornament. The chief architectural effect derives from the proportions of the powerful masses. It has one of the finest intact Beaux Arts interiors in New York, which revolves around a magnificent octagonal hall covered by an imposing sky-blue dome. The galleries and ambulatories originally contained library stacks and seminar rooms. Though built as the main library, the design proved impracticable, and the building was soon given over to administrative functions. Butler Library (to the south) and almost two dozen specialty libraries around campus now hold the university's collection. Seth Low, who was president of the university from 1890 to 1901 and subsequently mayor of New York, gave the library in honor of his father, Abiel Abbot Low, a merchant in the China Trade.

In 1907, Howells & Stokes completed St. Paul's Chapel, designed as a Greek cross and inspired by Byzantine and early Renaissance forms. The architects combined a variety of materials (red, blue, and burned black brick, Indiana limestone, tile, and terra-cotta) to create a subtly colored combination that moves from mosaic rigidity outside to warm, glowing tones within. Large wooden doors open into a breathtaking space. The dome and transept barrel vaults are made from self-supporting Guastavino tile, a Catalan system introduced into the United States after 1881. The stained glass was executed by Armstrong & Maitland, an English stained-and art-glass manufacturer, after designs by John La Farge.

Facing the apse of St. Paul's across Amsterdam Avenue is the Casa Italiana, designed by William M. Kendall (the successor to McKim, Mead & White's practice after 1915). It was built by the donations and labor of American, Italian, and Italian-American volunteers. Appropriately, it houses the university's Italian Department, and is designed as an adaptation of a fifteenth-century Roman palazzo. The subtly fenestrated Amsterdam Avenue façade rises six stories from a heavily rusticated base. The wrought-iron window grills and entrance doors and the finely carved stone balustrades are particularly handsome, and provide a happy contrast to the severe masonry.

HOLY TRINITY CHURCH, ST. CHRISTOPHER HOUSE, AND PARSONAGE, 1897
312–316, 332 East 88th Street, Manhattan
Architect: Barney & Chapman
Designated: February 15, 1967

The Holy Trinity Church complex was built by Serena Rhinelander as a memorial to her grandfather and father. The structures—which occupy a portion of the old Rhinelander Farm, purchased in 1798 by the first William Rhinelander—are an outstanding example of late-nineteenth-century brick and terra-cotta ecclesiastical architecture. The church is distinguished by its bell tower, perhaps the most beautiful in the city. The sculptural and decorative features of the entire complex are of terra-cotta, while the bodies of the buildings are Roman brick, mottled golden brown, made especially for the project. All three buildings have red tile roofs.

The tower of the church is accented vertically by open belfry slots consisting of deeply revealed concentric Gothic arches. It terminates in a cluster of turrets, pinnacles, and dormers, crowned by a simple eight-sided spire. The tympanum above the main doors, executed by the noted nineteenth-century sculptor Karl Bitter, depicts the Trinity and saints.

St. Christopher House looks like an elegant French Renaissance château and complements the French Gothic church. Three large arches grace a recessed ground-floor porch. The porch is repeated on the second story, while steep roofs intersected by pinnacled dormers rise above the third-floor façade. The three-story Parsonage, also French Renaissance in style, is notable for its relatively plain exterior walls, which contrast with elaborate gabled dormers, pinnacled terminations, elegant main entrance, and ornate bronze crestings.

BAYARD-CONDICT BUILDING, 1897–99
65–69 Bleecker Street, Manhattan
Architect: Louis H. Sullivan
Designated: November 25, 1975

The Bayard-Condict Building is the only New York City project of the great Chicago architect Louis H. Sullivan. Erected as a commercial building on the edge of the city's former printing district, the Bayard-Condict Building is an elegant expression of the most significant feature of a skyscraper, its great height. With the structural innovations of his Chicago School colleagues as a point of departure, Sullivan worked from the multiple-story arcaded buildings of the 1870s to develop a new aesthetic for the skyscraper.

In the Bayard-Condict Building, as in all of Sullivan's mature skyscraper designs, narrow piers rise the full height of the façade without a horizontal break. Here, Sullivan refined this system of structural expression further, making the piers that stand in front of vertical steel elements thicker than those that serve as window mullions. Both elements terminate in stylized Ionic columns at the cornice level, where elegant winged victories are arranged among intertwined geometric and natural forms.

Sullivan's reputation was built, to a certain extent, on his inimitable and inventive ornamentation. His highly stylized decorative elements were abstracted from a variety of sources: classical detailing, Celtic metalwork, medieval manuscript decoration, the English Arts and Crafts movement, Art Nouveau, and natural forms. These motifs help to clarify the organization of his skyscraper façades: the horizontal spandrels and vertical elements have different types of ornament, thus differentiating one system from another. The large-scale use of such intricate ornament is possible only with terra-cotta, mass-produced by casting in plaster molds.

After decades of partial occupation and neglect, the Bayard-Condict Building has at last been restored. Because of its architectural importance and its great beauty, the building has attracted many tenants involved in the arts, architecture, engineering, and publishing.

THE REGISTER / JAMAICA ARTS CENTER, 1898
161–04 Jamaica Avenue, Queens
Architect: A. S. Macgregor
Designated: November 12, 1974

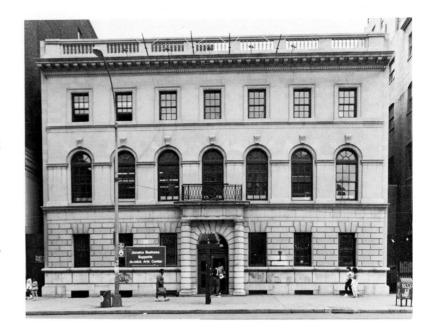

The Register / Jamaica Arts Center, an Italian Renaissance Revival building, was erected in 1898, the same year Queens was incorporated into Greater New York. The structure originally served as the office of the register, but has been adapted for use as a cultural center, with an art gallery, classrooms for York College, and offices of other arts organizations and the Greater Jamaica Development Corporation.

The building stands on a rusticated dark stone base that is separated from the first floor by a rolled molding, and the first floor is also rusticated, with smooth stone above. The focal point of the façade is the round-arched doorway, enframed by engaged columns. A classically inspired wrought-iron railing crowns the entrance. Console brackets at the roof support a dentiled stone cornice with egg-and-dart molding.

ERNEST FLAGG HOUSE, GATEHOUSE, AND GATE, 1898–1917
209 Flagg Place, Staten Island
Architect: Ernest Flagg
Designated: April 12, 1967; expanded landmark site designated, June 28, 1983

Ernest Flagg, the prominent, Brooklyn-born architect, trained at the Ecole des Beaux-Arts and in the atelier of Paul Blondel in Paris. Among his creations are the Singer Building, the Corcoran Art Gallery in Washington, D.C., and the U.S. Naval Academy at Annapolis, Maryland. Stone Court was his estate at Todt Hill, and includes a gatehouse, gardener's cottages, the Palm House, a swimming pool, stable, storage house, garage, and water towers.

For Stone Court, Flagg initially drew inspiration from local vernacular colonial architecture (although later revisions approximate classical Palladian villa architecture). The main house, constructed of local materials, had whitewashed fieldstone on the ground floor, shingles on the second story (now covered by aluminum siding), and a shingled gambrel roof, presently somewhat obscured by asphalt. The façade is dominated by a two-level veranda with a Tuscan columned entry porch on the first floor, surmounted by a projecting bay with three large windows on the second. A circular, balustraded widow's walk, twin brick chimneys with curved ventilator caps, and shed dormers accent the roof.

Surrounding this main house, Flagg arranged the other houses of the estate according to a modular system based upon mathematical principles of Greek architecture. These buildings, completed between 1898 and 1917, are likewise built of locally quarried fieldstone in the Colonial Revival style.

Stone Court was sold after Flagg's death in 1947, and today it serves as a seminary of the Pious Society of St. Charles.

Ernest Flagg House

Gatehouse and Gate

THE UNIVERSITY CLUB, 1897–99
1 West 54th Street, Manhattan
Architects: McKim, Mead & White
Designated: January 11, 1967

The University Club was founded in 1865 for "the promotion of Literature and Art." At the time, it was the only New York City club that required its members to have a college degree. In 1894 the club officers considered expanding their quarters in the Jerome Mansion at 26th Street and Madison Avenue. Unable to acquire the adjacent property, they purchased the five lots that make up the present site and hired Charles Follen McKim, himself a club member, to design their new building.

McKim turned to a venerable architectural type—the English gentleman's club, which evolved in the early Victorian period in the Pall Mall area of London. Sir Charles Barry, whose Travellers' Club (1829–32) inspired dozens of gentleman's clubs throughout England, had adapted the Florentine palazzo of the sixteenth century for the English clubhouse. His primary innovation was the increased scale of the palazzo's uppermost cornice. This feature, properly called a *cornicione*, enhances the effect of the building as a single mass.

McKim picked up this innovation, and then, to reinforce further the cubic form of the building, treated the corners as colossal, rusticated piers rising the full nine stories. He also grouped sets of three stories each between the stringcourses to "disguise" the nine-story building as a more typical Renaissance palazzo of three stories. Each grouping consists of a "major" story (actually two stories high, with a mezzanine in the back that does not show on the façade) and a full story above. As a result, the building appears lower than it actually is. The cornice friezes and balconies, with their delicate cast-bronze balustrades, have rich motifs derived directly from Italian Renaissance and Roman sources. McKim also added panels of carved and inscribed Knoxville marble, corresponding to the eighteen colleges and universities whose alumni then made up the majority of the membership; the carvings were designed by Daniel Chester French.

A stone balustrade originally ran around the base of the building at street level, softening the transition from the street to the building. It was removed in 1910 when the street was widened; McKim was quite bitter about the alteration.

Today representatives of more than 230 U.S. universities and 40 foreign institutions enjoy membership in this beautifully sited and elegant building. In June of 1987, the previously all-male club voted to admit women in accordance with a city ordinance.

ENGINE COMPANY 33, 1898
44 Great Jones Street, Manhattan
Architects: Ernest Flagg and W. B. Chambers
Designated: November 12, 1968

Firehouse, Engine Company 33, a flamboyant Beaux Arts building, was designed by the noted architect Ernest Flagg, with W. B. Chambers. Built in 1898, the structure is four stories high and constructed of brick and stone. The façade is dominated by an immense arch; beginning on the second floor, the deep, smooth arch rises from a strong rusticated stone base and swoops up three stories to an elegantly carved keystone above an ornate cartouche. The tall French windows on the second and fourth floors are enhanced by decorative metal railings. Two large doors for vehicles on the ground floor have three centered arches of graceful proportions. Crowning the structure is a very deep metal cornice ornamented with antefixes, fleurs-de-lis, and other classical forms. The firehouse is a superb example of rich civic architecture—full of flamboyance, but possessing dignity and order.

ESTONIAN HOUSE, formerly the Civic Club, 1898–99
243 East 34th Street, Manhattan
Architect: Thomas A. Gray
Designated: March 28, 1978

The Beaux Arts Civic Club building at 243 East 34th Street was designed by Brooklyn architect Thomas A. Gray. Built in 1898–99, it was commissioned by Frederick Norton Goddard, a leading social and political reformer, to house the Civic Club, which he founded to "render personal service as well as pecuniary aid to anybody needing it within the district [the members] regarded as their own, bordered by Fourth Avenue, 42nd Street, the East River and 23rd Street."

The façade of this handsome four-story limestone and brick building is enriched with a variety of decorative detail and distinguished by a rusticated first floor with three round-arched openings—a door and two windows. On the second level is a bowed central window with double French doors. Above a modillioned roof cornice crowned by a stone balustrade is a steeply pitched copper mansard roof.

The Civic Club remained in the building until 1946, when the Goddard family sold it to the Estonian Educational Society. The building now serves as a center for Estonian cultural and educational activities.

LYCEE FRANÇAIS DE NEW YORK, formerly the Oliver Gould Jennings Residence, 1898–99
7 East 72nd Street, Manhattan
Architects: Flagg & Chambers
Designated: January 11, 1977

The building at 7 East 72nd Street and the neighboring Sloane residence form an elegant pair of survivors from turn-of-the-century Manhattan. Historically known as the Oliver Gould Jennings residence, the house is an especially opulent example of a Beaux Arts town house. Ernest Flagg and Walter B. Chambers designed the house for Jennings, who was a director of the National Fuel Gas Company, Bethlehem Steel, and McKesson & Robbins. The architects worked to make the Jennings residence harmonize with the adjoining Sloane house by Carrère & Hastings, which was built two years earlier. Both are constructed of Indiana limestone, and they are further coordinated through the alignment of floor height and similar fenestration.

The Jennings house is three stories high above a basement and crowned by a tall convex mansard roof with ornate copper crestings. The variety of stone finishes of the façade creates visual interest, as do the iron railings. Other decorative elements consist of carved brackets, corbels, and scallop-shell motifs.

The Jennings and Sloane residences, which are truly Parisian in their elegance, are—appropriately—now part of the Lycée Français de New York, a private school with emphasis on French language, literature, and culture.

HAMILTON FISH PARK PLAY CENTER, 1898–1900
130 Pitt Street, Manhattan
Architects: Carrère & Hastings
Designated: December 21, 1982

Among the most notable small civic buildings in the city, the Hamilton Fish Play Center was designed in 1898 by the eminent firm of Carrère & Hastings. An outstanding example of the French Beaux Arts–inspired style favored by the firm, and designed in the manner of a small garden pavilion planned within a formal park, the building reflected the belief of the architects that utilitarian structures deserved a sophisticated architectural treatment. The park was built as part of a movement to add open space to the densely populated slums of the Lower East Side.

Inspired by Charles Girault's Petit Palais in Paris (1895), the pavilion is a symmetrically massed structure; the main focus is on the projecting centrally placed, round-arched entrance portal, constructed of limestone with brick trim. To each side of the entrance are three brick and stone bays set above a continuous high limestone basement.

The pavilion is used today for locker rooms and as an entrance to the swimming pool, which was added in 1935–36. Although the park itself has been redesigned twice since it was completed, the pavilion has remained a success, and stands as a monument to nineteenth-century notions of "civic betterment"—the belief that great architecture and design could help to endow the citizenry with outstanding moral character.

THE INDONESIAN PAVILION, formerly the William H. Moore House, 1898–1900
4 East 54th Street, Manhattan
Architects: McKim, Mead & White
Designated: January 11, 1967

The careful symmetry, order, and unity of structure, combined with the imaginative detail and ornamentation of this building, are typical of the work of McKim, Mead & White. Now the Indonesian Pavilion, this town house was built as a New York home for William H. Moore (1848–1923), a Chicago industrialist active in the foundation of the United States Steel Corporation, the American Can Company, and the National Biscuit Company. For many years it housed the America-Israel Cultural Foundation.

In a loose adaptation of Italian Renaissance design, the architects established order and stability through simple symmetrical fenestration. They then relieved any rigidity in the arrangement by successively reducing the volumes of the heavy window moldings from the first to the fifth floors. The surface is further enlivened by rustication on the first story and by the inclusion of ornate detail overall. The first-floor windows are graced with voluted keystones, while those of the floor above it are adorned with bracketed cornices; an elaborate dentiled entablature with a scallop-shell frieze rests above the windows of the fifth floor. Intricate carving ornaments an imposing second-floor balcony, and wrought-iron work is added to a smaller balcony above the central window head. Other decorative details include a cartouche carved on the door, a horizontal dentiled belt course between the fourth and fifth floors, and voluted brackets beneath the main cornice and balustrade.

In 1986, the building was renovated by the firm of Breger Terjesen Bermel.

NEW YORK PUBLIC LIBRARY, MAIN BRANCH, 1898–1911
476 Fifth Avenue at 42nd Street, Manhattan
Architects: Carrère & Hastings
Designated (exterior and interior): January 11, 1967

The New York Public Library was established in 1895, a consolidation of the Astor and Lenox libraries and a generous bequest of Samuel J. Tilden, former governor of New York, and an open competition was held among the city's most prominent architects to design its building. The rules of the competition were devised by John Shaw Billings (the library's first director), in collaboration with Bernard Green, the engineer who built the Library of Congress, and William R. Ware, founder of the school of architecture at Columbia University. Thomas Hastings of Carrère & Hastings submitted the winning design, and the cornerstone was laid in 1902.

Thomas Hastings's design was selected as much for its striking eighteenth-century French elevations as for its plan. Built of white Vermont marble, the Fifth Avenue façade is characterized by a contrast between finely executed detailing and broad, unrelieved surfaces. This contrast is especially noticeable in the main entrance, which sits atop an ample flight of steps. Here, Corinthian columns stand before three monumental arches, which form a deep porch with transverse barrel vaults. This section is connected to smaller, pedimented pavilions by colossal pilasters, and the whole rides on a massive rusticated base. The heavy masonry corners are the only unresolved elements in an otherwise flawless composition.

These and other aspects of the design troubled Hastings, who revised his plan repeatedly; he suggested alterations as late as 1927, and reportedly left money in his will to pay for alterations which were never made. The side façades repeat the window-over-arch motif from the main façade, with blank, barely molded piers replacing the Corinthian pilasters. The Bryant Park elevation, which contains the book stacks, is appropriately more modest, with simply molded arches, corner quoining, and piers executed in gray brick and limestone.

Four artists collaborated on the exterior sculpture: George Grey Barnard did the pediment; Paul W. Bartlett, the attic sculpture; Frederick MacMonnies, the fountains; and E. C. Potter, the now celebrated lions. At key points of the interior, many of the same muralists who had collaborated on the New York Court of Appeals building combined their talents with architect and sculptors to create superb decorative ensembles. The four murals and two lunettes in the Central Hall were painted by Edward Laning under the Artists Program of the WPA. They were completed in 1940. The ceiling, also by Laning, was finished in 1942.

An extensive restoration and renovation program is now under way. The work done in the Gottesman Exhibition Hall gives one a sense of the structure's original splendor and suggests what New Yorkers have to look forward to when the current restoration is completed.

NEW YORK YACHT CLUB, 1899–1900
37 West 44th Street, Manhattan
Architects: Warren & Wetmore
Designated: September 11, 1979

Whitney Warren's Yacht Club building is an expression of Baroque ingenuity adapted for recreational purposes: to house the country's most prestigious yachting institution, whose members wanted a showcase for their club. J. Pierpont Morgan, commodore of the Yacht Club, offered to purchase the necessary lots on the condition that the building display an impressive, seventy-five-foot front.

The resulting Beaux Arts structure includes elaborate decorations and an asymmetrical composition with external divisions that correspond to an internal plan. Grand arched windows mark each of the principal club rooms. The entire fine-grained, brick façade displays the base-shaft-capital separations of a classical column. This horizontal arrangement is offset by a vertical entrance pavilion divided into three external sections that in turn correspond to the different levels inside. Decorated with two stanchions and a lighted cartouche, the club's entrance occupies a single bay of the seven-story, four-bay front. Surrounding each of the remaining bay windows, a sculpted framework of sailing vessel sterns, shells, and seaweed announces the nautical theme of the private club inside. Grand in scale and romantic in tone, the Yacht Club building suggests the former elegance of New York's clubhouse district.

DUKE-SEMANS HOUSE, 1899–1901
1009 Fifth Avenue, Manhattan
Architects: Welch, Smith & Provot
Designated: February 19, 1974

This handsome Beaux Arts mansion, which was completed in 1901 and is prominently sited on the southeast corner of Fifth Avenue and 82nd Street, is one of the few survivors of the grand residences that once lined Fifth Avenue. Designed by Alexander M. Welch of the firm Welch, Smith & Provot, the house was built for S. W. Hall and T. W. Hall, speculative builders who specialized in the construction of large private residences.

The six-story limestone and brick mansion has a narrow façade facing Fifth Avenue, dominated by a broad, curved bay extending from the basement through the fourth floor. The roof, with two towers rising above the ends of the main block of the house, is covered with red tiling and crowned by handsome, boldly scaled copper crestings and finials. The 82nd Street façade is symmetrically composed; two slightly projecting corner pavilions flank a central four-story curved bay—a tripartite composition very typical of Beaux Arts design. The roof cornice is crowned by a balustrade behind which appear dormer windows with richly adorned arched pediments. Rich surface ornamentation, in the form of carved cartouches, wrought-iron railings, belt courses, and carved brackets, embellish the surface.

Shortly after its completion, 1009 Fifth was bought by the industrialist Benjamin N. Duke, a director and cofounder of the American Tobacco Company. In 1907, Benjamin sold the mansion to his brother and business partner, James B. Duke. After James's new residence at East 78th Street and Fifth Avenue was completed, 1009 was occupied by Angier Buchanan Duke, son of Benjamin Duke. The next resident was Angier's sister, Mrs. A. J. Drexel Biddle, and the house has remained in the Biddle family ever since. It has been fully restored, and is now known as the Duke-Semans House.

COOPER-HEWITT MUSEUM, formerly the Andrew Carnegie Mansion, 1899–1902
2 East 91st Street, Manhattan
Architects: Babb, Cook & Willard
Designated: February 19, 1974

Now the home of the Cooper-Hewitt Museum, Andrew Carnegie's sixty-four-room mansion on upper Fifth Avenue was one of New York's grandest private residences. Carnegie was born in Scotland in 1835 and immigrated to the United States with his family in 1848. He started as a full-time bobbin boy in a cotton mill, and over the next fifty years amassed a huge fortune from steamship and railroad lines, iron, coal, and steel companies. At his death in 1919, Carnegie was one of America's richest men and a noted philanthropist.

In 1898 Carnegie decided to build what he called the "most modest, plainest, and roomiest house in New York." In the 1860s and '70s, most affluent property owners built their sumptuous palaces on Fifth Avenue in the sixties and seventies, but Carnegie preferred the open space afforded by uptown living, and on his new grounds there was room for a magnificent garden filled with wisteria, azaleas, rhododendron, and ornamental trees. Carnegie's move encouraged other wealthy New Yorkers to follow suit, and the area became known as Carnegie Hill.

The architecture of the mansion is reminiscent of a Georgian-style English country house. In line with Carnegie's "modest" desires, the mansion is much more restrained than the "châteaus" and "palazzi" of his New York contemporaries. It is one of the few remaining freestanding houses in Manhattan. The four-story, symmetrical structure was constructed in red brick with limestone trim, and is typically Georgian in its use of heavy quoins and carved window frames, with a modillioned roof cornice beneath a balustrade. Segmental arches, copper-faced dormers, and tall, red-brick chimneys with limestone ornament add vitality at roof level. The main entrance on 91st Street was sheltered by a Tiffany-style copper and glass canopy.

The Carnegie mansion was not only inventive in architectural and geographical terms, but also contained several significant engineering techniques, including a heating and ventilation system that brought air inside, filtered it, heated and cooled it, and adjusted the humidity to the proper level. Carnegie even installed a filter system to purify the drinking water.

Carnegie's widow, Louise, lived in the house until her death in 1946, when it became part of Columbia University. In 1972, the building was given to the Smithsonian Institution to house its National Museum of Design. In 1976 it reopened to the public as the Cooper-Hewitt Museum.

CONSULATE GENERAL OF ARGENTINA,
formerly the Harry B. Hollins House, 1899–1901; addition, 1924
12–14 West 56th Street, Manhattan
Architects: McKim, Mead & White; addition, J. E. R. Carpenter
Designated: June 19, 1984

The building at 12–14 West 56th Street, designed by Stanford White as a residence for banker Harry B. Hollins, is one of the most elegant and well-proportioned Georgian Revival town houses of its time. Its strikingly simple façade is distinguished by a rusticated limestone ground floor; each of the three French windows on the second floor is fronted by a low, iron balcony and capped by a carved lunette, and the whole is crowned by a heavy limestone modillioned cornice with a parapet balustrade concealing the shape of the peaked roof. A small two-story, brick-faced extension on the east side of the building, added in 1924 by J.E.R. Carpenter, is set back from the street line behind a one-story aedicular entrance framed by fluted Corinthian pilasters; the original entrance is now the central ground-floor window.

The building has housed the Calumet Club, several commercial establishments, the Salvation Army, and, since 1947, the Argentine Consulate General.

ANSONIA HOTEL, 1899–1904
2101–2119 Broadway, Manhattan
Architect: Paul E. M. Duboy
Designated: March 14, 1972

The Ansonia Hotel, built between 1899 and 1904, embodies the standard of luxury applied to turn-of-the-century apartment buildings on Manhattan's Upper West Side. The hotel was designed by French architect Paul E. M. Duboy in the full flowering of the late Beaux Arts style—with the purely decorative aspects of the style given full expression in the building. The design was very much under the personal control of the owner-builder, William Earl Dodge Stokes, a real-estate developer who was responsible for much of the early growth of Riverside Drive and the Upper West Side. The hotel was named after the town of Ansonia, Connecticut, where Stokes's grandfather, Anson Greene Phelps, founded the Ansonia Brass & Copper Co.

Built with over 300 suites, the Ansonia rises seventeen stories; its façades are covered with ornament and balconies, marked by splendid corner towers, and topped by mansards in the very best French tradition. The effect is one of lightness, grace, and elegance, and the profuse surface ornament is never overbearing. The most striking features of this vast building are the corner towers, with their domes and railings, which rise slightly above and repeat the theme of the three-story convex mansard roof that tops the building. Another interesting feature is a series of recessed courts—two on the north, two on the south, and one on Broadway—that were intended to maximize light and air. The tiers of windows, recessed courts, and rounded towers establish a sense of verticality that is skillfully modulated by a series of horizontal balconies. The contrast of highly ornamented and delicate ironwork with terra-cotta and massive limestone details, and the contrast of quoins and rustication with smooth-paneled surfaces of brickwork, creates a highly dramatic and elegant surface.

The building, originally planned as a residential hotel, incorporated many of Stokes's own inventive ideas, such as heavy, all-masonry fireproof construction with heavy interior partitions to separate apartments. This construction was also virtually (and unintentionally) soundproof, a factor that has always made the building attractive to musicians. Indeed, it has numbered among its notable tenants Leopold Auer, Enrico Caruso, Bruno Castagna, Yehudi Menuhin, Lily Pons, Antonio Scotti, Igor Stravinsky, and Arturo Toscanini.

The Ansonia was always a highly individual enterprise; when it first opened, it included such unheard-of attractions as shops in the cellar, two swimming pools, and a roof garden where Stokes kept goats, ducks, chickens, and a pet bear. He sold eggs to the tenants at half-price until a lawsuit terminated this enterprise.

The Conservatory

BRONX PARK
The Bronx

Lorillard Snuff Mill, c. 1840
New York Botanical Garden
Architect: Unknown
Designated: April 19, 1966

The Conservatory, including Palm House and
wings, 1899–1902
New York Botanical Garden
Architect: William R. Cobb for Lord &
Burnham
Designated: October 16, 1973

Rockefeller Fountain, eighteenth century,
erected 1910
New York Zoological Park
Artist: Unknown
Designated: February 20, 1968

Rainey Memorial Gates, 1934
New York Zoological Park
Sculptor: Paul Manship
Designated: January 11, 1967

Bronx Park, containing the New York Botanical Garden and the New York Zoological Park, is
located on 661 acres purchased by the City of New York in 1884 from the Lorillard family and
other Bronx landowners. Among the more notable features of the Botanical Garden are the
original Lorillard Snuff Mill and the recently refurbished Enid A. Haupt Conservatory. Important
features of the Zoological Park include the Rockefeller Fountain and the Rainey Memorial Gates.

The Lorillard Snuff Mill was built about 1840 on the site of an earlier wooden gristmill. It is
one of the few surviving pre–Civil War industrial buildings that were once a common feature of
the landscape; the mill was in operation until about 1870. After the city acquired the property,
the Parks Department used the mill for a carpentry shop, leaving its machinery and its

Lorillard Snuff Mill

waterwheel unchanged until about 1900. Although the mill has been altered to serve as a café, its old fieldstone walls, brick trim, and century-old beams are still intact.

The Enid A. Haupt Conservatory, named in 1978 for the philanthropist who provided for its restoration by Edward Larrabee Barnes, was constructed in 1899–1902. Inspired by the Royal Botanic Gardens at Kew, England, and influenced by London's Crystal Palace of 1851, the structure was designed by William R. Cobb of the distinguished greenhouse firm of Lord & Burnham. The structure is C shaped in plan, and consists of the central Palm House (about one hundred feet in diameter) and ten connected houses, all built with steel posts bolted to stone foundations, which in turn support bowed steel ribs to form a curved roof.

Rockefeller Fountain

The eighteenth-century Rockefeller Fountain was purchased from Como, Italy, by William Rockefeller in 1902 and donated to the Zoological Park. It was moved to a circle in the garden's concourse in 1910. The marble sculpture is composed of an enormous bowl and a central shaft. Four large shells rest on the bowl, each containing a cherub playfully astride a sea horse. The sculpted shells, which are supported by mermaids and sea gods, alternate with grotesque bronze heads. The central shaft, supported by four sea monsters, is surmounted by a goose, from whose beak water spouts skyward to trickle down into the basin thirty feet below.

The Rainey Memorial Gates, located at the Concourse entrance to the Zoological Park, were completed in 1934 by sculptor Paul Manship. These monumental, freestanding Art Deco bronze gates with animal and plant motifs, which took five years to design and two to cast, were given to the Zoological Park by Grace Rainey Rogers as a memorial to her brother, Paul Rainey, a big-game hunter, who donated a number of exotic animals to the zoo. The central post that separates the gates' two openings is in the form of a tree trunk, modeled in ascending curves filled with figures of birds in profile; the tree is topped by a seated lion enframed by a soaring burst of stylized tree limbs that seem to metamorphose into birds' wings. Smaller trees flank each side of the gate, one topped by a panther and the other by a baboon.

Rainey Memorial Gates

SURROGATE'S COURT, formerly the Hall of Records, 1899–1907
31 Chambers Street, Manhattan
Architects: John R. Thomas (1899–1901); Horgan & Slattery (1901–11)
Designated: February 15, 1966; interior designated May 11, 1976

By 1888, the old eighteenth-century "gaol" in City Hall Park, which served as New York's first hall of records, had proved itself too small for the city's needs. The Sinking Fund Commission was formed to study the problem, and in 1892 it recommended razing City Hall and erecting a larger building that would combine both functions. An open competition drew over 130 entries; the winner was John R. Thomas, a Rochester-born architect with a wide New York City practice.

The public, however, was outraged at the proposal to destroy City Hall, and in 1894 the plan was abandoned. The current site was chosen in 1897 and Thomas retained the commission, but he died in 1901 before its completion. The Tammany Hall–connected construction firm of Horgan & Slattery finished the work largely according to Thomas's plans.

The building is of white Maine granite. Its high mansard roof and prominent chimneys are characteristic of French Second Empire design, but the pedimented central pavilion, colossal Corinthian colonnade, heavily rusticated base, and the division of the façade into three horizontal sections are all Beaux Arts features, as is the abundant architectural and figural sculpture. The figures in the roof area, representing the stages of man's development from childhood through old age, are the work of Henry K. Bush-Brown. The statues above the colonnade depict notable New Yorkers, from the founding of the Dutch settlement through 1888. These, as well as the Chambers Street groups portraying *New York in Its Infancy* and *New York in Revolutionary Times*, are by Philip Martiny.

Entered from the Chambers Street façade, the foyer and main lobby are among the most impressive interiors from this period in the entire city. The rusticated, polished yellow Siena marble and low-level lighting produce a glistening effect. The elliptical arched ceiling in the entrance foyer is covered with a mosaic by William de Leftwich Dodge, and bears symbols appropriate to a hall of records and the signs of the zodiac. The vault spandrels depict earlier instances of record keeping. The fine, white marble allegorical groups by Albert Weinert depict *The Consolidation of Greater New York* on the east, and on the west, *Recording of the Purchase of Manhattan Island*.

The original building was designed to include the Surrogate's Court, and the court's long association with the Hall of Records prompted the building's name change in 1963. In addition to the offices and courtrooms of the surrogate judges of Manhattan, the building is also occupied by the New York County Clerk, the City Register, the Office of the Public Administrator, the City Sheriff, and the New York City Department of Records and Information Services.

SOLDIERS AND SAILORS MONUMENT, 1900–02
Riverside Park at West 89th Street, Manhattan
Architects: Stoughton & Stoughton, with Paul Emile Marie Duboy
Designated: September 14, 1976

The Soldiers and Sailors Monument in Riverside Park pays tribute to the New York regiments that fought in the Civil War. The architects Stoughton & Stoughton won the competition for the design, which was judged by professors William R. Ware and A.D.F. Hamlin of Columbia University and architecture critic Russell Sturgis. The monument was originally intended to be erected at 59th Street and Fifth Avenue, but this plan was rejected by the Municipal Art Society.

To adapt their design to the new site, the architects invited Paul Emile Marie Duboy to collaborate with them. The cornerstone was laid on December 15, 1900, with Governor Theodore Roosevelt officiating. The monument's unveiling on Memorial Day, May 30, 1902, was followed by a parade of Civil War veterans.

The simple, white marble structure is based on the Choragic Monument of Lysicrates in Athens. One hundred feet high, it rests on a granite platform above a series of balustraded terraces. Twelve Corinthian columns, thirty-six feet high, form a colonnade that rises from a rusticated marble base adorned with laurel and oak leaves. Above the colonnade is a full entablature with a frieze containing the inscription, "To the Memory of the Brave Soldiers and Sailors who Saved the Union." A low conical roof decorated by an elaborate marble finial tops the building. The single entrance has a marble enframement crowned by a cornice supporting an eagle. Between 1961 and 1963 the monument was extensively rehabilitated at a cost of over $1 million.

GRAHAM COURT APARTMENTS, 1899–1901
1923–1937 Adam Clayton Powell, Jr., Boulevard, Manhattan
Architects: Clinton & Russell
Designated: October 16, 1984

Commissioned by William Waldorf Astor, the Graham Court Apartments were constructed in 1899–1901 as part of the great Harlem real-estate boom. Designed by the firm of Clinton & Russell, architects best known for their many apartment houses, hotels, and early commercial skyscrapers in New York City, the Graham Court Apartments were built as luxury apartments, and the building's design is one of the signal achievements in the history of the apartment house in the city. Graham Court is quadrangular in plan and built around a central courtyard—one of the few apartment houses of this type in New York City. In a conscious effort to evoke an image of luxury, the building recalls an Italian Renaissance palazzo; eight stories high with a projecting string course, the structure is divided horizontally into three parts with a two-story rusticated base. The whole is characterized by monumentality, symmetry, and restraint.

When Graham Court was built, West Harlem was developing into a prosperous and fashionable neighborhood; it attracted affluent people who had lived in attractive brownstones and luxury apartment buildings along Seventh and Lenox avenues. Graham Court, the largest and finest of the new buildings, was also one of the last major apartment buildings in Harlem to become integrated: it was not open to black residents until 1928. The building remained under the control of the William Waldorf Astor estate until 1933. It remains one of the most notable buildings in Harlem, a survivor from the neighborhood's heyday at the turn of the century.

THE DORILTON, 1900–02
171 West 71st Street, Manhattan
Architects: Janes & Leo
Designated: October 8, 1974

Located diagonally across Broadway from the famed Ansonia Hotel, this French Second Empire style apartment house was equally popular among local artists and musicians. Like the Ansonia, it has large, soundproof rooms; it also displays an exceptionally decorative exterior.

The base, topped by a balustrade, consists of two stories of rusticated limestone. The large main portion is accentuated by limestone quoins and alternating limestone brick bands; it also contains an impressive five-story bay window flanked by female figures at its base. This central shape is echoed on the 71st Street façade by the immense triple gateway, complete with high iron gates, leading to a deep entrance courtyard. The side portions of the gateway once served as a U-shaped carriage access drive, while the lower central portion was reserved for pedestrians. Deep voussoirs and an elaborate keystone compose the arch, nine stories over the gateway. The entire structure is capped by a two-and-one-half-story convex mansard roof with copper cresting.

1261 MADISON AVENUE, 1900–01
Manhattan
Architects: Buchman & Fox
Designated: July 23, 1974

Completed in 1901, this handsome Beaux Arts apartment house was commissioned by real-estate developer Gilbert Brown at a time when many wealthy New Yorkers were moving into the neighborhood soon to be known as Carnegie Hill, after Andrew Carnegie's 91st Street mansion. Erected on a site near the crest of the hill, 1261 Madison's generous proportions were intended to house only fourteen families.

The seven-story building has a two-story rusticated base and a three-story midsection. A heavy cornice serves as a balcony for the sixth floor, above which is a tiled mansard roof. The edges of the building's wide Madison Avenue façade are emphasized by slightly projecting bays flanked by pilasters and topped by arched pediments. The centerpiece of the Madison Avenue façade is a grand entrance portico. Its rusticated pilasters support a broken pediment beneath a cartouche inset with a marble medallion. The richly detailed exterior, coupled with the sense of spacious interiors imparted by the large windows and generous floor-to-floor distances, reveals the opulent expectations of the first generation of New York luxury apartment building dwellers.

REPUBLIC NATIONAL BANK,
formerly the Knox Building, 1901–02; alterations, 1964–65
452 Fifth Avenue, Manhattan
Architect: John H. Duncan
Designated: September 23, 1980

The Knox Building, one of the finest Beaux Arts–style commercial buildings in the city, was designed by New York architect John H. Duncan. Built in 1901–02 as the headquarters of the Knox Hat Company, the structure occupies an especially prominent midtown Manhattan location on Fifth Avenue at 40th Street, opposite the New York Public Library.

The ten-story façade is distinguished by full-height limestone rustication, large-scale ornament, and a two-story mansard roof—features carried over from Duncan's residential designs and skillfully applied to a large commercial building. Originally, the hat store was located on the first floor.

In 1964–65 the Knox Building was converted for use as the headquarters of the Republic National Bank. The architectural firm of Kahn & Jacobs altered the former hat store space into banking facilities. The overall effect is sensitive and compatible with the original character of the building.

GOUVERNEUR MORRIS HIGH SCHOOL INTERIOR, 1900–04
East 166th Street and Boston Road, The Bronx
Architect: C.B.J. Snyder
Designated: December 21, 1982

Gouverneur Morris High School, designed by C.B.J. Snyder in the Collegiate Gothic style, contains one of New York's most elaborate interiors designed for an educational facility. The Bronx's first major public secondary school, it occupies the area originally known as Morrisania, after the Morris family that included Lewis Morris, signer of the Declaration of Independence, and Gouverneur Morris, ambassador to France. In 1900, when construction began on the school building, it was called the Peter Cooper High School, but residents of Morrisania argued that the deeds of Gouverneur Morris were indelibly stamped on the minds of Morrisanians; thus in 1903, the name was officially changed to Morris High School.

The ornament of the Morris High School auditorium is consistent with Snyder's Gothic façade. The high-vaulted space is dominated by two-story Art Nouveau stained-glass windows that light the vast space. The interior surfaces are covered in elaborate Gothic plaster elements, including column capitals, foliate forms, and human masks. The monumental historical mural by Auguste F. M. Gorguet, *After Conflict Comes Peace*, which hangs over the stage, was completed in 1926. Together the windows, mural, organ, and architectural detail evoke the unity of the arts.

In 1956 the auditorium was renamed Duncan Hall in honor of Edith Duncan, who served as a teacher and principal of the school. Well-known Morris alumni include Dr. Herman Joseph Muller, who won the Nobel Prize for physiology or medicine in 1946, the cellist Wallinger Riegger, and the playwright Clifford Odets.

NEW YORK CHAMBER OF COMMERCE AND INDUSTRY BUILDING, 1901
65 Liberty Street, Manhattan
Architect: James B. Baker
Designated: January 18, 1966

The New York Chamber of Commerce and Industry, founded in 1768, never had its own building until the architect James B. Baker was commissioned to design this massive marble Beaux Arts structure, on the former site of the Real Estate Exchange, for the chamber and its remarkable picture collection, which includes portraits of business leaders such as John Jacob Astor, and a famous painting of the Atlantic cable crossing.

The front of the building is marked by a row of Ionic columns set on heavy masonry, surmounted by a handsome copper mansard roof with dormer windows. Three sculpture groups by Daniel Chester French—one of which depicted DeWitt Clinton standing next to a crouched worker, representing his support of the Erie Canal—were once framed by the columns, but erosion and pollution damaged the figures and they were removed. At the center of the façade, an arched entrance flanked by two arched windows permitted entry to a bank on the ground floor; a side entrance gave chamber members access to a large vestibule, where elevators and a monumental stairway led up to the main meeting room.

The chamber has moved to new headquarters on Madison Avenue. Currently a department store occupies one-half of the building and the other half is unoccupied.

KINGSBRIDGE HEIGHTS COMMUNITY CENTER,
formerly the 40th Police Precinct Station House, 1901–02
3101 Kingsbridge Terrace, The Bronx
Architects: Horgan & Slattery
Designated: July 15, 1986

A symbol of the presence of Kingsbridge's municipal government, this Beaux Arts building may have been associated with the City Beautiful Movement, a turn-of-the-century trend toward an urban aesthetic that resulted in the construction of many noteworthy public buildings.

One of Horgan & Slattery's best surviving works, the station house was headquarters first of the 40th Precinct and subsequently of the 50th Precinct. The building successfully integrates brick, terra-cotta ornament, tin, and stone. The U-shaped building, derived in plan from the fifteenth-century Italian palazzo, suggests security and monumentality—ideas appropriate to a police station headquarters.

The police moved to another Kingsbridge building in 1974. In 1975 the Kingsbridge Heights Community Center was established here and soon initiated major renovations which were completed in 1981. For safety reasons, the cornices were removed in early 1987; they will be recast when funding is available.

ST. NICHOLAS RUSSIAN ORTHODOX CATHEDRAL,
1901–02
15 East 97th Street, Manhattan
Architect: John Bergesen
Designated: December 18, 1973

St. Nicholas Russian Orthodox Cathedral was built in 1901–02 from the designs of John Bergesen, a New York City architect of Russian origin. Modeled after Muscovite Baroque architecture, the church was erected by the St. Nicholas congregation, which had formed in 1894. Unable to finance the building, the congregation was aided by the Synod of Russia, which was given Imperial permission to collect funds throughout the Russian Empire.

The cathedral and attached rectory present an impressive façade on East 97th Street. The broad front entrance to the sanctuary is contained within a central two-story gabled bay. Pendants with cherubs are set into the spandrels of the wide, segmental-arched entranceway. Above this, three tall, round-arched windows fill the gable. A terra-cotta frieze embellished by Greek crosses within linked circles ornaments the entablature. Wide brick pilasters, each surmounted by a small turret topped with an onion dome, flank this façade, which is trimmed by a blue and gold diamond-patterned band at the eaves. A flat platform, embellished by colorful panels, is set back from the sloping front roof. A dominant central onion dome, with ogee arches at the base and round-arched windows above, rises from the platform, surrounded by four smaller cupolas at the corners.

COLLECTORS CLUB BUILDING, formerly the Thomas B. Clarke House, 1901–02
22 East 35th Street, Manhattan
Architects: McKim, Mead & White
Designated: September 11, 1979

This beautiful and graceful building was erected as the home of Thomas Benedict Clarke in 1901–02. Located at 22 East 35th Street in the fashionable Murray Hill section, it is an especially notable example of Georgian Revival architecture, looking both to English and American precedents.

Thomas Benedict Clarke was a prominent New York City art collector, dealer, and decorator. His collection of American art was among the finest in the world in private hands. For a residence that would be a suitable showcase for his varied collections, Clarke turned to the prestigious firm of McKim, Mead & White; the design of Clarke's house has long been attributed to Stanford White, a personal friend of Clarke. In designing the new residence White altered an existing brownstone row house, adding an entirely new façade, extending the rear, and building an additional story.

The five-story building is faced with red and gray brick laid up in Flemish bond, with contrasting stone and metal detail. The rusticated ground floor is dominated by a classically inspired entrance portico, above which is a graceful two-story projecting bay window—the dominant feature of the façade. This Georgian Revival house is both unusual and delightful, looking both to English and American precedents, and is one of McKim, Mead & White's most outstanding residential designs in New York City.

In 1937, the house was purchased by the Collectors Club, an organization founded in 1896 and devoted to philately. Its library contains one of the world's largest and most comprehensive collections of philatelic literature. The organization has recently undertaken major repair and restoration of the façade and interior.

JAMES F. D. LANIER RESIDENCE, 1901–03
123 East 35th Street, Manhattan
Architects: Hoppin & Koen
Designated: September 11, 1979

At the turn of the century, the rows of brownstone houses in the Murray Hill district attracted wealthy and socially prominent New Yorkers such as James F. D. Lanier, A. T. Stewart, and J. P. Morgan. Lanier, a sportsman, pioneer automobile driver, and banker with one of the oldest private banking houses in the United States, commissioned this particularly handsome Beaux Arts structure.

Built on the site where two houses previously stood, the five-story building is a generous thirty-three feet wide. Its rusticated stone base creates an imposing ground floor with three arched openings—two window bays and an entrance—constructed from swagged and bracketed voussoirs. Carved paneled doors set beneath a bull's-eye window ornament the entranceway, which is also flanked by a cornucopia. Other decorative details include paneled newel posts topped by stone urns, which intersect both a stone balustrade and an elegant wrought-iron fence.

Colossal pilasters with swag-adorned Ionic capitals mark the three bays on the second and third floors. The openings on the second story have shallow cornices and French doors; those on the third, projecting sills and central keystones. On the fourth floor, the windows are screened by a lacy wrought-iron balustrade that echoes the stone balustrade on the second floor. The structure is balanced by a copper-covered mansard roof with pedimented dormers.

YESHIVA CHOFETZ CHAIM SCHOOL,
formerly the Isaac L. Rice Mansion, 1901–03,
additions and alterations, 1906–48
346 West 89th Street, Manhattan
Architects: Herts & Tallant, C. P. H. Gilbert (additions)
Designated: February 19, 1980

Erected in 1901–03, the Isaac L. Rice mansion is one of two freestanding mansions that survive on Riverside Drive. (The other is the Maurice Schinasi house at 351 Riverside Drive.) The mansion was designed by the noted theatrical architects Herts & Tallant and is one of their rare residential commissions in New York City. While it features elements of Georgian Revival and Beaux Arts design, the mansion displays the highly individualistic touch that Herts & Tallant brought to residential architecture.

Four stories high and faced with red brick laid up in Flemish bond with contrasting marble detail, the house is crowned by a hipped roof with broad eaves. Perhaps the most handsome features of the West 89th Street façade are a curved projection two stories high and a porte cochere, which was very unusual for Manhattan residences. The Riverside Drive façade is dominated by a series of broad entrance steps; a grand entrance at the second-floor level, encompassed by a bold arch that rises to the full height of the third story, gives vertical emphasis to the façade.

In 1907 Rice sold the house to tobacco importer Solomon Schinasi, brother of Maurice. Schinasi commissioned several compatible additions to the structure, and these were executed by the architect C.P.H. Gilbert. Because the house was long occupied by the Schinasi family, it survived while others on the drive were lost. Since 1954 it has housed the Yeshiva Chofetz Chaim School.

HOTEL BELLECLAIRE, 1901–03
2171–2179 Broadway, Manhattan
Architects: Stein, Cohen & Roth
Designated: February 10, 1987

The Hotel Belleclaire, located at the corner of Broadway and West 77th Street, was built in 1901–03 by architect Emery Roth of Stein, Cohen & Roth. Still a relatively unknown architect at this time, Emery Roth would play an important role in shaping the Manhattan skyline during his career of more than forty years, during which he completed more than 200 projects. The Belleclaire was one of a new breed of apartment hotels providing dwellings for both permanent and transient residents in single- or multiple-room units. These fashionable apartments were built without kitchen facilities or servants' quarters: all staff and services were provided by the hotel.

The owner, Albert Saxe, awarded Roth the Belleclaire commission after Saxe's successful 1899 collaboration with the architect on the Saxony Apartments at 250 West 82nd Street.

The Belleclaire is ten stories high and executed in red brick with limestone, terra-cotta, and metal detailing. It is composed of three symmetrically massed pavilions with an entrance court on West 77th Street and two deeply recessed light courts on the south façade; the eastern pavilion conforms to the angle of Broadway.

In designing the Belleclaire, the architect combined Beaux Arts principles with his own Art Nouveau–Secessionist style, seen in the profuse surface ornamentation. The strong horizontal design is dramatically counterbalanced by the verticals of the tower as well as by monumental pilasters in the main and side elevations. On Broadway, the pilasters enframe bays containing tripartite metal oriel windows that rise from the third to sixth stories, and also from the eighth to tenth stories. At the seventh story the pilasters enframe elliptically arched windows with curvilinear mullions. The stone pilasters are ornamented with pendants and stylized Indian heads.

THE ALGONQUIN HOTEL, 1902
59–61 West 44th Street, Manhattan
Architect: Goldwin Starrett
Designated: September 15, 1987

While the Algonquin's design is representative of architectural tastes at the turn of the century, it is the building's social history that distinguishes it from its contemporaries. Since its opening in 1902, the Algonquin has been associated with New York's literary and theatrical worlds. Under the proprietorship of Frank Case, the hotel was host to such notables as Sinclair Lewis, Douglas Fairbanks, Orson Welles, Tallulah Bankhead, Noël Coward, and dozens of other artists. After World War I, as home to the Round Table—a daily luncheon gathering of some of the city's brightest wits—the Algonquin's fame became national.

The twelve-story building is five bays wide, with a lightly rusticated, two-story limestone base. Above it are eight stories of brick with terra-cotta trim below a projecting cornice. Two stories at the top work together to function as an attic. The ten top stories have three sash windows in the center flanked by a pair of projecting bays on each side, except for the twelfth story where the bays are replaced with simple sash windows. The building was originally capped by a metal cornice, which has been removed.

NEW YORK STOCK EXCHANGE BUILDING, 1901–03
8–18 Broad Street, Manhattan
Architect: George B. Post
Designated: July 9, 1985

Since the early eighteenth century, Wall Street has been the focus of financial activity in New York City. The New York Stock Exchange, constituted March 8, 1817, as the New York Stock & Exchange Board, has been in its present location at 8–18 Broad Street since the completion of this building in 1903. Designed by George B. Post, one of America's most prominent nineteenth-century architects and engineers, this Greek Revival temple symbolizes the strength and security of the nation's financial community, and the position of New York at its center.

Post's exchange building is the second to stand on Broad Street. The Civil War had triggered a burst in securities trading, and with the growth of industrialization, the New York Stock & Exchange Board decided in 1863 to move out of rented quarters (at the Merchants Exchange Building on Wall Street) and commission its own building. This building, designed by John Kellum, was a four-story, marble-faced Italianate structure sited at 10–12 Broad Street. By the turn of the century even larger quarters were necessary for a rapidly expanding market. The adjacent land was bought, and construction began on the present Exchange Building in 1901.

The demands of the brokers and the site presented Post with a difficult challenge. The brokers wanted more space, greater convenience for business transactions, more light on the trading floor, and better ventilation. The site itself was irregular in both contour and incline, being located on a hill that rose to the north and northeast. Post anchored the structure on a two-story podium with a granite water table to overcome the incline, and set the activities of the exchange behind a massive façade of colossal Corinthian columns and pediment. He enhanced the interior lighting by designing the glass curtain wall that opens into the marble-walled, gilt-ceilinged trading room just behind the bank of columns. A similar but simpler façade faces New Street, surmounted by a cornice rather than a pediment.

The sculpture in the Broad Street pediment was designed by John Quincy Adams Ward and executed by Paul Wayland Bartlett. The eleven figures represent American commerce and industry; at the center stands *Integrity* with arms outstretched, protecting the works of men. On her left are *Agriculture* and *Mining*, on her right *Science*, *Industry*, and *Invention*—the products of the earth versus the means of invention.

Post's design continues to impart a sense of austerity, power, and security, and the building remains a potent symbol of one of this country's most important financial institutions.

HIGH PUMPING STATION, 1901–06
Jerome Avenue, south of the Mosholu Parkway, The Bronx
Architect: George W. Birdsall
Designated: July 28, 1981

The High Pumping Station was built to pump water from the Jerome Reservoir to consumers throughout the Bronx. Constructed in 1901–06 by George W. Birdsall, engineer for the Department of Water Supply, Gas and Electricity, the building is a major example of the contemporary belief that utilitarian structures were worthy of careful and sophisticated design treatment. The station also exhibits the technology that allowed water to be pumped to multistory buildings and other areas with poor service structures.

The pumping station is a long and narrow red-brick building crowned by a steeply pitched roof. Its façade is divided into a series of bays, each consisting of two arched windows flanked by shallow brick buttresses. This arrangement relieves the dominant horizontality of the design and creates a sense of rhythm. Capping each window is a semicircular corbeled brick lintel that adds texture and variety to the wall surface. Austerity of form coupled with a sensitive handling of detail is one of the hallmarks of the Romanesque Revival style; this style is beautifully expressed in the High Pumping Station.

Astor Place IRT Station, interior, downtown

IRT SUBWAY SYSTEM STATION INTERIORS, 1901–08
Manhattan
Architects: Heins & La Farge
Designated: October 23, 1979

Twelve of the original forty-five underground IRT subway stations are designated as interior landmarks, including portions of the stations at Borough Hall, Wall Street, Fulton Street, City Hall, Bleecker Street, Astor Place, 33rd Street, 59th Street–Columbus Circle, 72nd Street, 79th Street, 110th Street–Cathedral Parkway, and 116th Street–Columbia University. This status extends only to the wall elevations. The system engineer, William B. Parsons, a graduate of Columbia University School of Mines, planned each station. He studied Boston's subway and European underground systems in London and Vienna and combined what he felt were the best features of each. He devised two types of stations: the local stop, with platforms on either side of the tracks; and the express stop, with the platform between two tracks. In the spring of 1901, the Rapid Transit Commission selected Heins & La Farge to design the subway kiosks and control houses as well as the platform interiors.

George L. Heins and Christopher Grant La Farge had studied together at M.I.T. under the French architect Eugene Letang. (La Farge was the son of the noted painter and glass craftsman John La Farge; after M.I.T., he worked in the Brookline, Massachusetts, office of H. H. Richardson.) The firm is best known for the Cathedral Church of St. John the Divine, which they designed in 1891. All of the subway interiors followed a similar pattern. A coved, glazed terra-cotta molding serves as the wall base. Above this is a wainscoting of buff-colored Roman brick or rose-colored marble. White glazed or glass tiles cover the walls, which are divided into panels, usually by deep blue tiles. The panels correspond to the station columns, spaced fifteen feet off-center. The decorative treatment is particularized at the cornice level, where terra-cotta or faience plaques illustrate a local landmark or recall a historical event.

Many station interiors have lost their original splendor through insensitive modernization, poor maintenance, or vandalism. Fortunately, several stations are now being restored. The most successful restoration to date is the work completed at the Astor Place stop. Generally, the architects lavished the most care on the exterior kiosks and control houses. The best subway interiors are serviceable and compact, and retain their attractiveness with little maintenance.

QUEENSBORO BRIDGE, 1901–08
East River from 11th Street and Bridge Plaza North and Bridge Plaza South,
Queens, to Second Avenue and East 59th and 60th streets, Manhattan
Architect: Henry Hornbostel
Engineer: Gustav Lindenthal
Designated: April 16, 1974

The Queensboro Bridge was the first bridge built between Manhattan and Queens and the second between Manhattan and Long Island, after the Brooklyn Bridge. Completed in 1908, the bridge contributed significantly to the growth of Queens, whose population tripled in the first two decades of this century.

While emblematic of New York's growth and development, the Queensboro Bridge also represents an engineering accomplishment. It is one of the largest cantilever bridges in the world with no suspended spans. Engineered by Gustav Lindenthal, the bridge was designed by Henry Hornbostel; he appears to have been influenced by Jean Resal's Pont Mirabeau in Paris, which was completed while Hornbostel was a student at the Ecole des Beaux-Arts in 1895.

Today, the bridge's heavy steel frame contrasts visually with New York's more graceful suspension bridges. The piers are composed of rough-faced masonry with smooth quoins; spiky pinnacles crown its steel towers. Four of the original entrance kiosks still stand at the bridge's Manhattan entrance; the fifth, formerly in Queens, has been removed and now stands at the entrance to the Brooklyn Children's Museum.

NEW YORK PUBLIC LIBRARY, YORKVILLE BRANCH, 1902
222 East 79th Street, Manhattan
Architect: James Brown Lord
Designated: January 24, 1967

Built with funds contributed by Andrew Carnegie, the Yorkville Public Library is an elegant adaptation of the Palladian style. Symmetrical ordering coupled with a restrained use of ornament characterize this building as one of the few remaining examples of Italian Renaissance–style architecture in New York.

The three-story structure has a limestone façade divided into three bays. Ionic columns separate the windows, each containing another small oblong window framed with decorative garlands and resting above a triangular pediment. The round-arched opening of the first floor, crowned by lion's-head keystones, are set in rusticated stonework surmounted by a cornice. The low, second-floor balustrade is echoed by a simple baluster along the edge of the roof.

THE FLATIRON BUILDING, 1902
Broadway and Fifth Avenue at 23rd Street, Manhattan
Architects: D. H. Burnham & Co.
Designated: September 20, 1966

The Flatiron Building at 23rd Street remains one of New York's most distinguished and eccentric skyscrapers. Designed by D. H. Burnham & Co. of Chicago and completed in 1902, it was originally known as the Fuller Building; because of its triangular shape—determined by its site at the confluence of Broadway and Fifth Avenue—the building soon became widely known as the Flatiron. It was one of the earliest buildings in New York City to be supported by a complete steel cage; the non-visibility of its advanced structural support system, coupled with its soaring 285-foot height, created much skepticism among New Yorkers, who feared that high winds would topple it. When the building was viewed from uptown, the impression of fragility was increased by the remarkable, six-foot-wide apex at the crossing of Broadway and Fifth.

The building has a wonderful sense of drama. Its lyrical, romantic, and often haunting quality has provided inspiration to such photographers as Edward Steichen and Alfred Stieglitz. In comparison with other decorative skyscrapers of the period, such as the ornate 612-foot-tall Singer Building by Ernest Flagg (1908), the Flatiron's restrained and relatively uninterrupted wall treatment induces a sense of lightness and height. The building's twenty-one stories are divided along classical columnar lines of base, shaft, and capital, creating a visual impression of strength. The base, more heavily rusticated than the twelve-story shaft, gives the building a solid, well-anchored appearance. The more ornate treatment of the crowning four stories, accentuated by two-story rusticated pilasters and a heavy cornice, provides a satisfying visual stop to the upward sweep. The building's underlying steel frame made this kind of shoring up superfluous, but a combination of aesthetic and public prejudices made it necessary.

Despite initial public resistance, the Flatiron Building was an immediate success. Legend has it that the downdrafts generated by the tower and its location (supposedly the windiest corner in the city) created an even more agreeable spectacle—the billowing skirts of female passersby; the expression "twenty-three skiddoo" reputedly derived from the shouts of policemen posted at the corner to clear the gawkers. Whatever the attraction, the Flatiron Building became a symbol of the New York City skyline in its time.

OUR LADY OF LOURDES ROMAN CATHOLIC CHURCH, 1902–04
467 West 142nd Street, Manhattan
Architects: O'Reilly Brothers
Designated: July 22, 1975

In 1902–04, when Washington Heights consisted mainly of open fields, Our Lady of Lourdes was built. The church, however, was not entirely new; instead of obtaining freshly quarried stone, Father Joseph H. McMahon, the founding pastor, purchased ("at a bargain") stones salvaged from three of New York City's most famous nineteenth-century buildings: the National Academy of Design, the old St. Patrick's Cathedral, and the A. T. Stewart mansion—all of which were being demolished to make room for new structures.

From the outset, the superstructure of the new church was regarded as a notable artistic endeavor. Imaginatively combining the salvaged stones, the firm of O'Reilly Brothers of Paterson, New Jersey, reproduced in modified form the old Academy of Design, a Venetian Gothic–style building that dominated the corner of East 23rd Street and Park Avenue South until its demolition in 1901. The rear of the church, built with stones from St. Patrick's, was adorned with brilliant late Gothic stained-glass windows. The elaborately carved pedestals that flank the steps leading up to the entrance were taken from the Stewart mansion.

With its handsome marble and bluestone Gothic façade, Our Lady of Lourdes is a magnificent and regrettably rare example of urban rescue and reuse. The structure harmonizes well with the surrounding limestone houses, and the church continues today to serve its congregation.

CONSULATE OF THE POLISH PEOPLE'S REPUBLIC, formerly De Lamar Mansion, 1902–05
233 Madison Avenue, Manhattan
Architect: C.P.H. Gilbert
Designated: March 25, 1975

Designed by noted architect C.P.H. Gilbert, this imposing Beaux Arts edifice was built in 1902–05 for Dutch-born Raphael De Lamar, who amassed a fortune in Colorado's gold strike of the late 1870s. After De Lamar's death in 1918, the house was sold to the National Democratic Club; in 1973 the Polish People's Republic acquired the property for use as a consulate.

Conspicuous and dramatic on its Madison Avenue site, the De Lamar Mansion exhibits a towering and elegant mansard roof embellished by copper crestings with shell motifs. The main façade, which faces onto East 37th Street, is designed in a tripartite division, both vertically and horizontally. One of the building's most impressive features is the recessed entrance with double oak doors, crowned by a stone balcony with an imposing elliptical arched window, and capped by a handsome wrought-iron balcony.

THE CHATSWORTH APARTMENTS AND ANNEX
340–344 West 72nd Street, Manhattan
Architect: John E. Scharsmith
Designated: September 11, 1984

The Chatsworth Apartments, 1902–04

Annex, 1905–06

The Chatsworth Apartments and Annex were constructed in the Beaux Arts style as luxury "housekeeping apartments" for an affluent clientele. The original building consisted of two twelve-story blocks that shared a common base and entry. The annex was a separate, eight-story tower, linked to the original apartments at its base by a pavilion. Apartment houses at the beginning of the century had to overcome the middle-class belief that associated multiple-family dwellings with poverty and immorality. Naming an apartment house conferred upon it an appealing identity. Modern conveniences such as central heating, elevators, built-in bath and kitchen equipment, and building services—such as a sun parlor, billiard parlor, café, barbershop, valet, and tailor—satisfied the desire for comfort and created the impression that the apartment was a private home.

The Chatsworth exemplifies the inflated dimensions of classically inspired designs that had originally evolved for three- to five-story buildings. The rusticated limestone base rises three stories to a convex frieze and cornice. The midsection consists of seven stories faced in russet-colored brick with limestone trim. The attic and slate mansard roof occupy three stories, with the building's conservatory at the top.

The horizontal detail of the Annex works against its eight-story height to create the impression of a lower building. It is entered through a small, rusticated one-story pavilion, faced in limestone, that separates it from the main building.

FIRST CHURCH OF CHRIST, SCIENTIST, 1899–1903
1 West 96th Street, Manhattan
Architects: Carrère & Hastings
Designated: July 23, 1974

Carrère & Hastings' design for the First Church of Christ, Scientist, is a brilliant synthesis of historical precedents. The plain surfaces of the massive stone walls and the design and placement of the obelisk-capped spire are reminiscent of the Mannerist work of English architect Nicholas Hawksmoor. The rational articulation of the building's plan on its exterior—giving each aisle its own entrance pavilion, boldly exposing the windows of rooms above the sanctuary—reflect the architects' training at the Ecole des Beaux-Arts. The restrained use of classical forms was the means of bringing these two traditions together. Colossal engaged Ionic columns frame the stained-glass window above the entrance, while smaller engaged columns of the same order are used in the tower. A continuous, complete Ionic cornice ties the sanctuary to the tower, while a secondary cornice unites elements at the roof level of the aisles.

The Christian Science Society had organized a branch in New York by 1887; in 1896 the name changed to First Church of Christ, Scientist, New York City. Only the finest resources were used for the congregation's first building in the city. Carrère & Hastings were nationally known; the stained-glass window above the entrance was by John La Farge; the best Concord white granite was used for the exterior.

EAST 91ST STREET HOUSES
Manhattan

John Henry Hammond House, 1902–03
9 East 91st Street
Architects: Carrère & Hastings
Designated: July 23, 1974

John B. Trevor House, 1909–11
11 East 91st Street
Architects: Trowbridge & Livingston
Designated: July 23, 1974

Convent of the Sacred Heart, formerly the
James A. Burden House, 1902–05
7 East 91st Street
Architects: Warren & Wetmore
Designated: February 19, 1974

Convent of the Sacred Heart, formerly the Otto
Kahn House, 1913–18
1 East 91st Street
Architects: J. Armstrong Stenhouse and
C.P.H. Gilbert
Designated: February 19, 1974

7–11 East 91st Street

The East 91st Street Houses—palatial residences built between 1902 and 1918 for the city's affluent—are superb reminders of the Belle Epoque in New York City. Following the lead of Andrew Carnegie, who built himself a mansion at East 91st Street and Fifth Avenue, financier and banker Otto Kahn bought the site at 1 East 91st Street from Carnegie and had the architects C.P.H. Gilbert and J. Armstrong Stenhouse design a mansion that comes as close to a true Italian Renaissance palace as there is in the city, complete with a drive-through porte cochere and an interior courtyard, and the highest order of Renaissance-style detailing throughout. The house is now part of the Convent of the Sacred Heart.

Mr. and Mrs. William Sloane commissioned the noted architects Warren & Wetmore to design a palace at number 7 as a wedding present for their daughter when she married James Burden. Sloane had number 9 built for his second daughter, Mrs. John Henry Hammond, when she was married. Number 7, which is also today part of the Convent of the Sacred Heart, is a severe Italian Renaissance–style town house, noted for its magnificent circular marble staircase. Number 9 is an Italian Renaissance–style mansion designed by Carrère & Hastings, notable for its perfect symmetry and balance. The fenestration has clear roots in the works of Michelangelo, Vasari, and Bernini. Since 1976 the house has been the property of the Consulate of the U.S.S.R., although it has remained empty. John B. Trevor commissioned the firm of Trowbridge & Livingston to design his Beaux Arts–style town house at number 11.

1 East 91st Street

FRENCH EMBASSY, formerly Payne Whitney House, 1902–06
972 Fifth Avenue, Manhattan
Architects: McKim, Mead & White
Designated: September 15, 1970

The exquisite townhouse at 972 Fifth Avenue was designed in the style of the high Italian Renaissance by McKim, Mead & White. It was erected in 1902–06 for financier Payne Whitney and his wife, Helen, a poet and patron of the arts who lived in the house until her death in 1944. Since 1952, the mansion has served as a division of the French Embassy, and it now houses the embassy's cultural, press, and information services.

The gracious curve of the light gray granite front, covered with rich classical ornament, rises five stories. Entablatures delineate each story. The central doorway has an ornately carved marble enframement and double entrance doors of openwork bronze grills with an intricate floral motif. Winged cherubs fill the spandrels of the round arched parlor-floor windows, which are flanked with Ionic pilasters. The Renaissance treatment of the upper stories, with Corinthian pilasters and carved classical figures in low relief, is particularly handsome. The structure is topped by a pitched tile roof with a deep overhanging stone cornice supported by paired stone brackets.

The house was extensively restored in 1987, and the restoration uncovered a stained-glass window designed especially for the house by John La Farge.

EAST 79TH STREET HOUSES
Manhattan

63 East 79th Street, 1902–03; additions,
1945
Architects: Adams & Warren
Designated: May 19, 1981

67–69 East 79th Street, 1907–08;
Architects: Carrère & Hastings
Designated: May 19, 1981

59 East 79th Street, 1908–09
Architects: Foster, Gade & Graham
Designated: May 19, 1981

53 East 79th Street, 1916–17
Architects: Trowbridge & Livingston
Designated: February 15, 1967

The Upper East Side of Manhattan developed as a residential neighborhood in the 1860s, when simple brownstone row houses were constructed on speculation and sold to middle-class families. But during the twenty-five-year period between 1890 and the beginning of World War I, more opulent town houses, such as these on East 79th Street, replaced the older brownstone residences, reflecting the move uptown of the city's most elite families.

Number 53 was the residence of John S. Rogers until 1937, when the New York Society Library purchased the building; the association still occupies it today. This limestone structure, designed by Trowbridge & Livingston in 1916, has a front façade four stories high and three bays wide, terminating in a rich stone frieze and cornice topped by a balustrade. The fifth floor, set back a few feet behind this balustrade, has a tile roof with a wide overhang over an open terrace. Number 59 was designed for John H. Iselin by the firm of Foster, Gade & Graham in an eclectic mix of Northern Renaissance and French styles. The five-story structure is faced with buff brick enlivened by limestone detailing. Number 63, designed by architects Adams & Warren in an English Neoclassical style, is a five-story house with an Ionic entrance portico shading a Federal-style entranceway. The original mansard roof was removed when two stories were added in 1945. Number 67–69 was designed in 1907 by the prominent firm of Carrère & Hastings, the architects of the New York Public Library, in a late French Baroque style. The building now serves as the Greek Consulate and the offices of the Greek Orthodox Diocese of America.

EAST 90TH STREET HOUSES
Manhattan
Designated: July 23, 1974

11 East 90th Street, 1902–03
Architects: Barney & Chapman

17 East 90th Street, 1917–19
Architect: F. Burrall Hoffman, Jr.

15 East 90th Street, 1927–28
Architect: Mott B. Schmidt

These three dignified and elegant residences add considerable charm to the Carnegie Hill area of the Upper East Side. Number 11 is a handsome four-and-one-half-story limestone building designed in the best tradition of the French Beaux Arts and the eighteenth-century *hôtel particulier*. Number 15 is a charming Federal Revival house designed by Mott B. Schmidt, who was responsible for some of the most refined examples of this style in the city. Three and one-half stories high and of red brick laid in Flemish bond, its most notable feature is a handsome entrance portico composed of Corinthian columns supporting a full entablature that accents the paneled double doors. Number 17 combines a modified Georgian Revival style with an arcaded loggia in the Continental tradition; its most distinguishing features are the keystones of the arches of the loggia, embellished by decorative human masks, and the handsomely carved and paneled double doors.

CURTIS HIGH SCHOOL, 1902–04;
additions, 1922, 1925, 1937
Hamilton Avenue and St. Mark's Place, Staten Island
Architect: C.B.J. Snyder
Designated: October 12, 1982

Curtis High School, opened in 1904, was Staten Island's first public
secondary school. The campus—a broad lawn dotted with trees and
shrubs—provides the setting for C.B.J. Snyder's Collegiate Gothic–
style buildings. Snyder was the superintendent of school buildings
for New York City's Board of Education.

The original four-story building of brick and limestone is
rectangular in plan, with a central tower and gabled end pavilions.
Ornamentation is concentrated in the upper portions of the building;
a crenellated parapet wall adorns the roofline of the main block. The
centrally placed five-story English medieval–style tower contains the
main entrance, which is formed by a compound Tudor arch.

A south wing with workshops and classrooms was completed in
1922 and demonstrates an evolving Gothic sensibility in Snyder's
school designs. The brick and limestone construction and the Gothic
Revival ornament harmonize with the earlier building. The north
auditorium wing, with its tall, closely set windows and abundant
ornament, was completed in 1925. Later additions of 1937—the
swimming pool to the rear of the main building and the new
gymnasium wing—simplify and repeat the forms of the earlier
buildings.

RED HOUSE, 1903–04
350 West 85th Street, Manhattan
Architects: Harde & Short
Designated: September 14, 1982

Red House, an exceptionally handsome apartment building erected
in 1903-04, was one of the earliest buildings designed by the noted
New York architects Harde & Short. This lively six-story building
takes its name from the color of the brick facing, which
is set off by an abundant use of light-colored terra-cotta ornament.
The façade is organized into two pavilions, each with angled sides,
flanking a slightly recessed central window bay. The detailing of the
façade, which displays the concern for historicism typical of much of
the firm's work, is enhanced by a strong contrast between the red
brick and the cream-colored terra-cotta. Recalling the sixteenth-
century style of François I in its combination of French Gothic and
Renaissance elements, the detailing includes the use of the
salamander and crown motifs, baldachin canopies, and windows with
multi-paned sashes organized in bays.

The façade is crowned by an entablature composed of a corbeled
frieze supporting a projecting cornice and an architrave broken by
diamond-shaped panels that repeat the pattern of the window
spandrels. Elongated brackets terminate in terra-cotta pendants,
which display foliate motifs and the crown of François I.

NEW AMSTERDAM THEATER, 1902–03
214 West 42nd Street, Manhattan
Architects: Herts & Tallant
Designated (exterior and interior): October 23, 1979

The New Amsterdam Theater, built for the theatrical producers Klaw and Erlanger, was for many years the most prestigious theater in Times Square and home of the famous Ziegfeld Follies. Designed by the noted theatrical architects Herts & Tallant, it is one of the rare examples of Art Nouveau architecture in New York City.

At the request of the owners, the building was intended to be more than a theater. It incorporates two theatrical spaces—the auditorium and the Aerial Theater above—and an office tower for the administrative needs of the producers. The theaters are located on West 41st Street, but Klaw and Erlanger wanted the entrance on 42nd Street, sharing a façade with the office tower above. To meet the dual requirements of theater and offices, the architects made use of the relatively new structural steel frame.

The main ten-story façade united architecture and sculpture with an appropriate sense of drama. The entrance, modified drastically in 1937, spanned three floors, and was the most lavish feature of the exterior. A segmented triumphal arch entranceway was flanked by rusticated piers that supported paired marble columns at the second floor. Sculpture by George Grey Barnard, who probably also designed the various figures at roof level, rested on the cornice. Virtually all but the triumphal arch was removed to make way for a movie marquee and vertical electric sign. The second- and third-story windows are framed by Art Nouveau bronze flower motifs.

The interior is among the most sumptuous surviving the turn of the century. It expands on the restrained Art Nouveau sinuousness of the exterior entrance. It is distinguished by a synthesis of architecture, mural painting, sculpture, decorative panels, and continuous plaster and carved oak moldings. The auditorium is elliptical in plan and section—a form, pioneered in theaters by Herts & Tallant, that was considered to enhance acoustical properties. The firm also pioneered the use of cantilevered balconies, which allowed an unobstructed view from all seats and contributed to the effect of a merging and flowing of space and architecture in keeping with Art Nouveau theories.

HUDSON THEATER, 1902–04
139–141 West 44th Street, Manhattan
Architects: J. B. McElfatrick & Son and Israels & Harder
Designated (exterior and interior): November 17, 1987

The Hudson Theater was built in 1902–04 for Henry B. Harris, one of the top Broadway producers of the turn of the century. The design was begun by theater specialists J. B. McElfatrick & Son and completed by the firm of Israels & Harder. The reason for the change is unknown, and led to some confusion at the time, but it is clear that both firms were involved in the theater's construction.

The façade reflects the Beaux Arts classicism popular in New York at the turn of the century. Four stories high and five bays wide, the dignified composition focuses on the slightly projecting pavilion created by the three central bays. Medusa-head capitals decorate the pilasters on this inner segment, and an elaborate cartouche adorns the balustrade at the top.

In contrast to the theater's relatively simple exterior is the extraordinarily lavish interior. The ticket lobby has a grand coffered ceiling and elaborate plasterwork, and the inner lobby has a classical arcade and a ceiling embellished with domes of Tiffany glass. The ceiling of the auditorium has oval sections of plaster ornament, while floral reliefs and Corinthian columns enhance the walls.

The Hudson served as Harris's headquarters until his untimely death aboard the SS *Titanic*. The building continues today in the tradition of distinguished Broadway theaters.

LYCEUM THEATRE, 1902–03
149–157 West 45th Street, Manhattan
Architects: Herts & Tallant
Designated: November 26, 1974;
interior designated December 8, 1987

The oldest playhouse in New York City still serving the legitimate stage, the Lyceum Theatre opened on November 2, 1903, under the management of Daniel Frohman. Herts & Tallant, who designed the Beaux Arts theater, were to become well known as the architects of such theaters as the New Amsterdam, the Shubert, the Folies Bergère, and the Brooklyn Academy of Music. The Lyceum staged long-running productions rather than repertory; such performers as Ethel Barrymore, Leslie Howard, Judy Holiday, and Basil Rathbone starred here.

The façade is dominated by a row of tall, ornate columns rising above a soaring canopy that protects the entrances at street level. The columns terminate in composite capitals and support a massive entablature decorated with theatrical masks. A balustrade serves as a balcony for the three central pedimented windows of the penthouse. The sloping mansard roof with six oval dormer windows encloses a former rehearsal hall.

The interior continues the Beaux Arts themes of the exterior. The lobby contains a vaulted, domed ceiling and murals on canvas by James Wall Finn portraying actors Sarah Siddons and David Garrick. The auditorium has an elaborate proscenium arch decorated with figures representing Athena, music, and drama. Decorative plasterwork in a variety of motifs covers the boxes, balconies, and ceiling.

The Lyceum's modest size, with seating for about 900, promoted a sense of intimacy that Frohman felt was best suited to the realism in drama that was evolving at the time of the theater's construction. In recent years, productions of *Your Arm's Too Short to Box with God*, *Morning's at Seven*, and *As Is* have had long runs here.

NEW-YORK HISTORICAL SOCIETY, central section 1903–08; wings, 1937–38
170 Central Park West, Manhattan
Architects: York & Sawyer (central section); Walker & Gillette (wings)
Designated: July 19, 1966

In 1804 a score of prominent New York City residents established the New-York Historical Society. In the words of the society's first president, John Pintard, its purpose was to "collect and preserve whatever may relate to the natural, civil or ecclesiastical history of the U.S. in general, or of this state in particular." From 1804 until 1857 the society's collections changed location seven times, starting out at City Hall (1804–11) and finally settling at Town & Davis's New York University Building (1841–57). By 1857, charitable donations enabled the society to erect its first permanent building, at the corner of Second Avenue and East 11th Street.

In addition to holding conventional historical records, the society—as the only such public institution in the city—soon began to serve as the repository for several major art collections. Many of these collections were dispersed as various museums were established, but the society retains a strong collection of American art.

The 1857 building was soon hopelessly overcrowded. As art accumulated in the tightly packed quarters, society members called for the creation of a public museum in Central Park and became the first group to suggest the founding of the Metropolitan Museum of Art.

The fund-raising drive for a larger building began in 1887; the current site was chosen in 1891. The financial panic of 1893, however, postponed construction. In October, 1901, the New York firm of York & Sawyer won the commission for the current building in a sealed-bid competition. The central section was completed in 1908. With ample exhibition galleries planned from the very beginning, the society could provide free public access to the collection, as well as scholarly research facilities.

The 1901 design also allowed for the erection of two identical wings to the north and south as funds became available. A building extension fund was established in 1920 and York & Sawyer contracted to complete their original designs. Once again depression frustrated construction plans. In 1935, thanks to an enormous bequest from Mary Gardiner Thompson, Walker & Gillette received the commission to complete the building, adhering to Philip Sawyer's original designs fairly closely. Sawyer had designed colossal semi-detached colonnades for the wings, identical to the one on the Park façade. Ralph T. Walker preferred flat pilasters set into shallow spandrels and stylized Sawyer's heavily rusticated base. Walker did, however, match the original gray granite perfectly, and his additions are sensitive to the original design.

CARTIER, formerly Morton F. Plant House, 1903–05
651–653 Fifth Avenue and 4 East 52nd Street, Manhattan
Architects: Robert W. Gibson and C.P.H. Gilbert
Designated: July 14, 1970

This elegant, six-story Italian Renaissance–style building was designed for Morton F. Plant, a banker and yachtsman, and owner of two baseball teams. The East 52nd Street façade is dominated by an ornately carved balcony, supported by heavy console brackets at the second floor; four fluted Doric pilasters rise two stories above the balcony and support the low-pitched pediment. The fifth-floor attic windows are set in a profusely decorated frieze.

In 1917, Cartier acquired the building in an extraordinary manner: Mrs. Plant swapped the house for a necklace of perfectly matched, giant Oriental pearls that had been the pride of Pierre Cartier's collection. The jewelers have been located here ever since.

**PERMANENT MISSION OF YUGOSLAVIA
TO THE UNITED NATIONS,**
formerly the R. Livingston Beekman House, 1903–05
854 Fifth Avenue, Manhattan
Architects: Warren & Wetmore
Designated: January 14, 1969

This small yet elegant town house was designed by the Beaux Arts–trained firm of Warren & Wetmore and built in 1903–05 for R. Livingston Beekman. It is a superb example of Louis XV style, executed with vigor and authority.

Capped with a mansard roof containing two floors of dormers, the grand masonry façade is three stories high and two windows wide. The base of the house has two graceful round-arched openings with molded frames; the second-floor windows, pedimented at the top with balustraded balconies, are tall and dignified. The façade contains superior foliate ornamental detail in the Beaux Arts tradition. A low, open parapet, with a railing in front of the two fourth-floor dormers, rises above the cornice. The high mansard roof is covered with copper and has a richly molded cresting that crowns the house. This finest of extant small town houses on Fifth Avenue now serves as the Permanent Mission of Yugoslavia to the United Nations.

PIERPONT MORGAN LIBRARY AND ANNEX
29–33 East 36th Street, Manhattan
Designated: May 17, 1966; interior designated March 23, 1982

Pierpont Morgan Library, 1903–06
Architects: McKim, Mead & White

Annex, 1928
Architects: Benjamin W. Morris

In 1900 the great financier J. Pierpont Morgan began to make plans for a building to house his vast and important collection of paintings, sculpture, objets d'art, and rare books. He acquired land adjacent to his home on East 36th Street and hired the architect Whitney Warren to draw up plans. In 1902, however, he decided he wanted the firm of McKim, Mead & White—already established in the field of library architecture—to take over the project. With an enthusiasm that matched Morgan's sizable financial commitment, Charles McKim designed the Pierpont Morgan Library, considered by many to be his masterpiece.

Drawing stylistically upon the Italian Renaissance villa, the uncomplicated, classical library is the result of a close collaboration between client and architect. Morgan studied the plans for two years, often over breakfast meetings with McKim, working out details of structure and ornamentation. In the final version, three rooms open off a central rotunda. To the east is a library, and to the north a librarian's office; on the west is Morgan's personal office, the repository of his most prized artwork. The project also included a house on the same property for Morgan's daughter, Louisa Satterlee. The adjoining Florentine Renaissance–style Annex, designed by Benjamin W. Morris and built in 1928, exists in simple, subordinate harmony with the original library.

The main library entrance, on the south side, employs the Palladian motif of an archway with three openings. The four paired

Ionic columns (instead of the usual two) are backed by a deep porch with a beautifully decorated groin-vaulted ceiling. On each side of the doorway the side wings, flush with the entrance, are defined by pilasters and niches with sculpted figures. The exterior marble walls were assembled without mortar, and the blocks are set together so tightly that a penknife cannot be inserted into the joints. McKim had studied this technique at the Erechtheum on the Acropolis; this proof of structural longevity was enough to convince Morgan to spend an additional $50,000 on blocks of Tennessee marble.

The interior, richly turned out in materials and coverings from European sources, shows the same attention to detail. The rotunda, based on Renaissance prototypes, is distinguished by an allegorical vault painting by H. Siddons Mowbray. The marble floor of the central hall (the entrance hall today) is laid in a pattern modeled on a design in the Villa Pia in the Vatican.

The Pierpont Morgan Library is an influential example of studied form and consummate workmanship. In its careful design, which integrates sculpture, painting, and architecture, the library exemplifies the turn-of-the-century ideal of unity of the arts and creates a splendid showcase for Morgan's collection.

In April, 1988, the library announced its plan to purchase the old J. P. Morgan, Jr., mansion at 231 Madison Avenue to provide room for expansion.

STATEN ISLAND BOROUGH HALL, 1904–06
Richmond Terrace, Staten Island
Architects: Carrère & Hastings
Designated: March 23, 1982

The borough of Staten Island commissioned Carrère & Hastings, one of the leading firms in New York City, to design a new borough hall as a symbolic demonstration of the island's importance in the recently consolidated Greater New York. When constructed, the building rivaled the borough halls of Brooklyn and the Bronx as a significant public structure of its day.

The exuberant nature of the Louis XIII style chosen for the building by the architects is tempered by the rational planning inculcated by Beaux Arts training. The building is organized symmetrically on a five-part plan consisting of a five-bay central section, two recessed hyphens each one bay wide, and two projecting wings, each two bays wide. The ground floor of the building is limestone; above it are two stories of brick with limestone trim, surmounted by a two-story mansard roof. In the central section, the main entrance is recessed below a round arch flanked by four segmental arched windows. The base of the central section carries an engaged limestone hexastyle Doric colonnade between limestone piers. In the wings, the Flemish bond brickwork is further animated by limestone window enframements, spandrels, and an elaborate cornice. In the mansard, a variety of window styles are seen above the cornice; smaller shed dormers light the top floor.

When the building was completed, the *New York Times* lamented that it had "to hobnob with wooden and brick structures of no distinction whatever." Today it stands at the political center of a borough that is an increasingly vital element of New York City.

52ND POLICE PRECINCT STATION HOUSE, 1904–05
3016 Webster Avenue, The Bronx
Architects: Stoughton & Stoughton
Designated: June 18, 1974

Stoughton & Stoughton's 52nd Police Precinct Station House was built to serve the growing Norwood and Bedford Park neighborhoods following the 1898 consolidation of New York City. In detail and form, the three-story red-brick and terra-cotta building recalls Tuscan precedents. The south façade is governed by a centrally placed engaged tower. The base of the tower is a porte cochere where prisoners were delivered; its top is marked by polychromed terra-cotta clock faces beneath recessed arches on the three free sides. The first-floor walls are laid in Flemish bond and pierced by round-arched windows with square frames whose spandrels are decorated with blue terra-cotta panels. The second and third stories are separated by terra-cotta panels and distinguished by diaper-pattern brickwork. The main entrance to the building on Webster Avenue is marked by an Italianate porch. Above the porch is a terra-cotta plaque, embossed with the seal of the City of New York and the precinct number.

The precinct's former stable and patrol wagon garage remain behind the main building. This building, too, received careful detailing in the form of a belt course and diapered brickwork on the top story.

IRT BROADWAY LINE VIADUCT, former Manhattan Valley Viaduct, 1900–04
West 122nd Street to West 135th Street, Manhattan
Engineer: William Barclay Parsons
Designated: November 24, 1981

The Broadway Line Viaduct represents an elegant solution to the challenges that Manhattan's uneven topography presented to the construction of the city's transit system between 1900 and 1904. While most of the Interborough Rapid Transit (IRT) was built by the "cut-and-cover" method—entailing an open excavation, installation of the subway corridor, and replacement of surface ducts and fill—the topography of some locations made other construction techniques more practical. Some routes required tunneling. The route beneath Central Park between West 104th Street and West 110th Street at Lenox Avenue, for example, was so constructed.

The sloping Manhattan Valley, on the other hand, necessitated an elevated structure. William Barclay Parsons, Columbia University–trained and the Rapid Transit Commission's chief engineer in 1894, designed this viaduct, which was incorporated into the IRT system during its construction.

Parsons's structure not only carries the subway lines over West 125th Street, but also supports the steel- and wood-sheathed station centered above its arch. The viaduct's granite-faced brick foundations extend thirty feet below street level and support the steel towers, flanked by plate girders, that carry the tracks as the ground rises toward West 125th Street. Standard viaduct construction would have entailed costly realignment of the angled intersection of Broadway and West 125th Street, but Parsons's design used a double-hinged parabolic braced arch for the viaduct's center portion.

Decorative elements, including iron lampposts and scrolled railings, preserve the station's turn-of-the-century spirit. New escalators (the originals having been replaced) extend beyond the station, which is used by more than 6,600 passengers daily on both sides of the viaduct. The imposing masonry and elegant curves of the Broadway Line Viaduct and West 125th Street Station do justice to the skill and ingenuity of the engineers who designed New York City's first subway system.

72ND STREET SUBWAY KIOSK AND CONTROL HOUSE, 1904
West 72nd Street and Broadway, Manhattan
Architects: Heins & La Farge
Designated: January 9, 1979; interior designated October 23, 1979

The firm of Heins & La Farge developed two types of aboveground structures for the IRT—control houses and kiosks. Of the 130 original kiosks, each made of cast iron and glass, none remains, but a reconstructed one has recently been erected at the Astor Place station. The six original control houses—at West 103rd Street, West 116th Street, West 149th Street, Atlantic Avenue, Bowling Green, and this station—were of buff-colored Roman brick with limestone and terra-cotta trim. Their vaguely Flemish Renaissance style is an appropriate reference to New York's earliest Dutch settlement at Bowling Green. Two of the remaining three, this and the one at Bowling Green, are designated New York City landmarks.

The West 72nd Street Control House occupies the triangular site where Broadway crosses Amsterdam Avenue. The wrought-iron fence that surrounds it is original. The foundation is of granite; the trim is limestone, and the Flemish scroll gable coping and ball finials are terra-cotta. The brick is laid in the Flemish bond pattern. A louvered glass roof monitor and wrought-iron grills admit light and air. A fifth entry and magazine stalls are unfortunate additions to the north elevation. The south elevation, however, nicely preserves the character of this elegant little structure.

BATTERY PARK CONTROL HOUSE, 1904–05
State Street and Battery Place, Manhattan
Architects: Heins & La Farge
Designated: November 20, 1973

The Battery Park Control House is an entrance and exit for the Bowling Green Station of the Lexington Avenue IRT, the city's first subway, which was begun in 1900. Designed by the firm Heins & La Farge, this Beaux Arts structure of brick, stone, and glass is one of the last three remaining examples of the monumental subway entrances that expressed the city's pride in its first subway system.

The yellow-brick building has limestone quoins at each corner and a granite base. Smooth limestone banding encircles the building, above the plain brick walls pierced by simple high windows. The gable ends of the building are decorated with a central bull's-eye with elaborate moldings. The northern façade has a projecting limestone porch with engaged square columns supporting a stylized pediment on brackets. The southern façade has a brick extension, edged by plain stone quoins and topped with a copper entablature and roof.

SCHOMBURG CENTER FOR RESEARCH IN BLACK CULTURE,
formerly the New York Public Library, West 135th Street Branch, 1904–05
103 West 135th Street, Manhattan
Architect: Charles F. McKim of McKim, Mead & White
Designated: February 3, 1981

This three-story limestone library became a center of cultural, social, and political activity in Harlem. Franz Boas, W.E.B. DuBois, and Carl Van Doren lectured here; actors Harry Belafonte and Sidney Poitier made their acting debuts with the American Negro Theater on the building's basement stage. The library's collection of books about black literature and history was initially compiled by Ernestine Rose in the early 1920s; it increased dramatically with the acquisition of the Schomburg Collection, purchased in 1926 with the aid of a $10,000 Carnegie Corporation gift.

The symmetrically structured building has a rusticated ground floor pierced by square-headed openings. A wide belt course ornamented with a richly carved pattern of alternating wreaths and books divides the first story from the floors above. The second and third floors are broken into three bays by tall pilasters. Large double-hung windows with tiny windows above create the outer bays; the central bay is lit by a handsome Palladian window. The entire structure is topped by a broad, modillioned overhanging cornice containing a simple entablature, ornamented with round plaques and the inscription, "New York Public Library."

Plans are presently under way to convert the now-vacant structure into a museum in connection with the new Schomburg Center Building next door.

THE LAMBS, formerly the Lambs Club, 1904–05
128 West 44th Street, Manhattan
Architects: McKim, Mead & White
Designated: September 24, 1974

This handsome Georgian Revival clubhouse was built to house the Lambs Club, founded in 1874 for "the social intercourse of members of the dramatic and musical professions with men of the world." Henry J. Montague, one of the founders, had belonged to a similarly named club in London, and suggested the name for the New York group. The club became well known for its "Gambols"—satirical revues—that began in 1888. McKim, Mead & White, all members of the Lambs, were given the commission for the new building when the club outgrew its former quarters at 70 West 36th Street.

Stanford White was in charge of the design for the six-story brick, marble, and terra-cotta clubhouse. Its ground floor is faced with marble, while the upper stories are faced with red Flemish bond brickwork and flanked by stone quoins. A projecting cornice tops the fifth floor; a classical attic with a secondary cornice above the sixth floor is crowned by a roof balustrade. The fine decorative details include a belt course with Greek fret motif and identical doorways with Doric columns supporting full entablatures. At the second floor, graceful loggias with French doors are separated by Ionic columns, and enclosed by wrought-iron balcony railings. There are stylized lambs' heads between the spandrels of the windows, and a wall plaque flanked by lambs.

The club has moved to new quarters at 3 West 51st Street; the Manhattan Church of the Nazarene, also called "The Lambs," currently occupies the old clubhouse on West 44th Street.

PUBLIC BATHS, 1904–06
East 23rd Street and Asser Levy Place, Manhattan
Architects: Arnold W. Brunner and William Martin Aiken
Designated: March 19, 1974

In the late nineteenth century, charitable organizations and social reformers lobbied strongly for city governments to provide public sanitation and recreation facilities to help ameliorate living conditions in densely populated slums. The sanitation facilities in tenements were often inadequate or nonexistent. Reformers blamed overcrowded and filthy conditions for everything from periodic outbreaks of cholera and typhus to what was perceived as the decline of domestic values and morality.

Private organizations had provided bathing facilities based on contemporary European establishments since the 1850s, but these facilities proved insufficient by the 1890s. Lobbyists argued that only municipal funding for a citywide system could serve slum dwellers' needs. In 1894, the New York City Tenement House Commission, a special advisory board, concurred. The Panic of 1893, however, delayed appropriation of funds; these were allocated only through the intervention of newly elected Mayor Seth Low in 1901. Between 1902 and 1915, thirteen bathhouses were built for $2,000,000, making New York City's system the largest in the country. Today, nine bathhouses remain.

Arnold W. Brunner, who was associated with earlier sanitation reform movements and who also built community hospitals and public schools, based his design for the splendid East 23rd Street baths on ancient Roman models. The East 23rd Street bathhouse was also one of the first to provide both recreational and bathing facilities under one roof. It is a one-story brick and limestone building with four pairs of freestanding columns articulating three internal divisions. Men and women had separate waiting rooms and shower areas, marked by the large thermal windows facing East 23rd Street. A fountain, whose stonework simulates falling water, announces the building's function and marks the interior glazed pool area used by both sexes. A large swag-decorated shield, bearing the seal of New York City, rises above the balustrade.

Following the restrictive immigration laws of 1923 and the increasing number of tenements built with sanitation facilities, use of public baths dropped off; by the 1950s, the baths had been converted to community facilities or demolished. The East 23rd Street baths serve now as a recreation and community center.

SIXTY-NINTH REGIMENT ARMORY, 1904–06
68 Lexington Avenue, Manhattan
Architects: Hunt & Hunt
Designated: April 12, 1983

The Sixty-Ninth Regiment Armory was the first building of its type to reject the medieval fortress prototype typical of the Manhattan armories built between 1880 and 1906. Designed by the architectural firm of Hunt & Hunt, the armory synthesizes the classically inspired design principles of the Ecole des Beaux-Arts with a clear expression of military function. The armory, occupying much of the block bounded by East 25th and 26th streets and Lexington and Park avenues, is a comparatively unadorned brick structure, composed of two standard elements of armory design: an administrative building and a drill shed rising behind.

The armory served as a training and marshaling center for the National Guard. It is also the home of "The Fighting 69th," an Irish regiment that distinguished itself in the Civil War and the two World Wars. In 1913, the Sixty-Ninth Regiment Armory was the site of the International Exhibition of Modern Art, popularly known as the Armory Show. The exhibition changed the course of American art by making then-revolutionary European and American art forms available to a wider public.

SUPREME COURT OF THE STATE OF NEW YORK, QUEENS COUNTY, LONG ISLAND CITY BRANCH, 1872–76; rebuilt, 1904–08
25–10 Court Square, Queens
Architect: George Hathorne; reconstruction, Peter M. Coco
Designated: May 11, 1976

Constructed between 1872 and 1876 and rebuilt shortly after the turn of the century, the Long Island City Courthouse is a monument to the years when Long Island City served as the seat of Queens County. The building was also the setting for many important trials, notably the murder trial of Ruth Snyder and her lover, Henry Judd Gray, in 1927, and the trial of the notorious bank robber Willie Sutton.

Characterized by a bold fenestration and firm symmetry, the present English Renaissance–style building replaced a French Second Empire–style one designed by George Hathorne, the architect of Walker Hall at Amherst College. After a fire in 1904, the building was remodeled by architect Peter M. Coco who replaced its mansard roof with two additional stories, razed the two central towers, and removed the exterior detail. A huge stained-glass skylight decorates the third-floor courtroom reputed to be the largest in New York State. The Queens County Court was located in the courthouse until 1932, when it moved to accommodate the State Supreme Court. In addition, the building housed a variety of other judiciary services until the 1970s, when the Supreme Court took over the entire structure.

647 FIFTH AVENUE,
formerly the George W. Vanderbilt House, 1902–05; addition, 1917
Manhattan
Architects: Hunt & Hunt
Designated: March 22, 1977

In 1902, just a year after the architectural firm of Hunt & Hunt was formed, brothers Richard H. and Joseph Hunt began building the "Marble Twins," a pair of town houses at 645 and 647 Fifth Avenue, for George Washington Vanderbilt. The homes reflected both the longstanding patron-architect relationship between the Vanderbilts and the Hunts, and a continuation of the trend to build in the opulent French Renaissance style introduced to New York in 1879 by the architects' father, Richard Morris Hunt. Today, only one of the buildings, number 647, remains.

The town house is executed in the style of Louis XV. The first floor was originally rusticated, with round-arched openings; today a wide plate-glass window has been installed for a storefront. One of the most handsome features of the façade is a composite order of finely carved, fluted pilasters linking the second and third stories. The two top stories above the entablature were skillfully added in 1917.

When 647 was completed, the neighborhood was exclusively an area of Beaux Arts splendor—with the University Club two blocks away, the Plaza nearing completion up the street, and the handsome Union Club (now demolished) adjacent to the twins. One of the last reminders of the lavish mansions that once enhanced Fifth Avenue, 647 Fifth Avenue survives as a beautiful companion to 651–653, the former Morton A. Plant residence, which now houses Cartier.

POLICE HEADQUARTERS BUILDING, 1905–09
240 Centre Street, Manhattan
Architects: Hoppin, Koen & Huntington
Designated: September 26, 1978

On May 6, 1905, Mayor George B. McClellan, amid the ceremony of a police band and mounted troops, laid the cornerstone of the new police headquarters. Hailed by the press as the most up-to-date building of its kind, it was the result of police reform and reorganization begun in the late nineteenth century.

The Municipal Police Act of 1884 had abolished the antiquated "night watch" system and established the police force as we now know it. Under this act, the seventeen wards of the city were divided into precincts, each with its own station house, captain, and sergeant. Officers received a manual that outlined their duties and legal powers. They did not, however, accept their role as "public servant"; the officers refused to wear the proposed blue uniform, which was reminiscent of servants' livery. A star-shaped copper badge (from which the expression "cop" derives), was worn over the left breast, and identified the early police force.

By 1900 New York City's police force had become the most sophisticated and largest in the country, and clearly required new headquarters. In 1903 the firm of Francis L. V. Hoppin and Terence A. Koen designed the new headquarters for its wedge-shaped site, bounded by Grand, Centre Market Place, Centre, and Broome streets. The building is a monument both to the growing municipal consciousness of New York and the new, professional police force. The main façade is reminiscent of the English Baroque of Sir Christopher Wren. The colossal Corinthian columns in the main portico and end pavilions, the rustication carried through the attic story, and the vigorously plastic central dome produce lively contrasts of highlight and shadow.

In 1973, the Police Department left the building for new headquarters at 1 Police Plaza. The city tried to find new uses for the old structure through the late 1970s, but met with little success. Finally, in 1987, Fourth Jeffersonian Associates acquired the property, and the firm has begun extensive restoration as it renovates the building into luxury apartments.

AMERICAN ACADEMY OF DRAMATIC ARTS, formerly the Colony Club, 1905
120 Madison Avenue, Manhattan
Architects: McKim, Mead & White
Designated: May 17, 1966

The first private women's club in New York to build itself a clubhouse, the Colony Club was primarily a social club, with overtones of good works—namely, patronage of the arts. It was founded in 1901 by Anne Morgan (sister of J. P. Morgan), Mrs. J. Borden Harriman, and Helen Barney.

The clubhouse at 120 Madison Avenue, designed by Stanford White, opened in 1906, the year of the architect's death. It was built to accommodate a swimming pool, assembly rooms, a gymnasium, dining quarters, a roof garden, bedrooms, and a tea room—all within one six-story building that retains its domestic character. The graceful Federal Revival façade is constructed of grayish red brick with white limestone trim. The whole is dominated by five tall windows on the second floor, set within recessed arches. The beautiful stone cornice is crowned by a perforated railing separating the lower floors from the roof with its five small dormers.

In an admirable example of sympathetic reuse, the old clubhouse has served since 1963 as the home of the American Academy of Dramatic Arts. Founded in 1884, the academy is the oldest school of professional dramatic training in the English-speaking world. For over a century it has produced some of this country's most illustrious actors and actresses, among them Spencer Tracy, Kirk Douglas, Lauren Bacall, Rosalind Russell, and Edward G. Robinson.

B. ALTMAN & CO. DEPARTMENT STORE BUILDING, 1905–13
355–371 Fifth Avenue, Manhattan
Architects: Trowbridge & Livingston
Designated: March 12, 1985

Located on the northeast corner of East 34th Street and Fifth Avenue, the B. Altman & Co. department store building is a stately and elegant example of American commercial design and a landmark in the cultural history of New York City.

The present-day B. Altman & Co. evolved from a mid-nineteenth-century storefront dry-goods shop operated on Third Avenue and East 10th Street by Benjamin Altman and his father. In 1874 the family store moved to Sixth Avenue, at West 18th Street—the city's newly fashionable retail location. By the turn of the century, B. Altman & Co. had established itself as a world leader in fine dry goods, especially as a purveyor of exquisite silks, satins, and velvets. In a trend-setting move, the store acquired land in a newly commercial area—34th Street and Fifth Avenue—and Altman commissioned the architectural firm of Trowbridge & Livingston to design a new home for his company. Within a few years after the new building's 1906 opening, B. Altman was joined by such distinguished commercial establishments as W. & J. Sloane, Arnold Constable & Co., and Bergdorf Goodman. Fifth Avenue was quickly transformed from a street lined with town houses to a world-renowned commercial boulevard.

Trowbridge & Livingston employed an Italian Renaissance palazzo design that echoed the style of many of the residences that lined the avenue. Further, its façade of French limestone, a material previously used only on residential buildings, blended well with those of neighboring structures. The building's two-story limestone base is punctuated with tall, recessed-arch window bays separated by Corinthian pilasters; the entrances on Madison and Fifth avenues are marked by impressive projecting portals, each articulated by elegantly fluted Corinthian columns.

In June, 1988, the Landmarks Preservation Commission approved a six story addition to be constructed atop the taller, Madison Avenue end of B. Altman. Designed by Hardy, Holzman Pfeiffer Associates in a style compatible with the original building, the addition is scheduled for completion in 1991–92 if it receives the necessary approvals from the city.

131–135 EAST 66TH STREET, 1905–07
Manhattan
Architects: Charles A. Platt and Simonson, Pollard & Steinam
Designated: March 31, 1970

Located on the northeast corner of East 66th Street and Lexington Avenue, this distinguished apartment house was designed by Charles A. Platt. Eleven stories high, it was skillfully designed to make a relatively tall building seem hardly taller than its five-story neighbors. The heavily rusticated base is actually three stories high, and the fifth- and sixth-story windows are framed in stone to make them look as though they were one story. The great pedimented doorways run the full height of the three-story base.

A series of horizontal bands and cornices break up the remaining height of the building, while the windows of the entablature are lost within the shadows of the great overhanging cornice. This building is considered to be one of the finest examples of the Italian Renaissance style in an apartment house.

THE PLAZA, 1905–07
Fifth Avenue and West 59th Street, Manhattan
Architect: Henry J. Hardenbergh
Designated: December 9, 1969

The celebrated Plaza hotel sits majestically at the corner of Fifth Avenue and West 59th Street overlooking Central Park and Grand Army Plaza. Designed by Henry J. Hardenbergh—whose previous achievements included the Dakota Apartments, the old Waldorf-Astoria (on the present site of the Empire State Building), and the American Fine Arts Society building—the hotel opened on October 1, 1907, to great acclaim. It was described quite simply as "the greatest hotel in the world"; imposing, elegant, and opulent, it was destined to attract a fashionable and affluent clientele.

The Plaza was built at a cost of $12.5 million—an amazing sum at the time; it replaced a smaller (400-room) hotel designed by George W. DeCunha. Hardenbergh's new Plaza was much grander, with 800 rooms, 500 baths, private fourteen- to seventeen-room apartments (whose tenants included the George Jay Gould family and the Alfred Gwynne Vanderbilt family), two floors of public rooms, ten elevators, five marble staircases, and a two-story ballroom.

The Plaza's cast-iron skyscraper structure of eighteen stories is based stylistically on the French Renaissance château. The two main façades, one facing Central Park and the other Fifth Avenue, are organized along the lines of a classical column. A three-story marble base supports the ten-story white brick shaft. The capital, or crown, of the building, clearly demarcated by a horizontal band of balconies and a heavy cornice, consists of a mansard slate roof of five floors with gables and dormers and a cresting of green copper. The façades are unified vertically by recessed central bays and projecting corner towers. Hardenbergh claimed that the site on the park helped to determine the simplicity of his design.

To attract and impress its illustrious visitors and tenants, the Plaza was outfitted in rich woods and lavish ornamentation. Much of the interior decoration and furnishing came from Europe. Although the hotel has since undergone a series of renovations and refurbishings, most of its original grandeur remains. The Palm Court (formerly the Tea Room), just off the Fifth Avenue entrance, still has its four Italian caryatids representing the four seasons, and its mirrored walls; but the splendid Tiffany leaded-glass domelight was removed in the 1940s. The Plaza was purchased by Westin Hotels & Resorts in 1975, and the new owners immediately initiated a multimillion-dollar restoration program. In 1988 the hotel was again sold, to Donald Trump.

NEW YORK PUBLIC LIBRARY, HAMILTON GRANGE BRANCH, 1905–06; alterations, 1973–76
503–505 West 145th Street, Manhattan
Architects: McKim, Mead & White
Designated: March 31, 1970

The Hamilton Grange Branch of the New York Public Library is one of sixty-five branches built with funds donated by Andrew Carnegie for the development of a branch library circulation system.

In true Italian Renaissance style, the façade is symmetrical: the central entryway is emphasized by a cartouche bearing the seal of the City of New York, and the central second-floor window is surmounted by an arched pediment. The large, round-arched openings of the first floor give way to rectangular, pedimented windows on the second story; on both floors, the large windows alternate with narrower windows. On the third floor are five small windows of equal size. The strong verticality created by the narrow windows is balanced on the upper floors by the horizontal belt courses and on the first floor by the illusion of weightiness in the rustication.

The library was extensively rehabilitated between 1973 and 1976. Although the exterior remained largely unchanged, the main entrance was lowered to street level to provide easier access for the elderly and handicapped. The Hamilton Grange library has a particularly strong collection of books on black history and culture, and also contains many volumes in Spanish.

BRONX BOROUGH COURTHOUSE, 1905–15
East 161st Street between Brook and Third avenues, The Bronx
Architect: Michael J. Garvin
Designated: July 28, 1981

Designed by local architect Michael J. Garvin, the Bronx Borough Courthouse was erected to serve various borough courts. The building was officially opened in January of 1914, when the Bronx assumed the powers and responsibilities of a county in New York State.

The four-story granite Beaux Arts building occupies an entire block and can be seen from all sides. Its symmetrical classical design includes central pavilions that project from the structure's north and south elevations; these are punctuated by deeply recessed windows and double-height arched entrances.

The building's two-story base is faced with stone rustication; stylized voussoirs surmount the first-story windows, becoming archivolts at the building's arched entrances. The structure's upper stories form a single architectural unit and are faced with smooth granite bands. Two-story pilasters flank the window bays and form corner piers. On the East 161st Street elevation, two window bays flank monumental columns, which in turn frame a recessed central section with an arched window opening. An allegorical figure of Justice, the work of French-born sculptor J. E. Roine, sits in this alcove over the building's entrance.

VERDI SQUARE
Broadway at West 72nd Street, Manhattan
Designated: January 28, 1975

Verdi Square, a triangular lot in the northern part of Sherman Square, is a charming green that once lay within the old village of Harsenville—one of the many hamlets that arose along the old Bloomingdale Road, which was widened and renamed Broadway in 1849.

This small green honors the great Italian composer Giuseppe Verdi. The centrally located statue, sculpted by Pasquale Civiletti—brother of the noted Sicilian sculptor Benedetto Civiletti—was unveiled on October 12, 1906. The heroic *Verdi*, executed in Carrara marble, stands on a fifteen-foot base encircled by four lifesize figures from Verdi's operas: *Aïda*, *Falstaff*, *Otello*, and *La Forza del Destino*.

20 VESEY STREET, formerly the New York Evening Post Building, 1906
Manhattan
Architect: Robert D. Kohn
Designated: November 23, 1965

The former New York Evening Post Building is one of the few outstanding Art Nouveau buildings constructed in America, and more striking than Kohn's better-known Society for Ethical Culture on West 64th Street. The fourteen-story steel-frame structure, veneered with stone, is more Continental than American, reminiscent of the buildings that line the boulevards of Paris. Its ornamentation includes three gently bowed cast-iron bays framed by tall limestone piers, an elaborate patinated copper mansard roof two stories high, and four elongated sculpted figures on the front of the building. Two of these figures are the work of Gutzon Borglum, who is also noted for his heroic busts of presidents at Mount Rushmore.

The building originally served as the headquarters of the *New York Evening Post* during Oswald Garrison Villard's ownership. The New York Landmarks Preservation Commission was headquartered here from 1980 to 1987.

APTHORP APARTMENTS, 1906–08
2201–2219 Broadway, Manhattan
Architects: Clinton & Russell
Designated: September 9, 1969

The Apthorp Apartments is one of the Upper West Side's great courtyard apartment buildings. It was completed in 1908 by the firm of Clinton & Russell for the Astor Estate, and designed in the popular Italian Renaissance style.

The most conspicuous feature of this handsome, limestone-clad building is the use of rustication contrasted with the smooth ashlar masonry of the wall planes. Notable also is the adaptation of the three-story Renaissance palazzo design to a block-long, twelve-story edifice. The large wall planes of the façade are divided vertically into a three-story rusticated base, a smooth center portion, and two stories at the top with pilasters and windows just below the bold cornice. Instead of using quoins, the architects emphasized each corner by a wide band of rustication for its entire height. The monumental entrance archway, complete with ornate iron gateway and coffered ceilings and flanked by paired Corinthian pilasters capped with statues, creates a dramatic and commanding passageway to the drive-in courtyard. William Waldorf Astor named this apartment house after the very fine old Apthorp mansion that stood at West 91st Street and Columbus Avenue until 1892. At the time it was constructed, the building set a standard for luxury in apartment houses.

JEWISH MUSEUM, formerly the Felix M. Warburg Mansion, 1906–08
1109 Fifth Avenue, Manhattan
Architect: C.P.H. Gilbert
Designated: November 24, 1981

By the early 1900s Fifth Avenue facing Central Park had earned the nickname "Millionaires' Row"; the epitome of America's Gilded Age, the avenue was lined with magnificent mansions that proclaimed the owners' unabashed enthusiasm for the beauty money can create.

Few of the mansions have survived, and the Felix Warburg Mansion is among the finest left to us—an exceptionally handsome example of a "château" in the French Renaissance style. Constructed in 1906–08 for Felix and Frieda Schiff Warburg, the house was designed by C.P.H. Gilbert, one of the city's most eminent architects, who had designed a house for Felix's brother Paul. Felix Warburg admired the Isaac D. Fletcher house, an elaborate 1899 François I–style mansion by Gilbert at East 79th Street and Fifth Avenue. Over the objections of his father-in-law, Jacob Schiff, who thought such an ostentatious style would encourage anti-Semitism, Warburg commissioned Gilbert to design a similar mansion for himself.

The grand, lavishly ornamented building is faced in Indiana limestone, which allows for smooth wall surfaces and sharply defined ornate detailing. Above the five principal floors are steeply pitched slate roofs encircled by pinnacled stone gables, tall chimneys, copper crestings and finials, and a sixth story with small copper dormers. The windows are of various types, including square-headed and "basket-handle" arched, with ogee-arched enframements. Projecting bays and balconies further enliven the façades.

Members of an internationally renowned German banking family, the Warburg brothers emigrated from their native Hamburg to this country and joined the New York banking firm of Kuhn, Loeb & Co. While Paul devoted himself to banking, Felix's achievements were more diversified: a highly capable financier, he was also a bon vivant, art collector, philanthropist, and leader of the Jewish community. In fact, the entire family played an important role in Jewish causes in America. Mrs. Warburg donated the family mansion as a permanent home for the Jewish Museum, which opened in 1947. In May, 1988, the Jewish Museum announced a plan to build a seven-story French Renaissance–style addition, designed by Kevin Roche, John Dinkeloo & Associates, to the Felix Warburg Mansion. Construction would begin in 1991, pending the approval of the Landmarks Preservation Commission and other city agencies, and would require the demoliton of the present annex.

BELASCO THEATER, 1906–07; addition, 1909
111–121 West 44th Street, Manhattan
Architect: George Keister
Designated (exterior and interior): November 4, 1987

The sixth-oldest theater on Broadway, the Belasco is a monument to the genius and vision of its founder, David Belasco. One of the most important figures in the development of the American stage, Belasco was an actor, dramatist, manager, and director. He developed the Little Theater movement, which emphasized a close actor-audience contact best served in intimate, comfortable surroundings.

Designed by architect George Keister under Belasco's close supervision, the theater was built in the Georgian Revival style, which was more commonly seen in residences and civic buildings than in the typical, classical theater designs of the day. The pedimented façade has towers with Palladian windows. Also included were a four-story pavilion for offices, and a ten-room rooftop duplex, added in 1909, which became Belasco's personal residence.

The interior of the theater featured an entrance lobby and doors by John Rapp, light fixtures by the Tiffany Studios, and eighteen mural panels by Ash Can School artist Everett Shinn. Adding to the opulence of the interior was the colored glass ceiling, illuminated from behind to create the effect of daylight. The Belasco embodies its founder's vision of the ideal theater. Here he developed advanced methods of staging and lighting design that have had enduring significance in the modern theater.

PUBLIC BATH NUMBER 7, 1906–10
227–231 Fourth Avenue, Brooklyn
Architect: Raymond F. Almirall
Designated: September 11, 1984

Public Bath Number 7 is a survivor of what was once the largest system of public baths in the world. The bath system was an outgrowth of the mid-nineteenth-century tenement reform movement, whose goal was to improve slum conditions and to promote cleanliness in areas where only minimal sanitary facilities were provided. Bathing was viewed with some trepidation by many tenement dwellers, so the architectural expression of the bathhouses was of particular importance. The Classical Revival style chosen for many of these buildings, of which this is an especially flamboyant example, equated the bathhouses stylistically with banks, libraries, and other important public institutions.

The main façade has three large round arches, with a men's entrance on one side, a women's on the other, and a window in the center. The base of the building is a terra-cotta imitation of rusticated limestone; the upper portion of the façade is executed in white glazed brick. Raymond F. Almirall's signature use of color appears in the terra-cotta ornament of the building, much of which has aquatic themes. In the parapet, blue urns spill out green water; in the spandrels, blue T-shaped panels contain images of Triton and a trident.

Converted to a gymnasium in 1930 and abandoned briefly in the 1950s, the building has most recently served as a warehouse.

45 EAST 66TH STREET, 1906–08
Manhattan
Architects: Harde & Short
Designated: November 15, 1977

The building at 45 East 66th Street, designed by Harde & Short and erected in 1906–08, is a superb example of the luxury apartment houses that began to replace the opulent private mansions that lined the Upper East Side during the first decades of the twentieth century.

The picturesque building, with its distinctive corner tower, is among the earliest and most beautiful of its type to be built in the city. It rises ten stories with a penthouse above, and the ornate red-brick façade is trimmed with light-colored, Gothic-inspired terra-cotta details. The structure has an almost medieval quality that stands out in the neighborhood.

NEW YORK PUBLIC LIBRARY, 115TH STREET BRANCH, 1907–08
203 West 115th Street, Manhattan
Architects: McKim, Mead & White
Designated: July 12, 1967

This three-story Italian Renaissance–style structure was erected with funds from Andrew Carnegie's 1901 gift of more than $5 million to build branches of the public library throughout the city.

The façade is rusticated gray limestone with three widely spaced window bays. On the first and second floors, the round-headed windows are set beneath a belt course. On the first floor, a cartouche above the central window showing the city's coat of arms is supported by two cherubic angels bearing garlands. A projecting stone cornice, carried on ornate brackets, effectively terminates the façade at the top.

130–134 EAST 67TH STREET, 1907
Manhattan
Architect: Charles A. Platt for Rossiter & Wright
Designated: January 29, 1980

This apartment house was designed to complement another building
by Charles A. Platt—the nearly identical adjoining apartment house
at the corner of Lexington Avenue and East 66th Street. The building
is an important example of the luxury cooperative apartment house,
then a relatively new type of residence for wealthy urban dwellers.

Faced in finely worked limestone, 130–134 East 67th Street
reflects the common adaptation of the tripartite façade organization of
the Italian Renaissance palazzo to tall urban buildings in the late
nineteenth and early twentieth centuries. The first three of the
building's eleven stories are treated as a base, articulated by a
smooth-faced and shallow pattern of very regular rustication and
crowned by a bold ovolo molding. Molding courses also articulate the
upper stories into distinct horizontal bands. Among the building's
most prominent features are the twin porticoes that mark the main
entrances. Their baseless Doric columns support a full entablature
with crisply carved triglyphs and alternating lions' heads and
anthemia on the cornice. Above the third story, the façade is of very
closely laid smooth-faced limestone, and the window arrangement is
asymmetrical. A bold cornice crowns the structure.

ALWYN COURT APARTMENTS, 1907–09
182 West 58th Street, Manhattan
Architects: Harde & Short
Designated: June 7, 1966

The Alwyn Court Apartments is the finest of all of the turn-of-the-
century apartment houses to be decorated with terra-cotta, and one of
the most beautiful in Manhattan. The entire building is embellished
with decorative detail, leaving hardly any surface unadorned. Such
rich ornamentation, which would have been impossible in stone,
could be achieved with terra-cotta molds used repeatedly to produce
intricate designs in great quantity. The architects Harde & Short
were free to create an exterior of unparalleled sumptuousness.

In its departure from the design formula for apartment houses of
the time (base, plain shaft, and top story ornamented and crowned by
a projecting cornice), the Alwyn Court was quite radical. The first
four floors were treated as the base, the next five as the shaft, and the
final three as the crown. The tripartite divisions were separated
horizontally by strong projecting decorative bands, between which
Corinthian pilasters divide the Seventh Avenue elevation into four
bays and the West 58th Street elevation into five. In the best Parisian
tradition, a rounded bay marks the corner of the building. The shafts
of the pilasters, the belt courses, and all the windows are richly
decorated with intricate French Renaissance–inspired detail,
including the crowned salamander, symbol of François I of France.
The apartments provide a pleasing and refreshing contrast to the
neighboring glass and steel buildings of Seventh Avenue.

U.S. CUSTOM HOUSE, 1907
Bowling Green, Manhattan
Architect: Cass Gilbert
Designated: October 14, 1965; interior designated January 9, 1979

The Custom House, built at the lowest point of land in Manhattan, on what was once the shore of the Battery, has no difficulty in dominating the soaring contemporary towers that surround it. Though only seven stories high, the building is vast and monumental, enclosing a volume of space said to be fully a quarter of that of the Empire State Building.

The architect was Cass Gilbert, one of the ablest and most successful practitioners of his time. Gilbert's building was erected on the site of a much earlier custom house, destroyed by fire in 1814. One major source of revenue for the federal government in the days before taxes on income and corporations were tariffs on imported goods. As New York developed into America's largest port, the U.S. Custom Service acquired increasingly larger buildings; both Federal Hall and the Merchant's Exchange once served as custom houses. In 1892, due to the increasing demand for a new and larger building, the U.S. Treasury acquired the large plot of land at Bowling Green, and Gilbert was chosen over twenty other architects in a competition for the design of the new Custom House.

Gilbert said that the ideal for a public building like the Custom House was that it should encourage "just pride in the state, [be] an education to oncoming generations . . . [and] a symbol of the civilization, culture and ideals of our country." The Custom House was designed and constructed with these lofty purposes in mind. Indeed, Gilbert's building—a granite palace executed in a monumental Beaux Arts style—is a paean to trade, to the city's role as a great seaport, and to America's status as one of the leading commercial nations in the world.

The building was designed to turn its back upon the harbor, but its symbolic ornament is unquestionably marine: shells, snails, and dolphins embellish the walls of the façade. On the capitals of the forty-four stout columns that encircle the building is carved a head of Mercury, the Roman god of commerce; masks of different races decorate the keystones over the windows and a head of Columbus stares out from above the cavernous main entrance. On the broad stone sill of the sixth-story cornice rest twelve immense figures in white Tennessee marble, representing twelve of the most successful commercial nations and city-states in history: Greece, Rome, Phoenicia, Genoa, Venice, Spain, Holland, Portugal, Denmark, Germany, England, and France. The central cartouche at the top of the façade is the shield of the United States, supported by two winged figures. The four enormous white limestone sculptures, known as *The Continents*, rest on pedestals on the ground-floor level; the work of noted sculptor Daniel Chester French, they are among of the finest examples of Beaux Arts sculpture produced in America.

The interior of the Custom House is as majestic as its exterior. The main entrance leads to a grand, symmetrically designed two-story hall, finished in marbles of varying textures and colors with a spiral staircase rising the full height of the building at each end. Off the hall is one of the most splendid rooms in the city, paneled from floor to ceiling in oak and with a richly worked ceiling. Perhaps the most impressive feature of the interior is the rotunda, 135 feet long, 85 feet wide, and 48 feet high. The ceiling skylight is one of the curious tile-and-plaster vaulted masterpieces of the noted Spanish engineer Rafael Guastavino. Of special note in the rotunda are the sixteen frescoes by Reginald Marsh, executed in 1937; the small murals depict early explorers, while the larger panels follow the journey of a passenger liner through New York Harbor. By engaging the services of many nationally known artisans, Gilbert was to create a design that is unparalleled in public buildings of the period.

In 1973, the U.S. Custom Service abandoned the building for larger quarters, and in the last few years, the federal government has engaged in restoring the Beaux Arts masterpiece to house new federal offices. It is now scheduled to become the new home of the Museum of the American Indian.

RIZZOLI BUILDING, 1907–08
712 Fifth Avenue, Manhattan
Architect: Albert S. Gottlieb
Designated: January 29, 1985

Among the finest of the commercial buildings erected on Fifth Avenue in the early twentieth century is 712 Fifth Avenue, commonly known today as the Rizzoli Building. It was designed by Albert S. Gottlieb, an architect trained at the Ecole des Beaux-Arts in Paris and in the office of McKim, Mead & White.

Gottlieb's beautiful limestone building resembles an eighteenth-century Neoclassical town house with its balanced and restrained massing and elegantly executed detail. The ground floor has a rusticated base cut by the round-arched entrance to the upper floors. This entry is ornamented with a carved wreath set within a fanlight. Arched openings on the second floor have French doors and balustrade railings, above which are set Corinthian pilasters and delicately carved garland panels. A balustrade railing capped by urns runs above the cornice and shields a mansard attic.

The façades of the Rizzoli Building and the adjoining Coty Building are being incorporated into a mixed-use high-rise building, now under construction, whose bulk will be set back from Fifth Avenue. The Rizzoli Building will remain as one of the few surviving deluxe commercial establishments of the early twentieth century on this world-famous avenue.

FORMER COTY BUILDING, 1907–08
714 Fifth Avenue, Manhattan
Architect: Woodruff Leeming
Designated: January 29, 1985

The six-story limestone former Coty Building at 714 Fifth Avenue is a survivor from the earliest period of commercial development on Fifth Avenue south of 59th Street. It is significant because of the three stories of windows designed by the internationally acclaimed French craftsman René Lalique for the perfumer François Coty.

The history of the building extends back to 1871, when architect Charles Duggin designed a group of row houses for the west side of Fifth Avenue between 55th and 56th streets. In 1907 the building and its neighbor at 712 became the first commercial structures on this section of Fifth Avenue. The house at 712 was soon demolished and replaced by a French Neoclassical structure, the Rizzoli Building. Number 714 was only partially demolished; its old façade was removed and rebuilt. Architect Woodruff Leeming's design incorporated French design details that linked the building to its residential neighbors, but its large, multipaned windows clearly proclaimed its commercial function.

In 1910, François Coty, whose business had recently grown from a small concern into one of international renown, leased the building. Soon thereafter, he transformed the space into an elegant French shop. Interior designer L. Alavoine created a glamorous interior; René Lalique's workshop was commissioned to design and manufacture the windows for the façade.

The six-story façade consists of three floors unified within a single design concept. The horizontal window bands on each level are divided by vertical metal mullions into five sections, each filled by small panes of semiopaque glass. Four strands of intertwining poppies link each level to the next. These forms were created in three-dimensional molded glass with the flowers and vines on the exterior, recalling Lalique's early Art Nouveau work.

Coty remained at 714 Fifth Avenue until François Coty's death in 1934. In 1941 the City Investing Co. purchased the property, and it was used by a succession of commercial tenants. The façades of the Coty Building and the adjoining Rizzoli Building are being incorporated into a mixed-use high-rise building, now under construction. The glass will remain of great interest to many observant passersby and it is fitting that the world's art capital should have an intact Lalique shopfront.

SARA DELANO ROOSEVELT MEMORIAL HOUSE, 1907–08
47–49 East 65th Street, Manhattan
Architect: Charles A. Platt
Designated: September 25, 1973

The Sara Delano Roosevelt Memorial House at 47–49 East 65th Street is a superb example of an early-twentieth-century Georgian Revival town house. In 1905, Sara Roosevelt, Franklin Delano Roosevelt's mother, commissioned Charles A. Platt to design, as a wedding present for her recently married son, a double house that she could share with him. Sara Delano Roosevelt lived at number 47; Franklin and Eleanor Roosevelt moved into number 49 in 1908, and stayed there whenever they were in New York City, where he was a lawyer and an officer of an insurance firm. It was in this house in 1921 that he began his convalescence from his crippling attack of polio. After 1928, the year he was first elected governor of New York, Roosevelt spent only brief periods at number 49. His mother, Sara, continued to live at number 47 until her death in 1941. The following year, a group of citizens bought the double house for use by the students of nearby Hunter College as an interfaith social center.

COMMONWEALTH FUND, formerly the Edward S. Harkness House, 1907–09
1 East 75th Street, Manhattan
Architect: James Gamble Rogers
Designated: January 24, 1967

This marble mansion was commissioned from James Gamble Rogers by Edward S. Harkness, the son of Stephen Harkness, one of the founding partners of Standard Oil. In contrast to many of the mansions built on upper Fifth Avenue for wealthy clients, Gamble's design is notable for its combination of luxury and restraint. In 1910, the *Architectural Record* declared that "If there is any façade on upper Fifth Avenue which gives an effect of quiet elegance by worthier architectural means it has not been our good fortune to come across it." Rogers achieved this effect by turning to Renaissance models, and his design shows a profound instinct for their sense of proportion. The building's five stories are divided into a rusticated ground story, finely dressed ashlar upper stories with quoins, and a top floor disguised by a stone balustrade. A full cornice with an elaborate frieze articulates the transition from the body of the building to the top floor. The main entrance in the central bay of the East 75th Street façade features Tuscan columns supporting a balustraded balcony. In the tradition of the Renaissance palazzo, the important reception rooms form a *piano nobile*, expressed on the façades by large windows on the second story. In addition to the finely executed detail of the exterior, the house is also distinguished by the understated luxury of its rooms, which preserve the ambience of elegant life around the turn of the century.

In 1918 Edward Harkness's mother established the Commonwealth Fund, "to do something for the welfare of mankind." Edward and his wife, the former Mary Stillman, devoted most of their lives to the philanthropic programs of the fund. Harkness died in 1940, and his wife a decade later. In 1950 the house became the headquarters of the Commonwealth Fund, which today supports planning in the field of health and medical research, and provides fellowships to graduate students from the United Kingdom, Australia, and New Zealand. In 1987 the fund restored the house and its interior.

ORIGINAL MAURICE SCHINASI HOUSE, 1907–09
351 Riverside Drive, Manhattan
Architect: William B. Tuthill
Designated: March 19, 1974

The Maurice Schinasi residence was built in 1907–09 on the northeast corner of West 107th Street and Riverside Drive. A relatively small, freestanding mansion, it was designed by architect William B. Tuthill, who also designed Carnegie Hall. Schinasi was a member of the well-known tobacco-processing family and a partner in the firm of Schinasi Bros., Inc., which manufactured Natural brand cigarettes.

Tuthill designed an exquisite French Renaissance–style jewel box executed in pristine white marble, with a pitched roof of deep-green tiles, two spiked finials, and bronze grills on the balconies and at the main entrance. Two and one-half stories high and rectangular in plan, the house has a facade accented by an interplay of projected and recessed wall sections. Among its more distinctive features are high French windows on the second floor, a paneled frieze at the roofline, and boldly projecting dormer windows set above the modillioned roof cornice.

Schinasi so prized the whiteness of the façade that a special system of pumps was installed to allow every part of the exterior to be cleaned. The rich materials, wood paneling, mosaics, and stencil patterns used within contribute to a precious refinement unsurpassed on the Upper West Side, while mirrors and vistas between rooms enhanced the apparent spaciousness of the house.

MUNICIPAL BUILDING, 1907–14
Chambers and Centre streets, Manhattan
Architects: McKim, Mead & White
Designated: February 1, 1966

In undertaking to design the Municipal Building, the firm of McKim, Mead & White departed substantially from their usual practice. McKim in particular disliked designing tall buildings, which he felt were inevitably clumsy; moreover, their size was contrary to his vision of the city as a continuum of low-rise development punctuated by large public spaces and grand civic structures. The Municipal Building was the firm's first skyscraper; it reflects not so much a change in the original partners' attitudes as the influence of younger partners, including William Mitchell Kendall, who designed this structure.

It was also unusual for the firm to enter into competitions. McKim agreed to enter into the Municipal Building competition as a personal favor to Mayor George B. McClellan. The firm won the commission over designs by Carrère & Hastings, Clinton & Russell, and Howells & Stokes.

Kendall's first studies date from 1907–08 and change very little through the building's completion. The turrets and dome at the top, the most distinctive features, derive from three of the firm's earlier projects: the Rhode Island State Capitol, White's towers for Madison Square Garden (now demolished), and their Grand Central Terminal project, which was never built. The Federal period styling refers to Mangin & McComb's nearby City Hall. The Municipal Building influenced many later twentieth-century designs, including Albert Kahn's G.M. Building in Detroit, Carrère & Hastings's Tower of Jewels at the Panama Pacific Exposition in San Francisco (1915), and the main building at Moscow University (1949).

The roadway passage through the base, now closed, and the plaza that joined the newly completed IRT subway station to the building's entrances, demonstrated sensitivity to the requirements of the modern city. Several architects of the time—among them Cass Gilbert, whose Woolworth Building is diagonally across City Hall Park—tried to provide direct or sheltered entrances to buildings from the growing underground mass transit system, and this practice became fairly common in large office buildings through the 1920s.

BELNORD APARTMENTS, 1908–09
201–225 West 86th Street, Manhattan
Architect: H. Hobart Weekes
Designated: September 20, 1966

The end of pre–World War I development of the Upper West Side was marked by two large and very similar luxury apartment houses: the Apthorp at West 79th Street (1906–08) and the Belnord, begun one year later by H. Hobart Weekes. Both are in the style of sixteenth-century Italian Renaissance palazzi, with heavy rustication and elaborate wrought-iron grillwork; both are hollow squares in plan.

The central court of the Belnord was accessible to traffic from the south and to pedestrians from the east through monumental arched entries. Instead of the conventional, plain light court used in many contemporary apartment houses, this lovely courtyard with a fountain at the center lent a princely character to already luxurious multiple dwellings.

One of the Belnord's most distinctive features is the unusual treatment of the windows, which vary in size, enframement, and embellishment. Decorative panels link the corner windows vertically, and this sense of monumental verticality on the four long horizontal façades is enhanced by rusticated brickwork. An elaborate, over-scaled, projecting cornice terminates the elevations. Each courtyard entry has a coffered barrel vault.

The building's luxurious appointments, together with the elaborate services provided by the apartment management, quickly attracted tenants from row houses in other parts of Manhattan.

UNION THEOLOGICAL SEMINARY
Manhattan
Architects: Allen & Collins
Designated: November 15, 1967

Brown Memorial Tower, 1908–10
3041 Broadway at
Reinhold Niebuhr Place
(West 120th Street)

James Tower and James Memorial Chapel, 1908–10
Claremont Avenue between Reinhold
Niebuhr Place and Seminary Road
(West 120th and 122nd streets)

Union Theological Seminary, an independent, ecumenical graduate and professional school, was established in 1836. The seminary's first building, dedicated in 1838, was located near Washington Square at 9 University Place. In 1884 the seminary moved to its second home on Lenox Hill, with the central entrance at what is now 700 Park Avenue. The current seminary site is a complex of buildings between West 120th and 122nd streets, completed in 1910—a rectangle enclosing two city blocks and surrounding a landscaped inner quadrangle. Brown Memorial Tower, James Tower, and James Memorial Chapel were designed by the architects Allen & Collins, who won the commission in a competition.

Rising high above the lower buildings adjacent to them, Brown Memorial Tower in the southeast corner and James Tower in the middle of the Claremont Avenue side are among the finest examples of English Perpendicular Gothic–style architecture in New York City. At the base of these square towers, buttresses project from the corners, terminating at the top in pinnacles with delicate finials. Parapets at the roofline are paneled and ornately decorated. In the upper half of the Brown Memorial Tower, the tall windows are topped with handsome, intricate tracery. The windows in the James Tower, though shorter, have similar tracery.

The James Memorial Chapel on Claremont Avenue extends south from the tower of the same name. The walls of the east and west façades are evenly divided into seven bays, separated by stepped buttresses. Clerestory windows in both elevations are enframed within pointed arches, divided by two mullions that terminate in handsome tracery. On the Claremont Avenue side, buttresses rise above the crenellated parapet wall and terminate in finials.

PRATT–NEW YORK PHOENIX SCHOOL OF DESIGN,
formerly New York School of Applied Design for Women, 1908–09
160 Lexington Avenue, Manhattan
Architect: Harvey Wiley Corbett
Designated: May 10, 1977

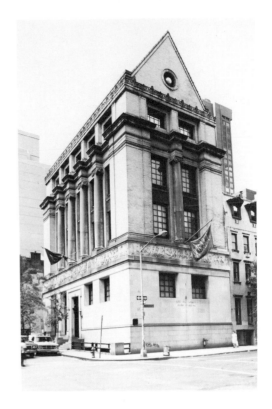

A highly imaginative Neoclassical design and an excellent combination of varied materials and textures in a unified composition, the Pratt–New York Phoenix School of Design is a veritable temple to the arts. Designed by Harvey Wiley Corbett (whose atelier of fledgling architects, it is said, worked on the drawings for the building), the structure is five stories high and built of terra-cotta and stone. The symmetrical building has its main façade on East 30th Street, with its most distinguishing feature the low-relief frieze above the high ashlar base; the frieze was composed from casts of portions of the Parthenon frieze. Four polished, unfluted granite Ionic columns rise above this frieze, emphasizing the strong verticality of the building. The boldly plastic entablature is executed in terra-cotta and ornamented with rich classical moldings. The steep gabled roof, of galvanized iron and tin painted green to imitate copper, continues the vertical emphasis. On the Lexington Avenue façade is a witty, single polished gray column.

The school was founded in 1892 with the purpose "of affording to women instruction which may enable them to earn a livelihood by the employment of their taste and manual dexterity in the application of ornamental design to manufacture and the arts." It was quite advanced for its time, demanding high-quality education for women. In 1944 the school merged with the Phoenix Art Institute, and in 1974 merged again with the Pratt Institute of Brooklyn. Since 1986, the building has been owned and occupied by a health rehabilitation agency.

CHURCH OF NOTRE DAME
Manhattan
Designated: January 24, 1967

Church of Notre Dame, 1909–10
Morningside Drive and West 114th Street
Architects: Dans & Otto (sanctuary);
completion, Cross & Cross

Rectory, 1913–14
409 West 114th Street
Architects: Cross & Cross

The firm of Dans & Otto designed and built the original section of this church—the sanctuary, which survives as an unusual grotto in the apse. In 1914 Cross & Cross continued the original plans for the chancel, but completed the church according to their own designs. In plan, the church is roughly a square, with a shallow Greek cross superimposed upon it. The cross is expressed in the portico on the east façade and slightly projecting pilastrade on the south elevation. A Corinthian portico dominates the façade. At the cornice level on the main body of the church is an elegant band of swags. The architects originally intended to raise a large dome over the crossing in a design closely based on Jacques-Germain Soufflot's dome on the Panthéon in Paris. In the carving and proportions, the whole seems inspired by French nineteenth-century architecture.

The gray brick and limestone Rectory on West 114th Street resembles a sixteenth-century Renaissance palazzo. The broad building is quite shallow, fitted onto a cramped site around the church. The most notable architectural features are the rounded corners, inset windows, and a two-story window set in a slightly projecting quoined central section. The wrought-iron fence surrounding the church creates a lively pattern against the austere façade.

Clock, 753 Manhattan Avenue   Clock, 783 Fifth Avenue   Clock, 522 Fifth Avenue   Clock, 200 Fifth Avenue   Clock, 30–78 Steinway Street

SIDEWALK CLOCKS
Designated: August 25, 1981

Clock at 753 Manhattan Avenue, Brooklyn, c. 1895
Maker: Unknown

Clock at 522 Fifth Avenue, Manhattan, 1907
Maker: Seth Thomas Clock Company

Clock at 200 Fifth Avenue, Manhattan, 1909
Maker: Hecla Iron Works

Clock at 30–78 Steinway Street, Queens, 1922
Maker: Unknown

Clock at 783 Fifth Avenue, Manhattan, c. 1927
Maker: E. Howard Clock Company

Although they enhance the cityscape and provide a public convenience, cast-iron street clocks were generally installed for advertising purposes. Introduced in the 1860s, these elegant timepieces were available from catalogues and sold for about $600. A merchant often painted his store's name on the clock face and installed the timepiece in front of his store to attract passersby. When a business moved, its clock was generally taken along. Originally, street clocks were operated by weights that descended gradually, and thus kept the clock running for about eight days. Today, they are mechanized and have secondary movements. Master clocks inside the buildings operate the clocks outside.

Though many were casualties of traffic mishaps and sidewalk ordinances, three clocks in Manhattan, one in Brooklyn, and one in Queens are designated city landmarks.

Manufactured in 1907 by the Seth Thomas Clock Company, the clock at 522 Fifth Avenue originally stood on Fifth Avenue and 43rd Street in front of the American Trust Company. When that bank and the Guaranty Trust Company merged in the 1930s, the clock was moved one block north to its present location. The nineteen-foot-tall clock features a fluted post and classically inspired ornamented base that support foliate scroll brackets. The clock's faces are marked with Roman numerals and rimmed with wreaths of acanthus leaf. An ornate pineapple motif crowns the clock.

The Hecla Iron Works manufactured the clock at 200 Fifth Avenue, which was installed in 1909 with the construction of the Fifth Avenue Building and features the building's name on its face. A stylish advertisement, the ornate cast-iron clock is composed of a rectangular, classically ornamented base and a fluted Ionic column with a Scammozzi capital. Its dials are marked with Roman numerals, framed by wreaths of oak leaves, and crowned by a cartouche.

The classically designed clock at 783 Fifth Avenue features a high, rectangular, beveled base with gilded panels that support the clock's slender fluted column and double-faced dial. Possibly installed in 1927 when the Sherry-Netherland Hotel was built, the clock was manufactured by the E. Howard Clock Company, a Massachusetts-based firm founded by Aaron L. Dennison and Edward Howard, creators of the first mass-produced pocket watch. The company introduced sidewalk clocks about 1870 and continued to produce them until 1964.

The cast-iron street clock at 753 Manhattan Avenue in Brooklyn was bought by Bomelsteins Jewelers and has a rectangular, beveled base, fluted column, and double-sided face. The clock surround has been obscured by a contemporary sign.

The tall cast-iron street clock at 30–78 Steinway Street in Queens has a large, round, double-faced dial, surmounted by an inverted triangular sign bearing the name Wagner Jewelers, and supported by a narrow, scroll-topped, fluted column on a beveled base. Erected in 1922, the clock was purchased secondhand in Manhattan by Edward Wagner, owner of the jewelry concern.

LIBERTY TOWER, 1909–10
55 Liberty Street, Manhattan
Architect: Henry Ives Cobb
Designated: August 24, 1982

Located at 55 Liberty Street in Lower Manhattan, Liberty Tower is a magnificent Gothic Revival skyscraper. When it was built, it had the distinction of being the "World's Tallest Building on so Small a Plot." Designed by Henry Ives Cobb, the thirty-three-story building was erected shortly before the Woolworth Building. Although only half as high as the latter, Liberty Tower anticipated much of the revolutionary character of its more famous contemporary by being almost entirely freestanding, clad largely in terra-cotta, and designed in a Gothic style.

Liberty Tower was one of the first early buildings to adapt a historic style to the newly emerging steel-cage method of construction, and it broke free, somewhat, of the tripartite system of skyscraper composition. It was also one of the first buildings to use terra-cotta as a primary cladding material—a style that soon became a trend in skyscraper construction. The high, sloping copper roof acquired a dull green patina that was intended to contrast with the white-glazed terra-cotta of the three main elevations. The prolific surface ornament is an adaptation of English Gothic. Pilasters at the corners of the roof are topped by pinnacles and crowned with finials. The dormers are flanked by small piers surmounted by terra-cotta animals.

The building was constructed according to the latest technological achievements of its time: The foundation was laid on caissons, resting on bedrock ninety feet below the curb, and the skeletal steel construction was fully fireproofed. The building was originally equipped with five high-speed elevators with wire glass enclosures.

The Garden City Company of Long Island bought Liberty Tower in 1916 and resold it to the Sinclair Building Company in 1919; the latter firm used it to house the main offices of the Sinclair Oil Company until 1945. For the next three decades, the building was owned by a real-estate company and rented out as offices. In 1979, the architect Joseph Pell Lombardi bought the building; he restored the exterior and public areas and converted it to a residential cooperative building. The residential space was sold unimproved, so that each of the eighty-nine apartments had its own architect, design, style, and layout.

GUATEMALAN PERMANENT MISSION TO THE UNITED NATIONS,
formerly the Adelaide L. T. Douglas Residence, 1909–11
57 Park Avenue, Manhattan
Architect: Horace Trumbauer
Designated: September 11, 1979

This elegant town house in the style of Louis XVI was designed for New York socialite Adelaide L. Townsend Douglas in 1909, a year after her divorce from William Proctor Douglas, a vice-commodore of the New York Yacht Club. The architect, Horace Trumbauer, had earned great prominence for his commissions from Peter A. B. Widener, including the Widener Memorial Library at Harvard University. He favored the stylistic prototypes of seventeenth- and eighteenth-century France, and the Adelaide Douglas house belongs to this mode.

The ground floor of the six-story granite and limestone structure is heavily rusticated. An impressive cornice, which also serves as a balcony, sets off the main portion of the façade at the second and third stories. The fourth story rises above a modillioned cornice with a grooved frieze decorated with bellflowers. A dentilled cornice and parapet sets off the slate-covered mansard roof that forms the fifth story. Shielded by a wrought-iron railing, only the parapet of the sixth floor, which is set back from the building line, is visible from the street. Wrought-iron railings also shield the windows, and a wrought-iron fence encloses the basement entryway. The Guatemalan Permanent Mission to the United Nations currently occupies the house.

NEW YORK CITY PARKING VIOLATIONS BUREAU, formerly the Emigrant Industrial Savings Bank Building, 1909–12
51 Chambers Street, Manhattan
Architect: Raymond F. Almirall
Designated (exterior and interior): July 9, 1985

Organized under the auspices of Bishop John Hughes and the Irish Emigrant Society, the Emigrant Industrial Savings Bank was incorporated in 1850 to protect the savings of people newly arrived in the United States. The bank grew rapidly with New York's growing immigrant population. In 1907 it acquired, for the second time, additional adjoining space and commissioned architect Raymond F. Almirall to design a new building for the expanded lot.

An intended backdrop to City Hall, Almirall's seventeen-story commercial building represents an early version of the New York skyscraper. The diffusion of sufficient interior light was a major preoccupation of the building's designers, who believed that a well-illuminated interior was crucial to healthy banking activity.

These goals were complicated by the strictures of Beaux Arts design, which called for heavy cornices to balance blocklike towers; these towers prevented light from reaching the building's upper stories. Some architects solved the problem by telescoping their towers to create a narrow main shaft that would permit light to reach a building's interior. Some developers responded by purchasing surrounding buildings to prevent the erection of light-blocking "spitescrapers."

Almirall's solution to the problem of interior light lay in his innovative H plan. Here, a series of double-height rusticated piers and engaged columns form nine bays that rest on a basement story and support an entablature. The long windows of these light bays illuminate the two-story banking halls within. Adorned with copper-framed, double-sash windows that lie recessed behind limestone piers, the building's twin towers create an unbroken line that emphasize the building's daring height. Though the solution was heralded in the *Real Estate Record and Guide* for having provided interior light, further use of the plan in other buildings was made impossible by a zoning law passed in 1916.

The majestic hall on the first floor remains one of New York's best banking rooms. Unlike better-known spaces, this formal hall achieves a gentle spaciousness through its repeated elliptical decorative motifs, which hint at the Art Nouveau style. Four stained-glass oval skylights portray figures that represent facets of the economy.

The Emigrant Industrial Savings Bank Building now houses municipal offices.

LUNT-FONTANNE THEATER,
formerly the Globe Theater, 1909–10
203–217 West 46th Street, Manhattan
Architects: Carrère & Hastings
Designated: December 8, 1987

The Lunt-Fontanne Theater, originally named the Globe, was designed by the distinguished architectural firm of Carrère & Hastings, and represents the theatrical vision of Charles Dillingham, who produced over 200 musicals and plays in his thirty-eight-year career on Broadway. Dillingham built the Globe as his headquarters, and named it for Shakespeare's theater as an honor to his central inspiration. Converted to a movie house in 1932, the Globe was renamed the Lunt-Fontanne in 1958, when it once more became a stage for the legitimate theater. Carrère & Hastings are best known for designing the New York Public Library and the Frick Collection and for their use of the Beaux Arts style. Characteristics of the Globe include a five-bay arcade of double-height Ionic columns, a deep cornice, and sculpted theatrical figures and masks. The extravagant design also included a large oval panel in the roof that could be removed to create an open-air auditorium. The lavish two-balcony interior was rebuilt in 1958, and none of the original remains. The Lunt-Fontanne is one of the oldest surviving Broadway theaters, and the only survivor of four designed by Carrère & Hastings.

NEW YORK SOCIETY FOR ETHICAL CULTURE BUILDING, 1909–10
2 West 64th Street, Manhattan
Architect: Robert D. Kohn
Designated: July 23, 1974

The New York Society for Ethical Culture building was designed in the Art Nouveau style by Robert D. Kohn. The society was founded in 1876 by Dr. Felix Adler, who intended the Ethical Culture Movement to bring together people interested in improving social morality. In 1897, after moving from Standard Hall to Chickering Hall and, in 1892, to Carnegie Hall, the movement attempted to find a permanent location. Kohn was a close friend of Adler's and served as a leader of the congregation and president of the society in 1921–44. His building reflects the influence of the Austrian Secession designs of Otto Wagner and Josef Hoffmann.

A quotation by Dr. Adler, engraved above the speaker's platform in the auditorium, articulates the philosophy of the institution: "The Place where Men meet to seek the Highest is Holy Ground." In keeping with this ideal, the prominent Central Park West front of the building's bright Indiana limestone façade combines large undecorated spaces with recessed openings to create a tremendous sense of scale. Each window group contains a shallow niche intended to hold sculpted figures of *Servants of Humanity*. The architect's wife, Estelle Rumbold Kohn, sculpted the figures that adorn a pedimented panel above the main entrance.

FIRST PRECINCT POLICE STATION, 1909–11
South Street and Old Slip, Manhattan
Architects: Hunt & Hunt
Designated: September 20, 1977

Old Slip, the site of the first official marketplace in New Amsterdam, became home to the First Precinct in 1884. The present station house was begun in 1909 and occupied by the First Precinct until 1973.

Despite its massive scale, the structure is simple in detail. Nine windows wide, with narrow, one-window ends, it follows the style of the Italian Renaissance Revival. The horizontal divisions include a molded granite base, a rusticated center section, and a smooth-faced attic story. A rhythmic series of arches pierces the center section; their square-headed first-floor windows and, in every third arch, a door, are separated by bronze spandrels from the arched voussoir windows on the second floor. Above the arches are square, paired voussoir windows. Approached by a short flight of steps, the central entrance has a recessed double door with leaded-glass panels, Doric columns, and a pediment supported by ornate brackets. Resting above a row of attic windows and a row of dentils, a roof cornice with console brackets crowns the building.

NEW YORK UNIVERSITY INSTITUTE OF FINE ARTS,
formerly the James B. Duke Mansion, 1909–12
1 East 78th Street, Manhattan
Architect: Horace Trumbauer
Designated: September 15, 1970

The Institute of Fine Arts is the southern cornerstone of the Metropolitan Museum Historic District. Designed by the noted Philadelphia architect Horace Trumbauer, this building is one of the last of the freestanding mansions that once lined "Millionaires' Row." James Buchanan Duke and his older brother amassed a fortune in their native Durham, North Carolina, in cigarette manufacture, and James owned real estate in many large cities, including New York, where he moved in 1884. Both of the Duke brothers contributed substantial funds to Trinity College in Durham, which was renamed Duke University in 1925 in their honor. Trumbauer was commissioned to design both of Duke University's Durham campuses between 1925 and his death in 1938.

Made from unusually fine-grained limestone, which looks like marble, the mansion is designed in the Louis XV style preferred by Trumbauer, who was fluent in several modes, for domestic commissions. James Duke died in 1925; his widow, Nanaline, and their only daughter, Doris, lived in the mansion until 1958, when Doris donated the house to New York University's Institute of Fine Arts, which is dedicated to the study of the history of art and architecture, archaeology, and conservation. Robert Venturi renovated the building in 1958 to accommodate the growing library. In 1977 more space was required, and Richard Foster and Michael Forstel were hired to increase the stack capacity of the library and restore the interiors to their original splendor.

BATTERY MARITIME BUILDING,
formerly Municipal Ferry Piers to South Brooklyn, 1909
11 South Street, Manhattan
Architect: Unknown
Designated: May 25, 1967

Ferry service, concentrated on the lower tip of the island, played an essential part in the life of early Manhattan. At the peak of the ferry era, seventeen lines ran between terminals in Manhattan and Brooklyn alone. Today, only the Municipal Ferry Terminal remains standing. In continuous operation since 1909, it is used by the Coast Guard for service to Governors Island and currently houses offices for the Bureau of Transit Operations.

Contrasting with the angular cityscape, arched three-hundred-foot openings mark the water side of the terminal. Embellished with latticework, raised moldings, and a variety of rivets and rosettes, these decorative arches are examples of Beaux Arts structural expressionism. They are set between colossal pilasters that appear to rise from the water's edge, their capitals transformed into scroll brackets.

An open promenade supported by low steel arches between piers resting on granite bases marks the land side of the terminal. Paired, tapered columns, also decorated with unusual capitals and scroll brackets, support the roof and cornice. Other features include a balcony ornamented with marine forms, a three-story curtain wall made of tall, tripartite framed windows, and swinging gates protecting the entrances to two of the ferry slips. The overall style, inclusive of these structural details, is reminiscent of turn-of-the-century French Exposition architecture.

MANHATTAN BRIDGE APPROACH, 1909–16
Manhattan Bridge Plaza, bounded by the Bowery and
Canal, Forsyth, and Bayard streets, Manhattan
Architects: Carrère & Hastings
Designated: May 10, 1968

The Manhattan Bridge, which opened in December of 1909, was the fourth bridge to span the East River. The monumental arch and colonnades on the Manhattan side of the bridge were designed by Carrère & Hastings. The arch is of light gray rusticated granite and its semicircular vaulting is richly coffered with rosettes and carved borders. The heavy cornice is surmounted by a balustrade with classical motifs, as is the colonnade. Originally, the approach had ornate sculptural decoration by Carl A. Heber and a frieze panel—called the *Buffalo Hunt*—by Charles Cary Rumsey. On the Brooklyn side were pylons with statues representing *New York* and *Brooklyn* by Daniel Chester French; these have been removed and now belong to the Brooklyn Museum.

In 1913 the commissioner of the Department of Bridges proposed building a grand boulevard to link the Brooklyn and Manhattan bridges in Manhattan. This boulevard was never developed; the arch and colonnades are all that remain of the original approach plan.

680–690 PARK AVENUE
Manhattan
Designated: November 10, 1970

Americas Society, 1909–11
680 Park Avenue
Architects: McKim, Mead & White

Italian Cultural Institute, 1916–19
686 Park Avenue
Architects: Delano & Aldrich

Consulate General of Italy, 1916–17
690 Park Avenue
Architects: Walker & Gillette

Spanish Institute, 1925–26
684 Park Avenue
Architects: McKim, Mead & White

This Park Avenue block is composed of four outstanding Federal Revival town houses. Built between 1909 and 1926, these residences have been adapted to serve as the headquarters of the Americas Society (formerly the Center for Inter-American Relations), the Spanish Institute, the Italian Cultural Institute, and the Consulate General of Italy.

Although the buildings were designed individually, the four present a uniform appearance: each house is red brick laid in Flemish bond, with rusticated limestone ground floors and stone cornice balustrades. Numbers 680 and 684 were designed by McKim, Mead & White, 686 is the work of Delano & Aldrich, and 690 was designed by Walker & Gillette.

Built for Percy R. Pyne, financier and philanthropist, number 680 achieved notoriety in 1960 when Soviet Premier Nikita S. Khrushchev gave a news conference from the iron balcony on the second floor. At the time, the building housed the Soviet Mission to the United Nations. The restoration of the house was begun by the Marquesa de Cuevas in 1965. The second-floor drawing room has an Adam ceiling panel by Angelica Kauffmann, the eighteenth-century decorative painter. On the ground floor, an art gallery has replaced servants' quarters and the kitchen.

Oliver D. Filley, Pyne's son-in-law, commissioned McKim, Mead & White to design his home at 684 Park Avenue. It was built on the site of the Pyne family's garden. The building was renovated in the 1960s to adapt it to its current function as headquarters of the Spanish Institute. The classic interior detail—a center staircase, an eighteenth-century paneled room, carved marble mantelpieces, vaulted ceilings, and plaster cornices—was retained. The rugs and furnishings from Spain are in the Spanish Neoclassical style, which parallels the Federal style of architecture.

Number 686 was built in 1916–19 for William Sloane. Some of the interior detailing was taken from Belton House, in Grantham, England, which was designed by Christopher Wren. The Italian Cultural Institute has occupied the building since 1959.

JAMES A. FARLEY BUILDING, formerly the U.S. General Post Office, 1910–13; addition, 1935
Eighth Avenue between West 31st and 33rd streets, Manhattan
Architects: McKim, Mead & White
Designated: May 17, 1966

On Labor Day, 1914, a new post office building at Eighth Avenue between West 31st and 33rd streets was opened to the public. Named Pennsylvania Terminal, it was designed by William Mitchell Kendall, who had joined the firm of McKim, Mead & White in 1906. On July 1, 1918, the facility became the U.S. General Post Office. The building was renamed in honor of James A. Farley, the 53rd postmaster general of the United States, in May of 1982.

A dignified and imposing urban structure, the building mirrored the Neoclassical magnificence of Pennsylvania Station across the street—until Penn Station was destroyed. An addition to the General Post Office—the West Building—was opened in December 1935. Together, the buildings cover an area of 1,561,600 square feet.

The original Kendall structure, the product of an important commission secured in 1908, was built between 1910 and 1913. The broad portico of twenty colossal Corinthian columns at the main entrance on Eighth Avenue is anchored at each end by massive, niched pavilions, and approached by a grand sweep of thirty-one steps. The scheme of the main colonnade is repeated with pilasters on all of the other elevations. An attic story surmounts a distinctive cornice.

The now-famous inscription occupying the entire height and length of the 280-foot frieze of the entablature was loosely adapted by Kendall from the Eighth Book of Herodotus. The motto, which has come to be familiarly associated with the aims of the U.S. Post Office, reads: "Neither snow nor rain nor heat nor gloom of night stays these couriers from the swift completion of their appointed rounds." Although such couriers carry out their appointed tasks in a very different manner today than in 1913, the Farley Building, seventy-five years later, continues to be both functional and elegant. It fulfills one of the chief objectives of McKim, Mead & White: to create a ceremonial public architecture related to its urban environment and reflecting the union of past and present.

CHEROKEE APARTMENTS,
formerly Shively Sanitary Tenements, 1910–11
507–515 and 517–523 East 77th Street and
508–514 and 516–522 East 78th Street, Manhattan
Architect: Henry Atterbury Smith
Designated: July 9, 1985

The Shively Sanitary Tenements, also known as the East River Homes, were conceived by Dr. Henry Shively, a prominent physician, and funded by philanthropist Mrs. William K. Vanderbilt. They were intended to house tuberculosis patients and their families in a clean, sanitary environment and to provide the city's poor and sick with the light and open space so important for recovery. Purchased by Mrs. Vanderbilt for $81,000, the site, between East 77th and 78th streets, York Avenue, and Cherokee Place, was selected for its proximity to the East River and consequent abundance of fresh air.

The architect chosen to design these four adjoining buildings was Henry Atterbury Smith, who in the early 1900s had developed a concept of the "open-stair" plan for apartment buildings as a healthful and economic form of housing for the working class. In the six-story Shively Sanitary Tenements, Smith had his first opportunity to put his open-stair plan into practice. He made use of other innovative architectural elements as well, including interior courtyards entered through Guastavino-tiled, barrel-vaulted passageways, roof gardens fitted with windbreaks and tiled floors, and such sensitive details as seats built into the outside stair railing at each level so that those ascending the stairs could rest along the way. The stairwells, rising to roof level from the interior corners of the courtyards, were shielded from inclement weather by glass canopies.

On each building's façade, Smith used a blend of materials—light stone, terra-cotta, and tan brick inset with green terra-cotta ornament—all topped by a projecting green tile roof. The triple-hung windows, meant to increase airflow to the rooms, were carefully and symmetrically arranged across each façade. They were fronted by cast-iron balconies supported by large curving brackets, which allowed people to sit or sleep outside.

The buildings were sold to the City and Suburban Homes Company for rental apartments in 1924.

998 FIFTH AVENUE, 1910–1912
Manhattan
Architects: McKim, Mead & White
Designated: February 19, 1974

The first large apartment house built north of 59th Street on the East Side, this expansive building at 998 Fifth Avenue dominated a neighborhood of smaller private homes. To promote the transition of potential occupants from private homes to apartment houses, it was filled with amenities, among them a refrigerated wine cellar, central vacuum cleaning, and three wall safes with combination locks for each apartment. In addition, the apartments were quite large, either seventeen-room single-floor apartments or slightly larger duplexes. The appeal of the building can be judged by the earliest client lists, which included such notables as Senator Elihu Root, former Governor Levi P. Morton, and Mr. and Mrs. Murray Guggenheim.

This building has long been recognized as the finest Italian Renaissance Revival apartment house in New York. The limestone exterior is divided into three superimposed, four-story sections separated by wide belt courses and balustrades. The base is heavily rusticated, while the upper two sections are more finely dressed ashlar with quoins. At the roofline, a large cornice with a deep overhang terminates this emphatically horizontal composition.

ST. THOMAS CHURCH AND PARISH HOUSE, 1909–14
1–3 West 53rd Street, Manhattan
Architects: Cram, Goodhue & Ferguson
Designated: October 19, 1966

The first church structure to house the St. Thomas parish, at Broadway and Houston streets, burned in 1851, and a second structure at the same location was closed in 1866 as the neighborhood around it deteriorated. The third church building, erected on this Fifth Avenue site, was built in 1870 and burned in 1905, to be replaced by the present church.

This massive limestone structure, although influenced by Gothic prototypes, is original in its design. The architectural firm of Cram, Goodhue & Ferguson won the commission with their plan for an asymmetrical single corner tower, and an off-center nave. This plan was a sensitive response to the problem of the corner site. Though the elevations are highly ornamented, the buttresses of the square tower are extremely simple and balance the elaborate main entrance and rose window above it. The delicate reredos, designed by Bertram G. Goodhue and the sculptor Lee Lawrie, offer relief from the massive solidity of the rest of the church.

ST. JEAN BAPTISTE CHURCH, 1910–13
1067–1071 Lexington Avenue, Manhattan
Architect: Nicholas Sirracino
Designated: November 19, 1969

The St. Jean Baptiste Church was built to serve the French-Canadian community of New York and was funded by the noted financier Thomas Fortune Ryan. Nicholas Sirracino, an Italian architect, designed the church in the Italian Renaissance style.

Renaissance and Baroque elements embellish the façade. Two slightly projecting bell towers, capped with small domes, are situated on each side of the front façade, and one large dome is situated over the crossing. A portico with four Corinthian columns marks the front entrance. Each of the towers is adorned with scrolls, swags, small pediments, and the heads and wings of cherubs. A globe, supported by angels, is located on the parapet between the bell towers; other angels are found just to the sides of the towers, standing on pedestals below the cornice.

EAST 70TH STREET HOUSES
Manhattan
Designated: July 23, 1974

11 East 70th Street, 1909–10
Architect: John H. Duncan

15 East 70th Street, 1909–10
Architect: Charles I. Berg

19 East 70th Street, 1909–10
Architect: Thornton Chard

17 East 70th Street, 1909–11
Architect: Arthur C. Jackson

21 East 70th Street, 1918–19
Architect: William J. Rogers

Built between 1909 and 1919, these houses on East 70th Street were inspired by the French classical and Italian Renaissance modes; although they were designed by five different architects, the buildings are unified by their splendid limestone façades. The properties on this block were held by the estate of James Lenox until 1907, when they were transferred to the New York Public Library. In 1909 the library began to sell the property to affluent New Yorkers, who bought these lots and erected elaborate houses for themselves.

The first house built here in 1909–10 was number 11, designed by John H. Duncan; number 15 was built in the same years and was designed by Charles I. Berg. Number 17, noted for its rusticated ground floor and boldly enframed central window, was designed by Arthur C. Jackson and built in 1909–11. Number 19, now occupied by the Knoedler Gallery, is an imposing house, designed by Thornton Chard in a simplified early Italian Renaissance style—complete with arched loggia, balconies, and prominent roof cornice. The simple yet elegant house at number 21, now Hirschl & Adler Galleries, was designed by William J. Rogers; the smooth ashlar limestone façade is pierced with two deeply recessed openings at each floor, which give the building its crisp and distinctive character.

SHELTER PAVILION AND ATTACHED BUILDINGS, 1910
Monsignor McGolrick Park, Nassau and Driggs avenues, Monitor and Russell streets, Brooklyn
Architects: Helmle & Huberty
Designated: February 8, 1966

This handsome, gently curving pavilion provides the focal point for this small park in the Greenpoint section of Brooklyn. Originally called Winthrop Park, it was officially renamed in 1941 to honor Monsignor Edward J. McGolrick, then pastor of St. Cecilia's Church. It was designed by Helmle & Huberty in the mode of seventeenth- and eighteenth-century French gardens, most notably the Grand Trianon at Versailles.

The crescent-shaped pavilion consists of an open arcade with a small building at each end. In the buildings, a central arched window is framed by engaged columns flanked by smaller, square-headed windows. The corners are accented by paired pilasters, and a handsome balustrade surmounts each of the two end buildings, while their cornices are carried through the full sweep of the colonnade—a strong unifying feature.

The park shelter controls the landscape plan around it. This type of radial landscaping—determined by the form of a building—is typically French and rarely encountered in America.

WOOLWORTH BUILDING, 1911–13
233 Broadway, Manhattan
Architect: Cass Gilbert
Designated (exterior and interior): April 12, 1983

The Woolworth Building is one of the most famous skyscrapers in the United States. Designed by Cass Gilbert and completed in 1913, it was the tallest building in the world until the Chrysler Building topped it in 1929. In terms of height, profile, corporate symbolism, and romantic presence, this graceful, Gothic-style tower became the prototype for the great skyscrapers that permanently transformed the skyline of New York City after World War I.

The Woolworth Building was commissioned in 1910 by Frank Winfield Woolworth, proprietor of a multimillion-dollar international chain of five-and-ten-cent stores. For the headquarters of his vast empire, Woolworth wanted a building that reflected not only his personal success but also the new twentieth-century phenomenon of mass commerce. Gilbert's building attained these goals, and at its inauguration, Woolworth nicknamed the building the "Cathedral of Commerce."

Cass Gilbert, the architect, objected to the frequently made ecclesiastical association between the Woolworth Building and a Gothic cathedral. He had great respect for the aesthetic significance of architectural historicism; but as a Midwesterner aware of the technological advances of the Chicago School, Gilbert was a keen advocate of the modern aesthetic of functionalism. He held that a building's surface should express its structure, and, in the case of the skyscraper, its construction around a steel cage.

The Woolworth Building is massive yet elegant in its soaring verticality. Unlike most earlier tall buildings, it avoids the traditional subdivision into base, shaft, and capital, presenting instead a silhouette based on two setbacks, creating three sections of progressively smaller dimensions culminating in a pyramidal roof (originally gilded) and four tourelles. Gilbert emphasized the skyscraper structure in three ways. The elevations of the thirty-story base and the narrower thirty-story tower are divided into continuous vertical bays of windows and Gothic-traceried spandrels, set off from one another by projecting piers that emphasize the underlying construction. Gilbert chose to cover the building in a skin of ornamental terra-cotta rather than masonry (except for the first four stories, which are limestone), to stress the fact that the walls themselves were not load-bearing. He used polychromy to enhance the shadows and accent the main structural lines. The overall color is cream, with highlights in buff, blue, and gold; the colors become stronger higher up on the tower.

The interior, designed as a monumental civic space, is divided into an arcade, a marble staircase hall in the center, and, beyond that, a smaller hall. The decoration continues the Gothic motif of the exterior. Rich in marble, bronze Gothic filigree, sculpted relief, mosaic vaults, glass ceilings, and painted decoration, the Woolworth Building has one of the most handsome publicly accessible interiors in the city.

The Woolworth Building is a key monument in the creation of New York as a skyscraper city because it established the basic principles for such construction after 1920. The tower continues to serve as the national company headquarters, celebrating both the Woolworth empire and the gilded age of New York City commerce.

1025 PARK AVENUE, 1911–12
Manhattan
Architect: John Russell Pope
Designated: October 7, 1986

The house at 1025 Park Avenue was designed in 1911 by John Russell Pope for Reginald DeKoven, a composer of light opera and popular music, and his wife, Anna. The building is a rare survivor of the private houses built on Park Avenue after the enclosure and electrification of its railroad tracks.

DeKoven established his reputation in the music world with *Robin Hood*, a light comic opera written in 1890 that included the favorite "O Promise Me." As a music critic, DeKoven joined with the Shuberts to build the Lyric Theater on West 42nd Street.

Pope's design for the couple's home took into consideration their musical life-style. The architect included a large, double-height front room to accommodate the DeKovens's traditional musical entertainments; this music room also served as a ballroom.

The design also reflected Mrs. DeKoven's love of early English design. The dominating, symmetrically arranged bay windows and solid brick façade with stone trim are reminiscent of British manor houses of the late sixteenth and early seventeenth centuries. Other features include three-sided bay windows with casements of leaded glass and stone mullions. The round-arched, classical doorway of Jacobean character supports a shield bearing the arms of the DeKoven family.

ROYAL CASTLE APARTMENTS, 1912–13
20–30 Gates Avenue, Brooklyn
Architects: Wortmann & Braun
Designated: December 22, 1981

An imposing Beaux Arts–style apartment house designed by the firm of Wortmann & Braun, the Royal Castle Apartments were built in 1912–13 for the development firm of Levy & Baird. Six stories high with stone decorative details, the Royal Castle is an imposing composition complementing the dignified and exclusive nature of Clinton Avenue, which was once known as Brooklyn's "Gold Coast."

The design of the Royal Castle was in keeping with the architectural character of the avenue. The flavor of the neighborhood was established by the freestanding mansions built in the latter half of the nineteenth century, spurred by oil magnate Charles Pratt's decision to erect his mansion here in 1875. The Beaux Arts style was associated with wealth and luxury; the name of this building was chosen to convey an image of luxury and social standing.

Built of brick above a rusticated limestone base, the structure commands the intersection of Gates and Clinton avenues. A deep central court on Gates Avenue marks the main entrance and divides the building into two pavilions; the building is entered through a one-story stone portico pierced by a broad, round arch with drip molding. The most dramatic feature is the striking silhouette of the sixth floor and roofline. The central bay at the sixth floor of each pavilion is designed as a large Venetian round-arched window with radiating keystones and a voussoir arrangement echoing the pilasters below. Ornate round pediments crown each pavilion.

CHURCH OF THE INTERCESSION AND VICARAGE, 1911–14
540–550 West 155th Street, Manhattan
Architects: Cram, Goodhue & Ferguson
Designated: August 16, 1966

In 1906 the Church of the Intercession—which was then located at West 158th Street and Grand Boulevard (now Broadway)—found itself in financial peril. The rector, Dr. Milo Hudson Gates, was aware that Trinity Church wished to establish a chapel near its uptown cemetery; he negotiated with Trinity, and the solution was that Intercession become a chapel of Trinity; the parent church, meantime, would build a new church building for the congregation on part of the cemetery's land. The cemetery had been landscaped by Calvert Vaux in the 1870s; a bridge designed by Vaux spanned Grand Boulevard at the time, and connected two halves of the cemetery.

In designing the new church, Bertram Grosvenor Goodhue took advantage of the dramatic site at the crest of a hill to create a wonderfully picturesque composition. A large western gable, emerging from buttresslike forms in Goodhue's characteristic manner, dominates the western façade. The design is reminiscent of English fourteenth-century Gothic, called Perpendicular, especially in the use of a tower with parapet, reticulated tracery, shallow buttresses, and generally broad proportions. The present steeple, installed in the 1950s, replaces the original, which was damaged. The tower is in an unusual position, and provides a smooth transition from church to vicarage, chapter house, and small cloister to the east. The random ashlar masonry (the stones were excavated on the site) is continued in this section; combined with Tudor hood moldings, windows, bays, and segmental arches, it creates a more secular image.

In plan, the church is a long rectangle with suppressed transepts and shallow aisles. The nave gives the impression of a single, sweeping space. The buff-colored, rough-cast plaster finish on the interior elevations is unusual. Against it, the stone arcades, window trim, and wall shafts stand out in strong relief. The most exciting interior feature is the brightly polychromed, wood hammerbeam roof. The church furnishings are exceptionally fine and worth a good look. Goodhue felt this was one of his greatest New York commissions, and asked to be interred here. His fine tomb, carved by Lee Lawrie, is in the north transept. Buried in the adjacent cemeteries are many other prominent New Yorkers, including Clement Clarke Moore, John James Audubon, and various members of the Astor family.

The vicarage is an integral part of the church complex. It is connected to the chapel by a cloister; the three elements surround a small courtyard. The vicarage is constructed of the same combination of rock-faced and ashlar stone as the chapel, and although its Tudor style differs from the Perpendicular Gothic of the chapel, the similarity in materials allows the two buildings to function as a unified whole.

Church of the Intercession vicarage

ADMINISTRATION BUILDING AT EAST 180TH STREET, 1912
481 Morris Park Avenue, The Bronx
Architects: Fellheimer & Long and Allen H. Stem
Designated: May 11, 1976

Originally designed as a railroad station serving the New York, Westchester & Boston Railroad, this building was constructed of concrete and operated by electricity—reflecting the trend toward modernized stations designed to serve the expanding suburban communities of the early twentieth century. Free from the heavy ornamentation of its wooden prototypes, the structure followed the simple style of an Italian villa.

The Morris Park façade contains a three-story central section with an arcaded loggia at the street level. It is flanked by four-story projecting end pavilions, resembling towers and marked by balustraded balconies. A narrow belt course with small square windows directly above it separates the first story from the upper portion of the façade. This rhythm is repeated on the third floor by paired arched windows set within shallow blind arches. Round plaques, recalling Tuscan originals, surround the street-level loggia. Other ornamentation includes the winged head of Mercury centered in the crowning broken pediment and picturesque red roof tiles.

The station was closed when service terminated in 1937. Since the 1940s, the building has functioned as an entrance to the East 180th Street subway station, with offices on the upper floors.

BOOTH THEATER, 1912–13
222–232 West 45th Street, Manhattan
Architect: Henry B. Herts
Designated (exterior and interior): November 4, 1987

Named for Edwin Booth, the great nineteenth-century Shakespearean actor (and brother of John Wilkes Booth), this theater was built in 1912–13 by architect Henry B. Herts for the Shubert brothers and independent producer Winthrop Ames. The city had stipulated that a space must exist between the two theaters and the Astor Hotel to the east. The creation of Shubert Alley allowed the theater to have two fully designed façades, making it an obvious showcase for the Shubert Organization. The two façades are joined by a projecting curved pavilion, which contains the central doorway, and decorated with Venetian Renaissance details, including low-relief sgraffito decoration below the cornice. The Booth and the Shubert contain the only known surviving examples of sgraffito in New York City.

Ames was an enthusiastic proponent of intimately scaled theaters. With the Booth—as with the Little Theater—he hoped to sell New York audiences on the style of drama that he had seen in Europe and elsewhere in the United States. The Booth contained just 785 seats—half as many as the Shubert Theater next door had. The design is similar to the Tudor-style theaters that Ames had seen in England, complete with wood paneling to enhance the acoustics and multipaned casement windows. The ceiling is decorated with latticework bands executed in plaster.

FORWARD BUILDING, 1912
173–175 East Broadway, Manhattan
Architect: George A. Boehm
Designated: March 18, 1986

The Forward Building was erected in 1912 to house the *Jewish Daily Forward*, a Yiddish paper founded in 1897 by a dissenting faction of the Socialist Labor Party. The editors argued for pragmatic socialism in the United States and called for cooperation among the labor left toward this common goal. The *Jewish Daily Forward* also published sensationalist stories similar to those printed in Joseph Pulitzer's *New York World*, and Yiddish literature by Morris Rosenfeld and Isaac Bashevis Singer, among others. More generally, the *Jewish Daily Forward* was one of several papers serving the large Eastern European Jewish community that grew rapidly from 1870 until 1925, when a federal law slowed immigration.

The newspaper offices occupied only four floors of the building; the rest were leased to labor organizations, including the Workmen's Circle and United Hebrew Trades. The staff and publishers decided to turn the building into a labor center, determined to erect a more imposing building than Josef Yarmalofsky's nearby twelve-story bank at Canal and Allen streets. Appropriately, the decoration in the first-floor frieze includes portraits of Karl Marx, Friedrich Engels, and two central European labor leaders, Ferdinand Lassalle and Friedrich Adler. Unfortunately, contemporary shop signs cover these portraits.

Not enough is known about the architect George Boehm to determine how and why he received this large commission from a socialist client early in his career. In the 1930s and '40s, however, Boehm criticized architects who catered to landlords and developers and argued for the introduction of public policy courses in architecture schools. He carried his social commitment further as a committee member both for the Citizens Housing and Planning Council and the Housing Section of the Welfare Council of New York.

The overall design follows that of the former Evening Post Building at 20 Vesey Street, completed in 1906 by Robert Kohn. Boehm trained in the Beaux Arts system, first at Columbia University (1893–97), then in Paris and Rome; the Forward Building's classical detailing reflects this background. The seven-story central section, clad in white terra-cotta and generously glazed, expresses the building's height especially well. The low, earlier structures on each side convey, perhaps better than at any other site in the city, the difference in height and design between construction from the 1870s and early '80s and the first generation of tall buildings.

STATEN ISLAND LIGHTHOUSE, 1912
Lighthouse Hill, Edinboro Road, Staten Island
Architect: Unknown
Designated: January 17, 1968

From Lighthouse Hill above historic Richmondtown, the Staten Island Lighthouse illuminates one of New York Harbor's many channels. Commonly known as the Richmond Light, this 350,000-candlepower beacon operates under the jurisdiction of the U.S. Coast Guard, in conjunction with the Ambrose Light Tower, to guide ships into the busy port.

The tall, octagonal, yellow-brick tower rises above a rusticated limestone base. Alternate faces of the shaft are set with rectangular stair windows framed by smooth stone beneath stepped lintels. From the cornice above, large ornate brackets support an octagonal widow's walk. Following the perimeter of the tower, this narrow walk is enclosed by a simple wrought-iron rail and is lined with bull's-eye windows. At the lighthouse's summit, glass-faced walls, beneath a low-pitched roof supporting a large ball and lightning rod, surround the powerful light. A small cantilevered balcony at this level echoes the widow's walk below.

MANHATTAN COUNTRY SCHOOL,
formerly the Ogden Codman, Jr., House, 1912–13
7 East 96th Street, Manhattan
Architect: Ogden Codman, Jr.
Designated: May 25, 1967

This Louis XVI house, built in 1912–13, was designed by the architect Ogden Codman, Jr., for his own use. Codman was a talented architect and decorator who practiced mainly in Boston, Newport, and New York from the 1890s through the first decades of the twentieth century. His work consisted mostly of interior decoration, although he designed twenty-two houses, creating stylish and elegant settings notable for their human scale and lack of excessive opulence.

His house at 7 East 96th Street, as well as the buildings at 12 and 15, were based on eighteenth-century French sources, and the façades are taken directly from plates from César Daly's *Motifs Historiques d'Architecture* (1880). The circular dining room was inspired by one taken from an eighteenth-century mansion in Bordeaux, now at the Metropolitan Museum of Art. (The rooms of Bordeaux houses were particularly useful models, because the houses occupy lots the same size as those of New York City town houses.)

The four-story structure with a limestone façade is distinguished by wrought-iron balconies, dormer windows, many shutters, a mansard roof, and a porte cochere leading to a courtyard and garage. Above a strong, rusticated first floor rests a second-floor stone balcony supported on carved brackets, with an exquisitely detailed wrought-iron railing extending the width of the entire façade. Completing the composition is a well-proportioned stone cornice, behind which rises a slate mansard roof with three unusual dormer windows.

After passing through the hands of several owners, including the Nippon Club, the mansion was bought by the Manhattan Country School in 1966.

CORT THEATER, 1912–13
138–146 West 48th Street, Manhattan
Architect: Thomas Lamb
Designated (exterior and interior): November 17, 1987

In the course of his career, architect Thomas Lamb designed more than 300 theaters throughout the world. The Cort is one of his oldest remaining New York theaters, built for producer and theater owner John Cort. Lamb's theaters, designed in historical styles popular with the wealthy, were accessible to the masses for the price of a ticket.

The façade of the Cort Theater is an adaptation of the Petit Trianon—the "playhouse" of Marie Antoinette at Versailles. This little house was a well-worn source of inspiration to architects of Lamb's generation. Although the theater is not an exact copy—Lamb used round-arched doors rather than square windows, and engaged columns instead of pilasters—the Cort still reflects the essence of its model.

The French theme is continued in the opulent interior. A replica of a bust of Marie Antoinette stands in a niche overlooking the ticket lobby, and plasterwork displaying French motifs, such as panels with cameos, decorates the entire interior. A mural above the proscenium arch depicts a garden dance that might have taken place during the reign of Louis XVI. The arch itself is the theater's most unusual feature; made of plaster and detailed with art glass, it was lighted during performances.

The Shubert organization purchased the palatial Cort in 1927, and continues to maintain it today.

LONGACRE THEATER, 1912–13
220–228 West 48th Street, Manhattan
Architect: Henry B. Herts
Designated (exterior and interior): December 8, 1987

The Longacre Theater, built in 1912–13, was designed by architect Henry B. Herts to house the productions of Harry H. Frazee, a Broadway producer and owner of the Boston Red Sox. Frazee had worked his way up from a movie-house usher to an influential Broadway producer in a very short time, and he opened the Longacre when he was only thirty-three years old.

Herts was one of Broadway's foremost theater architects and a longtime partner of Hugh Tallant, another theater architect. Herts and Tallant had met in Paris at the Ecole des Beaux-Arts, where Herts developed his French Neoclassical design; the Longacre is an outstanding example of this style. The façade has five bays, framed by six fluted pilasters. The three center bays form a large casement window, and the two outer bays are round-headed niches. Ornamentation includes carved fountains at the base of each pilaster, each topped by a personification of drama. A foliate cornice with projecting carved lions' heads, foliate vases, and strapwork escutcheons spans the top of the façade. In contrast to its architectural success, the Longacre had a history of failed productions and financial hardship.

HELEN HAYES THEATER, formerly the Little Theater, 1912; additions, 1917–20
238–244 West 44th Street, Manhattan
Architects: Ingalls & Hoffman; additions, Herbert J. Krapp
Designated: November 17, 1987

As part of his plan to popularize drama on an intimate scale in America, producer Winthrop Ames, along with architects Harry C. Ingalls and Francis B. Hoffman, Jr., built the Little Theater in 1912. When it opened, the theater had only 299 seats; in 1917–20 it was enlarged by the addition of a balcony according to a plan by the prolific theater architect Herbert J. Krapp. With 499 seats, today the Helen Hayes remains the smallest of the Broadway theaters.

The theater's red brick and limestone exterior resembles a home more than an ornate Broadway theater. The refined Georgian Revival exterior was paired with an equally refined Adamesque interior. The auditorium is enhanced by elaborate paneled wainscoting halfway up the walls, with tapestries above framed by Corinthian pilasters. The wood paneling not only aided the acoustics of the theater but also suggested the warmth and intimacy of a drawing room, thus realizing Ames's goal.

PALACE THEATER INTERIOR, 1912–13
1564–1566 Broadway, Manhattan
Architects: Kirchhoff & Rose
Designated: July 14, 1987

The Palace Era began when Sarah Bernhardt appeared on its vaudeville-style stage in 1913. She was immediately followed by a succession of famous entertainers, including Jack Benny, Ethel Barrymore, the Marx brothers, Mae West, and the great illusionist Harry Houdini.

Designed specifically for vaudeville, the grand lobby and spacious foyer were built to handle large crowds for several daily shows. Boxes, loggias, a high proscenium arch, and a large stage were all commonly found in such production spaces. Twenty tiered boxes were originally located at the ends of the double balconies that wrapped around the Palace's deeply splayed orchestra walls. While lavish ornamental plasterwork in high relief announced the entertainment in a boisterous fashion, the near-perfect sight lines and fine acoustics created an intimate relationship between the audience and the performers. Other interior decorations include Pavanzzo marble in the main lobby and an inner lobby constructed of Siena marble and containing bronze screen doors with stained glass. The building is in the shape of an L, with an eleven-story office complex connected to the theater.

Soon after its opening, the Palace began to feel the effects of the rapidly growing motion-picture industry; in 1932, the bill changed to include movies. Structural changes soon followed; the auditorium was renovated and modernized in the late 1930s and early '40s. Until its purchase in 1965 by the Nederlanders, the Palace fluctuated between a policy of mixed bills and straight film. The new owners, under the direction of designer Ralph Alswang, were successful in restoring the structure to its original splendor.

SHUBERT THEATER, 1912–13
221–233 West 44th Street, Manhattan
Architect: Henry B. Herts
Designated (exterior and interior): December 15, 1987

The Shubert Theater was built in 1912–13 by architect Henry B. Herts to be the headquarters of the Shubert Organization and a memorial to Sam S. Shubert, the leader of the business until his death. Designed to stage the organization's large musicals, the elaborate Shubert was built jointly with the smaller and more intimate Booth Theater in Shubert Alley.

Herts masterfully integrated the exteriors of both theaters into one design. Curved corner entrance doors are the most dramatic elements of the façade. Within, painted panels by J. Mortimer Lichtenauer represent classical figures; set in frames of various shapes and sizes, they create a sense of grandeur in the auditorium. Renaissance-inspired plasterwork outlines the main architectural elements of the interior. The Shubert Organization has its offices in this theater, which has been the home of *A Chorus Line* since 1975.

CHARLES SCRIBNER'S SONS, 1912–13
597 Fifth Avenue, Manhattan
Architect: Ernest Flagg
Designated: March 23, 1982

The Scribner Building, built in 1912–13, is an elegant Beaux Arts–style commercial structure by the eminent American architect Ernest Flagg. This was the second building Flagg designed for the prominent publishing firm of Charles Scribner's Sons and incorporated many of the design features of the earlier work, expanding and elaborating them for this new, more fashionable midtown location at Fifth Avenue near 48th Street.

The façade is divided into a base, midsection, and top and is crowned by a mansard roof with a large central dormer. Following Flagg's interpretation of the Beaux Arts dictum, the building is symmetrical from side to side: the three central bays form a distinct group, more elaborately decorated than the two end bays. The façade is dominated by the extensively glazed two-story storefront.

The Scribner Building was for many years an appropriate corporate symbol for the distinguished publishing firm of Charles Scribner's Sons. The Scribner Bookstore still occupies the building, which is now owned by Rizzoli International.

REGIS HIGH SCHOOL, 1912–14
55 East 84th Street, Manhattan
Architects: Maginnis & Walsh
Designated: November 19, 1969

Early in 1912, a group of Jesuit Fathers decided to erect a liberal-arts high school for gifted young men—a pilot project in Catholic education. When Regis High School opened two years later, *The Catholic News* reported that the school was "intended only for graduates from the parochial schools and is the first of its kind to be built in this city." The article also stated, "The general and private offices of the prefect of discipline will be given a commanding situation in reference to the entrances and stairways."

Designed by Maginnis & Walsh, distinguished architects of Boston, and constructed of limestone, the school was built to harmonize in scale with St. Ignatius Loyola Church directly across the street. The five-story building is characterized by monumental Ionic columns on the East 84th Street façade. On East 85th Street an exterior wall, designed in the classical manner, encloses a large auditorium on the first three stories; the style is enhanced by two stairways in slightly projecting end bays with imposing doors at street level and by a large blank wall that serves as the base for a row of Ionic columns on the two upper floors. The entablature carries the inscription "*Ad Maiorem Dei Gloriam*" ("To the Greater Glory of God"). The architects made maximum use of the available space and provided the seclusion desirable for effective education. Most of the classrooms open onto a central courtyard, which was once a playground.

With an annual enrollment of 500, the school has graduated 7,500 boys over its history. Most of its students rank nationally in the top 5 percent of the gifted. For the school's first fifty-five years, one family alone anonymously provided funds for the entire operation; today, the school receives donations from alumni and corporations.

KINGSBRIDGE ARMORY, Eighth Regiment Armory, 1912–17
29 West Kingsbridge Road and Jerome Avenue, The Bronx
Architects: Pilcher & Tachau
Designated: September 24, 1974

The Kingsbridge Armory, with its massive and crenellated parapets, gives the appearance of a medieval Romanesque fortress. Officially the home of the 258th Field Artillery (Eighth Regiment), it is reputedly the largest armory in the world, covering an entire city block. Designed by the firm of Pilcher & Tachau, which gained acclaim for their competition design of 1901 for the Squadron C Armory in Brooklyn, the Kingsbridge Armory was built on the site of the proposed eastern basin of the Jerome Park Reservoir. Excavation had begun for the eastern basin in the early 1900s, but the state legislature authorized the site for a National Guard Armory in 1911. A number of military relics were exposed during the excavation, reflecting the site's proximity to the sites of Fort Independence and Fort Number Five of the American Revolution.

The structure's red-brick walls are trimmed with stone and punctuated at regular intervals by slit window openings. Two semiengaged, tall, round towers crowned by conical roofs flank the main entrance. A stone stairway leads up to the round-arched doorway, where massive iron gates protect paneled doors. A metal and glass roof spans the enormous drill hall.

BROOKLYN CENTRAL OFFICE, BUREAU OF FIRE COMMUNICATIONS, 1913
35 Empire Boulevard, Brooklyn
Architects: Helmle & Huberty
Designated: April 19, 1966

The Brooklyn Central Office, Bureau of Fire Communications, was designed by the prominent Brooklyn architect Frank J. Helmle of Helmle & Huberty. Erected in 1913, the building serves as the central communications office for the Brooklyn Fire Department. One and one-half stories high, this brick and limestone pavilion is simple and utilitarian, and reminiscent of the magnificent Morgan Library in Manhattan. Both are Italian Renaissance–style structures that, for quite different reasons, required more wall space than windows. The architectural solution in both cases was to dramatize the contrast between the blank flanking wings and an open central loggia. The Brooklyn building is elegantly scaled and crowned by a plain cornice and tile roof. Three graceful arches with slender columns and a low balustrade frame the deep porch, or loggia, creating a fine entranceway.

GRAND ARMY PLAZA, 1913
Fifth Avenue and 59th Street, Manhattan
Architect: Carrère & Hastings
Designated: July 23, 1974

In their "Greensward Plan" of 1858, Frederick Law Olmsted and Calvert Vaux projected a plaza running from 58th to 60th Street along Fifth Avenue, in addition to "cuts" along Central Park South. These were to serve as standing areas for carriages, surrounded by trees and enclosed within railings. Several members of the City Board in Charge of Central Park were dissatisfied with this solution, and in 1863 a special committee selected designs for four plazas and gateways by Richard Morris Hunt, who had just returned from the Ecole des Beaux-Arts in Paris. Olmsted and Vaux were outraged by the monumental urban character of the gates, which they felt were completely foreign to their image of the park as a picturesque retreat.

Although Hunt's designs were rejected, the idea for an urban plaza—inspired by Napoleon III's reorganization of Paris—remained. Later, in the 1890s, Karl Bitter, a noted sculptor and member of the City Arts Council, returned to Hunt's ideas, which now found a wider audience thanks to the efforts of the City Beautiful Movement. No funds were available, however, until 1912, when Joseph Pulitzer bequeathed $50,000 to the city for the erection of a fountain "like those in the Place de la Concorde in Paris." Bitter then invited the Pulitzer estate to hold a limited competition, which Thomas Hastings (of Carrère & Hastings) won.

All parks, Hastings felt, should reflect their urban context by articulating the terminations and intersections of major arteries. He also felt that New York City's grid was too rigid and did not provide sufficient public areas. His plaza reflects these ideas. For the southern end, he designed a fountain rising in five concentric rings to Bitter's figure of *Abundance*. The architect took great care to align this fountain perfectly with the sculpture in the northern half of the plaza, Augustus Saint-Gaudens's *William Tecumseh Sherman*. The little park was officially named Grand Army Plaza in 1923.

MORGAN GUARANTY TRUST COMPANY OF NEW YORK, formerly J. P. Morgan & Co., 1913
23 Wall Street, Manhattan
Architects: Trowbridge & Livingston
Designated: December 21, 1965

This elegant building, designed by Trowbridge & Livingston, is an austere, four-story marble structure of massive strength and solidity that displays handsome classical details and proportions. The building is located where the north end of Broad Street widens to create the illusion of a small square. The building's chamfered corner enhances this illusion of openness, and the main entrance, with its heavy bronze grills, adds to the dignity of this intersection at the heart of New York City's financial district. The building served as the headquarters of J. P. Morgan & Co. and played a vital role in the commerce of New York City. It is now the home of the internationally renowned Morgan Guaranty Trust Company of New York.

RICHMOND COUNTY COURTHOUSE, 1913–19
Richmond Terrace, Staten Island
Architects: Carrère & Hastings
Designated: March 23, 1982

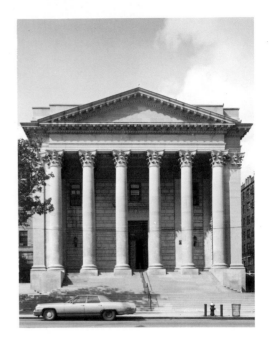

Reflecting the influence of Roman, Italian Renaissance, and Northern Renaissance architecture, this L-shaped limestone courthouse was built at the urging of Staten Island's first borough president, George Cromwell, as part of a grand scheme of governmental buildings.

The structure's classical details are derived from the Panthéon—the well-known symbol of justice. In addition to the little-used Corinthian front, these include alternating bands of wide and narrow rustication, upper-story pilasters, and rusticated wall surfaces with rhythmically placed pedimented windows. The rusticated rear façade, which is an impressive thirteen windows wide, now serves as the entrance. Its massive entry enframement contains a Northern Renaissance—inspired portico with banded columns, Doric frieze, and bracketed cornice. Wooden and bronze doors, framed by a round arch, are set into the rusticated wall surface directly behind the portico. Each side of the building is seven windows wide with a smooth limestone base. Rectangular windows mark the first floor of each side elevation; they appear in alternation with pedimented windows on the second story. A balustrade runs along the roofline.

Designed to enliven the long stretch of municipal buildings, a French garden lies along the courthouse's harbor front. A mélange of formal parterres, paved walks, sculpted elements, and fountains, it is geometrically arranged on three raised levels.

LYCEE FRANÇAIS DE NEW YORK, formerly the Mrs. Amory S. Carhart House, 1913–21
3 East 95th Street, Manhattan
Architect: Horace Trumbauer
Designated: July 23, 1974

Executed in the best tradition of eighteenth-century French classicism, the Mrs. Amory S. Carhart House resembles the residences of Louis XVI's Paris. The house, begun in 1913, was named for Mrs. Carhart, who commissioned its construction but never occupied it, as both she and her husband died before its completion in 1921. Architect Horace Trumbauer, noted for his many fine town houses, including the James B. Duke Mansion (now NYU's Institute of Fine Arts), was chosen to design the structure.

Ordered and formal in appearance, the building is a straightforward expression of the best of eighteenth-century French architecture. The façade, which is three bays wide, is divided horizontally into a one-story base, a two-story main section, and a crowning mansard roof. The boldly rusticated ground floor contains three tall, graceful arches that frame a central doorway with symmetrically placed windows on both sides.

Among other distinguishing features are a balcony with wrought-iron railings supported by large ornamental brackets on the second floor, and tall French doors with arched transoms enframed by arched openings.

GRAND CENTRAL TERMINAL, completed 1913
71–105 East 42nd Street, Manhattan
Architects: Reed & Stem and Warren & Wetmore
Designated: September 21, 1967; interior designated September 23, 1980

Grand Central Terminal, one of the great buildings in America, has been a symbol of New York City since its completion in 1913. It combines distinguished architecture with a brilliant engineering solution to the problem of accommodating under one roof a vast network of merging railway lines and the needs of the 400,000 people who pass through each day. This monumental building functions as well in the 1980s as it did when built. Its style represents the best of the French Beaux Arts—largely scaled spaces, imposing architecture, and grandly conceived sculptural decoration. Grand Central also operates as a modern urban nerve center. So extensive is the series of connections to nearby office buildings that many commuters can go to work without going outdoors. Grand Central has come to be associated with the mobility and nobility of New York City—the sometimes frenzied, but usually dignified, energy of its people.

The terminal was designed by two architectural firms. Reed & Stem devised the daring concept of using ramps to connect the various levels of the complex, as well as the separation of automobile, pedestrian, subway, and train traffic. The subsequent plans of Warren & Wetmore produced the rich Beaux Arts architectural details. The façade, largely the work of Whitney Warren, is based on a triumphal arch motif with three great windows, colossal columns grouped in pairs, and a dramatic sculptural group by Jules Coutan surmounting the cornice and clock over the central entranceway.

The interior of Grand Central, reminiscent of the huge vaulted spans of Roman baths, is truly a spatial triumph in the Beaux Arts tradition. It is 275 feet long, 120 feet wide, and 125 feet high,

and displays a remarkable unity of order, clarity, amplitude, and grandeur. The symmetrical and directionalized plan is characterized by a series of axially aligned major spaces connected by ramps and passageways that create a movement forward and downward, leading ultimately to the train platforms. The lateral ancillary spaces contribute to a sense of spatial flow and freedom within the tight, symmetrical plan. Covering the vault of the central hall is a magnificent zodiac mural by Paul Helleu.

Metro-North Commuter Railroad has operated Grand Central Terminal under lease for four years. The firm's ongoing restoration program has already called for a recent cleaning. Fortunately the U.S. Supreme Court upheld the city's right to declare the building a landmark in 1978, thereby ending plans to place a huge tower over the concourse. Grand Central Terminal will continue, in its original state, to monitor and mirror the pulse of New York City.

AUTOMATION HOUSE, AMERICAN FOUNDATION ON AUTOMATION AND EMPLOYMENT, formerly the Mrs. J. William Clark House, 1913–14
49 East 68th Street, Manhattan
Architects: Trowbridge & Livingston
Designated: November 10, 1970

Built in 1913–14, the Mrs. J. William Clark House was designed by the firm of Trowbridge & Livingston, architects responsible for such landmark structures as the B. Altman & Co. Building and the New York Stock Exchange. The building is part of an outstanding group of Federal Revival red-brick town houses known as the "Pyne-Davison Blockfront," which extends along Park Avenue between East 68th and 69th streets. The Clark house corresponds to 680 Park Avenue, the house on the corner; on both, the roof cornice, the belt course, and the height of the first story base are set at approximately the same level.

Four stories high and only two bays wide, the house has a red-brick façade laid up in English bond and a twin-arched loggia at the street level. Entry to the ground floor is gained through a doorway behind the right arch of the loggia. The arch on the left leads to the basement door, which is shielded by a low iron railing and gate. An effect of simplicity is created by the undecorated limestone cornice. The gambrel roof is clad in copper.

The house was built as a residence for J. William Clark, whose grandfather invented a form of cotton sewing thread that was first produced in Paisley, Scotland, in 1812. Clark's sewing thread was introduced to America in 1818, but during the Civil War, when importing became difficult, William Clark and his brother opened a thread mill in Newark, New Jersey; their six-cord thread, trademarked "O.N.T." (Our New Thread), soon became famous. Today, the building is occupied by the American Foundation on Automation and Employment.

APOLLO THEATER INTERIOR,
formerly Hurtig and Seamon's New Theater, 1913–14
235 West 125th Street, Manhattan
Architect: George Keister
Designated: June 28, 1983

Located on Harlem's main street and centered in the community's commercial district, the Apollo Theater is distinguished for having provided one of America's most important centers for the nurture of black talent and entertainment.

The theater spanned the two eras of Harlem's rich entertainment history: its construction in 1913–14 reflected the appeal that vaudeville and burlesque held for Harlem's middle-class white population in the late nineteenth century. The theater's later role as a center for black entertainment reflects the talent that blacks brought to Harlem as they settled in the community in the first decades of the twentieth century.

Hurtig and Seamon's New Theater still catered to white audiences in the early 1920s. In 1924 the theater installed a runway and featured some of the livelier "shimmy-shakers," including "Queen of the Runway" Erin Jackson and Isabelle Van and her Dancing Dolls. Billy Minsky, who was well known for having opened several of New York's burlesque houses, bought the theater in 1928, by which time the name had been changed to the Apollo. In an effort to quell mounting competition, Minsky negotiated an arrangement with neighboring theaters: they agreed not to schedule live performances, and Minsky promised not to show motion pictures.

In the 1930s, the Apollo changed hands twice. At Minsky's death in 1932, the theater was sold to Sidney Cohen, who presented black vaudeville. In 1935, after Cohen's death, Leo Brecher and Frank Schiffman assumed the theater's operation and instituted a permanent variety-show format that featured leading black entertainers. The Apollo thus presented a rich opportunity for black performers who, even as late as the 1950s, were excluded from many downtown establishments.

Throughout its history, the Apollo displayed every form of popular black entertainment, including comedy, drama, dance, gospel, blues, jazz, swing, bebop, rhythm and blues, rock and roll, and soul music. Bessie Smith, Billie Holiday, Louis Armstrong, Duke Ellington, Gladys Knight, and Bill Cosby are only a few of the distinguished entertainers who have performed here.

KNICKERBOCKER CLUB BUILDING, 1913–15
2 East 62nd Street, Manhattan
Architects: Delano & Aldrich
Designated: September 11, 1979

This building, the third home of the Knickerbocker Club, has long been recognized as one of the finest Federal Revival buildings in New York. Designed by William A. Delano, a distinguished architect as well as a club member, the structure was carefully scaled to a neighborhood then characterized by expansive single-family homes.

Organized on Halloween in 1871, the Knickerbocker Club was founded in reaction to a perceived relaxation of membership standards at the Union Club following the Civil War. Long a bastion of old New York families, the Union Club had begun to accept members whose family fortunes were more recently acquired. In an effort to retain their long-standing exclusivity, eighteen members of the Union Club, among them Alexander Hamilton, Jr., John L. Cadwalader, and John Jacob Astor, founded this new organization, which is still active in the city today.

Delano displayed a profound understanding of the tenets of Federal design in his composition of this three-story clubhouse. The seven-bay façade is divided into a rusticated limestone base surmounted by three stories of English bond brick, which are further divided by a stone belt course. The first and second stories are of approximately equal height, while the third story is diminished, suggesting an attic. Limestone lintels surmount all of the windows.

THE INTERNATIONAL CENTER OF PHOTOGRAPHY, formerly the Willard D. Straight House, 1913–15
1130 Fifth Avenue, Manhattan
Architects: Delano & Aldrich
Designated: May 15, 1968

The International Center of Photography today occupies the former Willard D. Straight House at Fifth Avenue and 94th Street—one of the last remaining examples of the great private houses that once lined upper Fifth Avenue.

Occupying a prominent and sunny corner lot, the house was built in 1913–15 for Straight, a diplomat, financier, and publicist, and his wife Dorothy Whitney, daughter of William C. Whitney, the Wall Street financier. They chose Delano & Aldrich, who also designed the Knickerbocker Club and the Colony Club, to design their residence.

William A. Delano, the chief architect, spoke of the building in his memoirs: "If I do say so, it's a well-planned and lovely house; once inside it seems much larger than it is." Delano was greatly influenced by both the Georgian and Federal styles of architecture, and used certain characteristics of each to create a highly individual style. The overall symmetry of the design and the use of red brick in a Flemish bond pattern are the key Georgian features. The house shows the influence of the Federal style in its decorative elements.

The Straight family lived in the house until 1927, and it was here that they founded *The New Republic*. Judge Elbert H. Gary was the second owner, but he died soon after making the purchase, and the mansion became the home of the legendary hostess Mrs. Harrison Williams, who maintained the city's most fashionable "salon."

Its days as a private residence ended in 1953, when the house became the headquarters of the National Audubon Society, one of the most important conservation organizations in America. In 1974 the newly established International Center of Photography acquired the house; the organization has gone to considerable effort to preserve and maintain the building.

NEW YORK STATE SUPREME COURT, formerly the New York County Courthouse, 1913–27
Foley Square, Manhattan
Architect: Guy Lowell
Designated: February 1, 1966; interior designated March 24, 1981

The New York State Supreme Court is a fine structure built on a grand scale, but it is in fact smaller and less ornate than the building called for in the original plan. Its long building history began in 1903, when the state legislature created a Courthouse Construction Board to oversee the construction of a new building to replace the Tweed Courthouse. Six different sites were considered through 1913, when Guy Lowell, a Boston architect, won a limited competition with a design for an enormous round building twice the size of the structure actually built. This design recalled the Colosseum in Rome and the work of the French visionary architects Etienne Louis Boullée and Claude Nicholas Ledoux. During excavation, however, engineers discovered underground springs that made the site unworkable and the board then purchased this smaller site.

A giant, fluted Corinthian portico dominates the main façade of the hexagonal building. The temple front is attached to a wall of rusticated masonry facing. Above this rustication is a stylized attic area, two stories high, and a service area recessed behind the simply carved cornice. The side elevations are identical: a colossal pilastrade is isolated by the rusticated wall. The heavy, almost blank corners mark the stairwells and elevators. This vigorous austerity is moderated inside by Tiffany-designed light fixtures, colored marbles, and murals by Attilio Pusterla on the theme of law and justice.

Critics here praised the structure on its completion. Europeans admired the building as well, less for its grandeur than for its innovative planning, which allows easy circulation of the public to specific courtrooms, and at the same time eliminates the crowd and street noise. The public enters by a rotunda placed at the center of six wings. From here each corridor leads to a specific courtroom. Each wing contains a single court and all the facilities relating to it, including separate entrances for the judges. Administrative offices are located above, and accessible by corner elevators. This arrangement is less interesting to the casual viewer, who is more likely to admire the simple nobility of the structure and the powerful urban space formed by this building, the state courthouse to the north, and the federal courthouse to the south.

FRICK COLLECTION AND FRICK ART REFERENCE LIBRARY
Manhattan
Designated: March 20, 1973

Frick Collection, 1913–14; addition, 1977
1 East 70th Street
Architects: Carrère & Hastings; addition,
Harry van Dyke, John Barrington Bayley, and
G. Frederick Poehler

Frick Art Reference Library, 1931–35
10 East 71st Street
Architect: John Russell Pope

Occupying the entire blockfront between East 70th and 71st streets along Fifth Avenue, where the Lenox Library once stood, the Frick Collection was constructed as the residence of coke and steel magnate Henry Clay Frick.

The building was designed in a restrained style reminiscent of that popular during the reign of Louis XVI. The three-story Fifth Avenue façade is set back from street level behind a broad, raised terrace. Centered on the eleven-bay-wide main block is a slightly projecting portico marked by four colossal Ionic pilasters with arched entrances between them. To the north of this block is a one-story loggia that extends forward along the East 71st Street edge of the terrace to Fifth Avenue, where it ends in a small, three-bay-deep, Ionic pavilion. A projecting two-story wing balances the composition on the south side of the terrace.

The Frick House was always intended to serve ultimately as a museum. Following the death of Frick's widow in 1931, John Russell Pope was hired to modify the original house and to design a new building to house the Frick Art Reference Library. Pope, one of the leading institutional architects of the twentieth century, created a library building that was stylistically very much in keeping with the original house.

In 1977 the P.A.B. Widener house, to the east of the galleries on East 70th Street, was demolished to make way for a wing designed by Harry van Dyke, John Barrington Bayley, and G. Frederick Poehler. The addition shares stylistic characteristics with the original building, and both are complemented by an adjoining garden designed by Russell Page.

NEW WORLD FOUNDATION, formerly the Lewis G. Morris House, 1914
100 East 85th Street, Manhattan
Architect: Ernest Flagg
Designated: April 19, 1973

Although Ernest Flagg was best known for his commercial buildings, the Beaux Arts–trained architect demonstrated his versatility with the design for this Federal Revival town house. The building appears to be two independent structures separated by a courtyard—a novel solution to the problem of building a house on a long, narrow lot.

The house rises three stories above a raised basement, with the larger western portion presenting the gable end of its slate roof to Park Avenue. Flagg used a variety of flat-arched lintels in the body of the house; five hipped-roof dormers above the modillioned cornice light the attic. The extra height required by the garage in the eastern wing necessitated raising the floor level half a story above that of the main house. Atop the garage, the first two stories are united behind superimposed bay windows, while the third story has the double-hung sash found in the western side. The two sections are connected by a staircase crossing the courtyard, which also contains the main exterior entrance stair and an elevator tower capped by a cupola.

The building was commissioned by Lewis Gouverneur Morris, whose family had been active in politics since before the Revolution. His daughters sold the house to the New World Foundation, hoping to preserve the structure. The foundation provides financial aid to groups working on education, civil rights, and peace issues.

HOUSE OF THE REDEEMER, formerly the Edith Fabbri House, 1914–16
7 East 95th Street, Manhattan
Architect: Grosvenor Atterbury
Designated: July 23, 1974

The Fabbri House, built in 1914–16 and designed by architect Grosvenor Atterbury, was the home of Edith Shepard Fabbri, great-granddaughter of Commodore Cornelius Vanderbilt and wife of Ernesto Fabbri.

The house is stylistically derived from Italian Renaissance sources and has many characteristics of an Italian palazzo. Five stories high, its distinguishing features include an L-shaped plan (with a rear wing at the western side of the main section of the house, forming a courtyard), fine architectural features such as rusticated pilasters set within a heavy rusticated stone frame comprising the impressive entrance, and elegant window treatment, in which the sizes and ornament vary at each floor level.

In 1949, Mrs. Fabbri transferred the building to the House of the Redeemer, and since that time it has been used continuously for religious retreats and operated by an independent Episcopal board of trustees.

RACQUET AND TENNIS CLUB BUILDING, 1916–18
370 Park Avenue, Manhattan
Architects: McKim, Mead & White
Designated: May 8, 1979

An architectural masterpiece by the firm of McKim, Mead & White, this building was erected in 1916–18 as the third home of the Racquet and Tennis Club, first organized in 1875 to "encourage all manly sports among its members"; from its beginnings, it was considered one of the most exclusive of New York's social and athletic organizations. Dominating the blockfront of Park Avenue between East 52nd and 53rd streets, the structure is a notable essay in Italian Renaissance Revival style, as taught at the Ecole des Beaux-Arts in Paris.

Based on sixteenth-century Italian palazzi, the Racquet and Tennis Club Building is an imposing structure noted for its refined and restrained detail and for the clarity with which its detail is expressed. A powerful rectangular block, fully visible on three sides, the building rises five stories on a rusticated granite base pierced by large arched openings. Stone quoins mark the corners of the building, contrasting with the smooth beige brick of the upper walls. A distinctive feature is a central loggia recessed behind three arched openings on the second floor, or *piano nobile*. The major courts for sports are located on the upper floors, indicated on the exterior by the large blind arches at the fourth-floor level. The terra-cotta frieze at the fifth floor incorporates racquets into the pattern. A balustraded roof parapet above a decorative cornice provides a fitting and scaled termination to the handsome design.

RUSSIAN ORTHODOX CATHEDRAL OF THE TRANSFIGURATION OF OUR LORD, 1916–21
228 North 12th Street, Brooklyn
Architect: Louis Allmendinger
Designated: November 19, 1969

The Russian Orthodox Cathedral of the Transfiguration of Our Lord was built between 1916 and 1921 by Louis Allmendinger. Although the building, at North 12th Street and Driggs Avenue, is claimed by residents of Greenpoint, Williamsburg, and Northside, it is technically in Williamsburg, by twenty-five feet. Monumental in scale and a striking example of eclectic ecclesiastical architecture, the church is a scholarly reproduction of the Byzantine style so characteristic of Russian churches, with a strong Renaissance flavor.

A Greek cross is surmounted by a great central onion dome on a drum. The four corners made by the arms of the cross are topped by small towers, each capped with a domed octagonal cupola housing the church's bells. The combination of the five copper-covered domes, each surmounted by a gilded patriarchal cross, makes a very picturesque silhouette against the sky. The main mass of the church is extremely severe; its light yellow-brick walls are pierced by simple round-arched windows and doors. The composition is tied together by a massive cornice that runs continuously around the entire structure.

LUCY D. DAHLGREN HOUSE, 1915
15 East 96th Street, Manhattan
Architect: Ogden Codman, Jr.
Designated; June 19, 1984

Built in 1915 for the socially prominent and wealthy Lucy Drexel Dahlgren, the house at 15 East 96th Street was designed by the well-known architect Ogden Codman, Jr., whose own house stood across the street at number 7. Codman, a Boston-born architect raised in France, practiced in Boston from the 1890s through the first decades of the twentieth century and then returned to France. A respected society decorator, he espoused a design philosophy that stressed the integration of architecture and interior decoration; he wrote on the subject in an 1897 book, *The Decoration of Houses*, which he coauthored with Edith Wharton.

The New York town houses of Ogden Codman are based on French and English eighteenth-century sources. The five-story Dahlgren house is a decorative, thirty-room Beaux Arts–style mansion, faced with rusticated limestone and ornamented with carved swags and an intricate wrought-iron balcony. Beaux Arts details include segmental-arched pediments crowning the second-floor window of the center bay and dormers, a slate mansard roof, Louis XIV–style volutes supporting the balcony, and original wooden casement windows with transoms. Elegantly detailed double-leaf wooden doors lead to a porte cochere and an interior court; the main entrance is off the court. Inside are a grand marble staircase and an octagonal dining room with two marble fountains.

The handsome mansion, with its seven fireplaces and eleven bathrooms, was bought in 1922 by the jeweler Pierre Cartier, who owned it until 1945. It was then sold to the St. Francis de Sales Convent, a Roman Catholic religious order. Barry Trupin, a financier, bought the house in 1981 for $3 million. It was recently sold for $5.7 million to Paul Singer, a New York businessman, and awaits a complete restoration.

BROADHURST THEATER, 1917–18
235–243 West 44th Street, Manhattan
Architect: Herbert J. Krapp
Designated: November 10, 1987; interior designated December 15, 1987

The Broadhurst Theater and its twin, the Plymouth, are among the earliest theaters built by the prominent architect Herbert J. Krapp, and the first of many theaters he built for the Shubert Organization. The Broadhurst was part of an area called Shubert Alley, which marked the heart of the Broadway theater district and already included two earlier Shubert theaters, the Booth and the Shubert. In an effort to maintain architectural consistency within the alley, Krapp incorporated into the Broadhurst many features common to the other theaters there.

The Broadhurst has a rounded corner that faces Broadway, the most accessible route for the audience. This corner includes an entrance with a broken-pediment enframement and an oval cartouche. The exterior is marked with diaper-patterned brickwork and Neoclassical details such as stone and terra-cotta trim—features that Krapp frequently employed.

The interior of the Broadhurst is designed in the Adamesque style. The walls are enframed by tall pilasters, and a plaster entablature covers the length of the wall above the proscenium arch. Relief panels based on the Parthenon frieze decorate the boxes, the front of the balconies, and the proscenium arch. The seating arrangement is flexible; a movable barrier and a false platform in the back of the theater permit expansion from 550 seats to 680, depending on the type of production. A single balcony is divided into two sections by means of a cross-over aisle.

The theater was leased by the prolific playwright George Broadhurst while it was still under construction. He named the building after himself, with the intention of staging chiefly his own productions there, although he did also put on a number of other plays throughout the years.

Bowcot

Wallcot

McCall Demonstration House

TODT HILL COTTAGES
Stone Court, Staten Island
Architect: Ernest Flagg
Designated: May 23, 1985

Bowcot, 1916–18
95 West Entry Road

Wallcot, 1918–21
285 Flagg Place

McCall Demonstration House, 1924–25
1929 Richmond Road

On the grounds of Stone Court, his country estate, the noted American architect Ernest Flagg constructed three remarkable small stone houses, now known as the Todt Hill Cottages, which expressed his aesthetic theories, as outlined in his widely regarded book *Small Houses: Their Economic Design and Construction*, published in 1922. Flagg considered these cottages to be of no less importance than his Singer Tower, which was the world's tallest building when completed in 1911. Employing the architect's inventive cost-saving design and construction techniques, they demonstrate Flagg's conviction that economy and good design are not mutually exclusive.

Bowcot was the first of the experimental stone cottages, built in 1916–18. Flagg observed that ". . . as the wall bends with the road, the house bends too": thus was Bowcot named. The cottage appears to nestle into the slope and surrounding landscape; this harmony of structure and topography is one of the most significant aspects of Bowcot's design. Constructed of mosaic rubble with an irregular rectangular plan, the cottage is distinguished by picturesque chimneys and gables.

Wallcot, known also as House-on-the-Wall, was built in 1918–21. Also of mosaic rubblestone, but with a less picturesque design than Bowcot's, the house consists of two rectangular sections, one and one-half stories high. The façade has an imposing main entrance with a wide, round-arched opening topped by a large gabled hood roof carried on enormous ornamental brackets. Wide-spreading roofs cover both sections of the house, and there is a lively variety of window types used.

The McCall Demonstration House was built in 1924–25 for *McCall's* magazine; in 1923, the publication asked the foremost architects of the country to design "a series of small houses planned not for beauty of design alone, but for the convenience of the homemaker, as well." Flagg wrote many articles in the magazine, discussing in detail his proposed design. The house illustrates Flagg's continuing experimentation with building technology, and incorporates such features as a combination slate/rubberoid roof and window frames flush with the walls, representing a pioneering example of passive solar design.

HENRY MILLER THEATER, 1917–18
124–130 West 43rd Street, Manhattan
Architects: Allen, Ingalls & Hoffman
Designated: December 8, 1987

The Henry Miller Theater was the creation of one of the most prominent figures of Broadway in the early twentieth century. First known as an actor, Miller eventually wrote and produced plays; after considerable success, he decided to build his own theater.

The building was designed according to Miller's idea that the theater should be an intimate and accessible environment in which to see drama. Built in 1917–18 by architects Allen, Ingalls & Hoffman, the structure is based on the Georgian Revival style, which was popular for smaller theaters at the time. The brick and terra-cotta façade features a classical colonnade, a terra-cotta entablature, and windows at the second and third stories. All of the windows, the cornice, and the pediments are trimmed with white terra-cotta.

Although the Henry Miller is currently a discotheque, it remains unchanged from its original form except for the addition of a new marquee.

PLYMOUTH THEATER, 1917–18
234–240 West 45th Street, Manhattan
Architect: Herbert J. Krapp
Designated: December 8, 1987; interior designated December 15, 1987

The Plymouth Theater, built in 1917–18, one of many constructed by the Shubert Organization and designed by Herbert J. Krapp. The Plymouth and the Broadhurst were built as a pair in Shubert Alley.

The Plymouth and the Broadhurst share many architectural characteristics. The façades, in diaper-patterned brickwork with Neoclassical detail, set the tone for Krapp's later designs based on a similar style. The interior of the Plymouth is in the Adamesque style. The low-relief plasterwork and friezes depict wreaths, urns, and classical figures holding musical instruments. These friezes outline all major elements in the theater—the balconies, ceiling, and proscenium arch.

After its construction, the Plymouth was immediately leased to manager/producer Arthur M. Hopkins, who was renowned for his pioneer productions of Ibsen plays on Broadway and his production of *Anna Christie*, Eugene O'Neill's first financial success. Hopkins was strongly identified with the Plymouth until his death in 1950. The theater still continues to run as a successful playhouse.

EAST 93RD STREET HOUSES, formerly the George F. Baker, Jr., House Complex
Manhattan
Architects: Delano & Aldrich

Synod of Bishops of the Russian Orthodox
Church Outside of Russia, 1917–18;
addition, 1928
69–75 East 93rd Street
Designated: January 14, 1969

67 East 93rd Street, 1931
Designated: July 23, 1974

Although each portion of the George F. Baker, Jr., House Complex was designed and built at a different time, the architectural firm of Delano & Aldrich was able to create an elegant, cohesive architectural unit. The earliest portion of the complex is the five-story brick house built in 1917–18 for Francis F. Palmer. The house is almost square with five evenly placed windows facing Park Avenue and four facing East 93rd Street. The decorative elements on the façade are spare and create an effective contrast with the plain brick walls.

In 1928, prominent banker George F. Baker, Jr., purchased the Palmer house and commissioned Delano & Aldrich to add a large, L-shaped ballroom wing. The addition was similar to the original design in scale, materials, and details. A courtyard was created between the addition and the original house.

In 1931 Baker once again asked Delano & Aldrich to add onto the complex by building a four-story house at 67 East 93rd Street for his father. This house is carefully designed to harmonize with the earlier buildings. A broad belt course separates the two lower floors from the upper ones and links the structure to the rest of the complex. The classical details and the carefully executed masonry of all three structures is exemplary of the Federal Revival style that Delano & Aldrich popularized.

In 1958 the Synod of the Bishops of the Russian Orthodox Church Outside of Russia purchased the original Palmer house and the ballroom addition to serve as its headquarters.

BARBARA RUTHERFORD HATCH HOUSE, 1917–19
153 East 63rd Street, Manhattan
Architect: Frederick J. Sterner
Designated: January 11, 1977

The house at 153 East 63rd Street is unusual and picturesque, adapting Spanish Colonial and Italian Renaissance styles to a sophisticated urban setting. Commissioned by Barbara Rutherford Hatch, a young socialite married to Cyril Hatch, the house was designed by the well-known town-house architect Frederick J. Sterner. The stucco walls, red tile roof, and ornate iron railings and grills of this three-story residence are all typically Spanish elements. U-shaped in plan, the house has two main wings parallel to the street that allowed for a spacious interior courtyard—a Mediterranean feature and a rarity in New York town houses.

Following the Hatches' divorce in 1920, the town house passed into the hands of a succession of illustrious owners, including Charles B. Dillingham, a prominent figure in the Broadway theater; Charles Lanier Lawrance, a pioneer aviation engineer; Gypsy Rose Lee, the entertainer; and most recently the distinguished American artist Jasper Johns.

PERSHING SQUARE VIADUCT, 1917–19
Park Avenue from 40th Street to Grand Central Terminal at 42nd Street, Manhattan
Architects: Warren & Wetmore
Designated: September 23, 1980

The Pershing Square Viaduct links upper and lower Park Avenue by way of elevated drives that make a circuit around Grand Central Terminal and descend to ground level at East 45th Street. Designed in 1912 by the architectural firm of Warren & Wetmore, it was conceived as part of the original 1903 plan for the station by the firm of Reed & Stem. The square was named in honor of General John J. Pershing.

In plan, the Pershing Square Viaduct reflects Beaux Arts design and planning: the overall design of Grand Central Terminal, including the connecting viaduct, was created with concern for monumental scale, axial planning, and a clearly defined system of circulation. French in character, the viaduct, almost 600 feet long, has three low, broad spanning arches and substantial granite supporting piers. Originally, all three arches were left open, with the trusses exposed, and at one time a trolley line ran underneath. The central arch was enclosed in 1939, when the New York City Convention and Visitors' Bureau was opened under the central section of the bridge. Today it temporarily serves as an employment office.

AMBASSADOR THEATER, 1919–21
215–223 West 49th Street, Manhattan
Architect: Herbert J. Krapp
Designated (exterior and interior): August 6, 1985

The Ambassador was designed by Herbert J. Krapp for the Shubert Organization and built in 1919–21. The very simple exterior is ornamented only by textured brick—a common building material in New York between the wars. A series of pilasters, shallow panels, and segmental arches articulate the façade; there is a rounded corner above the entrance—an element that Krapp also used at the Booth and Plymouth theaters. The unpretentious exterior hardly prepares us for the rich interior, an explosion of Adamesque fans, cameos, and swags—the mode in which nearly all Krapp's Shubert work is designed.

The Ambassador stage has a venerable history, and has featured such diverse talents as Claudette Colbert, Jason Robards, Jr., Sandy Duncan, Maureen Stapleton, and George C. Scott.

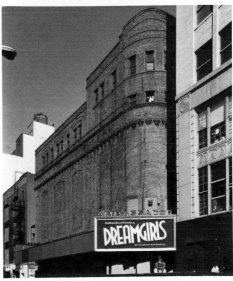

MUSIC BOX THEATER, 1920
239–247 West 45th Street, Manhattan
Architects: C. Howard Crane and E. George Kiehler
Designated (exterior and interior): December 8, 1987

In 1920 the Music Box Theater was built for the prolific producer Sam H. Harris and the legendary songwriter Irving Berlin. The theater was a rarity in the 1920s because it was not built by a large organization, but by an individual producer. Harris and Berlin asked architects C. Howard Crane and E. George Kiehler to design a theater that would stand out as the home of Berlin's famous "Music Box Revues."

The most prominent feature of the theater's façade is the limestone Ionic colonnade screening a gallery. A mansard roof tops the theater, and a decorative wrought-iron balustrade runs the length of the roof. A mixture of Georgian Revival and Palladian elements on both the exterior and interior suggests an opulent country manor.

The auditorium, embellished with Adamesque ornament in a color scheme of antique ivory and soft green, is one of the most handsome on Broadway. Elaborate boxes are the highlight of the design. Framed by Corinthian columns, they project at balcony level into the auditorium, with murals of bucolic classical ruins decorating the half-domes above the boxes.

TOWN HALL, 1919–21
113–123 West 43rd Street, Manhattan
Architects: McKim, Mead & White
Designated (exterior and interior): November 28, 1978

Characterized by one contemporary observer as "an idea with a roof over it," Town Hall was built in 1919–21 as a meeting hall for the city of New York. The League for Political Education, founded by six prominent suffragettes in 1894, commissioned the firm of McKim, Mead & White to design a structure versatile enough to accommodate a speaker's auditorium, a concert hall, a movie theater, and a clubhouse.

Town Hall began essentially as a forum to educate men and women in political issues. From its inception, it became a popular arena for airing many of the nation's most pressing and controversial issues, and over the years attracted such international speakers as Theodore Roosevelt, Winston Churchill, Thomas Mann, and Jane Addams. The building attained national importance in 1935 when its weekly Thursday evening meetings were broadcast by radio in a program entitled "America's Town Meeting of the Air." Town Hall has also become known for the excellent acoustics of its concert hall. In 1900 McKim, Mead & White had built the Boston Symphony Hall, one of the three or four acoustically superior auditoriums in the world, in conjunction with acoustical engineer Wallace C. Sabine of Harvard University. If Sabine, who died in 1919, did not directly advise on the Town Hall project, his previous collaboration with the firm certainly influenced the design of the auditorium.

Centrally located on the north side of West 43rd Street, Town Hall is a four-story adaptation of a Federal Revival design, a style frequently employed by McKim, Mead & White. Laid up in Flemish bond brick with contrasting limestone trim, the façade is punctuated by a seven-bay blind arcade, with theatrical canopies suspended over the double doors. In the middle of the façade is a large inscribed limestone plaque.

Inside, the roughly semicircular auditorium with cantilevered balcony has walls of rusticated artificial stone. The angles of the hall are accented by monumental gilded pilasters, and crystal chandeliers hang from a paneled plaster ceiling. Perhaps the most decorative features of the hall are the arched organ grills that flank the stage on the diagonal walls.

In 1958, Town Hall, Inc., merged with New York University, which for twenty years managed the hall and leased the auditorium for a variety of purposes. Town Hall is now used for various musical events.

ST. BARTHOLOMEW'S CHURCH AND COMMUNITY HOUSE
109 East 50th Street, Manhattan
Designated: March 16, 1967

St. Bartholomew's Church, 1917–19; porch
(from old St. Bartholomew's Church), 1902
Architects: Bertram G. Goodhue; McKim,
Mead & White (porch)

Community House, 1928
Architects: Bertram G. Goodhue and Mayers,
Murray & Philip

Flanked by the Waldorf-Astoria Hotel and the General Electric Building, St. Bartholomew's Church occupies a prominent Park Avenue site. The congregation was originally formed in a church at the corner of Lafayette Place and Great Jones Street; from 1872 until the early twentieth century, it occupied a Lombardic Revival structure by James Renwick, Jr., at the corner of Madison Avenue and East 44th Street. The Romanesque porch from Renwick's church was commissioned by Mrs. Cornelius Vanderbilt in her husband's memory and designed by Stanford White; it was removed from the old church and incorporated by Goodhue into his design for this building.

Goodhue was a noted church architect who preferred the Gothic style; St. Bartholomew's was his first church based exclusively on Byzantine forms. The design, both inside and out, shows the influence of John Francis Bentley's Westminster Cathedral in London. Stanford White's famous porch bears sculpture by gifted Americans: Henry Adams designed the north portal, and Philip Martiny the south portal; the central portal is the work of Daniel Chester French and Andrew O'Conor. Goodhue also reused marble columns from Renwick's church in the chapel to the south of the main nave.

St. Bartholomew's has a domed crossing resting on four reinforced concrete piers faced with stone. The shallow transepts and choir are barrel-vaulted with Rumford tile. The interior, completed in 1929, is a multicolored combination of brilliant mosaics and marble inlays. The gilded exterior of the dome adds a bright accent to skyscraper-lined Park Avenue.

The vestry of St. Bartholomew's has proposed that the Community House be removed and the land leased to a realtor for development. The Landmarks Preservation Commission is opposed to this plan and litigation is under way.

KAUFMAN ASTORIA STUDIOS, formerly Famous Players–Lasky Corporation Studios and Paramount Studios, Building No. 1, 1920–21
35–11 35th Avenue, Astoria, Queens
Architects: Fleischman Construction Company
Designated: March 14, 1978

The Kaufman Astoria Studios were built in 1920–21 as the eastern production headquarters for the Famous Players–Lasky Corporation, the forerunner of Paramount Pictures. Over 110 feature silent films were produced here between 1921 and 1927, with such stars as Gloria Swanson, Rudolph Valentino, W. C. Fields, and Dorothy Gish. In 1929, the studio's first sound feature was produced: *The Letter*, starring Jeanne Eagels. Soon such actors as the Marx brothers, Claudette Colbert, Tallulah Bankhead, George Burns, and Gracie Allen were associated with the studios. In 1932, Paramount moved all studio operations to California, and the Astoria studios were turned over to independent producers. A Works Progress Administration film, *One Third of a Nation*, was the last major motion picture produced at the studios before World War II.

In 1942 the buildings were transferred to the U.S. Army's Pictorial Center, and until 1970 the studios served as the production headquarters for army films. In 1970 the building was turned over to the City of New York. Since then, it has been rehabilitated and is in active use as a film production facility, handling an average of eight to twelve feature films each year as well as *The Cosby Show*.

The Fleischman Construction Company of New York designed and built the studios. Made of reinforced and cast concrete, with terra-cotta and masonry block used for decorative and facing materials, the main façade of Building No. 1 is three stories high, monumentally scaled, and distinguished by modified classical detail. The central portion is highlighted by a striking double-height porte cochere, five bays wide and flanked by end pylons. The building was designed around one large interior space—the Main Stage—that is spanned by a series of roof trusses. It is reportedly one of the four largest sound stages in the world, and the largest on the East Coast, historically important for its early use of such technological features as sound insulation and readily adaptable ceiling modules.

POMANDER WALK, 1921
Between West 94th and 95th streets, West End Avenue, and Broadway, Manhattan
Architects: King & Campbell
Designated: September 14, 1982

Pomander Walk extends from West 94th to West 95th Street in the middle of the block bounded by Broadway and West End Avenue; sixteen two-story buildings that face the private walk, and eleven buildings that face the cross streets, make up the complex. An unusual sense of place exists here; secluded from the street, Pomander Walk is an oasis of picturesque dwellings ornamented with Tudor Revival details. The romantic atmosphere created in this residential enclave reflects the intentions of restaurateur Thomas Healy, who commissioned King & Campbell to design a complex that evoked the village atmosphere of Lewis Parker's play *Pomander Walk*, which was then enjoying great success on Broadway.

The interiors and exteriors of the buildings in this displaced English village have remained essentially unchanged since their completion.

130 East 80th Street (Astor House)

124 East 80th Street (Dillon House)

120 East 80th Street (George Whitney House)

116 East 80th Street (Lewis Spencer Morris House)

EAST 80TH STREET HOUSES
Manhattan

116 East 80th Street, 1922–23
Architects: Cross & Cross
Designated: January 24, 1967

130 East 80th Street, 1927–28
Architect: Mott B. Schmidt
Designated: April 12, 1967

120 East 80th Street, 1929–30
Architects: Cross & Cross
Designated: November 12, 1968

124 East 80th Street, 1930
Architect: Mott B. Schmidt
Designated: January 24, 1967

This block of East 80th Street, between Park and Lexington avenues, was one of the earliest blocks in this neighborhood to have houses built upon it. Located on the south side of the street, the earliest town house is the Lewis Spencer Morris House, at number 116, which architects Cross & Cross designed in 1922–23 in the simple red brick of the Federal Revival style. In 1927–28 architect Mott B. Schmidt designed number 130 for Vincent Astor; it is now the home of the Junior League of New York. This Neoclassical building is carried out entirely in a mellow-toned limestone. Its sophistication suggests the Regency period in England.

The gap between the two houses was subsequently filled in by two more: the George Whitney House at number 120, designed by Cross & Cross, and the Clarence Dillon House at number 124, by Schmidt. Both were completed in 1930 and were considered to be the most elegant town houses of their day. The Whitney House, while still basically Federal Revival, is more elaborate than its neighbor at 116; the pedimented central window and the raising of the balustrade to the top of the slate roof above the dormers are Georgian features. The Dillon House, with its brick quoins, splayed lintels and keystones, and heavy pedimented doorway, is pure Georgian Revival. The two architects managed to achieve a handsome unity among the buildings, yet each one retains its own individual stamp.

369TH REGIMENT ARMORY DRILL SHED AND ADMINISTRATION BUILDING
2360 Fifth Avenue, Manhattan
Designated: May 14, 1985

369th Regiment Armory Drill Shed, 1921–24
Architects: Tachau & Vought

Administration Building, 1930–33
Architects: Van Wart & Wein

The 369th Regiment Armory, like other armories built in the city in the late nineteenth and early twentieth centuries, is a highly specialized structure built to serve as a training and marshaling center for the National Guard. The structure consists of two sections—the Drill Shed and the Administration Building—which were designed in two stages by the firms of Tachau & Vought in 1921–24 and Van Wart & Wein in 1930–33. The design of the building combines the medieval forms of earlier armories with contemporary Art Deco elements. In the Drill Shed, the reddish-brown brick walls are articulated with regularly spaced simulated buttresses with stone copings; they flank narrow window openings set within brick arches. The square-headed entrances are set in stone enframements below foliate spandrels and marked by overscaled, red sandstone pediments. The parapet terminates in a crenellated motif; a gabled roof rises above the parapets.

The Administration Building's forms and massing also recall medieval prototypes, but the setbacks and details are in the Art Deco mode, accented with appropriate military touches.

The 369th Regiment Armory is particularly noted as the home of the "Harlem Hell Fighters," New York's official black regiment, whose efforts in World War I brought military success and well-deserved accolades.

SAKS FIFTH AVENUE, 1922–24
611 Fifth Avenue, Manhattan
Architects: Starrett & Van Vleck
Designated: December 20, 1984

Representative of midtown Manhattan's premier shopping district, the handsome Saks Fifth Avenue building was an up-to-the-minute mélange of the latest in fashion design and Renaissance Revival architecture at the time of its construction. This dignified and elegant structure was the result of Horace Saks's timely decision to move from his father's original Herald Square site. The building's opening—part of the boom of the 1920s—created quite a stir, as throngs of patrons stampeded through the store.

In compliance with the city's strict new zoning resolution and the Fifth Avenue Association's neighborhood requirements, the upper stories were set back from the main portion of the building, and the restrained façades were sheathed in traditional stone and brick. Chamfered corners mark the transition from the main to the side-street façades. The ground floor of this ten-story structure is a rusticated granite base with entrances flanked by display windows. Carved spiral moldings decorate the entrances, which are topped by a plain cornice. Windows, set behind elegant detailed metal grills, surmount the doors.

Above the entrance level rises the main portion of the façade, with fluted pilasters supporting an architrave of Indiana limestone. Between the third and seventh floors the façade is brick with rectangular windows. The seventh-story level is set off by a sill molding; here, narrower windows alternate with stone roundels. Above the seventh floor rises a series of setbacks reserved for administrative offices. Their successive arrangement, marked by cornices and balustrades at the eighth through the tenth stories, completes the structure.

WINTER GARDEN THEATER INTERIOR, formerly the American Horse Exchange, c. 1885; rebuilt, 1896; conversions, 1910–11, 1922–23
1634–1646 Broadway, Manhattan
Architects: Unknown; W. Albert Swasey (1910–11 conversion); Herbert J. Krapp (1922–23 alteration)
Designated: January 5, 1988

Compared to most other Broadway theaters, the Winter Garden has an unusual history. It was erected about 1885 by William K. Vanderbilt as the American Horse Exchange; at the time, Long Acre Square (now Times Square) was the center of the horse and carriage trade in Manhattan.

By 1910 Times Square had become the center of the city's theater district. At this time, Lee Shubert approached Vanderbilt, who agreed to lease him the building. Shubert employed architect W. Albert Swasey to convert the building into a large vaudeville theater, which he named the Winter Garden, after such well-known European institutions as the Berlin Winter Garden. Al Jolson made his Broadway debut in *La Belle Paree*, the revue that opened the theater in 1911.

Swasey left the trusses of the ceiling exposed and added wooden latticework to the walls. Behind these elements a sky and landscape were painted, creating the illusion of being outside. A wraparound balcony was installed, and a grand runway was added in 1912—an unusual element in theater at the time, intended to break the barrier between the audience and the actors.

By the 1920s, the demand for the kind of theatrical spectacles that the Winter Garden staged was subsiding, and smaller, more intimate productions gained popularity. The Shuberts employed architect Herbert J. Krapp, who designed almost all of their theaters, to rework the Winter Garden's interior in 1922. Krapp lowered the ceiling of the auditorium, added two levels of triple boxes where a single balcony-level box had been, and added columns on each side of the balcony. He decorated the interior in the Adamesque style, a trademark of his designs. Low-relief, highly ornamental plasterwork outlined the proscenium arch of the stage, the boxes, and the ceiling trusses. Today the interior of the Winter Garden remains relatively unchanged, although the orchestra-level boxes have been removed. Over the years, the Winter Garden has housed productions of the *Ziegfeld Follies*, *Funny Girl* starring Barbra Streisand, *42nd Street*, which moved to the Majestic Theater after seven months, and *Cats*.

IMPERIAL THEATER INTERIOR, 1923
249 West 45th Street, Manhattan
Architect: Herbert J. Krapp
Designated: November 17, 1987

The Shubert Organizaton commissioned Herbert J. Krapp to design the Imperial Theater in 1923. Located in Shubert Alley, the Imperial was intended to be a premier showcase for the Shuberts' revues and musicals.

In contrast to the Imperial's plain and modest exterior, Krapp's Adamesque interior is quite elegant. Shallow pilasters line the walls, and the triple boxes are decorated with highly ornamental, low-relief plasterwork. Ornaments are placed on the ceiling and the walls contain friezes, floral and geometric motifs, and fairy figures holding the masks of comedy and tragedy.

In 1925, the Shuberts planned to add a fifteen-story residential hotel designed by Krapp on top of the Imperial; the plan was never executed. The Shubert Organization fell on hard times during the Depression, but was able to maintain management of the Imperial and make it into one of Broadway's most legendary musical theaters. It has housed successes such as *Gypsy*, *Carnival*, and *Fiddler on the Roof*.

AMERICAN STANDARD BUILDING,
formerly the American Radiator Building, 1923–24
40 West 40th Street, Manhattan
Architect: Raymond M. Hood
Designated: November 12, 1974

Raymond M. Hood established himself as one of the foremost architects in the United States with this, his first major commission in New York. Although the massing, setbacks, and Gothic ornament were not unusual architectural features in the 1920s, the black brick and gilded terra-cotta ornament startled both the profession and the public. This coloration was not present in the original design, and was added only after ground had been broken in early 1923. The black brick is particularly successful, giving the skyscraper a unified, slablike effect, much admired at the time of its completion. This effect had been achieved best by Louis Sullivan in his use of unbroken vertical piers; Hood created the same result through color and unaccented mass. Hood set the main body of the tower back from the east and west party walls, thus ensuring that the structure would always appear as a lone tower despite later construction of tall buildings in the area.

The entire ground floor once served as a showroom for American Radiator products; it now serves American Standard, Inc., in the same way. Hood's original display floor was distributed over three levels, with an almost clear view from the front to the rear of the building, made possible by an advanced form of the portal-braced steel frame. At the back of the showroom was a wrought-iron grill, based loosely on late Gothic metalwork, that led down to the building's boiler room where gleaming American Radiator heating equipment worked quietly and efficiently.

Every aspect of the structure was meant to attest to the high quality of the company's products. Dramatic nighttime lighting was added soon after the building's completion at the company's own initiative. The company was so pleased with its headquarters that Hood received the commission in 1928 for its European headquarters in Argyll Street, London.

MARTIN BECK THEATER, 1923–24
302–314 West 45th Street, Manhattan
Architect: G. Albert Lansburgh
Designated (exterior and interior): November 4, 1987

The Martin Beck is a monument to the man who conceived and built it. A Czech immigrant, Beck began his career in a vaudeville company. Eventually, he became involved in the Orpheum circuit, rising in 1920 to succeed his father-in-law as president of more than fifty Orpheum theaters.

The Orpheum merged with the East Coast–based Keith Circuit, and Beck was ousted in 1923. At this point, he decided to build his own theater. He hired G. Albert Lansburgh, whose designs for many of the Orpheum Circuit theaters had brought him national acclaim. Lansburgh looked on the Martin Beck Theater as his most notable accomplishment.

One of the most lavishly appointed theaters on Broadway, it met with immediate critical praise and success. The theater is done in a Moorish style, marked chiefly by a three-story arcade on West 45th Street. With its recessed entrances, exotically carved capitals, and angled piers, the arcade contrasts sharply with the more common flat façades and Neoclassical style of many other Broadway theaters.

The interior design echoes the elaborate façade, with an abundance of ornamentation, and the vaulted Romanesque ticket lobby; an inner lobby features three domes with mural paintings. One of the highlights of the interior is the ceiling designed by painter and illustrator Albert Herter.

EMBASSY I THEATER INTERIOR, 1925
1556–1560 Broadway, Manhattan
Architect: Thomas Lamb
Designated: November 17, 1987

The interior of the Embassy I, designed by Thomas Lamb, remains today as a reminder of the grandeur that was once part of the moviegoing experience. It was built in 1925 for the Metro-Goldwyn-Mayer corporation, and no expense was spared: noted muralist Arthur Crisp was commissioned for the murals, and the lighting fixtures and decorative elements were created by the Rambusch Studio.

The lobbies were decidedly French in style, with marble detailing in the outer lobby and rich blond wood paneling and Louis XV furniture—since removed—in the inner lobby. The French motifs were continued in the auditorium with its floral reliefs and oval insets, each in a different color and type of marble. The lighting fixtures are in the shape of vases supported on the backs of mermaids. These details were originally accompanied by tapestried chairs and silk damask curtains.

The Embassy was not a movie theater for the masses; it was designed for those wealthy enough to pay for reserved seats. The manager was Gloria Gould, an early feminist and darling of New York society, and the theater was staffed entirely by women, from the projectionists to the musicians.

The novelty of an exclusive movie theater run by women soon wore off, and the Embassy I was transformed into the first newsreel movie house in America in 1929. With the advent of television news, the newsreel became obsolete, and in 1949 the Embassy I began once more to show feature films.

CITY CENTER, formerly the Mecca Temple, 1924
131 West 55th Street, Manhattan
Architect: H. P. Knowles
Designated: April 12, 1983

The Mecca Temple began as an entertainment hall for New York City Shriners. The building's exterior reflects the organization's adopted heritage and includes elements from the Alhambra and Egyptian mosques, as well as Templar Church façades. Four main interior spaces—a lodge and club rooms, a stage, a large auditorium, and a banquet hall—are organized within a concrete-encased structural steel frame. Together, they form a massive cube covered in sandstone and surmounted by a tile dome.

The West 55th Street front, in a style deemed "modified Arabian" by the Shriners, is actually composed of two façades. One structurally merges with the upper dome, while the other is scaled to the pedestrian below. The façade on West 56th Street appears more classical and restrained than its Moorish counterpart. It is composed of five arches, of which the outer and central ones provide access to the stage, while those in between serve as public entrances. The large, decorative dome houses an exhaust fan eight feet in diameter.

The building changed hands several times during the Depression, until, in 1942, New York City acquired it. A year later, Mayor Fiorello LaGuardia was instrumental in reopening the temple as the City Center of Music and Drama, dedicated to the production of cultural events at affordable prices. Once home to the New York City Ballet and the New York City Opera, the theater has remained a vibrant center for dance and theater under the direction of the 55th Street Dance Theater Foundation, Inc. The Joffrey, Alvin Ailey, and Paul Taylor dance companies perform here on a regular basis.

46TH STREET THEATER, formerly Chanin's 46th Street Theater, 1924
226–236 West 46th Street, Manhattan
Architect: Herbert J. Krapp
Designated (exterior and interior): November 17, 1987

Built by Herbert J. Krapp in 1924, the 46th Street Theater was Irwin S. Chanin's first theatrical venture.

The brick and terra-cotta Renaissance-style façade of the theater is more elaborate than those of theaters that Krapp had previously designed. A triple-arched loggia placed between five Corinthian pilasters is the main design element. Terra-cotta embellishes the arches and on each side there are panels with theatrical masks.

The interior is designed in what Chanin called a stadium plan, which he believed would make theatergoing more democratic. All seats were reached through the same lobby, whether they were in the orchestra or in the balcony. The 1,500-seat auditorium was detailed with Adamesque plasterwork. The walls are decorated with pilasters and shell moldings that form arches, and the boxes are enhanced by wave friezes.

ARTHUR HAMMERSTEIN HOUSE, 1924; additions, 1924–30
168–11 Powell's Cove Boulevard, Queens
Architect: Dwight James Baum
Designated: July 27, 1982

Upon his marriage to film star Dorothy Dalton, and after the year-long success of his 1923 musical comedy *Wildflower*, Arthur Hammerstein, son of Oscar Hammerstein, built a mansion named Wildflower. Located in the Beechhurst-Whitestone neighborhood, Hammerstein's residence is a fine model of Tudor Revival architecture.

Dwight James Baum, the architect, designed an asymmetrically massed, two-and-one-half-story brick structure with peaked roofs and gables, steep chimneys, and projecting bays. Personal touches added by Hammerstein himself include a tile inscription in the entrance hall reading "AH. Thys Hovse was Bvilt in the Yere of owre Lorde MCMXXIV," and lead-inlaid windows by J. Scott Williams that depict Shakespearean characters. Modifications to the house, probably executed by Baum and certainly finished between 1924 and 1930, include a stone bay, gable, and one-story addition on the north elevation, and a regrouping of gables and openings on the south. Since 1930, the garage has been modified and the entrance set back into a vestibule, but the house remains otherwise largely unchanged.

With the onset of the Depression, Hammerstein was forced to sell Wildflower to raise funds to sustain his Hammerstein Theater, now the Ed Sullivan Theater, built in 1927. The house subsequently served as headquarters of the Clearview Yacht Club, then as a restaurant.

FEDERAL RESERVE BANK OF NEW YORK, 1924
33 Liberty Street, Manhattan
Architects: York & Sawyer
Designated: December 21, 1965

Fourteen stories high with five stories below ground, the Federal Reserve Bank of New York is an enormous building occupying an entire city block. Designed by the architects York & Sawyer and completed in 1924, the "Fed" building freely adapts Italian Renaissance precedents to twentieth-century demands. The stonework, arches, and ironwork recall the Strozzi Palace of 1489; the sheer monumentality suggests the Pitti Palace of the early 1400s; and the arching and façade molding closely follow the details of the Palazzo Vecchio. The size and shape of the building are unusual, as the building narrows to conform to an irregular site.

Among the building's finest features are its fortresslike rusticated façade, wrought-iron window grills and lanterns, fine proportions, and superb quality of construction. This building, worthy of the Fed's preeminent position in the financial life of the city and the nation, set a precedent for many other banks.

VIRGINIA THEATER, formerly the Guild Theater, 1924–25
243–259 West 52nd Street, Manhattan
Architects: Crane & Franzheim
Designated: August 6, 1985

The Virginia Theater was constructed for the Theater Guild as a subscription playhouse named the Guild Theater. The founding Guild members—including actors, playwrights, designers, attorneys, and bankers—formed the Theater Guild to present plays of high quality, which they believed would be artistically superior to the offerings of the commercial Broadway houses. The Guild Theater was designed to be a theater resource center as well, with classrooms, studios, and a library. The theater itself included the most up-to-date staging technology.

The Virginia's exterior, designed by prominent theater architect C. Howard Crane with Kenneth Franzheim, drew inspiration from fifteenth-century Tuscan villas. Differing markedly from the Beaux Arts–influenced Neoclassical styles of the majority of other theaters of the period, the building provoked as much admiration as the company's planned operations. Among its notable features are the stuccoed walls framed by rusticated stone quoins, a tiled roof overhanging the façade, and a small arched loggia.

In the 1930s, the Theater Guild was forced to give up its theater; in 1950 the building was taken over by ANTA, a similar theater group that had evolved from the Federal Theater Project. In 1981, ANTA moved to Washington and was rechristened the American National Theater Company. The building was purchased by the Jujamcyn Corporation in 1982 and renamed the Virginia Theater.

BILTMORE THEATER INTERIOR, 1925–26
261–265 West 47th Street, Manhattan
Architect: Herbert J. Krapp
Designated: November 10, 1987

Through its various theater projects, of which the Biltmore Theater is a fine example, the Chanin organization created much of the feeling of the Broadway district. Constructed in 1925–26, the Biltmore was designed by Herbert J. Krapp, the most prolific Broadway theater architect.

The interior of the Biltmore differs from other Broadway theaters in the design of its auditorium: it is horseshoe-shaped, with a single aisle. The interior is Adamesque, featuring highly ornamental, low-relief plasterwork. The auditorium is decorated with shallow pilasters, and its false boxes are adorned with Neoclassical aedicules. The ceiling is adorned with low-relief plasterwork, as are the panels on the walls. The Biltmore was the last of Krapp's Adamesque interiors.

EUGENE O'NEILL THEATER INTERIOR,
formerly the Forrest Theater, 1925–26
230–238 West 49th Street, Manhattan
Architect: Herbert J. Krapp
Designated: December 8, 1987

The Eugene O'Neill Theater was built in 1925–26 for the Shubert Organization; Herbert J. Krapp, the house architect for the Shuberts, was responsible for its design. The Eugene O'Neill is significant for being part of the first hotel-theater complex in Times Square. At that time, the buildings were known as the Forrest Hotel and Theater, after one of the greatest actors of the nineteenth century, Edwin Forrest.

One very unusual aspect of the building is the use of a structural steel skeleton, unheard of, until then, in theater construction. The most significant feature of the Eugene O'Neill, however, is its stunning Adamesque interior, with highly ornamental low-relief plasterwork based on ancient Roman decoration. The decor includes panels depicting classical scenes, cartouches with classically robed figures, and theatrical masks. Bands of plasterwork outline the ceiling and boxes.

The theater has had a succession of owners throughout its history, including playwright Neil Simon. In 1953 it was renamed the Eugene O'Neill by Lester Osterman, who was the owner at the time.

BROOKS ATKINSON THEATER, formerly the
Mansfield Theater, 1925–26
256–262 West 47th Street, Manhattan
Architect: Herbert J. Krapp
Designated (exterior and interior): November 4, 1987

This was the third theater designed by Herbert J. Krapp for Irwin S. Chanin, built in 1925–26. Originally named for Richard Mansfield, one of America's most famous nineteenth-century actors, the theater was renamed for critic Brooks Atkinson in 1960, when—after a ten-year stint as a radio and television studio—it reopened as a theater. The building is markedly different from the first two theaters that Krapp built for Chanin. The architect chose Spanish motifs, instead of the Neoclassical themes that were popular at the time. On the exterior, Palladian arches and windows, spiral Corinthian columns, a tiled roof, and flanking towers are combined with rich terra-cotta detailing to create a romantic effect.

The elaborate interior design echoes the Spanish exterior. Chanin brought in Roman Melzer, a former decorator and architect to Czar Nicholas II, as a consultant for the interior. The audience is brought close to the stage by an auditorium that is wider and more shallow than usual. Once seated, the audience is surrounded by ornate details, including murals depicting figures from the commedia dell'arte, muses by A. Battisti and G. Troombul, and ornamental low-relief plasterwork by sculptor Joseph F. Dujat.

FRED F. FRENCH BUILDING, 1926–27
551 Fifth Avenue, Manhattan
Architects: H. Douglas Ives and Sloan & Robertson
Designated (exterior and interior): March 18, 1986

Located on the northeast corner of 45th Street and Fifth Avenue, the Fred F. French Building was constructed in 1926–27 as the corporate headquarters of the prominent real-estate firm of the same name. The building—once described as an exotic "business palace"—was a collaborative design by H. Douglas Ives, the French company's skilled head architect, and Sloan & Robertson, a firm responsible for some of the most distinguished skyscrapers in New York, including the Chanin and the Graybar buildings. The architects chose to work in an eclectic blend of Near Eastern, Egyptian, ancient Greek, and early Art Deco forms.

The Near Eastern allusion is enhanced by a dramatic series of setbacks. Although mandated by the building code of 1916, these wedding-cake-like tiers had a romantic corollary in the ziggurats, or step pyramids, of ancient Assyria. The building has a tripartite configuration: a three-story limestone base, a pyramidal midsection with numerous setbacks, and a rectangular tower that rises straight to the thirty-fifth floor before setting back with a triplex penthouse. The tower terminates with a water tower, elaborately masked by large faience bas-reliefs depicting a rising sun flanked by griffins and bees—symbols, respectively, of progress, integrity, and watchfulness, and industry and thrift. On the ground floor the building's two entrances and fifteen commercial bays are crowned by a segmented bronze frieze whose metopes carry winged Assyrian beasts. The bronze and polychromatic decorative details throughout contrast to splendid effect with the building's limestone trim and russet-colored brick walls.

Inside, a similar Near Eastern effect is produced in the vaulted lobby and the enclosed vestibule on East 45th Street through the use of polychromatic ceiling ornament, decorative cornices of ancient inspiration, and elaborate wall fixtures. Most splendid of all are the twenty-five gilt-bronze doors, where inset panels of women and bearded Mesopotamian genies symbolize various aspects of commerce and industry.

The building was innovative from a technical standpoint as well, with such modern devices as an electric plumbing system, excellent lighting and ventilation systems, and, most notably, an automatic self-leveling elevator system. As one of the earliest and loftiest towers on Fifth Avenue above 42nd Street, the Fred F. French Building is important for its creative response to the new building ordinance, its accomplished blend of lingering historicism and vanguard modernism, and its use of architecture to establish a distinctive corporate image.

Golden Theater.

Majestic Theater

Royale Theater

ROYALE, MAJESTIC, AND GOLDEN THEATERS
Manhattan
Architect: Herbert J. Krapp

Royale Theater, 1926–27
242–250 West 45th Street
Designated (exterior and interior):
December 15, 1987

Majestic Theater, 1926–27
245–257 West 44th Street
Designated (exterior and interior):
December 8, 1987

Golden Theater, formerly the
Theater Masque, 1926–27
252–256 West 45th Street
Designated (exterior and interior):
November 17, 1987

Herbert J. Krapp designed the Royale Theater, the Majestic Theater, and the Golden Theater for the Chanin Construction Company as part of a complex that included the Lincoln Hotel (now the Milford Plaza). In this group of theaters, Krapp opted for a romantic and eclectic look, which he called "modern Spanish." The façades all shared a rusticated terra-cotta base with a Roman-brick wall above, and Spanish Renaissance-inspired ornamentation.

Each of the theaters was designed for a different purpose. The Royale was the medium-sized one; intended for musical comedy, it has as seating capacity of 1,200. The interior was designed by Roman Melzer, who had once served as architect to Czar Nicholas II of Russia. The groin-vaulted ceiling is supported by arches with lunettes, which are decorated with murals by Willy Pogany entitled *Lovers of Spain*. Joseph F. Dujat-inspired plasterwork outlines the major interior architectural elements. In 1937 the Royale became a broadcast studio for CBS, but three years later the Shubert Organization took over the building and converted it back to a legitimate theater.

The Majestic, with 1,800 seats, was the largest theater in the complex, intended for the production of musicals and revues. The highlights of the interior include a single entrance for ticket holders and the use of a stadium design, which allowed for a clear view of the stage from all seats. The lobby and auditorium are decorated with classically inspired ornament. During its heyday, the Majestic was considered one of the most desirable places to stage a show.

The Golden, originally the Theater Masque, was intended for intimate drama, seating only 800. In 1937 the theater was turned over to director and producer John Golden, who managed it for almost a decade and renamed it for himself.

ST. JAMES THEATER, formerly the Erlanger Theater, 1926–27
246–256 West 44th Street, Manhattan
Architects: Warren & Wetmore
Designated (exterior and interior): December 15, 1987

The St. James Theater, built in 1926–27, was originally known as the Erlanger in tribute to its builder, producer Abraham Erlanger. The theater was the first designed by the prestigious firm of Warren & Wetmore, which designed Grand Central Terminal. This commission is indicative of Erlanger's determination to make the house named for him as handsome as possible.

The St. James was the last theater to be built in the two-block cluster known as Shubert Alley. The façade is done in relatively simple finished stucco with a cornice decorated by theatrical masks; the visual highlight is an elaborate wrought-iron loggia located above the main entrance.

The interior of the theater is also simple in comparison to some of its neighbors. The ornamentation, which is mainly applied to the ceiling area and the side boxes, was done with paint rather than plasterwork. Each box is framed by fluted Corinthian columns and topped by a lunette adorned by murals. The ceiling is decorated with trompe l'oeil paintings of swags and musical instruments.

The Erlanger was renamed the St. James when it was sold in 1932, shortly after Erlanger's death. It is now owned by the Jujamcyn Corporation.

NEIL SIMON THEATER, formerly the Alvin Theater, 1926–27
244–254 West 52nd Street, Manhattan
Architect: Herbert J. Krapp
Designated (exterior and interior): August 6, 1985

The Alvin Theater was built to stage the productions and house the offices of producers Alex Aarons and Vinton Freedley, from whose names the acronym "Alvin" was derived. The theater opened on November 22, 1927, with George and Ira Gershwin's *Funny Face*, featuring Fred and Adele Astaire. It has since been home to countless plays and musicals.

Krapp designed a Georgian Revival façade, asymmetrically divided into two sections: a five-story auditorium section and a six-story stage section. The floors above the auditorium contain offices, and those above the stage contain dressing rooms. The red-brick façade is highlighted by terra-cotta elements: seashell niches, urns, quoins, pediments, pilasters, panels, belt courses, and window hoods. A small, one-story tower with arched openings and a balustraded parapet rises above the roofline.

Krapp's interior is as elegant as his façade. The exquisite Adamesque plasterwork on the ceiling, boxes, and walls features sunbursts, wreaths, urns, and fluted pilasters. Characteristic of Krapp's theaters is the single balcony divided into tiers and walls that curve in toward the proscenium.

APPLE BANK FOR SAVINGS, formerly Central Savings Bank, 1926–28
2100–2114 Broadway, Manhattan
Architects: York & Sawyer
Designated: January 28, 1975

This powerful structure of gray Indiana limestone is a welcome transition from the open area at the West 72nd Street subway kiosk to the high-rise apartment houses immediately to the north. The most striking feature of the six-story elevations is the rusticated facing, which is quite heavy at the ground story but becomes lighter above the fourth-story cornice. Large, arched windows with pointed voussoirs mark the main banking hall within. A Tuscan pilastrade applied over shallow rustication and a loggia above terminate the composition. The whole is capped by a roof of Spanish clay tile. The interior is richly ornamented and dramatically lit from four sides.

In designing the bank, the architect—probably Philip Sawyer—retained the form, but altered the proportions of an Italian Renaissance palazzo. The result is unique and highly expressive; the scale of the windows to the surrounding masonry is particularly successful. The appropriately massive wrought-iron grills and gates are the work of Samuel Yellin. During the 1920s, York & Sawyer established themselves as specialists in bank design. In this as in their other work, the fortresslike quality projects an image of reassuring stability.

DUNBAR APARTMENTS, 1926–28
West 149th Street to West 150th Street, between Seventh and Eighth avenues, Manhattan
Architect: Andrew J. Thomas
Designated: July 14, 1970

The Dunbar Apartments, named for the famous black poet Paul Laurence Dunbar, was the earliest cooperative garden apartment complex in the city. The project, financed by John D. Rockefeller, Jr., was immediately recognized for its architectural excellence with the award in 1927 of first prize, for walk-up apartments, by the New York Chapter of the American Institute of Architects. An average room rented for $14.50 a month and attracted such famous tenants as W.E.B. Du Bois, Countee Cullen, and Bill ("Bojangles") Robinson.

The complex, containing a total of 511 apartments, consists of six independent U-shaped buildings clustered around a large interior garden court. The buildings alternate in height between five and six stories, with adjoining units projected and recessed. The varicolored Holland brick, decorative limestone, wrought-iron balconies, and terra-cotta roof ornament complete the decoration.

ED SULLIVAN THEATER INTERIOR, formerly Hammerstein's, 1927
1697–1699 Broadway, Manhattan
Architect: Herbert J. Krapp
Designated: January 5, 1988

Originally named Hammerstein's, the Ed Sullivan Theater was built in 1927 by
Arthur Hammerstein as a monument to his father, opera impresario Oscar Hammerstein.
Hammerstein employed Herbert J. Krapp to design the theater.

Krapp designed the theater in the Gothic style, which established the building as
architecturally unique among New York's theaters. The interior is based on a Gothic
cathederal: the ceiling is vaulted, with panels bearing brightly colored heraldic designs.
The theater vestibule and lobby are finished with bronze grills and imitation Travertine stone.
The floors are of rich marble, and stained-glass panels depict scenes from Oscar
Hammerstein's operas. A large organ was built for the orchestra pit. A lifesize sculpture of
Oscar Hammerstein by Pompeo Coppini occupies the central foyer.

After the initial excitement of the theater's opening, Arthur Hammerstein met with
financial trouble and was forced to sell the theater in 1931. After a number of failed
ownerships, the theater was converted into a casino and nightclub in 1934, and renamed
Billy Rose's Music Hall, after the well-known producer of the period. In 1949, CBS
converted the building into a television studio, which became the set for *The Ed Sullivan
Show*. On December 10, 1967, after nearly twenty years as the set for the show, the theater
was renamed the Ed Sullivan, marking the first time a Broadway theater had been named for
a television figure. In 1993 CBS repurchased and refurbished the theater to accommodate
David Letterman's late-night television talk show.

BEACON THEATER INTERIOR, 1927–28
2124 Broadway, Manhattan
Architect: Walter W. Ahlschlager
Designated: December 11, 1979

The Beacon, which took its name from the airplane beacon on its roof, is one of the last grand
movie palaces from the first generation of motion pictures. Earlier movie houses were simple
structures, often inserted into spaces designed for a different purpose. In the 1920s, as
improvements in film technology and the advent of sound films attracted larger audiences,
movie-house owners and film distributors began to compete with the live theater. Movie houses
became more elaborate, emulating the ornate interiors of live theaters and often increasing their
decorative richness beyond what conventional theater owners deemed appropriate.

In the Beacon, Walter W. Ahlschlager, a Chicago architect, combined a wide variety of
classicizing motifs into an overwhelming decorative ensemble, using deliberate spatial
manipulations such as the contrast between the low ceiling in the ticket lobby and the high-
ceilinged rotunda beyond. This visual drama was crucial to the merchandising approach of the
Beacon's manager, Samuel L. Rothafel (known as "Roxy"), who felt that "the patron must begin
to feel what might be called the spell of the theater before he reaches his seat." (Roxy also
managed New York's Rialto, Rivoli, and Capitol movie houses.) In association with the Chanin
Construction Company, Roxy elaborated movie-house programs by introducing music and
dancing, novel lighting effects, hundred-piece orchestral accompaniment, and up-to-the-minute
technical devices such as elaborate systems of stage elevators. All this contributed to the
Beacon's enormous success and set the pattern for the grand movie palace through the 1930s.

Patrons enter the theater through an open-air ticket lobby, under multicolored, Renaissance-
inspired moldings and ornate light fixtures. Inside the three-level auditorium, the proscenium
arch is flanked by thirty-foot statues of armed Greek women. The ceiling simulates a brightly
colored tent, while above the side wall exits are large murals that depict caravans of elephants,
camels, and traders.

HELMSLEY BUILDING, formerly the New York Central Building, 1927–29
230 Park Avenue, Manhattan
Architects: Warren & Wetmore
Designated (exterior and interior): March 31, 1987

This skyscraper counterpart to Grand Central Terminal was part of the Terminal City project, Cornelius Vanderbilt's scheme to rid Park Avenue of the exposed railroad tracks whose smoke, noise, and cinders made the neighboring real estate uninhabitable. With the electrification of the rail lines, trains could be submerged below ground and the reclaimed acreage used for revenue-producing structures. The New York Central Building was erected to house the offices of the railroad companies that used Grand Central.

The design of the building was guided by circulation requirements. The terminal was built in the center of Park Avenue, with the Pershing Square Viaduct connecting the northern and southern segments of the boulevard. A system of ramps and winding one-way roads provided circulation around the terminal and through the base of this building, which includes two pedestrian walkways as well.

The New York Central Building added a distinctive accent to the skyline and provided a royal setting for the railroad barons, its lobby lavishly ornamented with industrial imagery. Harry B. Helmsley bought the building in 1977 and has extensively cleaned and restored much of the building's ornate splendor.

BERESFORD APARTMENTS, 1928–29
211 Central Park West, Manhattan
Architect: Emery Roth
Designated: September 15, 1987

One of the largest and most imposing apartment houses along Central Park West, Emery Roth's Beresford was completed in 1929. Roth was then at the height of his career as a master of apartment house architecture, and the prominently sited building, across West 81st Street from the American Museum of Natural History, takes full advantage of its location with two monumental façades crowned by corner towers.

Executed in brick, with limestone and terra-cotta trim, the Beresford is distinctively ornamented with sculpture derived from late Renaissance precedents. Animating the walls are winged cherubs, angels, dolphins, rams' heads, cartouches, and rosettes. Its vast scale and dramatic profile make the Beresford one of the most important elements of the Central Park West skyline, as well as a provocative reminder of the heights speculative building could reach in Manhattan.

CHANIN BUILDING, 1927–29
122 East 42nd Street, Manhattan
Architects: Sloan & Robertson
Designated: November 14, 1978

The Chanin Building was erected as the headquarters of the Chanin Construction Company, a well-known New York development firm. It is an excellent example of Art Deco architecture and was the first major skyscraper to be built in the area around Grand Central Terminal, anticipating a major shift in the business district of the city. Other notable skyscrapers such as the Chrysler and Daily News buildings soon followed. Built in 1927–29 by the Chanin Construction Company, it was thought to be an efficient, up-to-date, progressive structure that would attract businessmen of its day.

Designed by the prominent architectural firm of Sloan & Robertson, the Chanin Building stands at the corner of Lexington Avenue and East 42nd Street and rises fifty-six stories in a series of setbacks culminating in a tower—in accordance with the 1916 building code. As was customary in skyscraper design, the architects were concerned with establishing a clearly defined base, which here is marked by terra-cotta plant forms. The lobby contains remarkably intricate detail, designed by Jacques Delamarre; he collaborated with the noted architectural sculptor René Chambellan on the design of the sculptural reliefs and bronze grills adorning the vestibules inside the building entrances. Expressing the theme of New York as "the city of opportunity," they tell the story of the success and achievements of Irwin S. Chanin. Major setbacks begin above the seventeenth story, forming a pyramidal base for the tower, which rises uninterrupted from the thirtieth to the fifty-second floor. The upper four stories of the tower are further recessed and accented with buttresses. The steel frame is clad with buff brick, terra-cotta, and limestone.

The Chanin Building continues to function as an office building.

WILLIAMSBURGH SAVINGS BANK, 1927–29
1 Hanson Place, Brooklyn
Architects: Halsey, McCormack & Helmer
Designated: November 15, 1977

Soaring 512 feet above Hanson Place, the Williamsburgh Savings Bank, with its striking silhouette and famous four-faced clock, is the most prominent feature of the Brooklyn skyline and the tallest building on Long Island. Built in 1927–29, the building, designed by the firm of Halsey, McCormick & Helmer, is the third erected by the Williamsburgh Savings Bank—one of the oldest financial institutions in Brooklyn.

The setback and the fine ornamental details and rich carving of the lower two stories are the Byzantine building's most striking features. The base of the building is polished rainbow granite, the first floor is Indiana limestone laid up in random-coursed ashlar, and the shaft is buff-colored brick and terra-cotta, rising in a series of setbacks. The crowning gilded copper dome was intended to recall the dome of the bank's first building, at 175 Broadway in Brooklyn, designed by George B. Post. The setbacks are accented by contrasting limestone trim, with the thirteenth and the twenty-sixth floors set off by the use of round arches and a continuous decorative terra-cotta band. Beneath the dome is the famous illuminated four-faced dial clock, one of the largest in the world.

BARRYMORE THEATER, 1928
243–251 West 47th Street, Manhattan
Architect: Herbert J. Krapp
Designated: November 4, 1987; interior designated November 10, 1987

The Barrymore Theater is the latest of the surviving theaters built for the Shubert Organization in the Broadway district. Constructed in 1928, it was designed by Herbert J. Krapp. At the time of its construction, the Shubert Organization was the dominant force in theatrical production and ticket sales in the country; the theater was erected to honor the Shuberts' star performer, Ethel Barrymore.

Built during the pre-Depression prosperity of the 1920s, the Barrymore was a lavish and decorative theater. The façade features an enormous terra-cotta grillwork screen; at the base of this screen were two large bronze and glass canopies, which unfortunately no longer exist. The interior of the theater is designed in a mock-Elizabethan style. Raised plasterwork in a strapwork pattern, elaborate ornamental treatment of the theater boxes, and a coved ceiling with a thirty-six-foot-wide dome and cut-glass chandelier are the outstanding features.

The theater opened to rave reviews—both of the architecture and the initial production, *The Kingdom of God*, starring Ethel Barrymore.

MARK HELLINGER THEATER, formerly the Hollywood Theater, 1929
217–239 West 51st Street, Manhattan
Architect: Thomas Lamb
Designated: January 5, 1988; interior designated November 17, 1987

The Mark Hellinger Theater, formerly the Hollywood Theater, was built by Warner Brothers in 1929 at the advent of sound movie production. The Hellinger was the last of the grand movie palaces constructed in Times Square in the 1910s and '20s, and it is the only surviving theater of its type today.

Designed by Thomas Lamb in a grand, opulent style, the Hellinger—and other movie palaces like it—was intended to evoke the glamour of the world's most exotic locales, and to create an atmosphere of luxurious fantasy that would enhance the make-believe world of the cinema. The interior is based on Baroque church design. The grand foyer includes eight fluted Corinthian columns, gilded plasterwork, an oversized chandelier, and a ceiling mural of nymphs and clouds. The main auditorium is an extension of the foyer, also with elaborate plasterwork, murals, and chandeliers.

The exterior of the Hellinger shares no stylistic similarities with the Baroque interior; it is, instead, a reflection of the modernistic architectural trends of the period. Lamb used elements of early-twentieth-century buildings to construct a unique façade. The monumental paired sculptural figures at the entrance and the corbeling effect in the brick pattern of the façade are similar to those of Finnish architect Eliel Saarinen's well-known Helsinki Railroad Station. The flat, projecting overhang and ribbed corbels of the western wing are reminiscent of Frank Lloyd Wright's Unity Temple in Oak Park, Illinois, plans of which were published in architectural magazines in the late 1920s.

The theater opened in 1930 and was converted to a legitimate stage theater in 1934. It was renamed in 1949 in honor of the columnist, playwright, and former Warner Brothers producer, Mark Hellinger (1903–1947).

RKO KEITH'S FLUSHING THEATER INTERIOR, 1927–28
135–29 to 134–45 Northern Boulevard, Queens
Architect: Thomas Lamb
Designated: February 28, 1984

The RKO Keith's Flushing Theater is one of the few surviving buildings of the "movie palace" era, which reached its peak in the short period between World War I and the Depression. Part of the vaudeville circuit founded by B. F. Keith, later the Radio-Keith-Orpheum circuit (RKO), this theater opened in 1928 to an audience of subscription holders. Thomas Lamb, who designed hundreds of theaters, movie palaces, and auditoriums in almost every major American city, as well as in Canada, Europe, and Australia, designed the Keith's. This building is one of a handful that Lamb designed in the "atmospheric style"—a type of design for theaters that aimed at producing an illusion of open, outdoor spaces.

The grandeur of the 3,000-seat theater is seen not just in the auditorium, but also in the grand foyer, ticket booth hall, mezzanine promenade, and lounges. The walls of the auditorium—the theater's main interior space—were built up as stage sets representing a Spanish-style townscape in the "Mexican-Baroque" or so-called Churrigueresque style, an eighteenth-century modification of the Italian Baroque with Moorish and Gothic decorative elements. Among the Keith's elaborate "atmospheric" features are its murals, gilded wood and plasterwork, a bright blue ceiling with electric "stars," and a special machine projecting "clouds" moving across the ceiling—completing the illusion of a Spanish outdoor garden.

FULLER BUILDING, 1928–29
593–599 Madison Avenue, Manhattan
Architects: Walker & Gillette
Designated (exterior and interior): March 18, 1986

A fine example of the Art Deco skyscraper, the Fuller Building was designed by the prolific firm of Walker & Gillette and built in 1928–29 as the home office for one of the largest and most important construction firms in America. Of the many tall office towers erected in midtown during the late 1920s and early 1930s, the Fuller Building was one of the first to be located so far north in Manhattan.

In an unusual arrangement responding to the character of the neighborhood, the building's first six floors were designed to house high-quality shops and art galleries. The mixed use of the building is reflected in its design; the black granite cladding of the lower floors surrounds large display windows for retail shops, while above this the office floors are faced in light stone with smaller window openings. In a modernistic interpretation of classical forms, bold geometric patterns at the setbacks and at the top of the building take the place of cornices; these forms are complemented by a large sculpture over the front doors by the noted modern sculptor Elie Nadelman.

The richly decorated first-floor interior enhances this elegant Art Deco skyscraper. To symbolize the client's position in the construction field, as well as this building's place in the building boom, the architects used the theme of construction in their design of the magnificent lobby. Stylized classical motifs are joined with modernistic geometric patterns, executed in bronze and marble. On the floor of this elegant interior are promotional mosaics representing major monuments of the Fuller Company.

FILM CENTER BUILDING INTERIOR, 1928–29
630 Ninth Avenue, Manhattan
Architect: Ely Jacques Kahn
Designated: November 9, 1982

The Film Center Building's interiors are among New York City's most colorful and inventive surviving Art Deco ensembles. Walls and ceilings are treated as woven plaster tapestries, a motif that the architect, Ely Jacques Kahn, often used. He may have been influenced by Frank Lloyd Wright's California textile block houses, which were built in the mid-1920s; Kahn was in fact friendly with Wright. In any case, both shared an interest in Mayan architecture, which seems in a general way to lie behind their work.

One enters the rectangular outer vestibule from the Ninth Avenue façade. Here, an ornamental plaster band runs across the ceiling and down the two side walls in a stepped, upside-down triangle articulated in low-relief panels. The lobby is beyond a second set of doors. Its ceiling is articulated with a geometric pattern that also continues partway down the walls. The colors and shapes lead one to the elevator bays straight ahead. The walls in this area are horizontally banded with light and dark stone; this design is repeated on the elevator doors, directory board, and mailbox. The mosaic work is particularly noteworthy.

While New York has lost most of its Art Deco interiors, the Film Center Building lobby has survived largely intact, and is one of Kahn's most splendid productions. The exterior is less exciting, although the small touches of colored terra-cotta produce a subtle coloristic effect. Although much film industry activity has now left New York, this building continues to function in its original capacity.

GENERAL ELECTRIC BUILDING, formerly RCA Building, 1929–31
570 Lexington Avenue, Manhattan
Architects: Cross & Cross
Designated: July 9, 1985

The General Electric Building, famous for its pinnacled tower, is one of the monuments of the Art Deco style in New York City. Designed by Cross & Cross and erected in 1929–31, the fifty-story building exemplifies the Gothic mode of the Art Deco style; its design is expressive of its function as the headquarters of the Radio Victor Corporation of America (RCA), which by the late 1920s was at the forefront of the radio and communications industry.

The building is a tall, eight-sided tower, articulated with piers and recessed spandrels, rising from a base that completely fills the relatively small site. The symbolic signature of Cross & Cross, in imagery tailored to RCA, is found in the bolts and flashes that crackle from the building's surface and the monumental allegorical deities—expressing the power of radio—found just below the tower's pinnacled crown of gold-glazed tracery.

The primary material of the exterior is orange and buff brick, which harmonizes gracefully with the adjacent St. Bartholomew's Church. The streamlined piers, commencing at the base, send the eye upward. Patterns of electrical bolts adorn the spandrels, and the buttresses, pinnacles, tracery, and repeated Gothic features are executed in a streamlined Art Deco mode.

Over fifty years after its construction, the building continues as a striking corporate symbol—as appropriate to the General Electric Company as it was to RCA.

SAN REMO APARTMENTS, 1929–30
145–146 Central Park West, Manhattan
Architect: Emery Roth
Designated: March 31, 1987

One of New York's last grand apartment houses of the pre-Depression era, the San Remo was designed by Emery Roth, and is a distinctive feature of the Central Park West skyline. The Multiple Dwelling Act of 1929 allowed apartment houses of large ground area to rise to a greater height, and permitted the use of setbacks and towers. The San Remo, the first of the vast twin-towered West Side apartment houses, was designed in response to this law.

Emery Roth had received a number of important commissions prior to World War I, but it was the prosperity of the 1920s that carried him into a period of great achievement. Developers such as the Bing Brothers and Harris H. Uris retained Roth to design medium-height structures that the architect dubbed "skyscratchers." Originally designed to conceal water towers, Roth's towers evolved into a major element of his designs.

The main block of the San Remo is seventeen stories high, with terraced setbacks from the fourteenth to seventeenth floors. Two symmetrical towers, each ten stories high, are surmounted by elaborate structures that culminate in circular temples with lanterns to give the building a dramatic profile. The building is executed in light brick, over a three-story base of rusticated limestone. The architectural detailing in stone, terra-cotta, and metal is late Italian Renaissance in character. Balustrades, pilasters, engaged columns, broken pediments, garlands, urns, cartouches, scrolls, consoles, and rondoles are all employed to highlight entrance and window configurations.

The San Remo has had an illustrious sixty-year history, and today it continues in the tradition of New York's grand apartment houses.

ELDORADO APARTMENTS, 1929–30
300 Central Park West, Manhattan
Architects: Margon & Holder; Emery Roth (consultant)
Designated: July 9, 1985

The northernmost of the four twin-towered apartment houses that give Central Park West its distinctive skyline, the Eldorado extends along Central Park West between West 90th and 91st Streets. The Eldorado was designed in 1929 by the firm of Margon & Holder, with Emery Roth as consultant; it is one of the finest and most dramatically massed Art Deco residential buildings in the city.

The form of the building, with its massive base and twin towers set at the Central Park West corners, closely resembles the massing of Roth's San Remo, which was also completed in 1930. The Eldorado towers rise free of the base—seventeen stories, of which the bottom three are yellow cast stone—for twelve stories; each is six bays wide on Central Park West and faced with tan brick. Futuristic rocketlike pinnacles crown each tower, and an angular frieze runs above the third floor. There are stylized brick spandrel panels below many of the windows, and angular balconies with zigzag panels. The tripartite entrance on Central Park West consists of three faceted portals with bronze frames, each surmounted by a pair of ornamental plaques embossed with geometric and floral Art Deco motifs.

Construction of the Eldorado coincided with the stock market crash of 1929, which led to the collapse of the real-estate market. Despite financial and labor problems, the building was completed in 1930, but the owners experienced rental problems and finally defaulted on loan payments. The Eldorado has attracted many residents of note, particularly people associated with the arts, such as Milton Avery, Richard Dreyfuss, Faye Dunaway, Carrie Fisher, Tuesday Weld, Richard Estes, Groucho Marx, and Marilyn Monroe.

SOFIA APARTMENTS, formerly Kent Automatic Parking Garage, 1929–30
34–43 West 61st Street, Manhattan
Architects: Jardine, Hill & Murdock
Designated: April 12, 1983

This impressive brick and terra-cotta building was erected in 1929–30 as one of the two Kent Automatic Parking Garages, which used a patented automatic parking system with an electrical "parking machine" that engaged cars by their rear axles and towed them from the elevator platform to parking spots.

Designed by the firm of Jardine, Hill & Murdock, the Kent Automatic Parking Garage is a splendid Art Deco building. The client most likely chose the progressive style, with its implications of modernity, to indicate the innovative nature of the new parking garage housed within the building.

Twenty-four stories high with setbacks on the fifteenth, twenty-first, and twenty-third stories of its main Columbus Avenue façade, the building has an elaborate two-story entrance decorated with Aztec-inspired motifs in polychromatic terra-cotta. The upper stories are simply articulated with orange brickwork, black horizontal brick bands delineating the stories, and slightly projecting vertical brick piers defining the central window bays. The crenellated parapet areas of each setback, including the roof, are capped by cream and royal blue terra-cotta and cast-stone ornament, echoing the ornament of the main entrance.

The garage operated until 1943, when the Sofia Brothers Warehouse purchased the building. In 1983–84, the building was converted into apartments.

CENTURY APARTMENTS, 1930–31
25 Central Park West, Manhattan
Architect: Irwin S. Chanin
Designated: July 9, 1985

The Century Apartments, extending along Central Park West between West 62nd and 63rd streets, is one of four twin-towered apartment houses built along the west side of the park between 1929 and 1931. Together these give the avenue its distinctive silhouette. Irwin S. Chanin of the Chanin Construction Company developed two of them: the Century, and the Majestic (1930) at West 71st Street.

The Century was the last grand apartment house built during the redevelopment of Central Park West. Known as Eighth Avenue until 1880, Central Park West was first developed as a residential area after the building of Central Park; larger apartment houses were erected on the avenue, and row houses on the side streets. Building stopped around 1910. The second generation of Upper West Side apartments was erected in the 1920s; by 1931 the Depression had ended this boom.

In 1925 Chanin visited the Paris Exposition Internationale des Arts Décoratifs et Industriels Moderns—where the Art Deco style had its first major unveiling. On his return, he became one of the first American architects to apply the design sensibility espoused at the Exposition. The earliest Art Deco buildings by Chanin were commercial skyscrapers; the style was applied to apartment towers only late in the 1920s, the Century being among the first.

The thirty-story building shows a complex balance of horizontal and vertical elements. The horizontal banding of tan and light brown brick, the long corner windows, and the cantilevered balconies contrast with the vertically articulated bowed window bays in the towers. The sparse exterior ornament is used to highlight major points of emphasis in the design, such as the entrance, setbacks, and crowns.

CHRYSLER BUILDING, 1928–30
405 Lexington Avenue, Manhattan
Architect: William Van Alen
Designated (exterior and interior): September 12, 1978

The Chrysler Building, a stunning statement in the Art Deco style by architect William Van Alen, embodies the romantic essence of the New York skyscraper. Built in 1928–30 for Walter P. Chrysler, it was "dedicated to world commerce and industry." For a few months after it was built—until the completion of the Empire State Building in 1931—the 1,046-foot structure was the tallest building in the world.

The skyscraper originally designed for the site by Van Alen was an office-building project for William H. Reynolds, a real-estate developer and former New York state senator. Publicized as embodying the newest principles in skyscraper design, the Reynolds building was to rise sixty-seven stories (808 feet) and "to be surmounted by a glass dome, which when lighted from within, will give the effect of a great jewelled sphere."

In 1928 Chrysler, who was aggressively expanding his company and seeking to break into real estate, took over the project and lease. No corporate funds were used to finance the project, which Chrysler said he built so that his sons would have something for which to be responsible.

Work began on the Chrysler Building on October 15th of that year, and construction proceeded rapidly. Van Alen altered the original design of the building, doing away with the "jewelled sphere" and substituting a spire, which he called a "vertex." Chrysler himself took credit for suggesting that the building be taller than the 1,024½-foot Eiffel Tower; he also allegedly urged Van Alen to win the race to build the world's tallest building. It is suspected, however, that Van Alen had his own reasons for achieving this goal: his rival and former partner, H. Craig Severance, was at the time constructing the Bank of Manhattan (40 Wall Street) with the aim of making that the world's tallest building. Thinking that the Chrysler Building would be only 925 feet high, Severance added a fifty-foot flagpole to his project, making it 927 feet. Meanwhile, Van Alen had kept secret his design for the 185-foot Chrysler spire, which was delivered to the building in five sections and clandestinely assembled on the sixty-fifth floor. In November 1929 it was finally raised into position by a 20-ton derrick through a fire tower in the center of the building, then riveted into place; the whole operation took about ninety minutes.

The seventy-seven-story building, constructed in a series of setbacks in compliance with the building code of 1916, quickly captured the popular imagination. Some observers rejected it—Lewis Mumford criticized its "inane romanticism . . . meaningless voluptuousness, . . . [and] void symbolism"; but most saw it as Eugene Clute described it in the magazine *Architectural Forum*—as an "expression of the intense activity and vibrant life of [their] day . . . teeming with the spirit of modernism."

The ornamentation of the Chrysler Building is justly famous. A procession of idealized automobiles in white and gray brick, with mudguards, hubcaps, and winged radiator caps of polished steel, spans the frieze above the twenty-sixth floor of the façade. Other levels of the building also show automobiles, eagles, acorns, and gargoyles, all made of stainless steel. The walls and floor of the lobby are patterned in multicolored marble and granite from around the world. On the ceiling, a mural by Edward Trumball depicts the building itself, airplanes of the period, and scenes from the Chrysler Corporation's factory assembly line. There are thirty passenger elevators, with doors of wood veneer on steel; the interiors are decorated with wood inlays.

The Massachusetts Mutual Life Insurance Company purchased the Chrysler Building in 1975. The company invested $23 million in beginning a renovation that was completed by Jack Kent Cooke, the cable television and sports magnate, who bought the building in 1979. Once again, the Chrysler Building is the supreme Art Deco skyscraper, an aesthetic as well as commercial beacon of progress.

MUSEUM OF THE CITY OF NEW YORK, 1929–30
1220–1227 Fifth Avenue, Manhattan
Architect: Joseph H. Freedlander
Designated: January 24, 1967

Inspired by the Musée Carnavalet, which presents the history of Paris, the Museum of the City of New York was founded in 1923. The purpose of the museum was to create a love for, and interest in, all things particular to New York. Gracie Mansion was the first home of the museum, but the organization did not flourish there. So after over $2 million was raised—from such New Yorkers as John D. Rockefeller, Jr., and Edward S. Harkness—a new building was proposed on Fifth Avenue.

Joseph H. Freedlander's design for a five-story building in a modern adaptation of Georgian colonial architecture was selected from a competition of proposed designs. The finished building opened for inspection on December 17, 1930, and attracted a great deal of publicity. After receiving many gifts and collections, the museum opened to the public on January 11, 1932.

A short entrance walk leads from the street to a landscaped garden forecourt. A projecting four-story façade with a four-columned Ionic portico contains the main doorway. The columns support a low-pitched pediment containing the sculpted shield of the City of New York. White marble cornerstones accent the joints between the main building and its wings. The central portico is also distinguished from the surrounding brick mass by the use of elegant, white marble facing. Bronze sculptures of Alexander Hamilton and De Witt Clinton set into niches ornament the Fifth Avenue entrance of the building.

The Museum of the City of New York is one of the world's foremost museums of urban history and culture. It offers a wide variety of public programs, including walking tours and gallery displays of the extensive permanent collection.

PARK PLAZA APARTMENTS, 1929–31
1005 Jerome Avenue, The Bronx
Architects: Marvin Fine (elevations); Horace Ginsberg (layout)
Designated: May 12, 1981

The Park Plaza is one of the finest Art Deco apartment houses in the Bronx. Its designers, Marvin Fine and Horace Ginsberg, knew of and synthesized the major elements of the new skyscraper style being developed in Manhattan by Raymond M. Hood and William Van Alen, and adapted them to the low-rise apartment houses of the city's residential neighborhoods. The Park Plaza was a pioneering work, representing a major departure in scale and design from the surrounding buildings.

The eight-story building is divided into five sections, each six bays wide; the blocks are separated by recessed courtyards and connected by a continued section at the rear. Each block is defined by its window arrangement, brick patterns, small towerlike massings at the roofline, and terra-cotta banding. The Art Deco influence is apparent in the arrangement of brick and window bays as vertical shafts and in the use of polychromatic terra-cotta friezes with geometric decorative motifs. Traces of earlier building styles include the monochrome brick and the flat surface façade—with none of the later Art Deco curved wall surfaces or polychrome brick patterns. Large terra-cotta scenes under the windows show an architect presenting a model of his building to the Parthenon, as if to ask, "What do you think?" These scenes suggest that for the architect, the final judge was still classical antiquity.

DAILY NEWS BUILDING, 1929–30; addition, 1958
220 East 42nd Street, Manhattan
Architects: Howells & Hood; addition, Harrison & Abramovitz
Designated: July 28, 1981

Commissioned by the *Daily News*'s founder, Captain Joseph Patterson, the Daily News Building is home to this country's first successful tabloid. Dubbed the "servant girl's Bible" by competitors, the paper's circulation passed the one million mark in 1925, making it New York's best-selling paper.

Raymond M. Hood claimed that the Daily News Building's design was almost entirely determined by utility, but the façade is ornamented. The pattern of reddish-brown and black bricks in the horizontal spandrels evokes pre-Columbian art as well as contemporary Art Deco style. The white-brick piers echo those on earlier Gothic-style skyscrapers, such as Cass Gilbert's Woolworth Building. Unlike the designs of these and other tall buildings—which treat the elevation in three stages corresponding to the base, shaft, and capital of a classical column— the Daily News Building rises in a sequence of monolithic slabs. The termination of each setback is abrupt, without any cornice to interrupt the soaring vertical planes. As a result, the whole appears almost weightless, especially from a distance. Henry-Russell Hitchcock and Philip Johnson admired this effect, and included the building in the Museum of Modern Art's 1932 exhibition, "The International Style," among the more radically reductivist works of European modernists like Mies van der Rohe and Walter Gropius. The main entrance is set in a limestone slab, incised in low relief and lit up at night by neon light bars on each side.

The printing annex, added by Harrison & Abramovitz in 1958, is a sympathetic response to the older building. While the original building remains in excellent condition, Harrison & Abramovitz dramatically altered the splendid chrome and faceted black glass lobby in 1958. Inside, the large, slowly revolving globe and glass dome give some idea of Hood's futuristic concept.

LYCEE FRANÇAIS DE NEW YORK, formerly the
Mrs. Graham Fair Vanderbilt House, 1930–31
60 East 93rd Street, Manhattan
Architect: John Russell Pope
Designated: June 12, 1968

Designed in the manner of Louis XV, the Lycée Français building at 60 East 93rd Street is reminiscent of the small *maison particulière* at Versailles. Designed by John Russell Pope, the house is built entirely of finely detailed stone and is completely symmetrical except for the arched doorway, finished in rustic style and set back at the right side of the house. Details to note include the three high French windows crowned by keystones, each bearing the face of a different woman.

Mrs. Graham Fair Vanderbilt, the former wife of William K. Vanderbilt, Jr., occupied the house for a number of years before selling it in the late 1940s to Mrs. Byron C. Foy (Thelma Chrysler). For a time it served as the Romanian Permanent Mission to the United Nations, and it is now one of several landmark buildings that make up the Lycée Français de New York.

EMPIRE STATE BUILDING, 1930–31
350 Fifth Avenue, Manhattan
Architects: Shreve, Lamb & Harmon
Designated (exterior and interior): May 19, 1981

Its name, its profile, and the view from its summit are familiar around the world. The final and most celebrated product of the skyscraper frenzy produced by the economic boom of the 1920s, the Empire State Building was completed in 1931 on the former site of the Waldorf-Astoria Hotel; it marked the transformation of midtown from an affluent residential area into the commercial center of the metropolis. The building's design, engineering, and construction were remarkable accomplishments. Although it was in many ways shaped by constraints of time, cost, and structure, the Empire State Building is the finest work of architect William Lamb, designer for Shreve, Lamb & Harmon.

At 1,250 feet, the Empire State Building was the world's tallest tower until 1973 when the World Trade Center was erected. The Empire State was planned by John J. Raskob, multimillionaire executive of General Motors, as a speculative office building; unlike the Woolworth Building or the Chrysler Building, it was not meant to symbolize one man or one company, but simply to be a conglomerate of rentable commercial spaces. Raskob named Al Smith, four-time governor of New York State, to be president of the Empire State Company—an appointment that aroused extensive journalistic attention. The race to build the world's tallest structure had become somewhat of a publicity stunt in itself by the late 1920s, and the aggressive campaign created further sensation with the announcement that the mast atop the tower would be used as a mooring for dirigibles.

By the 1920s commercial architecture was being shaped largely by economic and engineering considerations. The aim was to have the maximum amount of rentable space. The spareness and economy of design of the Empire State Building reflected this new practicality. Its eighty-six-story elevation (the tower and mast add another fourteen) is organized around a series of setbacks whose general massing was determined by the elevator system. The exterior façade is covered in limestone, granite, aluminum, and nickel, with a minumum of Art Deco ornament.

The lobby, entrance halls, and elevator concourses are covered in restrained gray and red marble, heightened by bright metal and simply decorated silver ceilings. At the end of the main entrance hall on Fifth Avenue, an aluminum image of the Empire State Building with a rising sun behind it is superimposed on a map of New York State.

The Empire State Building is immensely imposing, epitomizing the enormous surge of skyscraper construction in New York City in the early part of the twentieth century. For most of the world, the Empire State Building remains the quintessential skyscraper.

NEW YORK COUNTY LAWYERS' ASSOCIATION BUILDING, 1930
14 Vesey Street, Manhattan
Architect: Cass Gilbert
Designated: November 23, 1965

The New York County Lawyers' Association Building is one of the lesser-known works of New York architect Cass Gilbert, designer of the U.S. Custom House. Constructed of stone in 1930, it is an example of Georgian Revival architecture.

The symmetry and bas-relief ornament of the front façade lend an imposing quality to the four-story structure. Above the smooth ashlar masonry base are five bays decorated by panels that incorporate garlands and classical figures. These bays are separated by pilasters with flattened capitals. The fourth story roof deck and attic are surrounded by a cornice crowned with a balustrade.

STARRETT-LEHIGH BUILDING, 1930–31
601–625 West 26th Street, Manhattan
Architects: Russell G. and Walter M. Cory
Associate Architect: Yasuo Matsui
Consulting Engineers: Purdy & Henderson
Designated: October 7, 1986

The Starrett-Lehigh is a massive factory building that occupies the entire block bounded by West 26th and 27th streets and Eleventh and Twelfth avenues. A cooperative venture of the Starrett Investing Corporation and the Lehigh Valley Railroad, the building originally served as a freight terminal for the railroad, with manufacturing and warehouse space above.

The Starrett-Lehigh Building is considered New York's great monument of Modernism. A structurally complex feat of engineering with an innovative interior arrangement, the nineteen-story building is most notable for its exterior design of horizontal ribbon windows alternating with brick and concrete spandrels. An irregular open framing system of steel columns and girders was used on the ground floor to accommodate curving railroad spurs and loading docks for trucks. Above the mezzanine level, the framing system consists of a regular arrangement of concrete mushroom columns carrying concrete floor slabs; these slabs are cantilevered beyond the outer columns, creating largely unobstructed spaces. Direct access was provided to each floor by truck elevators that exit to loading platforms. The specially designed, multipane steel sash windows provide maximum sunlight.

The railroad ended its association with the building in 1944, following the decline of freight railroads in the Northeast. The building continues to be used for warehousing, manufacturing, and office space.

162–24 JAMAICA AVENUE, formerly J. Kurtz & Sons Store Building, 1931
Queens
Architects: Allmendinger & Schlendorf
Designated: November 24, 1981

The old Kurtz Store is a striking Art Deco–style commercial building in downtown Jamaica, Queens. It was erected in 1931 as a retail store for the furniture chain of J. Kurtz & Sons, which occupied it until 1978. The company commissioned Allmendinger & Schlendorf to create a thoroughly modern and colorful building, to arrest the eye of those passing by on the elevated train, which then ran along Jamaica Avenue, and to reflect the contemporary quality of the furniture displayed there. A compact six stories high, the building bears decorative motifs in the form of tapered pylons in contrasting colors and materials that rise on the two main façades; these, and the skyscraperlike designs originally painted on the windows, show a clear connection to the Art Deco skyscrapers constructed in Manhattan at the same time. Despite the presence of strong horizontal lines, the vertical emphasis of the decoration dominates the façade, creating a building that is impressive beyond its size.

GROUP HEALTH INSURANCE BUILDING, formerly the McGraw-Hill Building, 1930–31
330 West 42nd Street, Manhattan
Architects: Hood, Godley & Fouilhoux
Designated: September 11, 1979

Sometimes affectionately referred to as the "jolly green giant," the McGraw-Hill Building is one of New York's great modern buildings, and one of the very few structures in the city to have been included in Henry-Russell Hitchcock and Philip Johnson's 1932 exhibition, "The International Style."

McGraw-Hill, the huge publishing company, decided to build its headquarters on 42nd Street west of Eighth Avenue partly in the hope of seeing land values rise there and partly out of the need to be in a neighborhood zoned for industrial use. Skyscrapers never caught on in the neighborhood, and the green tower has commanded the skyline of the far West Forties virtually alone for most of the building's life.

Raymond M. Hood designed the building with numerous setbacks on the north and south sides. From the east and west, the setbacks produce a stepped tower profile, but from the north and south they are invisible, creating the illusion that the building is a slab. Each story has a horizontal band of windows that look like "ribbon windows," but which are actually composed of seven sets of four double-hung windows each, separated by painted metal strips. The window bands are separated by continuous courses of blue-green terra-cotta blocks, the varying size and tone of which produce a somewhat shimmering effect.

The color of the terra-cotta sheathing was completely without precedent. The shade finally selected was said to be John Herbert McGraw's own choice. Above the thirty-fourth-story windows rise eleven-foot-high terra-cotta letters spelling out the name McGraw-Hill. The top two stories have horizontal ribs that form a distinctive pylonlike crown.

Apparently, Hood had no intention of designing a modern building. His emphasis on the practical, on utility and function, worked well given the building code of 1916 that applied to setbacks and towers on broad bases; the resulting masterpiece combines two separate profiles—one a graceful Art Deco tower and the other an International Style slab. Indeed, the building is a blend of Art Deco and the International Style, a transitional step between two approaches to architectural design.

McGraw-Hill left in 1970 and moved to new headquarters at Rockefeller Center. The building lay empty for four years, then was taken over by Group Health Insurance in 1974. It was, for five years, the location of the New York Landmarks Conservancy offices.

RCA Building

Sunken Plaza with Statue of *Prometheus*

RCA Building, interior

Maison Française

ROCKEFELLER CENTER

Manhattan

Architects: Hood, Godley & Fouilhoux; Corbett, Harrison & MacMurray;
Reinhard & Hofmeister; Carson & Lundin
Designated (exterior of entire complex): April 23, 1985

Radio City Music Hall, 1931–32
1260 Avenue of the Americas
Interior designated March 28, 1978

RCA Building, 1931–33
30 Rockefeller Plaza
Interior (ground floor) designated April 23,
1985

1270 Avenue of the Americas, formerly the
RKO Building, 1931–33

Promenade and Channel Gardens, 1931–34

Sunken Plaza with Skating Rink and statue of
Prometheus, 1931–34

British Building, formerly the British Empire
Building, 1932–33
620 Fifth Avenue

RCA Building West, 1932–33
1250 Avenue of the Americas

Maison Française, 1933
610 Fifth Avenue

International Building, including statue of
Atlas in courtyard, 1933–34
630 Fifth Avenue
Interior (ground floor) designated April 23,
1985

1 Rockefeller Plaza Building, formerly the
Time & Life Building, 1936–37

Associated Press Building, 1938
50 Rockefeller Plaza

10 Rockefeller Plaza Building, formerly the
Eastern Airlines Building, 1939

Simon & Schuster Building, including
addition, formerly the U.S. Rubber
Company, 1939, 1954–55
1230 Avenue of the Americas

Warner Communications Building, formerly
the Esso Building, 1946–47
75 Rockefeller Plaza

Radio City Music Hall

Rockefeller Center is the single greatest civic gesture of twentieth-century New York architecture. Its unprecedented scope, visionary plan, and brilliant integration of art and architecture have never been equaled. Initiated as a project to create a new home for the Metropolitan Opera Company, it was completed as an exclusively commercial project by John D. Rockefeller, Jr., after the stock market crash of 1929 forced the opera's withdrawal. Throughout the Depression, the construction of Rockefeller Center provided jobs for hundreds of laborers in the building industries.

The complex originally extended just over three full city blocks, from West 48th to 51st streets between Fifth and Sixth avenues. Within this area, three major axes define the circulation patterns. The first is along Fifth Avenue, and the second is the Promenade and Channel Gardens that run east to west from Fifth Avenue to Rockefeller Plaza. This planted alley slopes gently downhill to culminate in the Sunken Plaza with the statue of *Prometheus*. The intersection of these two axes forms the main façade of the complex and interacts with neighboring buildings to create a notably human-scaled space; the focus at one end is on the RCA Building and at the other on St. Patrick's Cathedral. The third important axis is Rockefeller Plaza, a private north-south street that was one of the first attempts (and the only successful one) to circumvent the grid system of streets that characterizes upper Manhattan. Rockefeller Plaza intersects the center at mid-block, providing functional access to the buildings at the heart of the complex. Minor axes run along West 49th and 50th streets and define the perimeter of Rockefeller Center at West 48th and 51st streets and the Avenue of the Americas.

Rockefeller Center is asymmetrical, its buildings designed to conform to the needs of the original tenants. Yet the control of materials and stylistic expression exercised ensured that even the most recent additions bear some contextual resemblance to the rest of the complex. This was Raymond M. Hood's triumph, a vindication of his belief in an expressive modern aesthetic that

Warner Communications Building

Simon & Schuster Building

International Building

did not refer to styles of the past. Here is the refinement of the slab style of skyscraper hinted at in his American Radiator and McGraw-Hill buildings. The structures are all sheathed in limestone with aluminum trim. The windows are grouped vertically in slightly recessed strips that emphasize the soaring quality of even the lowest building in the group. On the RCA Building, this soaring quality was enhanced by an elaborate series of setbacks and terraces, which allowed the building to conform to zoning regulations while giving it a profile distinct from those of its more Baroque contemporaries.

The architecture and the public spaces of Rockefeller Center are further enhanced by the works of art that were incorporated from the start. The statues of *Atlas* at the International Building and *Prometheus* in the Sunken Plaza, the tympanum panel of *Wisdom* at 30 Rockefeller Plaza, and the sculptural elements that terminate the vertical stone piers at the buildings' bases all combine to animate the exteriors of what might otherwise be austere compositions.

BRYANT PARK, renovated 1934, 1988–
Bounded by West 42nd Street, Avenue of the Americas, West 40th Street, and
New York Public Library, Manhattan
Architect: Lusby Simpson
Designated: November 12, 1974

Located just west of the New York Public Library, the land where Bryant Park is now has had a colorful history. The city used it during the 1820s as a potter's field. The Crystal Palace—which housed the New York Exhibition of 1853—was built on the site and burned spectacularly in 1858. During the Civil War, the site was used as a drilling and tenting ground. In 1847 the land was designated a park. In 1884 its name was changed from Reservoir Square, after the adjoining Croton Reservoir, to Bryant Park in honor of editor and abolitionist William Cullen Bryant. In the late 1890s the reservoir was removed from the adjacent plot and replaced with the New York Public Library, which opened in 1911. Thomas Hastings, one of the building's architects, designed the apselike structure that covers Herbert Adams's 1911 statue of Bryant and stands today at the park's east end.

Disturbance of the park by the construction of the subways prompted calls in the 1920s for its renovation. In 1933, the Architects' Emergency Commission sponsored a competition for a new park design. Lusby Simpson was awarded the $100 prize, and his design was implemented within six months. The park was dedicated on September 15, 1934.

Simpson's design included moving Lowell Fountain, which had been dedicated to the memory of Josephine Shaw Lowell by her sister in 1912, across the park to its present location at the west entrance. The fountain, which was designed by architect Charles A. Platt, is New York's first great public monument to a woman.

Today, Bryant Park is once again undergoing an extensive rehabilitation and redesign. Scheduled to reopen sometime in 1990, Bryant Park will have two restaurant pavilions and four kiosks, as well as new lighting and extensive perennial gardens. The architects for the renovation are Hardy Holzman Pfeiffer Assoc. and Hanna-Olin Limited. When the work is complete, Bryant Park will once again be a place where New Yorkers can find respite amid the towering structures and traffic of midtown Manhattan.

BRONX COUNTY COURTHOUSE, 1931–34
851 Grand Concourse, The Bronx
Architects: Joseph H. Freedlander and Max Hausle
Designated: July 13, 1976

The Bronx County Courthouse is a handsome example of government-funded architecture commissioned during the New Deal. Architects Max Hausle and Joseph H. Freedlander, in cooperation with sculptors and artisans, designed this building, which combines bold, modern massing with Neoclassical elements.

The nine-story courthouse stands on a massive, rusticated granite platform, which elevates it dramatically. A broad balustraded terrace surrounds the building on all sides. A monumental hexastyle portico is located in the center of each façade. The building is notable for its integration of a twentieth-century architectural style with figural sculptural adornment. A fine frieze sculpted by Charles Keck celebrates the activities of the universal working man. Flanking each entry are two freestanding figural groups, carved in pink marble, by Adolf A. Weinman.

LESCAZE HOUSE, 1933–34
211 East 48th Street, Manhattan
Architect: William Lescaze
Designated: January 27, 1976

Known as the first truly "modern" residence in New York City, the Lescaze House incorporated many elements indicative of later trends in urban planning. These include central air-conditioning, the use of glass bricks, and a large skylight to admit light to the living room, as well as the extension of outdoor living space to both the rooftop and rear of the house. Simplicity remains the dominant feature throughout; Lescaze was a devout follower of the French architect Le Corbusier, whose geometric precision, sharp edges, and smooth surfaces had a deep influence on his own work.

Set between deteriorating brownstones of the post–Civil War period, this building retains their modest scale and cornice line, but little else. Huge glass-block panels dominate the third and fourth floors; separated only by a narrow strip of wall, they encompass almost the entire width of the building. Ribbon windows with casements accentuate the elegant curve of an otherwise austere stucco front. On the ground floor, a solid glass-brick wall designates Lescaze's office. Designed to serve as both workplace and residence, the building reflects the architect's basic philosophy—to meet the needs of the individual from the inside out.

FIRST HOUSES, 1935–36
29–41 Avenue A, 112–138 East 3rd Street, Manhattan
Architect: Frederick L. Ackerman
Designated: November 12, 1974

First Houses was the first municipal housing project undertaken by the New York City Housing Authority and the first low-income, public housing project in the nation. Begun as a rehabilitation program to abolish the long-standing problems of the slums of the Lower East Side, First Houses commenced as an experiment in the partial demolition of existing tenements on the site.

Originally planned for 122 families, First Houses consists of eight four- and five-story brick buildings, largely rebuilt, laid out in an L-shaped plan around an inner yard. The apartments were designed to maximize light and air, and all had steam heat, hot water, and modern amenities. The minimal ornamentation is in a simplified Art Deco style. The paved courtyard is enlivened by freestanding and applied animal sculpture, designed by artists associated with the Federal Artists Program. Today, the First Houses continue to be a great source of pride to the city. The project attracts an ethnically and demographically mixed tenantry, and the rentals are still priced according to income.

FORT TRYON PARK, 1931–35
Manhattan
Architects: Olmsted Brothers
Landscape architect: Frederick Law Olmsted, Jr.
Designated: September 20, 1983

Fort Tryon Park, an outstanding example of landscape architecture in the English Romantic tradition by the notable firm of Olmsted Brothers, represents a continuation of the picturesque New York City public park legacy initiated with the construction of Central Park. The property was given to the city, along with the Cloisters, by philanthropist John D. Rockefeller, Jr. Built in 1931–35 on more than sixty acres, Fort Tryon has some of the highest open public land in the city, overlooking the Hudson River and the Palisades. Fort Tryon Park was the last park in the city designed by Olmsted.

The site is rich in history. It was named for General William Tryon, the last British colonial governor of New York. During the Revolution, the British built Fort Tryon here, clearing the hills for firewood. Evacuated in 1783, its military history came to an end, but the name remained. In the nineteenth century, several prominent persons built large estates on the land; Rockefeller purchased many of these in 1917 and donated them to the city.

Fort Tryon Park is a brilliant response to the geographical difficulties of its rocky site and represents a skillful integration of its various elements, including views of the Hudson River and the Palisades and remnants of nineteenth-century estates.

SMITHERS ALCOHOLISM TREATMENT AND TRAINING CENTER, formerly the
William Goadby Loew House, 1932
56 East 93rd Street, Manhattan
Architects: Walker & Gillette
Designated: March 14, 1972

Erected during the Depression, the Loew residence was the last of the large private town houses to be built in the city. Once home to wealthy socialite stockbroker William Goadby Loew, its restrained but elegant use of ornament recalls the English Regency style.

Although framed in steel, the three-story structure displays a smooth ashlar masonry façade with a rusticated English basement. Joined to the house are two-story projecting wings with arched Palladian windows. Together, they create a shallow forecourt at the center surrounded by an ornamental low stone wall.

Tall windows and an entrance portico accentuate the first floor, above which rests a slightly projecting central bay with a high, recessed arch. Within this arch, radial fluting enframes a bull's-eye window—a motif echoed in the Palladian windows as well. On the third floor, the smooth plane of the main mass contrasts strikingly with the sparse use of decorative detail. Four of the five rectangular windows have no ornament; the central window contains a crossetted frame and keystone. Set behind a parapet, a roof with dormer windows completes the structure.

The house is now the Smithers Alcoholism Treatment and Training Center, a division of St. Luke's–Roosevelt Hospital Center.

U.S. COURTHOUSE, 1933–36
Foley Square, Manhattan
Architect: Cass Gilbert
Designated: March 25, 1975

The U.S. Courthouse, begun in 1933, was the last building designed by noted American architect Cass Gilbert, designer of the Woolworth Building. Gilbert died in 1934 while the courthouse was under construction, and his son Cass Gilbert, Jr., completed it.

The thirty-one-story building is divided into three parts, reflecting the principal features of a column: base, shaft, and capital. The base of the building is irregularly shaped, expressing the shape of the lot. The back of the structure, facing Cardinal Place, is rounded. Ten four-story-high unfluted Corinthian columns make up the colonnaded portico on Foley Square. The square main tower is set back from the base and rises twenty stories above it. Surmounting the seventeenth story, a dentiled cornice sets three stories that are treated as a unit, and topped by a pierced stone parapet with urns at the corners, emphasizing the setback. A shallow cornice and low attic story crown the topmost section supporting the pyramidal roof, with eagles at the corners connected by simple low parapets.

Unfortunately, Gilbert died before the interior detail was completed; thus there are few spaces reflecting the sensitive use of color that appears in his watercolors, sketchbook, or previous buildings. Noteworthy, however, is the bronzework on the entry doors and elevators, which is compatible with the plaster and wood details.

One of the last Neoclassical office buildings erected in New York, and also one of the earliest skyscrapers built by the federal government, the U.S. Courthouse at Foley Square illustrates an important turning point in American architectural history.

THE BRONX POST OFFICE, 1935–37
560 Grand Concourse, The Bronx
Architect: Thomas Harlan Ellett
Designated: September 14, 1976

Thomas Harlan Ellett's design for the Bronx Post Office combines classical simplicity with the sleekness of Modernism. The approach to the building is marked by a broad, shallow staircase, flanked by bronze flagpoles, that mounts to a granite, balustrade-enclosed terrace. The building's plain, smooth exterior is lined with tall, elegant arched windows and doors in a manner that suggests a classical arcade. White marble enframes the openings, and a pale stone belt course crowns the structure to provide subtle contrast to the cool gray brick of the façade. Two monumental sculptures— *The Letter* by Henry Kreis and *Noah* by Charles Rudy—flank the three central arched entranceways, and are the façade's only ornamentation.

In contrast to the simple exterior, the interior lobby is richly decorated with thirteen murals of scenes with American workers, painted in 1939 by Ben Shahn and his wife, Bernarda Bryson.

THE CLOISTERS, 1934–38
Fort Tryon Park, Manhattan
Architect: Charles Collens
Designated: March 19, 1974

The Cloisters, which opened to the public in May of 1938, is a division of the Metropolitan Museum of Art, and houses a portion of the museum's medieval art collection. The noted sculptor George Grey Barnard acquired what would become the core of this collection in travels through Europe. He assembled, in addition to works in the decorative and fine arts, a large number of medieval architectural fragments. In 1925 John D. Rockefeller, Jr., made a donation to the Metropolitan Museum of Art to purchase this collection, and five years later he obtained the entire area that now forms Fort Tryon Park. After having set aside a four-acre site at the northern end for a museum building dedicated to medieval art, he gave all this property to the city.

Rockefeller hired Charles Collens, of the Boston firm of Allen, Collens & Willis, to design a structure that would integrate Barnard's collection within a sympathetic architectural setting. Earlier, Collens had designed Riverside Church for Rockefeller, as well as the additions to the adjacent Union Theological Seminary.

The Cloisters is not a copy of a particular medieval building. It is planned around the architectural elements of various buildings from the cloisters of five French monasteries that date from the twelfth to fifteenth centuries. At the center of the museum is the largest cloister, reconstructed with fragments from the monastery of St. Michel-de-Cuxa in southwestern France. The high tower overlooking this cloister is the most prominent feature of the entire complex; it was modeled after the tower at the same monastery. In May, 1988, the Cloisters celebrated its fiftieth anniversary with the opening of the Treasury.

The modern construction elements fit seamlessly with the ancient work: the finish and pattern of each new stone block were copied from medieval examples. The massive exterior walls are made of millstone granite from New London, Connecticut; the interior from Doria limestone, quarried outside Genoa, Italy.

The rocky outcrop on which the Cloisters stands is reminiscent of the remote and wild locations of many medieval monasteries. The plantings in the adjacent gardens and within the Cloisters are also based on medieval precedents. The museum's terraces provide excellent views of the Hudson River and the Palisades. The park and museum together create one of the most beautiful spots in all of Manhattan.

ROCKEFELLER APARTMENTS, 1935–37
17 West 54th Street and 24 West 55th Street, Manhattan
Architects: Harrison & Fouilhoux
Designated: June 19, 1984

The Rockefeller Apartments, built in 1935–37, were designed by the firm of Harrison & Fouilhoux and are a major example of the International Style, an architecture that synthesized the new currents in Europe—the functional aesthetic, new building techniques, and the use of industrial materials—with a concern for public housing.

Commissioned by John D. Rockefeller, Jr., and Nelson Rockefeller, the Rockefeller Apartments represent architect Wallace K. Harrison's first independent venture after the death of his former partner, Raymond M. Hood. The building is also the first of Harrison's many architectural collaborations with Nelson Rockefeller.

The apartments were built to provide accommodation near Rockefeller Center for well-to-do executives and professionals; their design displayed a concern for light and air unprecedented in apartment house design. The mid-block site, stretching from West 54th to 55th streets, is linked by a landscaped courtyard intended to ensure that sunlight reached all apartments. The complex is made up of two separate buildings, each eleven stories high; the buildings were designed to work as a unit, with slight variations in the façades creating a dramatic symmetry. The two façades differ in the number and height of the vertical cylindrical bows and in the orientation of these bows' glazed surfaces.

Harrison's window detailing of the Rockefeller Apartments is one of the buildings' most significant features. All of the steel casement windows are placed on the outer edge of the bond to ensure the continuity of the wall surface. The structural steel skeleton of these buildings is enclosed by smooth, tawny-colored bricks. The only adornment is the shadow cast by the unconventional vertical bows.

The Rockefeller Apartments changed the standards in New York City apartment house planning. The buildings allowed 15 percent more space for light and air than required by law and set a precedent of integrity and simple elegance in apartment design.

NORMANDY APARTMENTS, 1938–39
140 Riverside Drive, Manhattan
Architects: Emery Roth & Sons
Designated: November 12, 1985

The Normandy Apartments, overlooking the Hudson River, is one of the outstanding apartment buildings on Manhattan's Upper West Side. Erected in 1938–39 by Emery Roth, the Normandy is one of this noted architect's last works, as well as the last of the distinguished monumental apartment houses built prior to World War II.

The design of the Normandy shows the combined influence of the Italian Renaissance Revival and Art Deco styles of the 1930s. Occupying an entire blockfront on Riverside Drive, the nineteen-story Normandy is twin-towered (a Roth signature) and is characterized by streamlined curves and sweeping horizontal lines. The building is further defined by large, horizontally arranged rows of windows set close to the façade surfaces. The Renaissance-inspired detail includes a limestone base articulated with horizontal striations suggesting the rusticated stonework typical of Italian palazzi, flat pilasters with decorative capitals, and balustraded parapets. Original steel casements survive in most of the windows, and the placement of the corner windows follows the curve of the building.

Highly visible, meticulously designed, and still largely intact, the Normandy symbolizes the grand era of twentieth-century urbanism.

THE BRONX GRIT CHAMBER OF THE WARD'S ISLAND SEWAGE TREATMENT WORKS, 1935–37
158 Bruckner Boulevard, The Bronx
Architects: McKim, Mead & White
Engineers: Fuller & McClintock
Designated: June 8, 1982

The Bronx Grit Chamber is a primary component of the Ward's Island Sewage Treatment Works, New York City's first major project to alleviate the pollution of local waters. By the early twentieth century, pollution of the region's waters had become a serious problem, and in 1914 the Metropolitan Sewerage Commission recommended a sewage plant on Ward's Island in the East River. In 1928 the engineering firm of Fuller & McClintock, using the new technology of activated sludge, began the design for the sewage treatment plant, which was subsequently completed by the city. Construction commenced in 1931, was temporarily halted by the Depression, and resumed in late 1935 with a federal Public Works Administration grant.

The care and attention devoted to the exterior design of the grit chamber make it one of the most unusual industrial structures in the city. Hired as architectural consultants, McKim, Mead & White created an exterior within the tradition of monumental public buildings, for which the firm is best known. Four colossal rusticated pilasters flanking each side of a monumental arch dominate the symmetrical front façade on Bruckner Boulevard. The pedimented main entrance contains the seal of the City of New York.

The Grit Chamber still serves its original function, today under the jurisdiction of the New York City Bureau of Water Pollution Control.

MARINE AIR TERMINAL, 1939–40
La Guardia Airport, Queens
Architects: Delano & Aldrich
Designated (exterior and interior): November 25, 1980

The Marine Air Terminal and its accompanying hangar (now demolished) were built specifically to serve the Pan American Clippers—large seaplanes that made the first transatlantic flights from La Guardia after 1939. This explains the terminal's site, close to the water's edge, as well as the imagery of the exterior frieze of stylized flying fish. The airfield and terminal together were one of the most ambitious and expensive projects of the Works Progress Administration, which worked here in conjunction with the New York City Department of Docks and the architectural firm of Delano & Aldrich.

William A. Delano, who was responsible for the terminal's design, specialized in Federal and Renaissance Revival luxury residences. For such a thoroughly new building type he turned to a newer style. The use of colored terra-cotta, steel, abstract classical elements such as cornices, and a symmetrical plan and entrance façade are all typical of the Art Deco style. The simplified glazing bars and the austere, unmolded brick surfaces reflect tendencies commonly called Moderne; this style was particularly popular for transportation facilities and roadside architecture.

The main entrance to the south is the most monumental and stylish of the three projecting pavilions. At the rear, in a Y arrangement, are two lower wings that link the waiting room with the Clippers' boarding ramps. The waiting room, the central core of the building's circular plan, is decorated with rich materials: dark green marble walls, patterned gray marble floors, stainless-steel doors, and handsome wooden benches inlaid with a propeller blade motif lend this room extraordinary elegance. The uninterrupted span and curved walls produce the feeling of space greater than the room's actual size.

A magnificent mural, entitled *Flight*, rings the entire room; it is the work of James Brooks, the well-known WPA muralist and later Abstract Expressionist. The curved canvas panels depict the genesis of modern aviation in mythology and history, from Icarus and Daedalus to Leonardo da Vinci, the Wright Brothers, and the Pan Am Clippers themselves. The mural was covered over during a refurbishment in the 1950s. It has recently been restored and was rededicated on September 18, 1980.

HARLEM RIVER HOUSES, 1936–37
West 151st to 153rd streets, Macombs Place to Harlem River Drive, Manhattan
Architects: Archibald Manning Brown, with Charles F. Fuller, Horace Ginsberg, Frank J. Foster, Will Rice Amon, Richard W. Buckley, John Louis Wilson and Michael Rapuano. Landscape architect: Heinz Warnecke, assisted by sculptors T. Barbarossa, R. Barthe, and F. Steinberger
Designated: July 22, 1975

Harlem River Houses were the first housing project in New York City to be funded, built, and owned by the federal government. Erected in 1936–37, the complex consists of three complexes of four- and five-story buildings grouped around open, serpentine landscaped courts embellished with sculpture. It was made possible by the collaborative efforts of the New York City Housing Authority and the federal government, and was described as "a recognition in brick and mortar of the special and urgent needs of Harlem." Lewis Mumford exuberantly stated that the project offers "the equipment for decent living that every modern neighborhood needs: sunlight, air, safety, play space, meeting space, and living space. The families in the Harlem Houses have higher standards of housing, measured in tangible benefits, than most of those on Park Avenue."

Occupying nine acres, two-thirds of which were kept open, the simple, straightforward red-brick buildings are unornamented save for raised brick belt courses at the bases of the buildings and broad, steel-framed casement windows. The community-oriented project included a nursery school, health clinic, wading pool, stores, social rooms, and play areas. In the summer of 1937, more than 11,000 people applied for the 574 apartments available in the new project. About a dozen of the original tenants still live there. After fifty years, the Harlem River Houses are still a remarkably gentle oasis.

GEORGE AND ANNETTE MURPHY CENTER FOR SPORTS AND ARTS,
formerly the Municipal Asphalt Plant, 1941–44
Franklin D. Roosevelt Drive at East 90th to 91st streets, Manhattan
Architects: Kahn & Jacobs
Designated: January 27, 1976

Built in 1941–44, the former Municipal Asphalt Plant was designed by the prominent New York architects Ely Jacques Kahn and Robert Allan Jacobs. Constructed of reinforced concrete in the form of a parabolic arch, the asphalt plant was an innovative and radical design in its day—the first of its kind built in the United States.

The plant was built to produce asphalt for the streets of Manhattan and replaced another that had opened on the same site in 1914. Although it was to be an industrial structure, a standard industrial design was not desired; the Manhattan borough president wanted the new plant to be given an architectural treatment that would blend harmoniously with the East River Drive and the residential developments in the area. The architects began with the idea of a conventional rectangular building but the parabolic arch proved to be more economical. The four arched ribs are spaced twenty-two feet apart, each rising to a height of eighty-four feet and with a span of ninety feet. These support a barrel vault constructed of concrete panels. The side walls are pierced by steel sash windows about a third of the way up.

In 1968 when asphalt production for all five boroughs was consolidated at a plant in Queens, operations ceased at the plant. In 1972, the site—through the efforts of a community group called the Neighborhood Committee for the Asphalt Green—was converted into a much-needed youth center for sports, arts, and recreation. The plant was renamed the George and Annette Murphy Center for Sports and Arts, and the outdoor area, including an artificial-turf playing field, running track, and basketball courts, is called the Asphalt Green. On additional property to the north, the group plans to build a swimming pool and sports training center.

MANUFACTURERS HANOVER TRUST COMPANY BUILDING, 1950–52
600 Fifth Avenue, Manhattan
Architects: Carson & Lundin
Designated: April 23, 1985

The Manufacturers Hanover Trust Building, originally the 600 Fifth Avenue Building, was built in 1950–52. The last addition to the Rockefeller Center complex, it replaced the Collegiate Reformed Church of St. Nicholas. Designed by the firm of Carson & Lundin, this structure takes the form of a nineteen-story tower set on an L-shaped, seven-story base. In its scale, use of materials, detail, and setbacks, the architects created a design that is compatible with Rockefeller Center. The first major tenant was the Sinclair Oil Co., and the building was also known for many years as the Sinclair Building. Its purchase by Rockefeller interests in 1963 rounded out the center's site. In more recent years, the building has taken the name of its current tenant, the Manufacturers Hanover Trust Company.

LEVER HOUSE, 1950–52
**390 Park Avenue, Manhattan
Architects: Skidmore, Owings &
Merrill
Designated: November 9, 1982**

Lever House was the first skyscraper to use the postwar International Style in corporate architecture. Designed by Gordon Bunshaft of Skidmore, Owings & Merrill for the Lever Brothers Company, the building set a new standard for the modern steel and glass skyscraper.

Lever House is comprised of a vertical tower of steel and glass rising from a horizontal base of the same material; the overall effect is of a streamlined, minimal structure. Proponents of the International Style—including Le Corbusier, Walter Gropius, and Mies van der Rohe—stressed volume (as opposed to mass), sought regularity in design, and shunned the use of architectural ornamentation. The fixed window/walls of the building make up almost its entire exterior. Their horizontal direction, offset by the vertical stainless-steel mullions, creates a regular, boxlike pattern across each façade and achieves an exposed, skeletal effect. Because so much surface area is taken up by windows, the building is completely transformed from an opaque structure in daylight to a transparent one at night. Another innovative feature is the colonnaded space that extends from the sidewalk, creating open space for public use. The building was one of the first with a window-washing system that uses a small gondola suspended from miniature railroad tracks on top of the building.

In addition to its architectural interest, Lever House was significant for other reasons. Its construction marked the beginning of the transformation of Park Avenue from a boulevard of small masonry buildings to an imposing street of large glass and steel office buildings. Lever House is also a corporate symbol: Lever Brothers produced soaps and detergents, and the building was intended to convey an image of cleanliness characteristic of the company's products. Finally, Lever House also brought fame to Skidmore, Owings & Merrill, who were credited with developing a building both architecturally innovative and tailored to the needs of the client.

THE LANDMARKS OF NEW YORK, 1988 TO 1992

HENDRICK I. LOTT HOUSE, east wing, 1720; main section and west wing, 1800
1940 East 36th Street, Brooklyn
Architect: Unknown
Designated: October 3, 1989

Built eight years after his marriage into the socially prominent Brownjohn family, Hendrick Lott's new house integrated characteristics of the traditional Dutch Colonial frame house with the symmetrical composition and architectural details of the fashionable Federal style. For the east wing, Lott used the kitchen he had removed from the house built in the village of Flatlands in Kings County by his grandfather Johannes Lott, a prosperous farmer and member of the New York Colonial Assembly from 1727 to 1747. The older wing is readily identified by its low doorway, steeply pitched roof, twelve-over-eight window sashes, and small scale. The west wing's larger scale and porch, formed by posts that support the eaves, are typical of later construction.

Unlike many other houses of the period, this house retains its original southern orientation on the site, with sufficient surrounding property to give some sense of its original setting. Hendrick Lott's home contains some of the oldest surviving elements of any Dutch Colonial house in Brooklyn, with the exception of portions of the Pieter Claesen Wyckoff House. The house was occupied by members of the Lott family until the 1980s.

90–94 MAIDEN LANE BUILDING, c. 1810–30; new façades and internal alterations, 1870–71
Manhattan
Designers: Attributed to Charles Wright for Michael Grosz & Son, iron founders; iron elements cast by Architectural Iron Works of New York
Designated: August 1, 1989

This small and elegant building with a cast-iron façade is the sole remaining example of the French Second Empire style in a post–Civil War commercial building constructed in the financial district. It is the southernmost cast-iron building in Manhattan.

The building has long been associated with the Roosevelt family, which owned a store at 94 Maiden Lane from 1796 to the mid-nineteenth century. In 1810 James Roosevelt erected a mercantile structure next door, which has been incorporated into the present building. Under the direction of Cornelius Van Schaack Roosevelt, grandfather of future president Theodore (1901–9), the business—importing hardware, plate glass, and mirrors—prospered handsomely. In 1870, to accommodate the growing business, Roosevelt & Son—as the company was known—expanded into adjoining buildings at 90–92 Maiden Lane and 9–11 Cedar Street. A new cast-iron façade with a fish-scale mansard roof was erected on the Maiden Lane buildings, and a new brick-and-iron façade on the Cedar Street side. Charles Wright, an architect known for his cast-iron buildings, is credited with carrying out these alterations.

Since 1910 the building has undergone several modifications. The arrangement of windows and doors on the first story has changed several times, and the mansard roof was altered in the 1960s. The building is presently owned by the Fire Company's Corporation.

HENRY HOGG BIDDLE HOUSE, late 1840s
70 Satterlee Street, Staten Island
Architect: Unknown
Designated: May 1, 1990

Set high on a bluff, commanding panoramic views of Raritan Bay, this house is a superb example of the response of Staten Island builders to the high-style Greek Revival homes built by wealthy Manhattan merchants in the 1830s. Dramatic two-story, Doric-columned porticoes in the front and rear are combined with spring eaves, a design originating in France and used on Staten Island since the arrival in the seventeenth century of Huguenots fleeing religious persecution.

Henry Biddle Hogg, born in New York City around 1806, changed the order of his name in 1828 to become Henry Hogg Biddle, and soon after moved to Staten Island. There he married Harriet Butler, the daughter of a wealthy landowner, innkeeper, and ferry operator. Biddle's profession is unknown; it was his wife's inheritance that provided him with the means to become involved in a number of real-estate transactions. His fortunes fluctuated until the 1840s when he began to prosper from developing the village of Stapleton and by selling off small plots of land from the Butler farm.

Set back on two waterfront acres, Biddle's house reflects his improved financial status. The double-height porticoes used on the front and rear of his home create an imposing effect, whether approached from the street or the waterfront. The long approach drive, fences, and plantings further enhance the dramatic character of this unusual site.

5, 7, 9, 19, 21, 23 WEST 16TH STREET, c. 1845–46
Manhattan
Architect: Unknown
Designated: May 1, 1990

As Manhattan expanded northward in the 1840s, the area west of Union Square and above 14th Street, then delineating the city's upper limit, became a prosperous neighborhood of mansions and fine row houses. Built in the Greek Revival style that dominated American architecture in the 1840s, these elegantly proportioned brick-front row houses are distinguished by an eared and battered entrance surround. This feature, executed in stone, was initially derived from Egyptian sources and was a popular element of the Greek Revival style. A commanding presence on the street, numbers 5, 7, and 9 have generous street frontage and unusual curved bowfront exteriors, more commonly found on early-nineteenth-century houses in Boston.

At least a dozen houses on the block were planned and probably built by businessman Edward S. Mesier. A restrictive agreement regulated their appearance and use to ensure that the area developed as an enclave of fine residences. These elegant and simple houses, now divided into apartments, recall an early stage of a neighborhood that has since been largely transformed by commercial use.

359 BROADWAY BUILDING, 1852
Manhattan
Architect: Unknown
Designated: October 16, 1990

This early Italianate commercial building, constructed in the heart of a once-fashionable shopping district, the Ladies' Mile, is known for its most prominent occupant, photographer Mathew B. Brady. Later to become renowned for his photographs of the Civil War, Brady had previously operated one of New York's finest daguerreotype portrait studios in the top three stories of the building. Trained in photography by painter and inventor Samuel F. B. Morse, Brady—like the many other photographers along lower Broadway who capitalized on the novelty of the medium—catered to society ladies, who felt at ease amid the rosewood, velvet, and gilt appointments of his studio.

Equally lavish outside, this five-story building faced in stone was embellished with a profusion of ornamentation and set a precedent for picturesque stacked window openings, presaging their use in the cast-iron façades of the later 1850s, 60s, and 70s.

Toward the end of the century, as uptown became more fashionable, the neighborhood changed from a premier shopping district to a textile manufacturing and wholesaling zone. Today number 359 houses a textile concern and the Tibet Center, a religious and cultural organization.

160 EAST 92ND STREET HOUSE, 1852–53
Manhattan
Architect: Attributed to Albro Howell, carpenter-builder
Designated: June 7, 1988

This two-and-a-half-story clapboard dwelling is a rare remnant of the early years of Yorkville, a village that began as a stop along the Boston Post Road in the eighteenth century and was later settled by Irish immigrants who worked on Central Park and Manhattan's railroads. The structure is one of only six intact wooden frame houses on the east side of Manhattan. (While many houses built on the outskirts of the city during this period were of frame construction, the building of wooden structures in Manhattan itself was banned, due to fire hazard.) As development of the Upper East Side pushed northward in the 1880s–90s, masonry row houses and tenements filled in empty lots and replaced older frame buildings. Most probably built by Albro Howell, a local carpenter and builder who was active in developing this block in the heart of what was then a vigorous working-class community, the house comprises elements of both Greek Revival and Italianate styles.

In 1914 the house was purchased by Willard Dickerman Straight, a diplomat and financier, and his wife, the former Dorothy Paine Whitney, a philanthropist and social activist. Together they founded *The New Republic* in 1914, and the house served as living quarters for their staff until it was sold in 1942. The four fluted Corinthian columns of the front porch were replaced by the Straights in a 1929–31 renovation. Jean Schlumberger, an internationally prominent jewelry designer who maintained a salon at Tiffany & Co., owned the building from 1956 to 1987.

GUSTAVE A. MAYER HOUSE, 1855–56
2475 Richmond Road, Staten Island
Architect: Unknown
Designed: March 21, 1989

Situated on the crest of a hill, this Italianate villa overlooks grounds that recall the original landscaping. Originating in England as part of the Picturesque movement, the Italianate villa style had been introduced to the United States about twenty years before this house was built. The house was designed for the enjoyment of vistas. Its informal and secluded setting was in accordance with the Picturesque school's emphasis on texture, variety, and intricacy in landscape design. The structure consists of a two-and-half-story cube capped by a square belvedere and is encircled on three sides by a single-story timber porch. The construction typifies the then-revolutionary—and economical—balloon-framing system, which replaced hewn joints and massive timbers with quickly assembled nailed joints and boards. The importance of this well-preserved house is magnified by the scarcity of surviving rural residences in New York City.

Gustave Mayer, a German-born confectioner—known for inventing the Nabisco sugar wafer—bought the villa in 1889 and moved his family and small business there. Mayer used the basement for performing experiments, creating holiday decorations, making birch beer, and inventing a room humidifier that he later patented. Today his descendants still occupy the house.

ACTORS STUDIO, formerly the Seventh Associate Presbyterian Church, c. 1858
432 West 44th Street, Manhattan
Architect: Unknown
Designated: February 19, 1991

The Actors Studio building, with its painted brick façade adorned with smooth pilasters and topped by an undecorated pediment, is a fine and rare example of a vernacular Greek Revival structure. It was designed by an architect-builder for the Seventh Associate Presbyterian Church, a small working-class congregation formed in 1855.

In a period of expansion, 1825 to 1857, when Manhattan's population grew by 300,000, the number of churches in the city soared from 84 to 290. During this boom, the west side of Manhattan, particularly near the water's edge, seemed to attract the necessary but undesirable elements of urban life: garbage dumps, stables, slaughterhouses, factories, and distilleries. The nearby commerce from piers and railroad tracks also brought a rough crowd to the neighborhood which soon came to be known as Hell's Kitchen. There the small congregation—it began with only fifty-five members—maintained the building until 1944, when it officially disbanded.

The Actors Studio has occupied the building since 1955. The "Method" acting technique taught at the studio is based on the Moscow Art Theater director Konstantin Stanislavsky's teachings, which emphasize the use of an actor's personal experiences to portray dramatic characters. This acting style was promoted in the United States by Lee Strasberg, longtime artistic director of the Actors Studio. Distinguished studio graduates include Marlon Brando, Robert De Niro, Marilyn Monroe, Julie Harris, Paul Newman, Joanne Woodward, Montgomery Clift, and Eli Wallach.

CONDICT STORE, 1861
55 White Street, Manhattan
Architects: John Kellum & Son; iron components by Daniel D. Badger
Designated: March 22, 1988

Commissioned by cousins John Eliot and Samuel H. Condict as a store and warehouse for their saddlery business, this cast-iron Italianate building is among the dozen or so "sperm candle" designs remaining in New York, so-called because their tall, slender columns are reminiscent of candles made from sperm-whale oil. Its vertical and open design, unique to New York, was the forerunner of the modern skyscraper. The large plate-glass windows that allowed for well-lit interiors brought the term "window-shopping" into vogue. The structure's corner site permitted a unique one-bay return, which continues the articulation of the cast-iron façade fabricated by Daniel D. Badger. The utilitarian iron rolling shutters in the rear have been retained, as have the iron pilasters—bearing the illustrious Badger foundry plaques—that frame the basement and first floor.

Originally a blacksmith, Badger became second in importance only to James Bogardus as a manufacturer and promoter of this distinctively American building material and method of construction. Cast iron's strength, lightness, economy, durability, and fire-resistance won it popularity. Badger's firm began fabricating full cast-iron façades in 1856 and shipped them throughout the United States and abroad until Badger retired in 1873.

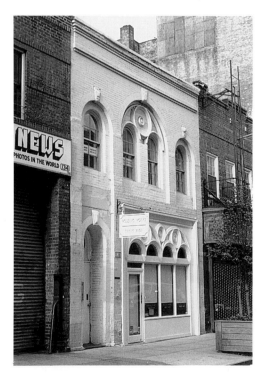

WEST 18TH STREET STABLES, 1864
126, 128, 130–132, 136, 140–142 West 18th Street, Manhattan
Architect: Unknown
Designated: December 11, 1990

For private transportation in New York, a horse and a carriage were necessities before Eli Olds began the mass production of automobiles in 1901. While most New Yorkers either rented horses or boarded their own in large commercial stables, the very wealthy maintained private stables built next to their homes. In the early 1860s, stables were usually erected a few blocks away from residential areas so the noises and smells would not disturb the character of exclusive neighborhoods. This remaining row of stables on 18th Street is an early example of the once-numerous streets devoted to private stables and commercial liveries during the late-nineteenth and early twentieth centuries.

All the stables in the row—there were originally thirteen—were designed in the *Rundbogenstil* (round-arched style), which came to the United States from Germany and central Europe in the 1840s with the immigration of German and central European architects. Incorporating Romanesque and Renaissance details, the style was characterized by an emphasis on flat wall surfaces and crisply executed architectural elements, such as the large central arch with a pair of inscribed arches and a bull's-eye tympanum that can be seen on this façade. The typical interior consisted of a ground-floor front room for carriages, a coachman's quarters above, and, in back, horse stalls topped by a hayloft.

319 BROADWAY BUILDING, 1869–70
Manhattan
Architects: D. & J. Jardine
Designated: August 19, 1989

This exquisite cast-iron building is the single survivor of a mirror-image pair built for Civil War hero and Croton Aqueduct engineer General Thomas A. Davies. Because of their location off Thomas Street, the pair of Italianate buildings was referred to as the Thomas Twins until number 317 was demolished in 1971. Characteristically, this Broadway building has a flat, corniced roof atop numerous arched windows, which—framed by colonettes and pilasters—create a lively façade.

The buildings were constructed to house a bank and offices on land leased by General Davies from the New York Hospital, which was formerly adjacent to this site. (Thomas Street was once the carriage drive into the grounds of the hospital.) Davies hired as architects David and John Jardine, brothers whose practice would gain special prominence in the 1880s. They modeled their design after the *Sun* building in Baltimore, which had introduced the Italianate style to the United States in 1850. The cast iron was manufactured by Daniel D. Badger's famous Architectural Iron Works.

Once a residential boulevard, this portion of Broadway became an important commercial center during the nineteenth century, after the opening of the Erie Canal in 1825 made New York City the country's most important port and trading center. The building stands as a landmark to this transformation.

287 BROADWAY BUILDING, 1871–72
Manhattan
Architect: John B. Snook
Designated: August 29, 1989

The family of Stephen Storm, a prominent wholesale grocer and tobacco merchant, erected this cast-iron building to house banks and offices at a time when lower Broadway was being transformed from a residential boulevard into the city's commercial center. Designed in a hybrid Italianate and French Second Empire style by John B. Snook, the building features a high mansard roof and an early Otis elevator—both signs of prestige associated with the rise of banking and insurance industries in the 1860s. Snook had first distinguished himself in 1846 with the Italian palazzo–style A. T. Stewart dry-goods store, which defined the character of cast-iron architecture for the rest of the nineteenth century.

The building's cast-iron façades and the ironwork on both Broadway and Reade Street were manufactured by Jackson, Burnet & Co. The façades are marked by large round-arched windows separated by Ionic columns at the second story and Corinthian columns above, each story crowned by a cornice. The arched window openings are a muted American adaptation of a motif derived from the Roman Colosseum and first used by architect R. G. Hatfield for the *Sun* building in Baltimore. The mansard roof—pierced by dormers with segmented pediments and round-arched windows and topped by lacy iron cresting—still boasts its original slate shingles.

While 287 Broadway continues to house commercial establishments, in recent years several upper floors have been converted to residential use.

175 WEST BROADWAY BUILDING, 1877
Manhattan
Architects: Scott & Umbach
Designated: November 12, 1991

An exceptional example of late-nineteenth-century polychromatic brick design, this small four-story office building was erected at a time when improved transportation spurred the construction of commercial buildings in the Tribeca area. During the 1870s the Metropolitan elevated railway was built at the Sixth Avenue line, drawing West Broadway into the city's transportation network. Although the area was initially residential—containing the houses and shops of blacksmiths, carpenters, and combmakers—its accessibility to Lower Manhattan, then the city's business center, quickly attracted four- and five-story loft and office buildings.

The building is typical of many others in the Tribeca area in the division of the façade into a cast-iron and brick first story and brick upper stories. It is distinguished, however, by the elaborate brick corbeling along the entablature and above the segmental arched windows. The corbeled moldings, stone imposts, and stone courses that enliven the façade show the influence of the *Rundbogenstil*, or "round-arched style"—first developed in Germany in the 1860s and 70s—particularly on those architects, like Umbach, of German descent. It is possible that the choice of brick was influenced as well by the major fires in Chicago and Boston in the 1870s, which had proved that brick façades were more fire-resistant than stone or iron.

THE YOUNG ADULTS INSTITUTE, formerly the
New York House and School of Industry, 1878
120 West 16th Street, Manhattan
Architect: Sidney V. Stratton
Designated: October 2, 1990

In 1850 political unrest in Europe, famine in Ireland, and the discovery of gold in California drew thousands of immigrants to this country. Most of them entered through New York, straining the city's existing social and political structures to the breaking point. Individual charities, like the New York House and School of Industry founded in that year, stepped in to provide assistance. Established and run by women from such leading merchant families as the Astors, Van Rensselaers, DePeysters, and Livingstons, the New York House and School of Industry employed "infirm and destitute females" in needlework, keeping "idle hands busy" and lessening "the chances for vice."

Commissioned for the institution, this building is one of the earliest in New York designed in the Queen Anne style. The asymmetrical massing, decorative plaques, projecting oriel, and recessed bays suggest the craftsman's hand—a design approach linked to the work of English designer and social reformer William Morris (1834–1896), who believed the preservation of the dignity of labor required a return to production by hand.

In 1951 the school merged with a settlement facility, Greenwich House, serving Greenwich Village. The Young Adults Institute, a not-for-profit organization that provides care and shelter for New Yorkers, uses the building today.

JEFFREY'S HOOK LIGHTHOUSE (Little Red Lighthouse), 1880; moved to current site and reconstructed, 1921
Fort Washington Park, Manhattan
Designated: May 14, 1991

Formerly the North Hook Beacon at Sandy Hook, New Jersey, Jeffrey's Hook Lighthouse is the only lighthouse on the island of Manhattan. The forty-foot cast-iron conical tower was erected in 1880 and moved to its current site in 1921, as part of a project to improve navigation on the Hudson River. The lighthouse, with a flashing red light and a fog signal, was in operation from 1921 to 1947, and became widely known through a celebrated 1942 children's book, *The Little Red Lighthouse and the Great Gray Bridge*, by Hildegarde H. Swift.

In 1931 the usefulness of the lighthouse was diminished by the construction, almost directly above it, of the George Washington Bridge, upon which an aeronautical beacon was placed in 1935. By 1951 the lighthouse was no longer needed as a navigational aid, but—thanks to the book's popularity—its impending loss aroused a public outcry, including editorials in the *New York Times* and the *New York Herald Tribune*; a four-year-old boy even offered to buy the lighthouse himself. In response to this overwhelming display of concern, Parks Commissioner Robert Moses requested that the lighthouse be given to the city, and in 1951 it was placed under the jurisdiction of the Department of Parks. In 1979 it was added to the National Register of Historic Places.

OSBORNE APARTMENTS, 1883–85, 1889; extension, 1906
205 West 57th Street, Manhattan
Architects: James Edward Ware; 1906 extension, Alfred S. G. Taylor
Designated: August 13, 1991

By the time the Osborne Apartments were erected, 57th Street had already begun to develop an air of exclusivity, confirmed in 1879–82 when Cornelius Vanderbilt built his enormous mansion on the corner of Fifth Avenue. The wide streets and the open expanse of nearby Central Park made possible the construction of larger buildings that could offer the level of privacy and spaciousness demanded by its upper-class residents. The Osborne was named for its original owner and builder, Thomas Osborne, who promoted his building as "absolutely fireproof; lighted throughout by electricity."

Architect James Edward Ware was known for his inventive tenement designs, including the "dumbbell plan"—a significant advance in rational planning that introduced more light and air into dark and overcrowded tenement buildings. In the Osborne Apartments Ware combined the rustication of the Romanesque Revival with the massing of a Renaissance palazzo in an original manner. The elaborate entrance and lobby areas were the work of Swiss-born and French-trained J. A. Holzer, with contributions by the renowned sculptor Augustus Saint-Gaudens and American Renaissance muralist John La Farge. The decor of the lobby was carried through in the apartments with marquetry floors, handcarved mantels, stained-glass transoms, and mahogany, oak, and walnut paneling.

In 1889 Ware raised the roof level, providing extra rooms for servants in the upper stories while creating fifteen additional stories at the rear of the building. A twenty-five-foot-wide extension designed by Alfred S. G. Taylor, a part-owner of the building, was added to the western side of the building in 1906.

ANTIOCH, formerly Greene Avenue, BAPTIST CHURCH, 1887–92; church house, c. 1892–93
828 and 826 Greene Avenue, Brooklyn
Architects: church, Lansing C. Holden; church house, Langston & Dahlander
Designated: November 20, 1990

A splendid example of the Queen Anne style detailed with Romanesque Revival elements, the Antioch Baptist Church gracefully harmonizes with the character, scale, and texture of neighboring row houses, which were designed in the same architectural spirit shortly after the completion of the church. A three-story brick-and-brownstone row house with raised basement, one of the original row of seven adjacent to the church, was bought by the church in 1961 for use as a church house.

The church features a modulated, symmetrical façade of projecting and recessed masses faced in contrasting colors of rock-faced and red-brown brick, russet slate shingles, and white rusticated limestone. The structure's robust horizontal expanse is balanced by the vertical thrust of stacked windows and the four crowned and capped towers. Romanesque Revival details, like the round-arched windows, carved stone bartizan bases, and serpentine iron strap door hinges, enhance the building's medieval appearance.

The church has played a prominent role in Brooklyn's religious history, first as the Greene Avenue Baptist Church, with a predominantly white congregation distinguished for local philanthropy and the dispatch of its members as missionaries to China, Cuba, and throughout the United States, then, beginning in 1950—as economic forces transformed the surrounding Bedford-Stuyvesant area into one of the city's largest African-American neighborhoods—as the Antioch Baptist Church. It remains a prominent African-American institution and has been host to many civil rights leaders, including the Rev. Dr. Martin Luther King, Jr., Rev. Ralph Abernathy, Rev. Dr. Adam Clayton Powell, Jr., Hazel Dukes (head of New York's NAACP), and Rosa Parks, as well as African-American politicians and celebrities in many fields.

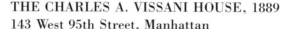

THE CHARLES A. VISSANI HOUSE, 1889
143 West 95th Street, Manhattan
Architect: James W. Cole
Designated: February 19, 1991

With a wealth of exuberant, Gothic-inspired details, this limestone-faced residence exemplifies the late Victorian version of the Gothic Revival style. An unusual choice for a city row house because of its picturesque yet space-consuming features, this style was considered more appropriate for places of worship, as Trinity Church, Grace Church, and St. Patrick's Cathedral so eloquently demonstrate.

The association between ecclesiastical and medieval, in fact, may have motivated the decision to use the Gothic style here. Commissioned by the Very Reverend Charles A. Vissani, the house was also to be used as headquarters for the religious work of the Franciscan priests who lived there; it even contained a chapel. Vissani had been appointed the first Commissary General of the Holy Land for the United States in 1880. The main tasks of the Commissariat—which moved to Washington, D.C., in 1889 and is still in operation today—are to increase public awareness about the holy places of Jerusalem and to preserve and recover the sanctuaries of Palestine.

Since 1946 the property has been used as a multi-unit residence. Nevertheless, the building's ecclesiastical overtones, heightened by pointed and ogee arches, pinnacles, trefoils, drip moldings, and lush foliated tympana, serve as an imposing reminder of the original residents' mission.

LINCOLN BUILDING, 1889–90
1–3 Union Square West, Manhattan
Architect: R. H. Robertson
Designated: July 12, 1988

When the Commissioners Map of 1807–11 first laid out Manhattan's grid plan, the acute angle where Bloomingdale Road (now Broadway) intersected the Bowery at 16th Street demarked an island of land that was dubbed Union Place. Initially the city's poor built their shanties there, but by 1839, Union Square (as it came to be known) had been graded, paved, and fenced in, and it was set aside for military and civic parades and festivities. By the 1850s, mansions had sprung up around the picturesque square. Within a few decades, tall commercial buildings, like the nine-story Lincoln, replaced the mansions as the city grew northward.

Combining metal-skeleton interior construction with masonry bearing walls, the Lincoln represents a transitional phase in skyscraper construction; eventually load-bearing walls were replaced by a steel skeleton that provides all the structural support—the essential criterion of a true skyscraper. Sheathed in Indiana limestone, granite, and brick, the Lincoln's Romanesque Revival arcades articulate the skeletal construction—though the massiveness of the walls is evident, and the horizontality of traditional masonry is further emphasized by the stacked fenestration. The building is ornamented with exceptional details: acanthus scrolls, Byzantine capitals, griffins, and human and lion heads, all carved in terra-cotta.

MECHANICS' AND TRADESMEN'S INSTITUTE, formerly the
Berkeley School, 1890; addition, 1903–05
20 West 44th Street, Manhattan
Architects: Lamb & Rich; addition, Ralph S. Townsend
Designated: October 18, 1988

Originally constructed as the Berkeley School for Boys, a private preparatory school, the building was acquired in 1899 by the General Society of Mechanics and Tradesmen. This organization had fostered building-trades education since 1785, offering free instruction and maintaining one of the city's three subscription libraries. Steel magnate Andrew Carnegie was initiated into the society in 1891, and it was a $250,000 grant from Carnegie that assured the society's survival and made it possible to alter the building significantly. Between 1903 and 1905 two wings were added to the rear and three new upper stories replaced an original fourth-floor gymnasium. The result is a sensitive design solution that blends monumental Beaux Arts classicism with Renaissance elements.

The building's exterior is a study in the tension between unifying and stratifying elements. The ten-foot-wide façade of seven symmetrical bays is variously composed of Indiana limestone, yellow Roman brick, and terra-cotta. The rusticated two-story base contrasts with the smooth-faced and elaborately ornamented upper floors. A wide frieze over the three central bays reproduces a portion of the Parthenon frieze, taken from casts at the Metropolitan Museum of Art, underscoring the importance of the front entrance.

In addition to housing a major collection of architectural books, the building now contains a museum, which features original manuscripts, coins, firearms, and a number of unusual locks.

329, 331, 333, 335, 337 WEST 85TH STREET, 1890–91
Manhattan
Architect: Ralph S. Townsend
Designated: April 16, 1991

This eclectic group of brownstone and red-brick row houses, originally built as prime single-family residences, demonstrates an unusual combination of divergent stylistic vocabularies. Designed for builder-speculator Perez M. Stuart, the buildings exemplify the architecture of the Aesthetic movement, a progressive trend in England and the United States that was popular in the 1880s. The arches, round-headed windows, and rustication recall the Romanesque Revival popularized by architect Henry Hobson Richardson. These forms are combined with elements of the Queen Anne style: the mullions of wood that cross the broad first-story windows; the smooth-faced basement and first-story arches; and the wide array of contrasting textures. The horizontal elements and tower-topped silhouettes visually unite the row, although each is distinguished by fanciful carvings of foliage, faces, or masks.

Architect Ralph S. Townsend is best known for his row houses and multiple dwellings in Greenwich Village, west Midtown, and the Upper West Side. His appealing designs sold quickly—four of these five on West 85th Street were purchased five days after completion; the fifth, ten days later. In 1988 the houses were converted into a cooperative apartment complex, entailing only minor modifications to the façades.

WILLIAM J. SYMS OPERATING THEATER, 1890–92
400 West 59th Street, Manhattan
Architect: William Wheeler Smith
Designated: July 11, 1989

By the late nineteenth century, surgery had become a common medical procedure. As operating theaters came to be constructed, they were modeled on the anatomical theaters that had been the centers of medical training since the Renaissance. When it opened in 1892, the Syms Operating Theater was the most advanced in the world and one of the first to be equipped for aseptic surgery. Dr. Charles McBurney, a prominent American surgeon who had achieved international recognition for identifying the diagnostic point on the abdomen for appendicitis, collaborated on its design with William Wheeler Smith, the architect. In an era when modern surgery was taking shape, numerous advances in surgical practice were developed here, including "McBurney's Incision," a method for removing the appendix.

The building forms part of Roosevelt Hospital, one of the earliest "pavilion plan" hospitals in America. First proposed in 1788 by the French Academy of Sciences, the pavilion plan emphasizes parallel two-story buildings positioned for maximum light and air to dispel the dirt, dampness, and vapors that were believed to carry infections. The theater was built with a $350,000 endowment from the city's largest gunmaker and dealer, William J. Syms. The subtly decorated flat brick walls with rounded corners, massive semi-conical roof, imposing entranceway, and overall monumentality are all expressive of the unusual functional demands of the building.

Syms remained an operating theater until 1941, and since then has functioned variously as a blood bank, mortuary, temporary emergency room, and office and laboratory space. Today the structure stands as built except for the removal of the south façade, now abutted by the Tower Building, and a few other minor alterations.

MACOMB'S DAM BRIDGE, formerly Central Bridge, AND
155TH STREET VIADUCT, 1890–95
From Jerome Avenue and East 162nd Street, The Bronx, crossing the Harlem
River to West 155th Street and St. Nicholas Place, Manhattan
Engineer: Alfred Pancoast Boller
Designated: January 14, 1992

Macomb's Dam Bridge is the third-oldest major bridge in New York City (after the Brooklyn
and Washington bridges) and the oldest intact metal-truss swing bridge, once common along
the Harlem River. At the time of its construction—which followed a succession of bridges
built at this site since 1815—the bridge's central swing span was thought to be the heaviest
moveable mass in the world. Alfred Pancoast Boller, an eminent structural engineer, had to
overcome daunting obstacles to successfully complete this significant engineering feat. Large
obstructing boulders were removed, and foundations varying in depth from twenty-four to one
hundred feet were sunk into marshland. The long, sloping 155th Street steel viaduct
provided a gradual descent toward the bridge from the heights of Harlem to the west. To
decorate the bridge, Boller added steel latticework, shelter towers, and ornamental iron
railings and lampposts, several of which are still intact.

Originally built to help spur development in northern Manhattan, Macomb's Dam Bridge
continues to provide an elegant and historically valuable connection between Upper
Manhattan and the Bronx.

316, 318, 320, 322, 324, 326 WEST 85TH STREET, 1892
Manhattan
Architect: Clarence F. True
Designated: April 16, 1991

While an intricately carved sandstone course spans the row, providing a visual link among
the six houses, Clarence F. True's arrangement of round-arched and rectangular windows,
classical ornamentation, and palazzo façades offers an urbane and varied example of the
Renaissance Revival style so successfully employed by the renowned architectural firm
McKim, Mead & White during the late nineteenth century. The restrained façades of the row
follow a rhythmic *a b a a b a* pattern, in a pleasing visual articulation of unity and diversity.
This approach is characteristic of True, who also used diverse polychrome materials in a
harmonious range of hues: Maynard red sandstone, light-orange Roman brick, and red
roofing tiles.

Though most of the streets on the Upper West Side, once known as Bloomingdale, had
been laid out following the Civil War, development crept along at a snail's pace until the
1880s, when improved public transportation stimulated real-estate speculation. True's group
of row houses was one of seven such projects he designed for the speculator-builder Charles
G. Judson before entering the speculative housing business himself in 1894.

CLAREMONT RIDING ACADEMY, formerly Claremont Stables, 1892
173–177 West 89th Street, Manhattan
Architect: Frank A. Rooke
Designated: August 14, 1990

Just six years before the automobile began to be seen negotiating the streets of New York, this handsome livery stable was built on the Upper West Side just two blocks from Central Park. One of 750 commercial stables at the turn of the century, it was a common building type then. Today it is a rare survivor. Claremont's fortuitous conversion to a riding academy in 1927, having easy access to Central Park's bridle trails and providing boarding facilities for horses, saved it from being turned into a garage. In 1965 the building was rescued from the wrecker's ball when demolition orders levied by the City of New York were canceled.

Built in the Romanesque Revival style that flourished on the Upper West Side in the 1880s, the stable was tucked away on a side street to keep the odor of horses at bay. The stable is distinguished by a dignified, symmetrical design that subtly expresses the utilitarian function within (it continues to operate today as a riding school). The façade, sheathed in contrasting beige Roman brick, limestone, and terra-cotta and articulated by a central bay with five round-arched openings, is characteristic of the style. The openings are formed of narrow brick voussoirs with narrow limestone keystones and are outlined by simple brick moldings. The symmetrical, restrained, and elegant effect of the building is due to the impressive balance of mass, volume, and scale, rather than to decorative details.

UNION BUILDING, formerly the Decker Building, 1892–93
33 Union Square West, Manhattan
Architect: John Edelmann
Designated: July 12, 1988

By the mid-nineteenth century, pianofortes had become increasingly popular, and, like many other businesses related to the arts, a number of piano makers had clustered around Union Square. Decker Brothers Piano Company appears to have been established originally in 1856 by John J. Decker, and the Decker Building was later commissioned by him for a prominent site he had leased from its owners.

An important example of the Moorish style, with Venetian touches (such as palazzo-style balconies), the building is profusely embellished with terra-cotta details that enliven and add variety to the façade. Naturalistic plant motifs ornament its enframements and intradosses (the interior curves of an arch), contributing to the overall impression of animation and movement. The limestone quoins that embellish the shaft and *alfiz* (the rectangular molding that frames a Moorish arch) and the pattern created by the loggia columns add to the aura of opulence. The building was an exterior complement to the Moorish look Louis Comfort Tiffany had employed in his interior designs of many nearby Fifth Avenue town houses.

Prompted by trade and exploration in the eighteenth and nineteenth centuries, the use of Islamic motifs was the longest-lived of exotic movements in design. In the Western context, Moorish details were often used to suggest relaxation, and they provided an escape from the mundane in the design of smoking rooms, cafés, theaters, and public baths. The pleasurable realms promised by a piano performance may have provided the architect of the Union Building with the inspiration to employ this ornate style for the Deckers.

PUBLIC SCHOOL 86 (Irvington School), 1891–93
220 Irving Avenue, Brooklyn
Architect: James W. Naughton
Designated: April 23, 1991

This four-story brick-and-stone school designed in the Romanesque Revival style is one of the few remaining nineteenth-century schools still being used for its original purpose. Located within the historical boundaries of the town of Bushwick, the school was constructed to meet the needs of a growing immigrant population. Thousands of Germans had fled to America, many settling in Bushwick, following the political upheavals in Europe in 1848.

Public School 86 was designed by James W. Naughton, who served as the superintendent of the Board of Education of the City of Brooklyn from 1879 until his death in 1898. During that time he designed and constructed more than one hundred schools—over two-thirds of the public school buildings erected in Brooklyn in the nineteenth century. Trained at the University of Wisconsin and at Cooper Union in Manhattan, Naughton used an amalgam of popular architectural styles in his school designs—combining, for example, Italianate layered palazzi with French Second Empire flanking pavilions and Gothic detailing. A picturesque silhouette distinguishes the handsome design of P.S. 86: a broad gable embraces a round arch, and prominent dormer windows punctuate the roofline.

WEST END AVENUE TOWN HOUSES AND WEST 102ND STREET TOWN HOUSE, 1892–93
854, 856, 858 West End Avenue and 254 West 102nd Street, Manhattan
Architects: Schneider & Herter
Designated: August 14, 1990

This group of four brownstone row houses was built as a speculative venture during a turn-of-the-century boom in residential development on West End Avenue. White-collar professionals were attracted to the area's landscaped suburb-like streets, its views of the Hudson River, and proximity to Frederick Law Olmsted's scenic Riverside Park. Highly variegated through the use of recessed entrances and balconies, these lively Queen Anne/Romanesque Revival–style houses typify West End Avenue's eclectic residential architecture of the 1890s. By detailing each building individually, the architects also expressed a reaction against the uniform look of the city's older Italianate row houses.

Featuring a prominent corner house and a house facing the side street behind the avenue, this three-story row house group is the only surviving example of a once-common site plan for corner lots on the avenue. Picturesque rooflines—punctuated by gables, pedimented parapets, carved panels, and cornices—distinguish the buildings. The centerpiece corner house, number 858, is dominated by a cylindrical tower that rises an extra story and is capped by a bell-shaped roof. A profusion of ornament, including asymmetrical pilasters with carved capitals and lion's-head supports, adorns the façades in the architects' distinctive mannerist style.

253, 256–257 BROADWAY, formerly the Home Life Insurance Company Building (incorporating the former Postal Telegraph Building), 1892–94
Manhattan
Architects: 253 Broadway, Harding & Gooch; 256–257 Broadway, Pierre L. LeBrun, of Napoleon LeBrun & Sons
Designated: November 12, 1991

Founded in Brooklyn in 1860, the Home Life Insurance Company moved its Manhattan branch office here in 1866. In 1890 several other insurance companies commissioned new buildings and established corporate headquarters nearby: Equitable at Broadway and Cedar Street; New York Life at Broadway and Leonard Street; and Metropolitan Life at Park Place and Church Street. In 1892, inspired by its business rivals, the company held a competition for the design of a new building. The contest was judged by William R. Ware, Columbia University's first professor of architecture.

Pierre LeBrun's winning entry is an early example of the tripartite formula in skyscraper design, a pioneering means of articulating verticality in the skyscraper. LeBrun visually mimicked the classical column, with its base, shaft, and capital, by concentrating the Renaissance-inspired ornamentation on the base and upper stories. The building's soaring eleven-story shaft stands in marked contrast to its neighbor, the former Postal Telegraph Building (purchased by the company in 1947 and connected through its interior), which—although only two stories smaller and also in the Renaissance idiom—emphasizes horizontality through distinct sill courses and a broad, copper-and-bronze cornice.

Believing that ornament should be appropriate to a building's function, LeBrun used the classical idiom to refer symbolically to the banking houses of Florence as a prototype, in an attempt to connect the foremost seat of commerce and entrepreneurship in the Renaissance to what was, at the time, the relatively young insurance business of the early twentieth century.

TRINITY SCHOOL AND THE FORMER ST. AGNES PARISH HOUSE; school, 1893–94; parish house, c. 1890–92
121–147 West 91st Street, Manhattan
Architects: school, Charles Coolidge Haight; parish house, William Appleton Potter
Designated: August 1, 1989

Trinity School is the oldest continuously operated school in Manhattan. Founded by Trinity Church in 1709 as the only coeducational school in the colonies for children from disadvantaged backgrounds, it was converted into a private preparatory school in 1827. In response to the needs of a growing urban population pushing northward at the end of the nineteenth century, Trinity Church, located on Wall Street, moved its school affiliate to the Upper West Side. Trinity Church also established next to the school the St. Agnes Chapel complex, of which only the parish house still exists. It was purchased by Trinity School in 1943 and has been remodeled into classrooms.

Trinity School's smooth-surfaced walls, tall bay divisions, and active roofline with steep gables and dormers reflect the English Collegiate Gothic style derived from the architecture of Oxford and Cambridge universities. Architect Charles Coolidge Haight later successfully employed the same style in his design of Yale University campus.

The parish house, a simply designed, massive three-story structure, was originally attached to the apse of a cruciform church. The alternating wide and narrow courses of brownstone and granite and deeply set windows reveal the influence of architect Henry Hobson Richardson. The house's Romanesque design was a common choice for ecclesiastical architecture in the 1890s.

THE FREE CHURCH OF ST. MARY-THE-VIRGIN (church, clergy house, mission house, rectory, and lady chapel), 1894–95
133–145 West 46th Street and 136–144 West 47th Street, Manhattan
Architect: Pierre L. LeBrun, of Napoleon LeBrun & Sons
Designated: December 19, 1989

The origins of this church complex can be traced to a High Church movement initiated in England in the 1830s. Led by a group of Oxford University theologians, the movement sought to enhance the spiritual lives of industrial workers. Ceremonial rituals were revived, church art and architecture began to follow the medieval style, and mission work in poor neighborhoods was fostered. In North America, the Episcopal Church echoed these developments.

St. Mary's, a complex of five connecting French Gothic–style buildings, was erected among working-class row houses and stables. Faced in limestone, the church is complemented by surrounding buildings of orange Tiffany brick. The group is distinguished throughout by John Massey Rhind's naturalistic ecclesiastical sculptures and abundant ornamentation. Keyed limestone surrounds and drip moldings frame doorways and windows. Inside are the long nave, lofty ceilings, side aisles, and deep chancels demanded by a highly ritualistic liturgy.

While St. Mary's looked backward to the ritual and art of pre-Reformation Catholicism, it was a pioneer in the use of the steel frame in church construction. The steel skeleton, associated at the time only with Chicago skyscrapers, enabled quick construction of the elaborate church complex and earned St. Mary's the nickname "the Chicago Church."

AHRENS BUILDING, 1894–95
70–76 Lafayette Street, Manhattan
Architect: George H. Griebel
Designated: January 14, 1992

The Ahrens Building is an elegant example of a successful marriage of state-of-the-art technology and historical ornamentation. This seven-story structure takes full advantage of its lightweight armature (thin walls, large windows) while allowing the façade sophisticated Romanesque Revival details. Among the many distinctive features of the building are the layered arcades of the two façades, which culminate in a crowning attic-story arcade, and the excellent craftsmanship evidenced in the bold metalwork of the patterned oriels and deep cornices. Architect George Griebel's building provided a handsome answer to the challenge that absorbed architects of the late nineteenth century—how to "dress" the skeleton of modern commercial buildings.

Griebel ingeniously adapted structural polychromy (the use of variously colored materials to highlight structural detail, a practice popularized by John Ruskin) to a pared-down cladding appropriate to the steel frame. Buff brick walls are punctuated by darker, rock-faced brown brick keys and terra-cotta moldings. The curved brick profiles of the windows accentuate the shallowness of the wall surface and gracefully evince the building's underlying construction.

Commissioned by liquor merchant Herman F. Ahrens, the building was a speculative investment that coincided with a municipal project to widen and improve Lafayette Street. Its original use was probably as a retail outlet for Ahrens' liquor business. The building remained family-owned until 1968, when it was acquired by Morris and Herbert Moskowitz. Fortunately, despite its varied uses (upper floors have been employed for storage, manufacturing, and office space), the structure has remained remarkably intact.

THE AMERICAN THEATER OF ACTORS, formerly the Eleventh Judicial
District Courthouse, 1894–96
314 West 54th Street, Manhattan
Architect: John H. Duncan
Designated: June 6, 1989

The Hell's Kitchen neighborhood served by this former courthouse in the late nineteenth and early twentieth centuries was reputed to be the most dangerous and crime-ridden spot in America. A notorious series of street riots in 1900 between the area's Irish and German residents, who represented the majority, and an African-American minority contributed to the exodus of African-Americans from the West Side to Harlem. Many of those who participated in the violence were arraigned at the West Side Court, as it was popularly known then. Proceedings at the courthouse played an integral role in the social history of the densely populated West Side. Senator George W. Plunkitt, a Tammany Hall politician and West Side "boss," was responsible for introducing a bill that enabled the construction of this public building, which housed both the Eleventh District Municipal Court and the Seventh District Magistrates' Court.

The court's design skillfully adapts the grandeur of the Renaissance Revival style to a small civic structure. (Some courthouses at the time were housed in former schools and firehouses.) A rusticated-stone, palazzo-inspired base supports the two brick upper stories, where the frontispiece of tripartite window groups and Corinthian pilasters denotes the location of the two courtrooms. In 1979 the building was subleased to the American Theater of Actors, which has converted the courtrooms into theaters.

GOLDOME BANK, formerly the New York Bank for Savings, AND INTERIOR, 1896–97
81 Eighth Avenue (also known as 301 West 14th Street), Manhattan
Architect: Robert H. Robertson
Designated: June 8, 1988

Although New York City became the nation's financial capital soon after the Civil War, its commercial banks were often located in unimpressive quarters—including converted residences—because of the high rents in the Wall Street area. Savings banks, however, dependent only on small private investors, took advantage of less expensive real estate farther uptown to build themselves monumental headquarters such as this one.

The bank is located on a prominent corner site and is a fine example of the Academic Classical style popularized by the 1893 World's Columbian Exposition in Chicago. Built on a monumental scale despite its small size, the L-shaped building embodies a classical architectural vocabulary sensitively molded to its institutional functions. The pedimented bay and dome on the building's 14th Street side, for instance, suggest the important public space within. The building's most striking features, however, are the copper-sheeted drum and dome and the grand Corinthian portico adorning the principal Eighth Avenue façade. Inside, rose-gray marble paves the landmark banking hall, which features majestic Corinthian columns on high plinths supporting the entablature and coffered ceiling. Siena marble wainscoting on many of the walls dates from a 1930 remodeling.

In 1940–41 a limestone-faced addition was built to the north of the banking hall to house expanded services. Upon merging with the Bank for Savings in 1964, the bank became the third-largest savings institution in the city. After a second merger, with the Buffalo Savings Bank in 1981, the building was closed to cut costs.

THE PHILIP AND MARIA KLEEBERG HOUSE, 1896–98
3 Riverside Drive, Manhattan
Architect: Charles Pierrepont H. Gilbert
Designated: January 8, 1991

Situated at the intersection of West 72nd Street and Riverside Drive, this refined five-story French Renaissance Revival–style town house is faced in limestone and brick and embellished with a generous application of classical motifs. Tall, faceted pilasters divide the windows of the three-story, four-sided bay, which projects out to the building line and is topped by a balustrade decorated with shields. Like the Francis I style that inspired it, Charles Pierrepont H. Gilbert's design of this residence blends Gothic and Renaissance details, combining picturesque dormers and steeply pitched rooflines with carved putti, gargoyles, shields, shells, wreaths, ribbons, and foliage. The house was considered so noteworthy that an 1899 prospectus put out by Clarence F. True, an Upper West Side architect and developer, included a photograph of the recently completed building as an example of the high-quality homes to be found in the area. It was the only structure not designed by True's office to be included in the prospectus.

Developers also stimulated the demand for houses by emphasizing the beautiful surroundings that made the area along Riverside Drive prime real estate. The original drive, designed by Frederick Law Olmsted, had been proposed as a formal park by Parks Commissioner William R. Martin in 1865. Today it stretches from 72nd to 129th streets.

PUBLIC SCHOOL 20 ANNEX, formerly the Northfield Township District School 6, 1891; 1897–98
160 Heberton Avenue, Staten Island
Architects: 1891, unknown; 1897–98 addition, James Warriner Moulton
Designated: March 22, 1988

Built in what was in the 1890s the rapidly growing shorefront village of Richmond, P.S. 20 Annex was one of the first schools on Staten Island to have more than one room. While primarily designed in the Romanesque Revival style, this modest, two-story brick structure combines diverse elements and stylistic features, such as the outsize clock faces that surmount the four-story, square bell tower.

The school's stylistic eclecticism predates the 1898 consolidation of Greater New York, which created a metropolis out of the area's scattered cities, towns, and villages and quickly standardized school construction throughout the region. The tower, for example, with its pyramidal roof atop a round-arched arcade, is in the Romanesque Revival style; its off-center placement, however, evokes Italian villa architecture. Diverse window treatments suggest Neo-Renaissance palaces, while decorative terra-cotta inset panels in the gable peaks and below the windows on the tower's eastern face are drawn from the American Queen Anne style.

A three-story addition, approved in 1897 to cope with increasing enrollment, follows the earlier Romanesque Revival style. Symmetrically disposed and simplified in design, the extension is less picturesque than the original, though terra-cotta ornaments—idealized female heads, putti, scrolled acanthus leaves, and reliefs depicting implements associated with learning—lavishly adorn its façade.

FIRE ENGINE COMPANY NO. 65, 1897–98
33 West 43rd Street, Manhattan
Architects: Hoppin & Koen
Designated: October 2, 1990

When West 43rd Street between Fifth and Sixth avenues underwent a fin-de-siècle character change, from a block of garages and horse stables for the Sixth Avenue Railroad Company to an enclave of luxury hotels and social clubs that sprang up as fashionable neighborhoods pushed northward, this firehouse was erected to protect the area's elite establishments. To complement the majestic neighboring façades and placate prestigious clubs objecting to the presence of an engine company in their midst, architects Frances L. V. Hoppin and Terence A. Koen—both classically trained at the renowned New York firm McKim, Mead & White—constructed a graceful, Renaissance-inspired exterior influenced by Beaux Arts architecture of the 1893 World's Columbian Exposition in Chicago. The Exposition had spawned the "City Beautiful" movement, which espoused a rational urban order based on classical Beaux Arts schemes—a civic aesthetic the firehouse graciously exemplifies. (Hoppin and Koen would later design the downtown landmark Beaux Arts palace, the Police Headquarters Building.)

The building's elegant proportions, despite the narrow lot, and stately white Roman brick façade embellished with symbolic ornament—the dragon-and-laurel motif signifying the battle between fire and water—clearly express the dignity of the civic fountain housed within and create an impression of monumentality.

The company started out with horse-drawn engines but progressed to the forefront of modern fire fighting and distinguished itself in battling such perilous blazes as that of the Ritz Tower Hotel (1932), the Empire State Building (in a 1945 bomber crash), and the Times Tower (1961).

THE UKRAINIAN ACADEMY OF ARTS AND SCIENCES, formerly the
New York Free Circulating Library, Bloomingdale Branch, 1898
206 West 100th Street, Manhattan
Architect: James Brown Lord
Designated: August 29, 1989

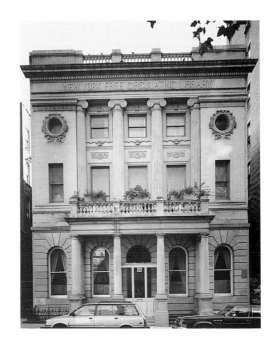

Among the wealthy patrons of this former circulating library—founded in 1880 to provide "moral and intellectual elevation of the masses"—were Andrew Carnegie, J. P. Morgan, and Cornelius Vanderbilt. Philanthropists were often actively involved in the management of libraries such as this one, which was devoted to the self-education of the poor. By 1901 the steady expansion of its services would be manifested in eleven branches. Prior to their consolidation with the New York Public Library, these free libraries were the only alternative to private, fee-charging institutions and the Astor and Lenox research libraries.

The building's eighteenth-century French Classic design, inspired by Renaissance models, appears to have been an influential prototype in the development of the urban branch library, as is evident in the Carnegie branch buildings constructed in the early twentieth century. A steel-framed, three-story structure, the library is faced in tan glazed Roman brick enlivened by terra-cotta and limestone. A shallow three-bay portico supported by Tuscan columns projects from a deeply rusticated limestone base featuring five round-arched openings. The architectural prominence of the center bays continues on the second and third stories with colossal Ionic terra-cotta elements framing slightly recessed windows. Since 1961 this handsome building has served as a library and research facility for the study of Ukrainian culture and sciences.

RIVERSIDE DRIVE HOUSES, 1898–99
103, 104, 105, 107–109 Riverside Drive, Manhattan
Architect: Clarence F. True
Designated: April 25, 1991

Clarence Fagan True, a prolific and well-known architect, whose 1893 and 1899 prospectuses for the Riverside Drive area feature more than 270 houses he designed, began to work as his own developer in 1894. In addition to promoting the Upper West Side, True's aim was to create buildings whose designs would be a departure from repetitive brownstone row houses. The varied architectural elements and materials for each building in the row (the brick is graduated in hue from tan to orange to red) demonstrate his philosophy of harmonious diversity.

The five extant row houses of an original group of six were built by True's development firm, the Riverside Building Company. They were designed in his signature "Elizabethan Revival" style, a picturesque style based on French and English Renaissance architecture and characterized by contrasting brick and limestone facing, dormers, decorative ironwork, chimneys, and crenellation. All the houses were also originally built with prominent projections, such as bowfronts and three-sided bays, but Charlotte Ackerman, a neighbor, sued True for blocking her view, light, and air, and in 1903 the New York State Court of Appeals ruled that no permanent encroachments would be allowed on the block. As a result, in 1911, all the façades facing Riverside Drive were removed and rebuilt by other architectural firms to strictly follow the property lines. Numbers 103 and 104, both altered by the architectural firm of Clinton & Russell, and number 107–109, altered by Tracy, Swartwout & Litchfield, were rebuilt with the original materials and retained many of their architectural details; Bosworth & Holden designed a new façade for number 105.

332 WEST 83RD STREET, 1898–99
Manhattan
Architect: Clarence F. True
Designated: April 16, 1991

One of a magnificent ensemble of row houses in True's idiosyncratic "Elizabethan Revival" style—readily identifiable by its asymmetrically placed bowfront, contrasting red Roman brick and limestone, decorative ironwork, and steeply pitched tile roof—this building is the only house of the group that remains unaltered. Unlike the four on Riverside Drive, its picturesque projections were not removed because it faced onto West 83rd Street. (The façades facing Riverside Drive were removed and set back after a neighbor brought a lawsuit against True for obstructing her view, light, and air.)

This house was purchased in 1900 by Robert E. Dowling, president of the prestigious real-estate firm City Investing Company. Dowling, who negotiated some of New York's largest real-estate transactions, lived in the house until his death in 1943. The following year the house was sold and converted to a multiple-unit residence.

CITY AND SUBURBAN HOMES COMPANY ESTATES
First Avenue and Avenue A, Manhattan
Designated: April 24, 1990

First Avenue Estate, 1898–1915
1168–1190 First Avenue (also known as 401 East 64th Street), 1194–1200 First Avenue (also known as 402 East 65th Street), 403–409, 411, 417, 419, 421, 423, 429 East 64th Street, 404–408, 410, 412, 414, 416, 430 East 65th Street
Architects: James E. Ware, James E. Ware & Son(s), and Philip H. Ohm

Avenue A (York Avenue) Estate, 1900–13
1470 York Avenue (also known as 501 East 78th Street), 1492 York Avenue (also known as 502 East 79th Street), 503–509, 511–517, 519–523, 527–531, 535–539, 541–555 East 78th Street, 504–508, 510–512, 516–520, 524–528, 530–534, 536–540 East 79th Street
Architects: Harde & Short, Percy Griffin, and Philip H. Ohm

These are the oldest projects executed by the City and Suburban Homes Company, the most successful privately financed company to address the housing problems of the city's working poor at the turn of the century. In the 1880s over two-thirds of New York's 3.5 million residents, many of them immigrants, were living in 90,000 tenements. To provide these wage-earners comfortable, safe, and hygienic housing at market rates, the company's investors—mainly wealthy philanthropists, including Cornelius Vanderbilt, Samuel B. Babcock, and Mrs. Alfred Corning Clark—agreed to limit their profits. The company established "a middle ground between pure philanthropy and pure business," said its president, E. R. L. Gould, and encouraged others to invest in model low-income housing. Both estates—each covering a full city block—are high-density developments: the First Avenue Estate has 1,059 apartments and the Avenue A Estate 1,257 plus 410 rooms, the largest low-income housing project in the world at the time of its completion in 1913.

Early Avenue A Estate buildings were executed in Neo-Renaissance and Georgian Revival designs. First Avenue Estate and later Avenue A Estate buildings were constructed in contemporary architectural styles, with such details as cartouches, heavy garlands, raised brickwork, and elaborately carved stone doorways; they are the product of the City and Suburban Homes Company's own architectural department, established in 1906 and headed by Philip H. Ohm. Ohm experimented with the configuration of courts, stairs, and halls to produce the most economical and efficient plans. The savings were used to augment the residents' amenities, adding public bathrooms, children's playrooms, and laundry rooms.

When the federal government began to establish a national housing policy in the 1930s, the large-scale development, management techniques, and financial structure of these model projects were worthy examples for the new programs.

BROADWAY CHAMBERS BUILDING, 1899–1900
273–277 Broadway, Manhattan
Architect: Cass Gilbert
Designated: January 14, 1992

Vibrant, unabashed color differentiates the Broadway Chambers Building from other contemporary tripartite structures. Architect Cass Gilbert eschewed the light monochrome materials fashionable at the time, preferring instead to use a pale-pink granite with deep-purple overtones for the base of his remarkable structure. He chose beige terra-cotta highlighted with brilliant Pompeian red, blue-green, and greenish yellow for the richly embellished capital. The Broadway Chambers Building exemplifies the classically inspired Beaux Arts style popularized by the 1893 World's Columbian Exposition in Chicago; the building's three-part vertical structure, which alludes to the three sections of a classical column, and its rich ornamentation—the Tuscan capitals are adorned with Hermes' and lions' heads, garlands, and wreaths—are characteristic of this lush, decorative style.

Still in use today as commercial office space, the Broadway Chambers Building remains remarkably intact. By and large, changes have been limited to ornamental detail: the copper cheneau was removed from the roof cornice in 1925, and later the decorative transom screen and flanking plinths which once had graced the main entrance were also removed.

The Broadway Chambers Building was the first of Gilbert's designs to be executed in New York City and was instrumental in establishing him as an important architectural force in the area. This formidable structure, along with later Gilbert creations—the U.S. Custom House and the Woolworth Building (both designated landmarks)—have left the architect's inimitable mark on New York's magnificent cityscape.

THE WILLIAM E. DILLER HOUSE, 1899–1901
309 West 72nd Street, Manhattan
Architect: Gilbert A. Schellenger
Designated: January 8, 1991

Faced in brick and limestone, this Renaissance Revival town house is one of four grand houses remaining at the intersection of 72nd Street and Riverside Drive. Designed during the resurgence of Neoclassicism in America, the building visually harmonizes with its neighbors, which display similar horizontal divisions, rounded bays, elaborate entrance porticoes, and ornate classical detailing. A low stoop leads to a central entrance framed by an Ionic portico whose columns and pilasters support a two-story bowed bay and an entablature lavishly adorned with carved vine details and moldings of anthemia (sculpted floral forms), beads, and reels.

In the 1880s grand mansions were the first types of dwellings constructed along Riverside Drive; skyrocketing real-estate prices later encouraged the construction of smaller row houses and town houses, such as this one, for greater numbers of less affluent tenants. The owner, William E. Diller, was a physician who, like many other well-to-do New Yorkers at the time, became involved in the real-estate market; from 1920 to his death in 1936 he constructed over one hundred single-family homes on the west side of Midtown Manhattan. Apparently this house was constructed for investment purposes also, for the Diller family sold the property only a year after construction was completed, and in 1927 it was converted to a multiple-unit dwelling.

THE FREDERICK AND LYDIA PRENTISS HOUSE, 1899–1901
1 Riverside Drive, Manhattan
Architect: Charles Pierrepont H. Gilbert
Designated: January 8, 1991

This imposing five-story residence, situated on a large, curved lot, was designed to take advantage of its prominent position at the intersection of West 72nd Street and Riverside Drive. With a dormered, copper-trimmed, slate mansard roof, the building is faced in limestone and features an entrance portico supported by Ionic columns and a turret topped with a conical roof. Curved bays project from the front and side façades. An architect for many prominent members of New York society, Charles Pierrepont H. Gilbert had attended the Ecole des Beaux-Arts in Paris, where he familiarized himself with interpretations of Renaissance and Baroque prototypes of Italian, French, and German architecture. His studies at the Ecole are evident in his treatment of this building's façade, which is replete with classical festoons, carved friezes, floral patterns, pilasters, balustrades, columns, and rustication.

The construction of the Prentiss residence took place during a remarkable period of real-estate speculation. Development of the area began slowly, but improved public transportation and the creation of Riverside Drive and Park contributed to its growth. By the 1880s the area was rife with speculative developers, whose advertisements focused on the area west of Broadway, emphasizing the easy access to transportation and the scenic setting.

In 1957 the building was purchased by the New York Mosque Foundation, which two years later modified the interior to accommodate a mosque on the first and second floors.

BRYANT PARK STUDIOS, 1900–1

80 West 40th Street (also known as 1054–1056 Avenue of the Americas),
Manhattan
Architect: Charles A. Rich
Designated: December 13, 1988

As New York's art community grew during the second half of the nineteenth century, it required more space for studios and meeting and exhibition rooms. Bryant Park Studios is one of the earliest buildings designed specifically to meet some of these needs, with generous windows facing the northern light preferred by artists and large work areas. Fernand Léger and Edward Steichen worked here, as did numerous other well-known artists. The studios were commissioned by the prominent American portraitist Abraham Archibald Anderson, who had experienced a lonely and difficult life in Paris as a young art student and was anxious to help others once he himself was established. Anderson occupied a penthouse apartment in the building until his death in 1940.

Executed in pink brick with terra-cotta and stone details, the building displays a tripartite organization. A banded brick and terra-cotta transitional story above a two-story base, grooved to simulate rusticated stone, leads to the main section, which displays a variety of window treatments and ornament—including some double-height windows grouped vertically in stone enframements for dramatic emphasis.

By locating the building just south of Bryant Park, Anderson felt assured that the desirable northern light would not be blocked by future tall buildings. Although the building is now surrounded by towering skyscrapers, it is still used as studio space; tenants today include several clothing and interior design firms.

THE WILLIAM AND CLARA BAUMGARTEN HOUSE, 1900–1

294 Riverside Drive, Manhattan
Architects: Schickel & Ditmars
Designated: February 19, 1991

At the turn of the century, the Upper West Side was experiencing a surge in growth due in large part to improved public transportation—especially following the completion of the Ninth Avenue Elevated Railway in 1879. Real-estate values soared as developers anticipated generous returns on their lots along Riverside Drive. This elegant Beaux Arts–style house harks back to the time when the Upper West Side was the site of intense real-estate development.

Unlike most of its neighbors, the house was not built on speculation but was commissioned by its owner, William Baumgarten, a successful German immigrant. The son of a master cabinetmaker, Baumgarten had arrived in America in 1865 and entered the field of furnishings and design. From 1881 to 1891 he headed the prestigious interior design firm Herter Brothers, which is credited with the interiors of houses belonging to J. P. Morgan, William Vanderbilt, and other wealthy clients. By the time he commissioned this residence for himself, Baumgarten had established his own decorating company and had worked with architect William Schickel, another German immigrant, on designs for numerous other New York City private residences.

The Baumgarten home, with its classical details—including an entrance portico supported by Ionic columns—exemplifies the popularity of the Beaux Arts style at the time, and the building's symmetrical design, slate mansard roof, limestone façade, carved ornament, and decorative ironwork express the affluence and taste of the client.

CAPITAL CITIES/ABC, INC. STUDIOS, formerly the First Battery Armory, 1900–03
56 West 66th Street, Manhattan
Architects: Horgan & Slattery
Designated: August 1, 1989

This looming, castlelike structure was designed by the firm of Horgan & Slattery, which achieved great commercial success through its close relationship with the administration of Mayor Cornelius Van Wyck (1898–1901). Following its refurbishing of the Democratic Club interior in 1897, the firm—commonly referred to as the Tammany architects—was awarded almost every contract for the Board of Health, the Department of Corrections, the Charities Department, and the Tax Department, ranging from landscaping and interior renovations to barge construction and machinery overhauling on city-owned boats.

Most of Horgan and Slattery's designs conformed to accepted principles of classical composition, planning, and vocabularies. Not surprisingly, their handling of the First Battery Armory adhered to the general architectural consensus that the medieval castle was the appropriate model for an armory, symbolizing military power and control in an urban environment. Indeed, the First Battery Armory was the seventh of ten armories built by the New York Armory Board as part of a general campaign—initiated with the State Armory Law of 1884—conducted in response to growing concern about urban riots.

THE JOHN AND MARY SUTPHEN HOUSE, 1901–2
311 West 72nd Street, Manhattan
Architect: Charles Pierrepont H. Gilbert
Designated: January 8, 1991

This is one of four remaining grand town houses designed for a notable site—the intersection of Riverside Drive and 72nd Street. Ionic columns at the entrance portico support a lavishly ornamental entablature decorated with egg-and-dart molding, volutes, and foliate carving. Curved bays grace the limestone front and side façades; the roof is an elaborately dormered mansard. Charles Pierrepont H. Gilbert, the architect, was known for his attention to detail and provision of generous interior spaces in the opulent residences popular among New York society during this period.

John Sutphen's father, John S. Sutphen, Sr., at one time owned the entire stretch of property along Riverside Drive between West 72nd and West 73rd streets. It is he who was responsible for establishing the restrictive covenants under which this neighborhood was developed. These codes stipulated the type of building that could be constructed—including the materials to be used—and prohibited the construction of slaughterhouses, nail factories, breweries, stables, or any other business "which may be in anywise dangerous, noxious, or offensive to the neighboring inhabitants." Through these restrictions Sutphen and other developers endeavored to ensure the future value and harmonious character of the neighborhood. An additional stipulation required the selection of Gilbert as the architect for three of the four town houses at this corner.

ST. REGIS HOTEL, 1901–4; 1927
699–703 Fifth Avenue, Manhattan
Architects: Trowbridge & Livingston; 1927 extension, Sloan & Robertson
Designated: November 1, 1988

Not the first of Colonel John Jacob Astor's New York hotels but his most ambitious, the St. Regis was constructed in the heart of what was then the most fashionable residential neighborhood in New York. The eighteen-story hotel was to be a home away from home for wealthy visitors, good enough to house the overflow of Astor's own guests. Named for the French monk who had been canonized for his hospitality to travelers, the St. Regis's elegance and service matched the grand European hotels Astor had visited, surpassing them in modern conveniences and technological inventions.

Distinctively Beaux Arts and reminiscent of the French apartment buildings of the period, the elegant limestone façade imitates a classical column, with the shaft of the building rising from a rusticated base and ending in a richly decorated capital. Equally lavish and commodious in its interior, there were a reported forty-seven Steinway pianos available for the use of the guests; the library, with its English oak paneling and three thousand leather-bound, gold-embossed volumes, was attended by a librarian who assisted guests with their selections. Even the engine and boiler rooms, sixty feet below Fifth Avenue, were lined in marble.

The first major renovation occurred in 1927, when the hotel was sold by Vincent Astor, John Jacob's son, to Duke Management. An extensive addition increased the number of guest rooms to 520, and two floors were added, including the famous St. Regis roof. The hotel was sold again in 1959 and subsequently changed hands several times until 1966, when it was purchased by the Sheraton Corporation. The most recent renovation of the St. Regis (begun in 1987 and completed in the fall of 1991) cost more than $100 million and included an upgrade of the operating systems, enabling the management to accommodate new demands for plumbing, electricity, and air circulation. In addition, the telephones were programmed in six languages and a fax machine was installed in each room. In true Astor tradition, the St. Regis renovation restored the opulence of the past while providing all the amenities of the present.

HELEN MILLER GOULD CARRIAGE HOUSE, 1902–3
213 West 58th Street, Manhattan
Architects: York & Sawyer
Designated: August 29, 1989

This elegant French Renaissance–influenced stable, which set an exceptionally high standard for carriage house design in New York, was built by the eldest daughter of transportation and communications tycoon Jay Gould. While her father's poor public reputation earned him the tag "robber baron," Helen Miller Gould was widely known for her generosity and unflagging support of worthy causes. (When she died in 1938, the *New York Times* called her "the best-loved woman in the country.") At the time of the stable's construction, the stretch of 58th Street between Fifth Avenue and Broadway resembled a mews. Area residents stabled their horses here, while those who enjoyed driving through nearby Central Park appreciated the convenience of liveries. Miss Gould, who lived in the Fifth Avenue mansion bequeathed to her by her father, demolished an existing stable to make way for this carriage house.

Architect Phillip Sawyer had studied for a year at the Ecole des Beaux-Arts in Paris, and elements of the Parisian-style façade suggest the uniform, symmetrical elevations of the seventeenth-century buildings that defined Henry IV's exclusive Place des Vosges. A suave, dignified effect is achieved by the building's subtle verticality, the attenuated hipped slate roof and tall flanking chimneys, and the limestone tethering rings at the arched entrance. Ornamentation, like the flat voussoirs (wedge-shaped pieces of an arch) of the third-story windows and the triglyph brackets supporting the cornice, imbue this chiefly utilitarian building—it housed horses, feed, a groom, and a coachman—with an unmistakable air of luxury.

BANK OF THE METROPOLIS, 1902–3
31 Union Square West (also known as 19–23 East 16th Street), Manhattan
Architect: Bruce Price
Designated: July 12, 1988

To attract the support of leading publishers and jewelry and other merchants located around fashionable Union Square, the Bank of the Metropolis' board of directors included such powerful neighborhood businessmen as decorator-glassmaker Louis Comfort Tiffany and publisher Charles Scribner. Sited on a commanding corner location, the building superbly demonstrates Bruce Price's ability to use the requirements of function, the dictates of site, and a classical vocabulary to create a skyscraper that emanates authority. The bank's Neo-Renaissance limestone-faced tower is enhanced by classical elements traditionally associated with American bank architecture—most notably, a bowed two-story portico with monumental polished-granite columns, lions' heads, consoles, and foliated spandrels.

The site demanded a long, thin building, and Price approached the bank's design with a vision that related the skyscraper to a classical column. The tripartite scheme—a rusticated base, a nine-story midsection, and a capital topped by a prominent copper cornice—is a commanding visual, rather than functional, solution to organizing a tall structure. Price, an influential architect of skyscrapers, once remarked that "their aerial aspect [is] of more value to the city as a whole than the distorted partial values . . . we can obtain from the street." His Neoclassical vocabulary fuses well here with the dictates of skyscraper construction to create a distinctly modern, urban building. Price also transformed the narrow façade into an imposing entrance with a two-story portico and classical ornament.

The bank operated until 1918, when it was absorbed by the Bank of the Manhattan Company; in 1955 the resulting entity merged with Chase to become the Chase Manhattan Bank. Today the banking floor is a restaurant, and many of the upper floors are apartments.

HOTEL MARSEILLES, 1902–5
2689–2693 Broadway, Manhattan
Architect: Harry Allan Jacobs
Designated: October 2, 1990

A handsome example of the wave of grand hotels that swept up Broadway in the first decade of the twentieth century, the Hotel Marseilles was built during a development boom that struck the Upper West Side when the IRT subway line opened in 1904. With its brick-and-limestone façade, terra-cotta and wrought-iron detail, and sloping mansard roof, this gracious apartment hotel illustrates the rise of "modern French" commercial and hotel architecture in New York. The fashionable, Beaux Arts–derivative style is representative of France's influence over late-nineteenth-century American architecture and the large number of important American architects who attended the Ecole des Beaux-Arts in Paris.

The apartment hotel was America's answer to space-conscious European-style apartment living without the intrusive presence of servants, to which well-to-do New Yorkers objected. Like its famous counterparts the Ansonia and the Hotel Belleclaire, the Marseilles provided a full-service staff, central kitchens, and restaurants for its residents (both permanent and temporary) so that personal servants could be dispensed with. Its six upper stories were divided into single rooms and suites, while the ground floor was rented out to retailers, an integral element of the apartment hotel design, in keeping with Broadway's early image as a flourishing residential boulevard dotted with storefronts.

Architect Harry Allan Jacobs, who specialized in elegant residences, lavishly adorned the U-plan Hotel Marseilles with Beaux Arts flourishes—wrought-iron balconies front the fourth-floor bay windows, and spandrel panels are carved with foliage and keystones.

The hotel is little changed today except for the roof, which has been resurfaced in asphalt shingles, and since 1980 it has been used as subsidized housing for the elderly.

PENINSULA HOTEL, formerly the Gotham Hotel, 1902–5
696–700 Fifth Avenue, Manhattan
Architects: Hiss & Weekes
Designated: June 6, 1989

The Gotham is among the oldest and finest "skyscraper" hotels erected at a time when Fifth Avenue was being transformed from an exclusive residential street to a fashionable commercial thoroughfare. This boldly rendered neo–Italian Renaissance rocket, rising twenty stories (with a modern rooftop addition), is a stylistic counterpart to the flamboyant Beaux Arts St. Regis Hotel directly across Fifth Avenue.

As former employees of McKim, Mead & White, the powerful architectural firm famed for the revival of Renaissance forms, Philip Hiss and H. Hobart Weekes brought many of the firm's stylistic concepts to their design. Yet they demonstrated originality in adapting Renaissance structures to the skyscraper form and enhancing the result with sculptural detail—the ornate main entrance is adorned with foliate-patterned architrave molding, swags, and crowning figures of Ceres and Diana. Faced in limestone, the Gotham is configured like a classical column: it features a monumental, rusticated base; a smooth-faced shaft, with stone-balustraded balconies at the end bays; and a capital. The capital boasts a garlanded cornice, scroll brackets, and wreathed corbels supporting a two-story arcade that echoes the arcade at the base, visually uniting top to bottom. The Gotham's architectural lines harmonize skillfully with the Renaissance lines of McKim, Mead & White's University Club, which adjoins it to the south.

KNICKERBOCKER HOTEL, 1902–6
1462–1470 Broadway, Manhattan
Architects: 1902, Marvin & Davis and Bruce Price; 1906 annex, Trowbridge & Livingston
Designated: October 18, 1988

When the Knickerbocker Hotel opened on October 24, 1906, it was deemed a great success, attracting such dignitaries as Woodrow Wilson, George M. Cohan, Enrico Caruso, and others to the theater district, all eager to see its elegantly furnished bars and restaurants featuring electric fountains by Frederick MacMonnies and murals by American artists Maxfield Parrish and Frederic Remington. One of several luxury hotels financed by John Jacob Astor at the turn of the century, the Beaux Arts–style, 556-room Knickerbocker, executed in red brick with French Renaissance ornament and a spectacular copper mansard roof, could accommodate nearly one thousand guests; the public rooms could serve two thousand.

Beginning with the Astor House of 1836 near City Hall, the Astor family enjoyed a reputation for building costly and well-appointed hotels. John Jacob's cousin William Waldorf Astor's many ventures included the Waldorf Hotel (1895), built on a site adjacent to John Jacob's Astoria Hotel (also 1895). (The Waldorf and Astoria were eventually joined to form the Waldorf-Astoria, considered among the first rank of American hostelry.)

Touted as "a Fifth Avenue hotel at Broadway prices," the success of the Knickerbocker abruptly ended with the onset of the Depression. The hotel was then converted to commercial and office use.

574 SIXTH AVENUE BUILDING, 1903–4
574 Avenue of the Americas (also known as 57–59 West 16th Street), Manhattan
Architect: Simeon B. Eisendrath
Designated: August 14, 1990

The Knickerbocker Jewelry Company built this four-story retail store during a resurgence of commercial activity in the Ladies' Mile area around the turn of the century. Located two blocks from where such prestigious stores as B. Altman and Siegel-Cooper once stood, the building is modeled on larger commercial structures of the period. Like the more prominent stores, the Knickerbocker featured large show windows around the base and mezzanine. Rusticated and smooth brick piers that project beyond the plane of the spandrels and lintels were allusions to the steel-frame construction of taller commercial buildings. The flamboyant sheet-metal cornice—falling forward in a scroll—and the baroque spandrels and window arches on the upper two stories were meant to attract the attention of passengers on the Sixth Avenue Elevated train that ran in front of the store. These flourishes, along with the large windows on the Sixth Avenue façade, suggest a glittering jewel box. Inside, the mezzanine gallery once surrounded a twenty-one-foot-high main showroom on the first floor.

Despite the effort to present the building as a commercial palace, the jewelry store was a short-lived venture; in 1905 it was taken over by a cloak maker and has since been repeatedly remodeled.

FORMER TIFFANY & CO. BUILDING, 1903–6
397–409 Fifth Avenue
Architects: McKim, Mead & White
Designated: February 16, 1988

When Tiffany & Co., America's premier jewelers, moved uptown from Union Square, it almost single-handedly established Fifth Avenue as the city's most exclusive shopping street. In April 1903 Charles Cook, Tiffany's president, instructed the renowned architectural firm McKim, Mead & White to "build me a palace." Noted for moving away from the Richardsonian Romanesque style prevalent at the time and favoring an Italian Renaissance vocabulary, the firm modeled Tiffany & Co.'s lavish new quarters on the majestic sixteenth-century Palazzo Grimani in Venice. (The Grimanis were once the richest family in Venice and thus were a fitting symbol for America's foremost purveyor of jewelry and luxury goods.) Sheathed in white marble, the building creates the illusion of being a three-story structure, although it is actually seven stories tall. Large plate-glass windows, Corinthian-order piers and columns, and an imposing entablature distinguish the façade; the result is one of the most elegant and sophisticated commercial buildings in New York.

The Tiffany building illustrates the success of McKim, Mead & White in the reintroduction of classical design in America, particularly in this prestigious retail district. The firm's vision of a Neoclassical city of monumental white buildings ushered in a new era in American planning, known as the "City Beautiful" movement, noted for its Roman rather than Renaissance inspiration. And, despite major ground-floor alterations, the former Tiffany & Co. store's exquisite proportions testify to the firm's enduring legacy of innovation.

FIRE ENGINE COMPANY NO. 23, 1905–6
215 West 58th Street, Manhattan
Architect: Alexander H. Stevens
Designated: August 29, 1989

This limestone and red-brick Beaux Arts–style firehouse served as a much-copied model for later firehouse design. Although the fire department continued to commission individual architects, by 1904 a program of in-house construction was instituted by the superintendent of buildings, Alexander H. Stevens. His plans for No. 23 were thus used as a prototype for future firehouses constructed through the 1920s. The building's symmetry, the height of its windows, and Stevens' choice of materials work together to suggest a sober, restrained official structure.

Engine Company No. 23 has been on West 58th Street for more than one hundred years; it moved from 69th Street to a new firehouse at 233 West 58th Street (now demolished) in 1884. The company has helped to put out some of the most notable fires in New York history: the steamship *Normandie* (1940); the Empire State Building airplane crash (1945); the Times Tower and the Mayflower Hotel (1960); and Trump Tower, during its construction (1980).

TRINITY BUILDING, 1905–7
111 Broadway, Manhattan
Architect: Francis Hatch Kimball
Designated: June 7, 1988

The Trinity Building's picturesque roofline, together with Trinity Church next door, the United States Realty Building, and the Woolworth tower, creates a striking Gothic silhouette on lower Broadway. The building extends the full length of the block between Broadway and Trinity Place. The United States Realty and Construction Company commissioned this skyscraper to use as speculative office space at a time when major American businesses were establishing themselves in Lower Manhattan. While the Gothic style suggested scholasticism and spirituality—both thought incompatible with the image of capitalism—a few massive, early neo-Gothic skyscrapers like this one made a great impact on Manhattan's skyline. The Gothic cathedral-type tower this building anticipated emerged a few years later, in 1911, with Cass Gilbert's soaring Woolworth Building.

Architect Francis Kimball, a prolific Gothic Revivalist who had studied medieval church architecture in England, decided the ecclesiastical style best suited a commercial building that would flank one side of Trinity Church. (To protect the consecrated churchyard during construction, Kimball thoughtfully surrounded the building with cantilevered scaffolding to contain workmen and materials.) The steel-framed, twenty-one-story building sheathed in Indiana limestone exemplifies Kimball's innovative skyscraper engineering techniques. Most impressive is the fact that the tower is set on fifty concrete caissons sunk into bedrock using an ingenious pneumatic process in order to avoid disturbing Manhattan's sandy soil. The building and its companion, the United States Realty Building (built by the same architect two years later), set world records for construction time and were, at a combined cost of over $15 million, the most expensive commercial buildings of their era.

UNITED STATES REALTY BUILDING, 1907
115 Broadway, Manhattan
Architect: Francis Hatch Kimball
Designated: June 7, 1988

Among the first Gothic-inspired skyscrapers in New York, the United States Realty Building and its near twin, the Trinity Building, were constructed at a time when insurance companies, conscious of public mistrust of monopolies and big business, were attempting to create positive images of prosperity. "Commercial Gothic," as the style came to be known, with its spiritual connotations, provided visual allusions to tradition, respectability, and integrity and suggested that big business was there to serve, rather than to sell. The vertical thrust of the Gothic cathedral was also viewed as an appropriate predecessor to a modern, vertical style. Kimball wanted to produce "a broad effect in stone, in one plane, unbroken by vertical lines of projection." The modeling along Gothic lines was no doubt also determined by Kimball's sensitivity to the site, adjacent to Trinity Church. In fact, Kimball adjusted the scale of the decorative ornament and arcaded windows of the lower stories to avoid overwhelming one of New York City's outstanding landmarks.

The United States Realty and Trinity buildings set world records for rapidity of construction and were considered the costliest commercial structures ever, together totaling over $15 million dollars (including land). A graceful finishing touch was applied in 1912, when Kimball erected a handsome footbridge of ornamental wrought iron to join the roofs of the two structures.

MANUFACTURERS HANOVER TRUST BUILDING, 1907
77–79 Eighth Avenue, Manhattan
Architects: De Lemos & Cordes and Rudolph L. Daus
Designated: June 7, 1988

Built for the New York County National Bank and situated on a prominent corner across the street from the New York Bank for Savings, this refined example of the Academic Classical movement is typical of bank design following the 1893 World's Columbian Exposition in Chicago. Stirred by the exposition's spectacular "White City," American architects strove to create a style characterized by order, clarity, and sobriety—qualities considered particularly appropriate for the design of banks. The siting and stylistic connection between the two banks on this important and busy crossway is also in keeping with late-nineteenth-century urban ideals, which valued the interplay of types and forms within the classical idiom.

Though small in scale, the elegant white marble–clad building reflects the gravity and importance of the bank's financial operations through a dignified classicism, superimposing two orders—trabeated and arcuate—in a unified and structurally expressive manner. The narrow façade forms a pedimented portico, while the four-bay, 100-foot side elevation reflects the large banking room behind it.

In 1921 New York County National Bank merged with Chatham and Phoenix National Bank; three years later, this institution merged with the Metropolitan Trust Company. The bank was subsequently acquired in 1932 by the Manufacturers Trust Company—later named the Manufacturers Hanover Trust Company—which continues to own and occupy the building today.

GAINSBOROUGH STUDIOS, 1907–8
222 Central Park South, Manhattan
Architect: Charles W. Buckham
Designated: February 16, 1988

Built during the heyday of artists' cooperative housing, the Gainsborough is a rare surviving example of this type of structure. While cooperatively owned buildings had existed in the cities of Europe since the early nineteenth century, it was not until one hundred years later that the idea was accepted in New York. Construction of cooperative studio buildings was motivated then by the return of young American artists from their studies abroad, which increased the already soaring demand for adequate living and working spaces. Mindful of artists' requirements, architect Charles W. Buckham designed the apartments so that the double-height studios on 59th Street faced the coveted northern light, and the smaller apartments were located to the rear of the building.

The brainchild of portrait painter August Franzen (a well-established member of the New York art world who cited eighteenth-century artist Thomas Gainsborough's work as a model for his own), the Gainsborough's most distinctive feature is the terra-cotta frieze, "Festival Procession," created by Austrian-born sculptor Isidore Konti, which depicts people of all ages carrying gifts to the altar of the arts. Located above the first story, the frieze, in conjunction with the other elements of the façade—the colorful tiles above the sixth story, the bust of Gainsborough, and the artist's palette over the entrance—effectively announces the building's purpose.

METROPOLITAN LIFE INSURANCE COMPANY TOWER, 1907–9;
renovation, 1960–64
1 Madison Avenue, Manhattan
Architects: Pierre L. LeBrun, of Napoleon LeBrun & Sons; renovation, Lloyd Morgan and Eugene V. Meroni
Designated: June 13, 1989

Metropolitan Life's third president, John Rogers Hegeman, realizing the value of corporate architectural imagery, took an avid interest in the construction of his company's home office. Indeed, it is Hegeman who is credited with conceiving the idea of a tower. During his tenure, from 1891 to 1919, the company expanded its complex to eight buildings, including the tower, all connected by corridors running east-west between avenues and north-south across streets. The vast complex covered two city blocks near Madison Square Park.

Recalling the famous campanile at Venice's Piazza San Marco, this 700-foot tower was the world's tallest building for four years after its completion. Architect Pierre LeBrun modeled its proportions on those of a Doric column, which was then translated by engineers into a fifty-story steel frame. The structure is distinguished by an arcaded capital that rises to a setback capped with a pyramidal spire, cupola, and glazed lantern. A major renovation by Morgan & Meroni in the early 1960s replaced the tower's original white-marble facing with limestone and eliminated much of the ornamental detail in order to harmonize with a new home office building. However, LeBrun's four great clock faces, featuring seventeen-foot-long minute hands weighing a thousand pounds each, continue to decorate the shaft.

EVERETT BUILDING, 1908
45 East 17th Street (also known as 200–218 Park Avenue South), Manhattan
Architects: Goldwin Starrett & Van Vleck
Designated: September 6, 1988

Built for the Everett Investing Company, this is a quintessential example of the commercial building type defined by A. C. David in the *Architectural Record* of 1910: functional, fireproof, and quickly constructed—the sixteen-story building was erected in just four months—while demonstrating a concern for "architectural decency." Prominently situated on a corner site at Union Square, the building, together with the monumental Germania Life Insurance Company Building, forms an imposing terminus to Park Avenue South.

In its frank expression of function, the tower recalls the Chicago style of commercial architecture. The appearance of a grid on the façade demonstrates the Chicago school's major tenet: to articulate the interior structure on the exterior. Here, the juxtaposition of verticals and horizontals, such as the crossings of ribbed mullions and textured panels on the eleven-story shaft, are surrogates for the concealed skeletal frame.

While a significant portion of the two upper stories appears to have been resurfaced, the structure remains largely unchanged. It continues to serve as an office building with retail stores on the ground floor.

SECOND BATTERY ARMORY, 1908–11; addition, c. 1928
1122 Franklin Avenue, The Bronx
Architects: Charles C. Haight; addition, Benjamin W. Levithan
Designated: June 2, 1992

The first permanent armory built in the Bronx, this medieval-looking building originally housed the Second Battery, a field artillery unit of the National Guard. The unit served during a number of major New York strikes and riots (including the Abolition Riot of 1834 and the draft riots of 1863) as well as in the Civil and Spanish-American Wars. Located in the Morrisania section of the Bronx, the armory reflects the rapid growth of the borough at the turn of the century, when it was formally annexed to the City of New York.

Designed by Charles C. Haight, a former member of the New York State militia and known for his public institutional buildings—many in the English Collegiate Gothic style, including eleven buildings at Yale University—the armory is notable for its bold massing, expressive brick forms, picturesque asymmetry, and restrained Gothic vocabulary. Haight's design is in keeping with the tradition of medieval imagery in earlier New York armory buildings, but refers also to Collegiate Gothic institutions. In 1917 the *Architectural Record* considered the Bronx armory the best building in the entire borough.

In addition to office space, the structure includes a rifle range, stables, a gun room, and a drill shed with 167-foot-wide iron roof trusses. Today the structure is managed by the Human Resources Administration of the City of New York and is used as a shelter for the homeless.

THE LOUIS ARMSTRONG HOUSE, 1910
34–56 107th Street, Queens
Architect: Robert W. Johnson
Designated: December 13, 1988

Louis Armstrong, born in New Orleans in 1901, began his musical career at the age of ten as the tenor in a children's street quartet, singing ragtime and comic songs. On New Year's Eve, 1912, he was arrested for firing a pistol in celebration and sent to the Colored Waifs' Home for eighteen months; there he learned to play the cornet. After his release, he continued to play with various New Orleans bands while working odd jobs. In 1930 Armstrong moved to New York, from there traveling more and more widely as he became increasingly well known.

In 1942 Armstrong married his third wife, Lucille Wilson; the following year she purchased and furnished this home in Corona, Queens. The modest, brick-clad frame structure was home to Armstrong from 1943 until his death in 1971. According to Lucille, when Louis first went to see it, he wasn't ready to settle down. "He left his bags in the cab and told the driver to wait for him. But, to his surprise, he fell in love with the house."

Lucille remained in this home until her death in 1983, whereupon the house and its contents were given by her to the City of New York to serve as a museum and study center devoted to Armstrong's career and the history of American jazz. The house appears the same today as when the Armstrongs lived there.

GUARDIAN LIFE BUILDING, formerly the
Germania Life Insurance Company Building, 1910–11
50 Union Square East, Manhattan
Architects: D'Oench & Yost
Designated: September 6, 1988

The unlikely founder of the Germania Life Insurance Company was Hugo Wesendonck, a former member of the Frankfurt parliament who fled a death sentence in Germany when the Revolution of 1848 failed and the parliament was disbanded. After dabbling in the silk business in Philadelphia, he decided "to bring the benefits of life insurance to the 'little people' of German extraction" in New York. Regarded highly for its ethical conduct and economical practices, the company flourished in the second half of the nineteenth century. The cost of this building, Germania's fourth headquarters, was a million dollars. (Anti-German sentiment during World War I led the owners to change the company's name to Guardian Life in 1918.)

While the building displays traditional European design elements—most prominently the four-story, Second Empire–style mansard roof and the masonry exterior—it also reflects the practical considerations of modern design. For instance, the architects provided the maximum amount of usable floor space, flooded with natural light, using a sophisticated system of fireproof floor construction. The ornamentation of the building, including garlanded keystones, links it with the "Cartouche" style, which distinguished Parisian architecture of the 1890s in its elaborate use of swags, garlands, and festoons. References to sixteenth-century German architecture, such as the interesting variety and arrangement of the dormer windows, can also be seen.

LONG DISTANCE BUILDING OF THE AMERICAN TELEPHONE & TELEGRAPH COMPANY AND FIRST FLOOR INTERIOR, 1911–14; 1914–16; 1930–32
32 Sixth Avenue, Manhattan
Architects: Cyrus L. W. Eidlitz and McKenzie, Voorhees & Gmelin; 1930–32, Ralph Walker, of Voorhees, Gmelin & Walker
Designated: October 1, 1991

This massive, brick Art Deco skyscraper was the result of three building campaigns, each undertaken in response to the remarkable growth of the early-twentieth-century long-distance communications industry. The first structure, a seventeen-story Romanesque Revival office building and telephone exchange, was prudently designed with a foundation and steel skeleton that would be able to accommodate additional stories. Only two months after completion, plans were filed to enlarge the structure to twenty-four stories; the seven-story addition extended the exterior architectural features of the original design. Still, within the next decade, the company required even more space. The last design added a multi-story penthouse and two large twenty-seven-story extensions. In its final state, the building—which was in use twenty-four hours a day—contained dormitories, a kitchen, three cafeterias, a five-hundred-seat auditorium, recreation spaces, and a medical department.

This "small city," with its overall sculptural quality and linear ornamentation, is united by the continuous polished Texas pink-granite water table, the vertical bands of brick, coherent fenestration patterns, and the faceted parapet of lighter colored brick. The earlier sections are faced in red-brown brick; the portions dating from the 1930–32 alteration are faced in a distinctive blend of red, orange, gray, brown, and dark-brown brick.

As he had done in the Barclay-Vesey building, architect Ralph Walker united the lobby with the exterior by echoing the building's architectural elements in his interior decorative program: the exterior brick curtain walls are reflected in the earth-colored tiles of the lobby, and the exterior vertical piers are recalled in the red tile pilasters set in the umber tile wall. Although broken into disjointed spaces because of the irregular building plan, the lobby is unified by a harmonious scheme of colors and textures and the consistent use of indirect lighting. Walker also used linear decorative motifs throughout to represent modern technology: patterns of terrazzo (mosaic flooring), tile, and glass are suggestive of the long-distance telephone lines and wires. In a less abstract fashion, the ceiling decoration includes allegorical figures of Australia, Asia, Africa, and Europe, reminding visitors of the building's function as a main hub of international communication: it was the crossroads of all main trunk routes in the Northeast, serving 360 cities and handling all transoceanic calls.

The building remains largely as it was in 1932, but it now also houses AT&T's television operations, as well as other departments and corporate offices.

CHARLES SCRIBNER'S SONS BUILDING INTERIOR, 1912–13
597 Fifth Avenue, Manhattan
Architect: Ernest Flagg
Designated: July 11, 1989

Today one of the most prominent publishing houses in the country, Scribner's began in 1846 with the publication of Edwin Hall's *The Puritans and Their Principles* and was soon established as a leading publisher of theological and philosophical books. Scribner's was also the first to publish the American edition of the *Encyclopedia Britannica*.

After occupying several offices in Lower Manhattan, the company followed commercial movement north to Midtown. Architect Ernest Flagg, Charles Scribner's brother-in-law and an eminent practitioner of Beaux Arts architecture, was asked to design the new headquarters. While adhering to the Beaux Arts tenet of logical planning, Flagg's two-story, plaster-paneled vaulted space—graced with a mezzanine, balconies, and a clerestory—resembles nothing so much as the well-tended library of a grand private home. The flamboyant ironwork framing the first-floor interior, and continuing in the staircase and balcony railings, exemplifies some of the best design and craftsmanship of the early twentieth century. Flagg's eye for spatial complexity and beautiful detail is apparent in the mirrored end wall, the graceful central staircase, and the iconography of the ceiling detail, which illuminates Scribner's world of publishing. The first-floor bookstore is now leased by Brentano, a division of Waldenbook Company. The building is owned by Edizione Realty Corporation, a subsidiary of the Benetton family.

41ST POLICE PRECINCT STATION HOUSE, formerly the
62nd Police Precinct Station House, 1912–14
1086 Simpson Street, The Bronx
Architects: Hazzard, Erskine & Blagden
Designated: June 2, 1992

Built in the West Farms area of the Bronx at a time of rapid development—due to the construction of the elevated portion of the subway—the station reflects the vision of the "City Beautiful" movement. Evoking the fifteenth- and early-sixteenth-century palaces of Florence and Rome, particularly Michelozzo Michelozzi's Palazzo Riccardi, built for Cosimo de' Medici in Florence, the style was considered appropriate for civic architecture. The three-story Simpson Street façade is faced with limestone ashlar—the ground story rusticated and the second and third stories smooth—and five large arches spring from the building's granite base. The structure is crowned with a richly ornamented terra-cotta cornice and a broad-eaved, hipped roof, originally covered in green tile.

When the station house first opened, the area still boasted the vestiges of gardens and orchards. World War II, however, drew thousands who had found employment in the war-related industries located nearby. By the 1960s many of these industries had relocated, causing unemployment to increase, housing maintenance to decline, and poverty to escalate. By the 1970s the majority of arrests made in the area were drug related, and for many residents the station house had become less a refuge and more a fortress; it was even nicknamed "Fort Apache" by the press. A new station house is under construction for the 41st precinct, and the once-admired station on Simpson Street will become a branch office of the Safe Streets program.

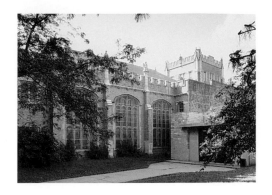

FLUSHING HIGH SCHOOL, 1912–15
35–01 Union Street, Queens
Architect: C. B. J. Snyder
Designated: January 8, 1991

Flushing High School, the city's oldest public high school, is located in one of the three colonial settlements that now comprise Queens. During the seventeenth century, this neighborhood began to develop into one of the most important centers for horticulture in the country. Nurseries in Flushing provided many of the trees in Central and Prospect Parks. The grounds of the school contain many rare trees and plants that recall the area's history. Less than a block from the high school stands a weeping beech tree that dates to 1847—also a designated New York City landmark.

Following the consolidation of New York City in 1898, Flushing residents, aware of the potential for rapid development in the area due to the proposed construction of the Queensborough Bridge and the extension of the subway into Queens, began to lobby for a new high school. This brick and gray-speckled terra-cotta building in its campus-like setting was the outstanding response of the newly formed city government. The school's monumental square entrance tower, picturesque silhouette, asymmetrical massing, and assorted Gothic-inspired details—crenellation, grotesque corbels, and heraldic statues of unicorns and griffins—echo the fanciful conjoining of styles typical of England's universities. This so-called Collegiate Gothic style was introduced to New York public school architecture by C. B. J. Snyder, superintendent of buildings for the Board of Education from 1891 to 1923.

RODIN STUDIOS, 1916–17
200 West 57th Street, Manhattan
Architect: Cass Gilbert
Designated: February 16, 1988

Like many of the studio buildings constructed in the 1880s, Rodin Studios was a cooperative venture undertaken by a group of artists who raised the necessary capital, elected officers, and formed a corporation. In return, each became an owner with the exclusive right to occupy or sublet one of the studio apartments in the building. The corporation chose as architect Cass Gilbert, whose patronage of artists for his own commissions perhaps guided the artists in their selection.

Named for the French sculptor considered by many to be the greatest living artist at the time, the Rodin Studios included stores on the first floor, offices on the second and third floors, and apartments and studios on the remaining eleven floors. The base of the building is comprised of five broad bays containing shop windows and a central entrance. The exterior is distinguished by rough-faced brick in richly colored hues ranging from buff to burnt-gold. As was also true of Gilbert's renowned "cathedral of commerce," the Woolworth Building, the Rodin had an extensive terra-cotta decorative program.

The building's design managed to combine the best contemporary technology with a graceful French Renaissance style. The studios are placed across the northern façade of the building, providing the maximum light necessary for a painter's work. The addition of handsome cast-iron canopies suspended between studio windows is another example of Gilbert's ability to marry elegantly form and function.

THE HOWARD E. AND JESSIE JONES HOUSE, 1916–17
8200 Narrows Avenue, Brooklyn
Architect: James Sarsfield Kennedy
Designated: March 8, 1988

One of the finest examples of the Arts and Crafts style of architecture in New York City, the Jones house is built of large, randomly laid, uncut rocks and boulders in assorted colors. One of the most unusual and appealing features of the house is the original asphalt roof; its tiles are scattered unevenly across the surface, and its sensuous curves and smooth molded edges are reminiscent of the thatched roofs of rural English cottages. Irregular terraced steps form a path to the main entrance through a central peak-roofed vestibule with a round-arched front. The varied heights of the house lead upward to a massive end-wall chimney, calling attention to the symbolic importance of the hearth as the center of the home.

The architect, James Sarsfield Kennedy, specialized in free-standing residences and worked in a variety of styles, frequently combining modern and historic sources. In this house, designed for shipping merchant Howard Jones, the architect created a late, yet sophisticated, version of the Arts and Crafts style, which advocated the handmade as a humanizing influence in the face of a rising tide of nineteenth-century industrialization. Kennedy's choice of rugged materials and avoidance of exact, crisp finishes effect the architectural "savagery" that John Ruskin, an early proponent of the movement, called for. Kennedy's finishing touch—a simple iron fence punctuated with widely spaced newels of roughly hewn stone—echoes and encloses this remarkable structure.

BUSH TOWER, 1916–18
130–132 West 42nd Street and 133–137 West 41st Street, Manhattan
Architects: Helmle & Corbett
Designated: October 18, 1988

Designed prior to the adoption of the 1916 New York City law that mandated setbacks for skyscrapers to allow sunlight to reach city streets, architect Harvey Wiley Corbett's Bush Tower incorporated setbacks as an aesthetic solution—the rooftop water tank and elevator housing unit were concealed on the recessed top story. And it soon became the prototype for the stepped-back buildings of the future.

The thirty-story buff brick and terra-cotta tower was named for Irving T. Bush, an oil company executive who established Brooklyn's Bush Terminal Company in 1902. The company later grew to occupy thirty city blocks of extensive lofts, warehouses, and piers for manufacturing, storing, and shipping goods. Bush Tower, in a prime location between the two major railroad terminals and readily accessible to out-of-town buyers, was created as a centralized merchandise showroom. While an unpartitioned display area was not an entirely new idea, the Bush project was much broader in scope than any other existing facility in New York. Lower floors housed a luxurious Buyers' Club decorated in an "Old English" style.

The Bush Terminal Company lost this property to the Metropolitan Life Insurance Company in 1938 foreclosure proceedings. Subsequent alterations to the building have been limited to changes in the street-level façade—reflecting the changing uses of the building—and the insertion of windows in the side walls between Corbett's handsome trompe l'oeil colored brick piers.

THE WONDER WHEEL, 1918–20
3059 West 12th Street, Brooklyn
Inventor: Charles Herman; manufactured and built by the Eccentric Ferris Wheel Amusement Company
Designated: May 23, 1989

The Wonder Wheel opened on Memorial Day, 1920, in "Sodom by the Sea," as Coney Island was known—a place synonymous with entertainment, fantasy, and fun for over one hundred years. Sigmund Freud said it was "the only place in the United States" that interested him.

The modern Ferris wheel is named for George W. G. Ferris (1859–1896), a civil engineer and head of the Pittsburgh Bridge Company. His giant, 264-foot-high wheel, erected for the 1893 Chicago World's Columbian Exposition, was developed from European and Oriental swing-like prototypes developed centuries ago at fairs and festivals. Though smaller (150 feet high), the Wonder Wheel's more sophisticated design was an improvement on the Ferris wheel. Of the twenty-four passenger cars, sixteen are swinging cars that slide along a serpentine track that leads each car either toward the hub or, as the wheel turns, toward the circumference. The wheel accommodates 160 passengers, weighs 200 tons, and is operated by a forty-horsepower motor. Since opening day the Wonder Wheel has carried approximately thirty million pleasure seekers. Offering panoramic views of Brooklyn, it is an important feature of the borough's skyline and, happily, has never caused an injury.

CROSSLAND FEDERAL SAVINGS BANK, formerly the
Greenwich Savings Bank, AND INTERIOR, 1922–24
1352–1362 Broadway (also known as 985 Sixth Avenue), Manhattan
Architects: York & Sawyer
Designated: March 3, 1992

One of the finest examples of the Academic Classical tradition in the country, this new
facility marked the success of the Greenwich Savings Bank in Greenwich Village and the
resultant desire of its trustees to move the headquarters to a more prominent Midtown
location, following the lead of the rest of the commercial district.

The bank's architects, Edward Palmer York and Philip Sawyer, had both worked for
McKim, Mead & White, and they carried the senior firm's trademark monumental classicism
into their designs. The Greenwich Savings Bank design was doubtless influenced by the two-
story, Italian Rennaisance Revival Herald Building, designed by McKim, Mead & White,
that once stood across the street, to the south. York was once Stanford White's assistant, and
Sawyer studied at the Ecole des Beaux-Arts in Paris; together they designed many hospital,
college, and federal buildings, although they are best known for their bank buildings.

Sawyer's knowledge of ancient Roman architecture is manifest in the manner in which the
three façades are articulated by a monumental Corinthian colonnade and a rusticated
podium. His knowledge and appreciation of eighteenth- and nineteenth-century French
planning and design are expressed in the elliptical floorplan of the main banking room. The
continuous elliptical screen, faced with Indiana limestone and Ohio sandstone, conceals the
fact that between this and the exterior wall there are six stories of offices and a basement.
For all of the building's historicism, the banking room is lit by a twentieth-century light
diffuser that hangs seventy-two feet above it.

Other than the change of signage on the exterior, the building has undergone few changes
since the day it opened. In 1981 it became the Metropolitan Savings Bank and two years
later, the Crossland Federal Savings Bank.

REFORMED CHURCH OF HUGUENOT PARK, 1923–24
5475 Amboy Road, Staten Island
Architects: Ernest Flagg; 1955 addition, James Whitford, Jr.
Designated: November 20, 1990

Library
906 Huguenot Avenue, c. 1903–5
Architect: Unknown

This church was built to commemorate the three-hundredth anniversary of the Huguenots settling on Staten Island after fleeing religious persecution in France. It stands on farmland that originally belonged to Benjamin T. Prall, a direct descendant of Pierre Billiou, leader of the first Huguenots to arrive on the island. Stylistically the church recalls medieval Romanesque and vernacular Norman architecture found in France and England. It is faced in concrete and mosaic serpentine stone quarried from architect Ernest Flagg's estate; Staten Island's rich-hued native serpentine stone—combined with Beaux Arts craftsmanship and technological innovations—is Flagg's trademark. Other features include a long nave articulated by a steeply pitched roof, gabled entrance pavilions on each side of the building's south end, a large square tower topped by a pyramidal roof at the north end, and a polygonal spire rising from the northwest corner. The massing of pared-down, abstract forms is the architect's personal interpretation of medievalism. A one-story assembly hall with a peaked roof, sympathetic in style to the original building, was added to the west side of the church by architect James Whitford, Jr., in 1955.

At the northeast corner of the site stands a diminutive, one-story frame building that was moved to its present location in the early twentieth century and served as the smallest branch of the New York Public Library until 1985.

In the mid-1980s an extensive restoration program repaired the asphalt shingle roof (originally seam metal strips) and replaced approximately twenty percent of the church's original crumbling stone with the same native serpentine stone Flagg had used.

BARCLAY-VESEY BUILDING AND FIRST FLOOR INTERIOR, 1923–27
140 West Street, Manhattan
Architect: Ralph Walker, of McKenzie, Voorhees & Gmelin
Designated: October 1, 1991

This stunning example of American Art Deco was built for the New York Telephone Company as their new central headquarters. Designed to be "as modern as the telephone activity it houses" and to symbolize the size and technological advances of the company, the building program mandated a facility large enough for six thousand employees serving 120,000 telephone lines. Hailed in its day as the ultimate modern skyscraper, the thirty-two-story building was awarded the Architectural League of New York's Gold Medal of Honor in 1927 and became a model for telephone headquarters later built throughout New York.

The company selected architects McKenzie, Voorhees & Gmelin, a firm that had a long history with New York Telephone. The critical success of the building quickly elevated architect Ralph Walker to partnership status in McKenzie, Voorhees & Gmelin, even though this was his first major project in association with the firm. Subsequent corporate commissions brought Walker recognition as a designer of Art Deco skyscrapers, earning him in 1957 the title "architect of the century" from the American Institute of Architects. Walker's approach to design was based on two precepts—that economy was the key to good design, and that machine technology was the road to modern style.

Walker's pragmatism is evident in both the design and the choice of building materials. Most of the façade is brick, which was selected for its texture and subtle color, with ornament for the upper stories fashioned in machine-cast stone. Occupying a parallelogram-shaped, 52,000-square-foot site, the massive base of the building was determined in part by the fact that many of the internal operations required only artificial light, thus eliminating the need for an interior court.

The dramatic first-floor interior is an integral component of the building. Serving as a long corridor between the two entrance vestibules, the lobby's design establishes continuity between exterior and interior by mirroring external elements, such as vertical piers, in the program of internal ornaments, like the marble pilasters. Walker also attempted to eliminate handwork in his interior design, choosing instead such materials as veneer, which celebrated machine technology. This machine-age emphasis was further underscored by a series of painted ceiling panels and bronze floor plaques that illustrate advancements in communications through the ages and, specifically, New York Telephone's role in these developments.

UNITED WORKERS' COOPERATIVE COLONY ("The Coops")
The Bronx
Designated: June 2, 1992

2700–2744 Bronx Park East, 1926–27
Architects: Springsteen & Goldhammer

2846–2870 Bronx Park East, 1927–29
Architect: Herman Jessor

These two residential complexes were erected by the United Workers' Cooperative Association (a group largely comprised of idealistic Jewish immigrant garment workers) in response to the appalling living conditions that many new immigrants faced on arrival in New York. Both projects were carefully sited and planned to maximize light, air, and privacy. Inspired in part by communist teachings, the colony encouraged cooperative activity in all aspects of life and was equipped with classrooms, a library, a gymnasium, and other facilities for social interaction. The workers organized their colony so that all residents shared equally in ownership and management and were prohibited from selling apartments at a profit.

The first complex, while incorporating neo-Tudor elements—such as pointed arches and half-timbering—also reflects a political view, with hammer-and-sickle motifs, symbols of learning, and smoking factories depicted in the spandrels of several of the pointed-arch entrances. The second complex was designed in an avant-garde Expressionist mode reminiscent of the progressive housing complexes that had recently been erected in northern Europe, especially in Amsterdam. Brick was used to create texture and pattern, a hallmark of the Amsterdam school of architecture.

The cooperative failed financially early in the Depression and became a rental complex in 1943. During Senator McCarthy's "witch-hunts" of the immediate post–World War II era, all residents of the colony became suspect. By the late 1970s, almost all of the original residents were gone, and in the mid-1980s, a new owner, Allerton Associates, rehabilitated the project.

PARAMOUNT BUILDING, 1926–27
1493–1501 Broadway, Manhattan
Architects: Rapp & Rapp
Designated: November 1, 1988

Situated in the heart of Times Square, this brick-clad setback skyscraper originally housed the Paramount Theater and served as the eastern headquarters for the Famous Players–Lasky Corporation, the forerunner of Paramount Pictures. Headed by Adolph Zukor and Jesse Lasky in the 1920s and 30s, Paramount could boast a roster of stars that included Rudolph Valentino, Clara Bow, Gloria Swanson, Gary Cooper, William Powell, Mae West, and Claudette Colbert.

The Paramount Building occupies the entire 200-foot block front on the west side of Broadway between 43rd and 44th streets and extends 207 feet on the side streets. Rising thirty-three stories, including a clock tower, it was the tallest structure north of the Woolworth Building on Broadway at the time it was built. Although the building's ornamental details are classical in style, its massing and setbacks were characteristic of the modern trend in 1920s office-building design.

Paramount Pictures, committed to creating a symbol of the company's role in the motion picture industry, added a number of aggrandizing elements: the setbacks were floodlit at each level; a globe was placed atop the clock tower to advertise the worldwide activities of Paramount; and the clocks' faces featured five-pointed stars, the Paramount trademark, to mark the hour. Not surprisingly, a film record of the building's construction was also made by the enthusiastic clients.

THE CYCLONE, 1927
834 Surf Avenue at West 10th Street, Brooklyn
Inventor: Harry C. Baker
Engineer: Vernon Keenan
Designated: July 12, 1988

By the time the Cyclone was introduced to Coney Island—New York's seaside Disneyland of the early twentieth century—the amusement park entertained nearly a million visitors every Sunday afternoon. While Irving Berlin and Mae West entertained the crowds in Coney Island's theaters, many were tempted to ride this thrilling coaster, a descendant of eighteenth-century Russian ice slides.

The world's first modern roller coaster was built at Coney Island in 1884, and the ride became popular here. The Cyclone is a rare species of wooden-track, twister-type coaster (resting on a steel framework) that is irreplaceable today because of the building code of the City of New York, which prohibits the construction of timber-supported roller coasters. The Cyclone hits a record-breaking speed of 68 miles per hour in order to maintain velocity over the course of its three thousand feet of looping, hilly track. (It is the tremendous weight of the old-fashioned cars that allows the Cyclone to reach its high speeds.) A chain carries the cars to the first plunge of ninety feet, after which they travel on their own momentum over six fan turns and eight more drops. Aviator Charles Lindbergh called the ride a "greater thrill than flying an airplane at top speed."

Today the Cyclone, one of the country's premier roller coasters, stands in Astroland amusement park—the only survivor of nearly two dozen roller coasters that once could be found in Coney Island.

HEARST MAGAZINE BUILDING, 1927–28
951–969 Eighth Avenue, Manhattan
Architects: Joseph Urban and George B. Post & Sons
Designated: February 16, 1988

Planned as the centerpiece of William Randolph Hearst's Plaza, this building is the sole surviving component of a grand scheme that would collapse because of the Depression and Hearst's own speculative and extravagant real-estate ventures. Hearst had moved to New York in 1895, seeking national prominence in politics. Initially he leased two floors in the Tribune Building in Printing House Square, but as other papers moved uptown, he began to envision a Midtown headquarters in the Columbus Circle area, a rapidly developing section of Manhattan already distinguished by several commercial buildings, as well as Carnegie Hall, the Art Students League, and numerous art galleries that Hearst frequented.

Encouraged by expectations for Columbus Circle's future as an extension of New York's theater district, Hearst, as early as 1895, purchased a small block between Columbus Circle and 56th Street. Plans for this block were abandoned when, in 1903, Hearst bought a larger block immediately south. He followed this pattern of buying blocks and abandoning plans until 1921, when he finally bought the largest lot in the area "for the headquarters of his eastern enterprises." Originally intended to hold a two-story structure housing stores, offices, and an auditorium, it ultimately became the site of the International Magazine Building.

Hearst's eventually ruinous pattern of speculative real-estate purchases and lack of follow-through may explain the unusual appearance of the building, created by noted architect and theater and stage designer Joseph Urban as a base for a projected, but never-completed, skyscraper. Hearst had been introduced to Urban by the noted impresario Florenz Ziegfeld, beginning a close association between the two lovers of spectacle. Urban's design is itself a theatrical tour de force, recalling the grandiosity of World's Fair architecture. Placed atop pylons, figures by German sculptor Henry Kreis dramatically break through a continuous second-story balustrade and are further accentuated by columns rising behind them.

BEAUX-ARTS INSTITUTE OF DESIGN, 1928
304 East 44th Street, Manhattan
Architect: Frederic C. Hirons, of Dennison & Hirons
Designated: August 23, 1988

Chartered in 1916 by the Society of Beaux-Arts Architects, the Beaux-Arts Institute of Design served as the national headquarters for architectural instruction modeled after the atelier system of the prestigious Ecole des Beaux-Arts in Paris, where students were trained in the studio of a practicing architect. The basis of the curriculum was a series of architectural competitions treating different design problems and increasing in difficulty as the student progressed. The institute established a nationwide standard of excellence in architectural education.

Appropriately, in 1927, when a new building was needed to meet the institute's growing enrollment, the board of trustees organized a competition open to all members of the institute and Society of Beaux-Arts Architects who were practicing architects. Participants included noted architects Frederic C. Hirons, Raymond Hood, Ralph Walker, Arthur Loomis Harmon, William Lamb, and Harvey Wiley Corbett.

Hirons's winning design combined modern, streamlined Art Deco elements with Beaux Arts principles of symmetry, axial planning, use of ornament to highlight important areas in the design, and the integration of architecture and the other fine arts. Vivid polychrome terra-cotta spandrel plaques by noted sculptor and model-maker René Chambellan depict the Parthenon, St. Peter's Church, and the Ecole des Beaux-Arts, recalling the institute's classical and architectural tradition. A series of allegorical figures in the relief panels alludes to the architectural profession, and bold block lettering dramatically surmounts the double-height entrance. The Atlantic Terra Cotta Company, then one of the largest and best-known manufacturers of terra-cotta in the world, executed the spandrel plaques on the façade.

MASTER BUILDING, 1928–29
310–312 Riverside Drive, Manhattan
Architects: Harvey Wiley Corbett, of Helmle, Corbett & Harrison, and Sugarman & Berger
Designated: December 5, 1989

Originally designed as a combination apartment hotel and museum, this Art Deco skyscraper was commissioned by foreign exchange broker Louis L. Horch and his wife, Nettie. They were both followers and patrons of the Russian artist and mystic Nicholas Roerich, to whom the museum was dedicated. The building has always played an important cultural role in New York City, housing first the Roerich Museum, in 1929, and later the Riverside Museum; an art school, the Master Institute of United Arts; and, since 1961, the Equity Library Theater, a showcase for New York artists.

One of the tallest residential structures on Riverside Drive, the building expresses its dual function in the design of the lower two stories—fewer windows and dramatically exaggerated entrances indicate their public character. The design also incorporates significant Art Deco elements, such as patterned brickwork that varies in color from dark at the base to light at the tower, setbacks, regular and faceted massing of the upper stories, and an ornamental cap. The most distinctive features are the corner windows, derived from modern European architecture and cited in contemporary accounts as the first use of this feature in a skyscraper in New York City; they are particularly appropriate for a building with views of Riverside Park and the Hudson River.

WESTERN UNION BUILDING AND FIRST FLOOR INTERIOR, 1928–30
60 Hudson Street, Manhattan
Architect: Ralph Walker, of Voorhees, Gmelin & Walker
Designated: October 1, 1991

This dramatically massed Art Deco skyscraper is characteristic of a group of communications buildings designed by Ralph Walker in the late 1920s. Like New York Telephone and other affiliates of AT&T, Western Union commissioned a modernistic skyscraper to both consolidate operations and establish a corporate identity compatible with advanced technology. Because of complex technical requirements, the "Telegraph Capitol of America," which housed seventy million feet of wire and thirty miles of conduit, took two years to complete. In addition to the continuously operating telegraph rooms, the building contained training rooms for operators, classrooms for high school study and mechanical trades, a library, and a gymnasium.

Walker's preference for brick as the material for his communications buildings is here fully indulged in a graded color scheme. Employing nineteen shades, from a deep rose-red at the base to a light, delicate yellowish pink at the top, the curtain walls of the façades part near street level to become a series of large proscenium-like openings, with fanned, pleated forms suggesting the folds of a drawn stage curtain.

Walker's style is also evident in the striking cliffed forms of the building and its faceted, vertical treatment. Further typical of Walker's design approach is a close visual connection between exterior and interior. This is displayed here in the repeated setback skyscraper shape seen in exterior doorway openings, a mailbox, and interior door designs. The all-brick exterior is recalled in the unusual, patterned brick corridor (which even contains a brick reception desk) that stretches between two entrance vestibules. Indirect lighting, the barrel-vaulted Guavastino tile ceiling, and corbel-arched doorways underscore the design's Expressionist aspects.

Sold in 1947, the building continued to be occupied by Western Union until 1983. It still serves as a communications center, housing both equipment and offices.

ANDREW FREEDMAN HOME, 1922–24; wings, 1928–31
1125 Grand Concourse, The Bronx
Architects: Joseph H. Freedlander and Harry Allan Jacobs; wings, David Levy
Designated: June 2, 1992

Successfully combining the manner of an urban Italian Renaissance palazzo with the setting and terraces of a rural villa, this home was built as a result of an unusual bequest in the will of wealthy capitalist Andrew Freedman, best known as the owner of the Giants, the New York baseball club. He asked that a home be established for "aged and indigent persons of both sexes" who were once wealthy.

Though this was architects Joseph Freedlander and Harry Allan Jacobs' only project together, both had attended the Ecole des Beaux-Arts in Paris and were well-known members of New York's architectural establishment. (Joseph Freedlander was one of the first three Americans to actually complete the Ecole curriculum and receive a diploma.) Freedlander's affinity for the Paris school's philosophy is obvious in the monumental massing of the home and its references to several traditions of European architecture. Its design features a recessed loggia, a balustraded terrace, fine stonework, and beautiful wrought-iron detail. While the design relies on historical sources, the home is a steel-frame, fireproof structure, with concrete floors and terra-cotta and brick partitions.

Referred to as a retreat for millionaires by the press, the early residents were actually doctors, dressmakers, and teachers. In the years before the home closed in 1983, many residents were German and Austrian Jewish refugees. The Mid-Bronx Senior Citizens Council bought the building in 1983, and the elegant rooms continue to serve the elderly.

BEAUX-ARTS APARTMENTS, 1929–30
307 and 310 East 44th Street, Manhattan
Architects: Kenneth M. Murchison and Raymond Hood, of Raymond Hood,
Godley & Fouilhoux
Designated: July 11, 1989

In 1928, facing a scheduled move to new headquarters at 304 East 44th Street, the board of the Beaux-Arts Institute of Design formed the Beaux-Arts Development Corporation with the intention of financing, designing, building, and managing its own real-estate venture, the Beaux-Arts Apartments. These apartments were intended to serve as adjuncts to the new institute, providing residential and studio accommodations for architects and artists.

Composed of some of the most prominent and well-connected architects of the day, the corporation included Raymond Hood, one of the most influential American architects of the twentieth century, and Kenneth Murchison. The two sixteen-story structures were among the first in New York City to reflect the horizontal emphasis of modernist European architecture and incorporate an Art Moderne convention of using industrial materials in a residential rather than commercial context—hence the bold massing, streamlined geometric metal railings, and corner windows. Originally constructed as "apartment hotels," the buildings' interiors, designed by Murchison, were fitted with such space-saving features as Murphy beds, custom-designed refrigerators, and smaller-than-standard bathroom fixtures.

The paired Beaux-Arts Apartments created a harmonious residential streetscape, even after the transformation of the Turtle Bay area by the construction of the United Nations (1947–53) and its many international agencies and missions.

MAJESTIC APARTMENTS, 1930–31
115 Central Park West, Manhattan
Architect: Irwin S. Chanin, of Chanin Construction Company
Designated: March 8, 1988

In the mid-nineteenth century, Central Park West was a rural outpost of run-down shanties and wandering goats. With the creation of Central Park and improvements in mass transportation, the Upper West Side experienced a period of major development, but real-estate prices on Central Park West rose to such heights that speculators were deterred from investing. Even in the 1890s more than half the blockfronts along the park from 60th to 96th streets remained vacant or contained modest frame houses.

The prosperity of the "roaring" 1920s brought to Central Park West an influx of aspiring Jewish immigrants, who, from their modest beginnings in the tenements of the Lower East Side or the cramped apartments of the other boroughs, viewed the Upper West Side as a cultural and architectural haven. By the mid-1930s, more than half of the residents of the Upper West Side were Jewish, and more than one-third of these families were headed by a parent born in Europe. Architect Irwin Chanin, born in Bensonhurst, Brooklyn, was himself the son of Ukrainian Jewish immigrants, a Cooper Union graduate, and an Upper West Sider who developed a real-estate and construction empire.

At thirty-one stories, the Majestic Apartments building reflects 1929 state legislature regulations permitting taller residential buildings with setbacks and towers. Though Chanin's first Art Deco residential design (he considered it to be "experimental"), the building is a sophisticated rendering of the later Art Deco style, eschewing elaborate decoration and relying on profile, tower terminations, and the interplay of vertical and horizontal elements for its impact.

HERMAN RIDDER JUNIOR HIGH SCHOOL, 1929–31
1619 Boston Post Road, The Bronx
Architect: Walter C. Martin
Designated: December 11, 1990

The 1920s saw dramatic changes in the design of American school buildings as the popularity of the Collegiate Gothic style declined and the specialization and standardization of classroom design increased. The result of a 1927 initiative to erect facilities specifically designed for junior high school programs, Herman Ridder Junior High School, named for the prominent newspaper publisher and philanthropist, is the first Art Deco public school building in New York. It was also the first junior high school to recognize the need for specialized classrooms and equipment for academic, industrial, athletic, and music curricula.

American school-building designers, seeking an efficient, modern aesthetic, turned to industrial and commercial buildings for inspiration—and to the machine. The design for Herman Ridder follows the Machine Age concept, suggesting—through its structural emphasis, the pier and window treatment, and the entrance tower—an industrial or commercial building. The square tower is modeled after a set-back skyscraper and displays a sculptural program of academic iconography: terra-cotta panels express allegories of the ideals of knowledge, music, and art.

SWISS CENTER, formerly the Goelet Building, AND
FIRST FLOOR INTERIOR, 1930–32
606–608 Fifth Avenue, Manhattan
Architect: Victor L. S. Hafner; engineer: Edward Hall Faile
Designated: January 14, 1992

Upon learning of the proposed development of Rockefeller Center, financial genius Robert Goelet decided to demolish his gracious home, which stood adjacent to the Rockefeller property, and erect a retail and office building in its place. Goelet insisted that the new commercial structure be as elegant and architecturally worthy as the mansion it replaced.

Goelet, a cofounder of the present-day Chemical Bank, was determined to offset the exorbitant real-estate taxes by maximizing his building's profits: since retail stores were more lucrative than office space, he stipulated that the plate-glass windows be as expansive as possible. (At the time the building was being designed, the show-window space was worth $3,000 a foot.) To meet this exacting requirement, the engineer devised a cantilevered, third-story platform to support the eight stories of office space above; he was thus able to conceal all supporting columns and provide uninterrupted show-window frontage.

It fell to Victor Hafner, the architect, to give this remarkable skeletal frame aesthetic distinction. To complement a design reflective of the transition between Art Deco and the International Style he chose a polychromatic scheme using two contrasting marbles—deep-green antique and white Dover cream. The colors and patterns distinguish the functions; the first two floors are faced with green marble, and eight horizontal bands of cream-colored marble distinguish the upper stories devoted to office space. Hafner's decorative flourishes include corbels with stylized Art Deco elements and an elegantly fluted, bronzed-aluminum frieze.

The entrance vestibule, outer lobby, and elevators all bear further witness to Hafner's discriminating use of color and his careful attention to the moods and uses of lobby space. The dark entrance vestibule—its walls are made of thinly veined black marble—was designed to suggest a transition between the frenzied pace of Fifth Avenue and the stately, serene interior. The illumination of the vestibule is dramatic: electric light glows through four vertical aluminum grills punctuated by stylized flowers and leaves. By way of contrast, the center of the outer lobby is designed with bands of variously colored marble that visually direct the visitor around and back to the elevator lobby. No surface left unfinished, each pair of elevator doors bears an octagonal medallion portraying two maidens, each attended by a gazelle, who part as the doors open. The structure stands little altered today—an enduring monument to one man's demanding aesthetic and pragmatic vision.

METRO THEATER, formerly the Midtown Theater, 1932–33
2624–2626 Broadway, Manhattan
Architects: Boak & Paris
Designated: July 11, 1989

This small, Art Deco movie theater is one of the four still open to the public out of eighteen that in 1934 lined Broadway between 59th and 110th streets. Constructed during the Depression, at a time when more than five hundred films were produced annually in the United States and a visit to the movie theater—costing only a nickel—was the most popular form of entertainment, the Midtown shows elements of both the Art Moderne and Art Deco styles.

The theater exemplifies the impact of the 1925 Paris Exposition Internationale on architects in New York City. Though the Exposition primarily influenced the design of skyscrapers, smaller commercial structures also began to boast vertical accents, colorful terra-cotta, stylized figures, and flat, patterned surfaces characteristic of the new mode. (The most impressive theater to be designed with the modernistic motifs of the new style was Radio City Music Hall, also constructed in 1932.)

With the capacity to seat 550 moviegoers, the Midtown's economy of design was particularly appropriate to the Depression-era construction budget. However, its ornate decorative program—a highly colored terra-cotta façade and bas-relief medallion enclosing figures representing comedy and tragedy—sets it apart from this period's more typical movie theater design, a marquee above a simple storefront.

F.W.I.L. LUNDY BROTHERS RESTAURANT BUILDING, 1934
1901–1929 Emmons Avenue, Brooklyn
Architects: Bloch & Hesse
Designated: March 3, 1992

Built during a government-sponsored renewal project in Sheepshead Bay, an area famous among fishermen and wildlife enthusiasts, this popular seafood restaurant could seat 1700 people; it was thought to be the biggest restaurant in the country when it first opened. It was owned by Frederick William Irving Lundy, whose grandfather, father, and uncle were all partners in the Lundy Brothers fish market, at the time the longest-operating (since 1880) and most successful seafood wholesaler in Brooklyn.

The restaurant is a freestanding structure designed in the Spanish Colonial Revival style, with sand-colored stucco walls, sloping tile roofs, and an arcaded second story (now concealed by enclosed porches). Details include arched corbeling on the Ocean Avenue side; carved wooden door lintels decorated with modillions (horizontal enscrolled brackets), anthemia, volutes, scallops, and dolphins; and large leaded-glass fanlights decorated with crabs and seahorses crowning the entrances.

During its heyday in the 1950s, Lundy's was the place of choice for Sunday dinner with the family, a first date, or even Sunday morning after church. A typical Sunday brought in ten thousand people, and a typical weekday, two thousand. In 1945 a one-story addition was constructed at the rear of the building. It was named the Theresa Brewer Room, after the popular singer who married Irving Lundy's nephew. Lundy's family continued to operate the restaurant for two years after his death in 1977. Since it closed, the building has been subject to vandalism and weathering.

LANE THEATER INTERIOR, 1937–38
168 New Dorp Lane, Staten Island
Architect: John Eberson
Designated: November 1, 1988

The Lane Theater is one of the few surviving examples of Depression-era, Art Moderne–
style theaters, and, in its size and decor, it typifies theater design of that period. While the
extravagant movie palaces of the 1920s and early 30s seated between two and six thousand
people, the Lane seats just under six hundred. Restrained in style as well as size, the Lane
departed from the rococo renditions of Moorish palaces, Egyptian temples, Italian villas, and
French boudoirs that characterized movie palaces in their heyday. Rather than mimicking
exotic locales, Art Moderne detailing suggested the excitement of travel and contemporary life
through intimations of speed, efficiency, and technological advancements. Streamlined
surfaces, curved planes, geometric forms, and horizontal bands or "speed lines" replaced
gilded plasterwork; these simple and relatively inexpensive ornamental elements were also
appropriate for the straitened budgets of the time.

    Architect John Eberson, one of the most prominent designers of theaters and opera houses
in the 1920s, had also introduced the popular "atmospheric theater" (a ceiling with a blue
plaster "sky" was dotted with electric lightbulbs simulating stars, and a hidden machine
projected "clouds" across the ceiling). His design for the Lane Theater interior is a variation
of these earlier atmospheric theaters, but in a more abstract mode, complete with stylized
murals that evoke a nighttime sky.

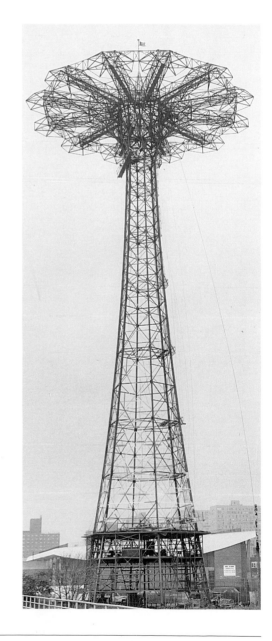

THE PARACHUTE JUMP, 1939
Southwest corner of the block between Surf Avenue, the Riegelmann Boardwalk,
West 16th Street, and West 19th Street, Brooklyn; moved to present site by
architect Michael Marlo and engineer Edwin W. Kleinert, 1941
Inventor: Commander James H. Strong
Engineers: Elwyn E. Seelye & Company
Designated: May 23, 1989

Originally erected for the 1939–40 New York World's Fair held in Flushing Meadows,
Queens, the Parachute Jump was inspired by the growing popularity of civilian parachuting
in the 1930s. It was invented by Commander James H. Strong, who received a patent for his
design in 1936. Although intended for military purposes, enthusiastic civilian interest during
testing prompted Strong to adapt his device for amusement: he added auxiliary cables to hold
the chutes open and prevent them from drifting. At 262 feet, the Parachute Jump was
surpassed in height only by the Trylon, the famous 610-foot, needle-like symbol of the fair.

    Following the close of the fair in October 1940, the jump was purchased by the Tilyou
Brothers and moved to their Steeplechase Park at Coney Island. A fire had damaged the park
in September 1939, providing space for the new attraction. During World War II the jump
was extremely popular, its double seats allowing couples to make the one-minute ascent and
ten-second descent together. However, Coney Island's popularity waned after World War II,
and Steeplechase Park closed in 1964. Leased to an amusement operator, the jump continued
to operate until 1968. Still in sound structural condition, the jump remains a prominent
feature of the Brooklyn skyline and a reminder of simpler pleasures of the past.

SEAGRAM BUILDING, INCLUDING THE PLAZA AND FIRST FLOOR INTERIOR, 1956–58
375 Park Avenue, Manhattan
Architects: Ludwig Mies van der Rohe, Philip Johnson, and Kahn & Jacobs
Designated: October 3, 1989

The only building in New York City designed by the renowned German-born architect Ludwig Mies van der Rohe, the Seagram Building embodies the quest of a successful corporation to enhance its public image through architectural patronage. The president of Joseph E. Seagram & Sons, Inc., Samuel Bronfman, guided by his daughter and architect-to-be Phyllis Lambert (who served as director of planning for this project), selected Mies van der Rohe to design a company headquarters in commemoration of the corporation's centennial anniversary.

At the end of the 1920s, Mies van der Rohe had emerged as one of Germany's leading architects, noted for his visionary skyscraper projects. After serving as director of the Bauhaus design school prior to its closure by the Nazis in 1933, he emigrated to the United States, where, in 1938, he was made a professor of architecture at Armour Institute (now Illinois Institute of Technology); the following year he designed a master plan and a complete new campus for the institute.

Mies became known as a proponent of the International style in architecture, a style that was rooted not in earlier vernacular or "national" vocabularies but in modern technological advances in construction. In its first manifestations in the early twentieth century, this style was characterized by asymmetrical composition, geometric shapes, absence of applied decoration, and large windows often in horizontal bands. In his work in the United States, Mies conceived of the steel frame as a skeleton, replacing the brick or stone-clad walls (imitative of supporting walls) of the earlier skyscrapers. Opaque walls were exchanged for glass, decorative ornamentation for cubic simplicity, and fixed interior plans for open plans.

The Seagram Building was designed by Mies in collaboration with architect Philip Johnson; working drawings were prepared by Kahn & Jacobs. In 1932 Johnson had coauthored (with historian Henry Russell-Hitchcock) *The International Style*, a manifesto for the avant-garde, radical architecture of Walter Gropius, Le Corbusier, and Mies van der Rohe. Having received a degree in architecture from Harvard in 1943, Johnson's association with Mies van der Rohe on the Seagram Building was one of the highlights of a prestigious career, resulting in what, due to its precisely crafted detailing, has been called the "Rolls-Royce" of buildings.

The thirty-eight-story tower, which occupies only fifty-two percent of the site, was the first fully modular office tower designed to accommodate standardized interior partitioning, thus permitting unobstructed views through the floor-to-ceiling windows. Mies' decision to situate the monumental tower in a broad, elevated plaza (with a radiant heating system to keep it free of ice) was in accordance with a push by progressive architectural firms for revisions of outdated zoning regulations mandating full-site set-back towers. The tranquility of the restrained plaza extends into the first-floor lobby, designed by Johnson. Unity is achieved through the use of continuous horizontal planes and transparent walls. While the traditional pink granite, travertine, and verd antique marble in the plaza contrast with the modern materials of the elegant curtain wall—bronze and pinkish-gray tinted glass—the bronze-clad columns and travertine floors and walls in the lobby provide a singleness of effect inside and out.

THE SOLOMON R. GUGGENHEIM MUSEUM AND INTERIOR, 1956–59
1071 Fifth Avenue, Manhattan
Architect: Frank Lloyd Wright
Designated: August 14, 1990

Frank Lloyd Wright's startlingly original, nautilus-shaped masterpiece was conceived with Solomon R. Guggenheim's need to find a permanent home for his equally radical collection of European works of art. In the years between the world wars, Guggenheim, a precious-metals mining magnate, amassed a vast collection of avant-garde, abstract works by such artists as Vasily Kandinsky, Piet Mondrian, Joan Miró, and Laszlo Moholy-Nagy. Guggenheim's adviser on emerging nonobjective European art was a French abstract painter, Hilla Rebay, who escorted him on numerous buying trips to the continent. Rebay worked to convert her benefactor's enthusiasm for abstract painting into a revolutionary institution of modern art that would not only house finished pieces but would offer studio and exhibition space to young artists.

In 1943 Rebay convinced Guggenheim to commission Frank Lloyd Wright, the nation's most celebrated architect, to design a museum. Based on his conception of an organic architecture replicating nature's holistic structures, Wright at first proposed a ziggurat-like building. Sixteen years elapsed between Wright's first vague evocation of an atmosphere appropriate to Guggenheim's art and the opening of this extraordinary and controversial museum.

The Guggenheim's sculpted, circular mass rises in ever-widening concrete bands separated by ribbons of square-paned aluminum skylights. The irreverent curvilinear form radically breaks the street wall of Fifth Avenue, and the ample plantings surrounding it correspond with Central Park across the street. The buff-colored vinyl paint on the exterior is a typical Wrightian innovation—it was originally used to protect the finish on guns and airplanes in World War II. Inside, Wright's prairie-house cantilevers become projecting balconies, and a quarter-mile-long ramp spirals in widening loops, allowing the visitor to follow an artist's chronological development.

"My Pantheon," is what Wright called the finished museum. It was completed only after he resolved numerous engineering challenges presented by the concrete, coiled-spring design and cleared most of the thirty-two objections initially raised by municipal building authorities. Many critics agree that the Guggenheim Museum, along with the Johnson Wax Building, are the crowning achievements of Wright's long, illustrious career.

After resolving a controversy between preservationists and expansionists, a ten-story, grid-patterned limestone annex by Gwathmey Siegel & Associates was approved and opened on June 28, 1992. It expanded the museum's exhibition facilities by 27,000 square feet, and more exhibition spaces were created from offices, laboratories, and storage areas. For the first time in years, areas that had been sectioned off now permit visitors to go to the top of the spiraling ramp and view the entire soaring atrium.

FOUR SEASONS RESTAURANT GROUND AND FIRST FLOOR INTERIORS, 1958–59
99 East 52nd Street, Manhattan
Designer: Philip Johnson
Designated: October 3, 1989

Reflecting architectural theories advanced by his mentor, Ludwig Mies van der Rohe, designer Philip Johnson, assisted by a team of consultants (interior designer William Pahlman as principal designer, lighting designer Richard Kelly, landscape architect Karl Linn, horticulturist Everett Lawson Conklin, weaver Marie Nichols, and artist Richard Lippold), here created a series of understated and elegantly proportioned dining rooms. Advantage is taken of the modular system of design through varied ceiling heights, an artful interplay of solids and voids, and a wealth of highly sophisticated detail—floor-to-ceiling "draperies" of anodized aluminum chains that ripple in the air blown in by ventilators, an innovative scheme of invisible recessed lighting, and designer accessories, including Charles Eames chairs. The use of rich materials throughout—travertine marble on the walls, grained French walnut paneling, and bronze mullions and bowl planters, all installed by expert craftsmen—made this, at $4.5 million, the costliest restaurant built in 1959.

The restaurant's focus is divided between two main dining spaces—the Pool Room and the Grill Room. A lofty square with twenty-foot-high ceilings, the Pool Room is dominated by a central, twenty-foot-square pool of white Carrara marble filled with burbling water. Four trees located one at each corner are changed seasonally, along with the menu, staff uniforms, and other decorative details. The Grill Room, a famous locale for publishers' "power lunches," is a theatrical, French walnut–paneled space with a balcony on the eastern side, a sleek central dining area, a lounge, and a laminated, "crackled" glass wall that sections off a majestic walnut bar. The square, solid bar stands in dramatic contrast to Richard Lippold's delicate overhead sculpture of gold-dipped brass rods that hangs from the ceiling on invisible wires. This juxtaposition is balanced by his smaller sculpture over the balcony. Critics have praised this restaurant, located in Mies Van Der Rohe's masterpiece Seagram Building, as one of the finest International-style interiors in the United States.

THE WILLIAM AND CATHERINE CASS HOUSE ("The Crimson Beech"), 1958–59
48 Manor Court, Staten Island
Architects: Frank Lloyd Wright, for Marshall Erdman & Associates, and Morton H. Delson
Designated: August 14, 1990

Aside from the famous Guggenheim Museum, this is Frank Lloyd Wright's only standing structure in New York City. An example of the master architect's prefabricated home designs, known as Prefab No. 1, it was created for the builder Marshall Erdman of Madison, Wisconsin. The Erdman prefabs were part of Wright's last major attempt to address the need for well-designed, moderately priced housing in America.

This residence was commissioned by a Corona, Queens, couple, Catherine and William Cass, after seeing Wright in a television interview. Components of the house were trucked from Madison and assembled on a steep three-quarter-acre site overlooking historic Richmondtown. The cost of the prefab materials was only $20,000, but local contractors added $35,000 to the total. The July 1959 opening of Crimson Beech (named for an ancient copper beech tree that once grew in the front yard) generated great fanfare.

Like Wright's other Utopian American or "Usonian" houses, Crimson Beech extends itself horizontally along the ground, emphasizing spatial fluidity. Full advantage is taken of the southern exposure, with clerestory windows in front and large expanses of glass that open onto two levels of terraces in the back.

At least eight other Prefab No. 1 homes were built, each with some variation in detail and plan. A swimming pool was created for the Casses by Wright's associate Morton Delson in 1970.

THE LANDMARKS OF NEW YORK, 1992 TO THE PRESENT

MOORE-JACKSON CEMETERY, est. by 1733
31–30 to 31–36 54th Street, Queens
Designated: March 19, 1997

In the mid-1650s, a group of English, nonconformist settlers negotiated with Governor Stuyvesant and the local Native Americans for the rights to land near Newtown Creek, in what is now Woodside. Among them was the Reverend John Moore (d. 1657), whose family became prominent farmers and married into such notable families as the Jacksons, Rikers, Rapelyes, and Blackwells. The Moores were ardent loyalists during the War of Independence, allowing the British to use their farmhouse to plan the capture of Manhattan, and to stockpile arms and quarter British and Hessian troops on their property.

The earliest gravestone in the Moore-Jackson Cemetery, located on what was the family's farmland, reads "SxR, dyed May [th]e 29, 1733"; the last recorded burial was in the 1880s.

As Queens became urbanized early in the twentieth century, most of its small cemeteries were obliterated. The Moore-Jackson Cemetery was one of the few catalogued by the Queens Topographical Bureau in 1919. The site became overgrown and was forgotten until 1935, when a WPA project uncovered grave markers; the fifteen surviving stones were then relocated to a small plot on the eastern end of the property. In the absence of surviving Moore heirs, the Surrogate Court of Queens County now holds the title to the cemetery.

ADRIAN AND ANN WYCKOFF ONDERDONK HOUSE,
c. 1750–75; reconstructed, 1980–82
1820–1836 Flushing Avenue, Queens
Architects: Unknown; reconstruction, Giorgio Cavaglieri Associates
Designated: March 21, 1995

Situated one block from the Queens-Brooklyn border, this is one of the few extant Dutch-American farmhouses in New York, and a rare example of a surviving stone house with a wood-framed gambrel roof. The main façade is one-and-a-half stories and symmetrical, and has an addition to the east. Also unusual for a New York City farmhouse, the house remains on its original site with a substantial parcel of land. The estate has yielded significant archaeological finds from both the prehistoric and historic periods.

In 1821, after a succession of farming families, the house and property were purchased by Adrian Onderdonk, a fifth-generation descendant of a Dutch Long Island family, and his new bride Ann Wyckoff, of a prominent Dutch Brooklyn family. The house remained in their family until 1912, and was then used for a variety of commercial and industrial purposes. Plans for demolition and a fire in 1975 threatened the house's survival, but extensive reconstruction in 1980–82, undertaken by the firm of Giorgio Cavaglieri in cooperation with the Greater Ridgewood Historical Society, restored the structure to its 1936 appearance. It is now open to the public as the Vander Ende–Onderdonk House.

FIRST REFORMED CHURCH OF JAMAICA, 1858–59; extension, 1902
153–10 Jamaica Avenue, Queens
Architects: Sidney J. Young; extension, Tuthill & Higgins
Designated: January 30, 1996

This building replaced a wooden structure from 1833 that was burned down in 1857 because its congregation had outgrown it. For the new building, the church settled on a design based on Richard Upjohn's Church of the Pilgrims in Brooklyn Heights. Designed and constructed by master carpenter Sidney J. Young, the First Reformed Church is one of the finest *Rundbogenstil* (a German variation of the Romanesque and Renaissance Revival style) buildings in New York. The church is faced in brick above a brownstone water table. The building's asymmetrical towers, round-arched openings, and corbel tables are characterized by complex brickwork.

New York City acquired the building in 1973 and, because it was in an urban renewal zone, slated it for demolition. Community pressure delayed the action and the site was granted landmark status in 1979. However, some officials from the Queens borough government objected, still hoping to have the building destroyed, and the New York City Board of Estimate reversed the designation. From 1982 until 1990 the Glorious Church of God in Christ occupied the building. It is currently vacant; the Greater Jamaica Development Corporation has rented the space from the city and plans to convert it into a performing arts center.

12 WEST 129th STREET HOUSE, c. 1863; additions and alterations, 1882–83, 1896, and c. 1920s
12 West 129th Street, Manhattan
Architects: c. 1863, unknown; 1882–83, Edward Gustaveson; 1896, Asbury Baker; c. 1920s, unknown
Designated: July 26, 1994

A rare survivor of Harlem's suburban past, this house has undergone many changes. Located in what was once an area of freestanding houses, this structure is now an anomaly, surrounded by apartments, tenements, and row houses. Originally a two-and-a-half-story frame structure, it was built circa 1863 for—and possibly by—two carpenters. Several owners later, in 1883, it acquired its eye-catching, ornamented porch, composed of eight Moorish-inspired arches; a third story was added in 1896, when the property was bought by Franciscan nuns. The final alterations to the building, including a stucco treatment and quoins, gave it the air of an Italian Renaissance villa. Currently the vacant property is owned by the neighboring Christ Temple Church, which intends to convert it into a senior citizens' home.

The house's most significant architectural feature is the wooden porch extending along the original front elevation and the eastern side elevation. At the time of designation, much of the porch had been removed because of deterioration. As it was built, the porch's arches rested on vertical supports and were ornamented with openwork quatrefoils and trefoils and separated by narrow pilasters with beaded edges. The design, created with a scroll saw, demonstrates the sophistication of nineteenth-century woodworking machinery.

FORMER CENTURY ASSOCIATION BUILDING, 1869
109–111 East 15th Street, Manhattan
Architects: Gambrill & Richardson
Designated: January 5, 1993

Of the many nineteenth-century clubhouses, the Century Association is the earliest surviving example. The then all-male Century Association, dedicated to "plain living and high thinking," was founded in 1847 to promote interest in literature and the arts. Its membership has been an eclectic mix of some of New York's cultural, business, and political leaders. While at its 15th Street home, the club's members included Stanford White, Charles C. Tiffany, J. P. Morgan, and Theodore Roosevelt. Since 1891, the Century Association has occupied the building at 7 West 43rd Street (q.v.), where its membership has included Alexander Calder, Benny Goodman, Dwight D. Eisenhower, and John Barrymore.

An earlier building on the 15th Street property was purchased in 1857, but in 1866 the club decided to replace it to accommodate its growing membership. Designed by the distinguished firm responsible for Trinity Church in Boston and the State Capitol in Albany, this building exemplifies the Neo-Grec style that became popular in the 1870s. An American interpretation of Parisian models, the façade is characterized by abstracted classical motifs, angular forms, and incised ornamentation. A mansard roof caps the symmetrical, three-bay, three-story building, and keyed quoins surround the windows on the basement level.

REPUBLIC NATIONAL BANK INTERIOR, formerly
Williamsburgh Savings Bank, 1870–75
175 Broadway, Brooklyn
Architect: George B. Post
Designer: Peter B. Wight
Designated: June 25, 1996

This venerable Brooklyn institution is one of the earliest structures designed by George B. Post, who also designed the New York Stock Exchange Building and the City College campus at 138th Street (both q.v.). The focus of the interior is the great banking hall, a rare extant example of a mid-nineteenth-century monumental public space from the post–Civil War era in New York. While most contemporary banks were designed in Italianate or French Second Empire styles, the Williamsburgh Bank and its interior, with Renaissance and Neo-Grec motifs, prefigure the "Greek temple" banks that became popular after the World's Columbian Exposition of 1893.

Before entering the central banking hall, one passes through a grand entrance vestibule with a balcony, on the far side of which is a massive vault. Dominating the banking hall is a soaring, 110-foot-high cast-iron dome capped by an interior vault. This vault is decorated with an abstract radial mural designed by architect and designer Peter B. Wight, who lost to Post in the initial competition for the commission. The mural, the only known surviving decoration by Wight, was influenced by the English Aesthetic Movement. It contains boldly outlined shapes intended to exaggerate the surface's two-dimensional quality. Stylized botanical details throughout the space complement the mural's forms.

JONATHAN W. ALLEN STABLE, 1871
148 East 40th Street, Manhattan
Architect: Charles E. Hadden
Designated: June 17, 1997

Until the early twentieth century, horses were used to pull coaches, fire-fighting equipment, delivery wagons, and private carriages, so during that period, the care and housing of horses was an integral part of the city landscape. This stable is a rare survivor from the era when horses were a vital part of everyday life in New York City. In 1896, it was reported that there were 4,649 stables accommodating 73,746 horses. After 1860, stables were commonly located in the less exclusive areas of the city, at least a block away from prime residential sections.

In 1871 Jonathan W. Allen, a broker living at 18 East 42nd Street, purchased an eighteen-foot-wide lot on East 40th Street for the purpose of building a private stable conveniently located near his home. At the time, the neighborhood of 40th Street east of Lexington Avenue was fully developed with small brick houses, factories, stables, and breweries.

The two-story stable was designed with room for Allen's carriage and horses on the ground floor and living space for the groom on the floor above. The structure is faced with brick and accented by stonework. The central carriage entrance has double wooden doors with large glass panels set beneath a segmental brick arch with a contrasting keystone and is flanked by two narrow, wood-paneled doors with glass transoms under round brick arches. The mansard roof has bold pedimented dormers, and is crowned with delicate iron cresting.

The stable was owned by Allen and his heirs until 1919, and records indicate the structure was still a stable in 1928. By 1946 the building had been converted to commercial use, with a storage area on the ground floor and an office above. It continues to be used for this purpose.

INTERNATIONAL MERCANTILE MARINE COMPANY BUILDING, 1882–87; redesigned and reclad, 1919–21
1 Broadway (also known as 1–3 Greenwich Street and 1 Battery Place), Manhattan
Architects: Edward Hale Kendall; alterations, Walter B. Chambers
Designated: May 16, 1995

In 1919, this thirteen-story, iron-frame structure had its Queen Anne façade removed, and it became the Neoclassical International Mercantile Marine Company (IMMC) Building. Organized by J. P. Morgan, the IMMC was created in 1902 by the merger of six of the leading American and British steamship companies. Contrary to expectations, however, it never received government subsidies and failed to eliminate the competition, thereby removing the threat of another monopoly. Until the Second World War, IMMC operated the largest American-owned merchant fleet in the world, and occupied one of the many shipping company buildings that gave the area north of Bowling Green the name "Steamship Row" in the 1920s.

Designed on a C-plan with chamfered corners, the building's two-story base is of granite, while the upper stories are clad in Indiana limestone with marble spandrels. IMMC's maritime affiliation is seen in the restrained carved stone details on the lower stories. Seaweed, seashells, ropes, and waves appear as decorative motifs, while Neptune, the god of the sea and Mercury, the messenger of the gods and the god of commerce, adorn the entrances. Shields from the company's major ports of call line the third-story balustrade. Currently owned by Allstate Life Insurance Co., the building underwent a major exterior restoration in 1993–94.

THE DOWN TOWN ASSOCIATION BUILDING, 1886–87; addition, 1910–11
60 Pine Street (also known as 60–64 Pine Street and 20–24 Cedar Street), Manhattan
Architects: Charles C. Haight; addition, Warren & Wetmore
Designated: February 11, 1997

At the close of the nineteenth century, New York's wealthiest families created luncheon and dinner clubs for men in particular fields: those in the shipping business met at the India Club; merchants gathered at the Merchants Club; and bankers, lawyers, and brokers assembled at the Down Town Association, which held its first meeting at the Astor House in 1859. The club's mission was to provide facilities for social interaction to people who were engaged in professional and commercial pursuits, especially while they were away from their homes, and to advance literature and art through the establishment of an on-site library, reading room, and art gallery.

In 1884 the Down Town Association purchased the lot at 60–62 Pine Street, and in 1886 club member Charles C. Haight was hired to design the new building. Haight's three-bay, red-brick Romanesque Revival façade features a prominent arched main entranceway. The building is ornamented with a modest frieze above the fourth story and terra-cotta details throughout. Large arched windows emphasize the third-story dining area, which was considered the club's most important space. In 1902 the Association leased the adjoining property at 64 Pine Street, replacing an earlier structure with Warren & Wetmore's 1910–11 two-bay addition echoing Haight's original façade in materials, fenestration, and details.

BENNETT BUILDING, 1872–73; additions, 1890–92, 1894; renovated, 1983
139 Fulton Street (also known as 135–139 Fulton Street, 93–99 Nassau Street, 28-34 Ann Street), Manhattan
Architects: Arthur D. Gilman; additions, James M. Farnsworth
Designated: November 21, 1995

The Bennett Building, among the tallest cast-iron buildings in New York City, is designed in the French Second Empire style that Arthur D. Gilman helped to make popular. It is Gilman's only surviving major office building, and one of only two Second Empire office structures left in lower Manhattan. Instead of the typical cast-iron, column-on-top-of-column design, the Bennett Building's three fully articulated façades are adorned with cornices, paneled pilasters, segmental arch window openings, and distinctive curved corners.

As commissioned by James Gordon Bennett, Jr., the publisher and editor of the *New York Herald* who financed Henry Stanley's expedition to Africa in search of David Livingstone, the building was originally six stories with a mansard roof. In 1889, John Pettit, a leading real-estate investor, acquired the building and commissioned architect James M. Farnsworth to enlarge it by adding four full stories and a two-story masonry penthouse, and to extend it twenty-five feet westward. The lower-story façades underwent significant renovations again when Haddad & Sons acquired it in 1983. In addition, the off-white façade was painted in pink, aqua, and cream, leading the *New York Times* to call it a "multicolored cast-iron confection," and to compare it to "an ice cream parlor at Disneyland." E.N.T. Realty bought the building in 1995.

SEVENTH REGIMENT ARMORY INTERIOR, 1877–78;
additions and alterations, 1909–11
643 Park Avenue, Manhattan
Architects: Charles W. Clinton; additions and alterations, Robinson & Knust
Designated: July 19, 1994

This palatial armory, among the nineteenth century's finest and costliest, was extremely influential in establishing the armory as a distinct building type, both in terms of functional design and architectural imagery. Besides being a military and police structure, the lavish armory was intended to serve as a social club for the prestigious "Silk Stocking Regiment," so called because of its ties to prominent New York families. Its Drill Room, approximately 200 by 300 feet, was one of the largest unobstructed interiors in New York City when it was built, and has the oldest extant "balloon shed" (a barrel-vaulted roof supported on visible arch trusses) in America.

Among the preeminent design and interior design firms that created the remarkable interiors were Louis C. Tiffany & Co. with Stanford White (Veterans' Room and Library), Herter Brothers (Board of Officers Room, Colonel's Room, Reception Room), Pottier & Stymus (Field and Staff Room), and George C. Flint & Co. (corridors, Entrance Hall, grand central Stair Hall). The armory interiors epitomize one of the high points of American interior design. They are exemplary of high-style, late-Victorian taste, possessing the decorative sensibilities of the Aesthetic Movement and using woodwork in the rich Renaissance Revival style. The interior is accessible on a regular basis during art and antique shows.

PUBLIC SCHOOL 1 ANNEX, formerly Westfield Township District School No. 5, 1878; enlarged, 1896–97
58 Summit Street, Tottenville, Staten Island
Architects: Unknown; enlargements, Pierce & Brun
Designated: May 16, 1995

The small town of Tottenville was named for the prominent family who built Totten's Landing wharf at the southern tip of Staten Island. In 1869, the town was connected to the rest of the island by rail for the first time, reorienting its economy toward land transportation and ending its dependence on the ferry. Tottenville became the largest, most populous, and most cohesive settlement on the southern part of the island, and to this day retains its character as a distinct suburban village.

Also called "Bay View Academy" for its impressive view of the New Jersey Hills and Sandy Hook, Tottenville's school is set on a T-plan around a central stairwell. The brick façade, with its temple-inspired forms, incorporates stylized classical elements and incised ornament; pilasters and window openings mark the side walls. Denticulated brick window heads, patterned bands, and a bracketed wood cornice stylistically unify the original building and the 1897 addition. Currently serving as Public School 1 Annex, this is the oldest public school building in use on Staten Island. It houses classrooms and a small gymnasium on the main floor of the original building.

FORMER PUBLIC SCHOOL 72, also known as the Julia de Burgos School, 1879–82; annex, 1921
1674 Lexington Avenue (also known as 1674–1686 Lexington Avenue, 129–131 East 105th Street), Manhattan
Architects: David I. Stagg; annex, C.B.J. Snyder
Designated: June 25, 1996

Named for a Puerto Rican poet who lived in East Harlem, the Julia de Burgos School (P.S. 72) is exemplary of the neo-Grec style that was prominent in New York City public school design during the 1870s and 1880s. David Stagg, superintendent of school buildings from 1872 to 1886, created a plan that includes airy classrooms and hallways, wide windows, and indoor bathrooms. The school is a symmetrically shaped, four- and five-story red-brick building characterized by angular and classically inspired brick-and-stone ornament and a dramatic entrance. The school's stair towers rise one story higher than the surrounding tenement neighborhood to ensure its visibility within the community.

The extension of the Second and Third Avenue elevated trains in 1879–80 precipitated a population boom in East Harlem, and P.S. 72 was part of a broad construction and renovation program to accommodate the increase. However, even with this program, the school was overcrowded when it opened, and by 1905 East Harlem was the most densely populated uptown district. Seventy years later, P.S. 72 closed due to declining enrollment. It has since been used by Touro College and as a vocational training center. The New York City Economic Development Corporation renovated it in 1994–95 for use as an artists' space, but that plan failed, and the structure remains unoccupied.

VAN SCHAICK FREE READING ROOM/ HUNTINGTON FREE LIBRARY AND READING ROOM, 1882–83; addition, 1890–92
9 Westchester Square, The Bronx
Architects: Frederick Clarke Withers; addition, William Anderson
Designated: April 5, 1994

The original Van Schaick Free Reading Room was the first library in the village of West Chester, which was later incorporated into the Borough of The Bronx. It was built with money bequeathed by local tobacco merchant Peter C. Van Schaick, but his estate did not provide enough funds for maintenance of the facility, so the building was left vacant after its completion. Eight years later, Collis Potter Huntington, who derived his fortune from the Southern Pacific Railroad, provided funding for the library's operations and an addition, which followed the architectural style of the original structure. He also renamed it in his own honor as the Huntington Free Library and Reading Room. Huntington's son, Archer, founded the Hispanic Society of America, one of the original components of the Audubon Terrace museum complex in Washington Heights, Manhattan.

The picturesque library has simple, monochromatic brickwork, asymmetrical massing, and varied rooflines derived from Gothic Revival designs. The round-arched tower entrance, terra-cotta tiled chimney, and overall simplicity of form evoke a hominess characteristic of late-eighteenth-century middle-class America. Today this private, independent, noncirculating library specializes in Bronx history, while a New York Public Library branch across the street houses general-interest materials.

FREE MAGYAR REFORMED CHURCH, PARISH HALL, AND RECTORY, formerly St. Peter's German Evangelical Church at Kreischerville
19–23 Winant Place and 25 Winant Place, Charleston, Staten Island
Architects: Church, Parish Hall: unknown; Rectory: Royal Daggett
Designated: July 26, 1994

Church, 1883
Parish Hall, 1898
Rectory, 1926

Representative of the small churches built for immigrant congregations during the latter 1800s, this church was constructed while the area was a quasi–company town centered around—and named for—Balthasar Kreischer's brick factory. Kreischerville's small German church was funded by Kreischer himself, who provided an organ, carved pews, and wainscoting. In 1919, a Hungarian congregation bought the church, renaming it the Magyar Reformed Church.

The small, wood-framed church has a front porch, making it residential in form and detailing, as well as a high foundation and steeply pitched roof with a spire, which also give it an institutional presence. Above the entrance is an arched enframement with a leaded rose window in its center. This building is a typical village church, but the architectural character reflects the involvement of a wealthy backer, whose tastes were even more evident in the church's interior. The Parish Hall consists of three parts: a dwelling, an entry connected to the church building, and a large hall. The rectory is a substantial building with a front porch spanning the façade, and a freestanding garage. Bricks from the Kreischer factory were used in the steps to the rectory, the church chimney, and brick piers on the church fence.

MOUNT MORRIS BANK BUILDING, 1883–84; enlargement, 1889–90; alteration, 1912
81–85 East 125th Street (also known as 1820 Park Avenue), Manhattan
Architects: Lamb & Rich; alteration, Frank A. Rooke
Designated: January 5, 1993

The six-story Mount Morris Bank Building was designed by Lamb & Rich, a firm known for its university designs, including buildings at Smith, Dartmouth, Colgate, Amherst, Barnard, and the Pratt Institute in Brooklyn. Before the construction of the adjacent elevated Park Avenue rail line, the prominent Mount Morris Bank Building was visible for some distance along 125th Street. The independent Mount Morris Bank was bought in 1913 by the Corn Exchange Bank, the first New York Bank to have local branches. The Corn Exchange merged with Chemical Bank in 1954, and this building remained a branch bank until Chemical sold it in 1964. Currently, New York City owns the structure, and it has been vacant since the late 1970s.

The Mount Morris Bank Building was a dual-purpose structure. The commercial function of the building's lower levels are reflected in a massive sandstone base with wide arched entrances, typical of the Romanesque Revival. Above, the residential character of the upper stories is indicated by red Philadelphia brick, ornate terra-cotta ornamentation, small squared windowpanes, and other classic Queen Anne motifs. The original structure sat on a single lot, but an 1890 addition, also designed by Lamb & Rich, doubled its size. In 1912 the entrances and stairs were altered.

WASHINGTON APARTMENTS, 1883–84
2034–2040 Adam Clayton Powell, Jr. Boulevard, Manhattan
Architect: Mortimer C. Merritt
Designated: January 5, 1993

The Washington Apartments is central Harlem's oldest apartment building, and one of the few in New York City that survives from the 1880s, when multifamily buildings were just gaining acceptance among the middle and upper classes. This building is one of the earliest examples of "French Flat" apartments, a reference to elegant Parisian multifamily dwellings that distinguished it from common tenements. It was designed by the prolific New York architect Mortimer C. Merritt, best known for his cast-iron commercial designs in the SoHo–Cast Iron and Ladies' Mile Historic Districts (q.v.). Built only two years after elevated trains had connected Harlem to lower Manhattan, the Washington was at one point the only building on its block.

The eight-story, Queen Anne–style brick building incorporates many neo-Grec details, such as engraved stone lintels and decorative side panels. The main façade is symmetrically arranged around a wide, projecting pavilion and is crowned by an overscaled Neo-Grec galvanized-iron frontispiece, consisting of a triangular pediment decorated with a sunburst motif. Other features, such as the delicately incised ornamentation on the impost blocks, are typical of New York Queen Anne buildings. The trim is made from stone, iron, and pressed brick, providing lively contrast and interesting textural dimensions.

POTTER BUILDING, 1883–86
36–38 Park Row, Manhattan
Architect: N. G. Starkweather
Designated: September 17, 1996

Orlando Potter was a prominent figure in New York State Democratic politics and served as a U.S. Congressman (1883–85), as well as being president of the Grover and Baker Sewing Machines Company. He commissioned this building to replace his World Building, which was destroyed by fire in 1882. The new Potter Building employed modern fireproofing techniques, including pressed-brick and terra-cotta walls and façade, and joists encased in flat-arch tile (fireproof bricks). In 1973, Pace University acquired the building, intending to demolish it. When this plan did not materialize, it became a cooperative apartment building.

The Potter Building was constructed after cast-iron framing and the express elevator made it possible to build structures of more than ten stories, but before the emergence of the true skyscraper. The eleven-story building is a flamboyant combination of Queen Anne, Neo-Grec, Renaissance Revival, and Colonial Revival styles, and it is characterized by a high degree of ornamentation throughout, especially in terra-cotta. Its two-story base is clad in cast iron, with brownstone-colored terra-cotta and red brick. The three façades are similarly articulated by continuous piers alternating with paired fenestration. Not surprisingly, Otis & Bros. Company elevators and the New York Architectural Terra Cotta Company were among the building's noteworthy tenants.

JOSEPH LOTH AND COMPANY SILK RIBBON MILL,
1885–86; additions and alterations, 1905
1818–1838 Amsterdam Avenue (also known as 491–497 West 150th Street and 500 West 151st Street), Manhattan
Architect: Hugo Kafka
Designated: September 21, 1993

This building was constructed during a post–Civil War boom in the American silk industry spurred by popular fashions and heavy import tariffs. The "Joseph Loth & Co. 'Fair and Square' Ribbon Manufactory" was one of the few silk mills to operate outside of Paterson, New Jersey, and one of the few factories of any kind located in Washington Heights. Austro-Hungarian émigré Hugo Kafka devised the unusual K-shaped floor plan, with the upright along Amsterdam Avenue, which satisfied building codes while creating an efficient work environment. The wings, less than thirty feet wide, were well lit by large windows on both sides and required neither interior columns nor fire walls, both of which would have interfered with the operation of driveshaft looms.

Instead of a featureless, industrial façade, the Loth Silk building displays architectural character, with rusticated corner pilasters organizing the brick façades in a visually engaging manner. The company name appears in raised brick above the factory's wings. A series of additions and changes were made beginning in 1905 to convert the building into commercial space. Currently only partially occupied, the building has housed a movie theater, a dance hall, a bowling alley, a skating rink, and a variety of small businesses.

LEWIS H. LATIMER HOUSE, 1887–89
34–41 137th Street, Flushing, Queens
Architect: Unknown
Designation: March 21, 1995

Lewis Latimer was an electrical engineer and inventor who worked briefly with Alexander Graham Bell and later, for twenty years, with Thomas Edison. Latimer's most important contribution was a process for making inexpensive, long-lasting carbon filaments, which reduced the production costs of lightbulbs and made them affordable for the average household. His patents proved profitable for Edison's Electric Light Company, but Latimer did not benefit personally. In addition to his engineering accomplishments, Latimer was also an activist member of the African-American community, and his house was a meeting place for civic and cultural leaders, including W.E.B. Du Bois and Paul Robeson.

This Queen Anne–style frame house, originally located on Holly Avenue in Queens, was bought by the Latimers in 1902, and was their home for twenty-six years. The house had several owners after Latimer's daughter's death in 1963. It was threatened with demolition by developers in 1988, but the combined efforts of the Ebenezer Baptist Church, the Borough of Queens, and Latimer's granddaughter, Dr. Winifred Norman, saved and relocated the Latimer House. Its present site abuts the Latimer Gardens houses, which were named for the inventor. Although it is currently unoccupied and boarded up, plans are in progress to restore the house and open it as a museum.

HOOK & LADDER COMPANY 14, now Engine Company 36, 1888–89
120 East 125th Street, Manhattan
Architects: Napoleon LeBrun & Sons

Between 1880 and 1895, the architectural firm of Napoleon LeBrun & Sons constructed forty-two firehouses in New York City, and helped to define the New York Fire Department's expression of civic architecture. This four-story, brick-and-stone Romanesque Revival firehouse reflects the firm's attention to setting, materials, and stylistic details.

The base of the building is dominated by a wood-paneled overhead door that is painted fire-engine red. Flanked by a door on the west side and a large window on the east side, the entrance is framed by cast iron and set in the center of a rusticated brownstone façade. Flame and fish-scale motifs decorate the cast-iron piers, transom bars, and lintel, and "Engine 36" is painted on the top center panel of the frame. The second and third floors, separated from the base by brownstone molding, are faced in brick and feature tripartite windows.

The fourth-story gable is the most detailed part of the structure. The stepped gable is trimmed in brownstone and capped with a finial and is set into a mansard roof with multicolored slate tiles. A wrought-iron jib, which was used to haul hay up to an attic storeroom, is still in place above the center window.

Hook & Ladder Company 14 relocated to 2282 Third Avenue in 1975. Since then this firehouse has been occupied by Engine Company 36, which relocated from 1849 Park Avenue.

ENGINE COMPANY 47, 1889–90
500 West 113th Street, Manhattan
Architects: Napoleon LeBrun & Sons
Designated: June 17, 1997

One of the first civic buildings in Morningside Heights, Engine Company 47 was built by the firm of Napoleon LeBrun & Sons during a fifteen-year period in which they designed over forty firehouses in New York City. This firehouse combines elements of Romanesque Revival and Classical Revival styles.

The twenty-five-foot-wide, three-story structure has a rusticated brownstone base, while the second and third stories are faced in orange brick with terra-cotta quoins. The one-over-one, double-hung, second-story windows are defined by a brownstone transom bar and lintel, and the round-arched windows on the third floor are outlined by decorative terra-cotta. Between the second and third stories is a brownstone plaque inscribed with the names of the fire commissioners and the architects. Beneath a heavy cornice is set an elaborately detailed terra-cotta entablature, below which are two large terra-cotta medallions with foliate patterns. Though it is a mid-block structure, the firehouse overlooks the Croton Aqueduct gatehouse immediately to the east, and so the architects were able to echo the appearance of the street façade in the articulation of the visible east elevation.

KREISCHERVILLE WORKERS' HOUSES, c. 1890
71–73 Kreischer Street, Charleston, Staten Island
Architect/builder: Unknown
Designated: July 26, 1994

The Kreischerville Workers' Houses, located in what is now the neighborhood of Charleston, are one in a group of four identical, two-story double houses. The houses were developed by Peter Androvette, a member of the prominent local shipping family that gave Charleston its original name, Androvetteville. Successful Manhattan brickmaker Balthasar Kreischer established a factory in the Staten Island town in 1857 because of its proximity to clay deposits and water transportation. As Kreischer's business grew, so did the village and its reliance on the brick industry. By the 1890s, Androvetteville—which by then was known as Kreischerville—was a quasi–company town; most of the population worked in the brick works and resided in rental housing built by either Kreischer or Androvette.

The workers' houses have four-bay façades, side porch entrances, masonry foundations, and stuccoed brick chimneys projecting from flat roofs. Originally, all four shared a single outhouse in back. They are characteristic semi-detached workers' cottages, and evoke the look of a late-nineteenth-century company town. Ironically, the Kreischerville houses, which were built as homes for brick workers, are constructed from inexpensive wood and shingle.

DELMONICO'S BUILDING, 1890–91

56 Beaver Street (also known as 2–6 South William Street and 56–58 Beaver Street), Manhattan
Architect: James Brown Lord
Designated: February 13, 1996

This Renaissance Revival building was the final location of the world-famous Delmonico's Restaurant. Swiss immigrants John and Peter Delmonico opened their first café in 1827 on William Street. During the 1870s and 1880s, the Delmonicos opened more cafés downtown, as well as several in the newly fashionable uptown districts. By 1890 the business was so successful that the present eight-story restaurant and office building was built on the site of an existing Delmonico's restaurant. Delmonico's went out of business in 1925, and the building has housed several tenants since then. The restaurant space is currently being renovated to house a brew pub.

The Delmonico's Building was the first major non-residential work by James Brown Lord, who later designed the Appellate Division Courthouse on Madison Square and the Yorkville Branch of the New York Public Library (both q.v.). The building's tripartite side façades feature giant arcades made of orange ironspot brick, brownstone, and terra-cotta. At the intersection of William and Beaver streets, the rounded corner housing the main entrance stands as an independent façade. The doorway, its flanking columns, and the marble cornice above are supposedly original to Pompeii. The columns were considered talismans of good luck for patrons who touched them as they passed through the door.

FORMER 19th PRECINCT STATION HOUSE AND STABLE, 1891–92
43 Herbert Street (also known as 512–518 Humboldt Street), Brooklyn
Architect: George Ingram
Designated: September 21, 1993

The assistant engineer for Brooklyn's Department of City Works designed this building to house Williamsburg's newly formed, and rapidly expanding, 19th Precinct. The sturdy structure, a Romanesque design that stands in sharp contrast to contemporary Italianate and French Second Empire law-enforcement architecture in New York City, became the archetype for later Brooklyn precinct houses. In the words of David A. Boody, Brooklyn's mayor in 1892, the 19th Precinct building was part of a broader program to provide Brooklyn with "station houses . . . as commodious and well-equipped as those in any city in the United States." Although it no longer houses a precinct, the building is currently in use by the New York Police Department for "special operations."

Inspired by H. H. Richardson's popular Romanesque civic designs, an arch defines the entrance porch of the complex, and the windows possess bold stone surrounds. The central window on the Humboldt Street façade is detailed with decorative spandrels and an ornamental grille. A two-story stable wing, which housed the cellblock and lodging rooms, is connected to the station house by a one-story passageway. A central tower rising above the entrance arch makes the building highly visible along the adjacent stretches of the Brooklyn-Queens Expressway.

56–58 PINE STREET BUILDING, formerly the Wallace Building, 1893–94; addition, 1919
56–58 Pine Street (also known as 26–28 Cedar Street), Manhattan
Architect: Oswald Wirz
Designated: February 11, 1997

Built as speculative real estate in what was then the city's insurance district, this originally twelve-story office building is representative of New York City's transition period between four- and five-story buildings and the massive commercial buildings that now fill the city's commercial spaces. When built, the Pine Street Building was among the tallest downtown structures. A 1919 addition, which does not relate to the rest of the building, is composed of two additional stories that are set back and hardly visible from street level.

The Pine Street Building was designed by Oswald Wirz, the in-house architect for the construction firm of James G. Wallace, for whom this building was originally named. The elaborate façade, although typical of the late nineteenth century, makes it distinctive in modern-day lower Manhattan. The four-bay façade is executed in brick, stone, and terra-cotta, and characterized by intricate Romanesque Revival detail, including round-arched openings and deeply set windows linked by groups of truncated, polished granite columns. Set on a raised granite basement, the building is also embellished with highly stylized foliate designs, fantastic visages, and grotesque heads, which merge with the other ornaments to create a unique façade.

HOME SAVINGS BANK OF AMERICA INTERIOR, formerly Bowery Savings Bank, 1893–95; alterations, 1980
130 Bowery, Manhattan
Architects: McKim, Mead & White; alterations, Swanke Hayden Connell & Partners
Designated: August 23, 1994

This interior design, principally credited to Stanford White, conveys both simplicity and grandeur. It is an early example of the august Roman Revival style, which reestablished the classical temple form as a standard for savings bank buildings. White employed several Roman prototypes: the colonnades are based on the Basilica Ulpia; the giant Corinthian columns are derived from the portico of the Pantheon; and the coved and coffered ceiling refers to the Basilica of Constantine.

The Bowery street entrance bears the inscription "YOUR FINANCIAL WELFARE IS THE BUSINESS OF THIS BANK" and opens onto the tellers' area of the waiting room, where a peninsular layout accommodates the once gender-specific counters. The eighty-foot-square, steel-framed banking room has a pyramidal skylight, and its axially symmetrical arrangement features a prominent, freestanding bank vault. This public space was innovative in offering customers a hygienic environment, as fresh air was introduced through open doors and windows, then vented through the skylight's louvers, creating a natural airflow. The marble wall surfaces and mosaic floors are durable and easy to clean. Despite a more recent series of adaptations, including artificial lighting and the reduction of the tellers' areas, the interior has retained its integrity. It now houses a branch of the Home Savings Bank of America.

FORMER SCHEFFEL HALL, 1894–95
190 Third Avenue, Manhattan
Architect: Weber & Drosser
Designated: June 24, 1997

Originally a renowned German rathskeller, Scheffel Hall is a legacy of *Kleindeutschland*, the German-American community that flourished on the Lower East Side during the last half of the nineteenth century. Founder Carl Goerwitz emigrated from Germany to the United States in 1873, and named his establishment after Josef Victor von Scheffel, a German poet, novelist, and lawyer.

Designed in German Renaissance Revival style, Scheffel Hall's elaborately detailed, unglazed terra-cotta façade is modeled after the famous Friedrichsbau at Heidelberg Castle, and is one of the earliest surviving examples of terra-cotta cladding in New York City. The ground-floor cast-iron storefront is ornamented with intricate strap-and-jewel work, diamond-point rustication, and cartouches. Richly embellished window surrounds and a curved front roof gable contribute to the unique character of the structure.

Though it changed hands a number of times, the building remained a popular gathering place for New Yorkers for over a century. The writer O. Henry, a regular patron, used Scheffel Hall as a setting for his 1909 short story "The Halberdier of the Little Rheinschloss," and from 1979 to 1995 the structure housed the renowned jazz club Fat Tuesday's. In 1995, the property was leased to the Highlander Brew Pub, which closed prior to designation. The building is now vacant.

AMERICAN SURETY COMPANY BUILDING, 1894–96; additions, 1920–22
100 Broadway, Manhattan
Architects: Bruce Price; additions, Herman Lee Meader
Designated: June 24, 1997

Built by one of the leading bond insurance companies in the nation, this was a key building in the evolution of the skyscraper, just as the insurance industry was crucial in the development of this section of Broadway. The second-tallest building in the city at the time of its erection, this was the first and most important skyscraper designed by the eminent architect Bruce Price. The twenty-three-story building was one of the first to incorporate such structural innovations as steel framing, curtain-wall construction, and caisson foundation piers carrying a cantilevered steel foundation structure, and was a prototype for the freestanding tower skyscrapers of the early twentieth century. Greek elements such as the Ionic entrance colonnade and classical sculptural figures on the third story—designed by J. Massey Rhind—indicate a neo-Renaissance decorative scheme.

Herman Lee Meader designed modifications that were added to the building between 1920 and 1922, including two penthouse levels, four bays on Broadway, and four bays on Pine Street. The new additions match Price's original design in material and articulation.

The building was bought by a group of investors in January 1962, and in 1973 was transferred to the Thomson Realty Company, which undertook a major renovation. In the mid-1980s, the interiors of the first thirteen stories were redesigned by the architectural firm of Kajima International for the Bank of Tokyo, and new windows, elevators, and mechanical systems were installed throughout the building.

BOHEMIAN NATIONAL HALL, 1895–97
321–325 East 73rd Street, Manhattan
Architect: William C. Frohne
Designated: July 19, 1994

The Bohemian National Hall (Národní Budova) is a rare survivor of the once numerous buildings that housed the benevolent societies organized by New York's immigrant communities. Czechs (Bohemians) and Slovaks, whose native lands were under Austro-Hungarian sovereignty, began immigrating in large numbers following the European revolutions of 1848. They first settled the Tompkins Square area of the Lower East Side, and in the 1880s and 1890s moved uptown to Yorkville. In their new neighborhood, called "Little Bohemia," they built the Bohemian National Hall.

The hall served the social, political, and economic needs of the community, housing meetings, lectures, dances, plays, and classes on various aspects of Czech and Slovak culture. During the First World War, the hall was the local base of the Slovak League, which actively petitioned for the creation of a binational Czech and Slovak state. The building has five stories organized into six bays, and is faced in stone, buff Roman brick, and terra-cotta. The bays are articulated with paired columns and pilasters, and the upper levels have a two-story arcade featuring lion's head bases supporting paired Ionic columns. The Bohemian Benevolent and Literary Society still owns the now vacant building and has plans to restore it.

**PUBLIC SCHOOL 27, formerly Public School 154,
also known as the St. Mary's Park School, 1895–97**
519 St. Ann's Avenue, The Bronx
Architect: C.B.J. Snyder
Designated: September 19, 1995

One of the earliest buildings designed by C.B.J. Snyder, New York City's superintendent of school buildings from 1891 to 1923, P.S. 27 is adjacent to St. Mary's Park in Mott Haven, in what was, at the time of construction, an Irish-immigrant working-class neighborhood. Snyder, who was very concerned with public health, set P.S. 27 on a C-shaped plan that provided ample light and ventilation, as well as created a semi-enclosed play area. The school was also unusual for its small classrooms and modern fire protection.

Not satisfied with simple utilitarianism, Snyder made the building handsome as well. The stepped gables refer to New York's Dutch heritage, while the polygonal bell crowning the center of the roof suggests early American Federal design. P.S. 27's main façade has thirteen bays, the central five composing a projecting pavilion. The five-story building is faced in buff brick with terra-cotta ornament and is covered with a hip roof. Limestone is used on the keyed window surrounds, the entrances, the corner quoins, and the stringcourses located above each floor. The building has continually served as a school.

**BOWLING GREEN OFFICES BUILDING, 1895–98;
alterations, 1912–13, 1917–20**
5–11 Broadway (also known as 5–11 Greenwich Street), Manhattan
Architects: William James and George Ashdown Audsley; alterations, Ludlow & Peabody
Designated: September 19, 1995

An enormous and beautifully crafted presence at the base of Broadway, the seventeen-story Bowling Green Offices Building was in the vanguard of New York commercial architecture when it was built. Its functional achievements included a large steel frame, a central light court, and provisions for electric service. The sheer mass of the building was also noteworthy—only the shorter Produce Exchange had a comparably large footprint, and only the much narrower Hudson Building was as tall.

The building's Hellenic Renaissance style is expressed in two nearly identical façades. The architects described the building as expressing "a free but pure treatment of ancient Greek architecture," meaning that their austere, rectilinear design avoided using specifically Greek forms, although it incorporated the proportions, spirit, and ornament of Greek architecture. The building is divided into a decoratively carved granite base, a white brick shaft, which solemnly reflects the rhythms of the structural skeleton, and an ornate terra-cotta capital. The bold, straightforward design shows the influence of the innovative architecture of the Chicago School. The original stoops on Broadway were reconfigured in 1912–13, and a seventeenth story and set-back, four-story tower were added in 1917–20.

PUBLIC SCHOOL 25, ANNEX D, formerly Westfield Township District
School No. 7, Public School No. 4, 1896; addition, 1906–07
4210–4212 Arthur Kill Road, Charleston, Staten Island
Architects: Unknown; addition, C.B.J. Snyder
Designated: May 16, 1995

During the second half of the nineteenth century, Kreischerville, which is the core
of modern-day Charleston, was a small, quasi–company town centered around the
Kreischer Brick Works. Following Staten Island's incorporation into New York City,
Kreischerville experienced a sharp increase in population. The Westfield School,
which was built to accommodate the children of the new residents, is one of the
borough's oldest surviving school buildings. Built with the intent of making it an
"ornament for the neighborhood," the school was the center of the town's civic life and
its most significant institutional building until 1984. It has since been under the
jurisdiction of the Division of Special Education.

   Standing two-and-a-half stories high, the Westfield School is set on a T-plan.
The narrow, gable-framed front façade prominently features the building's name and
construction date in light brick. The school's design incorporates classical elements
such as quoined corners and denticulated banding. An addition dating from 1906–07
stands two stories above a raised basement, and is set apart from the original structure
by a one-bay connector with entrances on the north and south sides. The walls facing
the street feature two tones of ironspot glazed face brick from Kreischerville's brick
factory.

ENGINE COMPANY 252, formerly Engine Company 52,
Engine Company 152, 1896–97
617 Central Avenue, Brooklyn
Architects: Parfitt Brothers
Designated: October 19, 1995

The City of Brooklyn established its professional Fire Department in 1869, four
years after New York City did. Between 1870 and 1900, concurrent with the opening
of the Brooklyn and Williamsburg bridges and the elevated trains over the East River,
Brooklyn's population tripled, surpassing one million. Also around this time, the
Brooklyn Fire Department's rival, the New York City Fire Department, built a number
of handsome and well-outfitted buildings, which led to the construction of twenty new
Brooklyn F.D. firehouses in the 1890s. Among them was this three-story Flemish
Revival building. One of the finest in Brooklyn, this firehouse has been in continuous
service since 1897.

   The walls are built of brick laid in a common bond, and Lake Superior red
sandstone surrounds the windows on the second and third stories. Stepped end gables
and a prominent scrolled front gable refer to the seventeenth-century Dutch settlement
in Bushwick. Fluted, cast-iron pilasters flank the entrance, where a rolling wood-and-
glass door has replaced the original double wooden doors. Above this, a wide stone
lintel with intricate botanical carvings incorporates the initials of the Brooklyn Fire
Department (B.F.D.), the company's name, the construction date, and shields carved
with "52."

STATEN ISLAND OFFICE OF PUBLIC BUILDING SERVICES, NEW YORK CITY BOARD OF EDUCATION, formerly Public School 15, Daniel D. Tompkins School, 1897–98
98 Grant Street, Staten Island
Architect: Edward A. Sargent
Designated: November 19, 1996

In 1897, due to an increase in Staten Island's student population, the Board of Trustees for the Middletown Township school district voted to replace its small 1883 schoolhouse with this three-story red-brick structure. New York City took over the school when Staten Island became a borough the following year. In 1916, the school was renamed for the founder of Tompkinsville, Daniel D. Tompkins (1774–1825), who served as governor of the state of New York from 1807 to 1817 and vice president of the United States from 1817 to 1825.

The Tompkins School is the only remaining Staten Island schoolhouse of the three designed by Edward A. Sargent, an English-born architect who also designed several hundred Staten Island residences. The main entrance on St. Paul's Avenue is flanked by projecting pavilions with hip roofs. Terra-cotta and stone trim accent the rough-textured, burnt red-brick façade. The building's most noteworthy feature is its four-faced clock tower, which rises a full story above the three-story structure. The school was closed in 1965, but two years later the Board of Education opened administrative offices in the building.

EMPIRE BUILDING, 1897–98; addition, 1928–30
71 Broadway, Manhattan
Architects: Kimball & Thompson; addition, J. C. Westervelt
Foundation Engineer: Charles Sooysmith
Builders: Marc Eidlitz & Son
Designated: June 25, 1996

The Empire Building is generally credited to Francis H. Kimball, "the father of the skyscraper," and it is his earliest extant building. Kimball also designed the nearby Trinity and U.S. Realty buildings (both q.v.). U.S. Steel located its headquarters in the Empire Building after it was formed by J. P. Morgan, who financed the merger of Carnegie Steel and seven other steel companies in 1901. This gigantic steel trust was soon the largest industrial concern in the world, and it dominated all aspects of the American steel industry. In 1919, U.S. Steel bought the Empire Building, which it owned until 1976. It has since had several owners, and has recently been converted into a luxury apartment building with 237 rental units, a health club, retail shops, and a rooftop sundeck.

Typical of early skyscrapers, the Empire's richly ornamented, Neoclassical granite façade is tripartite in its organization. The gray granite base is ornamented with arcades below paired, arched windows, the white shaft is organized horizontally with band courses and vertically with balconies, and the capital has colonnaded loggias below a heavy projecting cornice. The building has three articulated façades: polished granite columns capped by eagles on globes frame the two-story arched Broadway entrance; a narrow façade fronts Trinity Street; and the long Rector Street façade forms a backdrop to Trinity Church. The foundation is noteworthy for its early use of pneumatic caissons (sealed concrete cylinders sunk by mechanical means).

GREATER METROPOLITAN BAPTIST CHURCH, formerly St. Paul's German Evangelical Lutheran Church, 12th Church of Christ, Scientist, 1897–98
147–149 West 123rd Street, Manhattan
Architects: Schneider & Herter
Designated: March 8, 1994

Witness to a century of change in Harlem, this church was originally built to accommodate the growing German-immigrant congregation of St. Paul's German Evangelical Lutheran Church. The economic and social changes in Harlem from the late nineteenth through the early twentieth century saw the departure of the German community, and the church became home to the 12th Church of Christ, Scientist, the first African-American congregation of its denomination in New York City. In 1985, the building was bought by the Greater Metropolitan Baptist Church, which had broken off from the Metropolitan Baptist Church on West 128th Street, one of the oldest African-American churches in Harlem.

The building's neo-Gothic façade, executed in blue-gray Vermont marble, has a gabled center section with a recessed portal and gabled rose window. This is flanked by two square end towers containing secondary entrances, lancet windows, and finial-capped spires. The symmetrical design was chosen to project the church's architectural grandeur despite its mid-block location. The church's cornerstone, taken from the St. Paul's German Evangelical Lutheran Church building, which was demolished to make way for the current structure, reads *Christus Unser Eckstein* [German for "Christ our cornerstone"] / *1865 / 1897*. The east entrance now bears a sign including an illuminated cross and the name of the congregation.

NEW YORK PUBLIC LIBRARY, AGUILAR BRANCH, 1898–99; enlarged and refaced, 1904–05
172–174 East 110th Street, Manhattan
Architects: Herts & Tallant; enlargement and new façade, Herts & Tallant
Designated: June 25, 1996

This building, named for the British novelist and essayist Grace Aguilar (1816–47), who was of Spanish-Jewish descent and was widely known for her popular novels about the Spanish Inquisition, was originally the East Harlem branch of the Jewish community's broader Aguilar Free Library system. This library system was one of several programs that the small but established German-Jewish population created to educate and acculturate the huge numbers of newly arrived Eastern European Jews.

In 1899 Andrew Carnegie gave the city $5.2 million to establish a library system. Soon after, various independent libraries were consolidated into the Public Library, including the Aguilar building in 1903, when its original façade was replaced. The 1905 Classical Revival façade includes a three-story, three-bay, glass-and-galvanized-iron recessed screen, flanked by monumental fluted limestone piers. These end in Ionic capitals, which support a limestone entablature featuring the inscription "New York Public Library." This institutional building—which has been in continuous use, except for a 1993–96 renovation—is a rarity for Herts & Tallant, a firm renowned for their theater designs (including the Lyceum, the Shubert, and the Brooklyn Academy of Music, all q.v.).

ELLIS ISLAND, MAIN BUILDING INTERIOR, also known as the Registry Room, 1898–1900
Ellis Island, Island No. 1, Manhattan
Architects: Boring & Tilton
Designated: November 16, 1993

During the three decades between the opening of Ellis Island in 1892 and the restrictive Immigration Act of 1924, approximately twelve million Eastern and Southern European immigrants passed through this huge processing center. Today, the descendants of those who first set foot in the New World at Ellis Island represent more than one in every three Americans. As immigration slowed to a trickle in the 1920s, Ellis Island was adapted to serve a variety of governmental needs. It was finally closed in 1954, and abandoned until the late 1980s. In 1990 the National Park Service opened it as the Ellis Island Immigration Museum.

From 1986 to 1990, much of the Main Building was renovated, and the Registry Room was restored to its 1918–24 appearance; the space is now the centerpiece of the Immigration Museum. Designed in the Beaux-Arts classic style, its floor plan and use of space closely resemble the grand train stations of the era. The Registry Room has a two-story, fifty-six-foot, soaring barrel-vaulted ceiling in Guastavino tile, large, arched window openings at the clerestory, a perimeter balcony, and a 2,000-square-foot red Ludowici tile floor. This space offered an impressive—and intimidating—welcome to America to the up to 5,000 immigrants whom the room could accommodate daily.

MANHASSET APARTMENTS, 1899–1901; enlarged, 1901–05
2801–2825 Broadway, 301 West 108th Street, and 300 West 109th Street,
Manhattan
Architects: Joseph Wolf; enlargements, Janes & Leo
Designated: September 17, 1996

Around the turn of the century, rising Upper West Side real-estate prices—spurred by
an 1879 elevated train on Ninth Avenue (renamed Columbus Avenue in 1880) and the
Broadway subway line in 1901–04—effectively prohibited single-family dwellings for
all but the very wealthy. Meanwhile, the success of the 1880 Dakota Apartments (q.v.)
made multiple-unit living desirable for the upper-middle class, and led to an
apartment construction boom in the area. The Manhasset is an early example of the
type of speculative apartment building that would come to dominate the Upper West
Side.

The eight-story Manhasset was originally built as two contiguous buildings with a
flat roof. The brick-and-stone building was designed in the Beaux Arts style by Joseph
Wolf. The property was foreclosed before its opening, and the new owners added
entrance pavilions in the side street light courts, a ninth story, and a two-story mansard
roof—the building's most prominent feature—designed by Janes & Leo. The effect is
one large façade, asymmetrically massed, facing Broadway. The building has a two-
story limestone base, which is divided from a seven-story brick midsection by a
limestone sill. A metal cornice underlines the ninth story at the building's original
roofline. The Manhasset is now a cooperatively owned apartment building.

WADLEIGH SCHOOL, formerly the Wadleigh High School For Girls,
1901–02; restoration and addition, 1989–93
215 West 114th Street (also known as 203–249 West 114th Street
and 226–250 West 115th Street), Manhattan
Architect: C.B.J. Snyder; restoration and addition, URS Consultants
Designated: July 26, 1994

School construction was brisk at the turn of the century, due to mandatory children's
education and increasing immigration. The Wadleigh School, designed by C.B.J.
Snyder, the prominent superintendent of school buildings, was the first public girls'
school in New York City. In 1953–54, it was converted into a coeducational junior high
school and reopened in 1956 as I.S. 88. The school was named for women's education
pioneer Lydia Wadleigh (d. 1888), who founded the 12th Street Advanced School for
Girls in 1856 and achieved the position of Lady Superintendent at the New York
Normal College (now Hunter College).

The school is set on an H-plan and is steel framed, allowing for large banks of
windows, which give good light and ventilation. On a relatively small plot of land, the
five-story school has classrooms, laboratories, offices, gymnasiums, and study halls, all
accessible by some of the earliest electric elevators in a New York City public school.
Inspired by the Collegiate Gothic style, the red-brick and sandstone Wadleigh School
has gabled dormers and is ornamented with decorative terra-cotta shields. Its most
prominent feature is a 125-foot-high corner tower with a pyramidal roof, giving the
Wadleigh School a commanding presence despite its mid-block location. Between
1989 and 1993, the school was renovated, restored, and enlarged with a two-story
gymnasium annex.

GEORGE S. BOWDOIN STABLE, 1902
149 East 38th Street, Manhattan
Architect: Ralph S. Townsend
Designated: June 17, 1997

Until the early twentieth century, horse-drawn vehicles were the primary mode of transportation in New York City, and horses were a vital part of city life. This structure was built in 1902, during the last phase of stable construction in the city, for William H. Martin, a real-estate developer and senior partner in the clothing firm of Rogers, Peet & Company. The stable was purchased in 1907 by George S. Bowdoin, a partner in J. P. Morgan & Company, who lived at Park Avenue and East 36th Street.

The two-and-a-half-story Dutch Revival–style building alludes to New York City's history as the Dutch colony of New Amsterdam. Its configuration is typical of private stables of the era, with space for the carriage and horses on the ground floor and living quarters for the coachmen on the upper levels. Bold ornamentation and a strong roofline distinguish this building from others around it. Each of the three arched entries is defined by overscaled stone quoins and voussoirs. Sculpted stone horse heads accentuate each end of the narrow spandrel above the entryways, and in the center is a shield inscribed with the address number "149." Between the two square windows on the second story is a large stone panel with a shield citing the date of construction, "A.D. 1902."

An elaborate stepped gable rises from a mansard roof, with stone quoins marking each vertical edge of the gable, and a stone volute capping each step. A semicircular stone pediment tops the structure. In the center of the gable is an oval window with an ornate stone surround, above which sits a stone-carved bull dog's head.

In 1918, Edith Bowdoin inherited the stable from her father and converted it into a garage. She held ownership until 1944, and since then various owners have reconfigured the upper floors to house one or two families. It is currently a single-family dwelling.

PIKE STREET SYNAGOGUE (Congregation Sons of Israel Kalwarie), 1903–04
13–15 Pike Street, Manhattan
Architect: Alfred E. Badt
Designated: May 20, 1997

One of the few Lower East Side synagogues remaining from the era of Jewish immigration and settlement at the turn of the twentieth century, the Pike Street Synagogue served as a house of worship for the Congregation Sons of Israel Kalwarie for nearly one hundred years. Strongly influenced by Romanesque and German *Rundbogenstil* architecture, the three-story limestone building is distinct and impressive, with a columned portico above a raised basement. Its double lateral staircase leads to a recessed entrance with a small, round-arched corbel table above the windows, and a round-arched blind arcade encircles the top of the building.

The Pike Street Synagogue, one of the largest in its community, was also one of the few buildings designed specifically as a synagogue, rather than having been converted from an existing structure. Its congregation continued to worship in the synagogue well into the 1970s, when membership declined significantly. Abandoned, the building was vandalized and then fell into disrepair. Congregation members disagreed over whether to sell it, and only after a court battle was it sold in 1994. Today, the building's ground floor is used for commercial space, its main floor as a Buddhist temple, and its upper levels as apartments.

NEW YORK PUBLIC LIBRARY, TOTTENVILLE BRANCH, 1903–04
7430 Amboy Road, Tottenville, Staten Island
Architects: Carrère & Hastings
Designated: May 16, 1995

The Tottenville Branch dates back to 1899, when the Tottenville Free Library was established by the Tottenville Library Association. The village prospered from shipbuilding, oystering, and seaside resort tourism, and its Free Library was the first modern public library on Staten Island. The new building for the Tottenville Branch—one of the New York Public Library's oldest—housed a collection built around the Free Library's small holdings. It was the first of four Staten Island branch libraries funded by Andrew Carnegie's city-wide, $5 million public library project. This coincided with a larger trend that brought rural Staten Island into the realm of New York City's civic culture.

The Tottenville's architects, Carrère & Hastings, also designed the Main Branch of the Public Library and many other branch buildings. The one-story, classically inspired building is articulated in brick, stucco, and wood. It sits on a raised basement and its classical references include a Tuscan portico, quoins, and a modillioned raking cornice. The classical façade is softened by a hip roof, giving the building a graceful harmony with its landscaped site and village setting. The building has served the NYPL for more than ninety years.

NEW YORK COCOA EXCHANGE BUILDING, formerly the Beaver Building, 1903–04
82–92 Beaver Street (also known as 129–141 Pearl Street and 1 Wall Street Court), Manhattan
Architects: Clinton & Russell
Designated: February 13, 1996

This flatiron-shaped, fifteen-story structure was called the Beaver Building because of its address and the ornamental carved beaver-head decorations above the entrance. The building sits at the intersection of Beaver and Pearl streets, where an elevated railway line once curved around the Pearl Street façade. The building's Neo-Renaissance palazzo façade followed the 1890s trend to design New York City skyscrapers in a tripartite manner, using different materials to define the base, shaft, and capital areas. The three-story base is of granite and Indiana limestone, the middle section has alternating rows of tan and buff brick, and the top three stories are highlighted with polychromatic glazed terra-cotta of bright green, buff, and red.

Its first prominent tenant, the Munson Steamship Company, established in 1899 immediately after the United States occupied Cuba in the Spanish-American War, transported Cuban sugar. From 1931 to 1972, the building housed the world's first cocoa exchange, whose trading room occupied the building's double-height first story. Since 1979, the Cocoa Exchange has been part of the New York Coffee, Sugar & Cocoa Exchange, located at 127 John Street.

ENGINE COMPANY 7 AND HOOK & LADDER COMPANY 1 FIREHOUSE, 1904–05
100–104 Duane Street, Manhattan
Architects: Trowbridge & Livingston
Designated: September 21, 1993

While typical firehouses are composed of one bay on narrow lots, this three-story Beaux Arts–style building has three bays. The hook and ladder company occupied one bay, while the engine company occupied two for its two engines, which, in a neighborhood of tall buildings, were required to generate sufficient pressure for throwing water above eight stories. The companies, housed together since 1851, are among the oldest in New York (Hook & Ladder Company 1 was founded before the War of Independence), and together have protected both the City Hall area and the Financial District in lower Manhattan. The station's west bay became a museum in 1920, and then the Fire Department's Bureau of Fire Communications offices in 1987; the eastern bays still house Companies 7 and 1.

The symmetrically massed façade is visually unified by superimposed elements of an Anglicized Italian palazzo. Although it is actually two distinct buildings completely separated by a fire wall, the wide structure's façade is unified by a strong emphasis on horizontals. The ground floor, above a granite base, is boldly rusticated Indiana limestone ashlar with arched apparatus doorways, and the upper stories are gray brick with raised limestone bands. The building is topped by an entablature cornice and paneled parapet.

AMERICAN SAVINGS BANK, formerly the Union Square Savings Bank, 1905–07
20 Union Square West (also known as 101–103 East 15th Street), Manhattan
Architect: Henry Bacon
Designated: February 13, 1996

The Union Square Savings Bank, originally the Institution for Savings of Merchants' Clerks, was founded in 1848 to "encourage clerks . . . to take care of their earnings." Half a century later, the bank realized that its name was no longer suitable to an institution that had depositors of all professions, and so it changed its name to The Union Square Savings Bank. The building continues to serve as a bank, and its exterior has survived almost unchanged.

The Union Square Savings Bank building is one of the largest and best-known banks designed by Henry Bacon, who also designed the Lincoln Memorial in Washington, D.C. (1912–15). Bacon's work reflects the Academic Classic movement, which was popularized by the "Great White City"—the 1893 World's Columbian Exposition in Chicago. The Union Square Bank is a flat-roofed, four-story building covered in Troy white granite. The main façade design is a freestanding portico on four fluted Corinthian columns supporting the entablature and parapet. Above the columns is a cornice with dentils, egg-and-dart moldings, and carved faces of lions. A contemporary sign reading "American Savings Bank" now covers the frieze, which bore the original bank name, carved wreaths, and a beehive.

The building is currently undergoing exterior restoration and interior redesign. The site will house an off-Broadway theater, which will be named for its founding producer, Daryl Roth. The projected date for completion of the theater is late fall 1998.

FORMER STUYVESANT HIGH SCHOOL, 1905–07
354 East 15th Street (also known as 331–351 East 15th Street
and 326–344 East 16th Street), Manhattan
Architect: C.B.J. Snyder
Designated: May 20, 1997

Originally a "manual training" school for boys, designed to teach the practical application of science
and art to industry, the former Stuyvesant High School was one of the first built after the consolidation
of the New York City boroughs in 1898 and the subsequent creation of a citywide system of public
education. The five-story, H-plan building has two side courts that provide light and ventilation.
Designed in a Beaux Arts style with distinctive classical and Secessionist detail, the main façade on
East 15th Street is clad in tan brick and limestone with stone ornament, and is dominated by a
pedimented entrance pavilion flanked by three bays of windows. The East 16th Street façade is red
brick above a limestone base, with "Stuyvesant High School" inscribed above the entrance.

Stuyvesant quickly became one of the most prestigious high schools in the city, noted for mathemat-
ics, technology, and especially the sciences. Since the 1930s, admission has been based on a
competitive entrance examination. In 1967, a Brooklyn girl sued the Board of Education to gain
admission to Stuyvesant, and the subsequent court decision opened the school to girls in 1969. Among
the many notable Stuyvesant alumni are three Nobel Prize winners: Joshua Lederberg, class of '41, for
physiology and medicine; Robert W. Fogel, class of '44, for economics; and Roald Hoffmann, class of
'55, for chemistry.

In 1992, Stuyvesant High relocated to a new facility in Battery Park City. The original building
remains in use by the High School for Health Professionals, the Institute for Collaborative Education,
and P.S. 226, a special-education program.

MESSIAH HOME FOR CHILDREN, 1905–08; restoration, 1978
1771–1777 Andrews Avenue South, The Bronx
Architects: Charles Brigham; restoration, Castro-Blanco, Piscioneri & Feder
Designated: June 24, 1997

Constructed in 1905–08 for the Messiah Home for Children, a children's orphanage, this building
occupies a site donated by Standard Oil magnate Henry H. Rogers in 1902. The construction was
underwritten by Rogers and designed by Charles Brigham, a prominent Boston architect. Brigham
chose a Jacobethan Revival style marked by towers and turrets, numerous dormers, including some
with Flemish gables, and an array of deep-set, transomed windows for the elaborate structure.

The term *Jacobethan* is a combination of the terms *Elizabethan* and *Jacobean*. This architectural
style is a nineteenth-century revival of the Jacobean design style developed during the reign of King
James I (1603–25), which was essentially a later version of the style from the reign of Elizabeth. Originally developed during the High Renaissance in Italy, the Jacobethan style was revived in England in
the 1830s, becoming more elaborate toward the century's end. Around this time, American architects
were searching for design precedents for large institutional structures in the United States, and the
large estates of Europe proved useful as models. Bingham referred to these manor houses for his symmetrically composed and elaborately embellished early-twentieth-century designs.

The Salvation Army purchased the building in 1920 for use as a training college for cadets, adding
a temporary lecture hall in 1921. In 1958–60, the Salvation Army also constructed a five-story brick-
and-concrete dormitory building, connected by a one-story passageway, to the east of the original
structure. (This addition is not included in the designation.) The organization occupied the building
until 1975.

In 1978, the City of New York and the U.S. Department of Labor joined forces to rehabilitate the
structure for use as a Job Corps training center. Restoration, which included the repair and cleaning
of the masonry, the replacement of window sashes and roof shingles, and the re-creation of the original
copper trim with a new copper substitute, was executed by the architectural firm of Castro-Blanco,
Piscioneri & Feder. The City of New York still owns the building.

ENGINE COMPANY 84 AND HOOK & LADDER COMPANY 34, 1906–07
513–515 West 161st Street, Manhattan
Architect: Francis H. Kimball
Designated: June 17, 1997

This monumental, double-company firehouse was built in Washington Heights at a time when Manhattan's expansion northward was transforming the area from a rural respite to a residential neighborhood. The double-company firehouse was introduced in the early twentieth century, after New York City and its boroughs were consolidated in 1898 and municipal services were centralized.

The brick-and-limestone façade is an example of Beaux Arts civic architecture. Its grand scale, clearly articulated sections, and heavy ornamentation reflect the rational planning and urban-design principles of the City Beautiful Movement that influenced American urban planning at the turn of the century. Elaborate sculptural detail, overscaled window surrounds, and the use of rich materials create the firehouse's strong physical and symbolic presence. The two companies shared the building but operated separately, so the interior is divided by a fire wall. Two separate vehicular entrances reflect this division, while the second- and third-story three-bay organization unites the façade. Limestone panels inscribed with the name of each company are placed above the entrances. Ninety years later, Engine Company 84 and Hook & Ladder Company 34 continue to serve Washington Heights.

BANCA COMMERCIALE ITALIANA BUILDING,
formerly J. & W. Seligman & Company Building/Lehman Brothers Building, 1906–07; alterations, 1929; addition, 1982–86
1 William Street (also known as 1–9 William Street, 1–7 South William Street, and 63–67 Stone Street), Manhattan
Architects: Francis H. Kimball and Julian C. Levi; alterations, Harry R. Allen; addition, Gino Valle
Builder: George A. Fuller Co.
Designated: February 13, 1996

Originally the headquarters of J. & W. Seligman & Company, a prestigious investment-banking firm, this building is a rusticated, richly sculptural Neo-Renaissance–style structure, drawn from the contemporary Baroque Revival in England. It was designed by Francis H. Kimball, who is credited with New York's first skyscraper, in association with Julian C. Levi, a graduate of the Ecole des Beaux Arts and a nephew of the Seligmans. Viewed from Wall Street, this building's vertical focus is on the round, *tempietto*-form tower rising from an awkward, quadrilateral base atop the building.

Beginning in 1929, Lehman Brothers, another distinguished investment-banking firm, used this building as its headquarters. A new corner entrance was added, and the original arched South William Street entrance was replaced with windows matching the William Street façade. The current owner, Banca Commerciale Italiana, one of Italy's largest banks, built an eleven-story addition clad in banded limestone and black granite. The addition, completed in 1986, complements the original structure in a streamlined contemporary style, and is marked by an ornamental, round, openwork metal turret, echoing the *tempietto* tower on the opposite corner of the original building.

DIME SAVINGS BANK, 1906–08; addition, 1918; enlarged, 1931–32
9 DeKalb Avenue (also known as 9–31 DeKalb Avenue and 86 Albee Square), Brooklyn
Architects: Mawbray & Uffinger; addition, Russell Tracy Walker & Leroy P. Ward; enlargement, Halsey, McCormack & Helmer
Designated (exterior and interior): July 19, 1994

Founded in 1859, the Brooklyn-based Dime Savings Bank was named for its minimum required opening balance—one dime. In 1994, Dime merged with the Anchor Savings Bank, becoming Dime Bancorp, the nation's fourth-largest thrift institution. Dime's five-story, "Greek temple"–style building was the first structure in the United States to be clad in Pentelic marble, known to the ancient Greeks for its translucent quality. The main entrance, located on a chamfered corner, features a portico with fluted Ionic columns bearing a frieze with the bank's name. On the pediment above it is a clock and a sculpture with two figures, one depicting a youthful "Morning" anticipating work, and the other an older "Evening" reaping the fruits of his labor. A carved Mercury dime, the bank's symbol, is also above each entrance.

The bank's Neoclassical interior remains remarkably intact. The coffered ceiling and marble floor feature stars and hexagons, and six bronze chandeliers illuminate the marble tellers' counters. A central rotunda is composed of twelve marble Corinthian columns, an elaborate entablature, and a fifty-two-foot-diameter dome, which rises to 110 feet. In the 1931 enlargement, the use of a lightweight steel frame allowed an increase in floor space, from 14,000 to 29,000 square feet.

AMERICAN BANK NOTE COMPANY OFFICE BUILDING, 1907–08
70 Broad Street, Manhattan
Architects: Kirby, Petit & Green
Designated: June 24, 1997

This five-story, granite Neoclassical structure was constructed to house the corporate, administrative, and sales headquarters of the American Bank Note Company, which began producing the American Express Company's new "Travelers Cheques" in 1891. The company, which dominated the field of security engraving, resulted from a merger of seven banknote engraving firms in 1858, and became one of America's prominent producers of banknotes, stamps, stock certificates, and letters of credit by the late nineteenth century. When the company outgrew several smaller quarters, the administrative and sales functions were separated from the production facilities. This narrow Broad Street lot was chosen to house the administrative headquarters of the company because of its proximity to the financial institutions of lower Manhattan.

Banking institutions often favored distinctive, monumental buildings in classical styles to portray a solid and trustworthy image, and the American Bank Note Company commissioned the architectural firm of Kirby, Petit & Green to design a corporate headquarters that would reflect its prominence in the field. The building is distinguished by two overscaled, fluted Corinthian columns rising three stories above the entrance, which is capped with a carved eagle atop a medallion, the corporate symbol of the American Bank Note Company.

In 1988 the company offices moved to Blauvelt, New York, and the 70 Broad Street building was sold to real-estate investors. After serving several years as a fast-food facility, the building was again sold in 1995 and reopened as a restaurant.

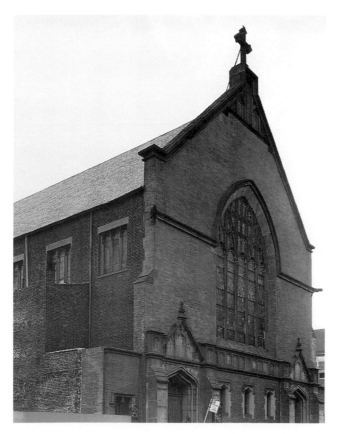

ST. PHILIP'S PROTESTANT EPISCOPAL CHURCH, 1910–11
210–216 West 134th Street, Manhattan
Architects: Vertner W. Tandy & George W. Foster, Jr.
Designated: July 13, 1993

This Neo-Gothic building is the fourth home of New York's oldest African-American Protestant Episcopal congregation, established as a parish in 1818. The congregation's original site, near the intersection of Chrystie and Stanton streets, was given by the Trinity Parish to be used as a burying ground for Trinity's African-American worshipers. Eventually, in 1818, St. Philips was recognized as an independent Episcopal parish. As mass transit made uptown living practical around the turn of the century, African-Americans migrated in large numbers to Harlem. St. Philip's was the first black church to move to central Harlem, and its move from lower Manhattan reflects the residential patterns of the African-American population in New York City. Its membership has included Thurgood Marshall, W.E.B. Du Bois, and Langston Hughes.

St. Philip's was designed by Vertner W. Tandy and George Washington Foster, Jr., who were among the first African-American architects to practice in the United States. The church's only true façade faces West 134th Street and is laid in orange Roman brick. It is symmetrically massed and dominated by an enormous stained-glass, pointed-arch window, below which are three small, street-level windows flanked by buttressed doorways. Gargoyles and a high-gabled roof complete the Gothic detail.

14 WALL STREET BUILDING, formerly Banker's Trust Building,
1910–12; addition, 1931–33
14 Wall Street (also known as 8–20 Wall Street, 1–11 Nassau Street,
and 7–15 Pine Street), Manhattan
Architects: Trowbridge & Livingston; addition, Shreve, Lamb &
Harmon
Designated: January 14, 1997

As monopolistic trusts grew in America's turn-of-the-century economy, New
York City's financiers defended their interests by forming the Banker's Trust.
Closely associated with J. P. Morgan, it was organized in 1903 with $1 million.
By 1912, the year in which its new building was completed, the Banker's Trust
was the second-largest trust in the country. It controlled $168 million, and its
board members held 113 interlocking directorships in fifty-five of the nation's
largest banking, insurance, transportation, manufacturing, trading, and utility
companies. In the same year, Congress discovered that more than three-
quarters of all American capital and credit was controlled by this small Wall
Street banking clique.

Capped by a seven-story, stepped pyramidal roof, this 539-foot-high
building—modeled on the campanile of San Marco in Venice—is a distinctive
element of the lower Manhattan skyline. Its much imitated profile became
a symbol of American capitalism, while its pointed top set a more general
precedent in skyscraper design. In the early 1930s, a twenty-five-story,
L-shaped addition articulated with a blend of Modern Classic and Art Deco
motifs was added north of the original tower. The Banker's Trust held the
building until 1987, and it is currently owned by General Electric.

FIORI RESTAURANT INTERIOR, formerly the Della Robbia Bar
and Grill, also known as the Crypt, 1910–13
4 Park Avenue, Manhattan
Architects: Warren & Wetmore
Vault construction: R. Guastavino Company
Architectural terra-cotta: Rookwood Pottery Company
Designated: April 5, 1994

A survivor from an opulent era, this restaurant was housed in the Vanderbilt Hotel,
which was designed by the prominent architectural firm of Warren & Wetmore,
which also designed Grand Central Terminal. The hotel was a personal project of
Cornelius Vanderbilt II's son Alfred, who occupied its luxurious penthouse
apartment. Along with 127 other Americans, Alfred met an early death aboard the
Lusitania, a British passenger ship that was torpedoed by a German U-boat in 1915;
the incident contributed to America's decision to enter the First World War. Today
the Vanderbilt Hotel building is office and storage space, and its façade has been
stripped of ornament.

The restaurant interior, however, remains largely unchanged. The bar (now the
front dining room) and two adjacent bays (now the rear dining room) have vaulted
ceilings. Elaborate terra-cotta dominates the decor, including flowers, keys, ropes,
and grotesque heads. The significance of ceramics in the Della Robbia is indicated
by the fact that it took its name from Luca della Robbia, a celebrated fifteenth-
century terra-cotta craftsman. Once frequented by such celebrities as Enrico
Caruso, Rudolph Valentino, and Diamond Jim Brady, the grotto-like ambience gave
the fashionable Della Robbia its nickname, "the Crypt."

THERESA TOWERS, formerly the Hotel Theresa, 1912–13
2082–2096 Adam Clayton Powell, Jr. Boulevard, Manhattan
Architects: George & Edward Blum
Designated: July 13, 1993

The thirteen-story Hotel Theresa opened in 1913 and maintained a strict policy of segregation. It was not until 1940 that the whites-only policy ended, and the Theresa—which came to be known as "the Waldorf of Harlem"—became the preferred hotel for prominent African-American writers, labor and business leaders, athletes, and bandleaders. The March on Washington Movement and Malcolm X's Organization of Afro-American Unity convened here. Fidel Castro also stayed at the Theresa in 1960, receiving such luminaries as C. Wright Mills, Allen Ginsberg, and Nikita Khrushchev. The father of Ron Brown, former U.S. secretary of commerce, was the hotel's manager.

The Theresa was constructed as a residence hotel, although the suites did not have full kitchens; residents could eat in the hotel dining room or have their meals delivered. When built, it was the tallest structure in Harlem, affording views of New Jersey and Long Island. The building's three façades have projecting bays, arched surrounds, and prominent gables. Using a variety of geometric shapes that create complex and ingenious patterns, the white façade exemplifies George & Edward Blum's singular approach to ornamentation and inventive use of terra-cotta. By 1966, the hotel had seriously deteriorated, but it was bought and converted into an office tower without alteration to the historic exterior.

FIRST CORINTHIAN BAPTIST CHURCH, formerly the Regent Theater, 1912–13
1906–1916 Adam Clayton Powell, Jr. Boulevard
(also known as 200–212 West 116th Street), Manhattan
Architect: Thomas Lamb
Designated: March 8, 1994

One of New York City's first—and most significant—motion-picture theaters, the Regent Theater building is among the few surviving local examples of the form, with one balcony and more than 1,800 seats. It was built during the motion-picture industry's transition from nickelodeons, which showed short silent pictures, to much larger theaters for viewing longer films. One critic remarked that the Regent initiated "an altogether new era in the moving picture world." Thomas Lamb, who was well known for his theaters and was responsible for many of the movie houses in Times Square, created the design. Among Lamb's extant theaters are the Mark Hellinger Theater, the Empire Theater, and Loew's 175th Street Theater and Ballroom.

The Regent followed the architectural example of existing dramatic theaters. It included a notable multicolored, terra-cotta façade and street-level commercial space that originally housed six stores. The exotic façades incorporate Italian, Neo-Renaissance, and Mannerist motifs. The Regent operated for fifty years as a venue for motion pictures and vaudeville, providing musical accompaniment, ushers, and an ornate and comfortable decor; it added air-conditioning in 1937. In 1964, the First Corinthian Baptist Church, an African-American congregation formed twenty-five years earlier, bought the building.

EQUITABLE BUILDING, 1913–15; restored 1980–87
120 Broadway (also known as 104–124 Broadway, 70–84 Cedar Street, 15–25 Nassau Street, and 2–16 Pine Street), Manhattan
Architects: Ernest R. Graham with Peirce Anderson; restoration, Ehrenkrantz, Eckstut & Whitelaw
Designated: June 25, 1996

New York City's concerns about unregulated skyscraper construction and shadows created by building mass culminated in the 1916 zoning law, which mandated setbacks to create "stepped façade" towers and stipulated that a building's total floor space could not exceed twelve times the area of its lot. The Equitable Building, whose commission predates the law, boldly illustrates what this regulation was designed to prevent: the massive structure rises forty-two stories from its property lines and is thirty times the area of its lot. It is capped by a two-story penthouse, which is not visible from the street. Upon completion, it was the largest office building in the world at 1.2 million square feet, and it could accommodate 16,000 workers.

The Equitable's six-story base and four-story capital are clad in granite and terra-cotta, and both feature Beaux Arts ornamentation with Classical details. The H plan, buff-brick shaft allows light and air to reach the offices. Double-height triumphal arches, flanked by three-story pilasters, define the main entrances on Broadway and Nassau Street. Although Equitable Life left the building in 1960, it continues to provide major office space in the financial center of lower Manhattan. In 1978 it was named a National Historic Landmark.

555 EDGECOMBE AVENUE APARTMENTS, also known as Roger Morris Apartments, 1914–16
555 Edgecombe Avenue, Manhattan
Architects: Schwartz & Gross
Designated: June 15, 1993

Facing Roger Morris Park and the historic Morris-Jumel Mansion, this thirteen-story building, known as "555" or "Triple Nickel," is one of the most impressive structures in Washington Heights. Created by the same firm that designed the 409 Edgecombe building (q.v.), the prestigious 555 was often considered to be part of the adjacent—and at one time more exclusive—neighborhood of Sugar Hill. Although much of the area around 555 was populated by African-Americans, the owners of the apartments refused to rent to them until 1939. One year after the race restriction was lifted, however, no white tenants remained in 555. Once available, the building's sizable apartments and fine views attracted a cross section of African-American professionals, as well as celebrities, including performer and activist Paul Robeson, social psychologist Kenneth Clark, and jazz musician Count Basie.

The apartments occupy a rectilinear, block-like building with a central court. Because of the slope of the plot, the building's Edgecombe Avenue façade has an exposed basement and cellar, which are faced in gray granite. This portion of the building also contains the arched main entrance. Above this, it is faced in beige and yellow brick, and the upper stories are separated from the lower by a terra-cotta beltway. Although the area has declined, 555 remains well maintained.

CHASE MANHATTAN BANK, formerly Brooklyn Trust Company, 1913–16
177–179 Montague Street and 134–138 Pierrepont Street, Brooklyn
Architects: York & Sawyer
Designated (exterior and interior): June 25, 1996

In the chaotic post–Civil War economy, America needed stable banks to help convey strong public images. One such bank was the Brooklyn Trust Company, founded in 1866. The bank occupied a former private residence from 1873 until 1913, when the trustees agreed a larger headquarters building was required. The Brooklyn Trust Company grew to thirty-one branches located throughout the city during the 1930s and, after a series of mergers, became Chase Manhattan Bank in 1996.

York & Sawyer designed this five-story urban palazzo in the sixteenth-century Italian High Renaissance style, reminiscent of the great banking houses of Florence and Verona. The building is composed of two limestone-clad sections: a rusticated and vermiculated base, and a *piano nobile* (upper section) with a smooth façade and a double-height colonnade of Corinthian columns. The bank has three façades but only two entrances. Mirror images of each other, the three-bay northern and southern elevations feature heavy, wrought-iron, double-height doors sided by torchères. The west elevation's seven-bay arcade lights the single-vaulted banking hall, whose fine materials and craftsmanship include a coffered ceiling and polychromatic marble mosaic floor. The building remains a bank, with only minimal alterations resulting from modern changes in banking procedures.

409 EDGECOMBE AVENUE APARTMENTS,
also known as Colonial Parkway Apartments, 1916–17
409 Edgecombe Avenue, Manhattan
Architects: Schwartz & Gross
Designated: June 15, 1993

Sugar Hill, the neighborhood between 145th and 155th streets, and Edgecombe and Amsterdam avenues, became home to many affluent African-Americans in the 1930s. This thirteen-story, E-shaped, Neo-Georgian and Neo-Renaissance apartment building, known simply as "409," was widely considered to be the most prestigious address in the area. The main entrance is marked by a stone enframement topped by a pedimented window surround. Faced in red-brown brick, the building's exterior has a tripartite design with terra-cotta detail at the base and capital. Set on the rocky ridge known as Coogan's Bluff, 409 overlooks Jackie Robinson Park—previously known as Colonial Park—which ensures an unobstructed view of the Harlem River and The Bronx.

During the late 1930s, some of the most well known and influential African-Americans of the period resided in this building. As *Ebony* magazine put it, "Legend, only slightly exaggerated, says bombing 409 would wipe out Negro leadership for the next 20 years." Residents included Jules Bledscoe, singer and actor; William Stanley Braithewaite, poet and critic; Aaron Douglas, painter and illustrator; W.E.B. Du Bois, scholar and activist; Thurgood Marshall, civil libertarian and the first African-American U.S. Supreme Court justice; Lucky Roberts, jazz musician; Walter White, executive secretary of the NAACP; and Roy Wilkins, White's successor.

AMERICAN EXPRESS COMPANY BUILDING, 1916–17
65 Broadway (also known as 63–65 Broadway and 43–49 Trinity Place), Manhattan
Architect: James L. Aspinwall of Renwick, Aspinwall & Tucker
Designated: December 12, 1995

This building served as American Express headquarters from 1874 until 1975, and continues to house its travel services. The American Express Company was formed in 1850 as a parcel-post business, transporting the mail and packages that the U.S. Post Office would not handle. The company made several major innovations involving the transfer of funds, initiating the money order in 1882, the travelers cheque in 1891, and the credit card in 1958. The building at 65 Broadway has also housed the headquarters of other prominent firms, including the investment bank of J. W. Seligman & Co., and the American Bureau of Shipping, a maritime concern.

The twenty-one-story (plus basement), Neoclassical, concrete and steel-framed structure, set on an H-plan, has light courts facing the street—an arrangement popularized by architect George B. Post. The design provides offices with ample light and air, and was widely employed from the 1880s through the 1910s. The building's façades, which are executed in white brick and terra-cotta above a granite base, are divided into a tripartite base-shaft-capital scheme. The building's massive stone walls are consistent with the masonry wall of its blockfront, contributing to the "canyon effect" that now characterizes lower Broadway, long known as "Express Row."

CUNARD BUILDING, 1920–21
25 Broadway (also known as 13–27 Broadway, 13–39 Greenwich Street,
and 1–9 Morris Street), Manhattan
Architect: Benjamin Wistar Morris
Consulting Architects: Carrère & Hastings
Designated (exterior and interior): September 19, 1995

Architect Benjamin Wistar Morris (of Seamen's Bank for Savings and Bank of New York & Trust Company Building) designed the twenty-two-story Cunard Building to conform to the zoning law of 1916, which mandated set-backs to create "stepped façade" towers and stipulated that a building's total floor space could not exceed twelve times the area of its lot. The building has subtle set-backs, and it is arranged on an H-plan with unusually long exposures to allow for ample light and ventilation. The Neo-Renaissance exterior has projecting end pavilions, but the façade is more noticeably separated into a rusticated base, central plane, and colonnaded crown; this tripartite division was characteristic of lower Manhattan's "canyon" walls. Nautically inspired details—representing sea horses, the four winds, and Neptune's head—animate the otherwise austere façade. The design conveys the prestige of the Cunard Steamship Line Ltd., then the premier transatlantic passenger line.

The Cunard Building housed a ticket office comparable in size to grand railway stations rather than steamship offices. The interiors are monumental public spaces modeled on Italian Renaissance and ancient Roman prototypes. Grandly proportioned and skylighted, the Great Hall consists of a central, domed octagonal space with square vault areas on either side, and a five-bay entrance lobby. Nautical iconography dominates the reliefs, ornaments, and painted surfaces. The U.S. Postal Service currently occupies the space.

GREENPOINT BANK, formerly the Bowery Savings Bank Building, 1921–23; addition, 1931–33
110 East 42nd Street, Manhattan
Architects: York & Sawyer, W. Louis Ayres design partner;
addition, W. Louis Ayres
Designated (exterior and interior): September 17, 1996

As one of New York's largest banks at the turn of the century, the Bowery Bank opened a midtown branch in the early 1920s, following the city's center of commerce as it shifted north from downtown. The building was designed by York & Sawyer, a firm known for its bank designs. The firm had inherited many of its aesthetic traditions—not to mention its staff—from the celebrated firm of McKim, Mead & White, which designed the first Bowery Bank (q.v.).

The 42nd Street property was too valuable to be occupied solely by a bank, so the planners created a dual-purpose building: a fourteen-story office tower superimposed over the monumental banking hall. The Romanesque façade, with its simple arches and expansive surfaces, breaks with the typical "Greek Temple" bank design. A deeply cut, four-story arched entrance on 42nd Street is the major element of the building's base, and the tower has a pier-and-spandrel system of four double bays. Immediately east of the original building, a six-story addition repeats the tower's motifs above an arcade.

Ayres's interior design is Italian Roman–Byzantine, recalling a basilica (a Roman court converted for Christian worship) with apselike areas along the side walls; the space celebrates thrift as a quasi-religious virtue. The simple Romanesque forms are constructed from a variety of lavish materials, including polished marble, limestone, sandstone, plaster, bronze, gold leaf, and wood.

In 1991, the Bowery Savings Bank was acquired by Home Savings of America, and in 1995 the banking spaces were transferred to GreenPoint Bank. The building remains in use as a bank and office building.

STANDARD OIL BUILDING, 1921–28
26 Broadway (also known as 10–30 Broadway, 1–11 Beaver Street, and 73–81 New Street), Manhattan
Architects: Carrère & Hastings
Associate Architects: Shreve, Lamb & Blake
Designated: September 19, 1995

A fine example of the new set-back style of skyscraper that emerged during the early 1920s, the Standard Oil Building supports one of the southernmost spires in the Manhattan skyline. The building's huge, sixteen-story base is articulated with Neo-Renaissance window bays and entrance portals, above which a thirteen-story, pyramid-capped tower rises at slight angles to both the Broadway and Beaver Street façades. The structure is clad in buff Indiana limestone. Its complex massing served to incorporate the earlier Standard Oil Building and fit into the irregular, five-sided site, while also allowing for subsequent building expansions. The Broadway entrance is ornamented with carved panels, above which is a glazed screen framed by spandrels, featuring the corporate iconography of triple torches merging into a single flame. Other images include globes showing both hemispheres, suggesting Standard Oil's powerful position in world commerce.

From this site, John D. Rockefeller and his associates saw Standard Oil monopolize the American oil industry. In 1911 the company withstood an antitrust decision that stripped it of its subsidiaries, though it managed to retain its dominant role in the international oil business. The building, constructed as the company approached its fiftieth year, reinforced its physical presence in New York City's center of commerce. In 1956, Standard Oil's successor sold the building, which remains an office tower.

ABYSSINIAN BAPTIST CHURCH AND COMMUNITY HOUSE, 1922–23
Church: 136–142 West 138th Street (Odell M. Clark Place), Manhattan
Community House: 132–134 West 138th Street (Odell M. Clark Place), Manhattan
Architects: Charles W. Bolton & Son
Designated: July 13, 1993

The Abyssinian Baptist Church was formed in 1808, when a small group of African-American worshipers broke with the predominantly white First Baptist Church on Gold Street. The church moved northward, following the residential patterns of New York's African-American community.

The Abyssinian Church and community house are constructed in the Neo-Gothic style, with a central gabled section serving as the focal point of the façade. The symmetrically massed church is faced with blocks of Manhattan schist in random ashlar with white terra-cotta trim. East of the church is the community house, faced with the same materials and designed to complement the style of the church.

In 1923, during the tenure of the Reverend Adam Clayton Powell, Sr. (1908–37), the church moved to its present Harlem location. Reverend Powell initiated the social-activist doctrine for which the church is known, and his son, Adam Clayton Powell, Jr., took over the ministry in 1937. He broadened the church's social mission in New York and in Washington, D.C., where he served as a United States congressman (1945–70), advocating civil rights legislation, federal aid for education, a minimum wage scale, and better unemployment benefits. In recent years, the church has supported social programs including AIDS awareness, economic aid to African communities, and the "Billboard Campaign," which has removed outdoor advertising for liquor and tobacco from the central Harlem area.

MOTHER AFRICAN METHODIST EPISCOPAL ZION CHURCH, 1923–25
140–148 West 137th Street, Manhattan
Architect: George W. Foster, Jr.
Designated: July 13, 1993

This church is the sixth home of New York City's first African-American congregation, and the founding church of the African Methodist Episcopal Zion Church. It was established in 1796, when the black members of the predominantly white John Street Methodist Congregation broke with their church, which refused to allow integrated communions. The new congregation withdrew from the Methodist Church denomination altogether and formed the Conference of A.M.E. Zion Churches in 1820.

During the nineteenth century, the A.M.E. Zion, known as the "Freedom Church," was noted for its outspoken abolitionism. It counted among its members Harriet Tubman, Sojourner Truth, and Frederick Douglass. Many of the Zion Churches were part of the Underground Railroad, which smuggled African-Americans out of the South. The A.M.E. Zion Church Conference continued its social activism in the twentieth century, and its membership included Langston Hughes, Marian Anderson, Joe Louis, and Paul Robeson.

Designed by one of the first African-American architects to be registered in the United States, this Neo-Gothic church is symmetrical, with a gray stone façade laid in random ashlar and trimmed in terra-cotta. Flanking a tall, central gable are pairs of narrow buttressed wings. A pointed-arch window dominates the center of the façade, above the entrance.

A. PHILIP RANDOLPH CAMPUS HIGH SCHOOL, formerly the New York Training School for Teachers / New York Model School, 1924–26
443–465 West 135th Street, Manhattan
Architect: William H. Gompert
Designated: June 24, 1997

The New York Training School for Teachers/New York Model School was the first building constructed expressly for the Training School, one of three municipal teacher-training schools maintained by the Board of Education to supply teachers to the city's school system. The facility, designed by William H. Gompert, architect and superintendent of school buildings for the Board of Education, was divided between the training school and its "model school" for practice teaching. The building was designed in an abstracted, contemporary Collegiate Gothic style, and the dual interior functions of the facility are differentiated by the exterior articulation. The five- and six-story (plus basement and central tower), L-shaped building is divided vertically by pavilions, buttresses, and square towers. Adjoining the training school portion of the building is a wing housing a two-story auditorium beneath a two-story gymnasium.

The Training School became the New York Teachers Training College from 1931 to 1933, after which it was abolished due to a surplus of teachers in the city school system during the Depression. In 1933, the model school portion of the building was devoted to Public School 193, followed in 1936 by the High School of Music and Art, established by Mayor Fiorello H. La Guardia. This was considered to be the first public high school in the United States that specialized in the study of music and art. The school merged with the High School of Performing Arts in 1984, becoming the Fiorello H. La Guardia High School of Music and Art and Performing Arts, and relocated to a building west of Lincoln Center. The 443–465 West 135th Street building has since housed the A. Philip Randolph Campus High School.

CITY CINEMAS VILLAGE EAST, formerly Phoenix Theater, Louis N. Jaffe Art Theater, Yiddish Art Theater, 1925–26
181–189 Second Avenue, Manhattan
Architect: Harrison G. Wiseman
Consultant for Interior Decoration: Willy Pogany
Designated (exterior and interior): February 9, 1993

By the 1920s, the Yiddish theater—arguably the most important part of Jewish immigrant culture—had begun a slow decline, as a second generation of Jews came of age and their linguistic particularity eroded. During this time, the Yiddish theater district moved from Grand Street ("the Yiddish Broadway") and the Bowery to Second Avenue.

Originally the Yiddish Art Theater, this building housed Yiddish productions until 1945 and staged Yiddish revivals in the 1970s and 1980s. The Phoenix Theater occupied the building in the 1950s, where, for affordable prices, audiences could see such well-known performers as Jessica Tandy, Hume Cronyn, Montgomery Clift, and Uta Hagen. Younger actors such as Larry Storch, Joel Grey, Carol Burnett, and Peter Falk also performed here. Over the next three decades, the building housed debut productions of *Grease*, *Oh! Calcutta!*, *The Best Little Whorehouse in Texas*, and *Joseph and the Amazing Technicolor Dreamcoat*.

The building's exterior is a 1920s Moorish Revival style that uses Judaic references such as half menorahs in its ornate entrance pavilion arch. The interior has lavishly ornamented tile and plaster ceilings containing six-pointed stars. In 1991, the building was converted into the seven-screen Village East cinema. Although the main room has been subdivided, much of the elaborate decor remains.

APPLE BANK FOR SAVINGS INTERIOR, formerly Central Savings
Bank, 1926–28
2100–2114 Broadway, Manhattan
Architects: York & Sawyer
Designated: December 21, 1993

This interior is housed in a designated landmark building (q.v.), whose name changed
from the German Savings Bank to the Central Savings Bank during the anti-German
hysteria of the First World War. An outstanding example of the academic classical
architectural tradition, this interior presents an early-twentieth-century design fusion of
Roman, Baroque, and High Renaissance prototypes, which are complemented by the
decorative ironwork designs of Samuel Yellin. One of this century's finest metalworkers,
Yellin was the subject of a 1911 Philadelphia Museum exhibition when he was only
twenty-six years old.

The accommodation of the great banking hall and its accessory areas to the irregular
four-sided site reflects the overall Beaux Arts organization and planning of the space.
The brilliance and monumentality of the banking hall are emphasized by the skillful
manipulation of scale between the low entrance sequence, the lofty banking hall, and the
mezzanine loggia. Outside, the Broadway entrance vestibule and foyer are walled with
simple sandstone. Inside, the banking hall is finished with rich materials and fine
interior details, highlighted by the polished polychromatic marbles of the floor. The main
banking room is dominated by the vast barrel-vaulted, coffered ceiling, from which hang
enormous chandeliers above a central tellers' cage.

REPUBLIC NATIONAL BANK INTERIOR, formerly Williamsburgh
Savings Bank, 1927–29
1 Hanson Place, Brooklyn
Architects: Halsey, McCormack & Helmer
Designated: June 25, 1996

Brooklyn's tallest building (q.v.), the only Brooklyn structure visible from the entire
borough, houses this interior. It is situated just off the intersection of the two main
thoroughfares, Flatbush and Atlantic avenues. Inside, a mosaic by the painter Angelo
Magnanti (d. 1969) portrays the stars and the signs of the zodiac with their mythological
figures. On the north wall of the bank is a mosaic in which the bank has a prominent
place in Brooklyn's skyline, reinforcing its general prominence in the borough.

The interior, a simple and elegant Romanesque Revival space, imagines banking as a
quasi-religious act. The great banking room—112 by 73 feet, and 63 feet high—is a
basilica-like, three-bay space set on a nave-and-aisles plan. Its walls and floors are
finished in polished exotic marbles, and it is highlighted with golden mosaic vaults and
enameled steel. Due to the prominence given the banking space, the elevators are
located in the southeast corner, not—as one would expect in a skyscraper—in the
building's center. The inclusion of a ladies' lounge in the original plan attested to the
growing role of women as depositors in the early twentieth century. The bank has
remained in continuous use, and is currently operated by the Republic National Bank.

LOEW'S PARADISE THEATER, 1928–29
2401–2419 Grand Concourse (also known as 2394–2408 Creston Avenue),
The Bronx
Architect: John Eberson
Designated: April 15, 1997

Marcus Loew, an Austrian-Jewish immigrant who settled on Manhattan's Lower East Side, began his company in 1909 with a single theater. By 1919 Loew's was a major nationwide chain. In 1920, Loew bought Louis B. Mayer's Metro Studio, which in turn acquired Samuel Goldwyn's studio in 1924, becoming Metro-Goldwyn-Mayer (MGM). Loew's Paradise Theater exemplifies the grand and eclectically themed movie palaces of the 1920s. It was one of five Loew's theaters built concurrently outside of midtown Manhattan: the others were in Flatbush, Brooklyn; Jamaica, Queens; Jersey City, New Jersey; and East 175th Street, Manhattan (q.v.).

The 4,000-seat Loew's Paradise is housed in a steel-framed structure. The façade is organized into three sections: a three-story lobby with an elaborate Italian Baroque terra-cotta frontispiece; a long, two-story section housing storefronts and office space; and a three-story stage house. The theater opened with a characteristically diverse program that included the national anthem, two musical performances, three short films, a stage presentation, and the feature-length talkie *The Mysterious Dr. Fu Manchu*; ticket prices ranged from 25¢ to $1. The interior space has been subdivided several times since 1973, but the theater continued to show films until 1994. Since then, the theater's future use has been the topic of contentious debate.

MANHATTAN COMPANY BUILDING, 1929–30
40 Wall Street (also known as 34–42 Wall Street and 25–39 Pine Street),
Manhattan
Architect: H. Craig Severance
Associate Architect: Yasuo Matsui
Consulting Architects: Shreve & Lamb
Consulting Engineers: Moran & Proctor
Builders: Starrett Brothers & Eken
Designated: December 12, 1995

Commissioned during the speculative real-estate boom of the 1920s and constructed in less than one year, this building was intended by H. Craig Severance to be the tallest in the world. Its rival was the concurrently built Chrysler Building (q.v.), designed by Severance's former partner, William Van Alen. The Manhattan Company Building soared to 927 feet, but Van Alen's addition of a 185-foot spire to the Chrysler Building—installed in sections under the cover of a single night—raised it to a total of 1,046 feet. One year later, the 1,250-foot Empire State Building (q.v.) exceeded both their heights, and decisively ended the record-setting height competition until the World Trade Center's twin towers were completed in 1973.

The overall massing of the Manhattan Company Building is characteristic of Art Deco–style skyscrapers. Consistent with the traditions of the Financial District, its base, which occupies almost the entire lot, is faced with granite and limestone and is articulated by a traditional classical colonnade. The building's midsection is defined by a series of setbacks as it rises into a freestanding tower, and spandrels with abstract Art Deco designs separate the windows. Topped by a seven-story, pyramidal steel roof and spire, the structure remains a distinctive element of the Manhattan skyline.

YESHIVA OF THE TELSHE ALUMNI,
formerly the Anthony Campagna Estate, 1929–30
640 West 249th Street, The Bronx
Architect: Dwight James Baum
Designated: November 16, 1993

Built as the home of Italian-born builder and philanthropist Anthony Campagna, this twenty-eight-room Italianate villa is a fine example of 1920s American architectural eclecticism. Dwight James Baum, who designed rural mansions for Count Alfonso and John Ringling, was commissioned for the project because he specialized in "historical" and European styles. The design suggests a Tuscan model, but is not based on a specific example. A rusticated limestone entrance portico is the central focus of the two-story façade, the remainder of which is faced in stucco. The frontal exposure also includes an off-center stair tower and a projecting east wing. The roof is handmade Italian tile.

The mansion is surrounded with formal landscape elements. A drive, starting at the stone-and-iron entrance on West 249th Street, leads into a walled forecourt with a center fountain. The grounds have a sunken garden area, a reflecting pool, fountains, and terraces. Secluded and forested in the Riverdale section of The Bronx, the estate has views of the Hudson River and the New Jersey Palisades. Campagna lived in the house until 1941, after which it had several owners. It is currently owned by an Orthodox Jewish boarding school, which plans to add two wings in the rear.

CITY BANK–FARMERS TRUST COMPANY BUILDING, 1930–31
20 Exchange Place (also known as 14–28 Exchange Place, 61–75 Beaver Street, 6 Hanover Street, and 16–26 William Street), Manhattan
Architects: Cross & Cross
Designated: June 25, 1996

This building was built as the new headquarters for City Bank–Farmers Trust Company, the predecessor of Citibank. The bank had been formed by a merger of Farmers Loan and Trust Company and National City Bank, the latter having been the largest bank in the country since 1894, as well as the first bank to offer interest on savings accounts. The building was one of several skyscrapers intended to secure the title of "world's tallest building" during the early 1930s. When it was completed in 1931, however, the sixty-story structure achieved only the uncertain distinction of being the tallest building with a predominantly stone façade.

Despite its massive base, the building achieves a vertical emphasis with two elements: widely spaced piers that rise to freestanding, stylized heroic figures believed to represent the "giants of finance," and a square tower that emerges at an angle slightly shifted from the base. Stylized coins, representing the countries in which City Bank had offices, surround the round-arched main entry on Exchange Place. The building lacks the profusion of Art Deco ornamentation characteristic of the period. Instead, the Modern Classic design emphasizes silhouettes, and the fine quality of the materials and ornaments.

THE NEW SCHOOL FOR SOCIAL RESEARCH, FIRST FLOOR INTERIOR, 1930–31; restoration, 1992
66 West 12th Street (also known as 66–70 West 12th Street), Manhattan
Architects: Joseph Urban; restoration, Prentice, Chan & Ohlhausen
Designated: June 3, 1997

The New School for Social Research was founded in 1919 by a group of academics that included Charles Beard, John Dewey, James Harvey Robinson, and Thorstein Veblen. Beard and Robinson had resigned from the faculty of Columbia University to protest the school's ban on antiwar demonstrations on the eve of World War I. The New School was designed to provide expanded learning opportunities for adults, and since its founding has been an important part of the intellectual life of New York City. In the 1930s and 1940s, the New School's "University in Exile" program provided employment for more than 150 European scholars who had fled the Nazis.

In 1928, the New School acquired four lots on West 12th Street and commissioned Joseph Urban, an architect born and trained in Vienna, to design a structure that would reflect the progressive ideals of the school. The seven-story brick-and-glass New School building, characterized by spare, simple forms and geometric patterns, was the first example of the International Style of architecture built in New York City. The first-floor interior houses a dramatic yet intimate auditorium. The oval plan of the room, as well as the color scheme of gray tones accented with red, give the space a sense of warmth and unity. At the center of the auditorium's rounded ceiling is a flat, oval panel, from which a series of concentric rings made of perforated plaster fan outward. This configuration was meant to improve acoustics, and influenced the design of Radio City Music Hall, which was built in 1932. In the lobby, graceful curves and hard, sleek materials such as polished stone and bronze complement the softer forms and materials of the auditorium.

The auditorium underwent restoration in 1992, and has since been named the John L. Tishman Auditorium. It provides an impressive setting for New School lectures, seminars, symposiums, film screenings, and theatrical productions.

JAMAICA BUSINESS RESOURCE CENTER, formerly La Casina, also known as La Casino, c. 1933; restoration, 1994–95
90–33 160th Street, Jamaica, Queens
Architects: Unknown; restoration, Li-Saltzman Architects
Designated: January 30, 1996

New York City nightclubs, once the romantic symbol of the city's nightlife, began growing in popularity as enforcement of Prohibition eased in the late 1920s, and continued to proliferate when Prohibition was repealed in 1933. Built at the twilight of the Jazz Age, La Casina Supper Club is one of the few surviving Streamlined Moderne buildings in the city. The style, which used dynamic massing and sleek, stripped forms, was a popular means of highlighting commercial structures in the 1930s, and was particularly beneficial for attracting attention to this small mid-block structure.

Horizontal bands of metal form a ziggurat cap over the smooth stucco plane, and the bright, projecting vertical neon sign helped attract business from nearby Jamaica Avenue. La Casina, one of the many clubs that made Jamaica an entertainment and commercial hub in the 1930s, served the traditional supper club mix of dining, dancing, and entertainment. By 1940 the club had closed, and it has since housed a church and a swimsuit and brassiere manufacturer. Since 1989, the Jamaica Business Resource Center, which provides information and capital access for small businesses, has owned and operated the building.

EMIGRANT SAVINGS BANK, formerly Dollar Savings Bank Building, 1932–33, 1937–38, 1949–52
2516–2530 Grand Concourse, The Bronx
Architect: Adolf L. Muller of Halsey, McCormack & Helmer
Designated (exterior and interior): July 19, 1994

This bank was built in three separate building campaigns spanning twenty years, yet it followed a single, coherent plan and retains its design integrity throughout. The easternmost bay was built in 1932–33; five years later, a one-hundred-foot expansion along the Grand Concourse completed a symmetrically massed, classicized Art Deco façade. Between 1949 and 1952, a ten-story office tower with a fifty-foot clock tower was added to the left of the existing façade, completing the building. It is still a bank, although the neighboring office tower was sold and converted into condominium space.

Twin entrances into the banking room, separated by three double-height windows, constitute the façade's main features. The exterior is clad in polished Texas pink granite ashlar, with red brick and terra-cotta on the upper tower stories. The attic is decorated with representations of "Liberty Head" silver dollars—now covered by the metal-and-plastic logo of the Emigrant Savings Bank, which acquired Dollar in 1992—and four inscribed tablets bearing advice on saving money. Inside, classical proportion and trabeation prevail in the monumental, unobstructed space, but the details and surfaces are Art Deco. Five murals by painter and mosaicist Angelo Magnanti, depicting the early history of The Bronx, further enhance the space.

BROOKLYN PUBLIC LIBRARY, CENTRAL BUILDING, 1935–41
Grand Army Plaza, also known as 2 Eastern Parkway and 415 Flatbush Avenue, Brooklyn
Architects: Alfred Morton Githens and Francis Keally
Designated: June 17, 1997

Initially proposed in 1888, when Brooklyn was still an independent city, plans for the municipally financed Central Building of the Brooklyn Public Library took more than fifty years to complete. The site was chosen in 1905 and ground was broken in 1911 for architect Raymond F. Almirall's Beaux Arts design. However, due to problems related to city politics and finances, the original plan was stalled and eventually abandoned. In 1935, Alfred Morton Githens and Francis Keally were commissioned to redesign the building, while retaining the existing foundation and steel skeleton from Almirall's original plan. The library finally opened to the public in 1941.

Set back on a terraced plaza at the intersection of Eastern Parkway and Flatbush Avenue, the three-story, limestone-clad library is a Modern Classic structure. The building is shaped like an open book, and the impressive Art Deco detailing created by the sculptors Thomas Hudson Jones and C. Paul Jennewein includes inscriptions and figures that express the institution's educational mission. One such inscription reads "The Brooklyn Public Library through the joining of municipal enterprise and private generosity offers to all people perpetual and free access to knowledge and the thought of the ages." A dramatic, fifty-foot-high entry portico is set into a concave façade, which reflects the elliptical configuration of Grand Army Plaza. The pylons flanking the entry are decorated with a series of gilded, curved bas-reliefs depicting the evolution of science and art. Above the triple doors is a forty-foot bronze screen with fifteen panels, each framing a figure from American literature, including Tom Sawyer, the Raven, and Moby Dick, as well as a portrait of Walt Whitman.

A book loading area and a garage added in 1964 mask the original rear exterior, and a two-floor addition was built in the early 1990s on top of the windowless extension that originally housed the Branch Distribution Room. However, the main façade of the library remains virtually unchanged. The Central Building of the Brooklyn Public Library endures as one of Brooklyn's best known and most frequently used civic buildings.

TWA TERMINAL A, formerly Trans World Airlines Flight Center, 1956–62
John F. Kennedy International Airport, Queens
Architects: Eero Saarinen & Associates (completed by Kevin Roche)
Designated (exterior and interior): July 19, 1994

For its new Idlewild Airport (now John F. Kennedy International Airport) terminal, TWA hired Eero Saarinen to design a distinctive building worthy of its highly visible site. Dissatisfied with the restrictive minimalism of the International Style, Saarinen saw each of his designs as a unique application of architectural technology. His often monumental designs (including the St. Louis Gateway Arch, Dulles International Airport outside of Washington, D.C., and the CBS Headquarters in New York City) are distinctive, organic, and integrated with their surroundings. Saarinen died while the TWA terminal was under construction, and his associate, Kevin Roche, completed the project.

The terminal is Saarinen's spatial rendering of "the sensation of flying." Through the use of soaring, sculpted organic forms, he created a sense of the excitement and drama—motion given shape. The roof of the center portion rises above low, sweeping wings that follow the airport service road. The massive, curved concrete buttresses and roof define the structure, while green-tinted glass walls give surface to the negative spaces. The interior presents a complex but unified vaulted space, which is divided into three levels and joined by a central curved staircase. Imaginative sculptural forms and glass-linked surfaces gracefully define the outdoor-like atrium. Although Saarinen de-emphasized the analogy, the structure is often seen as a bird in flight.

ABN-AMRO BUILDING, formerly the Pepsi-Cola Building, 1958–60
500 Park Avenue (also known as 62 East 59th Street), Manhattan
Architects: Skidmore, Owings & Merrill
Design Partner: Gordon Bunshaft
Senior Designer: Natalie de Blois
Designated: June 20, 1995

With a beverage originally formulated as a stomach tonic called "Pepsin Cola" (pepsin is a digestive enzyme) by pharmacist Caleb D. Bradham in 1898, the Pepsi-Cola Company was founded in 1902. The company expanded steadily until the Second World War, when its previously successful image as a bargain drink reminded too many people of the Depression, causing its profits to plummet. A sweeping reorganization in 1950, led by Alfred N. Steele, reversed Pepsi's fortunes, as sales jumped 112 percent in the following five years. With its increased profits, Pepsi-Cola built a new corporate headquarters in 1960.

Constructed during Manhattan's second wave of International Style architecture, the eleven-story Pepsi-Cola Building was smaller than other Park Avenue International buildings (Lever House and Seagram Building, both q.v.), but no less striking. Today it houses a branch of the Dutch bank ABN-AMRO. Occupying a corner lot, the structure is cantilevered over ten columns. The first-floor lobby is set back, giving the upper stories the appearance of floating. The nine floors of office space have a curtain wall of gray-green plate glass measuring nine feet by thirteen feet by one-half inch, separated by thin, polished aluminum mullions and spandrels. Top-floor penthouses are set back and barely visible from street level.

THE UNISPHERE, with surrounding pool and fountains, 1963–64
Flushing Meadows–Corona Park, Queens
Landscape Architect: Gilmore D. Clarke
Engineering and Fabrication: United States Steel Company
Designated: May 16, 1995

The Unisphere, a giant stainless-steel globe, was both the physical center and visual logo of the 1964–65 World's Fair. It embodied the fair's theme, "Peace through understanding in a shrinking globe and in an expanding universe." The Unisphere was designed by Gilmore D. Clarke, the noted landscape architect who also designed the grounds of the 1939–40 World's Fair, which took place on the same site. His 1964 plan set pavilions, sculptures, and fountains on axes radiating from the Unisphere in a geometric, Beaux Arts–inspired layout.

Towering over a circular reflecting pool punctuated with fountains, the Unisphere celebrates the dawn of the space age. Its structural steel cage is 140 feet high and 120 feet wide, and its more than 500 components weigh over 700,000 pounds. Winding steel members represent lines of latitude and longitude, curved shapes represent the continents, and suspended rings mark the first man-made satellite orbits. The world's capital cities are marked by lenses, which were backlit during the World's Fair.

The fair was a financial failure, ending more than $11 million in debt, and its remaining assets were spent on demolishing the exhibitions and restoring Corona Park. The Unisphere remained, but there was little money to maintain it, and by the 1970s the fountains had been shut down, the pool drained, and the site covered in graffiti. Beginning in 1989, the Parks Department cleaned and restored Corona Park; the Unisphere was restored in 1993–94 with funds from the Queens Borough President's Office.

Northeast corner of Broadway and 23rd Street, Manhattan

Sutton Place at East 58th Street, Manhattan

HISTORIC STREET LAMPPOSTS, various locations in Manhattan, Brooklyn, The Bronx, and Queens
Designated: June 17, 1997

Approximately one hundred historic, cast-iron lampposts survive in New York City. The precise dates these lampposts were erected, as well as the designers and fabricators of most of them, have not been determined.

Gas streetlights were introduced in New York City in 1825, and by May 1828, the New York Gas Light Co. had installed gas lines and cast-iron lampposts on every street between the East River and the Hudson River south of Grand and Canal streets. Two gas lampposts dating from the mid-nineteenth century are extant: one at Patchin Place in Greenwich Village and one at the northeast corner of 211th Street and Broadway.

In 1880, electric lights made their New York City debut along Broadway from 14th to 26th Street, and the first truly ornamental cast-iron lampposts were installed on Fifth Avenue in 1892. Called twin posts because they support two luminaires, these posts have a fluted base and shaft separated by a collar of acanthus leaves. Unusual spiral finials decorate each end of the crossarm, which is supported against the vertical shaft by C- and S-scrolls. Following this installation, a number of ornamental arc lamppost designs were introduced, the earliest and most ubiquitous of which is the bishop's crook, initiated circa 1900. Made from a single iron casting up to the arc, or "crook," it incorporates a garland motif that wraps around the shaft. The largest extant collection of bishop's crook lampposts can be found in City Hall Park.

By the 1930s, the city streets were lighted by a variety of lampposts, brackets, and pedestals. However, during the 1960s, most were replaced by modern, unadorned, steel-and-aluminum posts. The surviving historic lampposts continue to light the city streets, and are maintained by the Department of Transportation. Sixty-two lampposts and four wall brackets are included in this designation;[*] the remaining posts are already protected within designated historic districts.

*For exact locations of all lamppost and bracket designations, see page 528.

THE HISTORIC DISTRICTS OF NEW YORK, 1965 TO THE PRESENT

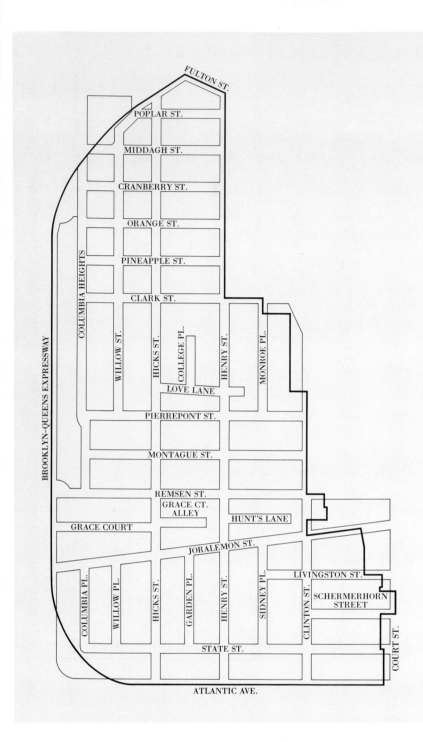

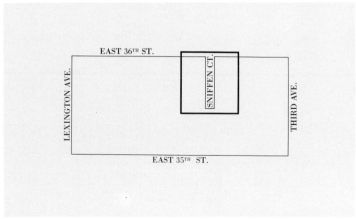

BROOKLYN HEIGHTS HISTORIC DISTRICT
Brooklyn
Designated: November 23, 1965

Brooklyn Heights is one of New York's best preserved and most attractive nineteenth-century historic districts. Occupying an elevated plateau just south of the Fulton Ferry Historic District and commanding dramatic views of Manhattan, Brooklyn Heights has been a residential community ever since it began to develop in the early 1800s. It is an area of dignified brownstone and brick houses and stately churches on streets bordered by stone sidewalks and lined with trees, as well as many carriage houses, preserved along picturesque and well-tended mews. Spared the constant restructuring that occurred in Manhattan, and left alone as Brooklyn expanded south, the configuration of streets and blocks in Brooklyn Heights is essentially the same as it was prior to the Civil War.

In 1965 Otis Pratt Pearsall, leader of the Historic Preservation Committee of the Brooklyn Heights Association, noted that of the 1,284 buildings fronting the streets of Brooklyn Heights, 684 were built before the Civil War, and 1,078 before the turn of the century. There are fine buildings in Federal, Greek Revival, Gothic Revival, and Anglo-Italianate styles. The district is particularly rich in Greek Revival architecture: there are more than 400 examples, including buildings by architects Richard Upjohn and Minard Lafever, two of the style's most distinguished practitioners. The opening of the Brooklyn Bridge in 1883 opened the rest of Brooklyn to development. Today, Brooklyn Heights remains a fashionable and elegant residential area.

SNIFFEN COURT HISTORIC DISTRICT
Manhattan
Designated: June 21, 1966

Built by John Sniffen in the 1850s, this charming group of ten two-story houses in a blind alley on East 36th Street between Lexington and Third avenues originally served as stables for families in Murray Hill. When automobiles began to replace carriages as transportation during the 1920s, most of the stables were converted into private residences.

The house at the south end of the court was used as a studio by the sculptor Malvina Hoffman from the 1920s through the 1960s. Its exterior wall, which she adorned with plaques of Greek horsemen, effectively terminates the narrow mews. Two of the stables were converted into a small theater by the Sniffen Court Dramatic Society, an amateur group that performed there in full evening dress.

Minor exterior details of the houses have been altered over the years, as evidenced by the filled-in arches and diverse window arrangements of some of the buildings. The overall effect, however, is still an unusually picturesque one, providing a well-preserved example of New York City during the Civil War era.

TURTLE BAY GARDENS HISTORIC DISTRICT
Manhattan
Designated: June 21, 1966

Turtle Bay Gardens, located near the United Nations, is named for a cove off the East River where turtles were once abundant. The cove, long since filled in, is now the site of the United Nations Park.

The twenty houses that surround the gardens were built during the 1860s; though no two have identical plans, most are four stories high, with English basements. On the garden side, they have delicate individual balconies and porches.

The interior gardens were created by Mrs. Walton Martin, who bought the property in 1919–20, filled in the swampy backyards, and redesigned the houses. The result is reminiscent of an intimate Italian garden. Low masonry walls separate each private garden and surround the shared central esplanade, which is graced by a fountain copied from the Villa Medici in Florence. The characteristic charm of 1920s architecture is expressed here, and the use of a cast-iron turtle on the gateposts of the entrance railing adds a touch of humor.

Over the years, the occupants of Turtle Bay Gardens have included Katharine Hepburn, Leopold Stokowski, and Tyrone Power.

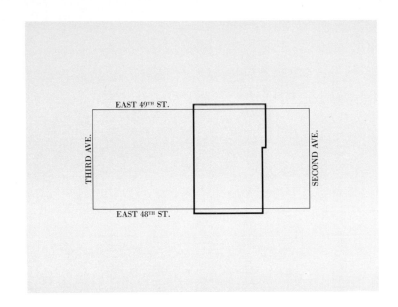

CHARLTON–KING–VANDAM HISTORIC DISTRICT
Manhattan
Designated: August 16, 1966

This site at the southwestern edge of Greenwich Village was the location of the famous Richmond Hill mansion, built in 1767, and used by George Washington during the Revolution as a headquarters. Situated on a hill four hundred feet high and surrounded by gardens and woods, it later became Vice President John Adams's mansion, and eventually passed first to Aaron Burr, who had the estate mapped out into lots in 1797, and then to John Jacob Astor, who began development in 1817. The mansion, moved off the hill, was used as a theater, and the land was leveled. The large majority of the houses were built in the decade of the 1820s. Thanks to Astor's hold over the land and its development, the houses display unusual architectural harmony. The area includes the largest and best preserved groupings of Federal town houses in the city, as well as Greek Revival, Roman Revival, Anglo-Italianate, and later-nineteenth-century buildings, mainly on King Street.

The houses were bought originally by merchants, lawyers, and builders. Many were kept within the same families for generations, which explains their remarkable state of preservation. The area was able to resist the modernization of the city and the commercialization of surrounding areas.

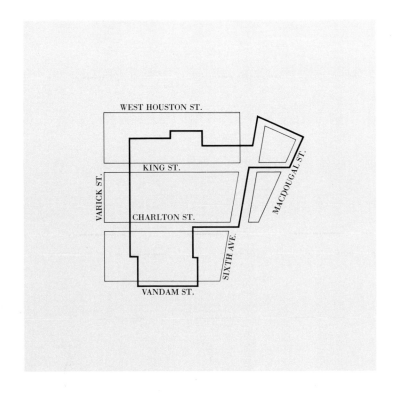

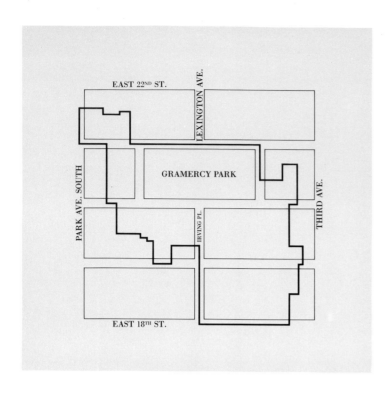

GRAMERCY PARK HISTORIC DISTRICT
Manhattan
Designated: September 20, 1966

Samuel B. Ruggles, a lawyer and real-estate operator, purchased the land for Gramercy Park, the only private park in the city, in 1831. It was originally part of the estate of James Duane, the first mayor of post-revolutionary New York. The original park was divided into sixty-six lots, each to be deeded to the owners of the surrounding property. An iron fence was built in 1832 and planting began in 1844. Private residences began to appear around the park and attract leading New Yorkers of the day, including Stuyvesant Fish, Samuel J. Tilden, and James Harper, who lived in the area in the 1860s and '70s.

The residences surrounding the park today represent a wide variety of architectural styles, ranging from Greek and Gothic Revival to Anglo-Italianate. There are also a number of notable non-residential buildings, including the National Arts Club (q.v.) and the Players Club (q.v.). Another notable building in the area is Pete's Tavern at 129 East 18th Street. Built in the mid-nineteenth century, it was frequented by the writer O. Henry and still remains intact. The Gramercy Park Historic District is unusual in that it is a serene, residential area in the midst of the city, and represents an early example of city planning.

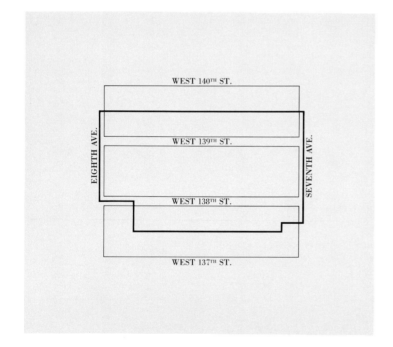

ST. NICHOLAS HISTORIC DISTRICT
Manhattan
Designated: March 16, 1967

These four rows of houses were built in 1891 by David H. King, Jr., who was the developer for the first Madison Square Garden, the Equitable Building, and the base of the Statue of Liberty (q.v.). King commissioned three prominent architectural firms to design these refined homes. They represent what was possibly the apex of the land speculation and investment in Harlem. Their location—on the heights overlooking St. Nicholas Park—allows unobstructed views and gives the district a feeling of openness. Though the rows of houses vary in design and detail, great care was taken by the architects to create a unified, distinct neighborhood, and the uniform block fronts add a cohesive element.

The twenty-five red-brick houses on the south side of West 138th Street were designed by James Brown Lord, in a restrained, rhythmic style derived from the Georgian tradition. Complete blocks of houses by Bruce Price and Clarence S. Luce extend along the north side of West 138th Street, the south side of West 139th Street, and Seventh and Eighth avenues. More detailed than the Lord houses, these are also Georgian inspired, incorporating buff-colored brick and Indiana limestone. The thirty-two Italian Renaissance–style houses on the north side of West 139th Street were designed by McKim, Mead & White; built of dark brown mottled brick with unusual window arrangements, they stand in pleasing contrast to the other two groups.

The King Model Houses became known as "Striver's Row" during the 1920s and '30s, in reference to the desirability of the neighborhood. Over the years, the district has been the home of many of Harlem's prominent doctors, in addition to such well-known entertainers as W. C. Handy and Eubie Blake.

MACDOUGAL–SULLIVAN GARDENS
HISTORIC DISTRICT
Manhattan
Designated: August 2, 1967

This block was purchased in 1796 by prominent New York merchant and financier Nicholas Low, whose estate built the twenty-two three-story Greek Revival houses that comprise the district in the 1840s and '50s. The Hearth and Home real-estate corporation bought the block in 1920. William Sloane Coffin, the president of Hearth and Home, and an experienced property developer, undertook the renovation of the block to preserve the charm of the neighborhood, and to provide moderately priced housing for middle-class professionals.

The houses were modernized, but changes to the façades were minimal. Architects Francis Y. Joannes and Maxwell Hyde removed the stoops and altered the basement entrances and doorways, adding Federal Revival elements, but retained the continuous cornice.

Coffin's plan included converting the open space in the center of the block into small private gardens and a large common area, with space specifically set aside for children's playground areas. A number of similar developments were inspired by MacDougal–Sullivan Gardens, including the Turtle Bay Gardens Historic District.

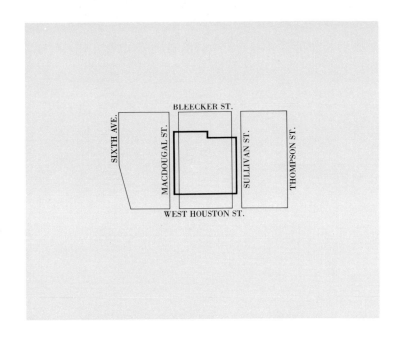

TREADWELL FARM HISTORIC DISTRICT
Manhattan
Designated: December 13, 1967

This charming residential neighborhood on the Upper East Side was originally part of the farms of Peter Van Zandt and William Beekman. The Van Zandt portion was sold at auction in 1815 to Adam Tredwell, or Treadwell, a wealthy fur merchant whose brother, Seabury Tredwell, owned what is now the Old Merchant's House at 29 East 4th Street (q.v.). After Adam Tredwell's death in 1852, his daughter Elizabeth purchased the Beekman holdings, and the land was divided into lots and sold to different buyers.

In 1868, the owners set standards for the dimensions of the buildings to be erected and specified the types of businesses that would be permitted in the area. As a result of their association, the neighborhood is architecturally uniform and quiet, with tree-lined streets and beautifully maintained houses. Most of the present buildings were constructed between 1868 and 1876, and are three- or four-story brownstones. A number of well-known architects were involved, including Richard Morris Hunt and James W. Pirrson. The handsome Victorian Gothic Church of Our Lady of Peace, at 239–241 East 62nd Street, dates from 1886–87.

Through the efforts of its residents, among whom have been such notables as Walter Lippmann, Tallulah Bankhead, Kim Novak, Montgomery Clift, and Eleanor Roosevelt, this district has retained its peaceful elegance.

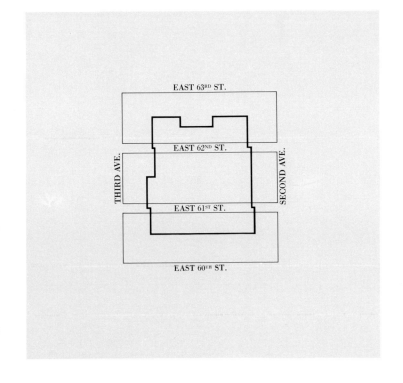

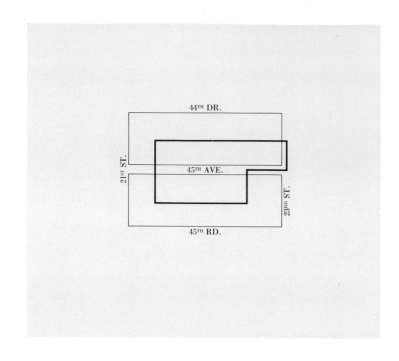

HUNTERS POINT HISTORIC DISTRICT
Queens
Designated: May 15, 1968

This dignified residential section of Long Island City was built on land that belonged to the Van Alst family for nearly two hundred years, until the trustees of Union College purchased the property in 1861. In that year, the Long Island Railroad moved its terminus to Hunters Point, and the area began to change as inns and taverns opened to accommodate the commuters. In 1870 the land was acquired by Spencer B. Root and John P. Rust, developers who built many of the surviving houses. Completed between 1871 and 1890, the forty-seven houses exhibit diverse architectural styles including the Italianate, French Second Empire, and Neo-Grec. A large number of the original stoops, lintels, pediments, and other architectural details are intact.

After the area was developed, the houses were occupied first by old American families, then by people of Irish descent. The most notable of these was the last mayor of Long Island City, "Battle-Axe" Gleason, who lived on Twelfth Street (now 45th Avenue) during the 1880s. When the elevated trains were extended to Long Island City early in the twentieth century, its noise caused many of the older families to move away. During the Depression, houses in the district were converted to multi-family dwellings, as most remain today.

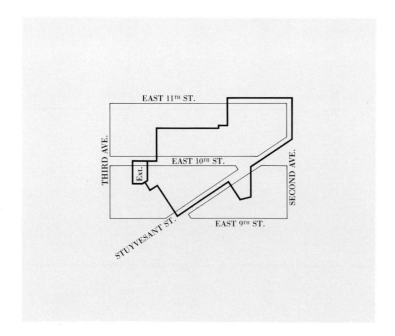

ST. MARK'S HISTORIC DISTRICT
Manhattan
Designated: January 14, 1969
Extension designated: June 19, 1984

The legendary Governor Peter Stuyvesant once owned the land comprising this historic district in the East Village, and Stuyvesant Street was originally a lane dividing two of his farms. His great-grandson, also named Peter, eventually acquired most of these properties. In 1787 the land was surveyed and laid out by Evert Bancker, Jr., who probably mapped out the street plan as well. The streets running east and west were named for male members of the family; those running north and south were named for Stuyvesant's four daughters.

St. Mark's-in-the-Bowery (q.v.), begun in 1795 on the oldest site of worship in Manhattan, is one of the three existing buildings in the district that date from the younger Stuyvesant's lifetime, the other two being the Stuyvesant-Fish House at 21 Stuyvesant Street (q.v.), and the house built in 1795 for Nicholas William Stuyvesant at 44 Stuyvesant Street. The lot once known as "Elizabeth Fish's Gardens" has since become "The Triangle," a group of houses, most completed in 1861, that extend around part of Stuyvesant and East 10th streets on an unusual triangular plot. Most of the other buildings in the district display variations of the Italianate style and date from the mid-nineteenth century.

GREENWICH VILLAGE HISTORIC DISTRICT
Manhattan
Designated: April 29, 1969

The history of Greenwich Village can be traced back to Indian and Dutch days. Originally tobacco farms, it was settled by prosperous colonists before the Revolution. After the Revolution, the population of the area grew enough to accommodate tradesmen and merchants, and it became known as a village. Greenwich Village developed separately from the city proper at the southern end of Manhattan, although yellow fever epidemics in the early 1800s caused many New Yorkers to relocate here. As the city expanded and modernized, the Village remained intact. The gridiron plan of 1807–11 bypassed the irregular streets of the Village, and the emphasis on low and uniform architecture created a strong residential community that was able to escape large-scale commercial and residential development. Greenwich Village is the only area in the city where all of the architectural styles of early New York row houses exist side by side, in a state of excellent preservation. The predominant styles are Federal, Greek Revival, Italianate, French Second Empire, Neo-Grec, and Queen Anne. Between the World Wars the Village expanded, with the construction of taller apartment buildings. Known then as a low-rent district, Greenwich Village had already become home to artists and writers and developed a bohemian reputation.

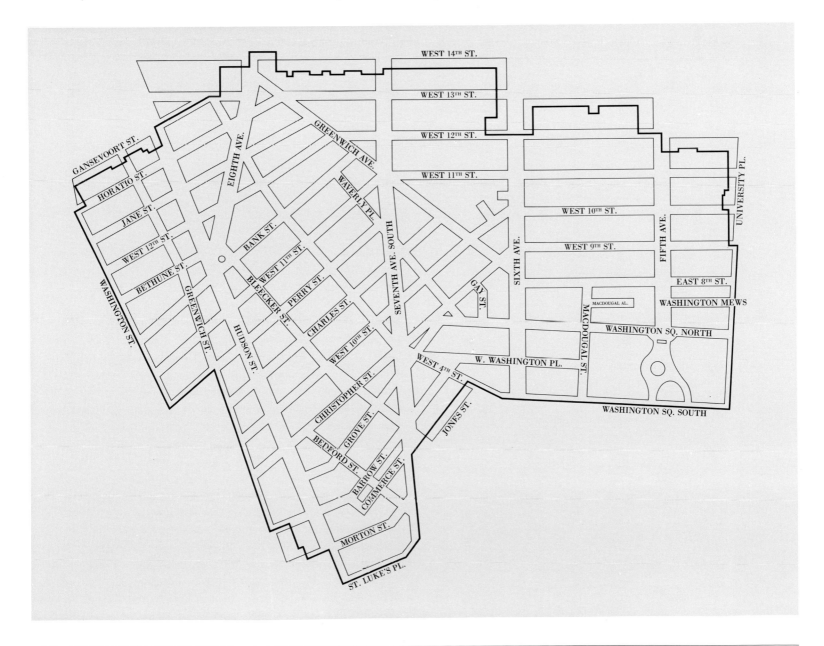

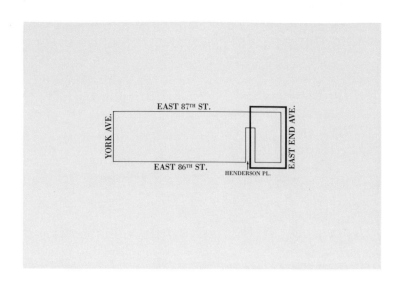

HENDERSON PLACE HISTORIC DISTRICT
Manhattan
Designated: February 11, 1969

During the eighteenth century, this compact residential neighborhood on the Upper East Side was part of William Waldron's farm. After the land was divided, following Waldron's death, the Yorkville block that comprises the historic district was acquired first by John Jacob Astor and Archibald Gracie, and later by John C. Henderson. Henderson, a wealthy fur importer, retained the architectural firm of Lamb & Rich to design two-story Queen Anne houses; twenty-four of the original thirty-two remain, and look for the most part as they did upon completion in 1882.

Many of the picturesque dwellings are set back, and the resulting front yards and basement areaways are graced with hedges and shrubs. The houses have such characteristic Queen Anne details as gables, dormers, and double-hung frame windows with the upper sashes divided into many panes of glass.

Gracie Mansion (q.v.), the mayor's residence, is just across East End Avenue from Henderson Place. Over the years, the carefully preserved houses in this half-acre district have been owned or occupied by a number of well-known people, among them Alfred Lunt and Lynn Fontanne.

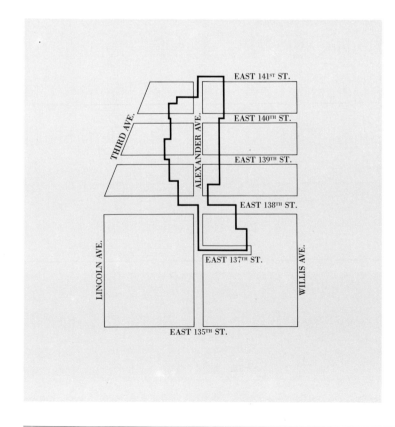

MOTT HAVEN HISTORIC DISTRICT
The Bronx
Designated: July 29, 1969

This district in the South Bronx derives its name from Jordan L. Mott, the first major industrialist to locate in the Bronx, who established an iron works on the Harlem River at East 134th Street in 1828 and called the surrounding area, which included his residence, Mott Haven.

Alexander Avenue, an airy, dignified thoroughfare once known as "The Irish Fifth Avenue," is home to two churches on the east side and two civic buildings on the west, as well as handsome row houses of the late nineteenth century. St. Jerome's Roman Catholic Church, built in 1898 by Dehli & Howard in the Italian Renaissance style, stands at the corner of East 138th Street; next to it are its French Neo-Grec rectory and Victorian Gothic school. The Tercera Iglesia Bautista terminates the northern end of the district at East 141st Street; designed by Ward & Davis, this stark, symmetrical structure was extremely modern at the time of its construction in 1900–02.

The Mott Haven Branch of the New York Public Library, opened in 1905, and the 40th Precinct Police Station, constructed in 1922–24, frame Alexander Avenue on its west side and effectively balance the two ecclesiastical buildings opposite.

COBBLE HILL HISTORIC DISTRICT
Brooklyn
Designated: December 30, 1969

The name Cobble Hill originally referred to a steep conical hill at the present intersection of Atlantic Avenue and Pacific Street with Court Street. One of the highest hills on Long Island, it served as a lookout for American forces at the beginning of the Revolution. Until the early nineteenth century, Cobble Hill was an area of large orchards and farms. Development of the neighborhood, which is separated from Brooklyn Heights by Atlantic Avenue, followed its incorporation into the independent city of Brooklyn in 1834 and the opening of the South Ferry two years later.

The first buildings in Cobble Hill were rural homesteads, and suburban mansions along the west side of Henry Street, which had excellent views of the harbor. None of these survive today. The earliest extant structures are Greek Revival row houses dating from around 1832. There are fine examples of most of the late-nineteenth-century architectural styles, as well as buildings designed by some of New York's most distinguished architects. The 1843 house at 296 Clinton Street is the work of Richard Upjohn, architect of Trinity Church (q.v.). The St. Frances Cabrini Chapel at Degraw Street and Strong Place was built in 1852 after a design by Minard Lafever. The Tower and Home buildings on Hicks, Warren, and Baltic streets, and the Workingmen's Cottages on Warren Place were designed by William Field & Son in the 1870s for laborers and their families; they are some of the nation's first planned low-income housing.

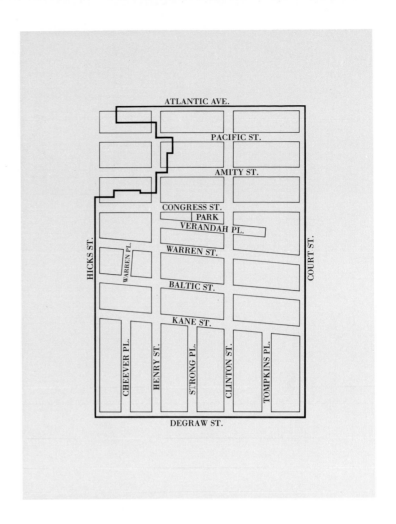

JUMEL TERRACE HISTORIC DISTRICT
Manhattan
Designated: August 18, 1970

The houses that comprise this district in Upper Manhattan provide an attractive setting for the Morris-Jumel Mansion (q.v.). They are the original and only buildings constructed on this land. The oldest group, dating from 1882, consists of two rows of wooden houses along Sylvan Terrace. The other row houses, bringing the total to just under fifty, were built between 1890 and 1902 in the Queen Anne, Romanesque Revival, and Classical Revival styles. The only apartment house in the district is a 1909 Federal Revival brick and limestone structure at the corner of Jumel Terrace and West 160th Street. That the buildings create a unified ensemble is owing mainly to the relatively brief period of their construction and the use of complementary materials in many of the structures.

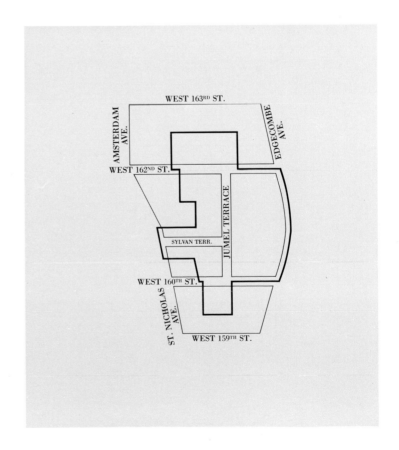

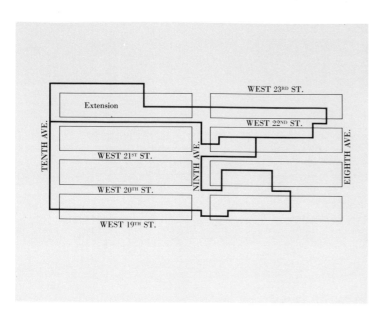

CHELSEA HISTORIC DISTRICT
Manhattan
Designated: September 15, 1970
Extension designated: February 3, 1981

In 1750 Captain Thomas Clarke purchased land for an estate which he named Chelsea, after the English village of Chelsea, now a part of London. In 1813 Chelsea was deeded to his grandson, Clement Clarke Moore, a poet, clergyman, and scholar. Moore first resisted the Commissioners' Plan of 1807–11, which called for a grid of roads and leveled land to replace the natural beauty of the estate. But he became a developer when his efforts were unsuccessful. Through the use of restrictive covenants stipulating conditions of building in his real-estate agreements, Moore was able to ensure that there would be open space in front of all of the houses, no stables or factories, as many trees as he deemed necessary, and houses constructed according to only the best designs.

The district today includes all of the land from Moore's former estate, showing his adaptation of the idea of the residential square. The center of the square is the General Theological Seminary, built between 1825 and 1902 on land donated by Moore; today it occupies the full city block bounded by Ninth and Tenth avenues, and West 20th and 21st streets. Around it remain a number of buildings erected in Moore's time. Notable among these is Cushman Row, 406–418 West 20th Street, one of the most handsome and well-preserved rows of Greek Revival town houses in New York. Chelsea also has some of the city's best Italianate buildings.

Chelsea's tradition of careful planning continued through the nineteenth century into the 1930s, affecting the design of the larger-scale apartment houses and tenement buildings on West 22nd and 23rd streets. As a result, the district preserves the human scale and attractive appearance Moore originally envisioned for it.

STUYVESANT HEIGHTS HISTORIC DISTRICT
Brooklyn
Designated: September 14, 1971

The ancestors of three of the original Dutch landowners held much of the farmland in this region of what is now Bedford-Stuyvesant for two centuries before it was acquired by developers and other investors, including the Brooklyn Railroad Company. The gridiron street plan that exists today was laid out in 1835, and the blocks lotted, although most of the streets were not opened until the 1860s. Until the late nineteenth century Stuyvesant Heights remained predominantly rural, save for a few freestanding houses on MacDonough Street. Two of these early country residences still stand: Number 97, built in 1861 for Charles W. Betts, and Number 87, erected two years later. The real development of the district spanned the years between 1870 and 1920, after Betts began to sell off his MacDonough Street properties in 1869. The Prosser family, who owned land in the southern portion of the district, relinquished much of their holdings to developers during the 1890s.

In the 1870s and '80s, rows of dignified masonry houses and brownstones, in a variety of styles, began to appear north of Decatur Street, creating a neighborhood whose appearance has changed little since that time. A number of well-designed four-story apartment houses were built between 1888 and 1903, marking the transition to an urban

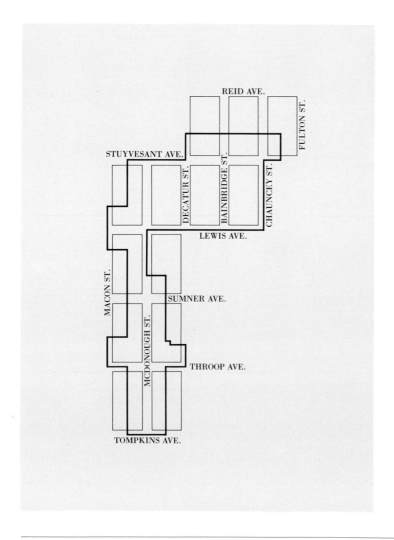

community and coinciding with the incorporation of Brooklyn within the City of New York in 1898. The district is almost entirely residential. There are three ecclesiastical groupings and only two buildings that were designed for commercial use: the two-story store and office building at 613 Throop Avenue, and the area's tallest structure, a five-story warehouse, also on Throop Avenue.

MOUNT MORRIS PARK HISTORIC DISTRICT
Manhattan
Designated: November 3, 1971

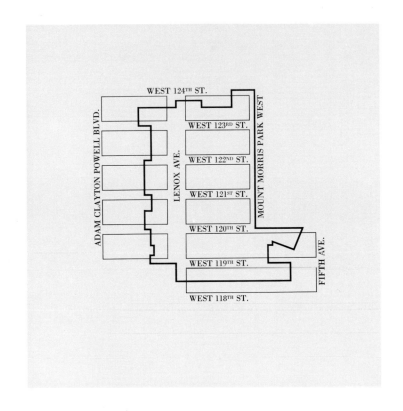

Until the mid-nineteenth century, Harlem remained a rural area, but the opening of the elevated railroad in 1872 encouraged speculative building around Mount Morris Park by William B. Astor, Oscar Hammerstein, and many others. The stately residences along Mount Morris Park West have been favorably compared with the mansions on Fifth Avenue, and the large town house at the northwest corner of West 123rd Street and Mount Morris Park West is an especially fine example of the Renaissance Revival style.

The churches in this district include St. Martin's Episcopal Church and Rectory (1888) on Lenox Avenue, one of the best representations of the Romanesque Revival style remaining in Manhattan. The modified Neoclassical Mount Morris Presbyterian Church and the Ephesus Seventh-Day Adventist Church, with its lofty spire, are also impressive.

The district's residential architecture, including both town houses and apartment buildings, ranges over diverse styles, including classical, French Neo-Grec, and Queen Anne.

CENTRAL PARK WEST–WEST 76TH STREET HISTORIC DISTRICT
Manhattan
Designated: April 19, 1973

Originally part of a large parcel of land stretching down to present-day 42nd Street that Governor Nicolls, the first English governor, granted to five farmers, by 1811 this district consisted of portions of farms owned by John Delaplaine and David Wagstaff. The latter initiated development of the area by subdividing his farm in 1852. Among the factors that made the area ripe for growth were the introduction of a stage line along Bloomingdale Road (now Broadway), the Commissioners' Plan for Central Park and neighboring streets of 1868, and the increasing congestion in other parts of the city. Slowed temporarily by the financial panic of 1873, the "Great West Side Movement" gathered momentum after the completion of the American Museum of Natural History (q.v.) in 1877. Construction on West 76th Street began with two rows of houses erected in 1887 by the realtor Leonard Beeckman, and was largely completed by 1898.

The district includes apartment houses, town houses, a museum, and a church. They display a wide variety of late-nineteenth-century styles, including the Neo-Grec, Renaissance Revival, Romanesque Revival, and Gothic Revival, but the French Beaux Arts style is particularly prominent and its influence is evident not only in the more orthodox Beaux Arts buildings but also in others that were designed in classicizing styles.

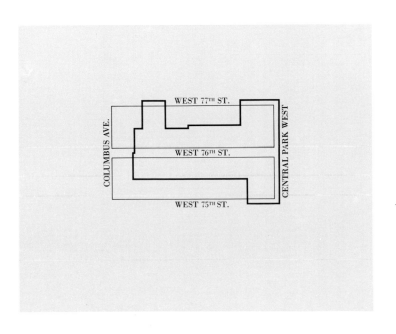

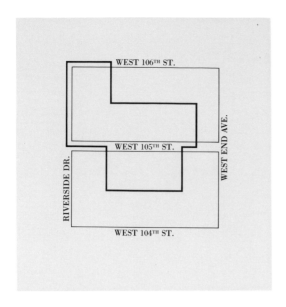

RIVERSIDE DRIVE–WEST 105TH STREET HISTORIC DISTRICT
Manhattan
Designated: April 19, 1973

Until the end of the nineteenth century, the Upper West Side of Manhattan was known as Bloomingdale, after Bloemendael, the flower-growing area of Holland. Although it was the site of two large building complexes—the Bloomingdale Insane Asylum and the Leake and Watts Orphanage—it was not until the 1890s that development began on a large scale. The town houses built between 1899 and 1902 on West 105th and 106th streets are the result of a period of great optimism, originally fueled by the hope that the proposed World's Columbian Exhibition of 1893 would be held in Riverside Park.

Built in the French Beaux Arts style, these houses were intended to lure wealthy residents from the Upper East Side, which by then had developed into New York's most fashionable neighborhood. Among the neighborhood's amenities were the park, with its views of the river and the hills of New Jersey, and the quiet atmosphere of its side streets. The neighborhood is notable for the visual harmony of the streetscapes—the result of deliberate planning in the form of restrictive covenants dictating the height of buildings and the character of their façades. The use of such horizontal elements as cornices, balconies, and mansard roofs carries the eye from one building to the next; the gently curved masonry bays on the façades add a rhythmic effect.

Many of these buildings have had unusually long occupancies, which helps explain their exceptional state of preservation today.

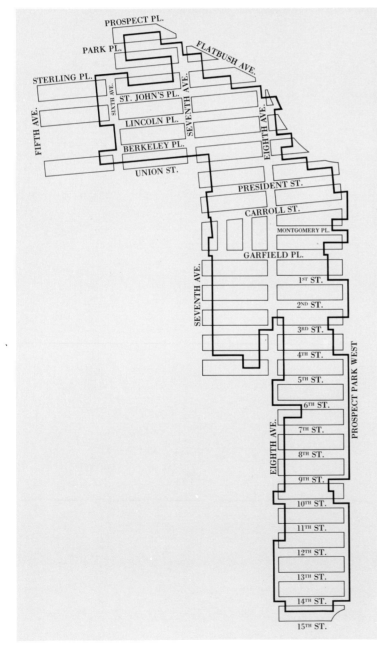

PARK SLOPE HISTORIC DISTRICT
Brooklyn
Designated: July 17, 1973

A semirural area until shortly before the Civil War, this district takes its name from the adjoining Prospect Park (q.v.), designed by Olmsted & Vaux in 1866, and completed around 1873. The park, with its large, open meadow, woods, and lake, attracted many builders, who erected houses for merchants, lawyers, physicians, and other professionals, many of whom commuted to Manhattan over the Brooklyn Bridge after it opened in 1883. Park Slope's tree-lined streets, wide avenues, and rows of brownstones preserve the turn-of-the-century Brooklyn that was known as "the city of homes and churches": The district is distinguished by long block fronts of harmonious two- and three-story buildings.

Built largely between the mid-1880s and World War 1, the houses exemplify practically every style of the late nineteenth century, including Italianate, French Second Empire, Queen Anne, Neo-Grec, Victorian Gothic, Romanesque Revival, Classical Revival, and early Modern. The Montauk Club, 25 Eighth Avenue, a Venetian Gothic palazzo of 1891 by Francis H. Kimball, and Montgomery Place, between Eighth Avenue and Prospect Park West, much of which was designed by C.P.H. Gilbert, are particularly notable. The Romanesque Revival had a long life in Park Slope, where it was practiced by many architects. With their broad, round entry arches and rugged stonework, these are some of the finest Romanesque Revival houses in the nation.

SOHO–CAST-IRON HISTORIC DISTRICT
Manhattan
Designated: August 14, 1973

The largest concentration of full and partial cast-iron façades anywhere in the world survives in the SoHo district. The earliest extant buildings within the district date from the first decade of the nineteenth century, when the area was exclusively residential. By mid-century, however, most of the early Federal houses had either been replaced or converted to commercial use. The commercial character of the area was firmly established by the 1870s, and the majority of buildings that incorporate full fronts of cast iron date from this decade.

The use of cast iron was an American architectural innovation. As a building material, it was cheaper than stone or brick: Architectural elements could be prefabricated in foundries from molds and used interchangeably for many buildings, while broken pieces could be easily replaced. A cast-iron building could be erected rapidly—some were completed in only four months' time. Previously, bronze had been the metal most often used for architectural detail. Architects now found that the relatively inexpensive cast iron could be formed into the most intricately designed patterns. Classical French and Italian architectural designs were often used as models for cast-iron building façades. And because stone was the material associated with architectural masterpieces, cast iron, painted in neutral tints such as beige, was used to simulate stone.

For the first sixty years of the twentieth century, SoHo was a limbo of small industrial and commercial enterprises. In the 1960s artists were attracted to the high-ceilinged, empty, and inexpensive lofts of SoHo. Eventually, with the help of city agencies, they were permitted to migrate into the area. The result, over two decades later, is that SoHo is now one of the most important centers of the production of fine art in the nation.

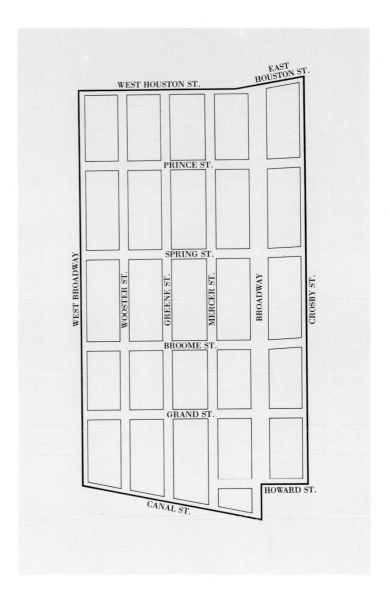

CARROLL GARDENS HISTORIC DISTRICT
Brooklyn
Designated: September 25, 1973

This quiet residential district adjacent to Cobble Hill, which includes over 160 buildings, was originally part of a tract of land purchased from the Mohawk Indians by the Dutch West India Company in 1636. Interest in the area was spurred by the opening of the Hamilton Avenue Ferry in 1846, the construction of the Gowanus Canal, begun in 1867, and the improvement of Carroll Park during the 1870s.

Carroll Gardens was laid out in 1846 by surveyor Richard Butts. He provided for blocks of unusual depth, so that the houses would be set back behind front yards between 25 and 39 feet deep. The result, when the rows of two- and three-story brownstones were completed between 1869 and 1884, was a neighborhood with a sense of remoteness and dignity.

The architectural unity of this district stems from the brevity and high standards of its construction period. The houses were built to accommodate both wealthy merchants and residents of more modest means. A number of popular styles are represented here, including the late Italianate and French Neo-Grec, and the varying arrangement of ornamental elements individualizes each house.

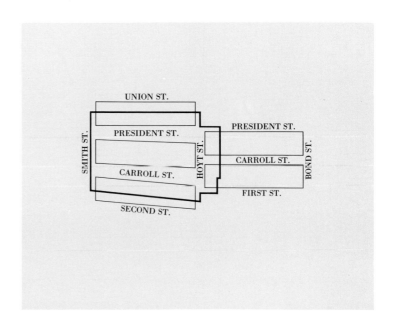

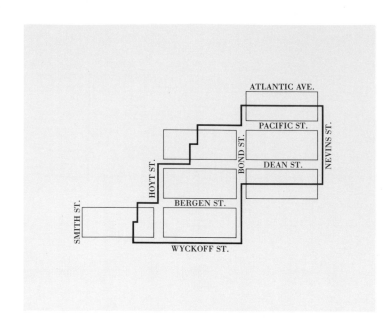

BOERUM HILL HISTORIC DISTRICT
Brooklyn
Designated: November 20, 1973

This district is part of the area, bounded by Fulton Avenue, and Smith and Nevins streets, that first acquired the name Breukelen, after the city in Holland with a similar topography. It was named after the Boerum family, who were prominent eighteenth-century farmers and civic leaders.

The construction of Boerum Hill began in the northeastern section during the 1840s. The rest of the district was developed in the 1860s and '70s. Like Brooklyn Heights, Park Slope, and other nearby areas, it was built as a residential community for professionals who worked in Manhattan and downtown Brooklyn. Its nearly 250 buildings run the gamut of nineteenth-century architectural styles. The earliest are Greek Revival, a style that remained popular through the 1850s. The majority are in the Italianate style, which was popular in Brooklyn even after the Civil War, by which time it had become outmoded in Manhattan.

Most of the houses are of brick, with brownstone used primarily for trim and decoration. Those built after the Civil War show a more lavish use of brownstone, although it was never used as extensively here as in other parts of Brooklyn. One of the most appealing features is the well-preserved ironwork used on stoops and in front of yards; in some instances it literally tied together the façades of the rows and gave a unity to the streetscape. Another unusual feature of houses in the district is the Queen Anne–style sunbursts and rosettes that were often incised in the 1880s on the brownstone basements of older houses.

CARNEGIE HILL HISTORIC DISTRICT
Manhattan
Designated: July 23, 1974

Throughout the nineteenth century, the villages of Harlem to the north and Yorkville to the south on what was to be the Upper East Side grew while Carnegie Hill lagged behind, retaining its semirural character. During this period, the area was comprised of churches and charitable organizations, shanties, squatters' shacks, and a few brownstones. With the construction of the New York Elevated Railroad on Third Avenue in 1881, the neighborhood began to change. As commerce pushed private residences out of midtown Manhattan, people moved farther uptown. During the late 1880s, luxury brownstones began to appear on the side streets. It was, however, the construction of Andrew Carnegie's mansion (q.v.) on Fifth Avenue between East 90th and 91st streets, completed in 1901, that established the neighborhood as prime residential property. Carnegie himself bought land surrounding his mansion and sold it to developers only when satisfied with their proposed plans.

Architecture in the district represents two periods of development. During the 1880s and '90s, the Neo-Grec, Romanesque, and Renaissance Revival styles dominated residential construction, echoing the styles of elegant mansions in other parts of the city. With the completion of the Carnegie mansion, larger private residences and apartment buildings replaced the row house construction of the preceding decades. The majority of these buildings were in the Federal Revival style.

HAMILTON HEIGHTS HISTORIC DISTRICT
Manhattan
Designated: November 26, 1974

This quiet, exclusively residential community on the Upper West Side
was named after Alexander Hamilton, who built his country house in
1801 near the corner of Amsterdam Avenue and West 143rd Street. The
Grange (q.v.), as Hamilton called it, was moved in 1889 to its present
location at 287 Convent Avenue.

The area remained mostly rural until 1879, when escalating real-estate
prices on the East Side, and the extension of the West Side elevated
railroad, helped speed Hamilton Heights toward development. Nearly all
of the row houses and low-rise apartment buildings in the district were
built between 1886 and 1906. The successive architectural styles of those
twenty years—Romanesque Revival, Flemish, Dutch, French and Italian
Renaissance, and Beaux Arts—are illustrated here.

St. Luke's Episcopal Church, built in 1892–95, is the earliest of the
three handsome churches that mark the boundaries of Hamilton Heights.
This massive Romanesque Revival structure, designed by Robert H.
Robertson, almost overshadows Hamilton Grange, now located alongside
it. The two other churches, both built in the Gothic Revival style, are the
graceful Convent Avenue Baptist Church of 1897–99 and the picturesque
St. James Presbyterian Church of 1904.

The unusual street pattern in this district (several of the streets
terminate in parks or dead ends) and its well-preserved turn-of-the-
century character create the impression of a protected enclave, separate
from the busy thoroughfares nearby.

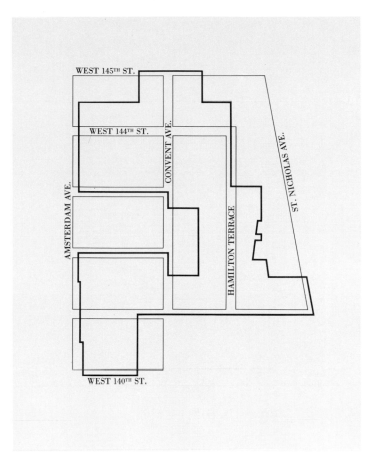

STUYVESANT SQUARE HISTORIC DISTRICT
Manhattan
Designated: September 23, 1975

Once owned by Governor Peter Stuyvesant, the land for Stuyvesant
Square remained a predominantly rural part of his family's holdings
until Peter Gerard Stuyvesant deeded it to New York City in 1836. The
square, laid out in that year, is a particularly handsome example of a
nineteenth-century park designed to relieve the gridiron pattern of city
streets; surrounded by a cast-iron fence and adorned by fountains, the
park also contains a statue of Antonín Dvořák by Ivan Meštrović. Most
of the houses in this fashionable neighborhood were built in the late
nineteenth century. The district's development quickened with the
construction of the Greek Revival Friends Meeting House and Seminary
(q.v.), built in 1860 on the west side of the square.

Nearly all of the residences are row houses, exemplifying a range of
architectural styles. Richard Morris Hunt designed 245 East 17th Street
in 1883 for Sidney Webster in a modified French Renaissance style; also
notable are the elegant four-story brick houses on East 16th Street,
especially fine representations of the Anglo-Italianate style, and the
Rainsford House at 208–210 East 16th Street with its elements of Tudor
and Flemish architecture. The several religious institutions in the district
include St. George's Church (q.v.).

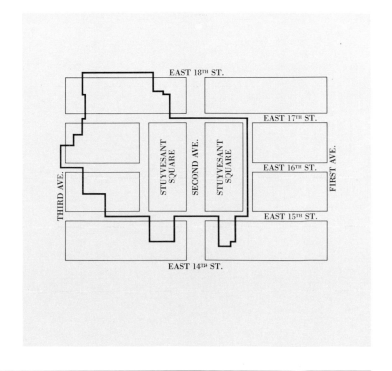

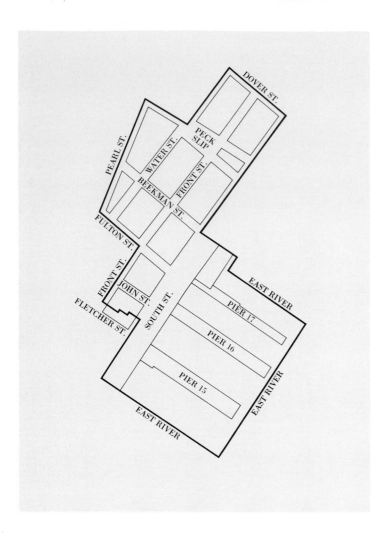

SOUTH STREET SEAPORT HISTORIC DISTRICT
Manhattan
Designated: May 10, 1977

The East River waterfront of Lower Manhattan was a boat landing as early as 1625, when the Dutch West India Company set up a trading post there. Over the next two hundred years, it developed into one of the most prosperous commercial districts in New York, and one of the largest ports in the world. With the completion in 1825 of the Erie Canal, which opened a navigable route to states on the Great Lakes, New York became the nation's foremost port, and the East River its busiest docks.

As the seaport began to prosper in the 1790s, the countinghouse became the standard commercial building type for merchant shipping companies in the area. The typical countinghouse consisted of three or four stories, topped by high-pitched slate or tile roofs and designed in the Georgian or Federal style, and contained storage lofts and a counting room for keeping accounts and records. It was from such buildings that great merchant families such as the Schermerhorns, the Macys, and the Lows conducted their businesses.

The great fire of 1835 strongly influenced subsequent development of the district, creating a demand for new warehouses and offices, which were constructed in the Greek Revival style. Many of the surviving buildings were remodeled in the new style, so that few retain much of their original Georgian detail.

FULTON FERRY HISTORIC DISTRICT
Brooklyn
Designated: June 28, 1977

Before it was extended with landfill in the mid-nineteenth century, this district was the waterfront site of the first ferry between Brooklyn and Manhattan. It was begun by the Dutch, who ran small, flat-bottomed boats between the two shores in the seventeenth century. In 1704 the "Road to the Ferry" was built, providing transportation to the port for farmers as far away as eastern Long Island. In 1814, a steam-propelled ferry was introduced by Robert Fulton, inventor of the new craft, and the street was renamed in his honor.

The first structures built in the district were seventeenth- and eighteenth-century ferry buildings and taverns; these no longer survive. Examples of surviving nineteenth-century buildings include Federal-style houses as well as well-preserved commercial buildings in Italianate, Greek Revival, and Romanesque Revival styles. The chief exponent of the latter was Frank Freeman, one of Brooklyn's most eminent early architects, whose Eagle Warehouse is at 28 Cadman Plaza West. (In the twentieth century, Fulton Street was renamed Cadman Plaza after the popular Brooklyn preacher S. Parkes Cadman, although it is still called Fulton Street as well where it ends at the river.)

With the opening of the Brooklyn Bridge in 1883, the ferry went into decline, finally closing in 1927. As a quiet backwater removed from the main channels of later development, the district has retained its nineteenth-century character. In the late 1960s it attracted the interest of a number of preservation-minded investors who renovated many of the building's exteriors.

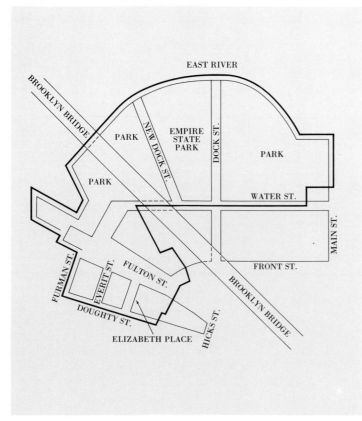

CENTRAL PARK WEST–WEST 73RD–74TH STREET HISTORIC DISTRICT
Manhattan
Designated: July 12, 1977

Originally part of a farm owned by Richard Somerindyck, the land in this district was subdivided into plots in 1835, although actual construction did not begin for almost fifty years. Edward Clark, president of the Singer Manufacturing Company, bought almost all of the land on this block between 1877 and 1881. At that time, the area was still predominantly rural, especially in contrast to the heavily populated East Side. Gas and water systems were underdeveloped and many cross streets remained unopened. The extension of the Ninth Avenue Elevated Railroad in 1879 brought more interest to the area and increased land values. A year later, construction was begun on Clark's Dakota (q.v.). Called "Clark's Folly" at the time because it was a luxury apartment building built in a then-undesirable location, the Dakota became the center of a residential community. The Clark family architect, Henry J. Hardenbergh, designed the Dakota, as well as the row of houses on West 73rd Street.

The houses along West 73rd and 74th streets display a variety of styles: German Renaissance, Georgian Revival, and Beaux Arts. Restrictive covenants specified the setbacks and the heights of the structures, resulting in a graceful achievement in community planning. The Langham, at 135 Central Park West, a massive Beaux Arts building of 1904–07, was one of the earliest luxury apartments on Central Park West.

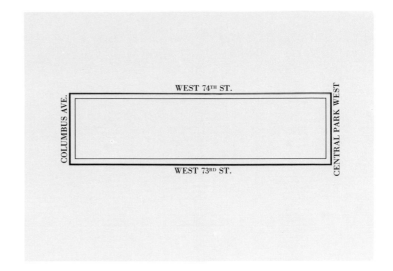

METROPOLITAN MUSEUM HISTORIC DISTRICT
Manhattan
Designated: September 20, 1977

Prior to the creation of Central Park (q.v.) in 1857, this land was an area of squatters' huts and squalid swamps. The park attracted residents, as did the Metropolitan Museum (q.v.), begun in 1874. Widespread development really began in the district with the extensions of the elevated railroads along Second, Third, Park, and Madison avenues. During this time, the area between 78th and 86th streets was completely built up with brownstone houses. These houses were designed in the Queen Anne and Neo-Grec styles, mostly by architects who were not formally trained and who had previously been builders. Many of these houses were replaced in the early twentieth century and few remain today. By the end of the 1890s, a number of mansions had been constructed along Fifth Avenue in the upper 70s and lower 80s for such wealthy individuals as Isaac D. Fletcher and Louis Stern. Built in the François I style of the French Renaissance, the mansions gave the name of "Millionaires' Mile" to this section of the avenue, and ushered in the era of large private residences designed by such architects as McKim, Mead & White and Carrère & Hastings. Meanwhile, major renovation of the older brownstones transformed their façades from the older Neo-Grec and Queen Anne styles to the more ornate and popular Beaux Arts and Renaissance Revival styles. Change came again to the area with the construction of Art Deco apartment buildings, predominantly in the 1920s, which replaced private residences and brownstones. Thus the variety of architectural styles shows the effects of change within a residential area.

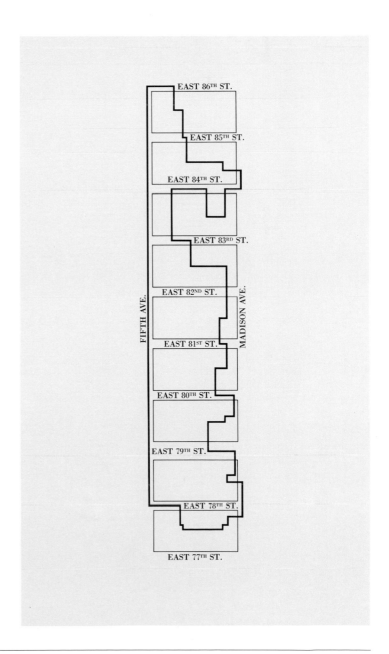

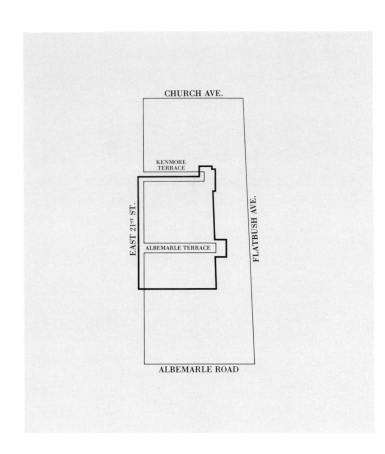

ALBEMARLE–KENMORE TERRACES HISTORIC DISTRICT
Brooklyn
Designated: July 11, 1978

The land on which these two quiet, residential courts now stand was owned by the Lott family from 1834 until 1916, when Mabel Bull acquired the property and chose the architectural firm of Slee & Bryson to develop it over the following four years. The property is in the most historic section of Flatbush, near the Flatbush Dutch Reformed Church (q.v.) and Erasmus Hall (q.v.), and it retains a tranquil character despite its proximity to the busy intersection of Church and Flatbush avenues.

The Federal Revival brick houses that line Albemarle Terrace are raised above street level and set back behind terraces or small gardens. The two-and-one-half- and three-story dwellings are arranged symmetrically, creating a pleasing ensemble, and trees are planted in the gardens rather than along the curbs, providing a feeling of seclusion from the street.

Kenmore Terrace, stylistically joined to Albemarle Terrace by the three-story Federal Revival house at its entrance, exhibits the English Garden City style in the six houses on its south side. The increasing popularity of the automobile provided a new challenge to urban planners—providing space for the storage and parking of family cars—and the architects of Kenmore Terrace responded by incorporating garages into the ground floors of the two-and-a-half-story houses.

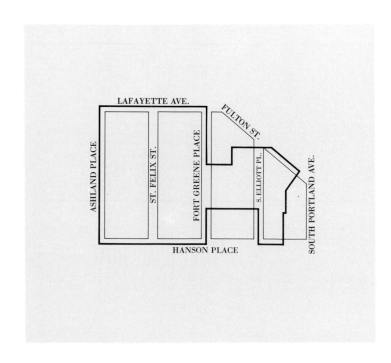

BROOKLYN ACADEMY OF MUSIC HISTORIC DISTRICT
Brooklyn
Designated: September 26, 1978

Once a thirty-acre farm owned by John Jackson, the land in this district was sold and residential development begun in the mid-nineteenth century. Many of the surviving row houses were built between 1855 and 1859 by local architects. Primarily three- or four-story brick and brownstone houses, they were built on speculation for the large numbers of people who were then relocating to Brooklyn. The majority exhibit a modified Italianate style, abundant in its use of architectural detail. A few houses in the area, built during the 1870s, incorporate Neo-Grec detail and have cast-iron façades, a rarity in residential architecture.

Change did not come to the area for almost fifty years after its initial development phase. In 1908, the Brooklyn Academy of Music moved to its present site at 30 Lafayette Avenue. The original Academy opened in 1861 but was destroyed by fire in 1903. The competition to design the new building was won by the firm of Herts & Tallant, which produced a large and richly detailed structure with an Italian Renaissance Revival façade. The other large-scale addition to the district was the 1929 Williamsburgh Savings Bank (q.v.), whose 512-foot tower still dominates the Brooklyn skyline.

FORT GREENE HISTORIC DISTRICT
Brooklyn
Designated: September 26, 1978

Until the mid-nineteenth century the Fort Greene area was dominated by four large farms that were subdivided for suburban "villas"—actually Greek Revival houses built from the same materials as the local farmhouses, which no longer survive. The major period of building took place between 1855 and 1875. Most of the buildings in the district are Italianate or closely related Anglo-Italianate and Queen Anne row houses, although one can also see the angular and geometric forms of the Neo-Grec style of the 1870s.

One of the prominent landmarks of the district is Fort Greene Park. The oldest urban park in America, it was the site of a fierce battle between the English and American forces at the beginning of the Revolution. Its conversion to a park is attributed to the poet Walt Whitman. As editor of the *Brooklyn Daily Eagle*, he argued persistently between 1848 and 1850 that the land be set aside for the enjoyment of the less affluent. The park, however, deteriorated so that in 1867 the City Commissioners felt obliged to redesign it. The commission was given to Frederick Law Olmsted and Calvert Vaux, whose plan emphasized the land's long, sloping fields and exceptional views of Manhattan through the use of elegant lawns and curved, intersecting walks. Within the park is the Prison Ship Martyrs' Monument, which contains the tombs of the many American prisoners who died in British prison ships during the Revolution. Designed by McKim, Mead & White, it has a monumental stairway leading to the vaults, which are surmounted by a 200-foot Doric column topped by a twenty-two-foot urn. It was inaugurated on November 14, 1908, by President-elect William Howard Taft.

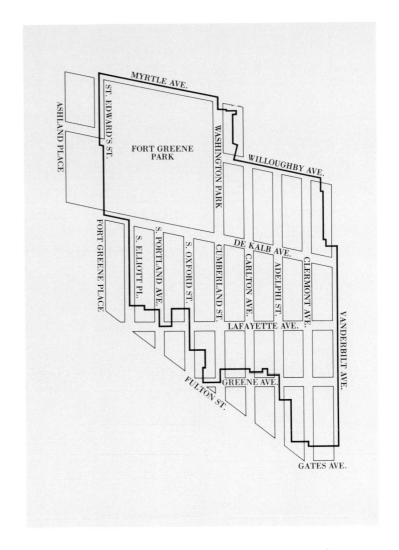

FRAUNCES TAVERN BLOCK HISTORIC DISTRICT
Manhattan
Designated: November 14, 1978

The block bounded by Pearl, Broad, and Water streets and Coenties Slip was built on landfill in 1689 and represents the first extension of the Manhattan shoreline for commercial purposes. The oldest surviving structure on the block is Fraunces Tavern (q.v.), built in 1719. The block was almost completely built up by 1728, and soon became dominated by commercial interests. After a period of bleak commercial prospects, the block saw a revival in 1827, shortly after the opening of the Erie Canal. Eleven of the sixteen present buildings were constructed between the years 1827 and 1833. The two most prominent styles on the block are the late Federal and Greek Revival. Red-brick façades and regularly spaced windows are characteristic of both styles. The Greek Revival commercial structures have large, open, granite storefronts featuring granite piers supporting a wide granite architrave. The red-brick façade begins above the architrave. Buildings with these characteristics are 3 Coenties Slip (1836–37), and 66 Pearl Street (1831). The New York City directory of 1851 lists the functions of various buildings on the block as freight forwarders, shipping agents, and wholesale merchants. The block retains its nineteenth-century character despite the presence of surrounding office towers.

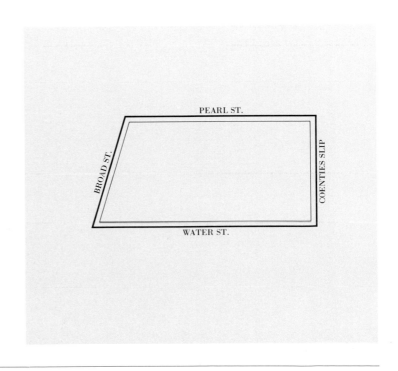

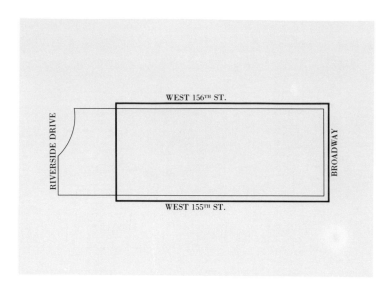

AUDUBON TERRACE HISTORIC DISTRICT
Manhattan
Designated: January 9, 1979

Audubon Terrace in Washington Heights is one of the foremost cultural centers in New York City and among the first of its kind in the country. Established on the former estate of the noted American artist and ornithologist John James Audubon, Audubon Terrace was conceived as a center for specialized research by Archer M. Huntington, a multimillionaire, philanthropist, and scholar. As a first step toward this goal, he founded the Hispanic Society of America in 1904. Buildings for the American Numismatic Society (1906–07), the American Geographical Society (1909–11), the Museum of the American Indian (1916–22), and the Church of Our Lady of Esperanza (1909–12) were soon added. The centralization of educational and cultural institutions outside of a university context was unique in America.

Huntington hoped that geographical closeness would promote cooperation among the various societies in their research fields. As a symbol of this cooperation and unity, he specified that all of the buildings be designed by his cousin, Charles Pratt Huntington, in an Italian Renaissance Revival style. Grouped around a central courtyard, their monumental Ionic colonnades are faced with Indiana limestone. The American Academy of Arts and Letters and the National Institute of Arts and Letters (1921–30) were designed in the same style after Huntington's death by William Mitchell Kendall of the firm of McKim, Mead & White with Cass Gilbert. The terrace is decorated with sculpture by Anna Vaughn Hyatt Huntington and others.

Though several of the institutions have relocated and attendance remains low for those that remain, Audubon Terrace retains an innocent charm: Grand in aspirations, it is small and friendly in scale.

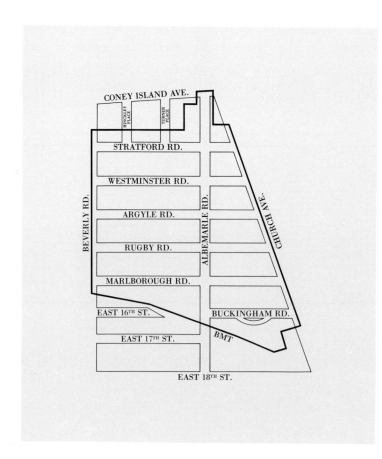

PROSPECT PARK SOUTH HISTORIC DISTRICT
Brooklyn
Designated: February 8, 1979

The development of this suburban district, the most architecturally significant in Flatbush, was spurred by the advancement of public transit, the construction of Prospect Park, and the opening of the Brooklyn Bridge, all of which contributed to the rapid growth of the City of Brooklyn. Approximately fifty acres of land, mostly belonging to the Dutch Reformed Church and the Bergen family, were purchased in 1899 by the real-estate developer Dean Alvord, who hoped that Prospect Park South would "illustrate how much of rural beauty can be incorporated within the rectangular limits of the conventional city block."

After Alvord sold his interest in Prospect Park South to the Chelsea Improvement Co. in 1905, the forty-five vacant lots were filled in with new frame houses. The juxtaposition of various architectural designs typify development convention around the turn of the twentieth century: houses were built in a wide range of styles including Spanish Mission, Italian Villa, Queen Anne, Colonial Revival, and Tudor Revival. Despite the alterations many of the homes have undergone, Prospect Park South retains much of its pastoral, turn-of-the-century ambiance.

PROSPECT LEFFERTS GARDENS HISTORIC DISTRICT
Brooklyn
Designated: October 9, 1979

Originally known as Midwout, the area along what is now Flatbush Avenue was the center of the Dutch farming colonies on Long Island. The Prospect Lefferts Gardens Historic District occupies a portion of the old estate of the Lefferts, a family prominent in Brooklyn since the seventeenth century. It was developed by James Lefferts between 1895 and 1925, with the greatest activity occurring in 1905–11, following the end of the financial panic of 1903, which slowed building throughout the city. Lefferts's plan was for a residential community of high quality; restrictive covenants still govern building heights, the setback from the streets, and other details intended to preserve the character of the neighborhood.

The houses in the district consist primarily of two- and three-story row houses interspersed with freestanding structures. The first were built in the Romanesque Revival style, although they represent a later, somewhat eclectic version of it; in addition to the customary rough-hewn stonework and round-arched windows and doorways, the houses often have such details as Palladian windows that reflect the classical revival at the turn of the century. There are also fine examples of the various Colonial Revival styles, such as the Federal and Georgian, as well as of the Tudor Revival style; the latter is unusual in that it may be found applied to row houses as well as freestanding ones. Among the individual landmarks of the district are the Lefferts Homestead (q.v.) and Flatbush Dutch Reformed Church (q.v.).

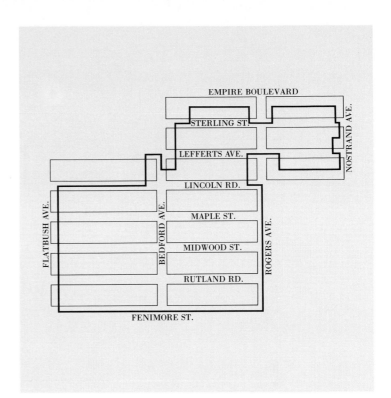

LONGWOOD HISTORIC DISTRICT
The Bronx
Designated: July 8, 1980
Extension designated: February 8, 1983

This district just west of Hunts Point in the South Bronx remained predominantly rural until it was transformed by plans to extend the IRT subway, which opened here in 1904. Located in a community now known as Pueblo de Mayaguez, the Longwood District was once part of Morrisania, a township of Westchester County established by the state legislature in 1788. George B. Johnson, who operated out of the S. B. White mansion (now the Patrolman Edward P. Lynch Center) at 734 Beck Street, developed almost the entire district.

Most of the houses in the primarily residential district were designed with elements of the Renaissance and Romanesque Revival styles by Warren C. Dickerson between 1897 and 1900. The semi-detached residences line Dawson, Kelly, Beck, and East 156th streets, and the north side of Marcy Place. Though house plans are repeated, the details are varied to dispel monotony.

The houses are set back from the street, a notable feature of Dickerson's designs, and the resulting fenced-in gardens and basement areas contribute a sense of openness to the neighborhood. The irregular street plan provides long and short views.

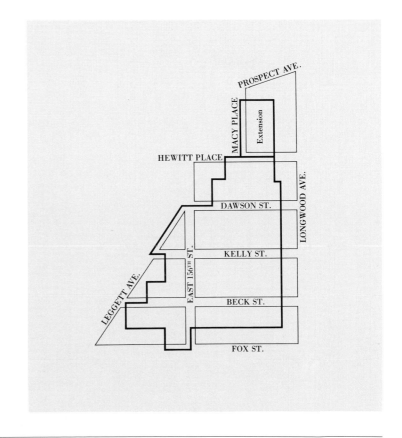

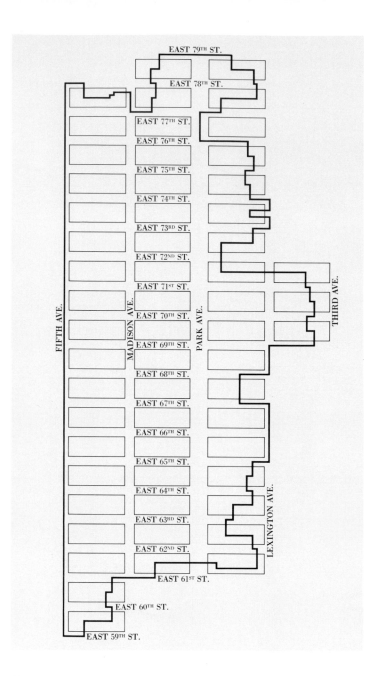

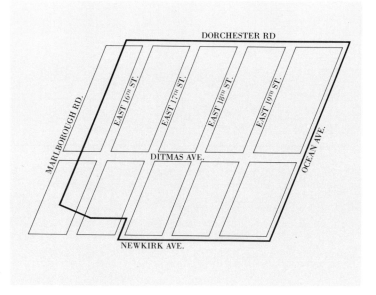

UPPER EAST SIDE HISTORIC DISTRICT
Manhattan
Designated: May 19, 1981

The Upper East Side, today one of the world's most elegant residential and shopping districts, was originally developed as a summer retreat for downtown New Yorkers, who built estates and private houses there during the late eighteenth and early nineteenth centuries. Following the creation of nearby Central Park (q.v.) between 1857 and 1877, the district went through several phases of development. The first houses were brownstones built in the Italianate and Greek Revival styles of the 1860s to '80s; examples of these may still be found on a number of side streets. There followed a period, lasting roughly from 1880 to 1910, when illustrious architectural firms such as McKim, Mead & White erected luxurious Beaux Arts palaces and French Renaissance châteaus for some of New York's wealthiest families. A third phase, from 1910 to 1930, saw a waning of the late-nineteenth-century taste for opulent and eclectic styles and a corresponding rise in the demand for classical forms. The Neoclassical Revival spurred many owners to redesign the façades of their buildings.

It was also during the early 1910s that the first luxury apartment buildings were constructed on the Upper East Side. These are distinguished by a sense of scale and proportion in relation to surrounding structures—the result of the builders' desire to preserve the high style of neighboring residences—thus imparting to the neighborhood a unique balance between the larger apartment buildings situated on major avenues and the smaller buildings on the side streets.

DITMAS PARK HISTORIC DISTRICT
Brooklyn
Designated: August 29, 1981

Ditmas Park is one of several suburban neighborhoods built on the old farms of Flatbush after the opening of the Brooklyn, Flatbush and Coney Island Railroad (now the Brighton Line of the BMT/IND) in the 1880s. It was created in 1902 by realtor Lewis H. Pounds, who purchased part of a large farm owned by the Ditmarsen family since the late seventeenth century. A land of high ridges, valleys, and no roads, it was leveled and divided according to a grid plan. Pounds's agreements included many restrictive covenants to preserve the suburban character of the area. All of the houses were originally single-family, two-story structures with attics, fronted by deep lawns and sidewalk malls with shrubs and flowers.

Most of the houses in Ditmas Park represent a free adaptation of colonial architecture, whose revival in the late nineteenth century was preceded by more than a decade of intense interest in seventeenth- and eighteenth-century traditions. Finished in clapboard and shingle, the houses are notable for the nostalgic adaptation of such elements as hipped and peaked roofs, dormer windows, columnar porches, splayed lintels, and Palladian windows. Among the later buildings are Tudor Revival houses with pseudo-half-timbered gables, brick siding, and leaded windows. The most unusual houses are thirteen bungalows on East 16th Street that adapt a Californian form to the eastern climate. Ditmas Park also contains the Flatbush-Tompkins Congregational Church, considered to be New York City's finest Georgian Revival religious building.

CLINTON HILL HISTORIC DISTRICT
Brooklyn
Designated: November 10, 1981

Clinton Hill was originally farmland, owned principally by the Ryerson family. In the 1830s it began to be divided and sold off for residential development. By 1880 it had become a suburban retreat, with villas encompassed by large lawns on Clinton and Washington avenues, surrounded by brownstone row houses, stables, and carriage houses.

In the late nineteenth and early twentieth centuries, the area began to attract some of Brooklyn's wealthiest residents. Mansions replaced the old suburban villas, which lacked modern conveniences and were considered unfashionable. This second period of growth began in 1874 when Charles Pratt, John D. Rockefeller's partner in the Standard Oil Company, erected a mansion for himself at 232 Clinton Avenue, and built four other residences as wedding presents for his sons. Other millionaires moved here, influenced by Pratt's commitment to the area, and Clinton Avenue became known as the "Gold Coast" of Brooklyn.

With the emergence of Manhattan as New York City's preeminent borough, the very wealthy left Clinton Hill. By the 1920s most of the old residences had been destroyed or divided into apartments and rooming houses. Four of the Pratt mansions still exist today, at 229, 232, 241, and 245 Clinton Avenue. Some of the finest residences in the area were purchased by or donated to the Pratt Institute (q.v.) and St. Joseph's College. Other nineteenth-century structures include row houses, churches, and carriage houses in a variety of styles.

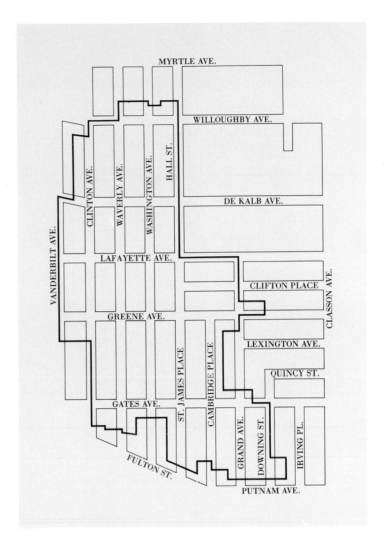

GREENPOINT HISTORIC DISTRICT
Brooklyn
Designated: September 14, 1982

The site of several large farms in the seventeenth and eighteenth centuries, Greenpoint became during the nineteenth century one of the most important industrial centers on the eastern seaboard. The mid-nineteenth century witnessed the flourishing of shipbuilding, as well as the growth of such related industries as iron and brass foundry. By the turn of the century, Greenpoint was a center not only for such major industries as china, glass, and oil, but also drugs, sugar refining, furniture, and many others.

In contrast to residents of Brooklyn Heights and Park Slope, who commuted to work, those who lived in Greenpoint worked in the plants and factories nearby. The neighborhood contains substantial row houses erected for owners of businesses, and more modest row houses and apartments built for factory workers. Most of these were designed by builders rather than professional architects, working from handbooks, and using standardized cornices, windows, doors, and other architectural elements that could be purchased ready-made. Their work typically represents the vernacular version of a contemporary style. Greenpoint's rows of Italianate, French Second Empire, Neo-Grec, and Queen Anne houses often have nearly identical lintels, iron railings, and shutters. In addition to the row houses, Greenpoint offers good examples of church architecture in both the Gothic and Romanesque Revival styles, and a number of frame houses, which were often built by ship carpenters.

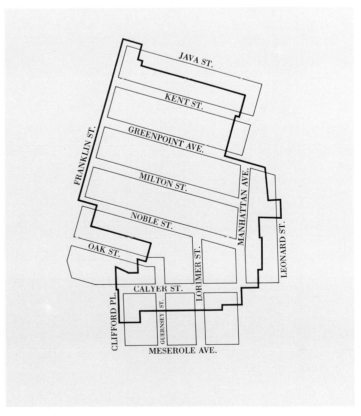

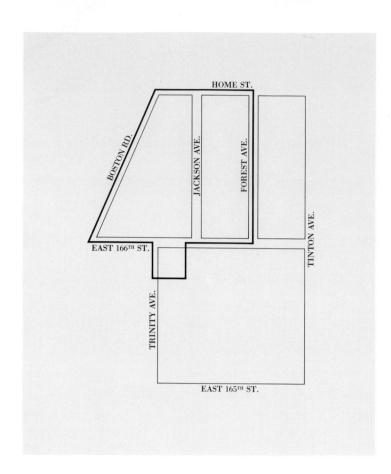

MORRIS HIGH SCHOOL HISTORIC DISTRICT
The Bronx
Designated: December 21, 1982

This section of the Bronx was once part of Morrisania, a township of Westchester County that was formally annexed to New York City in 1874. The region is named for two British officers, Colonel Lewis Morris and his brother Richard, who purchased a tract of land here in 1670. Though the construction of the Harlem and Hudson River Railroads and the creation of a brewing industry in the area helped populate Morrisania, the neighborhood remained largely rural until the beginning of the twentieth century. The real-estate boom that completed Morrisania's development was spurred by the extension of the subway into the district and the opening of Morris High School (q.v.) in 1904. The modest Trinity Episcopal Church, begun in 1874, across from the high school at the corner of Trinity Avenue and East 166th Street, is the oldest original structure in the district, but was redecorated in High Victorian Gothic style in 1906.

The residences in the district are mainly two- and three-story brick row houses, designed by local architects in a free classical manner, incorporating elements of the English, Flemish, and Italian Renaissance revivals, and built primarily between 1900 and 1904. Richly detailed with cohesive block fronts, these houses along Forest and Jackson avenues enhance the turn-of-the-century atmosphere of the district.

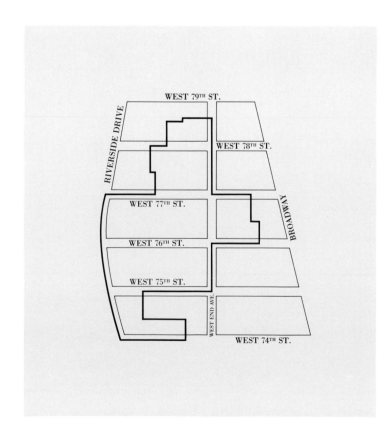

WEST END–COLLEGIATE HISTORIC DISTRICT
Manhattan
Designated: January 3, 1984

This area of the Upper West Side remained predominantly farmland until the 1880s, when the extension of the Ninth Avenue Elevated Railroad made it more accessible and the creation of Riverside Park (q.v.) provided an inducement to live there. Land speculation increased and the construction of private residences began. During this period, what is generally regarded as the most elaborate and eclectic collection of row houses in New York was built in the West End–Collegiate district. The houses derived their stylistic inspiration from Romanesque, Renaissance, Elizabethan, and François I designs. Particularly notable are the block front of houses by Lamb & Rich on West End Avenue between West 76th and 77th streets, and houses by Clarence F. True on Riverside Drive, West 75th Street, and West 77th Street.

The next phase of building in the area lasted from 1911 through 1931 and resulted in the construction of eight large apartment houses, whose architects—among them Emery Roth and Schwartz & Gross—emulated the styles and materials of the already existing row houses, providing a counterpoint to the lower-scale houses.

NEW YORK CITY FARM COLONY–SEAVIEW HOSPITAL HISTORIC DISTRICT
Staten Island
Designated: March 26, 1985

The New York City Farm Colony was built on the site of the former Richmond County Poor Farm in 1902. Established to house and aid the able-bodied poor, the institution was predicated on the idea of the exchange of labor for shelter and food, although work was not compulsory. The first dormitories opened in 1904. Although three architects were involved—Raymond F. Almirall, Frank H. Quimby, and William Flanagan—their designs share in common the vocabulary of the so-called Dutch Colonial Revival style. The use of brick and fieldstone, gambrel roofs, and classical porticoes evoke the Colony's past history as a farming community.

In 1915, the New York City Farm Colony was merged with Seaview Hospital, which had been constructed on adjacent land belonging to the Colony. When it opened in 1914, it was the largest institution in the world dedicated to the cure of tuberculosis. Its red tile roofs, stuccoed walls, and tile and mosaic decoration recall Spanish Mission architecture, but according to the architect, Raymond F. Almirall, were chosen without regard to their historical or geographical character. The eight pavilions— four survive—provided views of land and sea and sunlit rooms year-round, as contemporary medical theory stressed the importance of pleasant surroundings to tubercular patients. It is considered the finest of Almirall's buildings with a social purpose. After the discovery of a cure for tuberculosis in the late 1950s, Seaview was turned over to various community service offices.

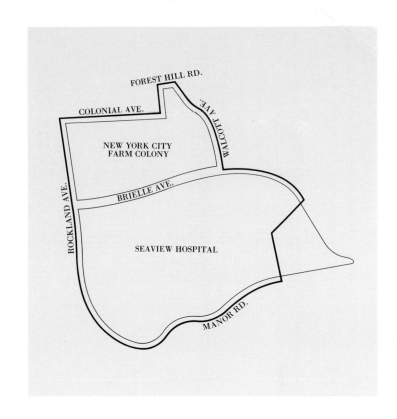

RIVERSIDE DRIVE–WEST 80TH–81ST STREET HISTORIC DISTRICT
Manhattan
Designated: March 26, 1985

Although it retained much of its rural atmosphere into the middle of the nineteenth century, the Upper West Side had been slated for development as early as 1811, when the engineer John Randel, Jr., drew up a street plan for the city's Board of Governors. Randel's plan, an extension of the grid plan of Lower Manhattan, was abandoned in 1867 when it became evident that the downtown street plan had dealt poorly with the congestion caused by increased development. Frederick Law Olmsted was given the task of designing Riverside Park and Drive, as well as some new streets and avenues. His plan took advantage of the contours of the land, creating gently curving roads and scenic perspectives. By the turn of the century, the area had become one of New York's most desirable neighborhoods.

The streets included within this district went relatively untouched by the wave of large apartment house construction in the area that followed World War I. Their buildings are largely the work of two architects, Charles H. Israels and Clarence F. True. Influenced by the Beaux Arts style of McKim, Mead & White, their designs are generally freer and more picturesque, utilizing such medievalizing details as bowfronts, oriels, parapets, and chimneys, and embellished with Roman brick, brownstone, limestone, leaded glass windows, terra-cotta, tile, and wrought iron.

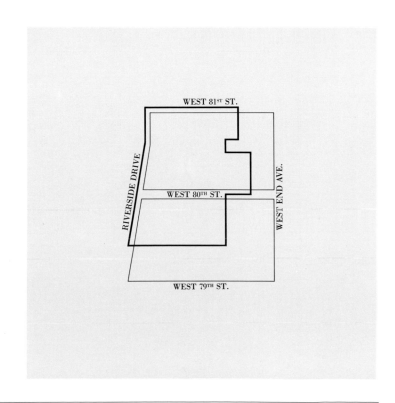

MORRIS AVENUE HISTORIC DISTRICT
The Bronx
Designated: July 15, 1986

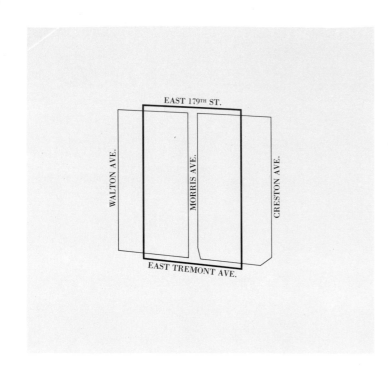

This double row of two-family row houses and tenements along Morris Avenue between East 179th Street and East Tremont Avenue was built over a four-year period by August Jacob. Vast real-estate speculation and a growing market for single-family dwellings developed in the Bronx with the extension of the IRT in 1904, and the Morris Avenue district was designed by architect John Hauser to fill the needs of people seeking to move out of the increasingly crowded borough of Manhattan.

The block of Morris Avenue that comprises this residential district was once a tiny portion of the 3,200-acre Manor of Fordham. After changing ownership several times, the property was purchased by Jacob from the United Real-Estate and Trust Company and developed in five building campaigns between 1906 and 1910. The mostly three-story, curved bow façade row houses are surprisingly homogeneous considering they were built in several stages. There are differences of detail, such as varying shades of brick and diverse patterns in the wrought-iron areaway railings. Along with the two tenement buildings on Tremont Avenue, these houses represent an intact early-twentieth-century neighborhood.

TUDOR CITY HISTORIC DISTRICT
Manhattan
Developer: Fred F. French Company
Architect: H. Douglas Ives
Designated: May 17, 1988

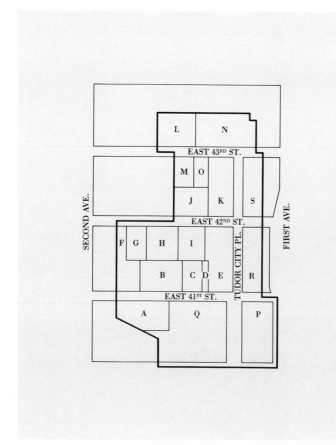

In a pioneering venture in urban renewal, Tudor City, a complex of apartment buildings overlooking the East River, was built to help ensure middle-class respectability in midtown Manhattan's East Side, a formerly working-class neighborhood of row houses and tenement buildings. The ten original residential buildings, conceived in 1925 by Fred F. French Company and designed by architects under the direction of H. Douglas Ives, are (with the exception of a transient hotel) in the Tudor Revival style, with elaborate skyline profiles complemented by scaled-down street levels and stained-glass windows, some illustrating scenes from New York's history.

Considered a "city within a city," the district provides a generous amount of open space, including two private greens, two open parks, and a landscaped core, called Tudor City Place, with shops and services for tenants. The original scheme even included a small eighteen-hole golf course, complete with traps, nighttime illumination, and a golf pro. Tudor City was a prophecy of subsequent twentieth-century planned urban communities.

COBBLE HILL HISTORIC DISTRICT EXTENSION
Brooklyn
Designated: June 7, 1988

The two Italianate houses in this three-building extension located at 354 and 356 Henry Street were identical when constructed and remain nearly so today. The buildings retain double-door, wooden entranceways flanked by projecting lintels, continuing the pattern of row houses along the block. The pair was part of the original Cobble Hill Historic District hearings before the Landmarks Commission in 1966 but was not designated at that time.

The third building of the extension, the Polhemus Building, replaced two other row houses in 1896–97 on the corner of the block. It served as a free clinic and training facility for nearby Long Island College Hospital. Its prominence—in size and French Renaissance Revival style—reflects the building's importance in the neighborhood. Designed by Marshall Emery, the clinic was founded by Caroline Herriman Polhemus in memory of her husband, Henry Ditmas Polhemus. Polhemus had been a regent of the Long Island College Hospital and was widely known in Brooklyn for his generosity and concern for others. The clinic was intended to provide medical services for the poor who lived near Brooklyn's waterfront.

The row houses were built in a group of eight in 1852–53; the other remaining four are within the boundaries of the original district.

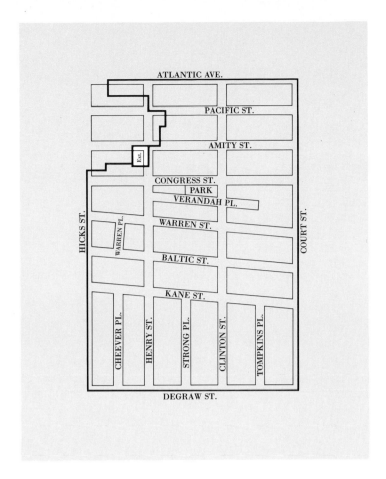

GRAMERCY PARK HISTORIC DISTRICT EXTENSION
36 Gramercy Park East Apartment Building, 1908–10
Manhattan
Architect: James Riely Gordon
Designated: July 12, 1988

Built on land originally owned by New York's first post-Revolutionary mayor, James Duane (1784–89), this district surrounds the only private park in New York City. Graceful nineteenth-century houses lend an air of refined elegance to the area, though some of the earlier structures on the north and east sides of the park have been replaced by apartment buildings such as 36 Gramercy Park East.

While maintaining the Gothic Revival style of the district, the apartment building at 36 Gramercy Park East also exemplifies the challenge posed to architects by the skyscraper—how to establish a style that best expresses the form and function of this new building type. The building's façade, covered in white glazed terra-cotta above a granite basement, is ornamented with an intricate Gothic tracery of trefoil moldings, pointed arches, thin colonnettes, heraldic shields, gargoyles, and putti.

Architectural terra-cotta gained popularity in this country during the 1870s, when, appreciated for being lightweight and fireproof, it was used extensively in the rebuilding of Chicago after the Great Fire. The ease with which inexpensive ornamentation could be reproduced in terra-cotta, rather than stone, also made it particularly well suited to the fine Gothic details that grace this handsome U-shaped building.

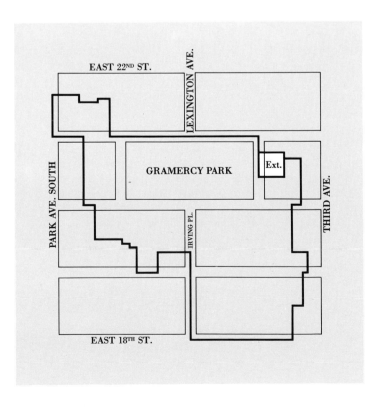

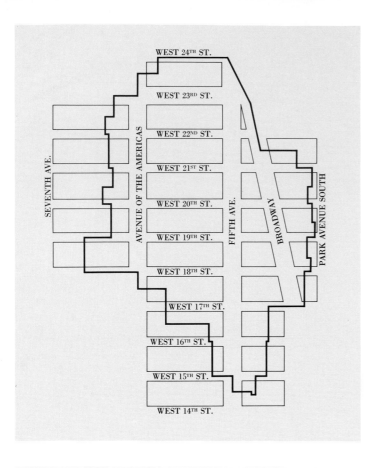

LADIES' MILE HISTORIC DISTRICT
Manhattan
Designated: May 2, 1989

Once the fashion center of New York's Gilded Age, this area was named for the stylish women who searched its streets tirelessly for French gloves, Japanese sunshades, bonbons, umbrellas, corsets, and other glamorous trifles. The area's financial success was ensured in 1860 by the Prince of Wales' stay at the Fifth Avenue Hotel on 23rd Street. Where princes led, there followed society, and the commercial rush began in the early 1860s with A. T. Stewart's cast-iron retailing palace at Broadway and 9th Street.

B. Altman, Lord & Taylor, Arnold Constable, W. & J. Sloane, Tiffany & Co., Gorham Silver, and Brooks Brothers all located their stores here to cater to the emerging "carriage trade." The opulence of the area drew America's first ladies, those from high society as well as the undeniably famous: Ethel Barrymore, Lillian Russell, Isabella Stewart Gardner, and Lillie Langtry. Restaurants, professional offices, piano showrooms, publishing houses, booksellers, the Academy of Music, Steinway Hall, and the first Metropolitan Museum of Art further enhanced the area's ambience.

The growing commercialization of the district eventually drove its more fashionable residents—Emily Post, Washington Irving, Samuel F. B. Morse, Edith Wharton, Horace Greeley, and the Roosevelt family—uptown. By the end of World War I, most of the department stores, too, had moved their operations further north, and the lavish buildings were converted to manufacturing use. However, the elegant structures remain as silent witness to a much-romanticized era—one characterized by gaslight, glitter, and glamour.

SOUTH STREET SEAPORT HISTORIC DISTRICT EXTENSION
Manhattan
Designated: July 11, 1989

The buildings that comprise the South Street Seaport Historic District Extension are, for the most part, utilitarian and straightforward, and as such they reflect the district's means of livelihood during the period of its fastest growth, from the early 1820s to the mid-1880s. Warehouses, lofts, and commercial storage spaces occupy this block bounded by Pearl Street, Water Street, Peck Slip, and Dover Street. While the block was originally designated along with the rest of the South Street Seaport Historic District in 1977, the Board of Estimate amended the designation to exclude the area; however, it remained as part of the district on the state and national registers of historic places.

The buildings on the block reflect several different trends in mercantile architecture during the nineteenth century, including Federal, Greek Revival, Italianate, and Romanesque Revival. Built by Ezra Hoyt in 1823–24 in the Federal style, 268 Water Street was originally a stove factory with residences upstairs. The 1829 building at 270 Water Street, with its monolithic ground-floor granite piers, follows the Greek Revival warehouse design popularized by noted New York architect Ithiel Town.

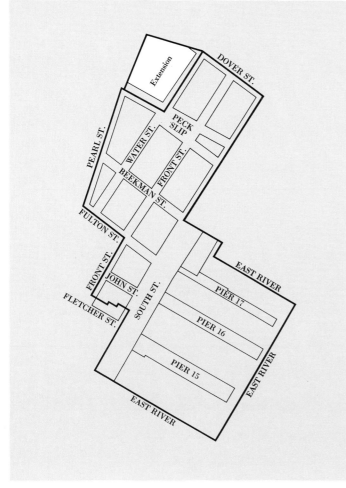

WEST 71ST STREET HISTORIC DISTRICT
Manhattan
Designated: August 29, 1989

The West 71st Street Historic District encompasses thirty-three buildings that occupy nearly an entire block between West End Avenue and the railroad tracks, shielded by a wall, to the west. It is significant both for its display of Upper West Side residential development and for the original Renaissance Revival details that remain on many of the individual buildings. Alterations over the years have been minimal.

The designs of the thirty-three houses along this street were primarily influenced by the Beaux Arts movement, and they display various interpretations of Renaissance prototypes in their decoration and detail. The regular rhythms of bays, cornices, and oriels along the buildings lining both sides of the street lend order and symmetry to this block, yet allow each building to retain its own distinct character.

The architects of these buildings include Horgan & Slattery, known for both institutional and residential designs; John C. Burne and Neville & Bagge, who were active throughout Manhattan; and George Keister, who is known for his theater designs as well as houses. The houses along this peaceful block have not been markedly altered over the years. The historic district remains a unique sampling of Renaissance Revival architecture from an active period of development on the Upper West Side.

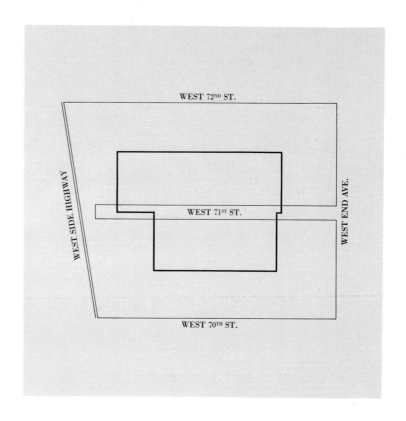

RIVERSIDE–WEST END HISTORIC DISTRICT
Manhattan
Designated: December 19, 1989

Once called the "Acropolis of the world's second city," this district is situated on a plateau and offers outstanding views of the Hudson River and Frederick Law Olmsted's Riverside Park, completed in 1879.

The early Upper West Side real-estate boom is recalled by the remaining harmonious groups of Renaissance Revival, Georgian Revival, and Beaux Arts row houses, many built by Clarence F. True, C. P. H. Gilbert, and Alexander Welch, architects who specialized in row house design at the end of the nineteenth century. The district also includes many pre- and post–World War I apartment buildings. These early six- and seven-story elevator flats, related in materials, style, and ornament to the row houses, reflect the growing acceptance of luxury apartment living for prosperous residents. Post-war construction in the district lined the avenues with fifteen-story apartment houses offering smaller, less expensive flats. Their modesty is reflected in the restrained façade treatments, with ornamental programs inspired by the Beaux Arts, Gothic, Renaissance, and Romanesque styles generally restricted to the base and upper levels. Only a few buildings in the district were constructed after the Depression, among them Emery Roth's 1939 Normandy, a notable combination of Italian Renaissance and Art Moderne.

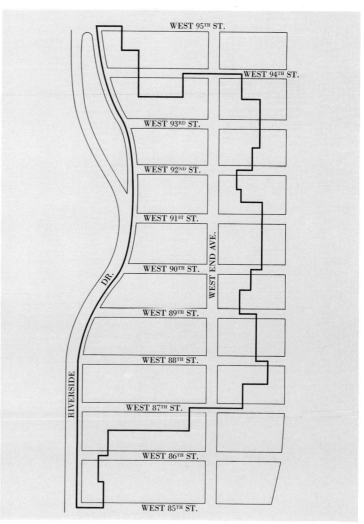

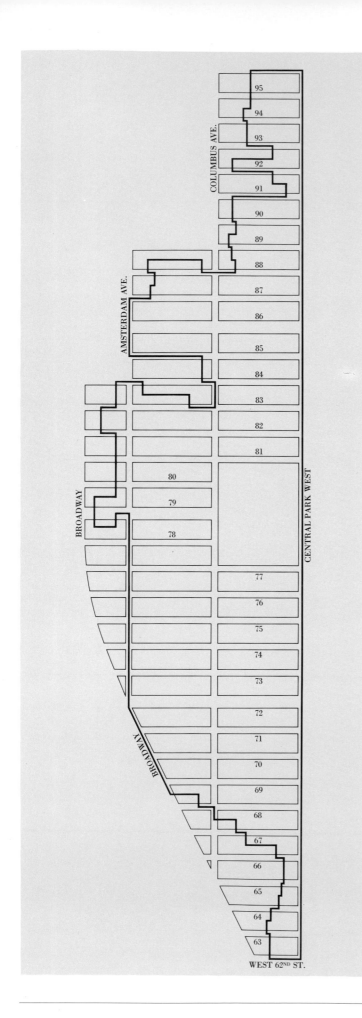

UPPER WEST SIDE–CENTRAL PARK WEST HISTORIC DISTRICT
Manhattan
Designated: April 24, 1990

This district incorporates two smaller, preexisting districts that focused on Central Park West and the adjacent side street blocks: Central Park West at West 73rd–74th streets and Central Park West at 76th Street. Known before its urbanization as "Bloomingdale" (by Dutch settlers recalling a flower-growing region of Holland), the area was developed primarily as a residential neighborhood over a fifty-year period beginning in the 1880s. Bloomingdale Road, later Broadway, followed an old Indian trail and was the northern route out of New York, past rural lodges and old shanties. Although working farms and small hamlets were established in the Bloomingdale area over the years, the area remained largely undeveloped until the 1880s, when the extension of horsecar lines up Broadway and Amsterdam Avenue and the completion of the Columbus Avenue elevated railway linked this once-remote area with New York City's commercial and financial centers.

The district's diverse building types and styles range from busy storefronts on Columbus Avenue to residences on quiet side streets to dramatic apartment towers along Central Park West. The first building boom in the area is reflected in the harmonious groups of multistory row houses that comprise the predominant genre of residential building in the district. Contemporaneous with these—and related in scale, fabric, and details—are the Neo-Grec and Romanesque Revival five- and six-story tenements and apartment buildings primarily located on Columbus and Amsterdam avenues.

Although later construction, particularly in the 1920s and 30s, replaced some of the original buildings, it added the distinctive skyline of tall apartment buildings along Central Park West that remain among the finest examples of three trends in twentieth-century residential architecture: Beaux Arts from the first decade, Neo-Renaissance from the 1920s, and Art Deco from the 1920s and 1930s. In fact, all of the Central Park West multitowered buildings within the latter two categories were designated New York City landmarks prior to the district's designation.

RIVERDALE HISTORIC DISTRICT
The Bronx
Designated: October 16, 1990

The Riverdale area, along the east bank of the Hudson River, was part of the large region inhabited by the Mahican Indians until 1646, when it came under control of Adriaen Van der Donck, a Dutch trader. Although the area remained relatively untouched, the land immediately acquired a higher speculative value upon the completion of the Hudson River Railroad in 1849. A group of influential and wealthy businessmen purchased a one hundred–acre parcel in 1852 and founded Riverdale, which was to serve as a suburban summer community center. Riverdale was for a time the only stop on the railroad between Spuyten Duyvil and Yonkers. The earliest known railway suburb of New York City, Riverdale was prototypical in its picturesque layout, which was conscientiously adapted to the topography.

The district itself corresponds to the seven original estates linked by a carriage alley, now Sycamore Avenue. Encompassing about fifteen acres of steeply sloping land overlooking the Hudson River and the Palisades, it comprises thirty-four buildings. These include villas of the 1850s with their later alterations; stables and carriage houses of the nineteenth and early twentieth centuries, later converted to residential use; and houses from the second and third quarters of the twentieth century designed in traditional architectural styles, such as Neo-Colonial and Neo-Federal, and built with traditional materials. All are situated to utilize and complement the original landscaping and topography of the seven estates, including stone borders and retaining walls, terraces, steps, paths and driveways, cobbled street gutters, individual specimen trees, and rows of trees and hedges.

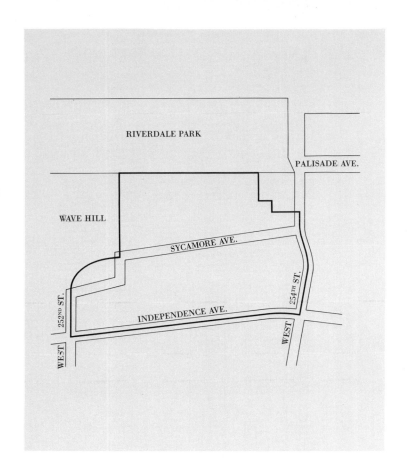

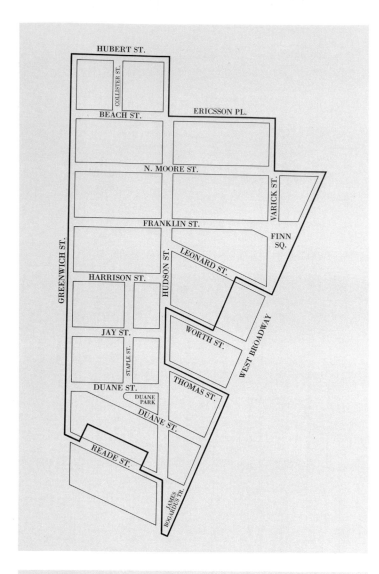

TRIBECA WEST HISTORIC DISTRICT
Manhattan
Designated: May 7, 1991

Upon the completion in 1825 of the Erie Canal, New York City became the preeminent port and trading center of the United States. Larger commercial ships that had once gingerly traversed the narrow East River could now be accommodated on the more easily navigable Hudson River. This new traffic also facilitated the development of markets for perishable goods on the west side of what is now known as Tribeca—the Triangle Below Canal Street.

The Washington Market, originally built in 1812 to the southwest, gradually expanded into this district and by the early 1880s had become New York's primary wholesale and retail produce outlet, offering imported cheeses, quail, squab, wild duck, swordfish, frogs' legs, venison, and bear steaks. The warehouses that were erected to store this bounty are the focal point of the Tribeca West Historic District.

The commercial vitality of the district is recalled by the buildings that form its dominant architectural character. Constructed between 1860 and 1910, these functional yet decorative stores and lofts include utilitarian structures derived from vernacular building traditions; others more consciously imitative of the popular period styles, such as Italianate, Neo-Grec, Romanesque Revival, and Renaissance Revival; and the later, high-style warehouses that reflect their architects' interest in creating a particularly American building type. The buildings are unified by scale, building material, and ground-floor treatment—cast-iron piers and canopies rise above stepped vaults and loading platforms. Folding iron shutters, massive wooden doors, granite-slab sidewalks, and Belgian-block street pavers enhance the district's unique architectural flavor.

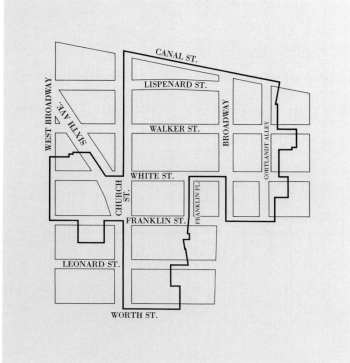

TRIBECA EAST HISTORIC DISTRICT
Manhattan
Designated: December 8, 1992

These imposing brick buildings symbolize how important the businesses and merchants in this area were to the flourishing city and nation. Though utilitarian in function, the structures borrowed materials and a style ordinarily reserved for more prestigious buildings. Executed in an Italianate manner and built largely in the mid-1800s, some of these five-story loft and store buildings demonstrate the greater degree of ornamentation then available to the metal fabricator. In contrast to earlier stone post-and-lintel storefronts, the new cast-iron and glass storefronts provided better illumination to the principal selling space on the first stories and enhanced the display of merchandise.

The façade designs suggest the profound impact made on New York architects by Italian Renaissance palazzo architectural devices introduced by Joseph Trench and John B. Snook in their design of a marble-faced department store for A. T. Stewart's highly successful dry-goods business.

TRIBECA SOUTH HISTORIC DISTRICT
Manhattan
Designated: December 8, 1992

This district is characterized by a row of well-preserved five-story store and loft buildings that were constructed in the mid-1800s. The buildings differ in their Italianate detailing—window openings are variously emphasized, for example, by pediments, arched hoods, or flat lintels. The widths of the buildings vary from three to six bays and collectively create continuous, strikingly unified streetscapes crowned by deep cornices. At street level they are linked by the rhythmic patterns created by the succession of columned cast-iron and glass storefronts.

The district's important cast-iron—fronted structures include the Cary Building, which has retained ornamental cast-iron façades on the Chambers and Reade Street elevations. Built in 1856–57, these façades are among the oldest still in existence. The 147 West Broadway Building, built in 1969, provides a rare example of cast-iron cladding designed to mimic ashlar construction.

The district is representative of the once-much-larger wholesale district, dominated by the textile and dry-goods trade, that developed northward from Cortlandt Street following the destruction of the earlier dry-goods district on Pearl Street in the fire of 1835.

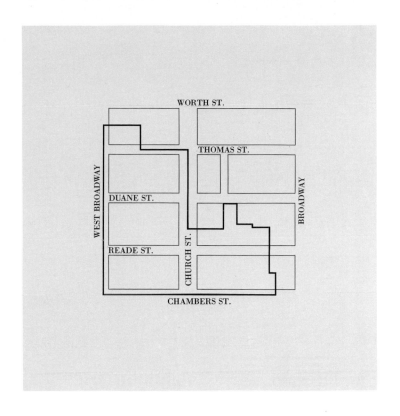

TRIBECA NORTH HISTORIC DISTRICT
Manhattan
Designated: December 8, 1992

Most of the buildings in this district were constructed between 1880 and 1913, and they represent the last remnants of the once-thriving warehouse and manufacturing industries on the Lower West Side, an area that played a major role in the emergence of New York City as an international port and a major industrial center.

The district contains some of New York's largest late-nineteenth-century brick warehouses and earliest surviving industrial buildings. Notable among these is a storage warehouse at 461–469 Greenwich Street that was built in 1880 in the Renaissance Revival style. One of the earliest storage warehouses, this six-story brick building is constructed in fireproof sections of approximately 30×100 feet, each section served by a separate lift. Currently being used as a warehouse, another massive brick structure on Laight Street, between West and Washington streets, appears to be a pre–Civil War sugar refinery.

Additional interesting buildings in the area include the ten-story Fairchild Brothers and Foster pharmaceutical factory—designed in 1899 by Thomas R. Jackson, at 76 Laight Street—and the 1913 Independent Warehouse Inc. and Erie Railroad Greenwich Street Station, at 415–427 Greenwich Street.

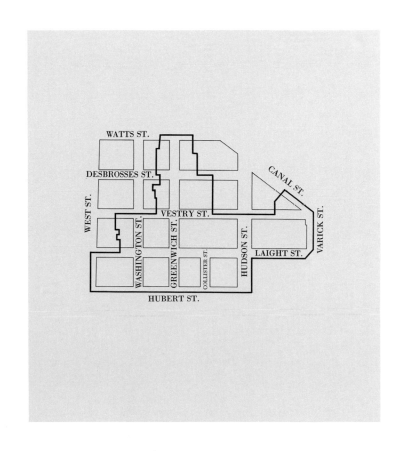

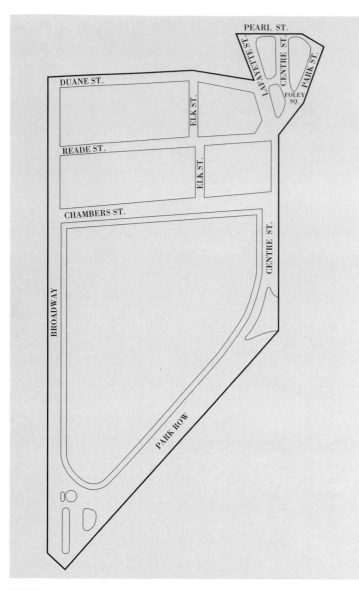

AFRICAN BURIAL GROUND
AND THE COMMONS HISTORIC DISTRICT
Manhattan
Designated: February 23, 1993

This district was designated for the historical and archaeological importance of the ground on which it is situated, as it contains material from the earliest Dutch, African, and English settlements. Currently, several landmark buildings (City Hall, 52 Chambers Street, a.k.a. New York County Courthouse, Surrogate's Court, a.k.a. Hall of Records, Sun Building, a.k.a. A. T. Stewart Store, and NYC Parking Violations Bureau, a.k.a. Emigrant Industrial Savings Bank, all q.v.) are located here.

Originally set aside as the Commons by the Dutch, this land has been one of the centers of New York's civic life since the seventeenth century. The English established the city's northern border—eventually with a palisades wall—midway through the Commons, at today's Chambers Street. Before the French and Indian War (1754–63), the southern half was converted into a military grounds, and, after independence, into City Hall Park and the seat of New York City government.

By the 1700s, New York City's African population, including freed slaves as well as domestic and skilled slaves, accounted for approximately one of every seven city residents. New York's emancipated Africans were forced to bury their dead outside of the city, on the north side of the palisades. In the early nineteenth century, as the city expanded northward, the African burial ground was built over with residential, commercial, industrial, and public buildings.

JACKSON HEIGHTS HISTORIC DISTRICT
Queens
Designated: October 19, 1993

The openings of the Queensboro Bridge in 1909 and the Roosevelt Avenue elevated subway line in 1917 encouraged the development and expansion of residential areas in northern Queens. About that time, Edward A. McDougall, president of the Queensboro Corporation real-estate development firm, initiated the construction of a planned community in Jackson Heights for the managerial and professional class, inspired by the Garden City movement in England and German suburban housing developments.

Eschewing the one-building-per-lot tenement configuration, the planners used the full city block as the unit of design for apartment houses surrounding spacious central gardens. These "garden apartments" allowed for more effective use of space within the units, as well as ample light and ventilation. The buildings are typically about six stories high, with simple façades and details that evoke English, Spanish, and Italian models. Later, designers created attached and semidetached single-family "garden homes," which are set back from the street and are typically finished in Georgian or Tudor Revival style.

The buildings in this thirty-eight-block district, most of which were erected between 1911 and 1950, demonstrate the integration of new types of housing with commercial, institutional, recreational, and transportation facilities. The area showcases many of the earliest examples of what became standard middle-class living, and it continues to be a vibrant community.

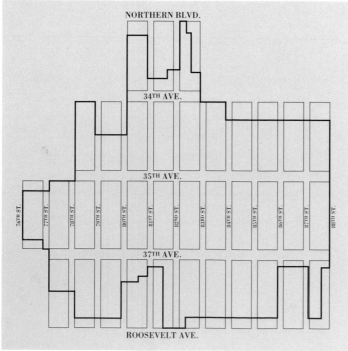

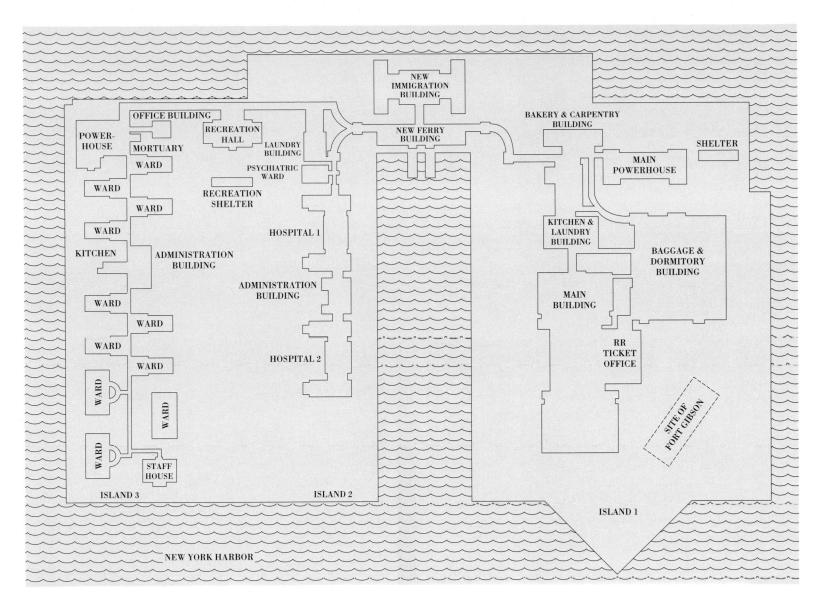

ELLIS ISLAND HISTORIC DISTRICT
Manhattan
Designated: November 16, 1993

As the flow of eastern and southern European immigration to the United States surged in the late nineteenth century, New York's modest processing center at Castle Garden (Castle Clinton, q.v.) in the Battery became inadequate. In 1892, the federal government assumed control of immigration and relocated to the site of Fort Gibson on Ellis Island. The massive complex that stands today was begun in 1897, after the original station was destroyed by fire.

This district, situated in New York Harbor, encompasses the Ellis Island Federal Immigration Station. Efficient control of immigration procedures dictated Ellis Island's design and architecture. The complex of some thirty interconnected structures, built between the 1890s and the 1930s, includes major portions designed in a monumental Beaux Arts style by the firm of Boring & Tilton, under the supervision of James Knox Taylor. One is the imposing brick-and-stone Main Building, which houses the Registry Room (q.v.). The structures rest on a largely artificial, twenty-seven-and-one-half acre, E-shaped island, which was created solely to accommodate the immigration station. The island is composed of three land masses: the original island on which the Main Building sits, and two manmade islands—now connected—made of subway tunnel fill, which support medical, administrative, and dormitory buildings.

Prior to the restrictive Immigration Act of 1924, Ellis Island processed approximately 12 million steerage-class (lower than third-class) immigrants; today, their descendants represent more than one-third of all Americans. Although immigration declined markedly after 1924, Ellis Island served an array of government functions until 1954. In 1965, it was made part of the Statue of Liberty National Monument, although it remained abandoned until the mid-1980s, when the Statue of Liberty centennial piqued interest in the island. In 1990, the National Park Service renovated and reopened the Main Building as the Ellis Island Immigration Museum, which it operates. Except for the restored portion, Ellis Island's structures are in very poor condition. On March 31, 1997, an arbitrator appointed by the Supreme Court deemed that the island be divided between New York and New Jersey, who have been at odds over its ownership for 200 years. If the ruling is sustained, the original island, including the museum, would remain under New York's jurisdiction, while New Jersey would gain control over the twenty-two acres of added landfill.

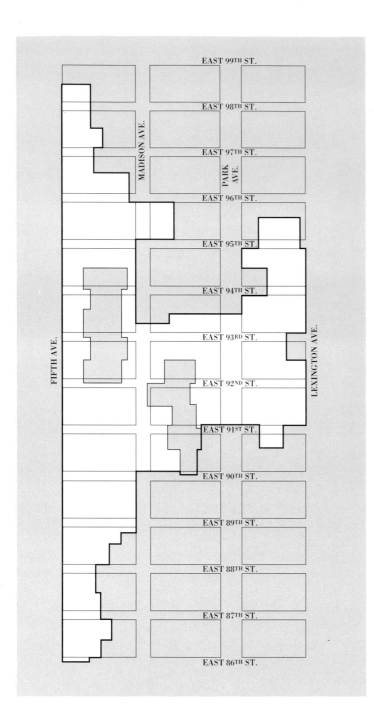

EAST 99TH ST.
EAST 98TH ST.
MADISON AVE.
EAST 97TH ST.
PARK AVE.
EAST 96TH ST.
EAST 95TH ST.
EAST 94TH ST.
FIFTH AVE.
EAST 93RD ST.
LEXINGTON AVE.
EAST 92ND ST.
EAST 91ST ST.
EAST 90TH ST.
EAST 89TH ST.
EAST 88TH ST.
EAST 87TH ST.
EAST 86TH ST.

EXPANDED CARNEGIE HILL HISTORIC DISTRICT
Manhattan
Designated: December 21, 1993

This seventeen-block district encompasses the original Carnegie Hill Historic District, designated in 1974. The district comprises a residential community built up over fifty-five years, presenting a wide variety of architectural styles and building types. While remaining predominantly a residential area, today many Carnegie Hill buildings are shops, museums, and schools.

The first railroad to the Upper East Side allowed industrial development in the 1830s, and several wood-framed row houses survive from the 1850s (including 120 and 122 East 92nd Street, q.v.). The Third Avenue elevated train spurred speculative residential construction following 1881. The side streets were developed with rows of elegant brownstone, limestone, brick, and stone houses in Neo-Grec, Queen Anne, Neo-Romanesque, and Neo-Renaissance styles. Along the longer avenue blocks, developers erected large apartment buildings and residence hotels. The Fifth Avenue lots, however, remained vacant due to their higher value.

When Andrew Carnegie purchased the lot on Fifth Avenue between 91st and 92nd streets in 1898, the neighborhood was an ordinary upper-middle-class district, and his new property was unoccupied except for squatters. When Carnegie's vast and luxurious Beaux Arts, Neo-Georgian mansion (q.v.) was finished in 1901, the district had become one of the most desirable locations in the city. Large mansions and town houses of great architectural distinction continued to be built in the district until the Depression hit in 1929. The Guggenheim Museum (q.v.), considered one of Frank Lloyd Wright's masterworks, is also situated in the district.

CLAY AVENUE HISTORIC DISTRICT
The Bronx
Designated: April 5, 1994

This district's land was once part of Fleetwood Park, an 1871 trotting track owned by William H. Morris of the landowning family for whom the Bronx town of Morrisania was named. The Fleetwood was maintained by the Driving Club of New York (whose members included the Vanderbilt, Rockefeller, and Whitney families), which was able to thwart the city's consistent efforts to develop the land. After the Third Avenue elevated train opened in 1888, however, property values rose and Morris's heirs closed the track in 1898, eventually selling the land in 1901.

This area is among The Bronx's most uniform streetscapes. Developer Ernest Wenigmann built twenty-eight semi-detached, two-family, Romanesque Revival houses dating from 1901. Intended to look like one-family buildings, they were rented primarily to white-collar professionals. A single one-family house from 1906 was built by hardware manufacturer Francis Keil. Wenigmann also put up three New Law tenement apartment buildings in 1909–10. Designed by the architectural firm of Neville & Bagge, they have Neo-Renaissance details, and were built for working-class renters. Over the years, many of the buildings have undergone interior renovations—especially subdivisions during the 1940s and 1950s—but the exteriors remain largely intact. Today, the tree-lined street remains fully occupied and well maintained amidst the general deterioration of the surrounding area.

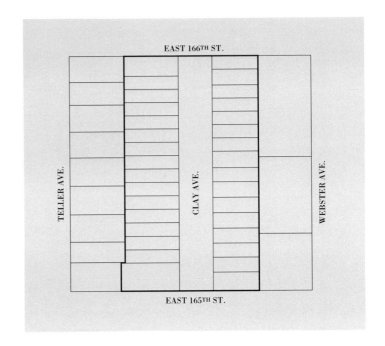

MOTT HAVEN EAST HISTORIC DISTRICT
The Bronx
Designated: April 5, 1994

This two-block district, a small enclave between East 139th and East 140th streets, is a rare island of original construction that survived the massive demolitions of the 1960s and 1970s in the economically depressed South Bronx. Mott Haven had been connected to Manhattan by rail as early as 1841, but it was the Third Avenue elevated train and several new bridges across the Harlem River in the 1880s that made real-estate development in The Bronx profitable. This district is composed of lower- and middle-income housing groups, constructed between 1887 and 1903, that comprise a sort of "museum" of late-nineteenth-century speculative housing. There are several groups of two-and-a-half-story Neo-Grec, Queen Anne, and Romanesque Revival row houses, as well as Romanesque and Renaissance Revival Old and New Law tenements.

The area was named for industrialist Jordan L. Mott, who located his home and his ironworks factory in the South Bronx in 1828. Most of Mott Haven's original population was of Irish- or other European-immigrant origins. It remained a European-immigrant enclave through much of the twentieth century, while the surrounding areas became populated mostly by African-Americans. The majority of the neighborhood is now of Latino descent. Despite the general decline of the surrounding neighborhoods, the blockfronts of this district retain a high degree of their architectural integrity.

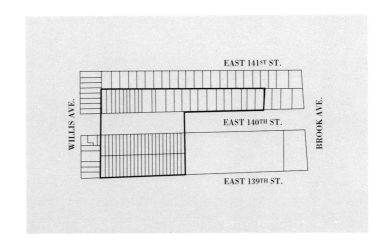

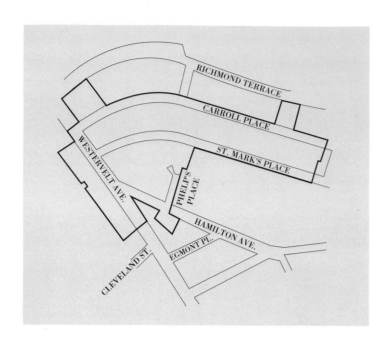

ST. GEORGE / NEW BRIGHTON HISTORIC DISTRICT
Staten Island
Designated: July 19, 1994

This seventy-eight-building district, developed in distinct phases, lies along Staten Island's northern shore. The New Brighton Association began construction in the 1830s, hoping to take advantage of the new steamboat ferry service. Although that venture collapsed, the name has remained, along with four Greek Revival houses, and a distinctive crescent street plan, which follows the curves of a steep incline. Several Italianate and Second Empire structures also survive from the post–Civil War period.

In the 1880s, the ferry lines were consolidated, and the St. George terminal became the sole landing, giving the neighborhood its current name. Reportedly, ferry and railroad magnate Erastus Wiman derived the name from George Law, a financier for whom he promised canonization in return for backing the terminal plan. The majority of the district's houses were constructed in the 1880s and 1890s, and reflect a combination of Queen Anne, Colonial Revival, and Shingle styles.

The five boroughs were consolidated into New York City in 1898, and in 1906 Staten Island moved its borough government from Richmondtown to St. George. This, coupled with the municipal takeover of the ferry in 1905, focused attention on the district. The historical significance of the St. George district comes in part from the prominence of some of its early residents, including the founders of such important local institutions as the Staten Island Institute of Arts and Sciences and the Staten Island Women's Club. By the 1950s, however, middle-class residents were abandoning St. George. In the 1970s, houses that had been multiple dwellings were restored to one- or two-family use, and it has again become a vibrant neighborhood.

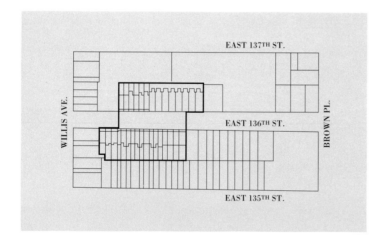

BERTINE BLOCK HISTORIC DISTRICT
The Bronx
Designated: April 5, 1996

In the 1890s, developer Edward Bertine and prominent Manhattan architect George Keister (who also designed The Gerard, the Belasco Theater, and Harlem's Apollo Theater, all q.v.) built several groups of row houses in this once industrial South Bronx neighborhood. Among these is the Queen Anne–style Bertine Block, for which this district is named. This group of buildings is constructed of brick, stone, slate, and stained glass. Most have tall chimneys rising above such diverse rooflines as mansards and flat roofs, pediments, and steeped and scrolled gables. The Bertine Block's brickwork is highly patterned, and the fenestration is varied. The district also contains eight low-income tenement buildings, erected in 1897 and 1899, which have Renaissance-inspired details and five-room, railroad-flat layouts.

The district was physically unchanged from 1900 until the Second World War. After the war, however, many of the town houses were subdivided, and several adjacent apartment buildings were combined. By the 1970s, entire neighborhoods, including those adjacent to the Bertine Block Historic District, were being demolished to make space for warehouses and housing projects. Today, the surviving thirty-one buildings that compose this district occupy less than one-half of a block in economically depressed Mott Haven. Several of the buildings are currently unoccupied, and many of the structures are in disrepair.

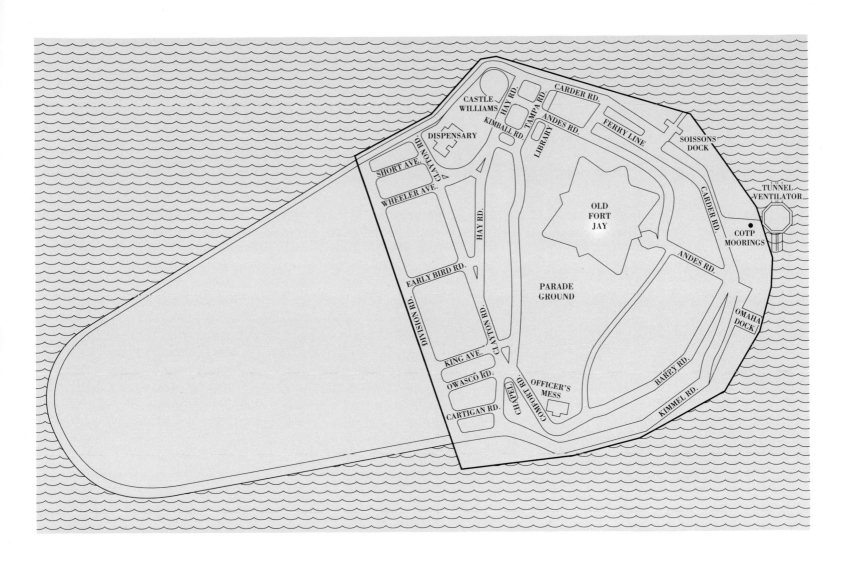

GOVERNORS ISLAND HISTORIC DISTRICT
Manhattan
Designated: June 18, 1996

The first Europeans to occupy this island, located one-half mile south of Manhattan, were the directors of the Dutch New Netherland Colony. Its name derives from its similar function as the estate of the Governors of the English Colony of New York. The U.S. Army maintained a base on the island from 1821 until 1966, and it has since been the U.S. Coast Guard's largest installation. The Coast Guard will cease operations on the island by the end of 1998; the Government Services Administration is conducting a study that will help determine the island's future use.

Between 1902 and 1912, the area of Governors Island was doubled to a quarter square mile using landfill from subway construction. This historic district covers 70 percent of the island, including the entire original island and a portion of the fill area. It also contains one hundred buildings dating from the early eighteenth century to the 1980s, five of which are individually designated: Governor's House (early 1700s), Fort Jay (1794–98), Castle Williams (1807–11), Admiral's House (1840), and Block House (1843). McKim, Mead & White's Building 400 (1929–30) is also noteworthy. It was the first structure built to house an entire regiment (1,375 men), making it the largest military building in the world at that time.

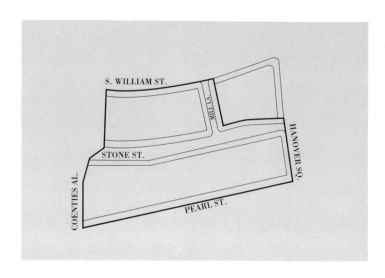

STONE STREET HISTORIC DISTRICT
Manhattan
Designated: June 25, 1996

Built on the original Dutch colony street plan, the Stone Street district's two blocks wind through a rare surviving cluster of fifteen buildings, dating primarily from the 1830s, amidst the skyscrapers of the Financial District. When England seized the colony in 1664, this area became the "English Quarter" in what remained essentially a Dutch city. The colony's Jewish population also lived here, and it is the site where North America's oldest Jewish congregation, Shearith Israel, held its first services—clandestinely—in 1654.

The neighborhood was gutted by the Great Fire of 1835, and the reconstruction, prototypical of nineteenth-century mercantile architecture, reflected the increasing commercialization of lower Manhattan. Adhering to the then ubiquitous Greek Revival style, the buildings are austere four- and five-story brick structures with simple granite pier-and-lintel storefronts. A later structure, the 1851 India House, a.k.a. Hanover Bank (q.v.), is a rare example of the Anglo-Italianate style that once typified the Financial District.

The area was largely ignored during the later 1800s as commerce moved toward Midtown. At the turn of the century, an eclectic Neo–Dutch Renaissance and Neo-Tudor block emerged along the back of many of the Stone Street buildings, reorienting their addresses to South William Street. By the 1970s, the area was again commercially depressed and on the verge of changes that challenged the historic integrity of the area.

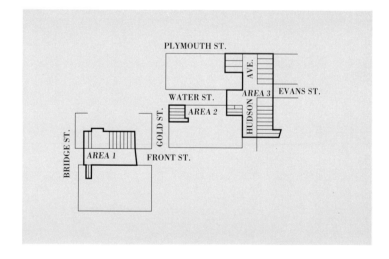

VINEGAR HILL HISTORIC DISTRICT
Brooklyn
Designated: January 14, 1997

In 1798, the British Army crushed an Irish revolution at the Battle of Vinegar Hill in County Wexford, Ireland. Many Irish immigrated to New York in the aftermath, and a significant number of them settled between the current sites of the Brooklyn Bridge and the Navy Yard. John Jackson, a wealthy shipbuilder who owned that land, renamed it Vinegar Hill in honor of the Irish patriots. In 1801, the U.S. Government established the Navy Yard. During the War of 1812 it grew rapidly, as did neighboring Vinegar Hill, where most of the workers lived. By the turn of the century, the district was a dense residential, industrial, and commercial neighborhood.

In the first half of the twentieth century, however, industry and transportation completely transformed Vinegar Hill, as the Manhattan Bridge approach, new warehouses and factories, and the Brooklyn-Queens Expressway all but obliterated the existing neighborhood by the 1950s. The Navy Yard closed in 1966, resulting in the demise of many nearby warehouses and factories. But starting in the 1970s, diverse newcomers began to arrive in the all but abandoned area, rehabilitating homes and converting many warehouses into loft space.

This designation covers three isolated pockets containing thirty-nine buildings, mostly Greek Revival row houses, dating from 1830 to 1850. In Vinegar Hill, the style is expressed with pedimented windows and doors, denticulated cornices, and acanthus-leaf ironwork.

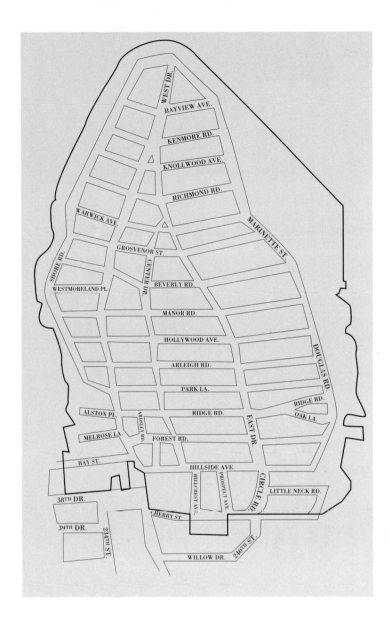

DOUGLASTON HISTORIC DISTRICT
Queens
Designated: June 24, 1997

The Douglaston Historic District reflects three centuries of Queens history and development and provides an important example of an early-twentieth-century planned suburb adapted to the site of a nineteenth-century estate. The property, seized by Thomas Hicks in the 1660s, was passed down through several family members and was subsequently sold to several other families before being acquired for agricultural use by Wynant Van Zandt, a prominent New York City merchant and city alderman, in 1813. George Douglas, a wealthy Scottish immigrant, acquired the estate from Robert B. Van Zandt in May of 1835. Much of the landscaping, including a variety of exotic specimen trees, survives from the Douglas Manor estate, which was inherited by Douglas's son, William Proctor Douglas, after his father's death in 1862.

Most of the more than 600 houses in the historic district were constructed in the early twentieth century as part of a planned suburb, also called Douglas Manor. It was developed by the Rickert-Finlay Company as part of the residential redevelopment of the Borough of Queens, following its creation and annexation to the City of Greater New York in 1898. The twentieth-century residential architecture reflects a variety of styles, including variants of Colonial Revival, Tudor Revival, English cottage, and Mediterranean Revival. Most of the houses were designed by local Queens architects, a number of whom were Douglaston residents. One of America's first successful female architects, Josephine Wright Chapman, designed eight of the houses in the 1910s and 1920s. The Cornelius Van Wyck House (q.v.), built c. 1735 as a farmstead for an Early Dutch settler, is the oldest extant house in the district and one of the oldest in New York City.

INDIVIDUALLY DESIGNATED LAMPPOSTS AND BRACKET LIGHTS

These lampposts and bracket lights are those included in the June 17, 1997 landmark designation.

Borough of The Bronx

Lamppost 70: north side of Kazimiroff Boulevard, by the entrance to the Haupt Conservatory, New York Botanical Garden

Lamppost 71: north side of Kazimiroff Boulevard, by the entrance to the Haupt Conservatory, New York Botanical Garden

Lamppost 83: west side of Broadway between 230th Street and Kimberly Place, adjacent to 5517 Broadway

Lamppost 96: southeast corner of Mosholu Avenue and Post Road, adjacent to 5802 Mosholu Avenue

Lampposts 101 and 102: flanking the steps on West 256th Street, leading from the west side of Post Road to the east side of Sylvan Avenue

Borough of Brooklyn

Lamppost 73: southern side of the pedestrian bridge crossing the Belt Parkway (Leif Erikson Drive) between Exit 4 (Bay 8th Street) and Exit 5 (Bay Parkway)

Lampposts 97, 98, 99, and 100: Dyker Beach Park Golf Course on Park Drive east of 7th Avenue, opposite 88th Street

Lamppost 103: southern side of the pedestrian bridge crossing the Belt Parkway (Leif Erikson Drive) between Exit 5 (Bay Parkway) and Exit 6 (Coney Island Avenue)

Borough of Manhattan

Lamppost 1: southeast corner of 1 Battery Park Plaza (State and Bridge streets)

Lamppost 3: adjacent to 24 Beaver Street between Broad and New streets

Lamppost 4: adjacent to 50 Broadway

Lamppost 5: adjacent to 80 Broadway

Lamppost 6: adjacent to 10 Pine Street, The Equitable Building

Lamppost 7: west side of Greenwich Street between Battery Place and Morris Street

Lamppost 8: east side of Greenwich Street between Battery Place and Morris Street, adjacent to the Cunard Building

Lamppost 9: intersection of Greenwich Street, the foot of Battery Place, and Trinity Place

Lamppost 10: adjacent to 1–9 Trinity Place, a.k.a. 29 Broadway

Lamppost 11: west side of Trinity Place overlooking depressed exit ramp of the Brooklyn Battery Tunnel

Lamppost 12: west side of Trinity Place overlooking depressed exit ramp of the Brooklyn Battery Tunnel, near Rector Street subway entrance

Lamppost 13: west side of Trinity Place on the traffic island

Lamppost 14: adjacent to 34–38 Western Union International Plaza

Lamppost 15: adjacent to 21–23 Morris Street

Lamppost 35: southeast corner of Canal and Lafayette streets

Lamppost 45: north side of Gansevoort Street at the foot of Little West 12th Street

Lamppost 51: northeast corner of Broadway and 23rd Street, adjacent to Madison Square Park

Lamppost 53: adjacent to 314 Fifth Avenue

Lamppost 54: southeast corner of Park Avenue and East 46th Street

Lamppost 55: southwest corner of Park Avenue and East 46th Street

Lamppost 56: southeast corner of Beekman Place at 51st Street, adjacent to 39 Beekman Place

Lamppost 57: Sutton Place at East 58th Street, east side of Sutton Square north of Riverview Terrace

Lamppost 58: southeast corner of West 139th Street at Edgecombe Avenue, adjacent to 90–96 Edgecombe Avenue

Lamppost 59: intersection of Amsterdam Avenue, Hamilton Place, and West 143rd Street, within Alexander Hamilton Square

Lampposts 60 and 61: on the paths of Colonel Charles Young Triangle, at the intersection of West 153rd Street at Macomb's Place

Lampposts 63, 64, 65, 66, 67, and 68: lining both sides of the entrance ramp to Harlem River Drive on Adam Clayton Powell, Jr. Boulevard, south of West 153rd Street

Lamppost 77 (wall bracket): on 147 Nassau Street between Bruce and Beekman streets

Lamppost 78: east side of the Western Union International Plaza between Morris Street and Battery Place

Lamppost 79: northeast corner of Albany and West streets

Lamppost 80: adjacent to 107 and 109 Washington Street, between Rector and Carlisle streets

Lamppost 81: south side of 48th Street between Park and Lexington avenues, adjacent to the 48th Street side of 277 Park Avenue

Lamppost 82: south side of 49th Street between Park and Lexington avenues, adjacent to the 49th Street side of 279 Park Avenue

Lamppost 84: former intersection of Broome and Sheriff streets

Lamppost 85: northeast corner of West 211th Street and Broadway, adjacent to 4980–4988 Broadway

Lampposts 86, 87, and 88: on the West 215th Street step street from Broadway to Park Terrace, west of Broadway

Lamppost 89: southeast corner of Washington and Warren streets

Lamppost 90: southwest corner of Fifth Avenue and 28th Street, adjacent to Madison Square Park

Lamppost 91: southwest corner of Walker Street and Sixth Avenue

Lamppost 92: adjacent to 303 West 10th Street between West and Washington streets

Lamppost 93 (wall bracket): on 33–43 Gold Street, Excelsior Power Company Building

Lamppost 94 (wall bracket): on 153 East 26th Street, at northwest corner of East 26th Street and Broadway alley

Lampposts 105 and 106: in Highbridge Park at the foot of West 187th Street and Laurel Hill Terrace

Lamppost 107: east side of Riverside Drive at West 163rd Street, inside Fort Washington playground

Borough of Queens

Lamppost 72: south side of 53rd Avenue step street between 64th Street and 65th Place, Maspeth

Lamppost 95: Rockaway Boulevard near 150th Street by Baisley Pond Park

SCENIC AND INTERIOR LANDMARKS

Scenic Landmarks

Bryant Park
Central Park
Eastern Parkway
Fort Tryon Park
Grand Army Plaza
Ocean Parkway
Prospect Park
Riverside Park and Drive
Verdi Square

Interior Landmarks

Ambassador Theater
American Museum of Natural History
Apollo Theater
Appellate Division of the Supreme Court of the State of
    New York
Apple Bank for Savings
Barclay-Vesey Building
Barrymore Theater
Bartow-Pell Mansion Museum
Beacon Theater
Belasco Theater
Biltmore Theater
Booth Theater
Broadhurst Theater
Bronx Community College, C.U.N.Y., Gould
    Memorial Library
Brooklyn Historical Society Building
Brooks Atkinson Theater
Charles Scribner's Sons Building
Chase Manhattan Bank
Chrysler Building
City Cinemas Village East
City Hall
Columbia University, Low Memorial Library
Cort Theater
Crossland Savings Bank
Cunard Building
Dime Savings Bank
Ed Sullivan Theater
Ellis Island, Main Building
Embassy I Theater
Emigrant Savings Bank
Empire State Building
Eugene O'Neill Theater
Federal Hall National Memorial
52 Chambers Street
Film Center Building
Fiori Restaurant
Ford Foundation Building
46th Street Theater
Four Seasons Restaurant
Fred F. French Building
Fuller Building
Gage & Tollner Restaurant
General Grant National Memorial
Golden Theater
Goldome Bank

Gouverneur Morris High School
Grand Central Terminal
Greenpoint Bank
Helen Hayes Theater
Helmsley Building
Home Savings Bank of America
Hudson Theater
Imperial Theater
IRT Subway System Stations
King Mansion
Lane Theater
Longacre Theater
Long Distance Building of the American Telephone
    and Telegraph Company
Lyceum Theater
Majestic Theater
Marine Air Terminal
Mark Hellinger Theater
Martin Beck Theater
Metropolitan Museum of Art
Morris-Jumel Mansion
Music Box Theater
Neil Simon Theater
New Amsterdam Theater
New School for Social Research
New York City Parking Violations Bureau
New York Life Insurance Building
New York Public Library, Main Branch
New York Public Library, Ottendorfer Branch
New York State Supreme Court
Old Merchant's House
Palace Theater
Pierpont Morgan Library and Annex
Plymouth Theater
Republic National Bank (175 Broadway, Brooklyn)
Republic National Bank (1 Hanson Place, Brooklyn)
RKO Keith's Flushing Theater
Rockefeller Center, Radio City Music Hall, RCA
    Building; International Building
Royale Theater
Sailor's Snug Harbor, Building C; Veterans
    Memorial Hall
St. James Theater
Seagram Building
Seventh Regiment Armory
72nd Street Subway Kiosk and Control House
Shubert Theater
Solomon R. Guggenheim Museum
Surrogate's Court
Swiss Center Building
Town Hall
TWA Terminal A
U.S. Custom House
Van Cortlandt Mansion
Western Union Building
Winter Garden Theater
Woolworth Building

SITES DESIGNATED FROM AUGUST THROUGH NOVEMBER 1997

September

John and Elizabeth Truslow House, 1887–88
96 Brooklyn Avenue, a.k.a. 1331–1343 Dean Street,
    Brooklyn
Architects: Parfitt Brothers
Designated: September 16, 1997

October

The CBS Headquarters, 1965
51 West 52nd Street, Manhattan
Architect: Eero Saarinen
Designated: October 21, 1997

Chase Bank, formerly Manufacturers Trust
    Building, 1954
510 Fifth Avenue, Manhattan
Architects: Skidmore, Owings & Merrill
Designated: October 21, 1997

The Ford Foundation Building (exterior and
    interior), 1967
321 East 42nd Street
Architect: Kevin Roche/John Dinkeloo Associates
Designated: October 21, 1997

DESIGNATION RESCINDED

Poillon-Seguine-Britton House, 1695; additions, 1730,
    1845, 1930
361 Great Kills Road, Staten Island
Designated: August 25, 1981
Designation rescinded: November 18, 1997
Destroyed by fire

SITES HEARD BUT NOT DESIGNATED BY THE NEW YORK CITY LANDMARKS PRESERVATION COMMISSION, JANUARY 1982–JULY 1997

American Bank Note Company Printing Plant
1201–1239 Lafayette Avenue (a.k.a. 890 Garrison
    Avenue), The Bronx
Heard: 6/2/92, 9/8/92, 12/8/92

American Female Guardian Society Home for the
    Friendless
936 Woodycrest Avenue, The Bronx
Heard: 6/2/92

122 Androvette Street
Staten Island
Heard: 10/1/91

Astoria Play Center
19th Street, Queens
Heard: 4/3/90, 7/10/90, 9/11/90

Bedford Stuyvesant/Bed-Stuy Heights Historic
    District expansion
Brooklyn
Heard: 9/21/93

The Beekman Tower Hotel
(Former Panhellenic Tower Hotel)
1–7 Mitchell Place, Manhattan
Heard: 4/12/83, 6/14/83, 7/10/90, 7/21/97

Bernheimer & Schwartz Pilsener Brewing Company
(Formerly D.G. Yuengling Brewing Co. Complex
    Buildings)
1361–1369 Amsterdam Avenue (a.k.a. 461–467,
    473–479 West 126th Street, a.k.a. 423–427,
    433–437, 439–449 West 127th Street, a.k.a.
    454–458, 460–470, 484–490 West 128th Street),
    Manhattan
Heard: 7/15/91, 10/29/91

Betsy Head Play Center
Hopkinson Avenue between Livonia and Dumont
    avenues, Brooklyn
Heard: 4/3/90

Joseph Bicknell Residence
Post Road and West 243rd Street, The Bronx
Heard: 2/10/82, 4/13/82, 1/5/93

Biltmore Theater Exterior
261–265 West 47th Street, Manhattan
Heard: 10/19/82

183–195 Broadway Building
Brooklyn
Heard: 6/12/84, 7/10/90

311 Broadway Building
Manhattan
Heard: 12/12/89

315 Broadway Building
Manhattan
Heard: 12/12/89, 4/3/90

325–331 Broadway Building
Manhattan
Heard: 12/12/89, 4/3/90

Broadway Fashion Building
2309–2315 Broadway (a.k.a. 250–256 West 84th
    Street), Manhattan
Heard: 11/18/86, 5/5/87

Broadway Theater (exterior and interior)
Manhattan
Heard: 10/19/82

Brooklyn Clay Retort and Fire Brick Works
76–86, 99–113 Van Dyke Street and
    106–116 Beard Street, Brooklyn
Heard: 9/11/90

Canal Street Houses
502–508 Canal Street, Manhattan
Heard: 6/14/83, 9/13/83, 9/19/89

Carnegie Hall Interior
881–893 Seventh Avenue, Manhattan
Heard: 9/17/85, 11/12/85

Catholic Apostolic Church
417 West 57th Street, Manhattan
Heard: 12/10/85

Century Theater Interior
111 East 15th Street, Manhattan
Heard: 10/19/82

120–122 Chambers Street Building (a.k.a. 50–52
    Warren Street)
Manhattan
Heard: 9/19/89

143 Chambers Street Building
Manhattan
Heard: 9/19/89

Church of the Transfiguration
1 East 29th Street, Manhattan
Heard: 9/11/94

Consolidated Edison Powerhouse
(Former Interborough Rapid Transit Powerhouse)
Eleventh Avenue between 58th and 59th streets (a.k.a.
    850 Twelfth Avenue), Manhattan
Heard: 7/10/90

Former Convent of the Church of the Annunciation
56–64 Havemeyer Street, Brooklyn
Heard: 6/12/84

Coogan Building
(Former Racquet and Tennis Club)
776–782 Sixth Avenue, Manhattan
Heard: 11/12/85, 2/7/89, 6/13/89

Crotona Park Play Center and Bath House Interior
Fulton Avenue and East 173rd Street, The Bronx
Heard: 4/13/90

Drake-Dehart House
134 Main Street, Staten Island
Heard: 11/1/91

Christian Duryea House
562 Jerome Street, Brooklyn
Heard: 1/8/85
(Destroyed by fire)

East River Savings Bank
743–749 Amsterdam Avenue, Manhattan
Heard: 7/12/88

Empire Theater (exterior and interior)
(Former Eltinge Theater)
236–242 West 42nd Street, Manhattan
Heard: 6/14/82, 10/19/82

Engine Co. 70
(Former Engine Co. 79)
160 Chambers Street, Manhattan
Heard: 9/19/89

Erasmus Hall High School
911 Flatbush Avenue, Brooklyn
Heard: 7/10/90

Estey Piano Factory
112–128 Lincoln Avenue (a.k.a. 15–21 Bruckner
    Boulevard, a.k.a. 270–278 East 134th Street),
    The Bronx
Heard: 6/2/92

Fairway Apartments
76–09 34th Street, Queens
Heard: 12/4/90

Fiss, Doerr & Carroll Horse Co. Building
139–151 East 24th Street, Manhattan
Heard: 2/7/89, 5/16/89

66–45 Forest Avenue House
Queens
Heard: 12/4/90

Frost Building of the S.R. Smith Infirmary–Staten
    Island Hospital
101 Stanley Avenue, Staten Island
Heard: 10/12/82, 1/11/83, 2/8/83

General William B. Ward House
631 Howard Avenue, Staten Island
Heard: 1/31/91

The Guastavino Houses
118, 121, 123, 124, 125, 127, 128, 130, 132, 134 West
   78th Street, Manhattan
Heard: 11/15/83

Guild ANTA Theater Interior
33 West 50th Street, Manhattan
Heard: 8/6/85

Harris Theater Interior
226 West 42nd Street, Manhattan
Heard: 6/14/82, 6/15/82, 10/19/82

71 Harvard Avenue House
Staten Island
Heard: 11/10/81

Highbridge Play Center
Amsterdam Avenue and West 173rd Street, Manhattan
Heard: 4/3/90

191–01 Hollis Avenue House
Queens
Heard: 9/13/83, 11/15/83

Hope Community Hall
(Former 28th Police Precinct Station House)
177–179 East 104th Street, Manhattan
Heard: 7/15/91

Horton's Row
411–417 Westervelt Avenue, Staten Island
Heard: 10/1/91

Hotel Churchill
252 West 76th Street, Manhattan
Heard: 6/12/84

Thomas Jefferson Play Center
First Avenue between East 111th and East 114th
   streets, Manhattan
Heard: 4/3/90

Nicholas Killmeyer Store and Residence
4321 Arthur Kill Road, Staten Island
Heard: 10/1/91

94–100 Lafayette Street Building
Manhattan
Heard: 12/12/89, 4/3/90

Leggett-Fish House
150–10 Powells Cove Boulevard, Queens
Heard: 11/10/81

Level Club
(Former Phoenix House, Hotel Riverside Plaza)
253–263 West 79th Street, Manhattan
Heard: 4/13/82

Loew's Paradise Theater Interior
2405–2419 Grand Concourse, The Bronx
Heard: 6/12/84

2251–2259 Loring Place Houses
The Bronx
Heard: 9/13/83

Luchow's Restaurant (exterior and interior)
110 East 14th Street, Manhattan
Heard: 6/8/82, 9/14/82
(Demolished)

Lyric Theater
213 West 42nd Street, Manhattan
Heard: 6/14/82, 6/15/82, 10/19/82

McCarren Play Center
Lorimer and Bayard streets, Brooklyn
Heard: 4/3/90

174 Meserole Street House
Brooklyn
Heard: 6/12/84, 7/10/90

I. Miller Building
167 West 46th Street (a.k.a. 1552–1554 Broadway),
   Manhattan
Heard: 11/12/85, 9/11/90

Morningside Park
Manhattan
Heard: 2/19/91

Murray Street and Warren Street Buildings
41–43, 45–47, 51, 53 Warren Street; 41, 43, 45, 49, 51,
   53, 55 Murray Street, Manhattan
Heard: 9/19/89

Mutual Reserve Fund Building
305 Broadway, Manhattan
Heard: 12/12/89, 4/3/90

Nederlander Theater
208 West 41st Street, Manhattan
Heard: 2/15/87

New Apollo Theater (exterior and interior)
228–238 West 43rd Street, Manhattan
Heard: 6/14/82, 6/15/82, 10/19/82

Newtown High School
48–01 90th Street, Queens
Heard: 9/15/87

The New York Times Building
217–247 West 43rd Street, Manhattan
Heard: 11/12/85, 7/19/91

Noonan Plaza Apartments
105–145 West 168th Street, Manhattan
Heard: 6/2/92

Eugene O'Neill Theater
230–238 West 49th Street, Manhattan
Heard: 12/8/87

Orchard Beach Bath House and Promenade
The Bronx
Heard: 6/2/92

Palace Theater
1564 Broadway, Manhattan
Heard: 7/14/87

23–25 Park Place Building (a.k.a. 20–22
   Murray Street)
Manhattan
Heard: 12/12/89, 4/3/90, 7/10/90

45–47 Park Place Building
Manhattan
Heard: 9/19/89

Pepsi-Cola Sign
4600 Fifth Street, Queens
Heard: 7/12/88

28th Police Precinct Station House
177–179 East 104th Street, Manhattan
Heard: 7/15/91

Former Public School 90
2274–2286 Church Avenue, Brooklyn
Heard: 2/7/89

Public School 166
132 West 89th Street, Manhattan
Heard: 7/12/88, 1/5/93

Red Hook Play Center
Bay Street between Clinton and Henry streets,
   Brooklyn
Heard: 4/3/90

Renaissance Theater and Casino
2341–2349 and 2351–2359 Adam Clayton Powell, Jr.
   Boulevard, Manhattan
Heard: 7/15/91, 10/29/91

Ritz Theater (exterior and interior)
225 West 48th Street, Manhattan
Heard: 12/15/87

Riverside/West End 107–108th Streets Historic
   District
Manhattan
Heard: 7/12/88

Jackie Robinson Youth Center YMCA
181 West 135th Street, Manhattan
Heard: 7/15/91, 7/21/97

Rockefeller Townhouse
242 East 52nd Street, Manhattan
Heard: 6/15/93

Rogers Peet & Co. Building
258 Broadway, Manhattan
Heard: 12/12/89

Rutan-Journeay House
7647 Amboy Road, Staten Island
Heard: 10/1/91

Sacred Heart of Jesus Roman Catholic Church
    and Rectory
451–457 West 51st Street, Manhattan
Heard: 12/10/85, 3/11/86, 4/4/92

Sailor's Snug Harbor Historic District
Staten Island
Heard: 9/11/84

St. Ann's Church Interior
117–131 Clinton Street, Brooklyn
Heard: 7/19/91

St. Benedict the Moor Roman Catholic Church
(Former Second Church of the Evangelical Association
    of North America)
342 West 53rd Street, Manhattan
Heard: 12/10/85, 4/14/92

103 St. Mark's Place House
Staten Island
Heard: 11/10/81, 2/9/82

St. Mary's Protestant Episcopal Church
    (Manhattanville) Parish House and Sunday School
517–523 West 126th Street, Manhattan
Heard: 7/15/91

St. Paul's Methodist Episcopal Church
7558 Amboy Road, Staten Island
Heard: 10/1/91

Salvation Army Territorial Headquarters Building
120 West 14th Street (a.k.a. 123 West 13th Street),
    Manhattan
Heard: 4/13/82, 7/10/90, 9/11/90

August Schoverling House
344 Westervelt Avenue, Staten Island
Heard: 10/1/91

Gustav Schwab House
University Avenue, The Bronx
Heard: 1/31/91

Sea Gate Chapel
3700 Surf Avenue, Brooklyn
Heard: 12/12/89, 4/3/90, 4/14/92

Second Church of Christ, Scientist
10 West 68th Street, Manhattan
Heard: 6/8/82, 9/14/82
(Now absorbed into Upper West Side/Central Park
    West H.D.)

Selwyn Theater (exterior and interior)
229–231 West 42nd Street, Manhattan
Heard: 6/14/82, 6/15/82, 10/19/82

Siegel-Cooper Building
616–632 Avenue of the Americas (a.k.a. 25–27 West
    18th Street, a.k.a. 30 West 19th Street), Manhattan
Heard: 2/7/89
(Now absorbed into Ladies' Mile H.D.)

Governor Alfred E. Smith House
25 Oliver Street, Manhattan
Heard: 1/31/91

Sohmer & Co. Piano Factory Building
31–01 Vernon Boulevard, Queens
Heard: 11/15/83, 6/12/84, 7/10/90, 9/11/90

Studio 54 Interior
254 West 54th Street, Manhattan
Heard: 10/19/82

Sunset Play Center and Bath House Interior
77th Avenue between 41st and 44th streets, Brooklyn
Heard: 4/3/90

Times Square Theater (exterior and interior)
215–223 West 42nd Street, Manhattan
Heard: 6/14/82, 6/15/82, 10/19/82

Tompkinsville Play Center (Joseph H. Lyons Pool)
    and Bath House Interior
Murray Hulbert Avenue, Staten Island
Heard: 10/12/82, 4/3/90

The 21 Club Building
21 West 52nd Street, Manhattan
Heard: 9/17/85, 11/12/85

Unification Church Headquarters
(Former Columbia University Club)
4 West 43rd Street, Manhattan
Heard: 9/13/83, 11/15/83

Victory Theater (exterior and interior)
(Former Republic Theater)
207–211 West 42nd Street, Manhattan
Heard: 6/14/82, 6/15/82, 10/19/82

416–424 Washington Street Building
Manhattan
Heard: 1/8/91, 3/12/91, 5/7/91, 7/9/91

177 West Broadway House
Manhattan
Heard: 9/19/89

232 West End Avenue House
Manhattan
Heard: 7/12/88, 10/21/90

West 16th Street Buildings
3, 11–15, 25, 27–29, 31–41, 43–47 West 16th Street,
    Manhattan
Heard: 6/10/86

35, 41 West 54th Street Houses
Manhattan
Heard: 9/17/85, 1/31/90

West 82nd Street Historic District
305–357, 328–346 West 84th Street, Manhattan
Heard: 11/18/86, 4/14/92

West 89th Street Stable
167–171 West 89th Street, Manhattan
Heard: 4/18/88

West 101st Street Historic District
310–332, 319–327 West 101st Street, Manhattan
Heard: 11/18/86

Windmere Apartments
400–406 West 57th Street, Manhattan
Heard: 10/6/88

Winter Garden Theater
1634 Broadway, Manhattan
Heard: 1/5/88

Wolcott Hotel
4–10 West 31st Street, Manhattan
Heard: 4/12/83, 6/14/83, 1/3/91

39, 41 Worth Street Buildings
Manhattan
Heard: 9/19/89

Young Men's Christian Association Building,
    Harlem Branch
180, 181 West 135th Street, Manhattan
Heard: 7/15/91, 7/21/91

ACKNOWLEDGMENTS

This book is the result of a collaborative effort involving many people, including the Historic Landmarks Preservation Center's staff and Board, the owners, occupants, and managing agents of landmark buildings, concerned citizens, photographers, architects, preservationists, and a wide range of individual and institutional sources that focus upon New York City's architecture. My special thanks to Paul Gottlieb, Marybeth Kavanagh, Michael Stewart, Ciorsdan Conran, Hal Cohen, Jared Knowles, Adele Westbrook, Amy Vinchesi, Judith Michael, and Carl Spielvogel.

Space prohibits the inclusion on this list of numerous others who lent their time, knowledge, and support to this project. To those whose names might have inadvertently been omitted, and those who wished to remain anonymous, I extend my thanks. Without their invaluable assistance, *The Landmarks of New York III* would not have been possible.

BARBARALEE DIAMONSTEIN
27 September 1997

PHOTOGRAPH CREDITS

David Allen: 30 top, 31 top, 31 bottom, 35 top, 36 bottom, 49 top, 82 top, 87 center, 90 bottom, 94 top, 102 bottom, 111 top, 117 bottom, 125 top, 136, 143 bottom, 145 bottom, 148 center, 157 bottom, 199 bottom, 235 left, 237 center, 265 top, 296 right, 349 bottom, 351 bottom.

Stephen Barker: 370 bottom.

Kaija Berzins: 111 bottom, 144 bottom, 240 top, 372 top.

Olivia Biddle: 384 bottom, 389 bottom, 392 bottom, 398 bottom, 404 both, 408 top, 409 both, 411 top, 413 top, 420 bottom, 430 bottom, 435 right.

Julio A. Bofill: 439 bottom, 446 both, 447 bottom, 454 top, 458 top, 468 top, 469 bottom, 471 top, 475 both, 479 top.

Andrew Bordwin: 44 top, 54, 64 top, 68 center, 68 bottom, 69 bottom, 71 top, 72 bottom, 73 both, 80 bottom, 92 bottom, 108 top, 109 top, 114 top, 123 top, 159, 177, 183, 196 bottom, 200 top, 205 bottom, 231, 238 bottom, 244, 257, 258 center, 258 bottom, 289 both, 295 top, 300 bottom, 325 both, 326 all, 335 bottom, 364, 365 bottom, 425 bottom.

Richard Cappelluti: 382 top, 383 top, 385 top, 400 bottom, 421 top, 422, 424 both, 427 top, 432 bottom, 433 bottom, 436 bottom.

Matthew Cazier: 388 bottom, 392 top, 393 bottom, 394 top, 397 top, 399 left, 400 top, 402 all, 403, 406 both, 408 bottom, 414 bottom, 431 center.

Alan Chin and Jorge Roldan: 390 top, 391 top, 394 bottom, 395 both, 401 bottom, 410 both, 415 bottom, 416 bottom, 417 bottom, 419 both, 426 top, 428 bottom, 429 bottom, 432 top.

Eric C. Chung: 438 both, 439 top, 441 bottom, 442 top, 444 bottom, 445 top, 448 top, 454 bottom, 456 bottom, 457, 458 bottom, 460 bottom, 461 bottom, 468 top, 472 both, 474, 478 top, 479 bottom, 480 bottom, 483 both, 484 bottom.

Carin Drechsler-Marx: 32 all, 52 all, 53 top, 61 top, 86 bottom, 161 bottom, 164, 167 top, 193 bottom, 216 top, 217 bottom, 220, 243, 245, 250 bottom, 262 top, 266 bottom, 268, 284 top, 294 both, 300 top, 310 bottom, 311 center, 313 center, 314 top, 315 center, 331 top, 331 center, 334 top, 337 bottom, 342 top, 343 center, 346 left, 348 top left, 348 top center, 348 top right, 349 top, 354 center, 358 bottom, 373 top.

Nathaniel Feldman: 50 top, 56, 71 top, 97, 118 bottom, 126, 144 top, 146 top, 147 all, 152 bottom, 168 top, 204 top, 205 top, 211 both, 227 bottom, 234, 235 top right, 235 bottom right, 241 bottom, 249 bottom, 254 bottom, 255 right, 263 top, 263 center, 269 bottom, 271 top, 274 top, 283 top, 308 bottom, 309 left, 313 top, 316 bottom, 318 top, 321 both, 327 bottom, 329 top, 333 bottom, 345 top, 349 third from top, 350 top, 357 bottom, 368 center right.

Stephen Fischer: 36 top, 38, 71 bottom, 116 top, 118 top, 119 top, 124 bottom, 132 top, 137 bottom, 140 top, 141 both, 155 bottom, 161 top, 193 top, 206 top, 208 right, 215 bottom, 225 top, 232, 251 top, 258 top, 261 bottom, 282 top, 286 bottom, 297 bottom, 305 top, 317 top, 338 all, 344 top, 357 top, 376, 378 right.

Karen Fried: 53 bottom, 197 bottom, 328 top.

Andrew Garn: 3 right, 39 top, 59 all, 64 center, 66 bottom, 68 top, 74 bottom, 76, 77, 93, 100 bottom, 102 top, 102 center, 104 bottom, 125 bottom, 131, 152 center, 153 bottom, 157 top, 162, 168 bottom, 178 top, 178 center, 186 bottom, 188 both, 189 bottom, 191 top, 192 bottom, 194 top, 208 left, 209 bottom, 210 bottom, 213 top, 214 both, 219 right, 223 center, 223 bottom, 226 top, 229 bottom, 236 top, 239 top, 242 top, 261 top, 262 bottom, 263 bottom, 279 top, 296 left, 302 top, 302 center, 305 bottom, 309 right, 316 top, 319 bottom, 343 top, 344 bottom, 347, 350 bottom, 356, 358 top, 359 top, 375 top, 377 both, 378 left, 434 top.

Jerry Ghiraldi: 415 top, 416 top, 418 right, 421 bottom, 428 top, 429 center, 431 bottom, 434 bottom, 436 top.

Lesley-Ann Gliedman: 133, 238 top.

Timothy Dlyn Haft: 383 bottom, 385 bottom, 386 bottom, 389 top, 393 top, 397 bottom, 401 top, 412 top, 431 top.

Serge Hambourg: 151 top, 184 top, 185 bottom, 227 top, 273, 292 top, 297 top, 370 top right, 371 bottom.

Jeanne Hamilton: 24 top, 25 top row, 25 second row, 26 bottom, 27 top, 27 bottom, 29, 33 both, 34, 37 both, 40, 42 top, 43 bottom, 44 bottom, 45, 47 both, 48 top, 55 both, 60 bottom, 146 bottom, 181.

Kristin Holcomb: 440 top, 441 top, 444 top, 448 bottom, 449 top, 453 top, 455 top, 459 both, 460 top, 463 bottom, 464 top, 466 top, 473 both, 476 all, 480 top, 481 both, 484 top, 485 both.

Liz Hunter: 61 bottom, 62 center, 80 top, 81 all, 87 top, 222 all, 223 top, 282, 361 bottom, 371 top, 373 bottom.

Claudia Joskowitz: 442 bottom, 447 top, 450, 451 bottom, 464 bottom, 467 top, 469 top, 471 bottom, 478 bottom.

Abby Weitman Karp: 24 center, 24 bottom, 25 third from top, 25 bottom, 26 top center, 26 top right, 26 center left, 39 bottom, 63 bottom, 79 center, 90 top, 98 bottom, 99 all, 113 bottom, 135 bottom, 140 bottom, 142 both, 148 top, 158, 172 both, 175 top, 189 top, 198 left, 237 bottom, 247 center, 247 bottom, 272, 330 all.

Jeff Kaufman: 241 top, 259 bottom, 303, 323, 363, 374.

Michael Kingsford: 96, 154 top, 230, 277 top, 281, 341, 353, 362, 365 top, 367, 368 left, 368 top right, 368 bottom right, 369 both, 370 top left, 380, 381.

Robert Kozma: 84 bottom, 135 top, 149 top, 170 bottom, 185 top, 191 bottom, 192 top, 206 bottom, 225 bottom, 254 top, 269 top, 291 bottom.

James Lane: 382 bottom, 384 top, 386 top, 387 both, 388 top, 396, 398 top, 405, 413 bottom, 414 top, 418 left, 425 top, 429 top.

Cynthia Larson: 26 top left, 103 top right, 103 bottom right, 117 top, 137 top, 285 bottom, 312 bottom, 317 bottom.

Barbara Mensch: 2 left, 2 right, 46 bottom, 50 bottom, 58 both, 78 bottom, 85 top, 139, 150, 169 both, 195 top, 249 top, 274 bottom, 295 bottom, 298, 301 top, 310 top, 322 top.

Brian L. Mikesell: 440 bottom, 445 bottom, 449 bottom, 451 top, 455 top, 456 top, 461 top, 465 both, 470 both, 477 bottom, 482.

Fred Miller: 178 bottom, 286 top, 290 both.

New York City Landmarks Preservation Commission: 463 top, 466 bottom, 477 top.

Miwa Nishio: 443 all, 452 both, 453 bottom, 462 both, 467 bottom.

Christine Osinski: 35 bottom, 46 top, 78 top, 78 center, 84 center, 85 center, 92 top, 103 left, 106 left, 109 bottom, 116 bottom, 132 bottom, 154 bottom, 319 top.

Cosmo Prete: 62 top, 62 bottom, 63 top, 65 top, 85 bottom, 95 bottom, 100 top, 112 top, 113 top, 124 top, 130, 174 top, 190 all, 194 bottom, 195 bottom, 198 right, 221 top, 283 bottom, 307 bottom, 328 bottom, 354.

Nina Rappaport: 3 left, 30 bottom, 86 top, 100 center, 120 top, 143 top, 148 bottom, 152 top, 156 bottom, 180, 202, 203, 209 bottom, 237 top, 255 left, 259 top, 265 bottom, 277 bottom, 287 top, 287 bottom, 332 bottom, 337 top, 359 bottom, 371 center.

Andrea Robbins and Max Becher: 42 bottom, 48 bottom, 67 bottom, 105 top, 110 top, 120 bottom, 121 bottom, 149 bottom, 155 top, 170 top, 179, 197 top, 207 bottom, 213 bottom, 216 bottom, 224 bottom, 242 bottom, 264 bottom, 280, 299, 332 bottom, 335 top, 361 top, 366 bottom, 372 bottom.

Steven Tucker: 2 center, 3 center, 22 top, 22 bottom, 43 top, 51 top, 57 top, 60 top, 64 bottom, 66 top, 69 top, 70 top, 74 top, 83, 84 top, 88 bottom, 91 bottom, 94 bottom, 95 top, 101, 104 top, 107, 112 bottom, 115, 118 top, 119 bottom, 123, 127 all, 128, 134 both, 138, 145 top, 151 bottom, 156 top, 160 bottom, 173, 174 bottom, 175 bottom, 182, 186 top, 187, 199 top, 200 bottom, 201 both, 207 top, 212 right, 215 top, 217 top, 218 left, 221 bottom, 224 top, 226 bottom, 228, 229 top, 233 both, 236 bottom, 239 bottom, 240 bottom, 246, 247 top, 248, 250 top, 251 bottom, 253 top, 256, 260, 262, 264 top, 266 top, 267 top, 270, 276, 278 both, 279 bottom, 284 bottom, 285 top, 288, 291 top, 293, 301 bottom, 302 bottom, 304, 307 top, 308 top, 311 top, 312 top, 314 third from top, 318 bottom, 320, 322 bottom, 324, 327 top, 329 center, 333 top, 339 bottom, 352 both, 355 top, 360, 366 top, 375 bottom, 427 bottom.

Rene Velez: 390 bottom, 407 both, 411 bottom, 412 bottom, 417 top, 420 top, 423 left, 426 bottom, 430 top.

Bill Wallace: 51 bottom, 57 center, 57 bottom, 63 center, 65 bottom, 67 top, 72 top, 72 center, 75 all, 79 top, 79 bottom, 87 bottom, 89, 91 top, 98 top, 105 bottom, 106 right, 108 bottom, 110 bottom, 114 bottom, 129, 153 top, 160 top, 171, 176, 184 center, 184 bottom, 196 top, 204 bottom, 210 top, 218 right, 219 left, 253 bottom, 271 bottom, 275 top, 275 bottom, 296 second from left, 296 third from left, 296 fourth from left, 306 both, 336, 339 top.

In addition to the above, the author and publisher would like to thank the following for providing archival photographs of landmarks where access for the purpose of photography could not be arranged:

The American Museum of Natural History, New York: 165. **The Metropolitan Museum of Art,** New York: 167 bottom. Courtesy of the **National Society of Colonial Dames in the State of New York:** 41. **New York City Landmarks Preservation Commission:** 355 center; John B. Bayley: 423 right; Carl Forster: 206 bottom, 252 top, 267 bottom, 285 center, 311 bottom, 313 bottom, 314 second from top, 314 fourth from top, 315 top, 315 bottom, 329 bottom, 331 bottom, 333 center, 334 bottom, 340 both, 342 center, 342 bottom, 343 bottom, 345 bottom right, 346 top, 346 bottom right, 348 bottom left, 348 bottom center, 348 bottom right, 349 second from top, 351 top, 354 bottom, 355 bottom, 399 right, 433 top; Kevin McHugh: 391 bottom. **Solomon R. Guggenheim Museum,** New York: 435 left.